Human Diversity in Education

An Intercultural Approach

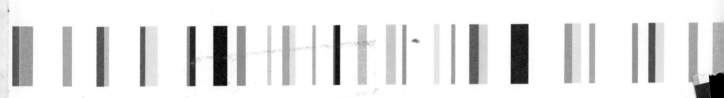

Human Diversity in Education

An Intercultural Approach

Kenneth Cushner, Averil McClelland

Kent State University

Philip Safford

Case Western Reserve University

(7)

McGraw Hill

Connect
Learn
Succeed™

HUMAN DIVERSITY IN EDUCATION: AN INTERCULTURAL APPROACH,
SEVENTH EDITION

Published by McGraw-Hill, a business unit of The McGraw-Hill Companies, Inc., 1221 Avenue of the
Americas, New York, NY 10020. Copyright © 2012 by The McGraw-Hill Companies, Inc. All rights
reserved. Previous editions © 2009, 2006, and 2003. No part of this publication may be reproduced
or distributed in any form or by any means, or stored in a database or retrieval system, without the
prior written consent of The McGraw-Hill Companies, Inc., including, but not limited to, in any
network or other electronic storage or transmission, or broadcast for distance learning.

Some ancillaries, including electronic and print components, may not be available to customers
outside the United States.

This book is printed on acid-free paper.

2 3 4 5 6 7 8 9 0 RJE/RJE 1 0 9 8 7 6 5 4 3 2 1

ISBN 978-0-07-811027-6   978-0-07-737789-2 (Florida Edition)
MHID 0-07-811027-0   0-07-737789-3 (Florida Edition)

Vice President & Editor-in-Chief: *Michael Ryan*
Vice President EDP/Central Publishing Services: *Kimberly Meriwether David*
Publisher: *Beth Mejia*
Senior Sponsoring Editor: *Allison McNamara*
Executive Marketing Manager: *Pamela S. Cooper*
Editorial Coordinator: *Marley Magaziner*
Project Manager: *Erin Melloy*
Design Coordinator: *Brenda A. Rolwes*
Cover Designer: *Studio Montage, St. Louis, Missouri*
Cover Images: *Two pupils Working On Computer:* © *Stockbyte/Getty Images RF; Student Doing A Written
Assignment:* © *BananaStock/PictureQuest RF; Group Of Children Getting On School Bus:* © *SW Productions/
Getty Images RF; Girl Writing In Classroom:* © *Getty Images RF.*
Buyer: *Susan K. Culbertson*
Media Project Manager: *Sridevi Palani*
Compositor: *Glyph International*
Typeface: *10/12 Berthold Baskerville*
Printer: *R. R. Donnelley*

Library of Congress Cataloging-in-Publication Data

Cushner, Kenneth.
    Human diversity in education: an intercultural approach/Kenneth
Cushner, Averil McClelland, Philip Safford.
      p. cm.
    ISBN-13: 978-0-07-811027-6 (alk. paper)
    ISBN-10: 0-07-811027-0 (alk. paper)
    1. Multicultural education–United States. 2. Individual differences in
children–United States. 3. Sex differences in education–United States.
  I. McClelland, Averil. II. Safford, Philip L. III. Title.
    LC1099.3.C87 2011
    370.1170973–dc22

                                                    2010052299

Brief Contents

Contents

Chapter 3   Culture and the Culture-Learning Process 65

Chapter 4   Classrooms and Schools as Cultural Crossroads 109

Chapter 5   Intercultural Development: Considering the Growth of Self and Others 145

② Multicultural Teaching in Action 173

Chapter 6   Creating Classrooms That Address Race and Ethnicity 175

Chapter 7   The Classroom as a Global Community: Nationality and Region   211

Chapter 8 Developing Learning Communities: Language and Learning Style 255

Chapter 9   Religious Pluralism in Secular Classrooms 291

Chapter 10 Developing a Collaborative Classroom:
Gender and Sexual Orientation 327

Chapter 13   Improving Schools for All Children:
The Role of Social Class and Social
Status in Teaching and Learning 433

About the Authors

Kenneth Cushner is Professor of Education in the College and Graduate School of Education, Health and Human Services at Kent State University, Kent, Ohio. In addition to this text, Dr. Cushner is author or editor of several books and articles in the field of intercultural education and training, including: *Intercultural Student Teaching: A Bridge to Global Competence,* (2007, Rowman Littlefield); *Human Diversity in Action: Developing Multicultural Competencies in the Classroom, 3rd edition* (2006, McGraw-Hill); *International Perspectives on Intercultural Education* (1998, Lawrence Erlbaum Associates); *Improving Intercultural Interactions: Modules for Cross-Cultural Training Programs, volume 2* (with Richard Brislin, Sage Publications, 1997), and *Intercultural Interactions: A Practical Guide, 2nd edition* (with Richard Brislin, Sage Publications, 1996). A former East-West Center Scholar, he is a frequent contributor to the professional development of educators through writing, workshop presentations, and travel program development. He is a Founding Fellow and Past-President of the International Academy for Intercultural Research, and past Director of COST–the Consortium for Overseas Student Teaching, which regularly sends students to student teach in 16 countries. In his spare time, Dr. Cushner enjoys music (percussion and guitar), photography, and travel. He has developed and led intercultural programs on all seven continents.

Averil McClelland is currently Associate Professor and Coordinator of the Cultural Foundations of Education program in the College and Graduate School at Kent State University, from which she received her Ph.D. Dr. McClelland has had extensive experience in curriculum design and program evaluation, as well as experience with addressing issues of gender and education and cultural diversity in education. In addition to this text, she is the author of *The Education of Women in the United States: A Guide to Theory, Teaching, and Research* (Garland, 1992), as well as a number of articles in scholarly journals. She received the Distinguished Teaching award from Kent State University in 1996, and has a long-standing relationship with the National First Ladies Library, where she develops Web-based curricula based on the lives of the nation's 44 First Ladies. Her special interests are the history, sociology, and politics of education, the reconstruction of teacher education, and internationalizing the college curriculum for pre-service and practicing teachers.

Philip Safford, Adjunct Professor of Psychology at Case Western Reserve University, is Emeritus Professor and former chair of Special Education at Kent State University. Prior to earning his Ph.D. through the Combined Program in Education and Psychology at the University of Michigan, with specialization in special education and child development, he had been a teacher and administrator in residential treatment programs for children with emotional disorders. Dr. Safford has authored or edited six books and numerous articles dealing with special education history, early intervention for young children with disabilities, and related topics. He has directed or co-directed a number of training, research, and demonstration projects in special education supported by federal and state grants.

Preface

People the world over continue to marvel at both the complexity as well as rapidity of change that confronts them in many aspects of their lives. The changes, problems, and subsequent challenges faced by humankind today cross national borders, span cultural differences, and increasingly affect all people regardless of nationality, race, ethnicity, religion, gender, or socioeconomic status. It is not only that such problems are encountered in our increasingly culturally diverse classrooms and communities, but that in order to solve these problems people must have the knowledge, skills, and motivations to reach beyond their own cultural boundaries and collaborate with others–or today's problems will not be solved. Intercultural understanding must ultimately become content that is actively addressed throughout the school curriculum.

It is attention to this reality that continues be at the foundation of this book and explains the slight modification in its title. The seventh edition of *Human Diversity in Education: An Intercultural Approach* focuses on the preparation of teachers and other human-service providers for teaching and interacting effectively with the wide diversity of students they are certain to encounter in their classrooms, schools, and communities. As world events continue to evolve, it is increasingly important that teachers provide young people with a foundation that will assist them to better understand the complex nature of their world while developing the skills that will enable them to be proactive problem solvers in an interdependent, global society.

Much has happened in the three years since the previous edition of *Human Diversity in Education,* both on the domestic as well as international fronts, although it is becoming increasingly difficult to separate one from the other. On the domestic front, we elected our first African American president that, in turn, brought about a swift shift in attitude from others toward the United States. We experienced our most severe economic downturn since the Great Depression, which continues to impact markets and economies around the world. The environmental disaster in the Gulf of Mexico reminds us that our emphasis on cost-cutting can have a disastrous impact on both people and nature that will be felt for years to come. Other recent events that significantly impact us include the passage of the health reform legislation; our prolonged military presence in the Middle East and the Central Asian region; the increased number of natural disasters, including Hurricane Katrina and the earthquake in Haiti; the continued rise in income and global reach of the nations of India and China; the on-going debate about immigration in the United States; diseases such as HIV-AIDS continue to affect an ever-growing number of people worldwide; we prepared for global pandemics from SARS and H1N1; and the increased identification and prevalence of autism affecting young children.

New to This Edition

This book continues to receive overwhelmingly positive feedback from users around the world, and because of this we have maintained much of the familiar format. Regular users, however, will notice some changes in this seventh edition.

The book continues to provide a broad treatment of the various forms of diversity common in today's schools, including nationality, ethnicity, race, religion, gender, social class, language acquisition and use, sexual orientation, health concerns, and disabilities. We also maintain its research-based approach, with an increased cross-cultural and intercultural emphasis. Because attention to diversity is not unique to the United States, and because we can learn quite a bit from others, we have maintained the International Perspectives that are featured beginning in Chapter 5. Scholars and practitioners from around the world bring another voice to the discussion, sharing their perspectives on how similar issues are addressed in their home countries of Australia, Canada, China, the Republic of Georgia, Germany, Ghana, Kenya, and South Africa.

We continue to stress that it is at the level of the individual teacher and the organizational structure of the school that significant change must occur with regard to how diversity is understood and accommodated. Little institutional or systematic change will occur until individuals fully understand the role that culture plays in determining their thoughts and actions and how they can go about altering its powerful influence. Culture learning of both teacher and student, along with intercultural interaction, remain central to this book.

We also recognize that today's generation of young people has been exposed to greater diversity, both global and domestic, through the influence of global media, demographic changes that have occurred in many local communities, as well as through the increased use of technology by both individuals and schools. This edition, thus, sees greater attention to the role that technology plays both in teaching and learning as well as the international socialization of young people. In the previous edition we added Active Exercises at the end of each chapter. In this edition we have added a section of Classroom Activities designed to demonstrate how the concepts introduced in the chapter can be applied at both the elementary and secondary classrooms. Links to the Online Learning Center continue to provide students with additional activities and active exercises.

Case Studies and Critical Incidents continue to be integral teaching devices throughout the book. Each chapter begins with a Case Study that introduces major concepts and sets the context for that chapter. A number of related Critical Incidents can be found at the end of each chapter. Each chapter also identifies an expanded number of updated references and websites that students can access for more information. An icon in the margin identifies these websites. A teacher's guide and other online learning resources are also available that provide directions for instructors as well as classroom activities and test questions.

The general format of this edition remains similar to the previous one with a few modifications. Part One provides background to the broad social, cultural and economic changes that confront society today (Chapter 1), with a historical overview of past multicultural effort (Chapter 2). We place particular emphasis on culture learning and intercultural interaction in Chapters 3 and 4. Chapter 5 explores the concept of intercultural development and provides a model that teachers can use to gauge their own growth as well as that of their students.

Part Two examines what teachers can do to make their classrooms and schools more responsive to diversity and more effective learning communities; that is, how to structure classrooms that are collaborative, inclusive, developmentally appropriate, globally oriented, and religiously pluralistic. Each of the chapters in Part Two centers on a major aspects of diversity: race and ethnicity (Chapter 6), global understanding (Chapter 7), language and learning style (Chapter 8), religious pluralism (Chapter 9), gender and sexual orientation (Chapter 10), age and development (Chapter 11), exceptionality and ability (Chapter 12), and social class and social status (Chapter 13).

We hope you continue to find benefit from this edition, and we welcome feedback from you.

Kenneth Cushner
Averil McClelland
Philip Safford

Supplemental Material

The seventh edition of *Human Diversity in Education* is accompanied by a supplemental website, www.mhhe.com/cushner7e. Instructor's materials are offered on a password-protected section of the site and include an Instructor's Manual and a Test Bank. Instructors can contact their local McGraw-Hill sales representative for a username and password to access the site. Students will find study resources including an online glossary, PowerPoint presentations, and the *Diversity in Action* workbook

This text is available as an eTextbook from CourseSmart, a new way for faculty to find and review eTextbooks. It's also a great option for students who are interested in accessing their course materials digitally and saving money. CourseSmart offers thousands of the most commonly adopted textbooks across hundreds of courses from a wide variety of higher education publishers. It is the only place for faculty to review and compare the full text of a textbook online, providing immediate access without the environmental impact of requesting a print exam copy. At CourseSmart, students can save up to 50% off the cost of a print book, reduce their impact on the environment, and gain access to powerful web tools for learning including full text search, notes and highlighting, and email tools for sharing notes between classmates. For further details contact your sales representative or go to www.coursesmart.com.

McGraw-Hill Create
www.mcgrawhillcreate.com

Craft your teaching resources to match the way you teach! With McGraw-Hill Create you can easily rearrange chapters, combine material from other content sources, and quickly upload content you have written like your course syllabus or teaching notes. Find the content you need in Create by searching through thousands of leading McGraw-Hill textbooks. Arrange your book to fit your teaching style. Create even allows you to personalize your book's appearance by selecting the cover and adding your name, school, and course information. Order a Create book and you'll receive a complimentary print review copy in 3–5 business days or a complimentary electronic review copy (eComp) via email in about one hour. Go to www.mcgrawhillcreate.com today and register. Experience how McGraw-Hill Create empowers you to teach *your* students *your* way.

Foundations for Multicultural Teaching

Education in a Changing Society

Focus Questions

1. What is the rationale for attention to diversity and intercultural competence in education?

2. What are some of the fundamental changes influencing American society and the world, including issues in the broad categories of globalization, changing demographics, rapidly expanding technologies, and consequent changing experiences, attitudes, and values among the generations?

3. What are some differences between schools designed to prepare students for an industrial age and schools designed to prepare students for an informational, global age?

4. Why do you think real, substantial change is so difficult? Or do you?

" Education is integral to maintaining the cultural and structural stability of society. Society, whether it is viewed on a local, national, or global scale, is in a perpetual state of flux. An effective education system is one that is adaptable to change. "

WILLARD R. DAGGETT

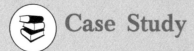

Case Study

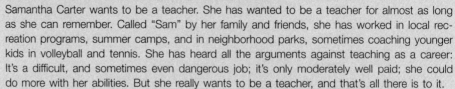

Samantha Carter's Diversity Class

Samantha Carter wants to be a teacher. She has wanted to be a teacher for almost as long as she can remember. Called "Sam" by her family and friends, she has worked in local recreation programs, summer camps, and in neighborhood parks, sometimes coaching younger kids in volleyball and tennis. She has heard all the arguments against teaching as a career: It's a difficult, and sometimes even dangerous job; it's only moderately well paid; she could do more with her abilities. But she really wants to be a teacher, and that's all there is to it.

Sam is also a volleyball player. She has a full athletic scholarship to the university and hopes to coach volleyball in the high school where she has already been hired to teach social studies in the fall. She has it all planned out: graduation in a few months, spend the summer using her new laptop (an early graduation present!) designing websites and interactive assignments and recording podcasts for the classes she'll be teaching, and finally, starting her new job in a suburban school system just far enough from her parents' home to give her a real sense of independence. American history...World history...Economics...Government... and, of course, volleyball! She can hardly wait!

Except...except, here she is, sitting in a required diversity course, wondering why in the world everyone is making such a fuss about all this "diversity stuff." Haven't we gotten past all that? On the Internet, after all, no one knows what your color is, or your religion, or your gender. Indeed, she and her friends often use "alternate" personalities while surfing the net, and clearly, people on MySpace and Facebook can also give themselves "other" faces and personalities. The important thing is what people have to say, not what they look like!

Still, she recalls that the superintendent told her that the district she will be teaching in is changing rapidly in terms of race and social class—did he tell her that because it might be a problem? Well, it isn't as if she has never spent any time with people who are different from her. Her volleyball team looks like the United Nations, and they all get along fine. She knows all their parents and siblings, and they will be friends forever. And it certainly isn't as if she doesn't already know that some groups of people still suffer from discrimination—some of her college community service credits have been spent working with kids in a low-income urban neighborhood, and she spent one whole summer helping rebuild houses in flood-damaged New Orleans. She really liked the people she worked with and wished she could have done more to help them.

Why, Sam thinks to herself, she could probably teach this course! And anyway, she thinks, teaching social studies will give her great opportunities to introduce her students to issues of difference. Yet, she thinks with a little pang of doubt, the urban kids she worked with had zero interest in history. And some of the people in New Orleans spoke with such an accent she could hardly understand them. And she doesn't feel too well prepared to deal with children with disabilities either, and no doubt there will be students with both medical and developmental disabilities in her classes.

Sam is learning that society is changing—in lots of ways. If there is one thing she has found in the past few years, it's that schools aren't like they used to be, even when she was in school. Her older brother teaches sixth-, seventh-, and eighth-grade social studies in a school not too far from the district where she will be teaching, and half of the students in his classes live in families headed by a single parent (some of them, fathers), one third are reading below grade level, and two thirds are eligible for free lunches. And his classes are far from being all white or even all native-born: he has African American students, East Indian, Vietnamese, and Central American students, as well as students who are the children of immigrants from the Middle East and the Sudan. His students include fundamentalist Christians, some are Catholic, a growing number are Muslims, several are Jewish, and one belongs to the Jehovah's Witness denomination. He has one student in a wheelchair after surviving a bad automobile accident, two students with breathing apparatuses because of asthma, and at least six who are waiting (after 6 months) to be tested to determine their eligibility for the severe behavior disorders class, which soon is going to be eliminated altogether because the school is moving to full inclusion.

Activity 1:
Mental Maps of Culture: An Ice Breaker

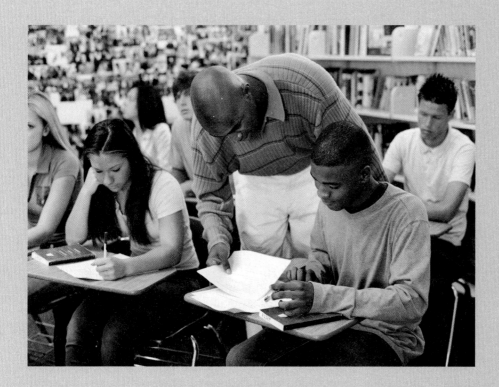

Other changes are taking place as well, both for her brother and for herself in her new school. The principal of her new high school announced proudly that every teacher will have a smart board by fall, and that there will be at least five computers in each room. He also mentioned, though, that the needs and expectations of students seem to be changing, even from just a few years ago. Growing up with technology as they have, today's students seem easily bored, have shorter attention spans, want things done quickly, and don't like to read long assignments, even if they are good readers. What's going on here?

In addition, 10 years after implementation of the No Child Left Behind Act, the performance of students, teachers, and school districts is being measured as never before. "The good news," says her professor, "is that the proponents of accountability really want all children to learn. The bad news is that we have never before really tried to educate all children to the same standard, and we are still not altogether sure how to do that."

A classmate raises his hand. "What," he asks, "about kids with really bad family problems, or kids whose parents aren't even there for them? What about kids with ADHD, or kids who just hate school? What about kids who are working 20 hours a week, or kids who just can't 'get it'? What about kids who don't speak English? What about kids who act out in violent ways?"

"Yes," says another classmate, "how are we supposed to teach everyone?"

"Perhaps," says the professor, "we'd be better off asking it another way: How are we to think about our practice of teaching so that everyone learns? The scene has shifted in schools today from an emphasis on teaching to an emphasis on learning. That's what accountability is about, and that's the reason for testing—to see what's been learned. This change in focus makes it all the more important that we understand differences among students—all kinds of differences, visible and invisible, because those differences may influence a student's learning, and our job is to create classrooms in which everyone learns."

Sam sighs. She really does want to be a teacher, but it seems to be a lot more complicated than she thought it would be. As the world around her changes, perhaps she, too, will have to make some significant changes if she is going to be as effective an educator as she hopes to be.

The Reality of Social Change

As we get used to living in the 21st century, Samantha, along with all of us, is witnessing changing circumstances in many areas of life that have widespread importance for the future of our country and our schools. Taken together, these changed circumstances are resulting in profound shifts in the nature of some of our basic social institutions, such as the economy, politics, religion, the family, and, of course, education.

Institutions in Transition

The term **social institution** has been defined as a formal, recognized, established, and stabilized way of pursuing some activity in society (Bierstedt, 1974). Another way to define a social institution is to think of it as a set of rules, or **norms**, that enable us to get through the day without having to figure out how to behave toward others, or whether to brush our teeth, or if, in fact, we should go to school or to work. In this society, as in all societies, we have rules that pattern the way we interact with family members, friends, people we see often, such as neighbors, teachers, or doctors, and even strangers who fill certain roles–the bus driver, the clerk in the store, the server in a restaurant. We know these rules because we have internalized them as children, and in a stable society we can depend on the rules staying relatively the same over time. All societies, including nonliterate ones, create social institutions–or sets of norms–that govern at least five basic areas of social need: *economics* (ways of exchanging goods and services), *politics* (ways of governing), *religion* (ways of worshiping one or more deities), *the family* (ways of ensuring the survival of children), and *education* (ways of bringing up and educating the younger generation so that the society will continue to exist).

In our society, and indeed in most of the world, people are witnessing profound changes in the nature of these basic institutions; in other words, the rules–or norms–are changing. Many scholars who study the past as a way to understand the future assert that these changes are so fundamental as to constitute a shift in the very nature of our civilization. Alvin Toffler (1980) was among the first scholar-futurists to warn that our institutions (what is normative in society) are changing in specific and characteristic ways and to hint at the rise and the effect of globalization on us all. Many of today's changes, Toffler suggested, are neither random nor independent of one another. He identified a number of events that *seem* to be independent from one another–the "breakdown" of the nuclear family, the global energy crisis, the influence of cable television, the loss of manufacturing jobs in the United States, and the emergence of separatist movements within national borders of many nations–and suggested that the reverse may, in fact, be true. These and many other seemingly unrelated events are interconnected and may be part of a much larger phenomenon that Toffler described as the death of industrialism and the rise of a new civilization that he called "the Third Wave."

Toffler is not the only one to have perceived these changes before most people were aware of them. In the early 1980s, John Naisbett's (1982) book *Megatrends: Ten New Directions Transforming Our Lives* added a new word to the language. In this work Naisbett accurately predicted the move toward globalization, the shift from an industrial economy to an "information" economy, and the growth of networks as a way of managing information (although he didn't even mention the Internet or the World

Alvin Toffler

Wide Web!). Later Naisbett and Patricia Aburdene (1990) wrote *Megatrends 2000: Ten New Directions for the 1990s*, in which they discussed the evolution of telecommunications, the rise of China as a competing power, and a growing need to "look below the surface" to find the meaning of these changes for real human beings and real organizations. Indeed, Aburdene (2005) now believes that our society is reaching a new phase in which the ideas of social responsibility, environmental values, and a spiritual dimension are beginning to reshape capitalism in interesting ways.

Although we cannot take all these predictions as absolute fact (predicting the future is a precarious occupation), it is worth thinking about our changing circumstances and the impact these changes are having (and will continue to have) on the way we live, work, play, govern ourselves, worship, and learn.

The Impact of Specific Changes on Basic Institutions

It is useful to think in terms of four different sets of specific changes that, taken together, seem to be reshaping our basic institutions. These areas, suggested by Willard Daggett (2005), are *globalization, demographics, technology*, and *changing values and attitudes among the generations*. New circumstances in each of these areas are having an impact on the way we think about and accomplish our purposes as a society. And each of these provides a rationale for greater cross-cultural knowledge and understanding. Let's take a closer look at how each of these areas may be changing the basic social institutions in our society.

Factors Influencing the Institution of Economics

1. From National to Global   For much of our nation's history, the U.S. economy has been based on manufacturing done by companies whose production could be found within the borders of the country. Today, our economy is firmly global. Indeed, the much-revered American corporation can hardly be said to exist any longer: The acquisition of raw material, manufacturing processes, and distribution of goods by such giants as Ford Motor Company, General Motors, or General Electric is done worldwide. In large measure because of advances in computer technology and high-speed travel, we find ourselves looking more and more often beyond our own borders for goods and services. Robert Reich (1992), former Secretary of Labor, described this reality almost two decades ago in the following terms:

> Consider some examples: Precision ice hockey equipment is designed in Sweden, financed in Canada, and assembled in Cleveland and Denmark for distribution in North America and Europe, respectively, out of alloys whose molecular structure was researched and patented in Delaware and fabricated in Japan. An advertising campaign is conceived in Britain; film footage for it is shot in Canada, dubbed in Britain, and edited in New York. A sports car is financed in Japan, designed in Italy, and assembled in Indiana, Mexico, and France, using advanced electronic components invented in New Jersey and fabricated in Japan. A microprocessor is designed in California and financed in America and West Germany, containing dynamic random-access memories fabricated in South Korea. A jet airplane is designed in the state of Washington and in Japan, and assembled in Seattle, with tail engines from Britain, special tail sections from China and Italy, and engines from Britain. A space satellite designed in California, manufactured in France, and financed by Australians is launched from a rocket made in the Soviet Union. Which of these is an American product? Which a foreign? How does one decide? Does it matter? (p. 112)

The effects of globalization are now increasingly encountered by each and every individual. Call the help desk with a problem with your computer, or have a question about your cable TV, and it is likely that the person you are speaking with on the other end of the phone is in India or Costa Rica. In your daily interactions, whether on campus or in your local stores, hospitals, and community in general, you are almost certain to encounter people who have immigrated to the United States and who speak a language other than English. And while there are many positive aspects to globalization, this is not always the case; and certainly not so for everybody on the planet. While you may be able to buy your favorite fruits and vegetables almost any time of the year relatively inexpensively and flown in from countries around the globe (currently, about 13% of our food is imported), we then encounter the possibility of large-scale salmonella outbreaks, as was experienced across the United States in 2008 from contaminated jalapeno peppers imported from Mexico. And the importation of inexpensive goods and services from outside our own borders oftentimes keeps others in poverty—both those overseas who are forced to work in substandard conditions and for minimal pay, and our own citizens who may lose their jobs.

Arguing that globalization is not new, Thomas Friedman (2006) writes that, in fact, there have been three phases of globalization. The era he calls *Globalization 1.0* began at the end of the 15th century when Columbus opened trade between Europe and the Americas and lasted until around the beginning of the 19th century. This was the era of national competition—often incited by religion or the lure of conquest—that began the process of integrating the countries of the world. *Globalization 2.0*, he asserts, lasted from the beginning of the 19th century to the beginning of the 21st century and was an era characterized not by *national* entities in competition but by the formation of *multinational* entities—usually companies and corporations—driving global integration. He writes:

**Globalization 101:
What Is Globalization?**

> These multinationals went global for markets and labor, spearheaded first by the expansion of the Dutch and English joint-stock companies and the Industrial Revolution. In the first half of this era, global integration was powered by falling transportation costs, thanks to the steam engine and the railroad, and in the second half by falling telecommunication costs—thanks to the diffusion of the telegraph, telephones, the PC, satellites, fiber-optic cable, and the early version of the World Wide Web. (p. 9)

Beginning around the year 2000, Friedman claims that *Globalization 3.0* emerged, a product of the convergence of three elements:

> the personal computer (which allowed every individual suddenly to become the author of his or her own content in digital form) with fiber-optic cable (which suddenly allowed all those individuals to access more and more digital content around the world for next to nothing) with the rise of work flow software (which enabled individuals all over the world to collaborate on that same digital content from anywhere, regardless of the distances between them). (pp. 10–11)

The differences between the first two eras of globalization and Globalization 3.0 are striking. Whereas the first two empowered national and multinational companies and corporations, Globalization 3.0 empowers *individuals* to "go global." Furthermore, while the first two eras of globalization were largely the product of European and American explorers, entrepreneurs, and companies, Globalization 3.0 is seeing the rise of individuals literally from everywhere, exercising their initiative in both competition and collaboration with other individuals around the planet, forming networks of communication and shared work that hold the possibility of competing effectively with–and sometimes superseding– both nation-states and national and multinational companies and corporations.

2. *A Growing Discrepancy Between the Rich and the Poor* In a special issue of *Time Magazine* titled "America at 300 Million" (2006), data from the Bureau of Labor Statistics and the IRS indicated that 50% of American workers report income of less that $30,000; 70% report income of less than $50,000; and 90% report income of less than $100,000. Of the remaining 10%, 9.5% report income of less than $500,000, and the top 0.5% report income between $500,000 and $10 million.

Another way to look at the discrepancy between the rich and the poor is by examining the ratio of CEO compensation to the compensation of the average nonmanagement worker. In 1982, the average CEO made 42 times the pay of the average worker; in 1990, about 107 times more. The highest discrepancy occurred in 2001, when the average CEO took in $525 for every $1 of worker pay. In 2004, that ratio had been reduced to 431:1 (Sahadi, 2005).

3. *A Change in the Work We Do* It will come as no surprise that manufactur- ing jobs in the United States are giving way to so-called service jobs. On the global scale, people around the world are increasingly divided by vast differences between rich and poor, and this discrepancy has widened in the past decade. The average U. S. citizen earns about $104.10 per day. This compares to those living in the poorest countries of the world (e.g., the Republic of Congo, Somalia, Haiti, Niger), who take home less than $1.00 per day. In 2006, for example, services provided by private businesses amounted to 67.8% of the U.S. domestic product. Financial services such as banking, insurance, and investment lead the way, as do real estate services. Other growing service industries are transporta- tion, health care, legal, scientific, and management services, education, wholesale and retail sales, arts, recreational services, hotels, restaurants, and other food and beverage services (USA Economy, 2007).

At the same time, the Council on Competitiveness notes that "Low value, commodity-based manufacturing is disappearing from the United States, moving to developing nations where routine manufacturing can be performed at low cost" (USA Economy, 2007). Because service jobs–especially in sales, recre- ational services, hotels, restaurants, and so forth–do not generally pay as well as manufacturing jobs have in the past, these shifts in the economy disproportion- ately affect lower-income families. Rachleff (2006) notes that this was also the case in the first third of the 20th century, when the great mining and manufac- turing companies had total control of workers. That situation changed when the labor movement of the 1930s and 1940s and "their contracts brought them not only improved wages and working conditions but also benefits including indi- vidual, family, and retiree healthcare coverage, paid vacations, and pensions. These benefits are not available to low-paid service workers in our economy today; moreover, the idea of unionism is not popular in jobs where workers are encouraged to put their patients and customers first, to see themselves as 'unskilled,' and to expect little reward for their work" (Rachleff, 2006).

In the past, labor unions and the contracts they negotiated provided the scaffolding for working-class families to rise into the middle class; that "ladder" doesn't exist today in many service industries, which employ–probably disproportionately–many minority, immigrant, and poor individuals. One of the tasks ahead, then, is to create conditions in the service sector such that people can "move up" the social ladder into the middle class.

Recent trends in globalization, like the growth of China and India, have increased the number of U.S. jobs "outsourced" to other countries. Between 1984 and 2004 more than 30 million U.S. workers lost their jobs, mostly in high import-competing manufacturing industries such as clothing, autos, and electronics. These industries account for only 30% of all manufacturing jobs in the United States, but 38% of manufacturing job loss. Of those workers displaced, about one in three moved into new jobs with equal or better incomes, but one in four suffered earnings losses of more than 30%. This trend will continue, with one estimate putting the number of white-collar job losses at 3.3 million by 2015–and this was predicted before the global economic downturn experienced in 2008. There are spin-off effects as well. Nearly 70% of Americans who have health insurance get their coverage through their employers, so losing a job can be extremely costly to families, with lost health coverage as well as lost wages (CDF, 2009).

4. A Change in Generational Attitudes About Work Until not too long ago, the norm was that folks went to work for a particular company and stayed there throughout their working lives. Indeed, as recently as 30 years ago, people who changed jobs too many times were considered quite undependable. Today, however, it's a different story. Although workers may frequently change jobs because their companies are moving production to another country, or eliminating jobs altogether, it is also the case that workers move to enhance their own prospects, and it is more likely today that workers will not work for the same company for 30 years.

Moreover, the so-called Millennial Generation has other characteristics that are likely to have an impact on economic reality. According to many observers, the generation born between 1980 and 2000 are "optimistic, talented, well-educated, collaborative, open-minded, influential and achievement-oriented" (Raines, 2002).

As all generations are, these new workers are shaped by the times in which they grow up. In the Millennials' case, *and for the middle class*, those times included, among other things, unprecedented affluence, scheduled lives, terrorism, and parent advocacy. As Raines (2002) notes, they have been bombarded with a unique set of messages since birth:

Be smart–you are special. They've been catered to since they were tiny. Think Nickolodeon, Baby Gap, and *Sports Illustrated for Kids*.

Leave no one behind. They were taught to be inclusive and tolerant of other races, religions, and sexual orientations.

Connect 24/7. They learned to be interdependent–on family, friends, and teachers. More Millennials say they can live without the television than without the computer. Many prefer chatting online to talking on the phone.

Achieve now! Some parents hired private agents to line up the right college; others got started choosing the right preschool while the child was still in the womb.

Serve your community. Fifty percent of high school students reported volunteering in their communities, many of their high schools requiring community service hours for graduation. On one Roper Survey, when Millennials were asked for the major cause of problems in the United States, they answered *selfishness*.

As a result of their upbringing, many young workers in this generation are looking for role models in the workplace, want more learning opportunities, want to work with friends, have fun at work, get respect for their ideas, even if they are young, and have time flexibility to pursue family and interest activities.

Factors Influencing the Institution of Politics

1. International Agreements Changes affecting economics have their counterparts in the political sphere as well. As we increasingly interact with people from other nations in matters of trade, we also increasingly interact with them politically, and political events occurring in other countries have a much more profound effect on our own political agenda than they used to. For example, the realization of the North American Free Trade Agreement (NAFTA), the Central American-Dominican Republic Free Trade Agreement (CAFTA-DR), the General Agreement on Tariffs and Trade (GATT) Treaty–as well as its successor, the World Trade Organization–are political responses to the facts of international trade. The end of the Cold War and the dissolution of the Soviet Union in 1989 was a defining feature of international politics as the 20th century drew to a close (see Chapter 7). Today, the recurring ethnic and religious wars around the world, as well as the recent terrorist attacks on American soil and on Western interests around the world, are expressions of new realities with which the United States must contend. Clearly, a day does not go by without some news of our entanglement with other countries that has political consequences for the United States. The norms have changed–we are doing politics differently.

North American Free Trade Agreement and the World Trade Organization

2. Increasing Debate Between So-Called Conservative and Liberal Voters
Over the past 20 years, conservative political ideas have come to the forefront on both economic and social issues. In part, this probably reflects a resistance to the very rapid change that characterizes the times in which we live. However, the blue state/red state dichotomy has been shown to be both overstated and simplistic. Indeed, an interesting series of political maps, called *cartograms,* showing voting patterns by states according to their populations rather than their geographical locations provides evidence that American voters are more "purple" than red or blue (Maps and Cartograms, 2004).

In some ways, these data indicate a decline in the power of the two major political parties in the United States and provide some intriguing questions about the future. For example, will we see a rise in third parties? Will there be a greater emphasis on the difference between economic and social issues in the political marketplace of ideas? Will a new generation of voters be more interested in the electoral process than their parents have been?

3. Political Participation It is often noted that less than 50% of Americans actually vote in any given election. This is not quite the case: 35% of eligible voters do vote regularly, and another 20% are registered but don't always vote. In 2008, both the number and percentage of so-called youth voters, ages 18 to 29, were up, and the total turnout of eligible voters in that presidential election was nearly 62% (United States Election Project). If current projections about the interest of the next generation in civic affairs prove to be accurate, it is possible that participation in elections will improve in the next few decades.

4. Change in Voting Technologies   Another change in the political landscape with respect to voting is the advent of electronic voting machines, which replace voting with pencil or stylus and the hand-counting of ballots. Debates center around the following issues: security, lack of a paper trail of votes cast, interference with the transmission of results, inability to conduct an independent recount, vulnerability to tampering with the machines before the vote, and machine malfunction (Wang, 2004).

Given that younger generations of Americans have been and are growing up accustomed to technological innovations, it is interesting to speculate on how long this debate may continue. On the other hand, younger generations are also, theoretically at least, more likely to be engaged in civic affairs. Clearly, there is going to continue to be a large role for education in giving young people both the knowledge and the judgment to support this engagement.

Factors Influencing the Institution of Religion

Religious Diversity

1. Increasing Diversity of Religious Ideas   In times of transition such as we are experiencing today, organized religion can serve as a stabilizing influence. However, the institutionalized churches of all faiths are undergoing change as well. Once largely a nation steeped in the Judeo-Christian heritage, the United States is now home to a growing number of faiths that are unfamiliar to many people. Buddhism, Islam, and other religions of the East and Middle East are growing as new immigrants bring their religious ideas and practices with them, with Islam being among the fastest growing religions in the nation. Similarly, a wide variety of relatively small but active congregations built around scientific, philosophical, and psychological ideas are appearing to proliferate—the so-called New Age religious sects.

Although demographic studies of the religious makeup of the American population vary according to both the time in which they were done and the methods used, in general about 80% of Americans follow some form of Christianity,

nearly 2% are Jewish, a bit more than 1% are Muslim, and at least 14% are unchurched. Within Christianity, however, there are multiple denominations, and often both conservative and liberal attitudes within each denomination, as well as differences within some denominations that speak to more or less evangelical beliefs and practices. Added to that are a growing number of African American Protestant churches, some of which are the historically black denominations and others that are essentially evangelical ministries claiming no denomination.

2. *The Rise of Fundamentalism in Many Religious Contexts* Conservative branches of mainline Protestant, Catholic, Jewish, and Muslim religions serve as havens for people for whom social change seems too rapid and too chaotic, and fundamentalist denominations (usually Protestant) are both the fastest growing religious organizations in the nation and, often, the most politically aware and active. Fundamentalism is not limited to Christianity but is also growing among young Jews and Muslims.

In Britain, for example, a recent study of young Muslims found a growing number to be in favor of the more orthodox practices of Islam, including wearing the *hijab* in public places, a stronger preference for Islamic schools, and *sharia* law. The report notes that "Religiosity amongst young Muslims is not about following their parents' cultural traditions, but rather, their interest in religion is more politicized" (Mirza, Senthilkumaran, & Ja'far, 2007). In Western societies, at least, fundamentalism seems to represent both a desire for order–or, as John Dewey called it, "a quest for certainty"–and a desire for a well-defined identity. That young people are increasingly attracted to fundamentalism in its various forms is also, perhaps, an indication of a generation of children who have been brought up to be conventional, sheltered by their parents in a period of affluence and of many choices.

3. *The Marriage of Religion and Politics* The founders of the United States were firm in their belief that religion and politics, or church and state, should be separate. Indeed, the nature of the separation of church and state written into the First Amendment of the Constitution is there not so much to involve religion in public affairs but to protect religious groups from interference by the state.

Nevertheless, we have nearly always carried religious ideas into the public (or political) sphere. Organized religions have, at various times in our history, been more or less important in the carrying out of public business. Today, and for the past two decades or so, some religious groups–notably conservative Protestant Christian groups–have become important "players" on the political scene, not only by putting forth agendas for public policy, but also by systematically organizing and supporting their members in elections, from school boards to Congress.

This is not, however, just an American phenomenon, but a global one, as can be seen by the involvement of religiously backed political (and military) forces in eastern Europe and the Middle East in the past 20 years. The same technological revolution that has provided innovative individuals and groups with the means to author their own digital content and link to others around the world for very little money has also provided the mechanism for individuals and groups to organize and carry their message (sometimes based on religious ideas) to others who, without this technology, would be unreachable. As Friedman (2006) cautions, "the playing field is not being leveled only in ways that draw in and superempower a whole new group of innovators. It's being leveled in a way that draws in and superempowers a whole new group of angry, frustrated, and humiliated men and women" (p. 8).

4. Generational Differences and the Role of Electronic Culture   Another shift that is having an impact on religion is the presence of a generation of young people who have been raised in a technologically rich environment and who are looking to all the major institutions, including religion, for new ways of understanding traditional messages and new forms of worship.

While issues and solutions vary, the next generation of church-goers appears to be giving its elders pause for reflection. For example, a new study of college students who identify as Jewish, sponsored by Hillel, the Foundation for Jewish Campus Life, shows that these students "are increasingly likely to be products of interfaith marriages, to have non-Jewish boyfriends and girlfriends, and to shun denominational labels" (Birkner, 2005). Indicating that this generation has a different understanding of identity, the director of the study's online student survey notes that

> they see their identity as a set of windows on a computer screen, and any number of screens can be open simultaneously. For them, it's not just a question of am I a Jewish American or an American Jew. They see themselves as American, Jewish, heterosexual and a volleyball player all at once. They don't feel the need for one of those windows to take over the whole desktop. (Birkner, 2005)

Similarly, two sociological studies of young Catholics note that this generation "is more individualistic, more tolerant of religious diversity and far less committed to the practices of their faith than older Catholics" (Heffern, 2007). And Arthur Jones (2001) of the *National Catholic Reporter*, writes:

> Millennial youth, in a nutshell, look and sound more like 1950s Catholics than anything since the '50s. But they're not.

Researchers Thomas and Rita Tyson Walters, in a study for St. Meinrad's Seminary focusing on priestly vocations among Millennial youth, show that Catholic high school students graduating in the year 2000 were optimistic; consider themselves religious; are in danger of being theologically illiterate; are "televiliterate"; trust their parents; and find themselves in a church of mixed messages. And they are not thinking about becoming priests or sisters.

Finally, Protestant Christian denominations are increasingly interested in framing the religious message in ways that the "wired generation" can understand. Typical of the language used by those who advocate meeting the religious needs of the newest generation by learning from the electronic culture to which they are so attuned is a passage from an exhortation on the Millennials from a youth ministry in St. Kitts and Nevis in the Caribbean:

> It's time to shift gears. The next generation is the net generation. They've grown up on the Internet. They've grown up networking. In my parents' generation they focused on buildings and institutions. Thank goodness, or we'd have nothing to stand on. . . . For the next generation, you must shift your emphasis from programs to relationships—from organization to networking—from committees to connecting—from boards to teams—from elections to spiritual gifts. (Youth-Impact Ministries, n.d.)

Factors Influencing the Institution of the Family

1. Increasing Age of Men and Women at the Time of Marriage and Childbirth   The age at which men and women marry in any society varies over time, and that is the case in the United States as well. In 1900, the average marriage age for men was 26 and for women, 22; by midcentury, it had fallen to

23 for men and 20 for women; but by 2005, it had reached the all-time high of 27 for men and nearly 26 for women (Lehrer, 2007).

Some authors believe that this phenomenon bodes well for marriage because marrying later in one's 20s often means that the partners have higher educational levels, which is, itself, a stabilizing factor in marriage. Moreover, since the overall life span is increasing—in 2003 the average life expectancy in the United States was 77.4 years (Arias, 2007)—ages for marriage and childbirth might be expected to rise. Debates still exist, however, about the relation between age of marriage and first children to divorce, health care, work life, religious affiliation, and other family and social issues. It is safe to say, though, that increasing the age at which typical couples marry will have some effects on the society as a whole.

2. *Increasing Diversity of Family Forms* In the family, too, we are witnessing profound changes in structure and organization. For the first time in 150 years, the number of households headed by single adults and unmarried couples is greater than those headed by married couples (Coontz, 2006). Recent research on the changing demographics of our families graphically portrays the changing nature of family life. For instance, in 1942, 60% of families could be described as nuclear families consisting of two parents and their children. Furthermore, if one believes the images that until relatively recently were often portrayed in basal readers, this nuclear family includes a dog and a cat all living happily together in a white house surrounded by a neat picket fence. In these families, the father's role was to leave home every day to earn the money to support the family, and the mother's role was to stay at home and raise the children. Those were the norms. Today, fewer than 10% of American families match that picture. The norms, again, have changed.

Examples in Children's Readers of the "Traditional" American Family

It is estimated today that about half of all marriages in the United States will be disrupted through divorce or separation. More than 10 different configurations are represented by the families of children in today's classrooms—a most significant one being the single-parent family, often a mother and child or children living in poverty. Increasingly, this single parent is a teenage mother. Another increasing family configuration, and a hotly debated topic, is one in which two adults of the same sex, committed to one another over time, are raising children who may be biologically related to one or the other adult, or who may have been adopted by them.

3. *Increasing Intermarriage Across Racial and Religious Boundaries* There has also been a corresponding increase in intermarriage between individuals from different ethnic or religious groups. Nearly one third of Latinos born in the United States, for instance, now intermarry, as do about 10% of African Americans. In some Asian American groups (Japanese Americans, for instance), more people marry outside the group than marry within the group (Cortes, 1999), and roughly 50% of American Jews marry outside their religion. For the first time in our history, the 2000 census allowed people to identify themselves with multiple race identifications. Only 2.4% of the population identified themselves as mixed, but it is estimated that at least 40% of the American citizenry has some racial mixing in the last three generations, including former president Bill Clinton and Martin Luther King (Hodgkinson, 2000–2001). Children of these mixed marriages will increasingly find themselves in our schools, as is evident in the 6.8% of young people under the age of 18 who claim similar multiple racial identities.

4. Increasing Effects of Poverty in a Globalized America   Poverty and its effects on children is not limited to so-called Third World societies. Consider these facts about children collected by the Children's Defense Fund (2003): 1 in 3 children is born to unmarried parents, half will live in a single parent family at some point in childhood, 1 in 4 lives with only one parent, 1 in 8 is born to a teenage mother, 1 in 13 was born with low birth weight, 1 in 15 lives at less than half the poverty level, 1 in 24 lives with neither parent, 1 in 60 sees their parents divorce in any year, 1 in 139 will die before their first birthday, and 1 in 1,056 will be killed by guns before age 20. In addition, 1 in 5 was born poor, 1 in 3 will be poor at some point in childhood, and 1 in 6 is born to a mother who did not receive prenatal care in the first trimester of pregnancy. One in 5 is born to a mother who did not graduate from high school, 1 in 5 has a foreign-born mother, 1 in 3 is behind a year or more in school, 2 in 5 never complete a single year of college, 1 in 7 has no health insurance, 1 in 7 has at least one worker in their family but still is poor, 1 in 8 lives in a family receiving food stamps, 1 in 8 never graduates from high school, and 1 in 12 has a disability. Clearly, the family pattern once considered the norm, that provided the image of the "right" and "proper" kind of family, and that guided the policies of our other institutions has changed.

Factors That Influence the Institution of Education

1. Changing Demographics of the School-Age Population and the Population as a Whole   All the institutional changes discussed thus far are inevitably reflected in the institution of schooling—its purposes, policies, and practices. For example, demographic changes with respect to the total population of the United States are first seen in our schools. It is projected that by the year 2040, children of color will comprise more than half the children in classrooms, up from approximately one third at the beginning of the 21st century (U.S. Census Bureau, 2007). Startling changes are already occurring in a number of places in the country. For example, more than a decade ago, students from minority groups comprised more than 50% of the school populations in California, Arizona, New Mexico, Texas, and New York. In these states, minority children soon may find themselves in the uncomfortable position of being the majority in a world whose rules are set by a more powerful minority. And recent census figures for California show that there is currently no majority cultural group in the state!

Demographics

Three factors are of primary importance in the shifting **demographics** of our population. First, immigration from non-European countries currently rivals the great immigrations from Europe that this country experienced at the turn of the 20th century. There is an important difference, however. In the early part of the 20th century, the majority of immigrants (87%) arrived from Europe. Except for language, it was relatively easy for these new immigrants to fit into the cultural landscape of the country; after all, many of these people looked similar to the majority of people around them. Today, 85% of the roughly 1 million immigrants who come to the United States each year come from Latin America and Asia (Cortes, 1999). Most look somewhat different from the mainstream, which immediately sets them apart. Indeed, many communities are becoming increasingly international as the phenomenon of globalization extends its reach.

Demographics for School Enrollment

Second, while birthrates among Americans as a whole are just holding their own, birthrates among nonwhite populations are considerably higher than they are among whites. Among European Americans, for instance, birthrates have dropped to 1.4 for every 2 people, well below the 2.1 replacement level. Birthrates for all other groups have remained the same or increased slightly. When most current teacher education students were born (the late 1980s to early 1990s), approximately 1 in 4 schoolchildren was a child of color (traditionally referred to as minority students). By the year 2020, it is likely that this figure will increase to 1 in 2, and many of these children will be poor. By midcentury, people of color will become the majority of Americans. By 1998, European Americans had become a numerical minority in 243 U.S. counties, with 42 of those counties making the transition since 1994 (Cortes, 1999). And in 1994, in the 25 largest school districts in the United States, children of color comprised about 72% of the total school enrollment (National Center for Educational Statistics [NCES], 2007). By 2056, the average U.S. resident will trace his or her descent to Africa, Asia, Central and South America, the Pacific Islands, or the Middle East—almost anywhere but white Europe (U.S. Census Bureau, 2010).

Third, the total population of children in relation to adults in the United States is changing as the public grows older. Although the number of school-age children will increase from now until the year 2025, the number of American youth compared to citizens age 65 and older will continue to shrink (U.S. Census Bureau, 2010). An increasing concern is that there will not be enough workers to support the aging baby boom population, who will be a tremendous drain on the nation's Social Security system at a time when the system itself may be in jeopardy. In addition, emerging medical technology is enabling people to live longer lives, and the health care needs of an aging population are projected to strain the government's Medicare program to its limits unless adjustments are made. Both of these concerns mean that public resources for school-age populations will be in direct and serious competition with the needs of older Americans.

2. Increasing Language Diversity Among Schoolchildren

Along with ethnic and racial diversity often comes linguistic diversity. For the first time in our history, the 2000 Census Bureau printed questionnaires in languages other than English, including Spanish, Chinese, Vietnamese, Korean, and Tagalog (the major language of the Philippines). Increasing numbers of children are entering school from minority language backgrounds and have little or no competence in the English language. Nearly 1 in 5 Americans, some 47 million individuals age 5 and older, speak a language other than English at home, reflecting an increase of approximately 50% during the past decade (U.S. Census Bureau, 2007). It is estimated that there

National Association of Bilingual Education

are approximately 4.5 million Limited English Proficient (LEP) students, or 9% of the school age population, in schools in the United States, many of whom speak Spanish as their primary language (Baca, 2000), making the United States the fifth largest Spanish-speaking country in the world. The majority of these students (67%) can be found in the five states of California, Texas, New York, Florida, and Illinois, with the greatest percentage of increases being in Delaware, Kentucky, and south Carolina, but most school districts in the country have LEP students. Spanish is the most common second language spoken in America's classrooms, spoken by 75% of English language learners, although an increasing number of students are entering the schools speaking Arabic, Chinese, Russian, Hmong, Khmer, Lao, Thai, and Vietnamese. More than 50% of LEP students are in grades K–4, with 77% coming from poor backgrounds. A relatively high dropout rate characterizes this group of children in spite of all our efforts at bilingual education. Since a person's language provides the symbols used to understand the world, children whose symbol systems differ from those of the dominant group are likely to see the world from a different perspective, to look for meaning in different ways, and to attribute different meanings to common objects and processes. Although these students may be perceived as a challenge to our educational system in the years ahead, one consequence of successfully accommodating this diversity is that all of us–students, teachers, and communities alike–will become more knowledgeable, more accepting, and better skilled at communicating with people from different backgrounds.

3. Increasing Concern About Gender Differences in School Outcomes   In the 1970s and 1980s, there emerged an increasing awareness in many classrooms of a difference among children that is so fundamental that it has been overlooked as a matter of inquiry throughout most of our history. That difference is gender. Because we have included both girls and boys, at least in elementary education, since the very beginning of the common school, and because our political and educational ideals assume that school is gender neutral, the effect of gender on children's education has not been analyzed until recently. In the past 35 years, however, considerable research has been done on differences in the social and educational lives and academic outcomes of boys and girls in school. In the earlier years, the focus was on girls–the "stereotypical" roles they saw themselves playing in textbooks, the way in which they were counseled away from math and science courses, the ways in which teachers interacted with them, and ways in which the "culture of the school" tended to channel them in certain directions, both socially and vocationally.

Today, there are some who are equally concerned with the educational lives and outcomes of boys–the fact that they are dropping out of school at a higher rate, that their success in literacy is lower, and that fewer are academically prepared for college (and, in fact, are attending college in reduced numbers). Whatever the case, it is true that gender roles have changed in our society and that these changes have an effect on all our institutions, including, of course, education.

4. An Increasing "Clash of Cultures" Between Teachers and Students
A considerable discrepancy continues to exist between the makeup of the student population in most schools and that of the teaching force. Most of our nation's teachers continue to come from a rather homogeneous group, with approximately 85% being European American and middle class (U.S. Census Bureau, 2004). Indeed, the profile of the teacher education student that emerged from Zimpher's (1989) study has not changed appreciably. Typically, the teacher education student

is a monolingual white female from a low-middle- or middle-class suburban or rural home who wants to teach children who are just like herself. Women outnumber men by 3 to 1 in the teaching force, with nearly 90% of Pre K–6, and 59% of high school teachers being women (U.S. Census Bureau, 2010).

These figures contrast sharply with the student diversity that currently exists in schools and that is projected to increase in the years ahead. A considerable number of children are thus missing important role models who represent their background within the school setting–boys in the early years, and children of color throughout the educational experience in general. Majority students as well miss having role models who represent groups other than their own.

Equally critical is the fact that teachers (like many other people) tend to be culture-bound, to have little knowledge or experience with people from other cultures, which limits their ability to interact effectively with students who are different from them. Indeed, in Zimpher's study, 69% of white teacher education students reported spending all or most of their free time with people of their own racial or ethnic background. This, too, has not changed appreciably in recent years. More disturbing, this same study reported that a substantial number of teacher education students do not believe that low-income and minority learners are capable of grasping high-level concepts in the subjects they are preparing to teach. Finally, the traditional identification of teaching as women's work means that even multiculturally sophisticated teachers are usually powerless to make their school's culture more accommodating to female and underrepresented students because white males are usually in key decision-making roles.

Rethinking Schools and Learning: The Effort to Reform Our Schools

In terms of traditional definitions of social order, it appears that most of our social institutions are not working very well in the beginning of this new millennium. Another way to state this observation is to say that the norms governed by our institutions have changed. In this context, the principle values of democratic equality, liberty, and community are once again called into question. What does equality mean when people from a variety of cultures around the world are competing for the same jobs? What does liberty mean when language barriers prevent common understanding? What does community mean when allegiance to one's group prevents commonality with people in other groups?

Some scholars have argued that the changes we are experiencing require a shift from the ideals of a Jeffersonian political democracy (in which democratic principles are defined by individualism) to the ideals of a cultural democracy in which democratic principles are defined by cultural pluralism (McClelland & Bernier, 1993). Such a shift involves a radical change in our beliefs about how we are to get along with one another, what kinds of information and skills we need to develop, and how we are to interpret our national ideals and goals. Among other changes, this cultural view of democracy requires a fundamental rethinking of our national goals and how we structure or organize schools in relation to those goals. Schooling is, after all, the institution charged not only with imparting necessary information and skills but also with ensuring that young people develop long-cherished democratic attitudes and values. Schooling alone cannot completely alter the larger society in which it exists, but schooling can influence as well as reflect its parent society. And since teachers can engender or stifle new ideas and new ways of doing things with their students, they are in a position to influence both the direction and pace of change in our society.

As Sam is learning in her teacher education program, one of the most significant results of rethinking schools and teaching is the testing and accountability movement. Although there is considerable debate about both the means and ends of the movement, taken at face value it signals a major change not only in the way we think about schools but also in the way we think about teaching and learning. It is no longer acceptable to eliminate certain children from the ranks of the educable. Nor is it acceptable to think that it's all right if some children don't measure up to standards, or that you just can't "teach everyone." Indeed, the emphasis is now squarely on learning outcomes for *all* children.

Fortunately, some teachers have accepted this challenge and are learning to think about their practice in more inclusive ways. They work in classrooms in all regions of the country, and, increasingly, in schools around the world—sometimes alone and sometimes with colleagues who are also excited about new possibilities. They work with students of all backgrounds: white and nonwhite, wealthy and poor, boys and girls, rural and urban, domestic and international. They work with students of varied religions and of no particular religion, with students who have vastly different abilities, and with students who have different sexual orientations. They work in wealthy districts that spend a great deal of money on each student and in poor districts that have little in the way of resources. But most important, their classrooms reflect their belief that all children can succeed. In 21st-century schools and classrooms, teachers see change as an opportunity rather than a problem and difference as a resource rather than a deficit.

The Difficulty of Change

Change is difficult, particularly when it deals with the fundamental beliefs, attitudes, and values around which we organize our lives. Attempts at such change often result in hostility or in an effort to preserve, at any cost, our familiar ways of doing things and thinking about the world around us. The universal nature of such resistance to change is illustrated in the following parable.

The Wheat Religion: A Parable

Once upon a time there was a group of people who lived in the mountains in an isolated region. One day a stranger passed through their area and dropped some wheat grains in their field. The wheat grew. After a number of years, people noticed the new plant and decided to collect its seeds and chew them. Someone noticed that when a cart had accidentally ridden over some of the seeds, a harder outer covering separated from the seed and what was inside was sweeter. Someone else noticed that when it rained, the grains that had been run over expanded a little, and the hot sun cooked them. So, people started making wheat cereal and cracked wheat and other wheat dishes. Wheat became the staple of their diet.

Years passed. Because these people did not know anything about crop rotation, fertilizers, and cross-pollination, the wheat crop eventually began to fail.

About this time, another stranger happened by. He was carrying two sacks of barley. He saw the people starving and planted some of his grain. The barley grew well. He presented it to the people and showed them how to make bread and soup and many other dishes from barley. But they called him a heretic.

"You are trying to undermine our way of life and force us into accepting you as our king." They saw his trick. "You can't fool us. You are trying to weaken us and make us accept your ways. Our wheat will not let us starve. Your barley is evil."

He stayed in the area, but the people avoided him. Years passed. The wheat crop failed again and again. The children suffered from malnutrition. One day the stranger came to the market and said, "Wheat is a grain. My barley has a similar quality. It is also a grain. Why don't we just call the barley grain?"

Now since they were suffering so much, the people took the grain, except for a few who staunchly refused. They loudly proclaimed that they were the only remaining followers of the True Way, the Religion of Wheat. A few new people joined the Wheat Religion from time to time, but most began to eat barley. They called themselves The Grainers.

For generations, the Wheat Religion people brought up their children to remember the true food called wheat. A few of them hoarded some wheat grains to keep it safe and sacred. Others sent their children off in search of wheat, because they felt that if one person could happen by with barley, wheat might be known somewhere else too.

And so it went for decades, until the barley crop began to fail. The last few Wheat Religion people planted their wheat again. It grew beautifully, and because it grew so well, they grew bold and began to proclaim that their wheat was the only true food. Most people resisted and called them heretics. A few people said, "Why don't you just admit that wheat is a grain?"

The wheat growers agreed, thinking that they could get many more wheat followers if they called it grain. But by this time, some of the children of the Wheat Religion people began to return from their adventures with new seed, not just wheat, but rye and buckwheat and millet. Now people began to enjoy the taste of many different grains. They took turns planting them and trading the seed with each other. In this way, everyone came to have enough sustenance and lived happily ever after.

This parable carries many metaphorical messages: It applauds diversity and recognizes that a society cannot function to its fullest when it ignores the ideas, contributions, efforts, and concerns of any of its people. The parable illustrates some of the consequences of unreasonable prejudice but also recognizes the powerful emotions that underlie a prejudiced attitude. It also indicates the power of naming something in a way that is familiar and comfortable to those who are uncomfortable about accepting something new.

But perhaps most important, the parable recognizes the tendency people have to resist change. People are creatures of habit who find it difficult to change, whether at the individual level, the institutional level, or the societal level. People often work from one set of assumptions, one pattern of behavior. Because of the way in which people are socialized, these habits of thought and behavior are so much a part of them that they find it very difficult to think that things can be done in any other way. Some habits people develop are positive and constructive; others are negative and limiting. The story shows us that sometimes even a society's strengths can become weaknesses. And yet new circumstances and opportunities arise in each generation that demand that new perspectives, attitudes, and solutions be sought. Such circumstances are evident today in the changing face of the American classroom, and much of the responsibility for change must lie with teachers and teacher educators.

How prepared are *you* to accept the reality of change? How ready are *you* to examine some of your own beliefs and ideas about others? About yourself? About how *you* can interact with others? Are you at a point where, like Sam in the case study, you can begin to see how critical it is that you may have to change?

Ideological Perspectives on Multicultural Education

Attention to social differences among students has a relatively long history in this society, beginning at least with the arguments for the common school (which was intended to give students of different social class backgrounds a "common" educational experience that would enable the society to continue to be governed by "we, the people"). During some periods of our history, the focus was also on assimilation to a "common culture," by which was meant a dominant, largely Anglo society. During other periods–notably in the early years of the 20th century, when black scholars began to develop curricular materials on the African American experience in America, and in the 1940s, when the Intergroup Education movement had as its main objective the reduction of prejudice and discrimination in the U.S. population–various attempts have been made to perceive difference as a strength rather than as a problem.

The field now known as multicultural education emerged in the aftermath of the civil rights movement in the 1960s, first with the ethnic studies movement and later with a somewhat broader "multicultural" education effort. Within that effort (and outside it as well), there are a variety of perspectives on both the definition and the goals of multicultural education, which will be discussed in greater detail later in the book. Essentially, **multicultural education** can be defined as a process of educational reform that assures that students from all groups (racial, ethnic, socioeconomic, ability, gender, etc.) experience educational equality, success, and social mobility.

Some important questions emerge from what is in fact a healthy debate about our ability to provide educational opportunity and success for all children. Some of these questions have existed from the beginning; others have emerged as knowledge has increased and times have changed. Consider the following:

- Is multicultural education for everyone, or for minority students alone?
- Should multicultural education focus on the individual student, on the student as a member of a group, or on both?
- If multicultural education takes as its focus the study of group identity and experience, which groups should be included?
- To what extent should multicultural education include the study of relationships of power along with the history and contributions of all people?
- Is multicultural education academic or political or both?
- Will multicultural education, as an ideological movement, divide us as a people or bring us closer together?
- Are multicultural teaching practices good for everyone?
- To what extent should multicultural education have as a goal the reconstruction of the whole society?
- Is multicultural education centered on domestic (i.e., American) issues of diversity, or should it take as its central idea a more global understanding of difference?

All of these questions are important, in part because they are inexorably related.

Given the interdependent nature of the world in which we live, it is becoming less and less possible to think about purely American (or, to be more accurate, 'United Statesian') issues of difference. If the students being taught happen to belong mostly to one group or another, it is still the case that all of them, at some point in their lives, will need to learn how to understand and work with those who are different from themselves. If you think that local issues of inequality, poverty, and unequal access to education, housing, and jobs are central to

Multicultural Education

Americans' work concerns, consider that well over half the world's population is struggling with the same issues (Cushner, 1998). Americans work to preserve and protect democratic institutions in this society while millions of people around the world try to understand what democracy really is.

Multicultural education, both as an organized field of study and practice and as an ideological perspective, has witnessed a continued broadening of its scope and interests over the years. Increasingly, the field and its ideologies are turning toward a more global sensibility. This change does not mean that local or national issues are no longer important; it means that what Americans have and continue to learn locally has important implications for global action. It also means that, inasmuch as we are not the only society struggling with issues of difference, there is much we can learn from others around the world. For instance, what can we learn from the French as they struggle with the question of whether or not to allow Muslim girls to wear the hijab, or head scarf, in public schools? What can we learn from the way Arabs and Jews are portrayed in textbooks in Palestinian and Israeli schools?

This book is based in part on a notion of intercultural interactions and their cognitive, emotional, and developmental aspects. An intercultural interaction can be domestic–that is, between two (or more) people within the same nation that come from different cultural backgrounds–or it can be international, between two (or more) people from different countries. The cultural identity of the parties involved in an interaction may come from a limited and mutually reinforcing set of experiences or from more complex and sometimes conflicting elements. The significant difference in an interaction may be race or class or religion or gender or language or sexual orientation; it may be physical or attitudinal in origin; it may be age-related or status-related; or any combination of these.

Regardless of the kind of differences involved, all people tend to approach significant differences in similar, oftentimes negative, ways. That is, to understand the processes involved is a first step toward overcoming these differences; and both culture-specific knowledge and culture-general knowledge are prerequisites on the road to social justice.

Goals of This Book

This book is about change, especially as it relates to diversity. It is about teaching all children in a society that is growing more diverse each year. It is about changes in classrooms and in the act of teaching within those classrooms. It is about changes in schools and in the larger society in which these schools are embedded. It is equally about change within oneself, for change in the larger dimensions of society cannot occur without significant changes in one's own perception, attitudes, and skills. All these environments (self, classrooms, schools, and society) are connected, so that changes in any one of them produce disequilibrium and change in the others. Their connectedness, and the mutual influence that each one exerts on the others, is visually depicted in Figure 1.1.

As a teacher in the 21st century, you will spend your career in ever-changing schools, schools whose mission will be to help society make an orderly transition from one kind of civilization to another. Your ability to feel comfortable and

Figure 1.1
Interconnected
Environments

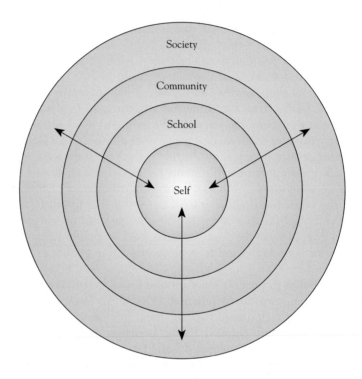

operate effectively within such a changing environment will require a unique set of cultural understandings and interpersonal skills that go beyond traditional pedagogy. These skills, perspectives, and attitudes that you as a teacher must adopt in order to coalesce diverse students into an effective learning community must also be transmitted to the students in your charge, who will live their lives in the same kind of highly interconnected and interdependent world. You are thus walking both sides of a double-edged sword, so to speak. The process that you undergo to become more effective working across cultures must ultimately become content that you teach to students. This feat will not be easy!

Figure 1.2 illustrates four basic goals of this book, which can be viewed as steps in understanding intercultural education and your role as an educator in an inclusive system. A word about each goal follows.

Goal 1: To Recognize Social and Cultural Change

The first step in providing an education that is truly multicultural is to improve students' understanding of the concept of pluralism in American society. Pluralism in this context must consider such sources of cultural identity as nationality, ethnicity, race, gender, socioeconomic status, religion, sexual orientation, geographic region, health, and ability/disability, and must look particularly at how each of these identities has had an impact on the individual as well as the group. This step requires that teachers understand the social changes that have historically and are currently taking place in our pluralistic society; these social changes provide the underlying rationale for multicultural education and are found in Chapters 1 and 2 as well as throughout the book.

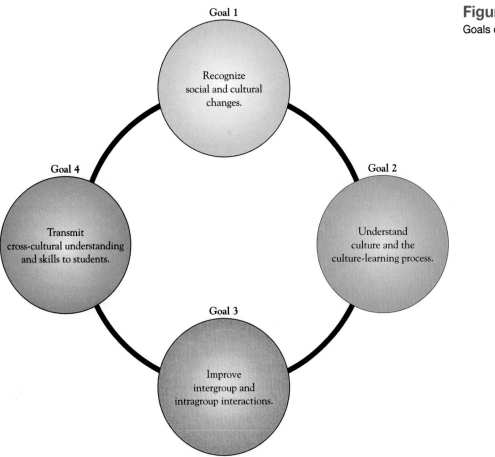

Figure 1.2
Goals of This Book

Goal 2: To Understand Culture, Learning, and the Culture-Learning Process

After establishing the need for an education that is multicultural, it is necessary to understand just what is meant by that term. What does the term *culture* refer to, and how do people come to acquire different cultural identities? With what knowledge do children already come to school? Too often schools do not legitimize the experiences children bring with them to the school; instead schools label some children as failures because their backgrounds, including their language and culture, are not seen as adequate or legitimate. Teachers must thus expand their knowledge base of culture and the different groups found in the United States as well as abroad. This means that curriculum content must be expanded and pedagogy adapted to include the experiences of all students. Chapter 3 examines these issues and in the process provides models of the sources of cultural learning and of the culture-learning process. An important recognition here is that differences within groups are often as important as differences between groups. Individuals belong simultaneously to many different groups, and their behavior can be understood only in terms of their simultaneous affiliation with these many groups. These models illustrate how culture filters down to the individual learner who actively engages with it, accepting and absorbing certain elements and rejecting and modifying others.

Goal 3: To Improve Intergroup and Intragroup Interactions

While Goal 2 is to examine how individuals come to acquire their particular cultural identity; Goal 3 is to show how culturally different people interact with one another and how these interactions can be improved. We must work to improve intergroup as well as intragroup interactions. We must also learn how individuals develop intercultural competence and improve their interactions with other cultures. Goal 3 demands attention to such issues as development of intercultural sensitivity, cross-cultural understanding and interaction, attribution and assessment across groups, and conflict management. Teachers, in particular, must broaden their instructional repertoire so that it reflects an understanding of the various groups with whom they will interact. To help teachers understand the interaction between culturally different individuals (whether from different groups or from the same group), Chapter 4 presents a model of intercultural interaction that applies culture learning to ourselves as well as to our students and that develops a culture-general model of behavior. These models help us analyze the nature of intercultural interaction, and they show how key concepts can be applied to various types of school situations. Chapter 5 offers some useful models of development and synthesizes them with a new and somewhat more sophisticated model of intercultural development that helps increase the number of concepts as well as the language with which we can profitably understand and discuss these issues.

Goal 4: To Transmit Intercultural Understanding and Skills to Students

The book's final goal is to help teachers transmit to students the same understandings and skills that are contained in (1) the model for explaining cultural differences and (2) the model for improving intercultural interaction in order to prepare multicultural citizen-actors who are able and willing to participate in an interdependent world. That is, this book strives to empower action-oriented, reflective decision makers who are able and willing to be socially and politically active in the school, community, nation, and world. This book is concerned not only with developing the knowledge and skill of practicing teachers, but also with transferring this knowledge to the pupils in their charge. Thus, individuals become proactive teachers and reflective practitioners who can ultimately prepare reflective citizen-actors (their students) for an interdependent world. The content of these models is universal. It applies to all intercultural situations, not just those confronted by teachers in classrooms and schools. Teaching these understandings and skills to students can be accomplished both through teacher modeling and through explicit instruction, and both methods are illustrated in the remaining chapters of the book.

The Role of Stories, Cases, and Activities

Stories

This book contains many stories because stories help us visualize and talk about new ideas and experiences. Some stories are about real people and events, while others, like the story of the wheat people, are folktales and parables. Stories contain the power to speak about complex human experiences; in this book, stories speak about how people experience the fact of human diversity. Stories help us to see the universals within the experience. Everyone, no matter what his or her cultural or biological differences, goes through similar stages of experience when confronted with change. Stories, like no other literary device, help us cut through the morass of individual and cultural differences that separate us and enable us to focus on the universals of the experience as we come to grips with those changes.

Case Studies and Critical Incidents

Because it is difficult to imagine situations with which you have had little experience, this book develops a series of Case Studies and Critical Incidents describing multicultural teaching situations that you might encounter. These scenarios are actual or synthesized real-life situations that have been described by a number of researchers and practitioners. Think of them as scenes in a play about schools with a multicultural student population. Most cases have been generated from multiple sources, each of which is noted in the list of references.

Because the cases cover a variety of communities and classrooms with diverse kinds of people in them, multiple issues are embedded in most of the cases. Although each case is designed to illustrate one or more particular issues related to the topic at hand, the portraits of people, places, ideas, and activities are rich enough that they can also be used to discuss topics in other chapters. Taken together, these cases illustrate a number of complex classroom realities that defy simple right-and-wrong solutions. Rather, they present small dramas in which a number of interpretations are possible and in which a number of ideas can be used to develop plans of action and fallback positions. Each chapter begins with a Case Study that introduces many of the concepts that will be further developed. Critical Incidents can be found at the end of many of the chapters that ask you to give further consideration to the topics presented.

Summary

This chapter provides an overview of some of the factors that are undergoing change in American society and that have an influence in the lives of children and teachers in schools. Such rapid social change has resulted in schools being caught in the transition from the Second Wave, an earlier factory model that offered a standardized curriculum for all, to the Third Wave, a more globally oriented dynamic model that attempts to address social change and prepare a citizenry that is more inclusive, integrative, and proactive. This book is designed to assist pre-service and in-service teachers to (1) recognize social and cultural change, (2) understand culture and the culture-learning process in self and others, (3) improve intergroup and intragroup interactions, and (4) transmit cross-cultural understandings and skills to students. The chapter also recognizes that change is difficult, yet is a force that we all must understand and accommodate—both as individuals and as institutions.

Chapter Review

Go to the Online Learning Center at www.mhhe.com/cushner7e to review important content from the chapter, practice with key terms, take a chapter quiz, and find the Web links listed in this chapter.

Key Terms

demographics 16

multicultural education 22

norms 6

social institution 6

Reflective Questions

1. Identify three changes that American society is undergoing, and discuss how those changes are reflected in schools.

2. Think back to your experiences in elementary or high school. What indication do you have that your school was attempting to become a different kind of school? What indication do you have that your school was reflective of an information-age school?

3. In the case study, Sam questions why she needs to be in a diversity course. What experiences have you had that might lead you to say that you are well prepared for diversity? In what areas do you not feel as well prepared?

References

Aburdene, P. (2005). *Megatrends, 2010: The rise of conscious capitalism.* Charlottesville, VA: Hampton Roads.

America at 300 million. What we earn. (2006, October 30). *Time Magazine, 168*(18), 47–48.

Arias, E. (2007). Statistics from United States life tables, 2003. *National Vital Statistics Reports, 54*(14). Retrieved from http://www.cdc.gov/nchs/data/nvsr/nvsr54/nvsr54_14.pdf

Baca, L. (2000, November 15). *The status and future of bilingual education.* Paper presented at the 10th annual conference of the National Association for Multicultural Education, Orlando, FL.

Bierstedt, R. (1974). *The social order.* New York: McGraw-Hill.

Birkner, G. (2005, November 4). Millennials forcing big changes at Hillel. *The Jewish Week* [Electronic version]. Retrieved from http://www.jewishweek.org/news/newscontent.php3?artid=11622

Children's Defense Fund. (2003). *American children's yearbook.* Retrieved from http://childrensdefense.org

Children's Defense Fund. (2009). Retrieved from http://childrensdefense.org.

Coontz, S. (2006, October 22). Marriage as a social contract. *The Philadelphia Inquirer* [Electronic version]. Retrieved from http://www.contemporaryfamilies.org/subtemplate.php?t=inTheNews&ext=marriageascontract

Cortes, C. (1999, May). The accelerating change of American diversity. *The School Administrator,* 12–14.

Cushner, K. (1998). *International perspectives on intercultural education.* Lanham, MD: Lawrence Erlbaum.

Daggett, W. R. (2005). Preparing students for their future [White paper]. Retrieved from http://www.icle.net/pdf/Preparing%20Students%20for%20Their%20Future%206-05.pdf

Friedman, T. L. (2006). *The world is flat: A brief history of the twenty-first century, updated and expanded.* New York: Farrar, Strauss, & Giroux.

Heffern, R. (2007, March 6). 'Bookend' generations–Studies point to much smaller U.S. church. *National Catholic Reporter Online.* Retrieved from http://www.catholic.org/national/national_story.php?id=23289

Hodgkinson, H. (2000–2001). Educational demographics: What teachers should know. *Educational Leadership, 58*(4), 6–11.

Jones, A. (2001, March 30). Engaging, keeping new Catholic generations. *National Catholic Reporter Online.* Retrieved from http://www.natcath.com/NCR_Online/archives/033001/033001s.htm#TOP

Lehrer, E. (2007, May 28). Are individuals who marry later too set in their ways to make their marriages work? *Council on Contemporary Families.* Retrieved from http://www.contemporaryfamilies.org/subtemplate.php?t=pressReleases&ext=marryolder

Maps and cartograms of the 2004 U.S. presidential election results. (2004). Retrieved from http://www.cscs.umich.edu/~crshalizi/election/

McClelland, A., & Bernier, N. (1993). A rejoinder to Steve Tozer's "Toward a New Consensus Among Social Foundations Educators." *Educational Foundations, 7*(4), 61.

Mirza, M., Senthilkumaran, A., & Ja'far, Z. (2007). *Living apart together: British Muslims and the paradox of multiculturalism.* London: Policy Exchange.

Naisbett, J. (1982). *Megatrends: Ten new directions transforming our lives.* New York: Warner Books.

Naisbett, J., & Aburdene, P. (1990). *Megatrends 2000: Ten new directions for the 1990s.* New York: Morrow.

National Center for Educational Statistics. (2007, May 22). Retrieved from http://nces.ed.gov

Rachleff, P. (2006). *Welcome to the service economy.* Retrieved from http://www.zmag.org/content/showarticle.cfm?ItemID=10876

Raines, C. (2002). *Managing millennials. Generations at work.* Retrieved from http://www.generationsatwork.com/articles/millenials.htm

Reich, R. (1992). *The work of nations.* New York: Vintage Books.

Sahadi, J. (2005, August 30). *CEO pay: The sky gets even higher.* Retrieved from http://money.cnn.com/2005/08/26/news/economy/ceo_pay/

Toffler, A. (1980). *The third wave.* New York: William Morrow.

U.S. Census Bureau. (2001). Retrieved from http://www.census.gov/population/ceb2000

USA Economy in Brief. (2007). *A service economy.* International Information Programs, U.S. Department of State. Retrieved from http://usinfo.state.gov/products/pubs/economy-in-brief/page3.html

U.S. Census Bureau. (2010). *American Fact Finder.* Retrieved from http://factfinder.census.gov, and http://www.census.gov/hhes/www/ioindex/reports.html

United States Election Project. (2006). Retrieved from http://elections.gmu.edu/Voter_Turnout_2004.htm

Wang, T. A. (2004). Understanding the debate over electronic voting machines. *Reform Elections.org.* Retrieved from http://www.reformelections.org/publications.asp?pubid=475

Youth-Impact Ministries. (n/d). Retrieved from http://www.youth-impact.org/millenials.htm

Zimpher, N. L. (1989). The RATE project: A profile of teacher education students. *Journal of Teacher Education, 40*(6), 27–30.

Chapter 2

Multicultural Education

Historical and Theoretical Perspectives

Focus Questions

1. As a matter of principle, do you think that differences in language, religion, and culture should be recognized and taken into account in schools, or should schools be the central place in American society where all students are "made into" good Americans?

2. What do you think the phrase "good American" means?

3. What are some challenges and benefits to the idea of religious pluralism today?

4. Do you think faith-based schools should receive support from federal and state tax funds?

5. On balance, do you believe that recent waves of immigration into the United States are a major problem or a major benefit to the society as a whole?

❝ Scholars describe the United States as one of history's first universal or world nations—its people are a microcosm of humanity with biological, cultural, and social ties to all other parts of the earth. **❞**

NATIONAL COUNCIL FOR THE SOCIAL STUDIES

When Noah Webster observed that "our national character is not yet formed," he identified a central dilemma that still faces the United States, as well as many other multiethnic nations (as cited in Frost, 1942, p. 1.41.1). This land of immigrants is, indeed, a land in which it is not all that difficult for many people to feel like strangers in their own country.

In the United States, one major instrument for attempting to create unity out of diversity has been the public school system, which has been used as a powerful tool for socializing us into a common culture. Resistance to this attempt at socialization has also been a part of our history, either by those who have not wanted to be "melted," or those who believe their vision of the "American way of life" should be the model to which all others must be formed. Thus the public schools have always been a battleground where various groups have sought to control the public school and its curriculum and, by so doing, shape our common culture. The way schools should address American pluralism has been publicly debated from the beginning of our Republic and continues unabated today, particularly in light of our position as one leading player in the global community of nations.

Educational literature over the past 170 years reflects profound disagreement about how to educate the young while forging a nation-state from a multiethnic population. Should differences of language and culture be recognized and taken into account? Or should we work as hard and fast as we can to assimilate newcomers to "the American way of life"? Indeed, as our nation becomes increasingly diverse and increasingly a part of an interdependent global community, many question whether or not there really is any longer something called the "American way of life." What *is* certain is that advocates on all sides of the debate have never been fully satisfied with the role played by the school and the way it carries out its socializing mission. And there have been many times when dissatisfaction grew into violent action.

If, as we argued in the preceding chapter, fundamental changes must be undertaken in the way we "do school" for an increasingly diversified population, then it will be helpful for us to examine the history, not only of specific incidents in the struggle for equal educational opportunity, but also of the debate surrounding multicultural or intercultural education. What follows is a somewhat abbreviated but, we hope, clear account of how educators have reached their current place with respect to this debate and what the major issues are today.

Historical Perspectives on Pluralism in the United States

We Have Been Different From the Beginning

The Taino People

One might argue that intolerance toward differences in the Americas began with the introduction of European culture in the 1490s. There is considerable evidence that the Native American populations that lived in the Americas before European settlement exhibited far greater tolerance toward diversity of thought and lifestyle than did the arriving Europeans. The Taino people, for instance, greeted Columbus with food, shelter, and open festivity when the Spaniards first arrived on their small Caribbean island in 1492. At first intrigued with the Taino, Columbus wrote that "their manner is both decorous and praiseworthy" (as cited

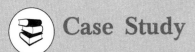

Case Study

Central High School, Little Rock, Arkansas, 1957

On September 4, 1957, nine black teenagers attempting to enter Central High School in Little Rock, Arkansas, for the first time were turned away by the National Guard, which was called out by Governor Orval Faubus "to preserve the peace and avert violence." This event was not the final chapter in the story of the integration of Central High School, but it was not the first chapter either. It was, however, one that—shown widely on national television—riveted the nation. If any episode in the history of the civil rights movement in public education can be said to remain in the public mind, it is this one.

Contrary to what many people believe, the state of Arkansas and the city of Little Rock had made some strides in desegregating its public facilities prior to the integration of Central High School. As early as 1949, the School of Law at the University of Arkansas was integrated, and in 1951 the Little Rock Public Library board approved the integration of its facilities. In 1956, the city's public buses were quietly desegregated with little fuss. However, as in many other places in the United States, integrating schools was a more difficult—and emotional—matter.

In May of 1954, five days after the Supreme Court decision in *Brown v. Board of Education of Topeka,* the Little Rock School Board issued a policy statement offering to comply with the *Brown* decision "when the Court outlines the method to be followed and the time to be allowed." Two days later, the board voted unanimously to adopt the superintendent's plan of gradual integration beginning in September 1957 at the high school level and adding the lower grades over the next 6 years. But for those who yearned for faster action, this plan was insufficient.

In January 1956, 27 students attempted to register in all-white Little Rock schools and were turned down. One month later, the National Association for the Advancement of Colored People (NAACP) filed suit on behalf of 33 black children denied admittance to four white schools, and in August of that year, a federal judge dismissed the suit, ruling that the Little Rock School Board had acted in good faith in proposing its plan. The students would have to wait.

As the fall of 1957 approached, those opposed to integration began to organize. Specifically, a member of the Mother's League of Central High School attempted to block integration by asking for an injunction, which was granted in a local court on August 27, and then nullified in a federal court 3 days later. Central High School would be integrated in September.

But it was not that simple. On September 23, surrounded by an angry crowd of about 1,000 people, nine students again tried to enter the school—this time through a side door. When the crowd discovered that the students were inside, it became unruly and police feared that they could not maintain control. The black students were taken out of the school, again through a side door. The next day, the mayor of Little Rock asked President Eisenhower for federal troops to maintain order; the President sent 1,000 members of the 101st Airborne Division to Little Rock and federalized the Arkansas National Guard. On September 25, escorted by federal troops, the nine black students were escorted back into Central High School.

During the 1957–58 school year, the "Little Rock Nine" (as the students came to be called) tried to maintain their composure and their studies in an atmosphere of student unrest and adult confrontations—in court and outside of it. In December, one of the nine students, at the end of her patience with taunting by white students, dumped a bowl of chili on her tormentors in the cafeteria; she was suspended for 6 days, and, after further altercations, ultimately for the rest of the year. She transferred to a high school in New York City.

In February 1958, the Little Rock School Board filed a request to delay integration until the concept "all deliberate speed" was defined. In June, a federal judge granted the delay, writing

(continued)

that although black students had a constitutional right to attend white schools, the "time has not come for them to enjoy that right." The NAACP appealed that decision, and in August it was reversed by a federal court of appeals.

Over the summer of 1958, the school board asked for a stay of the appeals court ruling to enable them to appeal to the Supreme Court; the Supreme Court called a special session to discuss the Little Rock case; Governor Faubus asked the Arkansas legislature for a law enabling him to close public schools to avoid integration and lease the closed schools to private school corporations; the Supreme Court ruled that Little Rock must continue with its integration plan; the school board announced the opening of the city's high schools on September 15; Governor Faubus ordered Little Rock's three high schools closed. At the end of September, voters overwhelmingly opposed integration by a vote of 129,470 to 7,561. Public high schools in Little Rock were closed for the year.

In November 1958, five of the six members of the Little Rock School Board resigned in frustration, having been ordered to proceed with integration of the high schools even though it had no high schools to integrate. In December, a new school board was elected, evenly divided between "pro" and "con" factions. In May of 1959, segregationist members of the school board attempted to fire 44 teachers and administrators suspected of integrationist sympathies. Three moderates on the board walked out, refusing to participate. In June 1959, a federal court declared the state's school-closing law unconstitutional, and the new school board announced it would reopen the schools in the fall of 1959.

Fifteen years later, in the fall of 1972, all grades in Little Rock public schools were finally integrated. Forty years later, in the fall of 1997, President Clinton—who was an 11-year-old student in a nearby town when the first attempt to integrate Central High School occurred—held the door to the high school open for the returning members of the Class of 1957, including most of the "Little Rock Nine." One of those students, Ernest Green (who was the first of the nine to graduate from the high school), spoke for all of them and, perhaps, for all those involved in this drama, when he said: "We were a part not just of civil rights history, but of American history. . . . It's something to see your name in your kid's history book."

Source: Much of the material in this case study was taken from a timeline on the "History of Little Rock Public Schools Desegregation," and other articles on World Wide Web pages regarding the incident in Little Rock. See, especially, www.centralhigh57.org.

in Brown, 1970, p. 1). The Taino's hospitality, however, was soon met with severe cruelty by the Spaniards. Within 20 years of Columbus's landing, the Taino were extinct as a people. In fact, this tendency toward intolerance for both religious and cultural diversity on the part of the Spaniards may have prevented them from becoming the dominant culture in North America. So much energy was spent repressing and fighting the native populations that the northern spread of Spanish culture was halted in the southwest.

The emergence of the English as the dominant force in the new lands may be partially attributed to their somewhat greater tolerance, born, perhaps, of their own need for religious freedom. However, even though the English government allowed, even encouraged, immigrants from a variety of ethnic backgrounds to settle in America, it was the white, English-born Protestants who, by the time the United States became a nation in 1776, had emerged as the dominant group. This group, too, was fearful of "different" kinds of immigrants. In 1698, for example, South Carolina passed an act exempting Irish and Roman Catholics from new bounties (Dinnerstein & Reiners, 1975). In 1729, Pennsylvania placed a duty on all servants of Scotch-Irish descent. One official at the time wrote, "The common fear is that if they continue to come, they will make themselves proprietors of the province" (p. 2). Ironically, the very people who originally had come to the New World to escape religious persecution were among those who actively engaged in the persecution of others for their beliefs, values, and lifestyles.

Industrialization, Immigration, and Religious Pluralism

In the early years of the 19th century, an influx of European immigrants followed the industrial revolution across the Atlantic. At the same time, the United States was developing the idea of the "common school," heralded in part as a way to give all children, no matter what their cultural, religious, or economic backgrounds, a common experience that would help them understand one another and provide the common basis for citizenship in a democracy. Despite a growing network of public elementary schools, the increasing diversity within the United States began to be viewed as a "problem" for public schooling. The first battles within these pluralistic common schools were not waged around the issue of race or ethnicity, as is common today, but around the issue of religion.

Many new immigrants in this period were Catholic and, to native-born Protestants, represented a threat to the stability of the republic–as well as competition for newly created industrial jobs. Many suspected that newly arrived Catholics owed a greater allegiance to the pope than to the U.S. government, an issue that was not finally settled until the election of John F. Kennedy to the presidency in 1960. Second-, third-, and fourth-generation Protestants also opposed the emergence of Catholic schools, believing that they were intended to instill undemocratic values in Catholic children. Catholic parents, on the other hand, felt that a Catholic education was necessary to preserve their children's religious faith and an important vehicle for maintaining Catholic communities.

Opposition to Catholic schooling often became violent both in word and deed. Political cartoonists had a field day with caricatures of the pope as an ogre attempting to "swallow" the United States. More serious, however, were physical attacks on Catholic schools, exemplified by the burning of the Ursuline convent in Charleston, Massachusetts, by a Protestant mob in 1834 (Provenzo, 1986, pp. 90–91).

In the 1830s, the common school movement, which was supposedly nonsectarian but was largely Protestant driven, came into dramatic conflict with those who wished to educate their children in religious-based schools. If the emphasis in Catholic schools was toward a religious faith, the emphasis in the common school was toward a secular government that would maintain the new forms of democracy being developed in the United States. The democracy that was taking shape was rapidly becoming a kind of civil religion, and the development of loyalty to that idea was one of the foundations of public schooling. Thus, Catholics had some justification for the belief that the common school might socialize their children away from their religious faith. As the number of Catholic immigrants increased, and the network of Catholic schools grew, Catholic parents began to insist that public funds raised through taxation to support public schools should also be used to fund private Catholic institutions. That debate continues to this day.

Catholics were not the only group who were feared and persecuted. In 1835, the Indian Removal Act saw the last vestige of Native American culture in the eastern United States swept westward across the Mississippi River in the tragic roundup known today as the Trail of Tears. In the case of Jews, the last barrier to their voting rights was not abolished in New Hampshire until 1877. And in 1882, the immigration department passed an act that prohibited the entry of Chinese into the country.

The Civil War: Freedmen's Schools and the Issue of Race

Issues of race in *public* education became important only after the Civil War. In the pre–Civil War South it was against the law to educate black slave children, so no racial *educational* problem existed in southern schools. In the North, blacks who had bought or had been given their freedom achieved some education in the common schools, in African American church communities, and through

abolitionist efforts. After the Civil War, the education of black children was still not perceived to be a "national problem" by most whites because, where African Americans were educated at all, they were educated in separate schools.

Southern states, notably resistant to providing public education for blacks, were not above taxing them for white schools. In some places—Florida, Texas, and Kentucky, for example—black schools were built only after black citizens paid a second tax to build their own schools (Webb & Sherman, 1989, p. 524).

In 1865, Congress established the **Freedmen's Bureau** to help freed slaves with the transition to citizenship. In 1866, the law was amended to assist in the provision of black schools. Many of the teachers in these schools were northern white women, often daughters of abolitionist families. Indeed, the story of the women, both black and white, who taught in the "Freedmen's Schools" is among the proudest in the history of teaching. By 1870, nearly 7,000 white and black "schoolmarms" were teaching 250,000 black students, and learning to cross the barriers of race and class that have characterized American history. The legacy of these teachers was enormous. Not only did they educate the children who later became the teachers in segregated schools, but they educated a generation of free black leaders who are too seldom talked about today (Hoffman, 2003).

Violence characterized the development of black schools after the Civil War as it had the development of Catholic schools earlier. Burning buildings and harassment of black teachers and students were commonplace. However, passage of the Fourteenth Amendment to the Constitution in 1868 made responsibility for civil rights a federal rather than a state function and, as a result, African Americans began to gain more access to public education. Fully aware that education was a way out of poverty, black parents saw that their children got to

The Freedmen's Bureau

school, one way or another. When they were needed on the farm, they alternated between school and work, as this Alabama boy describes:

> I took turns with my brother at the plow and in school; one day I plowed and he went to school, the next day he plowed and I went to school; what was learned on his school day he taught me at night and I did the same for him. (Weinberg, 1977, p. 46)

Plessy v. Ferguson

Black children remained in segregated schools that were funded at minimal rates and often open for only part of the year. Indeed, despite efforts through the courts to equalize the rights of blacks in all spheres of public life, in 1896 in the *Plessy v. Ferguson* decision, the Supreme Court held that segregation was not prohibited by the Constitution. *Plessy v. Ferguson,* which upheld the doctrine that "separate but equal" facilities for blacks and whites were constitutionally permissible, justified separate (usually inferior) education of African American children in both the North and South until 1954, when *Brown v. Board of Education* made such unequal facilities illegal.

Very few African American children with disabilities received any schooling at all in the 19th century, but the tiny number who did, mainly those with visual impairments, experienced double segregation. Among the 30 public and private residential schools for blind pupils established in the United States between 1832 and 1875 was the first school for "the colored blind," in North Carolina (Wallin, 1914). By 1931 there were five such separate schools for black children and youth. Ten other black schools maintained separate (inferior) departments for blind students, most of which used second-hand materials such as badly worn Braille books that were virtually impossible to read. Moreover, "segregation not only kept black children in separate schools staffed by black teachers, but prevented those teachers from attending courses given at white southern colleges" (Koestler, 1967). Their lower salaries made attendance at northern colleges prohibitive.

Anglo-Conformity and Assimilationist Ideology

The issue of diversity as a problem for public schools is not a new phenomenon. During the earlier years of massive immigration, from about 1870 to perhaps 1920, the "problem" of diversity in the schools was largely perceived as a problem of how to assimilate children of other nationalities. In short, it was thought to be the school's task to make immigrant children as much like white, middle-class, Anglo-Saxon Protestants as possible in as short a time as possible.

Interestingly, a key strategy employed by public schools to accomplish this goal involved establishing the field of speech therapy (formally termed speech/language pathology). Immigrant children placed in New York's "vestibule" or "steamer classes" were instructed in the proper use of English by speech teachers, who very soon, at parents' requests, were also assigned to work with children who had medically impaired articulation or fluency. Described as **Anglo-conformity,** or the **assimilationist model,** the rationale for this strategy was typified by these words of Ellwood Cubberly, a prominent educator at the turn of the 20th century:

> Everywhere these people settle in groups or settlements to set up their national manners, customs, and observances. Our task is to break up these groups or settlements, to assimilate and amalgamate these people as part of our American race and to implant in their children so far as can be done, the Anglo-Saxon conception of righteousness, law and order, and our popular government and to awaken in them a reverence for our democratic institutions and for those things in our national life which we as a people hold to be of abiding worth. (as cited in Trujillo, 1973, p. 21)

The assimilationist strategy was applied to each new ethnic group as immigrants poured through Ellis Island and other ports of entry. Jews, Poles, Slavs, Asians, and Latin Americans all became the "raw material" from which the "new American" would be made. Between 1860 and 1920, 37 million immigrants became naturalized citizens. Their sheer numbers changed the ethnic makeup of America. By 1916, for example, only 28% of San Francisco's population claimed English as its first language.

Yet despite the high number of immigrants, the *dominant* American culture retained its English, Protestant identity. The nation's public schools, staffed largely by white, middle-class, Protestant women, did little or nothing to encourage the expression of ethnicity or address the special needs of an increasingly diverse student population. Indeed, in the eyes of the nativist population, the schools were supposed to prevent such expression. The idea of a melting pot was used to describe the process of helping immigrants shed their native languages, learn English, and assimilate into the dominant American culture.

The term *melting pot* actually came from the name of a play written by Israel Zangwill (1909). The goal of creating one homogeneous culture from the many that arrived on the shores of the United States is captured in the following speech from that play:

Israel Zangwill and
The Melting Pot

> America is God's Crucible, the great Melting Pot where all the races of Europe are melting and reforming! Here you stand, good folk, think I, when I see them at Ellis Island, here you stand in your fifty groups with your fifty languages and histories, and your fifty hatreds and rivalries, but you won't be long like that, brothers, for these are the fires of God. A fig for your feuds and vendettas! Germans and Frenchmen, Irishmen and Englishmen, Jews and Russians—into the Crucible with you all! God is making the American. . . . The real American has not yet arrived. He is only in the Crucible. I tell you—he will be the fusion of all races, the coming superman. (p. 37)

**Activity and
Reading 7:
Cultural Values in
American Society**

James Banks (1988) suggests that assimilationists believe that one's identification with an ethnic group should be short-lived and temporary as it presents an obstacle to an individual's long-term interests and needs. Assimilationists believe that, for a society to advance, individuals must give up their ethnic identities, languages, and ideologies in favor of the norms and values of the larger, national society. The goal of the school, from an assimilationist perspective, should be to socialize individuals into the society at large so all can function in an "appropriate" manner; that is, in a manner that supports the goals of the nation as expressed through its leaders. Ethnic group identification, if it is to be developed, should be confined to small community organizations. In short, the goal for assimilationists is to make it possible for everyone to be "melted" into a homogeneous whole.

The assimilationist view, sometimes called a *monocultural* perspective, shares an *image* or *model* of American culture. In this view there is a core "American" culture composed of common knowledge, habits, values, and attitudes. For people who think of American culture this way, these common characteristics might include the following: "real" Americans are mostly white, middle-class adults (or are trying to be); they are heterosexual, married, go to church (mostly Protestant but sometimes Catholic). They live in single-family houses (which they own, or are trying to); they work hard, eat well, stand on "their own two feet"; they expect their children to behave themselves; they wash themselves a good deal, and generally try to smell "good"; they are patriotic and honor the flag; they are often charitable and, in return, expect only that those receiving their charity will try to "shape up"; and they are not very interested in "highfalutin" ideas found in books written by overly educated people; instead they believe in "good, old-fashioned common sense."

Of course, this is a composite picture. Not all monoculturalists fit neatly into this view of "real" Americans. But most share many of these characteristics, and divergence from some of them (for example, heterosexuality) almost automatically disqualifies a person even if that is the only way in which he or she differs. For people who see American culture in this narrow way, those who do not share these characteristics are clearly not "real" Americans, whether they happen to have been born here or not. Moreover, their difference makes them dangerous to the maintenance of America as it is "supposed" to be. It is therefore a primary role of schooling to make the children of the culturally different into "American" children; that is, to teach these children those ways of thinking, behaving, and valuing that will help them to fit harmoniously into the monoculturalists' culture. Children of monoculturalists, of course, do not need such help because they already match the model.

Although exceptional individuals, those who have disabilities and those who are intellectually or otherwise gifted, may be considered "real" Americans, they too have been viewed in some sense as "others." Beginning in the 1870s, large urban school districts formed separate classes for "unrulies" and for "backward" or "dull" pupils. In actuality, most such classes were repositories for children who, for one reason or another, "didn't fit" the regular program. From these beginnings, special education emerged as a separate, smaller system within the public school.

Multiculturalism and the Pluralist Ideology

Those who believed strongly in the idea of the melting pot have been both bemused and angered by the fact that the contents of the pot never melted.

Eventually, in opposition to the assimilationist ideology, came the call for **cultural pluralism** by a small group of philosophers and writers who argued that a political democracy must also be a cultural democracy (Banks, 1988). To these pluralists, immigrant groups were entitled to maintain their ethnic cultures and institutions within the greater society. The analogy they used was that of a salad bowl, and in order to have a rich, nutritious salad (society), it was necessary to include a variety of cultures. In short, American society would be strengthened, not weakened, by the presence of different cultures.

Cultural Pluralism

Pluralists view one's social group as critical to the socialization process in modern society. The group provides the individual with identity, a sense of belonging or psychological support, particularly when faced with discrimination by the larger society. It is through one's group, usually the ethnic group, that one develops a primary language, values, and interpersonal relationships, as well as a particular lifestyle. Pluralists believe the identity group (racial/ethnic, religious, and so forth) to be so important that the schools should actively promote their interests and recognize their importance in the life of the individual. Because pluralists assume a "difference" rather than a "deficit" orientation, they stress the importance of a curriculum addressing different learning styles and patterns of interaction, and fully recognize students' cultural histories. The assumption is that the more congruent the school experience is with the other experiences of the child, the better the child's chance of success.

Legislative and Judicial Landmarks

The Civil Rights Movement and the Schools

Six decades after *Plessy*, diversity in American society and in its schools again became the subject of major social turmoil. During the 1960s and 1970s, fueled by the general social ferment of the civil rights movement and the war in Vietnam, educational reform legislation was enacted in the following areas: desegregation, multicultural and bilingual education, mainstreaming students with special needs into regular classrooms, and gender-sensitive education. These programs recognized the pluralistic nature of this society in a positive rather than a negative sense. Each one attempted to help some educationally disadvantaged group to receive a better education within a pluralistic framework.

It is important to realize that these educational mandates were not achieved in isolation but as part of the larger human and civil rights struggles of the 1960s and 1970s. During this period, Congress passed a number of antidiscriminatory statutes: the *Voting Rights Act* (1963), dealing with voter registration; the *Equal Pay Act* (1963), which required that males and females occupying the same position be paid equally; the *Civil Rights Act* (1964), dealing with housing and job discrimination as well as with education; the *Bilingual Education Act of 1968* (Title VII of the *Elementary and Secondary Education Act*), which established programs for children whose first language was not English; *Title IX of the Education Amendments* (1972), prohibiting sex discrimination against students and employees of educational institutions; and the *Education of All Handicapped Children Act* (1975), requiring schools to assume the responsibility for educating all children in the least restrictive environment possible. It was, in the words of one partisan observer, a period of "intensity of concern and commitment to do something about the problems in America stemming from the continued growth of its pluralistic character" (Hunter, 1975, p. 17).

In education the chief concerns were for access and equity: access to public education for excluded groups and a guarantee that such education would be equitable; that is, that it would be commensurate with the best that public education could offer. All these efforts rested on the belief that previously excluded groups had an inherent *right* to educational equity. Why was it important to emphasize the *rights* of racial and ethnic minorities, women, and persons with disabilities? Why was it important to enact legislation that protects their rights? Quite simply, because these rights had not been recognized in the past, and large numbers of people had experienced discrimination and unequal opportunity in a society that rests on the principle that *all* citizens are equal under the law. The civil rights movement was a reaffirmation of beliefs that form the very basis of American society and an insistence that we live up to our ideals in education as well as in other aspects of social life. Specifically, Spanish-speaking Americans in the Southwest, Puerto Ricans on the East Coast, Asian Americans on the West Coast, Native Americans on reservations and in urban settlements, and African Americans throughout the United States began to seek their fair share of what America had to offer and demand that the nation live up to the ideals it professed. The powerful buildup of unrest and frustration born of the discrepancy between American ideals and American practices sought an outlet. From the *Brown v. Board of Education* decision in 1954 through the Civil Rights Act of 1964 and through the Vietnam War, those groups marched out of the ghettos and into the courts.

Judicial and Legislative Mandates Regarding Equity

The start of these events is usually marked by the 1954 Supreme Court decision in *Brown v. Board of Education*. This landmark decision stated that segregated schools were inherently unequal and that state laws that allowed separate schools for black and white students were unconstitutional.

In 1967, the U.S. Commission on Civil Rights was established primarily to investigate complaints alleging the denial of people's right to vote by reason of race, color, religion, sex, or national origin. About the same time (1966), the National Education Association issued a study supporting the teaching of Spanish to Mexican Americans in Tucson and the American Association of Colleges of Teacher Education produced a policy statement on pluralism entitled, "No One Model American." These and other investigative, judicial, and legislative moves were directed toward ending educational discrimination and the comfortable middle-class perceptions about cultural assimilation that supported discrimination. Together, these reports and judicial proceedings began to dim the embers under the American melting pot.

In the 12-year period from 1963 to 1975, private and government studies and hearings and a series of lawsuits regarding rights to native language instruction, placement of children with disabilities, and desegregation produced many mandates for the schooling of minority students. Concurrently, new educational strategies and curricula, especially in bilingual and bicultural education, appeared in districts across the nation.

The Civil Rights Act of 1964 made it illegal for public schools that received federal or state funds to assign students to schools based on their color, race, religion, or country of origin. The Bilingual Education Act was passed in 1968 as Title VII of the Elementary and Secondary Education Act. President Lyndon Johnson clarified the intent of this law in the following words:

> This bill authorizes a new effort to prevent dropouts; new programs for handicapped children; new planning help for rural schools. It also contains a special provision establishing bilingual education programs for children whose first language is not English. Thousands of children of Latin descent, young Indians, and others will get a better start—a better chance—in school. (Tiedt & Tiedt, 1990, p. 9)

In 1970, the Office of Civil Rights Guidelines tried to make special training for non–English-speaking students a requirement for public schools that receive federal aid. The office stated:

> Where inability to speak and understand the English language excludes national origin-minority group children from effective participation in the education program offered by a school district, the district must take affirmative steps to rectify the language deficiency in order to open its instructional program to these students. (Tiedt & Tiedt, 1990, p. 9)

Also during the 1960s and early 1970s, members of the women's movement began to pressure Congress to enact legislation that would guarantee equitable educational experience for girls and women. The result was Title IX of the Education Amendments of 1972. Intending to prohibit discrimination in elementary and secondary schools on the basis of sex, the preamble to this statute reads, in part:

> No person in the United States shall, on the basis of sex, be excluded from participation in, be denied the benefits of, or be subjected to discrimination under any education program or activity receiving federal financial assistance.

It was not until 1975, however, that the rules and regulations enforcing Title IX were published and sent to state departments of education and to school districts. In the interim, there was heated controversy, as well as 10,000 written comments from citizens (Carelli, 1988, p. 85).

Similarly, the Education of All Handicapped Children Act of 1975 (P.L. 94-142) became the basis for the educational rights of children and youth with disabilities. Like other educational equity efforts, P.L. 94-142 was not enacted in a vacuum but was the culmination of a long-lived movement. In 1948, for example, prior to the *Brown* decision, Congress prohibited discrimination against people with disabilities by the U.S. Civil Service Commission. In 1968, the Architectural Barriers Act prohibited the use of government funds to construct facilities that were inaccessible to the handicapped. With enactment of amendments to the Vocational Rehabilitation Act of 1973 (P.L. 93-112) and amended by P.L. 93-516, even more far-reaching policies were established. The most familiar part of this legislation, Section 504, specifically prohibits any form of discrimination against persons with disabilities on the part of any agency receiving government funds. Enactment of the Americans with Disabilities Act of 1991 extended that prohibition to the private sector. Table 2.1 summarizes the chronology of the major civil rights legislation that sought to redress the education disadvantages experienced by various groups in the United States.

Table 2.1   Major Civil Rights Legislation Chronology

ISSUES OF RACE	
1896	In *Plessy v. Ferguson* (163 U.S. 537), a case about a man who was ejected from a train because he, being one-eighth African American, refused to move to a segregated train car, the Supreme Court found that the doctrine of "separate but equal" in the state of Louisiana did not violate either the Thirteenth or Fourteenth Amendments to the Constitution. This case became the basis for segregated schools in the South.
1954	In *Brown v. Board of Education of Topeka* (349 U.S. 294), the Supreme Court rescinded the Court's view in *Plessy v. Ferguson* (1896) that supported the "separate but equal" doctrine. The Court declared that "separate but equal has no place in public education" and that "separate facilities are inherently unequal."
1954	In *Brown v. Board of Education of Topeka II* (349 U.S. 294), the Supreme Court affirmed its original decision in *Brown I,* acknowledged that local school districts had differing conditions but added that all districts should desegregate "with all deliberate speed."
1964	Title VI of the Civil Rights Act (P.L. 88-352) prohibits discrimination on the basis of race, color, or national origin against students of any school receiving federal financial assistance.
1964	Title VII or the Civil Rights Act (P.L. 88-352) prohibits discrimination on the basis of race, color, or national origin against employees of any school receiving federal financial assistance.
1964	The Voting Rights Act (P.L. 89-110) prohibits discrimination on the basis of race, color, or national origin against U.S. citizens' right to vote.
1968	In *Green v. County School Board of New Kent County* (391 U.S. 430), the Supreme Court ruled that the New Kent County School Board in Virginia could not use a "freedom of choice" plan to create a dual school system for blacks and whites, and that school districts must avoid segregation in student assignment, faculty, facilities, staff, transportation, and extracurricular activities. These aspects of school life become the "Green factors" used by courts to decide whether school districts had, indeed, met the requirement to desegregate given in *Brown I* and *II.*
1971	In *Swann v. Charlotte-Mecklenburg Board of Education* (402 U.S. 1), the Supreme Court authorized mandatory busing, redrawn attendance areas, and a limited use of racial-balance quotas as tools of desegregation.
1971	In *Larry P. v. Riles* (793 F2d 969, 9th Cir.), a California state court found that some African American children placed in special education classes have been inappropriately placed. The case changed the assessment and placement practices in California and has had an impact throughout the nation.
1971	In *Keyes v. Denver School District No. 1* (413 U.S. 921), the Supreme Court ruled that de facto segregation (the result of housing patterns, for example) was insufficient grounds for judicial intervention.
1974	*Milliken v. Bradley I* (418 U.S. 717), the Detroit school district was not allowed to require cross-district busing to desegregate its schools. The Court said that "It must first be shown that there has been a constitutional violation within one district that produces a significant segregative effect in another school district." This case is generally thought to be the beginning of the end of school busing as a tool of desegregation.
1976	In *Pasadena City Board of Education v. Spangler* (427 U.S. 424), the Supreme Court ruled that once a racially neutral system of student assignment is established, courts cannot require school districts to rearrange their attendance zones each year to ensure desirable racial balance in schools.
1976	In *Milliken v. Bradley II* (418 U.S. 717), also in Detroit, the Supreme Court ruled that remedial education for students subjected to past segregation may be part of a desegregation order.
1976	In *Regents of the University of California v. Bakke* (438 U.S. 265), the Supreme Court ruled that race could be one of the factors considered in university admissions decisions, but that quotas, such as those in affirmative action programs, were not permissible.

Table 2.1 *Continued*

1991	In *Board of Education of Oklahoma City v. Dowell* (498 U.S. 237), the Supreme Court ruled that court-ordered busing could be eliminated if school districts became resegregated because of private choices (such as housing) and all practical efforts were taken to eliminate segregation.
1991	In *Freeman v. Pitts* (503 U.S. 467), the Supreme Court again ruled against intervention for racial balance in the schools "where resegregation is a product not of state action but of private choices," on the grounds that it was beyond the authority of the Court to try to counteract "continuous and massive demographic shifts."
1991	In *United States v. Fordice, Governor of Mississippi* (505 U.S. 717), the Supreme Court ruled that the State of Mississippi had to take "affirmative steps" to dismantle the discriminatory system of higher education in which five predominantly white institutions and three black institutions continued to exist.
1995	In *Missouri v. Jenkins* (515 U.S. 70), the Supreme Court ruled that a lower court exceeded its authority by mandating salary increases for school personnel in Kansas City, and "reasoned that asking whether student achievement levels were at or below national norms was inappropriate to determine whether the district had achieved unitary status."
2003	In *Gratz v. Bollinger* (539 U.S. 244), the Supreme Court ruled that the University of Michigan's point system for undergraduate admissions (which included race as a factor) was too "mechanistic" and therefore unconstitutional.
2003	In *Grutter v. Bollinger* (539 U.S. 306), on the other hand, the Supreme Court upheld the University of Michigan Law School's narrow use of race, holding that the Constitution "does not prohibit the law school's narrowly tailored use of race in admissions decisions to further a compelling interest in obtaining the educational benefits that flow from a diverse student body."
2007	In *Parents Involved in Community Schools v. Seattle School District No. 1, et al.* (413 U.S. 189), the Supreme Court declares invalid programs in Seattle and metropolitan Louisville, Kentucky, that sought to maintain diversity in its schools by using race as one criterion for assignment to schools.
ISSUES OF RELIGION, OR SEPARATION OF CHURCH AND STATE	
1925	In *Pierce v. Society of Sisters* (268 U.S. 510), the Supreme Court ruled that an Oregon law requiring all children to attend public schools was unconstitutional because it infringed on parents' rights to control the education of their children. This case, in effect, established the legitimacy of parochial and other private schools.
1930	In *Cochran v. Louisiana State Board of Education* (281 U.S. 370), the Court upheld a lower court's decision that providing schoolbooks to children in parochial and private schools did not violate the Constitution.
1943	In *West Virginia State Board of Education v. Barnette* (391 U.S. 264), the Supreme Court declared unconstitutional a West Virginia law that compelled children of the Jehovah's Witness faith to salute the American flag.
1947	In *Everson v. Board of Education* (330 U.S. 1), the Court found that a New Jersey law allowing reimbursement for transportation to parents of parochial school students was constitutional. Of even more importance, this decision reflected the broad interpretation of the Establishment Clause of the First Amendment that would guide the Court for decades.
1947	In *McCollum v. Board of Education* (333 U.S. 203), the Supreme Court disallowed the Illinois practice of providing religious instruction in public school classrooms during the school day.
1952	In *Zorach v. Clausen* (343 U.S. 306), the U.S. Supreme Court ruled that religious instruction during school hours does not violate the First Amendment of the Constitution as long as it takes place off school grounds and is conducted by teachers or religious figures independent of and not paid by the school.
1962	In *Engle v. Vitale* (370 U.S. 421), the Supreme Court ruled that it was unconstitutional for government agents such as schools to require public school students to recite an official prayer in the classroom.

(continued)

Table 2.1 *Continued*

1962	In *Abington School District v. Schempp* (374 U.S. 203), the Supreme Court ruled that public schools cannot start the day with required prayer or Bible reading.
1968	In *Epperson v. State of Arkansas* (393 U.S. 97), the Supreme Court found that to forbid the teaching of evolution as a theory violated the First Amendment free speech clause.
1971	In *Lemon v. Kurtzman* (403 U.S. 602), the Supreme Court found that direct government assistance to religious schools was unconstitutional.
1971	In *Wisconsin v. Yoder* (406 U.S. 205), the Supreme Court held that Amish children may be excused from compulsory schooling after the eighth grade.
1980	In *Palmer v. Board of Education*, (444 U.S. 1026) the Supreme Court ruled that a teacher's right to religious beliefs must be respected, but those beliefs cannot be required of students. Thus, teachers must follow district curricula, even though portions of such curricula may include matters to which they have religious objections.
1985	In *Wallace v. Jaffee* (466 U.S. 924), the Supreme Court held that state legislation authorizing a minute of silence for prayer or meditation, led by teachers, was unconstitutional.
1987	In *Edwards v. Aguillard* (482 U.S. 578), the Supreme Court found that no state can require that schools teach the biblical version of creation.
1990	In *Board of Education of Westside Community Schools v. Mergens* (496 U.S. 226), the Supreme Court held that the organizing of a Christian Club by students who wished to meet after school did not violate the Establishment Clause of the First Amendment.
1992	In *Lee v. Weisman* (505 U.S. 577), the Supreme Court upheld a ban on prayers at high school graduation ceremonies.
2005	In *Kitzmiller v. Dover Area School District* (Case No. 04cv2688), a Pennsylvania federal court judge ruled that requiring the teaching of "intelligent design" as an alternative theory to evolution was unconstitutional on the grounds that intelligent design was a form of creationism and thus violated the Establishment Clause of the First Amendment. This case was the first direct challenge to intelligent design brought in a federal court.
	ISSUES OF LANGUAGE
1967	In the Elementary and Secondary Education Act (P.L. 90-222), the U.S. Congress provided federal funds for schools that wished to implement bilingual education programs designed for language minority students.
1968	With the Bilingual Education Act, (Title VII, ESEA), the U.S. Congress established that language and cultural heritage are basic means by which a child learns, and provided funding for bilingual programs. This law was reauthorized in 1974, 1978, 1984, 1988, and 1990.
1968	In *Diana v. State Board of Education* (CA 70 RFT/N.D. Cal. 1970), a suit brought on behalf of Mexican American, Spanish-speaking children who had been placed in special education classes based on IQ tests in English, the U.S. Supreme Court ruled that testing for eligibility for special education services must be done in the dominant language of the student.
1972	In *Guadalupe Organization, Inc. v. Tempe Elementary School District No. 3* (587 F2d. 1022), a suit brought in an Arizona state court on behalf of Yaquii Indian and Mexican American children disproportionately placed in special education classes based on IQ tests given in English, an out-of-court settlement involved reevaluation of these students and testing in their primary language.
1974	The Equal Educational Opportunities Act (20 USC Sec. 1703) reaffirmed that the failure of any educational agency to take action to overcome language barriers that impeded equal participation by students is a denial of equal educational opportunity.
1974	In *Lau v. Nichols* (414 U.S. 563), a suit brought on behalf of Chinese-speaking children in California who had been disproportionately placed in special education classes, the U.S. Supreme Court ruled that affirmative steps must be taken by a school district to rectify language deficiency.

Table 2.1 *Continued*

1979	In *Martin Luther King, Jr. Elementary School Children v. Ann Arbor School District Board of Education* (73 F.Supp. 1371/E.D. Mich.), filed on behalf of Black English-speaking children in Ann Arbor by parents demanding that their children be taught standard English, a U.S. district court in Michigan found for the parents and mandated linguistic instruction for teachers on Black English as a legitimate dialect.
1981	In *Castañeda v. Pickard* (648 F2d 989), the Fifth Circuit Court of Appeals provided the criteria for determining whether a school district is in compliance with the Equal Educational Opportunity Act of 1974. Briefly, the criteria are: (1) a pedagogically sound program for LEP students; (2) enough qualified staff to actually implement the plan; and (3) an evaluation system for the plan. It did not mandate a bilingual education program but required that "appropriate action be taken to overcome language barriers" through well-constructed programs.
1982	In *Plyler v. Doe* (457 U.S. 202), the Supreme Court held that children of undocumented immigrants, while illegally in this country, were still people, and thus entitled to protections—including education—under the Fourteenth Amendment; thus, school districts had to educate them.
1987	In *Gomez v. Illinois* (811 F2d 1030), the Seventh Circuit Court of Appeals ruled that State Education Agencies are required under EEOA to ensure that language minority students' educational needs are met.
1988	The Bilingual Education Act of 1988 reauthorized bilingual education but added a "three-year enrollment rule" implying that 3 years of bilingual education was sufficient for most students with limited English proficiency.
1990	In *League of Latin American Citizens (LULAC) v. State Board of Education Consent Degree, Southern Florida* (Case No. 90-1913), the decree ensured the equal treatment of English Language Learning (ELL) students under the Civil Rights Act of 1964.
2002	Title VII—the Bilingual Education Act of the Elementary and Secondary Education Act expired.
ISSUES OF GENDER	
1963	With the Vocational Education Act (as amended by the Education Amendment of 1976), the U.S. Congress required states to make efforts to overcome sex discrimination and stereotyping in vocational education.
1972	In *Title IX of the Education Amendments* (P.L. 92-318), the U.S. Congress prohibited discrimination on the basis of sex against students and employees of any school receiving federal financial assistance.
1978	With the Pregnancy Discrimination Act (P.L. 95-555), the U.S. Congress prohibited discrimination on the basis of pregnancy, childbirth, or related medical conditions as unlawful under Title VII of the Civil Rights Act.
1992	In *Franklin v. Gwinnett County Public Schools* (503 U.S. 60), the Supreme Court held that any school supported by federal funds can be sued for sex discrimination and sexual harassment.
1998	In *Alida Star Gebser and Alida Jean McCullough v. Lago Vista Independent School District* (524 U.S. 274), the Supreme Court ruled that damages may not be recovered for sexual harassment of a student by a teacher unless an official of the school district who at a minimum has authority to institute corrective measures on the district's behalf has actual notice of, and is deliberately indifferent to, the teacher's misconduct.
2005	In *Jackson v. Birmingham Board of Education* (No. 02-1672), the Supreme Court ruled that Title IX also covers those who report violations to Title IX, thus allowing them to sue for remedy against retaliation by school districts.
2006	The U.S. Department of Education relaxed rules regarding the enforcement of Title IX by allowing communities more flexibility in the creation and maintenance of single-sex schools and classrooms.

(continued)

Table 2.1 *Continued*

ISSUES OF DISABILITY
1973	With the Rehabilitation Act of 1973, the U.S. Congress expanded opportunities available to persons with disabilities. Section 502 requires accessibility in all buildings built after 1968 and financed with federal funds. Section 503 requires affirmative action and nondiscrimination clauses in all contracts valued at more than $2,500. Section 504 provides equal educational opportunity (including accessibility) for "otherwise qualified handicapped individuals" in all educational programs.
1976	In the Education of All Handicapped Children Act, the U.S. Congress established that all school districts are responsible for education "in the least restrictive environment for all children, regardless of handicapping condition."
1982	In *Board of Education of Hendrick Hudson Central School District v. Rowley* (458 U.S. 156), the Supreme Court found that the requirement for a "free, appropriate, public education" in the Educational of All Handicapped Children Act is satisfied when "the state provides specialized instruction with sufficient support services to permit the handicapped child to benefit educationally from the instruction." It does not require that any service that would guarantee such a child's education to his or her "fullest potential" be provided.
1984	In *Irving Independent School District v. Tatro* (468 U.S. 883), the Supreme Court ruled that CIC (clean intermittent catheterization) was a legitimate support service that should be provided by the school when necessary, as it enabled the child to stay in school and was no less a support service than transportation.
1984	In *Smith v. Robinson* (468 U.S. 992), the Supreme Court held that parents were not entitled to reimbursement for attorneys' fees in litigation over special education services even when the petitioners (parents) won the case, on the grounds that since such reimbursements were not written into the Education of All Handicapped Children Act, Congress must have intended that they be excluded.
1986	In response to the Supreme Court's decision in *Smith v. Robinson* (above), Congress passed the Handicapped Children's Protection Act of 1986 (P.L. 99-372), which provided for the award of attorneys' fees, under stated conditions, to parents if they prevailed.
1988	In *Honig v. Doe* (484 U.S. 305), the Supreme Court held that schools may temporarily exclude a handicapped student for up to 10 days who poses an immediate threat to himself/herself or others. During this 10-day period, the school should initiate an IEP review to determine placement after the suspension is over.
1990	With the Individuals with Disabilities Education Act (I.D.E.A.; P.L. 101-476), the U.S. Congress introduced the phrase "individuals with disabilities" as language more appropriate and realistic than "handicapped persons," and extended its provisions to serve individuals until age 21.
1992	With the Americans with Disabilities Act (ADA), the U.S. Congress extended to the private sector provisions to ensure the rights of access and freedom from discrimination for persons with disabilities that had previously applied only to agencies and settings receiving federal funds.
1993	In *Florence County School District Four v. Shannon Carter* (510 U.S. 7), the Supreme Court held that if a public school program does not provide an appropriate education and the parents place the child into a private program where the child does receive an appropriate education, the parents are entitled to reimbursement for the child's education.
1999	In *Cedar Rapids Community School District v. Garrett F.* (526 U.S. 66), the Supreme Court ruled that school districts are required to provide nursing services when such supportive services are necessary for students to access and benefit from their educational program.
2005	In *Schaffer v. Weast* (546 U.S. 49), the Supreme Court ruled that the burden of proof in contesting a school district's IEP for a child with a disability lies with the parents.
2007	In *Winkleman v. Parma City School District* (No. 05-983), the Supreme Court held that parents of children with disabilities may go into court without a lawyer to challenge their school district's decisions on special education services for their child or children, on the grounds not to be able to do so compromised the rights of parents who could not find or afford an appropriate attorney.

Table 2.1 *Continued*

ISSUES OF SOCIAL CLASS (SCHOOL FUNDING CASES)	
1971	In *Serrano v. Priest* (5 C3rd 584), the California Supreme Court found that the state formula for distributing school aid unconstitutionally discriminated against students in low-income districts.
1973	In *San Antonio Independent School District v. Rodriguez* (No. 71-1332), the Supreme Court found that despite local disparities in school aid and differences in tax effort throughout Texas, the state's system of school aid did not violate the equal protection clause of the Fourteenth Amendment, thus "permitting and encouraging vital local participation and control of schools through district taxation."
1977	In *Horton v. Meskill* (376 A.2d 359), the Connecticut Supreme Court found that the Connecticut Constitution requires the state to "provide a substantially equal educational opportunity" and declared the existing system unconstitutional because it was based primarily on local property taxes with no significant equalizing state support and, therefore, generated large per-pupil spending disparities.
1982	In *Lujan v. Colorado State Board of Education* (649 P.2d 1005), the Colorado Supreme Court found that the state's education clause did not require "absolute equality in educational services or expenditures." In addition, the court ruled that the goal of local school control was a legitimate state purpose that justified the state's school financing system under the equal protection clause.
1989	In *Rose v. Council for a Better Education* (790 S.W. 2d 186, 60 Ed. Law Rep. 1289), the Supreme Court of Kentucky found that legislative initiatives for funding schools were insufficient to provide equal educational opportunity, and ordered wide changes in school funding, which were, in fact, put into law.
1996	In *Sheff v. O'Neill* (678 A.2d 1267), the Connecticut Supreme Court held that students in the Hartford public schools were racially, ethnically, and economically isolated and that, as a result, Hartford public school students had not been provided a substantially equal educational opportunity under the state constitution. A settlement determined that at least 30% of Hartford students should receive an educational experience with reduced isolation by using interdistrict magnet schools, the Open Choice program, and interdistrict cooperative programs.
1997	In *DeRolph v. State of Ohio* (678 N.E.2d 886), the Ohio Supreme Court found four times that the way in which schools were funded in the state, based on property taxes, was unconstitutional. The state has allocated more funds for K–12 education since these decisions, but has done nothing to address the court's remedy, which was to change the basis of school funding.

Theoretical Approaches to Multicultural Education

One set of programs responsive to cultural and other forms of diversity fell under the umbrella term **multicultural education**. Growing out of the civil rights movement of the 1960s, these programs tried to address the needs of racial, ethnic, and linguistic minorities. In their analysis of multicultural education in the United States, Sleeter and Grant (1987) find five distinct categories of efforts described under the label multicultural education that are commonly found in schools. Although there is clearly some overlap among them, they represent the variety of approaches that have been used by educational pluralists in attempting to advance the cause of a positive approach to cultural diversity.

Multicultural Education

Teaching the Culturally Different

The main purposes of these approaches are to counter a cultural deficiency orientation while assisting individuals to develop and maintain their own cultural identity. Such efforts attempt to help individuals develop competence in the culture of the dominant group while developing a positive self-identity. The focus of such efforts tends to be on aspects of the culture and language of specific target groups that a teacher can build upon, not on issues of social and power relationships. Few of these efforts extend beyond attention to culture (in the traditional sense), race, and ethnicity and, therefore, exclude attention to gender, exceptionality, and social class.

Such approaches are evident in situations where the majority group is rather homogeneous and of a different background from the teacher. Also characteristic of such approaches is an emphasis on the transmission of mainstream curriculum content. Examples of such efforts include the extensive KEEP (Kamehameha Early Education Program) project in Hawaii, which aims to modify the school context so that it is more congruent with the culture of the child. Teacher training efforts that teach "all there is to know about teaching the _____ child" reflect such an orientation. Such efforts can transmit a considerable amount of culture-specific information; however, they may mask an assimilationist ideology.

Human Relations

This category views multicultural education as a means by which students of different backgrounds learn to communicate more effectively with others while learning to feel good about themselves. Such efforts provide practical ideas for how teachers can improve their communications with others while at the same time helping students understand their culturally different peers.

It is essential that individuals in a pluralistic nation learn to communicate more effectively with one another, but this emphasis on communication is only part of the solution. An education that effectively addresses diversity goes well beyond such a limited scope to include attention to such factors as curriculum expansion and inclusion and empowerment.

Single-Group Studies

This category addresses instruction that focuses on the experiences and cultures of one specific group. In response to the early demands by those seeking inclusion in the curriculum, specific courses that reflected the heritage, contributions, and perspectives of these "forgotten" groups were developed in many schools and universities across the nation. Such courses as African American History, Chicano Literature, and Native American Culture, typically monoethnic courses, were developed and taught, for the most part, by members of that particular group. Those who took such courses were typically members of the target ethnic group. The primary goals of these courses are twofold: (1) to develop a content dimension because exclusion from mainstream material typically resulted in a lack of information readily available about certain groups, and (2) to help individuals develop a more positive perception and self-image.

Although such efforts are needed, they may have the tendency to perpetuate a rather ethnocentric orientation, albeit from a different group's perspective. Addressing diversity effectively today demands that *multiple* perspectives be considered. The efforts of all who have contributed to the single-group studies can assist those working to expand the curriculum content for today's students.

Inclusive Multicultural Education

It soon became apparent that the adoption of single-group courses in and of themselves was not sufficient to enable many minority students to achieve in school at levels comparable to most of their majority counterparts, nor to advance along such a hierarchy. These early efforts seemed to be more akin to educational practices for minorities rather than practices for an inclusive multicultural education.

A slow shift in direction began to occur that offered a new approach, a new way of looking at the question of what is appropriate multicultural education. Attention began to be paid to broader issues of school reform that focused on the total school environment. As more and more ethnic groups began to make similar demands, the pressure on schools and universities to develop and deliver courses that reflected the experiences of many different groups increased. As similarities in people's experience and perspective became evident, schools, colleges, and universities began to offer courses that attempted to link the experiences of ethnic groups from a variety of perspectives while developing a conceptual core. Such course offerings as Ethnic Minority Music, Minority Literature, and The History of Minorities in America became popular.

These courses helped to raise the consciousness of a number of people concerning the perspectives and contributions of various groups to a variety of disciplines and causes. Underlying all these approaches was a focus on such issues as the strength and value of diversity in a pluralistic nation, human rights as a basic tenet for all, the acceptability of alternative life choices, social justice and equal opportunity, and equitable distribution of power among members of all ethnic groups.

Still others became interested in educational reform that would consider the educational problems beyond those of ethnic minority groups. Such efforts attempted to address the needs of women, religious groups, individuals with handicaps, and those from particular regions of the country, such as white Appalachia. Teachers who employed such a multicultural approach in their teaching would utilize material, concepts, and perspectives of many different individuals from diverse groups. English literature, for instance, would not be limited to a study of the literature of the so-called dead white men but also would include pieces written by women as well as by individuals from a variety of ethnic and cultural groups. In addition, the pieces selected for study would be ones identified as relevant by members of that particular group.

Education That Is Multicultural and Social Reconstructionist

None of the approaches identified previously seemed to have sufficient impact on the experiences of many, at least to the degree that people were empowered to make a difference in their lives. A significant mismatch between the curriculum of the school and the daily experiences and cultural backgrounds of many people of color is assumed to exist, which is nearly impossible for many to transcend. Essentially, the schools succeed at placing certain individuals at an advantage while effectively suppressing many others.

Sleeter and Grant (1986) spoke of providing education that is multicultural and social reconstructionist. This approach goes beyond multicultural education

in its attempt to help students critically analyze their circumstances and the social stratification that keeps them from full participation in the society at large. The phrase "education that is multicultural" means that the entire education program should be designed to address the needs of diverse groups regardless of race, ethnicity, culture, religion, exceptionality, or gender. This approach also strives to provide students with the skills necessary to become socially active in creating the necessary changes. Such an effort is designed to enable individuals to shape their own destinies, hence the term *social reconstructionist*.

Outcomes of Multicultural Education

Student Outcomes

Since the middle part of the 20th century social scientists have known that children as young as 3 years of age are able to differentiate human physical characteristics such as skin color. Children also, from about age 5, make attributions about others based on their skin color, associating black as having negative value and white as having positive value (Frenkel-Brunswick, 1948). So, if children come to school already identifying differences in skin color and making judgments about others based on this, what kind of impact can multicultural education have?

Relatively little has been written about the impact of most multicultural education programs. Banks (1990) provided a comprehensive survey of the effects of multicultural education on the racial attitudes of children. Positive effects of multicultural education efforts have been observed through the use of a variety of strategies, including curriculum units and courses developed around specific ethnic or cultural groups (e.g., African American History); multiethnic readings in the social studies; integrating multicultural activities into social studies, English, and reading; the use of multiethnic readers in the language arts program, as well as in the particular instructional strategy that is used.

Studies in cooperative learning rather consistently suggest that positive racial attitudes can result among students of different ethnic groups when they utilize cooperative learning activities (Cooper & Slavin, 2004). The lessons learned from the cooperative learning studies suggest that the particular content taught may not be as important as how it is taught and how the concepts are communicated to students, parents, and the community. You will read more about cooperative learning, as well as other strategies, later in this book.

In response to this dearth of studies assessing the impact of multicultural education, Stephan, Renfro, and Stephan (2004) conducted a meta-analysis of 35 published articles evaluating multicultural education programs that were diverse in terms of location (across the United States and abroad) and ranging from 4 to 80 hours in length. Findings of this analysis support Banks's earlier analysis, suggesting that, in general, multicultural education programs have been successful in changing people's attitudes and behaviors. However, the results of such studies have not been consistent. Some possible reasons for such inconsistent findings include the nature and structure of the intervention, duration of exposure, individual student characteristics, such school characteristics as degree of cooperation versus competitiveness, characteristics of the community where the school is located, as well as aspects of the individual teachers.

Program Outcomes

It is instructive to reflect on the very different outcomes of the different mandates for equal educational opportunity legislated in the 1960s and 1970s. Why, for example, did P.L. 94-142 take root while bilingual education programs and anti-sex discrimination policies have had less success? Although a number of factors may be involved—economic recession, a resurgence of nativism, a backlash against feminism—the success of P.L. 94-142 and its later amendments is due largely to the actions of vocal parents and other advocacy groups supporting individuals with disabilities. Such advocacy on the part of parents, especially, has also led to an increasing awareness of the importance of community and family involvement in schools and classrooms.

The decade of the 1980s saw a powerful resurgence of the academic (as opposed to the social) mission of schools. That is, the primary function of schooling was seen as the transmission of knowledge rather than the transformation of society. Moreover, as people begin to understand the magnitude of the demographic changes taking place in the United States, schools are once again being viewed as potential agencies of assimilation, not just for exceptional (handicapped and gifted) students, but also for minority culture groups, the lower classes, and females. In short, the reality of social and demographic changes is forcing schools to reexamine both their academic and social missions and, in the process, to acknowledge that these two missions cannot really be separated. Many teachers and administrators are coming to the realization that curricula that are not attuned to the life experiences, values, and cognitive styles of the student population have little hope of producing desired academic outcomes.

James Banks (Banks & Banks, 2003) asserts that "if multicultural education is to become better understood and implemented in ways more consistent with theory, its various dimensions must be more clearly described, conceptualized, and researched." He describes five such dimensions for the field: *content integration* (the extent to which teachers present multiple perspectives on issues, concepts, and problems to their students); *knowledge construction* (the extent to which teachers instruct their students on the ways in which the social, behavioral, and natural sciences construct knowledge and the social and cultural factors that contribute to shaping it); *prejudice reduction* (the extent to which teachers use strategies that will help students develop more democratic attitudes and values); *equity pedagogy* (the extent to which teachers use methods and approaches to enhance the academic achievement of all students, regardless of race, ethnicity, gender, or social class); and *empowering school culture* (the extent to which the culture of the American school is restructured so that students from diverse racial, ethnic, language, and social class groups may experience true educational equality).

Where We Are Today

Public Responses to Multicultural and Bilingual Education Reforms

Passage of civil rights laws and educational mandates, however, did not guarantee equality of educational opportunity to all American children. Frequently court assistance was needed to ensure compliance with congressional mandates. A significant case in the development of multicultural and bilingual education was *Lau v. Nichols* decided by a 1974 Supreme Court ruling. This decision declared that a San Francisco school district violated a non–English-speaking Chinese student's right to equal educational opportunity when it failed to provide needed English language instruction and other special programs. An important consequence of the *Lau* decision was the declaration that school districts across the country must provide students an education in languages that meets their needs.

Although *Lau v. Nichols,* filed on behalf of 1,800 Chinese American pupils, did not involve special education directly, the ruling underscored the responsibility of schools to address language differences in making decisions about placing students, as well as in teaching them. Two previous judicial decisions in class action suits brought by parents had directly addressed the issue of overrepresentation of minority children in special education. In 1970, in *Diana v. State Board of Education,* parents charged that the number of Hispanic students placed in special classes for children with mental retardation in California was approximately twice what would be expected based on the proportion of Hispanic children enrolled in that state. In *Larry P. v. Riles* (1971), similar overrepresentation of black children was found in the San Francisco Unified School District.

In both cases, disproportions were attributed to invalid use of IQ tests as the basis for placement decisions; *Diana* revealed that Spanish-speaking children were administered tests in English and that African American pupils in *Larry P. v. Riles* were found to score within the normal range when retested.

In terms of schooling mandates, educators and the public have responded (and still respond) to multicultural efforts in various ways. In direct conflict are those who advocate special programs such as bilingual and multicultural education and those who oppose them. Opponents of special programs fall into two categories. First, there are those who believe the American educational system in its "traditional" form has always provided for the upward mobility of culturally diverse peoples who are "willing to work." Other opponents believe that the nation-state will be destroyed if the schools do not continue offering a monocultural and monolinguistic education. In the latter group, some moralize that pluralistic approaches to education, especially bilingualism, only serve to delay students in learning the English that will help them in the everyday world. Others worry that "ethnics" will now be mandated for available (and scarcer) teaching positions. Still others warn that ethnic (and racial) identity movements serve to weaken the cultural "glue" that holds the nation together, thereby aggravating tensions rather than diminishing differences among groups.

A third group, composed primarily of educators and speaking in a somewhat softer voice, assert that pluralism in education should not be viewed as a remedial effort, nor a form of reparation, but rather as the long overdue affirmation of a social reality. Pluralism, in their view, is not an ethnic or racial property but a national characteristic, long ignored in education. Rudolf Schmerl (1977) at the University of Michigan, for example, observes:

> Intercontinental origin is still much more apparent in our electoral process than in our educational system. Our politics cultivate the immigrant and ethnic ethos as a matter of simple realism. Our educational system seems to be capable, so far, of no more than cursory, half-embarrassed hints about the diversity of our origins and experience, memories, and loyalties, fears, hopes, bitterness, and pride. (p. 45)

Recent Reaction to Multicultural Education

The 1980s saw a retrenchment from the ideals of educational equity and equality and resurgence of old assimilationist arguments in new costumes. In particular, we have heard these arguments masked by a call for "excellence" in the face of "mediocrity." Those calling for excellence generally advocate curricula based on the old European-, white-, male-oriented classics. Frequently, these calls for the traditional model of education have explicitly deplored the attention given to diversity. President Ronald Reagan, for example,

> claimed that one reason that the schools were failing was the attention that had been focused on female, minority, and handicapped students. He asserted that, if the federal government and educators had not been so preoccupied with the needs of these special groups of students, education in the U.S. might not have succumbed to the "rising tide of mediocrity." What the President failed to note is that, if these three groups of students are eliminated, only about 15 percent of the school population remains. (Shakeshaft, 1986, p. 499)

National Association
of Multicultural
Education

During this period, programs in multicultural education, global or international education, gender-equitable education, and education for exceptional individuals continued to develop, although in a political climate that was far from congenial. Unfortunately, children from diverse backgrounds are still, more often than not, forced into a single, more manageable class group by teachers who are stressed from the demands of a difficult job. Still, the model for the students in these classes is one in which they are usually treated as if they are Anglo, middle class, and experientially enriched.

Proponents of multicultural education in the past decade have continued to pursue the goal of equal educational opportunity, and to argue that a truly equitable education will also be truly excellent. Scholars in multicultural education have looked both within the field and outside it for ideas and concepts that will broaden the field, taking interest especially in areas of gender research and of inclusionary practices in special education. The past decade has also witnessed the publication of the second handbook of research in multicultural education, as well as the first systematic dictionary of multicultural terms and concepts. With these publications, the field of multicultural education has made a strong claim to being not just an advocacy but a disciplined field of study.

It is safe to say, however, that current media and other attention to perceived deficits in schooling in general have sometimes come into conflict with the development of multicultural practice. Thus the efforts of those who believe strongly in the affirmation of multicultural principles as principles of good teaching for all students must continue with as much energy and dedication as before.

Resegregation: The Legacy of Neighborhood Schools

It is perhaps ironic that the story behind the original impetus for the *Brown v. Board of Education* case concerned a third-grader—Linda Brown—who had to walk six blocks from her home to a school bus stop to ride a bus one mile to her segregated black elementary school, passing, as she walked, a white elementary school that was only seven blocks from her house.

As an adult, Linda Brown Thompson (2004) recalled her happiness at the thought that she might be able to attend the neighborhood school with all her friends:

> well, like I say, we lived in an integrated neighborhood and I had all of these playmates of different nationalities. And so when I found out that day that I might be able to go to their school, I was just thrilled, you know. And I remember walking over to Sumner school with my dad that day and going up the steps of the school and the school looked so big to a smaller child. And I remember going inside and my dad spoke with someone and then he went into the inner office with the principal and they left me out...to sit outside with the secretary. And while he was in the inner office, I could hear voices and hear his voice raised, you know, as the conversation went on. And then he immediately came out of the office, took me by the hand and we walked home from the school. I just couldn't understand what was happening because I was so sure that I was going to go to school with Mona and Guinevere, Wanda, and all of my playmates.

In the 56 years since the *Brown* case, the concept of the neighborhood school—a (usually elementary) school that children of the neighborhood attend—has undergone considerable stretching and twisting; indeed, sometimes it has disappeared altogether. Linda Brown had to pass up her neighborhood school in order to attend a segregated school, and the case brought by her father and the parents of other black children argued that she should be allowed to attend her neighborhood school. The issue was segregation, and the Supreme Court ruling that segregated schools were inherently unequal, and thus unconstitutional under the terms of the Fourteenth Amendment. A remedy, however, was not so easily articulated, and the case ended with Chief Justice Warren asking for the Attorney General of the United States and the attorney generals of the 17 states that required segregation and the 16 states that permitted it to appear before the Court to submit briefs and to argue for specific appropriate relief.

Over time, the original interest in *desegregation,* the process of ending segregation in schools, became an overriding interest in *integration,* the process of bringing students of different races together in schools. Proponents of desegregation used the law to make segregation illegal; proponents of integration used the law to make bringing students together mandatory. Lost in the many attempts to accomplish *integration*—voluntary and involuntary busing, magnet schools, reorganized districts—was the idea of the neighborhood school, and, indeed, sometimes the idea of equal educational opportunity, itself. As Tolson (2004) notes, "the great tragedy of *Brown,* many commentators agree, is that its original emphasis on racial integration as a means toward equal education somehow shifted toward an emphasis on integration as an end itself."

Between 1971, when the *Swann* decision (see Table 2.1) ordered the creation of a more racially diverse school district, and 1999, when a U.S. district court overturned it, a whole series of district court and Supreme Court decisions served to move the nation away from mandated integration of schools. In the past several years, the Supreme Court has, in fact, forbidden the use of race for admission to college or assignment to K–12 schools in a number of cases. Most recently, in its June 28, 2007, decision in *Parents Involved in Community Schools v. Seattle School District No. 1, et al.,* the Court "invalidated programs in Seattle and metropolitan Louisville, Kentucky, that sought to maintain school-by-school diversity by limited transfers on the basis of race or using race as a 'tiebreaker' for admission to particular schools" (as cited in Greenhouse, 2007).

Today, the notion of school choice has also provided a countervailing pressure to mandated integration of schools. Whether parents of any race choose schools because they are "in the neighborhood," have high test scores, or are in some other way desirable for their children, the fact remains that choice can either bolster the neighborhood school idea or shatter it.

Moreover, many black as well as white parents are emphatic in the belief that they should have good quality schools in their own neighborhoods. Indeed, there is considerable thought among black parents and black leaders that neither segregation nor integration are as important as having their children in schools with the resources to help them succeed. In addition, some believe that there is a cultural benefit to black children to be in schools together. Elizabeth Eckford

(Tolson, 2004), for example, one of the original nine students to integrate Central High School in Little Rock, says,

> There was a time when I thought integration was one of the most desired things. . . . I appreciate blackness more [now] than I did then.

Resegregation

So, after six decades, the issue of desegregated or integrated schools has resulted, in many cases, in the resegregation of schools, mostly because of housing patterns. To the extent that resegregated schools result in a significant pattern of discrimination and unequal education because such schools receive fewer and older textbooks, have teachers who are less highly qualified, and provide no vision of success to poor and minority children, the resegregation of schools is a tragedy. As Jonathan Kozol (2005), one of the most articulate advocates for justice for urban poor and minority children notes,

> Look, the school district in the South Bronx in which I've spent so much of the past 15 years has 11,000 students in elementary and middle schools, of whom 26 are White. That's a segregation rate of 99.8 percent. Two-tenths of 1 percent mark the difference between legally enforced apartheid in Mississippi 50 years ago, and socially and economically enforced apartheid in New York today. To the children we cordon off from the mainstream of America, it doesn't matter a single jot whether this is the consequence of a state law, or state and city demographic practices and policies. It makes no difference at all.

While the debate continues, there are some for whom there is a bottom line. Damien Jackson (2002), for example, quotes Steve Johnston, executive director of a nonprofit organization in North Carolina dedicated to advancing the value of diversity in public education, who notes that "integrated neighborhoods produce integrated schools." Jackson goes further:

> Johnston contends that until white people and the institutions they control pay equitable wages to people of color and allow for the kind of educational institutions that can produce economic parity, the onus will always be on whites to make neighborhoods and schools integrated. "Economic diversity in housing patterns will create diverse schools," he says.

The Impact of Global Perspectives on Inequitable Education

Currently, as the impact of globalization makes itself felt in American schools, we are entering a new phase of the ongoing effort to provide an equitable education to all our students—native-born or immigrant, English language speaking or English language learners, rural or urban, economically comfortable or the children of poverty. The impact of global perspectives changes, somewhat, the emphasis on domestic multicultural education, giving it a more international perspective and tending toward a focus on the idea of *intercultural education* as relating to both native-born and internationally-born students in American schools.

For one thing, many states and districts around the country are working very hard to internationalize their curricula—to add to and integrate global content, global perspectives, and global language instruction (primarily Chinese and

Farsi) with traditional curricula so as to provide American students with the necessary foundation for living in an increasing global context in the 21st century.

These efforts are closely tied to the acknowledgment, made by many policymakers, that American students are not doing very well in internationally competitive tests of knowledge and skills. This reality, should it be allowed to continue, will have significant consequences in a global marketplace. As noted by The New Commission on the Skills of the American Workforce (2007),

> The best employers the world over will be looking for the most competent, most creative, and most innovating people on the face of the earth and will be willing to pay them top dollar for their services.... Beyond [strong skills in English, mathematics, technology, and science], candidates will have to be comfortable with ideas and abstractions, good at both analysis and synthesis, creative and innovative, self-disciplined and well organized, able to learn very quickly and work well as a member of a team and have the flexibility to adapt quickly to frequent changes in the labor marker as the shifts in the economy become ever faster and more dramatic. If we continue on our current course, and the number of nations outpacing us in the education race continues to grow at its current rate, the American standard of living will steadily fall relative to those nations, rich and poor, that are doing a better job. The core problem is that our education and training systems were built for another era, an era in which most workers needed only a rudimentary education. It is not possible to get where we have to go by patching that system. We can get where we must go only by changing the system itself.

The good news, for those who champion a strong commitment to equity in American education is that one of the changes we need to make involves refusing to allow American schools to be as hugely inequitable as they currently are. Scholars who study education systems in high performing countries note that these societies are actively transforming their schooling systems for all students by infusing resources across the board, by encouraging and then acting on teacher recommendations on curriculum development and pedagogy, and by emphasizing the importance of the development of human capital to their future (Darling-Hammond, 2010).

How these things will be accomplished will depend, in part, on a strong collaboration between the nation's teachers and the nation's policymakers and legislators. Clearly, this process will write a new chapter in the history of attention to diversity in American education.

Summary

The history of multicultural education has its roots in a debate between those who think that American schooling should provide a common education to all children based on the history and culture of European Americans and Western civilization, and those who think that American schooling must recognize and affirm the rich historical and cultural backgrounds and perspectives of a population that has always been diverse and is becoming ever more so.

Chapter Review

Go to the Online Learning Center at www.mhhe.com/cushner7e to review important content from the chapter, practice with key terms, take a chapter quiz, and find the Web links listed in this chapter.

Key Terms

Anglo-conformity 38
assimilationist
   model 38

cultural pluralism 41
Freedmen's Bureau 37

multicultural
   education 49

Active Exercise

Additional Active Exercises are available online at www.mhhe.com/cushner7e.

Family Tree: Tracing One's Roots and Family Experiences

Purpose: To discover your family's experiences in past generations and compare them to immigrants and refugees today.

Instructions: Most of us in the United States can trace our family history, or roots, to someplace other than where we currently reside. Speak with family members and look through old family photographs (if you have any) to trace your family's heritage as far back as possible. If you are adopted or do not know your ancestors, respond in terms of an adoptive or foster family, or one to which you closely identify. Respond to the following questions as best you can, and share your responses with others.

1. From what parts of the world did your family (or families) originate?

2. What motivated your ancestors to leave their homeland for a new world? When did they leave? If your ancestors were always in North America, what was their life like prior to European contact?

3. What hardships did your ancestors face in previous generations, either when they first arrived or soon after contact? What did they do to overcome any hardships? Do they recall any prejudice that was experienced?

4. What did your ancestors do in the previous two to three generations? How did this influence what the family does today?

5. What languages did your ancestors speak? What has happened to these languages in your family today?

6. What family traditions or practices have been carried out over the years that are special or unique to your family?

7. What do you know of the meaning behind your family name? How, if at all, has it changed over the years? Do you know the reason for any changes?

8. How are the experiences of your family similar to, or different from, those faced by various immigrants or refugees today?

9. In what ways was this exercise easy or difficult for you to do? Under what circumstances might an exercise like this be difficult for a student to do? What might you do as a teacher to modify it in special circumstances?

Reflective Questions

1. In the case study about the desegregation of Central High School in Little Rock, Arkansas, it is suggested that this episode in the history of the civil rights movement remains in the public mind. Do you think this is the case, and if so, why?

2. One of the difficulties in the Little Rock situation was that members of the school board wanted to take a gradual road to integration, and others, largely families of black children, were impatient with waiting, something they had been doing, for all practical purposes, since the Civil War. Do you think that a gradual or a relatively rapid approach to significant change would be the most effective? Why?

3. How would you have liked to be one of the "Little Rock Nine"? How do you think you would have reacted to the fact that you needed armed guards to enter school? How would you have reacted to the shouts and slurs of those on the streets who didn't want to see you enter that building?

4. Why do you think it took 15 years to finally integrate all the schools in Little Rock? Think about some factors that probably contributed to the long, slow process of integration.

References

Banks, J. A. (1988). *Multiethnic education: Theory and practice* (2nd ed.). Boston: Allyn & Bacon.

Banks, J. A. (1990). Multicultural education: Its effects on students' racial and gender role attitudes. In James Shaver (Ed.), *Handbook of research on social studies teaching and learning*. New York: Macmillan.

Banks, J. A., & Banks, C. A. (2003). *Handbook of research on multicultural education* (2nd ed.). New York: Macmillan.

Brown, D. A. (1970). *Bury my heart at Wounded Knee*. New York: Holt, Rinehart, & Winston.

Brown v. Board of Education of Topeka, 347 U.S. 483 (1954).

Carelli, A. O'B. (1988). What is Title IX? In A. O'B Carelli (Ed.), *Sex equity in education: Readings and strategies*. Springfield, IL: Charles C Thomas.

Cooper, R., & Slavin, R. (2004). Cooperative learning: An instructional strategy to improve intergroup relations. In W. Stephen & P. Vogt (Eds.), *Education programs for improving intergroup relations: Theory, research, and practice*. New York: Teachers College Press.

Darling-Hammond, L. (2010). *The flat world and education: How America's commitment to equity will determine our future*. New York: Teachers College and Columbia University, p. 5.

Diana v. State Board of Education, CA 70 RFT/N.D. Cal (1970).

Dinnerstein, L., & Reiners, D. M. (1975). *Ethnic Americans: A history of immigration and assimilation*. New York: Harper & Row.

Executive Summary, *Tough choices or tough times: The report of the new commission on the skills of the American workforce* (2007). National Center on Education and the Economy, pp. 7–8. Accessed on April 26, 2010 at http://www.skillscommission.org/pdf/exec_sum/ToughChoices_EXECSUM.pdf.

Frenkel-Brunswick, E. (1948). A study of prejudice in children. *Human Relations, 1*(3), 295–306.

Frost, R. (1942). The gift outright. In *The witness tree* (p. 1.41.1). New York: Henry Holt.

Greenhouse, L. (2007, June 29). Justices limit the use of race in school plans for integration. *New York Times* [Electronic version]. Retrieved from http://www.nytimes.com/2007/06/29/washington/29scotus.html

Hoffman, N. (Ed.). (2003). *Women's "true" profession: Voices from the history of teaching* (2nd ed.). Cambridge, MA: Harvard Education Press.

Hunter, W. A. (Ed.). (1975). *Multicultural education through competency-based teacher education.* Washington, DC: American Association of Colleges of Teacher Education.

Jackson, D. (2002, December 20). Here comes the neighborhood: Charlotte and the resegregation of America's public schools. *In These Times.* Retrieved from http://www.inthesetimes.com/issue/27/04/feature1.shtml

Koestler, F. (1967). *The unseen minority: A social history of blindness in the United States.* New York: David McKay.

Kozol, J. (2005, November). Resegregation in America's schools. *NEAtoday.* Retrieved from http://www.nea.org/neatoday/0511/kozol.html

Larry P. v. Riles, 793 F2d 969, 9th Cir. (1971).

Lau v. Nichols, 414 U.S. 563 (1974).

Parents Involved in Community Schools v. Seattle School District No. 1, et al., 413 U.S. 189 (2007).

Plessy v. Ferguson, 163 U.S. 537 (1896).

Provenzo, E. F., Jr. (1986). *An introduction to education in American society.* Columbus, OH: Charles E. Merrill.

Schmerl, R. B. (1977). The student as immigrant. In D. E. Gross, G. C. Baker, & L. J. Stiles (Eds.), *Teaching in a multicultural society* (p. 45). New York: Free Press.

Shakeshaft, C. (1986). A gender at risk. *Phi Delta Kappan, 67*(7).

Sleeter, C., & Grant, C. (1986). Educational equity, education that is multicultural and social reconstructionist. *Journal of Educational Equity and Leadership, 6*(2), 105–118.

Sleeter, C., & Grant, C. (1987). An analysis of multicultural education in the United States. *Harvard Educational Review, 57*(4), 421–444.

Stephan, C., Renfro, L., & Stephan, W. (2004). The evaluation of multicultural education programs: Techniques and a meta-analysis. In W. Stephen & P. Vogt (Eds.), *Education programs for improving intergroup relations: Theory, research, and practice* (pp. 227–242). New York: Teachers College Press.

Thompson, L. B. (2004). *Black, white, and brown.* Transcript of program produced by KTWU Channel 11 in Topeka, Kansas. (Originally aired May 3). Retrieved from http://brownvboard.org/video/blackwhitebrown

Tiedt, P. L., & Tiedt, I. M. (1990). *Multicultural teaching: A handbook of activities, information, and resources* (3rd ed.). Boston: Allyn & Bacon.

Tolson, J. (2004, March 14). Chain reaction: Resegregation, reverse discrimination, busing, and white flight: What happened after Brown? *U.S. News and World Report* [Electronic version]. Retrieved from http://www.usnews.com/usnews/news/articles/040322/22after_print.htm

Trujillo, R. (1973). Bilingual-bicultural education: A necessary strategy for American public education. In National Bilingual Bicultural Institute, *A relook at Tucson '66 and beyond*. Washington, DC: National Education Association.

Wallin, J.E.W. (1914). *The mental health of the school child: The psychoeducational clinic in relation to child welfare*. New Haven, CT: Yale University Press.

Webb, R. B., & Sherman, R. R. (1989). *Schooling and society* (2nd ed.). New York: Macmillan.

Weinberg, M. (1977). *A chance to learn: A history of race and education in the United States*. New York: Cambridge University Press.

Zangwill, I. (1909). *The melting pot*. New York: Macmillan.

Culture and the Culture-Learning Process

Focus Questions

1. How is it that you became the cultural being that you are today?
2. How have different individuals and institutions you have come into contact with influenced you?
3. How has the media influenced your cultural identity? Your religion? Your community? What other forces operate to influence your cultural identity?
4. What do you know about your own culture that you can use to better understand another culture, or that will enable you to talk intelligently about cultural differences with someone who is different from you?

" The first month or two in class I was always saying, 'Look at me when I talk to you,' and the (Navajo) kids simply wouldn't do it. They would always look at their hands, or the blackboard, or anywhere except looking me in the face. And finally, one of the other teachers told me it was a cultural thing. They should warn us about things like that. Odd things. It makes children seem evasive. "

TONY HILLERMAN,
The Skinwalkers

The word *education* is derived from the Latin word *edu-care,* meaning "to lead forth." If we are to seriously engage in the education of students who will be contributing, collaborative, and proactive citizens in a multicultural and global society, we must lead our students in such a manner that they understand the cultural basis of their own as well as others' behavior; are cognizant of the conditions, both present and past, that affect people around the world; and are able to take the necessary steps to adjust to change, both in themselves and in the world around them.

Clearly, *education* is a broader term than *schooling.* Indeed, one of the difficulties we all encounter in talking about education is that it is pervasive in human life. Not often emphasized, however, are the actual settings, apart from schools, in which education occurs and the precise nature of teaching and learning in those settings. Yet it is in these settings–particularly in the home, the neighborhood, and our houses of worship–that we acquire the language, knowledge, attitudes, and values that enable us to engage in the dramatic conversation called "culture." It is in these settings that people develop the cultural identities they bring to their interactions with others, both within as well as outside of school. And it is through these settings that we must work to lead our students forward into the future.

Giroux and Simon (1989) speak directly to the importance of teachers understanding their own cultural identities and those of their students:

> By ignoring the cultural and social forms that are authorized by youth and simultaneously empower and disempower them, educators risk complicity in silencing and negating their students. This is unwittingly accomplished by refusing to recognize the importance of those sites and social practices outside of the schools that actively shape student experiences and through which students often define and construct their sense of identity, politics, and culture. (p. 3)

These ideas can be clarified through the use of a "thought experiment"–a community you can enter in your imagination, so as to consider the educational implications of living there. In this experiment, imagine a medium-sized suburban city of about 100,000 people that is a first-ring suburb of a major city of about half a million people. The entire metropolitan area has a population of about 1.5 million people and is an hour or so from two other midsized cities. Let's call this city Beechland Heights. Now, conditions in such a city will vary depending on its ethnic and religious composition, its economic base, and its location (Is it in New England? The deep South? The Midwest? The mountain states of the West? The Southwest? The Northwest?). The size of Beechland Heights is also a factor to consider. If it were a city of several million, or a village of several hundred (or thousand) people, conditions might be different. In this thought experiment, Beechland Heights may assume a variety of characteristics. Read on and see what you can surmise.

Exploring the Concept of Culture

One of the greatest difficulties people have when they begin to explore concepts related to culture and culture learning is that of agreement on what it is they are talking about. This chapter looks closely at the concept of culture and the culture-learning process; that is, how we acquire a cultural identity. The chapter begins with some definitions of culture and with some of the analytical concepts devised

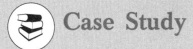

Case Study

Beechland Heights: A Thought Experiment

The imaginary city of Beechland Heights is clearly a geographical community in the sense that it is in some ways like a small city and in other ways like the larger city adjacent to it. It has city limits, a mayor, and a city council. It has its own set of laws and is also under the jurisdiction of its county, its state, and the nation. Importantly, a major highway bisects the city, a fact that the residents acknowledge by using the terms "north side" and "south side."

The city of Beechland Heights has a rather wealthy residential section, a number of middle-class neighborhoods, and a few neighborhoods that are rather poor. It has some manufacturing industries, a number of churches, two synagogues–one conservative and one reform–as well as a mosque. There is a Buddhist temple in a neighboring community. Throughout the area are numerous day-care centers, a number of quality museums, a relatively large public library system with several smaller branch libraries, three local television stations and several radio stations, one daily newspaper, and two smaller community weekly papers. There are numerous hospitals in the area–one of them Catholic and one Jewish–and numerous "neighborhood" medical drop-in centers. It has department stores, discount stores, bars, neighborhood convenience stores, and several commercial and service businesses. It has a municipal park, its own ice rink, and semi-professional baseball, basketball, and football teams, a large YM/YWCA as well as a Jewish Community Center, a welfare department, a children's services department, and a juvenile detention center. It has a professional theater, a dance company on the brink of collapse due to lack of funding, several malls, and a downtown business district. It has an adequate number of lawyers, doctors, dentists, accountants, architects, and other professionals. It has both public and private elementary, middle, and high schools. There are a few Catholic schools as well as one small Jewish day school. There are three well-established, well-endowed private schools in neigboring suburbs just outside the city limits. Beechland Heights has one state university, one large private university, and a community college, all of which interact well with the community.

Within the geographical community that is Beechland Heights, there is also a set of educational communities–groups of people who are actively engaged in instruction and learning (formal and informal) as well as those organizations and settings in which deliberate and systematic teaching and learning occurs. It is in these educational communities that the dramatic conversations of culture take place in particular ways—in families, neighborhoods, businesses, religious settings, and voluntary associations. So the particular combination of settings in Beechland Heights sets the tone, so to speak, of the community itself and of the educational messages–both coherent and conflicting–available to its people.

Say, for the sake of the experiment, that Beechland Heights is in upstate New York and is a largely Protestant city (of all denominations, including three good-sized black churches). It also has a considerable number of Catholic families, enough to support several churches, as well as a few Catholic schools, 13 public elementary schools that feed into six middle schools, and four comprehensive high schools. There is a significant Jewish community that supports one K–8 Jewish day school, and relatively small groups of Islamic and Buddhist families.

Say, further, that for the most part, Beechland Heights is a historically white, working- and middle-class city that has undergone significant ethnic changes due to the migration of people from the inner city over the past 20 years. The African Americans who live in the neighboring city have been there for at least 75 years, and they comprise about 40% of the population, most having migrated from the deep South between the World Wars to work in the city's factories. People of color now comprise about 20% of Beechland Heights. Let's further suppose that the area industries are suffering from severe competition, both domestic and foreign. Business is not good, and the residents of Beechland Heights are fearful that many jobs could be lost, thus creating a depressed economic situation for all income-producing businesses.

As in all communities, the cultural conversations of Beechland Heights have their roots in the economic, religious, socioeconomic class, and family life of the town. The particular education received by an individual growing up in Beechland Heights depends, in large

(continued)

part, on the ethnic, religious, social class, and occupational character of the individual's family and the character of the housing and neighborhoods in which the individual lives, works, and plays. These factors—as well as others, such as the age of the individual, the individual's health, and the size and composition of the family of which the individual is a member—also have a great deal to do with the access the individual has to a broad or narrow range of educational resources and experiences available both within and outside the school.

Take a look, now, at five 16-year-old high school students who live in Beechland Heights. What cultural conversations do you think have meaning for them?

Michael Williams is an African American young man who has lived his entire life with his grandmother and grandfather (retired and at home), his mother (an assembly line worker at the lightbulb factory), his aunt (who works evenings cleaning at the museum), two brothers, and a sister in a house on the northeast side of the city. He doesn't know who or where his father is. His older brother never went to college after he graduated from high school, and works in a local factory—although he is thinking about joining the army. The family regularly attends the local Baptist church. As a child, Michael played basketball at the community house near his home and continues to help out there with younger children. He attends the public high school and is in the college prep academic program, where he earns excellent grades. He has a steady girlfriend; is a member of the high school golf team, which practices at the local golf course; is on the school newspaper staff, which is advised by an editor of the Beechland Heights newspaper; and works after school and weekends at the golf course.

Dinorah Rodriguez lives in a pleasant, but small ranch house on a cul-de-sac on the south side of town. She is the youngest of a large, extended Mexican family; her parents having come to the United States initially as migrant workers before she was born. Although she attended Catholic parochial school through the eighth grade, she currently attends the public high school, where she is taking business-related subjects and is planning to become a secretary—perhaps in one of the local banks. Her family has always been very involved in the local Mexican community as well as in the church, and Dinorah gained a considerable amount of attention (not all of it positive) when she became the first altar girl at St. Mary's. Her family keeps in close contact via e-mail with the extended family members who remain in Mexico, and still sends money to support one of her aunts who is a nun. At home, the family speaks a fair amount of Spanish, something that Dinorah finds rather embarrassing when her friends are around. In school, she earns reasonably good grades, is on the cheerleading squad, and is a scorekeeper for the wrestling team. She dates a number of boys, mostly athletes, and works on weekends at a department store in a local shopping mall.

Steven Wong lives in a large, comfortable house on The Hill, on the west side of town, with his parents and a younger sister. His father is a successful businessman, and his mother, an artist, is in charge of the adult volunteers (called docents) at the museum where Steve sometimes works as a guide for special exhibits. His family does not belong to any religious group. He attends a private high school located in a neighboring community, where he struggles a bit for average grades, and is a member of the tennis and debate teams. As a child, Steven played Little League baseball, belonged to the Boy Scouts, and traveled extensively in the United States and to Hong Kong to visit family. He doesn't date much, and when he does it is usually with non-Asian girls who are children of his parents' friends. He is not certain that he wants to go to college, much to his parents' dismay.

Jacob Goldsmith lives with both of his parents in the same neighborhood as Steven Wong on The Hill. When Jacob was younger, he attended the one small Jewish day school that drew children from Beechland Heights as well as three or four other communities.

Jacob's father is a pediatrician with a fairly successful practice in town. His mother is a professor of English literature and teaches at a private college located about half an hour away. Jacob is an avid reader, plays tennis and golf on the school teams, and one day hopes to be a doctor like his father. His family is affiliated with Temple Israel, a reform synagogue near the school, but is not highly observant. For Jacob's Bar Mitzvah, his family took him on his first international trip–a 2-week trip to Israel. Since then he has remained active with a small group of Jewish high school students that meet Wednesday afternoons at the Temple. He hopes to return to Israel one day–perhaps to study for a year during college.

Shameka Collins is living in one of only three African American families on her street, which is on the south side of town. Shameka lives with her parents, an African American mother who works as a bookkeeper for a local department store, and a European American father, who spends much of his time working out of state. She sees him only occasionally–perhaps once or twice a month. Shameka is the only biracial student in her school, although most other students are not aware that her father is white. She has an older brother who is stationed on a nuclear submarine presently on duty in the Persian Gulf. As a child, Shameka was a Girl Scout for a while but dropped out. She has gone to Sunday school at the local Presbyterian church all her life. After school and on Saturdays she works at the main branch of the public library downtown, saving most of the money she makes for college. She does not have either the time or the inclination to date much, but she does find time to go to all the exhibitions at the museum and to all the local community theater productions. Once she even had a small part in a play there. Since Shameka and her mother are generally alone, they spend as much time together as possible. Her mother has taught her to sew, and she makes almost all her own clothes. She worries about leaving home when she goes to college and is trying to decide whether to attend the local community college for 2 years before actually leaving home. Because she takes advanced placement courses in high school, she will be eligible for courses at the college in her senior year and will probably become a student there. She thinks perhaps she will become a doctor.

Each of these students, lifelong residents of Beechland Heights, participates in a particular pattern of educational life, out of which has emerged a cultural identity. The cultural knowledge, beliefs, attitudes, and values of these students, like those of most Americans, are multiple– none identifies with a single cultural group. Yet their cultural and educational patterns are different and sometimes surprising. How do you see their various cultural influences affecting their lives? What aspects of their upbringing do you think influences them most today? In what ways are they similar or different to one another? In what ways are they similar or different to you? Can you put yourself in Beechland Heights?

by social scientists in their attempts to understand cultural similarities and differences among groups of people as well as individuals. This discussion sets the stage for subsequent analysis of cross-cultural interaction and intercultural development that occurs in the context of schools.

Defining Culture

Culture is studied by many different disciplines, including anthropology, sociology, education, psychology, health, business, and the military. If you were to peruse the literature of these various disciplines looking for the concept of culture, you would find literally hundreds of definitions. Some of these definitions are more useful than others in an examination of how culture influences the teaching-learning process. What all these definitions seem to have in common is the idea that culture refers to a human-made part of the environment as opposed to aspects that occur in nature. Culture determines, to a large extent, people's thoughts, ideas, patterns of interaction, and material adaptations to the world around them.

Coon (2000) refers to culture as "the totality of socially transmitted behavior patterns, arts, beliefs, institutions, and all other products of human work and thought characteristic of a community or a population" (p. 53). He likens culture to the act of cooking. When cooking, you begin with some basic ingredients, but then you add a few condiments, include a little bit more or less of certain items, adjust the cooking time, and so forth.

The criteria by which cultures define themselves, and differentiate themselves from one another, vary a great deal. The basic ingredients determining a culture may be geography, ethnicity, language, religion, and history. The factors that divide cultures can consist of any combination of these elements plus the "condiments" of the local scene. In Iraq, for instance, the population is divided religiously between Muslims and Christians; among Muslims between Shia and Sunni Muslims; and ethnically between Arabs and Kurds, as well as a number of other, smaller ethnic and religious groups. The situation is similar in India, where religion divides Muslim and Hindus; however, the Hindu majority is further split according to the caste to which one is born. In the United States and other modern nation-states, group loyalties based on cultural differences exist, but more or less as subsets of an overarching group loyalty called nationalism or patriotism. Ethnicity further divides these groups.

A culturally defined group can be as small as a group of Aborigines in the outback of Australia or as large as a nation-state. It can exist in a small, defined territory, or its members can share a territory with other culturally defined groups. It can be a closed system, or it can be open to new ideas introduced from other cultures. The only real requirement is that people who share the culture sense that they are different from those who do not belong to their group.

Activity and
Reading 5:
**Understanding
Cultural Complexity**

Culture in Everyday Use

Sociologists, who study culture in terms of various competing social groups within a society, have developed a number of concepts that are useful in discussions of cultural pluralism. Some of these terms are used interchangeably and often cause confusion. Five terms commonly used to describe social groups that share important cultural elements but that are smaller than a whole society are subculture, microculture, ethnic group, minority group, and people of color.

Subculture

The term **subculture** refers to a social group with shared characteristics that distinguish it in some way from the larger group in which it is embedded. Generally, a subculture is distinguished either by a unifying set of ideas and practices, such as the corporate culture or the drug culture, or by some demographic characteristic, such as the adolescent culture (Bullivant, 1993).

Microculture

The term **microculture** also refers to a social group that shares distinctive traits, values, and behaviors that set it apart from the parent macroculture of which it is a part. Although the terms *microculture* and *subculture* are often used interchangeably, *microculture* seems to imply a greater linkage with the parent culture. Microcultures often mediate–that is, interpret and transmit–the ideas, values, and institutions of the larger political community (Banks, 1989). Thus, for example, the family, the workplace, or the classroom can each be thought of as a microculture embedded in the larger culture of the neighborhood, the business, or the school. These larger macrocultures are themselves embedded in larger professional, regional, or national cultures. Thus a particular entity, such as the school, may be simultaneously both a macroculture (the culture of the school as a model of society) and a microculture (the culture of the particular school).

Minority Group

This term refers to a social group that occupies a subordinate position in a society. In 1978 Wagley and Harris defined a minority group as one that experiences discrimination and subordination within a society, is separated by physical or cultural traits disapproved of by the dominant group, shares a sense of collective identity and common burdens, and is characterized by marriage within the group (as cited in Bennett, 1990, p. 42). However, characterizing minority groups based on these criteria sometimes leads to confusion and inaccuracy. For example, women are often referred to as a minority group because they are thought to be oppressed, even though they constitute more than half the general population and do not, as a rule, marry within their group. Similarly, when students who are African American, Native American, or Latino constitute a majority of the population in a particular school, the school is often referred to as a "majority-minority school." The term *minority* can also be used in different ways in different countries. In the Netherlands, for instance, *minority* refers to immigrant groups that occupy a low socioeconomic status. Chinese, for instance, are considered minorities in the United States and Canada, but not in the Netherlands because they do not have low socioeconomic status (Cushner, 1998).

Ethnic Group

The term **ethnic group** refers to groups who share a common heritage. When asked to complete the statement, "I am _____" using as many descriptors as possible to define yourself, those statements that reflect identification with a collective or reference group are often indicative of one's ethnic identity. When people respond that they are African American, Jewish, or Polish, they are identifying with a group of people who share a common heritage, history, celebrations, and traditions, who enjoy similar foods, and who might speak a common language other than English. A sense of peoplehood, or the feeling that a person's own destiny is somehow linked with others who share this same knowledge, reflects identification with an ethnic group. Thus people can live in one nation and claim one nationality, yet maintain ancestral ties to another.

Activity 9:
Who Am I?

People of Color

The phrase **people of color** refers to nonwhite minority group members, such as African Americans, Mexican Americans, Puerto Ricans, and Native Americans, but reflects recent demographic realities of the United States. This phrase is preferred over *ethnic minority* by many people because these groups are, in many schools and communities, the majority rather than the minority.

As the United States and its schools grow increasingly complex with respect to cultural difference, many voices are beginning to criticize the use of collective terminology like people of color. These voices call for awareness and understanding of specific ethnic, racial, religious, and other groups. In this effort, it is recognized that the terms *Hispanic* or *Latino,* for example, are only umbrella terms for a number of Spanish-speaking ethnic groups, including Puerto Rican, Spanish, Salvadoran, and Mexican. Similarly, the term *Native American* is an umbrella term for an enormous variety of tribal or ethnic identities (over 400 officially recognized by the Bureau of Indian Affairs), including the indigenous people of Alaska and Hawaii. Clearly, these groups can be as different from one another as they can be from the mainstream society.

Commonalities in Definitions of Culture

Many definitions of culture ask the question, "What do all cultures have in common?" Some try to answer this question by examining the functions or purposes of culture. Webb and Sherman (1989), for example, describe culture in a functional way:

> Cultures solve the common problems of human beings, but they solve them in different ways. . . . Each provides its people with a means of communication (*language*). Each determines who wields power and under what circumstances power can be used (*status*). Each provides for the regulation of reproduction (*family*) and supplies a system of rules (*government*). These rules may be written (*laws*) or unwritten (*custom*), but they are always present. Cultures supply human beings with an explanation of their relationship to nature (*magic, myth, religion,* and *science*). They provide their people with some conception of time (*temporality*). They supply a system by which significant lessons of the culture (*history*) can be given a physical representation and stored and passed on to future generations. The representation usually comes in the form of dance, song, poetry, architecture, handicrafts, story, design, or painting (*art*). What makes cultures similar is the problems they solve, not the methods they devise to solve them. (pp. 49–50)

Culture can also be understood in terms of the assumptions or ideas inherent in the concept itself. Four of these assumptions seem particularly important.

Humans Construct Culture

Humans Construct Culture

Human beings are born with certain genetically determined predispositions, some of which underlie behavior and others that direct physical features. Although these predispositions are not precise, they do help to determine the parameters under which humans develop. Humans have fewer biological instincts (e.g., breathing, swallowing) than any other species does, which means that we are born relatively helpless and remain so for a considerable amount of time, longer than any other organism in the animal kingdom.

Unlike most members of the animal world, people are not biologically programmed so that they automatically know how to utilize the environment to find food and shelter. In short, we do not know how to survive without other people to care for us and to teach us. Therefore, humans must discover ways of effectively interacting both with their environment and with each other. They must learn how to *construct* the knowledge, including rules of living, that will enable them to survive. This knowledge, the manner in which it is presented (in the family, in the neighborhood, in literature, art, school lessons, etc.), and the meaning it has for us is called culture. Culture, then, is the one factor that determines the kinds of guidelines to which the individual is exposed.

The concept of culture usually refers to things (both physical and mental) that are made or constructed by human beings rather than to things that naturally occur in the environment. When you look out over a body of water, for instance, neither the water itself, the undeveloped beachfront, nor the horizon is considered culture. These items are naturally occurring components of the environment. How we *think about* and what we *do* with the natural environment, however, is usually dependent on our culture. Thus, a beachfront along Miami Beach in the United States has been viewed as a good place to build condominiums, hotels, piers, a boardwalk, and a marina. Similarly, in Sharm el Sheikh, located along the Red Sea on the Sinai Peninsula in Egypt, one of the world's greatest beach resorts can be found in this otherwise parched desert region. In another culture, this same beachfront might be regarded as a sacred space with little human intervention allowed.

The physical artifacts of any culture are expressions of people's underlying knowledge, attitudes, and values toward a part of the natural environment. Other expressions of culture include behavioral patterns–for example, people's tendency to litter the oceans and beaches with various kinds of waste. Traditional societies in many parts of the world, on the other hand, have an entirely different view of the natural environment. Rather than seeing themselves as controllers of nature, many Native Americans, for instance, believe strongly that human beings are an integral part of the natural world. And since in their view we live within rather than outside nature, they believe we should not interfere with it too much.

This example is interesting because it not only shows that different sociocultural groups perceive the world in very different terms but also that cultural beliefs and attitudes can and do change. Western peoples are now beginning to see the damage they have caused to the environment and to consider not only ways to clean it up but also ways of rethinking the very basis of the relation of human beings to nature.

Culture Is Shared

Culture is not only constructed, it is *socially constructed* by human beings in interaction with one another. Cultural ideas and understandings are shared by a group of people who recognize the knowledge, attitudes, and values of one another. Moreover, they agree on which cultural elements are better than others, arranging these in a hierarchy of value that may change over time. Mainstream

American attitudes about children's place in the economy provides a good example. Before the middle of the 19th century, children in the United States were regarded as economic assets to their families and to the community. That is, they worked not only on the farm or in the shop but also often outside the family for money that went to help support the family. Zelizer (1985) makes a distinction between the "useful" and the "useless" child in talking about the change that occurred during the last half of the previous century:

> By 1900 middle-class reformers began indicting children's economic cooperation as unjustified parental exploitation, and child labor emerged for the first time as a major social problem in the United States.... By 1930, most children under fourteen were out of the labor market and into schools. (p. 61)

This example illustrates the changing nature of cultural ideas. The notion that children do not belong in the labor market and that parents whose children bring income into the family may be exploiting them has become a highly valued idea in our society, but it is one that is relatively new. In contrast to early-19th-century families, we believe that children should be in school when they are young. Moreover, when we encounter families that do send their children out to work, whether it be in the United States or elsewhere, we have a sense that they are doing something wrong. Thus, in contemporary mainstream U.S. culture, until our children are in midadolescence, we place a greater value on the "useless" (nonworking) child than we do on the "useful" one who works. Indeed, although many people find ways around it, in this country there are legal restrictions on the age at which children can be employed. In some parts of the world, however, many families are still highly dependent upon their children to generate income–even in the face of strong criticism from outsiders.

Culture of the Deaf

In nearly all instances, shared cultural identification is transmitted from one generation to the next. One exception to this cultural transmission process, however, can be seen in the case of deaf persons whose primary language is a manual system, ASL (American Sign Language) in North America. Although most deaf persons have hearing parents, the Deaf normally form strong ties to their own community and tend to marry a deaf partner. Thus, cultural transmission in this instance is deferred until entry into the Deaf community occurs through instruction in schools for the Deaf and through a network of social clubs, theater, political organizations, and publications. For some young people, their first enculturation into the Deaf community may come through enrollment at the world-famous Gallaudet University and its related centers and school, which provides schooling from preschool levels through college.

Culture Is Both Objective and Subjective

A third common feature of culture is that it is comprised of two components: objective elements and subjective elements (Triandis, 1972). The **objective** components of culture consist of the visible, tangible elements of a group; that is, the endless array of physical artifacts the people produce, the language they speak, the clothes they wear, the food they eat, and the unending stream of decorative and ritual objects they create. These elements are relatively easy to pick up or observe, and all people would describe them in a similar manner. It is the objective elements of culture that are most commonly thought of when

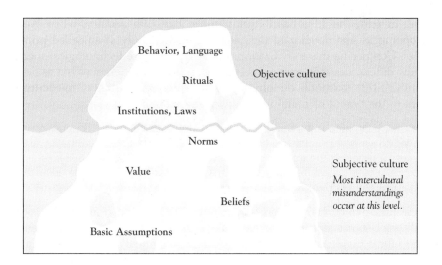

Figure 3.1
Iceberg Model of Culture

cultural differences are considered. **Subjective** components of culture are the invisible, less tangible aspects of culture, such as the attitudes people hold, the values they defend, their norms of behavior, the manner in which they learn, and the hierarchy of social roles–in short, the *meaning* that the more objective components of culture have for individuals and groups.

In this respect, culture can be likened to an iceberg: only 10% of the whole is seen above the surface of the water (Figure 3.1). It is the 90% of the iceberg that is hidden beneath the surface of the water that most concerns the ship's captain who must navigate the water. Like an iceberg, the most meaningful (and potentially dangerous) part of culture is the invisible or subjective part that is continually operating at the unconscious level and shapes people's perceptions and their responses to those perceptions. It is this aspect of culture that leads to most intercultural misunderstandings, and that requires the most emphasis in good multicultural or intercultural education.

Culture Is Nurtured

A final assumption about culture is the idea that it involves nurturing and growth, similar to the nurturing of plants. In the case of humans, however, the growing process involves teaching the young, both formally and informally. Thus, to **enculturate** a child is to help that child become a member of her or his social groups. In the United States, as elsewhere, enculturation may mean helping a child negotiate the different cultural perspectives found among the various social groups in which he or she participates.

Activity 4:
Childhood Experiences

Culture is also related to growth through the fine arts (music, dance, literature, and the visual arts) as well as through social behavior. A "cultured" person is one who has been nurtured (helped to grow) by participation in such activities. However, observation tells us that it is people of comfortable circumstances who most frequently have the time, energy, and inclination to devote to such pursuits. Thus is born the notion of an elite (high-status) group.

The idea that culture "belongs" to an elite group also carries with it the notion that this kind of "high culture" has more value than what we might call "folk"

High Culture

culture. In part, this idea has its roots in the late 19th century, when Western anthropologists first developed their ideas from the study of so-called primitive peoples. Comparing these civilizations to their own more technological societies, they saw differences that were perceived not simply as differences but as deficits. Warren's (1873) textbook on physical geography, for instance, introduced its readers to the "races of man" in the following manner:

> The Caucasian race is the truly cosmopolitan and historical race. The leading nations of the world, those who have reached the highest state of civilization and possess a history in the true sense of the word, belong to it. It has, therefore, not improperly been called the active race; while the others, embracing the uncivilized or half-civilized peoples, have been termed the passive races. (p. 86)

Such quasi-evolutionary theories of culture have even been invoked to explain disabilities. Down syndrome, for example, is named for John Haydon Langdon Down's ethnic classification, according to which individuals with "mongolian" features, whatever the "race" of their parents might be, represented regression to a more primitive state of evolutionary development. Tragically, before the discovery of its chromosomal basis in the 1950s, a newborn with Down syndrome was often described as a "throwback," as were infants with a variety of congenital anomalies.

Western anthropologists' notion of cultural evolution was directed mainly at other (non-Western) societies. At the top of the cultural hierarchy were the highly "civilized" peoples, mostly the Europeans and Americans who popularized the concept. At the bottom were the more primitive "savages" or "natives." Everyone else was placed somewhere in between and thought of as having the potential to climb up the cultural ladder. Inherent in this and other cultural models was the anthropologists' assumption that the natural progression of culture is upward. Indeed, the idea of a hierarchy of cultures existed well before anthropology was even accepted as a scientific discipline. In 1824, half a century before Warren wrote his textbook, Thomas Jefferson wrote:

> Let a philosophic observer commence a journey from the *savages* of the Rocky Mountains, eastwardly towards the seacoast. These he would observe in the earliest stages of association, living under no law but that of nature, subsisting and covering themselves with the flesh and skins of wild beasts. He would next find those on the frontiers in the *pastoral stage,* raising domestic animals to supply the defects of hunting. Then succeed our own *semi-barbarous* citizens, the pioneers of the advance of *civilization,* and so in his progress he would meet the gradual shades of *improving* man until he would reach his, as yet, most improved state in our seaport towns. This, in fact, is equivalent to a survey, in time, of the progress of man from the infancy of creation to the present day. (as cited in Pearce, 1965, p. 155)

Jefferson's categories foreshadow those of the early anthropologists. And in many ways our thinking has not moved very far beyond this framework. Books with such titles as *Affable Savages* (Huxley, 1957) and commonly used terms such as *underdeveloped* and *developed nations,* or *Third World* versus *First World* perpetuate the idea of cultural movement toward something perceived as more ideal or better or more civilized. Moreover, the direction of this movement is generally toward a culture that looks a great deal like our own. While these ideas are largely discredited among modern anthropologists, they continue to exist in the minds of many Americans when contrasting U.S. society with other societies, particularly those that are less technological. And this is increasingly becoming a dangerous idea to sustain because, in the past 30 years or so, other nations have made great strides in the world marketplace—economically, socially, and educationally. As Fareed Zakaria (2008) notes, this is

> not so much about the decline of America but rather about the rise of everyone else. It is about the great transformation taking place around the world, a transformation that, though often discussed, remains poorly understood.

Traditionally, Americans have expected their schools to socialize all students into traditional European American, upper- and middle-class culture, generally referred to as "the best of Western civilization." Although it is true that great art, beautiful music, and meaningful literature have been given to the world by Western peoples, it is equally clear that Western contributions do not represent all that is great and beautiful in the world.

Applying the Concept of Culture

When school programs are instituted to increase awareness and understanding of specific groups, they are called group-specific or **culture-specific approaches** and stress information about a particular group of people, usually identified by a single characteristic such as race, ethnicity, religion, or gender. Although these approaches have much to offer, several problems are associated with them. First, while they attend to differences *between* one group and another, these approaches do not attend to important differences *within* groups. Consequently, they tend to give the impression that all people identified as belonging to a group (all Latinos or all Jews, for instance) are alike, which is clearly not

Cross-Cultural Psychology

the case. Second, because these programs usually rely on students of certain *samples* of the larger group (e.g., *urban* African Americans, *white* middle-class girls, Navajo *who live on reservations*), they may promote stereotypes. Third, group-specific programs, because of their intentionally narrow focus, cannot attend to the wide array of differences that collectively control the teaching–learning process.

In contrast to the group-specific approach to understanding diversity is another, more inclusive approach that attempts to deal directly with the complex nature of cultural phenomena. Called a **culture-general approach,** it derives mainly from principles developed in the field of cross-cultural psychology and training. Cross-cultural psychologists are mostly interested in the effect of

culture on the *individual* and on the interface or interaction between individuals of different groups. In addition to describing how culture affects an individual, these psychologists have also been developing a variety of training strategies to help individuals anticipate and deal effectively with problems that may arise in intercultural interaction.

Culture-Specific Versus Culture-General Frameworks

It is important to understand the distinction between culture-specific and culture-general knowledge. A culture-general concept is one that is universal and applies to *all* cultural groups, as seen in the following example.

The way an individual "learns how to learn" depends on the socialization processes used by his or her culture. That is, learning style is related to socialization processes. This very general statement can be regarded as a cultural universal, or culture-general concept. It doesn't tell us anything about an individual's preferred learning style, but it does tell us that everyone has one and that it is formed by socialization experiences. Thus, knowing that socialization experiences vary from culture to culture, it follows that learning styles will also vary among cultures. Such a culture-general concept is valuable to teachers in that it warns them of the possibility that there will be many variations in learning style among their students, perhaps as many as there are cultural groups represented in their classroom. So informed, a teacher presiding over a multicultural classroom would be alert for signs of learning style differences and would attempt to develop alternative lesson plans or instructional approaches that match these differences.

A culture- or group-specific concept, on the other hand, is one that applies to a specific cultural group. For example, both Hawaiian and Native American children have historically acquired most of their knowledge, values, and attitudes about the world through direct participation in real-world events. Traditionally, their teachers were usually other members of their family or ethnic group who were also participating in those events. Thus direct participation, or **in-context learning,** became their familiar and preferred learning style.

Contrast in-context learning with the more formal schooling given to most urban and suburban middle-class European American children. These children are sent to a captive learning environment (schools) where specially trained teachers who are usually total strangers use books and other abstract learning tools to provide indirect participation, or **out-of-context learning,** about real-world events. In a classroom where both cultural groups are present, the teacher should anticipate learning style differences (culture-general knowledge), try to assess the culture-specific learning styles that are present, and then adapt instruction accordingly.

In short, teachers in multicultural classrooms need to have both culture-general and culture-specific knowledge. That is, they need to know that certain cultural universals (e.g., learning style differences, patterns of communication, value orientation) are at work in every multicultural classroom, and then they need to gather–through observation, inquiry, and study–the particulars of those variations so that they can plan and deliver instruction that is appropriate for *all* their students. To focus solely on culture-specific knowledge, which is always based on *samples* taken from some target culture, is to ignore not only individual differences within that group but also the cultural universals that cut across groups. Likewise, to focus solely on culture-general knowledge is to ignore the very real differences that separate groups and that provide a map for assessing and adapting instruction.

The Culture-Learning Process

Individuals tend to identify themselves in a broad manner and in terms of many physical and social attributes. For example, a young man might identify himself as an attractive, athletic, Asian American who intends to be a doctor and live in upper-class society. Other people also identify individuals according to these attributes, and interactions among individuals are often shaped by such identifications. Figure 3.2 shows 12 sources of cultural identity that influence teaching and learning. Who learns what, and how and when it is learned, is briefly described here and is further illustrated and discussed in later chapters.

Activity and
Reading 10:
The Culture-Learning Process

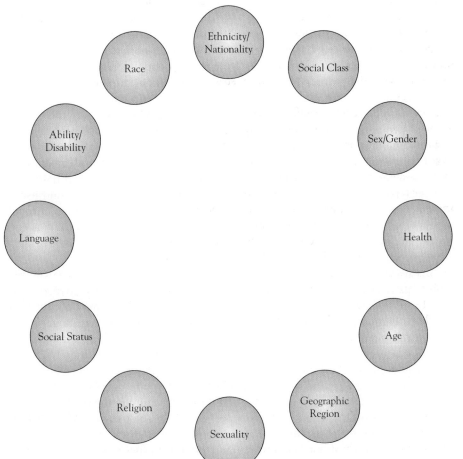

Figure 3.2
Sources of Cultural Identity

What Is Learned: The Sources of Cultural Knowledge

Race is a very amorphous term. Biologically speaking, it refers to the clustering of inherited physical characteristics that favor adaptation to a particular ecological area. However, race is culturally defined in the sense that different societies emphasize different sets of physical characteristics when referring to the same race. In fact, the term is so imprecise that it has even been used to refer to a wide variety of categories that are not physical, for instance, linguistic categories (the *English-speaking race*), religious categories (the *Jewish race*), national categories (the *Italian race*), and even to somewhat mythological categories (the *Teutonic race*) (Yetman, 1991). Although race has often been defined as a biological category, it has been argued that race as a biological concept is of little use because there are no "pure" races. As Yetman notes:

> Many groups possess physically identifiable characteristics that do not become the basis for racial distinctions [and] . . . criteria selected to make racial distinctions in one society may be overlooked or considered insignificant or irrelevant by another. For instance, in much of Latin America skin color and the shape of the lips, important differentiating criteria in the United States, are much less important than are hair texture, eye color, and stature. A person defined as black in Georgia or Michigan might be considered white in Peru. (p. 3)

The use of the term *race* is not based on biology; rather, it is socially defined on the basis of physical criteria such as skin color. Historically, the term has its roots in classifying groups of people by class inequalities, not skin color, with the British referring to the Irish as a "lower race." Then, during European colonial expansion, race began to be defined in terms of skin color where nonwhite people were considered "lower" races. Recent research in mapping the genetic code of five people of different races demonstrates that the concept of race has no scientific basis (Ah, But the Mystery, 2000). Thus, race is an important social characteristic not because of its biology but because of its cultural meaning in any given social group or society. In the United States, race is judged largely on the basis of skin color, which some people consider very meaningful and use as a criterion for extending or withholding privileges of various kinds. Through subtle yet effective socializing influences, group members can be taught to accept as "social fact" myriad myths and stereotypes regarding skin color, stature, facial features, and so forth.

The use of the term *race* continues to change, even from one census to another. The United States Census Bureau, for instance, uses the federal government's definitions of race when performing a census. The question asking about race in the 2000 census was different from the one used in the 1990 census in several ways. Most significantly, for the first time, respondents were given the option of selecting one *or more* race categories to indicate their racial identities.

Racism results from the transformation of race prejudice and/or ethnocentrism through the exercise of power against a racial group defined as inferior by individuals or by institutions, with the intentional or unintentional support of an entire culture. Simply stated, racism is preference for, or belief in, the superiority of one's own racial group over any other.

Sex/gender is also culturally defined on the basis of a particular set of physical characteristics. In this case, however, the characteristics are related to male and female reproduction. Cultural meanings associated with gender are expressed in terms of socially valued behaviors (e.g., nurturing the young and providing food) that are assigned according to sex. Such culturally assigned behaviors eventually become so accepted that they are thought of as natural to that sex. Thus, gender is what it *means* to be male or female in a society, and gender roles are those sets of behaviors thought by a particular people to be "normal" and "good" when carried out by the assigned sex.

In all sociocultural groups, gender includes knowledge of a large set of rules and expectations governing what boys and girls should wear, how they should act and express themselves, and their "place" in the overall social structure. Beardsley (1977) noted that any social or psychological trait can be "genderized" in favor of one sex or the other. Thus, in the dominant society of the United States, active traits such as aggressiveness are genderized in favor of males and against females, whereas more passive traits such as submissiveness are genderized in favor of females and against males.

Like cultural definitions of race, the specific set of traits assigned to males and females may vary by society. And within a society, these traits may vary by ethnicity, class, or religion. For instance, on a continuum of submissiveness to males (a norm in U.S. society), many African American females might be located closer to the less submissive end of the scale, many Hispanic females might be located closer to the more submissive end, and many European American females would probably be located somewhere in between.

Geert Hofstede (2001), who conducted the world's largest investigation into cross-cultural differences on a global scale, named one of the five dimensions he identified as Masculinity versus Femininity, referring to the distribution of roles between the genders. His studies revealed that (a) women's values differ less among societies than men's values, and that (b) men's values from one country to another contain a dimension from very assertive and competitive and maximally different from women's values on the one side, to modest and caring and similar to women's values on the other. The assertive pole has been called "masculine" and the modest, caring pole "feminine." The women in feminine countries have the same modest, caring values as the men; in the masculine countries they are somewhat assertive and competitive, but not as much as the men, so that these countries show a gap between men's values and women's values.

Health is culturally defined according to a particular group's view of what physical, mental, and emotional states constitute a healthy person. The expert opinion of the medical profession usually guides a society's view of health. Although a medical model has dominated cultural definitions of health, most disabilities (mental retardation, deafness, blindness, etc.) are not judged in terms of this model's norms. Thus, just as a person with cerebral palsy would not be considered sick, it is possible to be a healthy blind person or person with mental retardation.

In the United States and most of the industrialized world, the prevailing health system is almost totally biomedical. However, alternative systems such as acupuncture, holistic medicine, and faith healing are available, and the acceptance of alternative systems varies widely both within and between social groups. In other societies (e.g., China), what we deem alternative medicine may in fact be the dominant model, and our ideas of biomedicine may be operating at the fringes. The cultural meanings associated with health depend on which model, or which combination of models, an individual or family group accepts. For example, a 4-year-old Russian child, who had recently immigrated with her family to the United States, suddenly suffered a high fever and flu symptoms. The child's middle-class European American nursery school teacher wanted the family to take the child to the doctor immediately for an antibiotic. The child's grandmother, on the other hand, who was the family expert on medical matters, prescribed a traditional treatment: the child should be put to bed, surrounded by lit candles and family members engaged in prayer. In this case, the grandmother was the final authority, and the child got better.

Ability/disability, like the term *health,* is culturally defined according to society's view about what it means to be physically, emotionally, and mentally "able." The categories of ability and disability refer to a wide variety of mental and physical characteristics: intelligence, emotional stability, impairment of sensory and neural systems, impairment of movement. The social significance of these characteristics may vary by setting as well. For example, the terms *learning disability* or *learning disabled* are primarily used with reference to schooling and are rarely used outside of school. Indeed, it may be that the current emphasis on learning disability in American schools is primarily a reflection of a technologically complex society's concern about literacy. In other nations, specific learning disabilities among people who are otherwise unimpaired are of little concern. In fact, this "condition," as a category of exceptional individuals, is nonexistent in most of the world.

The cultural meaning of *ability* and *disability* is related to both the needs and the public perception of the ability or disability itself. For example, the culture of the Deaf "needs" a shared, rule-bound system of communication (sign language) as well as shared traditions and values among its members. However, the public acceptance of deaf individuals is far less positive than for those who are gifted. This lack of acceptance can be seen in the privileges accorded each group in schools. School experience might enhance the self-esteem of a gifted student while it threatens that of a student who is deaf. In the United States, the reaction to ability/disability hovers closely around a socially defined norm: We favor bright individuals but often exclude those who show evidence of extreme intelligence; we favor individuals who "overcome" their disabilities but often exclude those who, for one reason or another, cannot.

Social class is culturally defined on the basis of those criteria on which a person or social group may be ranked in relation to others in a stratified, or layered, society. There is considerable debate about the criteria that determine social class. Some criteria identify class membership primarily in terms of wealth and its origin (inherited or newly earned). Other commonly used criteria include education, power, and influence over others. Class structures vary widely among societies and social groups in terms of their rigidity and their importance to an individual's life chances. In some societies, such as Britain and India, for example, the class structure is fairly rigid and determines to a large extent the opportunities each person will have. In these societies, a person is truly born into a particular social class and tends to remain there. In other societies, the structure is not so rigid, and although individuals may be born into a particular social class, it is expected that they may move up by virtue of their achievements. Societies also vary according to the value placed on leaving one's social class. In the United States, upward mobility is a value; in Britain it is not so highly valued. The consequences of these attitudes are not always salutary. In the United States, for example, if individuals do not succeed in moving up, the perception may be that something is wrong with them.

Social class differences are also tied to a person's social expectations and cultural tastes. For example, individuals who exhibit the child-rearing practices, speech, and general tastes of the upper classes in matters such as dress, food, and housing can affect their social image and thereby their chances for upward mobility.

Ethnicity/nationality are culturally defined according to the knowledge, beliefs, and behavior patterns shared by a group of people with the same history and perhaps the same language. Ethnicity carries a strong sense of "peoplehood"–that is, of loyalty to a "community of memory" (Bellah, Madsen, Sullivan, Swidler, & Tipton, 1985). It is also related to the ecological niche in which an ethnic group has found itself and to adaptations people make to those environmental conditions.

The category of *nationality* is culturally defined on the basis of shared citizenship, which may or may not include a shared ethnicity. In the contemporary world, the population of most nations includes citizens (and resident noncitizens) who vary in ethnicity. Although we are accustomed to this idea in the United States, we are sometimes unaware that it is also true in other nations. Thus we tend to identify all people from Japan as Japanese, all people from France as French, and so forth. Similarly, when American citizens of varying ethnic identities go abroad, they tend to be identified as "American." A tragic example of this misconception is the recent history of ethnic warfare in the former Yugoslavia and Iraq. Americans in general are unaware of the role that ethnicity may play in dividing people. Most of the conflicts that occur across the planet are the result of long-held ethnic strife and are not limited by national boundaries.

Religion/spirituality are culturally defined on the basis of a shared set of ideas about the relationship of the earth and the people on it to a deity or deities and a shared set of rules for living moral values that will enhance that relationship. A set of behaviors identified with worship is also commonly shared. Religious identity may include membership in a worldwide organized religion (e.g., Islam, Christianity, Judaism, Buddhism, Taoism) or in smaller (but also worldwide) sects belonging to each of the larger religions (e.g., Catholic or Protestant Christianity, or Conservative, Reformed, or Hasidic Judaism). Religious identity may also include a large variety of spiritualistic religions, sometimes called pagan or "godless" religions, that are often but not always associated with indigenous peoples in the Americas and other parts of the world. Like ethnicity, religious affiliation can engender intense loyalty, as witnessed through the actions of members of Osama bin Laden's Al Qaeda network in their attempts to live out their perceived religious missions. Religion also engenders a sense of belonging or community and pride in a people's shared history. Because religious identity involves individuals' relationship with the earth and with forces perceived to be greater than themselves, the cultural meaning of religion is often expressed in terms of a rigid sense of righteousness and virtue that is linked to a belief in salvation or the possibility of an eternal life after death. It is thus often an extremely powerful determiner of behavior.

Geographic location/region are culturally defined by the characteristics (topographical features, natural resources) of the ecological environment in which a person lives. Geographic location may include the characteristics of a neighborhood or community (rural, suburban, urban) and/or the natural and climatic features of a region (mountainous, desert, plains, coastal, hot, cold, wet, dry). It has been argued that, in the United States, people's regional identity functions in the same way as their national heritage. Thus, southerners, westerners, and midwesterners are identified and often identify themselves as members of ethniclike groups, with the same kinds of loyalties, sense of community, and language traits. This type of regional identity can also be found in some other countries of the world.

The cultural meanings of geographic location are expressed in terms of the knowledge a person has of how to survive in and use the resources of a particular area. This knowledge may include what foods are "good" (and how to grow and harvest them), how to protect oneself from the natural elements and common dangers of the locality, even how to spend leisure time. This kind of knowledge also applies to the type of community a person lives in. It is commonly acknowledged, for example, that "city people," "country people," and "suburban people" can be quite different from one another. The nature of that difference stems in part from their familiarity with and knowledge about how to live in a particular kind of community with its particular resources and dangers.

Age is culturally defined according to the length of time an individual has lived and the state of physical and mental development that individual has attained. Chronological age is measured in different ways by different social groups or societies. Some calculate it in calendar years, others by natural cycles such as phases of the moon, and still others by the marking of major natural or social events.

Mental and physical development is also measured differentially, in much the same way and under many of the same circumstances that health is determined. Most humans view such development as a matter of stages, but the nature and particular characteristics of each stage may differ widely. In most Western societies, for example, age cohort groups are usually identified as infancy, childhood, adolescence, adulthood, and old age. "Normal" development markers include the acquisition of motor and language skills (infancy and childhood), the ability to understand and use abstract concepts (childhood and adolescence), and the ability to assume responsibility for oneself and others (adolescence and adulthood). In other societies, these cohort groups may differ. For example, in many non-Western societies, the cohort group we define as adolescents may not exist at all, and the classifications of childhood and old age may be longer or shorter.

The cultural meaning of age is usually expressed in terms of the abilities and responsibilities attributed to it. Thus, in the United States, childhood is prolonged (hence the category of adolescence), and adult responsibilities are not expected until at least age 18, if not age 21 or beyond. In other societies (and indeed in the United States prior to the 20th century), childhood is shorter, and adult responsibilities are assumed at younger ages.

Sexuality is culturally defined on the basis of particular patterns of sexual self-identification, behavior, and interpersonal relationships (Herek, 1986). There is growing evidence that a person's sexual orientation is, in part, a function of that person's innate biological characteristics (LeVay & Hamer, 1994). Culturally speaking, sexuality is tied to a number of factors, including sexual behavior, gender identity (both internal and external), affiliation, and role behavior. Like health, sexuality has a variety of orientations. Because sexuality is frequently linked to a person's deepest, most meaningful experiences (both religious and interpersonal), those who deviate from socially approved norms are often socially ostracized and sometimes physically abused or even killed, as in the case of the Matthew Shepard murder. In mainstream U.S. culture, the prevailing view of sexuality is bimodal: only male and female are identified as possibilities. In other societies, additional possibilities are available. The Lakota Sioux, for example, approve four sexual orientations: biological males who possess largely masculine traits, biological males who possess largely feminine traits, biological females who possess largely feminine traits, and biological females who possess largely masculine traits. The female-identified male in Lakota society is called *berdache* and is accorded high honor because he possesses multiple traits and characteristics. Berdache tend to be teachers and artists, and if a berdache takes an interest in one's child or children, it is considered to be an advantage.

Other Approaches to Sexuality

Language is often defined as a system of shared vocal sounds and nonverbal behaviors that enables members of a particular group to communicate with one another. Language may be the most significant source of cultural learning because it is through language that most other cultural knowledge is acquired. Indeed, some researchers consider language and the category systems available in language to be *the* determiner of culture (Sapir, 1949; Vygotsky, 1962; Whorf, 1968).

Considerable research on the relation of brain function to language gives evidence that human beings are hardwired for language development at a particular stage in brain development (Chomsky, 1966). That is, children who are in the company of other people appear to be programmed to learn whatever spoken language or sign system is used around them. Children even appear to invent their own language systems, complete with syntactical structures, if no other language is available (Chomsky, 1966). It may also be that this ability decreases or disappears altogether at a certain point, which helps to explain why it may be more difficult for older children and adults to acquire a new language. Language is meaningful in terms of both its verbal properties (what we name things, people, ideas) and its nonverbal properties (its norms regarding interpersonal distance, meaningful gestures, and so forth). Because language literally represents reality, the types and meanings of verbal and nonverbal behavior in any society or social group will reflect people's experience with their surroundings and the ways in which they interact with it. More than any other characteristic, language is a window into another person's life.

Social status is culturally defined on the basis of the prestige, social esteem, and honor accorded an individual or group by other social groups or by society (Berger & Berger, 1972). Social status cuts across the other categories. Every social group or society appears to construct hierarchies of honor, prestige, and value with which to "sort out" its members, often on the basis of such attributes as race, age, gender, ability, and so forth. In some cases, social status varies with social class; in many other cases, however, social class does not explain a person's status in a social group or society. Thus persons may occupy a high place in the class system in terms of income and power but not be accorded prestige or honor. The children of a newly wealthy family who can well afford to send

Figure 3.3
Socializing Agents That
Transmit Culture

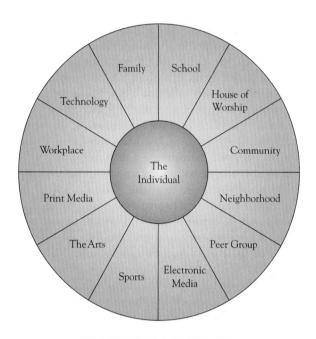

them to Harvard, for example, may have little prestige among the sons and daughters of inherited wealth. Similarly, there may be people accorded high status in the society who occupy relatively low-class positions. In U.S. society, many entertainers and sports figures fit this description. Social status is normally expressed through social roles. Thus, status assigned to a person's gender may determine the role that person plays in any situation; an individual's health status may determine the role he or she plays as a "sick" person; an individual's social class status may determine the role that person plays as a member of the upper, middle, or working class; and so forth.

While there is some overlap among these 12 attributes of culture, the important point to remember is that a particular society or social group culturally defines each of them. The cultural identity of all individuals (i.e., their knowledge, attitudes, values, and skills) is formed through their experience with these 12 attributes. Such experience is gained through contact with socializing agents such as family, house of worship, workplace, peer group, and the various forms of mass media. These socializing agents can be thought of as transmitters of cultural attributes. It is through these socializing agents (depicted in Figure 3.3) that individuals acquire the cultural knowledge that is defined by race, ethnicity, gender, language, and social class.

How Culture Is Learned:
The Socializing Agents

We acquire the specific knowledge, attitudes, skills, and values that form our cultural identity through a variety of socializing agents that mediate the sources of cultural identity and give them a particular "cultural spin." Thus a person's understanding of race, gender, social class, disability, age, sexuality, and so forth depends in part on how that socializing agent is interpreted by those particular families, schools, neighborhoods, peer groups, workplaces, houses of worship, and communities that the person affiliates with at a particular time. Each of these socializing agents has its own slightly different interpretation of a particular cultural attribute, which it passes on to its members.

In contemporary social life, some socializing agents, such as families and peer groups, operate face-to-face, while others, such as the mass media, use technology to operate from a distance. Television, DVDs, the Internet, and the music industry, for example, exert significant influence on the self-perceived identity of many young people. Referred to by some researchers as the "third educator" (following family and school), television influences young people's acquisition of basic language and visual and aural skills. It also influences their ideas of "appropriate" dress, language, attitudes, and values.

Cortes (2000) suggests that the media functions much like the school curriculum, serving as a powerful teaching medium. Especially with regard to intercultural understanding and the school curriculum, he says, "the media curriculum is chaotic, inconsistent, multivocal, in many respects unplanned and uncoordinated, laden with conflicting messages, and offering myriad perspectives" (p. 19). In addition, media often blurs information with entertainment, creating confusion in the minds of many people. For example, a survey of viewers of the television show *America's Most Wanted* revealed that 50% considered it to be a news program while 28% considered it entertainment (Rosenstiel, 1989). Where do we draw the line on many of the more popular reality shows broadcast almost daily? How much of them are, in fact, reality, and how much is scripted entertainment? These media lessons not only may affect young people's picture of themselves and others, but also may affect the picture that adults have of them.

The media also teaches about older people, and again with conflicting messages. The visual image of the woman who has "fallen and can't get up" describes older people as weak, helpless, and slightly hysterical–and in need of a product that will alert some caregiving agency that she needs help. Conversely, commercials for vitamins for older adults often depict them as active people–hiking, swimming, traveling–no doubt as a result of taking the promoted vitamins. Because we live in a nation that is growing older, we can expect more commercials defining older people as active rather than passive.

Other technological tools, such as computers, microwave ovens, and cell phones appear to exert significant influence on our notions of time. Teachers and other human service providers have noticed, for example, that over the last 30 years or so both children and adults have exhibited shorter attention spans. People seem to have become accustomed to receiving information and accomplishing tasks in shorter periods of time and are unwilling or unable to persevere in tasks that take a long time (Cottrell, 1990).

Other socializing agents of note include the performing and visual arts and, in the United States at least, sports. These widely available carriers of cultural messages help to shape people's attitudes, values, and behavior. The aesthetic value of design, language, music, dance, and theatre, as well as ideals of moral and ethical behavior, are presented through the arts. Likewise, behavioral ideals such as fair play, personal achievement, and competition are taught through sports. It is also true that other qualities may be taught through these media, violence, for example, being an increasing part of movies, television, and sports. The contemporary nature of national sports teams as bottom-line businesses comes increasingly into competition with our cultural interest in providing a level playing field for all competitors.

Figure 3.3 provides a visual overview of how cultural knowledge is filtered by a variety of socializing agents to individuals through experience. Although sources of cultural knowledge (race, language, sexuality, etc.) are universal and appear in all cultures, the socializing agents (family, schools, media, etc.) that transmit them vary considerably from one culture to another. In most industrialized societies, for example, a wide variety of socializing agents bombard people daily, often with contradictory messages. In agriculturally oriented societies, on the other hand, a few primary socializing agents (e.g., family and gender group) may share the bulk of the culture-filtering process. As a result, individuals in different cultures develop very different worldviews.

When Culture Is Learned: The Process of Socialization

One way to begin to understand how individuals acquire cultural knowledge, attitudes, values, and skills from the social groups with whom they have meaningful contact is to look closely at the concept of **socialization.** From the point of view of the outside observer (including such people as sociologists and anthropologists who use the term more than most people), *socialization* is the process by which people learn the norms that are expected of them by a particular group. These patterns may include the acquisition of a particular language, knowledge of social roles and role behavior, and particular understandings of all aspects of the physical and social environment and normative behaviors toward it. Berger and Berger (1972) note that "the socialized part of the self is commonly called identity" (p. 62).

There is some consensus that the processes of socialization can occur at three stages of life: (1) primary socialization, which involves the socialization of infants and young children by families and other early caregivers; (2) secondary socialization, which in most contemporary societies involves the neighborhood, the religious affiliation, the peer group, and the school as well as television and other influences that surround and come into the home; and (3) adult socialization, which involves the socialization of adults into roles, settings, and situations for which they may have been unprepared by primary and secondary socialization. Some examples of adult socialization include taking a new job, marrying, moving to a new area, or becoming a parent (Sheehy, 1994).

These stages of the socialization process are not entirely discrete but rather interact with one another in our lives. What we learn as children can be reinforced or modified, for good or ill, by what we learn as we grow up and have more experiences. In each of its three stages, the purpose of socialization is to teach the learner those habits of mind and action that will make him or her a loyal and functional member of a particular group. The use of the word *habits* in this context is important, for it points to another aspect of socialization, which is that the learner should internalize socially approved patterns of behavior so that he or she will voluntarily–and with little thought or effort–think and behave in an appropriate manner.

One important aspect of the internalization of particular knowledge, beliefs, attitudes, values, and behaviors is that the process by which they are acquired is, in a sense, a secret. Most people remember very little about their own socialization, the assumptions they make about the world, what has conditioned them, and the various cultural patterns that have become so ingrained in their makeup as to become nearly invisible.

Primary Socialization and Cultural Similarities

Most people share some aspects of primary socialization that are common to all or most of the people of their primary group. The primary group "Americans," for instance, traditionally would include those who have been born in the United States and speak English as a native language. Consider, for example, the rules they have learned about eating. When food is put before most Americans, they expect that it will be placed on a plate or in a bowl on a table at which they expect to sit on chairs. Once seated, the American automatically reaches for utensils called forks, knives, and spoons; cuts meat with the fork in the left hand and the knife in the right hand (except for left-handed folks); and then switches the fork to the right hand to carry the food to the mouth. In the same situation, a British person expects the plates, bowls, table, and chairs; cuts meat with the fork and knife in the same hands as an American; but then does *not* switch the fork to the right hand but continues to use it in the left hand. In the same situation, a Japanese person may expect the food to be placed on a low table, at which he or she will kneel, and the utensils used to carry food to the mouth will be two long, slender wooden or plastic implements that many Westerners call chopsticks. And in yet other cultural contexts, the hand and fingers (particularly the right hand) would be used to pick up or scoop food. On a global scale, approximately one third of people eat with knives and forks, one third with chopsticks, and one third with their hands. In all cases, the people eating will not consciously think about these expectations and behaviors, they will simply expect and do them because they are "right," "appropriate," and "proper." Friedman's (1984) book *How My Parents Learned to Eat* is an interesting children's story that discusses Japanese and American eating customs and can be used to introduce such similarities and differences to children.

Within this general "American" set of rules for eating (as within any large nation-state), however, are many variations. How formally we set our tables, how many utensils we use, whether our plates are served for us or we serve ourselves (and how many different plates we use), what kinds of food we eat, what we commonly use as a beverage (water, milk, wine, soda or pop, coffee, tea), and whether we bring the beverage to the table in its original container or in a pitcher, all depend somewhat on the region in which we live; the ethnic, social class, and religious origins of our parents; our ages; and so forth. No matter what the particulars are of our personal and family rules for eating, however, we believe they are "normal" in part because we have internalized them.

Here is another example of both the secret nature of primary socialization and the degree to which knowledge acquired through primary socialization is internalized: the way people learn to speak. Do you remember how you learned to talk? If you have taken another language in school, perhaps it was difficult for you–but your *own* language, now that was easy! Or so it seems. It might, however, be very difficult for you to teach a non-English speaker to correctly pronounce the sentence "Can you tell me the time?" when that person might more easily say "Can you dell me the dime?" What might you tell this person about English that would correct his or her pronunciation? Go ahead; try it. How would you teach someone to make the correct sounds?

Most people begin to play with their tongue, noting supposed differences in where it is placed in relation to the teeth. But that is not where the distinction lies. If you have determined that a little puff of air passes out of the mouth when the *t* sound is made in such words as *tell* and *time* that is not passed in words beginning with the letter *d,* you are on the right track to discovering the secret. Correct speakers of English aspirate their stops; that is, some air passes out of the mouth when such letters as *t, p,* or *k* are spoken. This aspect of pronunciation is considered a secret because even though most of us differentiate these sounds quite regularly and easily, you probably were not able to describe the difference to others. This practice has become so much a part of your behavior that you take it for granted; you must consciously think about it in order to describe it to others. This is not the end of the secret, however. If you think about it some more, you will realize that English speakers aspirate their stops only at the beginning and in the middle of words, not at the end. We do not aspirate the *t* in *hit, bit,* or *cat.*

That you have learned these rules is quite clear; you use them all the time. How these rules were learned, however, is considerably less clear. They were probably not taught in formal sessions with your parents or by reading appropriate language texts. Indeed, you may not have been able to talk about them at all because you did not have the language to use words such as *aspirate* or *stops.* Rather, you probably learned these rules through trial and error and with much reinforcement while you learned to speak your native language. This particular language pattern is often hidden, as are its results. The same is true for other aspects of cultural learning; they, too, can be conceived as patterns that are hidden from our conscious thought and behavior.

Few people receive formal instruction in how to be an appropriate member of any particular cultural group. Rather, people are culturally socialized by observing others, by trial and error, and by continuous reinforcement. In other words, cultural knowledge such as the rules for speaking and eating are learned experientially, not cognitively. Consequently, it becomes difficult for many people to speak comfortably about the cross-cultural problems they might encounter. One of the difficulties people often face in their intercultural encounters, then, is that while they may feel uncomfortable or unsure in a given situation, they may be unable to talk about the problem. Thus, as is natural to most, people may try to avoid situations in which they feel discomfort–certainly *not* one of the long-term goals of multicultural or intercultural education. A reasonable goal is for people to become more knowledgeable and thus conversant about the issues at play in cross-cultural interaction so that when problems or misunderstandings arise, we have the cognitive and linguistic tools, as well as the comfort level, to inquire into and talk about our differences.

Secondary Socialization

Perhaps the most important source of secondary socialization in most people's lives is the school. It is in school that individuals are often introduced to ideas and values that differ from those they acquired at home. In fact, one of the purposes of education is to "lead forth" or "liberate" individuals from the narrow confines of their primary socialization–in a sense, to expand their cultural identities. The difficulties of this process of alteration, however, should not be minimized, especially in situations where the cultural knowledge, beliefs, values, and skills required by the school may be in conflict with those of the home. Still, teachers often find themselves attempting to serve as "change agents" of their students' cultural identities.

The main goal of most school socialization in the United States has traditionally been to teach the rules of middle-class attitudes, values, and behavior. This cultural socialization to the middle class is no less a secret than the varied cultural socialization of individual families. The school, like the family, does not make cultural socialization explicit; it is simply taken for granted as "normal." Few people ever take a formal course in the variations of cultural knowledge that exist, and they almost never examine their own cultural patterns in contrast to others. Few ever learn why they behave the way they do, or why they think many of the things they think. Fewer still ever evaluate the assumptions they make. People thus generally lack the concepts and vocabulary with which to talk about these things. Yet cultural patterns that are a given, along with the assumptions, beliefs, and behavior associated with them, often do guide us along whether we are aware of it or not.

There is yet another aspect of socialization that must be analyzed: the power of early socialization when viewed from the inside. It is certainly true that as we grow up and meet people outside our childhood social groups, we learn that there are a variety of ways to interact with the physical and social environment. As children, however, we experience the imposition of patterns of socialization as absolute (Berger & Berger, 1972). There are two simple reasons for this absoluteness: (1) the power of adults in relation to young children, and (2) ignorance of any other possibilities. Berger and Berger describe the nature of this experience in the following way:

> Psychologists differ in their view as to whether the child experiences the adults at this stage of life as being very much under his control (because they are generally so responsive to his needs) or whether he feels continually threatened by them (because he is so dependent upon them). However this may be, there can be no question that, objectively speaking, adults have overwhelming power in the situation. The child can, of course, resist them, but the probable outcome of any conflict is a victory on the part of the adults. It is they who control most of the rewards that he craves and most of the sanctions that he fears. Indeed, the simple fact that most children are eventually socialized affords simple proof of this proposition. At the same time, it is obvious that the small child is ignorant of any alternatives to the patterns that are being imposed upon him. The adults confront him with a world–for him, it is *the* world. It is only much later that he discovers that there are alternatives to this particular world, that his parents' world is relative in space and time, and that quite different patterns are possible. (p. 51)

Some Consequences of Socialization

Ethnocentrism

Because of the absoluteness with which the child experiences socialization, he or she begins, early on, to share the human tendency to view the world from his or her own perspective and to begin to believe that his or her way is, if not the only way to view the world, certainly the *best* way. This perspective, called **ethnocentrism**, refers to the tendency people have to evaluate others according to their own standards, and it is an almost universal result of socialization. Think again about the example of eating behaviors: When confronted by someone from Bangladesh who eats with his or her fingers, most Americans will consider such behavior not as simply different but as *beneath* their own, and may make negative judgments about the person. While a certain degree of ethnocentrism serves to bind people together, it can also become a serious obstacle when those who have internalized different ideas and behaviors begin to interact with one another.

The Metric System

One major expression of ethnocentrism is a strong *resistance to change*. People have a tendency to resist change, even under the best of circumstances, as illustrated in the story of the Wheat Religion people in Chapter 1. If people believe that their way of doing things is best and if they have the power to choose to continue in familiar ways, why should they change? Consider the case of the United States and the adoption of metrics. At this time, all countries of the world have adopted the metric system as their primary means of measurement except the United States, Liberia, and Myanmar. We continue to resist this change despite the difficulties it causes travelers, manufacturers, and others who must interact in a variety of ways with people from other nations. Failure to convert English measures to metric values by NASA scientists was the cause of the September 1999 loss of the Mars planet orbiter, a spacecraft that smashed into the planet Mars instead of reaching a safe orbit. This oversight resulted in the destruction of a $125 million spacecraft and jeopardized the entire Mars program.

While this example comes from life outside of schools, other examples of ethnocentric behavior do not. There is, for example, continued insistence on the part of some educators and politicians that we need to strengthen a Eurocentric curriculum in our schools on the grounds that a curriculum based on "the best of Western civilization" is the most valuable preparation any student could have. However, there is increasing interest among some educators to consider alternative perspectives. Consider this response to American educators in the 1700s about sending Native American children to American schools:

> You who are wise must know that different Nations have different Conceptions of things and you will therefore not take it amiss if our Ideas of this kind of Education happen not to be the same as yours. We have had some Experiences of it. Several of our Young People were formally brought up at the Colleges of the Northern Provinces: they were instructed in all your Sciences, but when they came back to us they were bad Runners, ignorant of every means of living in the woods . . . neither fit for Hunters, Warriors, nor Councellors, they were totally good for nothing.
>
> We are, however, not the less obliged by your kind Offer, though we decline accepting it. And to show our grateful Sense of it, if the Gentlemen of Virginia will send us a Dozen of their Sons, we will take Care of their Education, instruct them in all we know, and make Men of them. (as cited in Blaisdell, 2000)

More recently, the debate over Afrocentric curriculum efforts is, for example, one that should be examined quite closely. Can a school experience that embraces an African perspective effectively reach African American children better than the standard Eurocentric curriculum? Is this curriculum worth embracing and evaluating? After eight years of emphasis on common curriculum content, evaluated by standardized tests that are close to national in scope, and renewed pressure for the adoption of common curriculum standards across the nation, American policy-makers (and many educators) are increasingly less open to variations in curriculum driven by differences in the cultural backgrounds of American students. Yet, if culturally driven curricula are to continue to be a part of our educational system, expressions of ethnocentricity on the part of all sides in that debate must become more aware of ways in which their ethnocentric attitudes become a barrier to finding the "good" in diverse approaches to knowledge and skills.

Afrocentric Curricula

Perception and Categorization

Another result of socialization is that we learn to *perceive* the world and to *categorize* information about people and things in our environment in particular ways. Perception and categorization are both cognitive processes that are shaped by socialization. People receive millions of bits of information each and every day through their senses. To think that people can respond to each individual piece of information is expecting too much; a person's physical and emotional systems would be overwhelmed. Because of the need to simplify things, people organize their world into categories; into each category they put items that share similar characteristics. People then generally respond to the category to which an individual item belongs.

Perception refers to the stimulation of the sense organs; that is, to what people immediately report seeing, hearing, feeling, tasting, and smelling. While no two people have exactly the same physiological structure and therefore no two people perceive stimuli identically, those with healthy nervous systems tend to perceive similar things in the environment in similar ways. Physicists, for example, tell us that the human eye can discern more than 8 million colors as distinguished by variations in wavelength. There is no practical reason, nor is it humanly possible, even to consider all these fine variations of shade and hue let alone to react to each individual color. Individuals, therefore, need some schema with which to group colors, the most familiar probably being the one based on the spectrum in which red, orange, yellow, green, blue, indigo, and violet are the major colors. When asked about the color of the sky, a Westerner's response typically is "blue." A sapphire is blue, oceans depicted on a map are blue, and robin's eggs are blue. Grass, however, is green, as are the leaves of most trees and the inside of a kiwi fruit.

In traditional Japanese language, however, the term *aoi* refers to colors that span blue and green wavelengths. When asked the color of the sky, a Japanese individual's response would be "aoi." When asked the color of grass, the response would again be "aoi." How would you explain these responses? Certainly the entire Japanese population is not color-blind! Rather, whereas European Americans have learned to place these particular stimuli into different schemata, traditional Japanese have learned to place them in the same one.

Clearly, sense perception alone is not sufficient. We also need to make sense out of the busy world around us, and to do so, we utilize schemata. Another term for such schemata is *category*. **Categorization** is the cognitive process through which human beings simplify their world by putting similar stimuli into the same group. What kind of categories we use, how narrow or broad they are, and what meanings are attached to them are all shaped by culture and acquired through socialization. A good example of the relation between perception and categorization is the dog: how people perceive the animal, and how they have learned to respond to the stimuli. All people will see, or perceive, the dog in a similar way, but they will certainly think about it differently. Most Westerners think of dogs as pets, as companions, and in some cases, as important members of their families. A traditional Muslim, confronted by the same creature, might consider the dog filthy, a lowly animal, and something to be avoided at all costs–similar to the reaction a North American might have to a pig. People in some Asian or Pacific Island nations might place a dog in the category of food. It is not uncommon to find dog meat as part of the human diet in many parts of the world.

The concept of a *prototype image* is critical in the analysis of categories. For most categories that humans create, there is one set of attributes or criteria that best characterizes the members of that category. In other words, there is a clear example of what the category encompasses. This example becomes a "summary" of the group and is the image most often thought of when the category is mentioned. If you were asked to think about a bird, for instance, you might conjure up an image of a creature about 8 or 9 inches long (beak to tail feathers), brown or perhaps reddish in color, that has feathers, flies, and nests in trees. You probably did not think of a turkey, penguin, ostrich, or even a chicken. For someone socialized in or near the jungles of South America, the prototypic image of a bird might be larger and more colorful because those birds that we call exotic (e.g., parrots) are part of their everyday world. Yet robins, parrots, and penguins have all the critical attributes that characterize members of the bird family; they all have feathers, beaks, and hollow or lightweight bones, and they all lay eggs. Teachers must examine what their own prototype image of a student is and how they will respond to those who do not fit neatly into this image.

Stereotypes

Activity 17:
Stereotypes and Their Impact on Interaction and Learning

Stereotypes

Categories help people to simplify the world around them. That is, people put stimuli that have common characteristics into one category and then respond to the group. People do not, for instance, respond to each and every chair or table when they walk into a room but refer to them in their broader context of chairs, tables, or furniture.

People respond in a similar manner in their interactions with people. **Stereotypes** are examples of categories of people. Socially constructed categories designed to simplify the identification of individuals who are in some way "other" frequently become negative stereotypes associated with groups. Here we find that the processes of perception and categorization along with ethnocentrism combine to create a potentially harmful situation. Although any cultural group may teach its members to categorize other groups either positively or negatively, most stereotypes end up as negative labels placed on individuals simply because they are members of a particular group.

In the most general sense, the word *stereotype* refers to any sort of summary representation (or prototypic image) that obscures the differences *within* a group (Brislin, 1993). Stereotypes obtain their power by providing categories that appear to encode a significant amount of information in a concise manner and that help us avoid having to pay serious attention to all the sensory data that is available. Negative stereotypes also enable us to keep our ethnocentric ideas intact by preventing us from seeing contradictory evidence before our very eyes. For example, it is much easier and quicker for us to think of all girls as stereotypically weak or passive than it is to notice that at least some of the girls in our classroom are stronger and more aggressive than the boys. Indeed, if we do notice such a thing, we tend to label those particular girls as "unfeminine," which helps us avoid the larger task of accurately differentiating one girl from another and also allows us to maintain a cultural value that teaches that boys are supposed to be strong and aggressive while girls are not. Stereotypic conceptions of others can be acquired through both early and later socialization and are powerful insofar as they promote group solidarity and ethnocentric beliefs.

Some Limits on Socialization

Although perception and categorization both depend in part on the cultural knowledge and meanings associated with the physical and social environment in which a child is socialized, and although early socialization is a powerful factor in the development of identity, it is also true that the power of socialization has limits. Three of these limitations are particularly important to educators. First, socialization is limited to some extent by the nature of the child's physical organism. For example, it is true that an infant or very young child can learn any language and any particular pattern of living, but it is not true that any child can be taught beyond his or her biological limits. Socialization to color wavelength categories, for example, may be limited by color blindness to red and green. Similarly, socialization to musical sounds will not necessarily produce an operatic singer. However, sensory limits in one area may be, and often are, compensated for by increased attention to other senses, as in people with hearing limitations.

Second, because socialization is an unending process that is never completely finished, its powers of control are never absolute. Because a child is socialized according to one set of patterns (language, situational behavior, understanding of role, categorization) does not mean that he or she cannot learn new patterns. Indeed, the extension of socialization beyond childhood knowledge is one of the chief purposes of formal schooling.

Third, socialization is limited in its power because human beings are not simply passive recipients of socialization; they always act on that socialization in some way. Individuals resist or reject accepted norms, they reinterpret accepted norms, and they create new kinds of normative behavior. Thus socialization can be seen not as an all-powerful force that totally molds the human creature but rather as a transactional process through which individuals are shaped but not totally determined. Your future students might become Nobel Prize winners, shuttle astronauts, or famous inventors.

Each of these limits on socialization is a resource on which educators can build. However, as Dewey (1916/1966) noted repeatedly, the most effective learning takes place when it begins with what the child already knows and moves on from there. It is important for teachers to understand not only the nature and purpose of cultural socialization in general but also the specifics of the cultural patterns to which they and their students have been socialized.

Understanding Cultural Differences

Variations in Cultural Environments: Returning to Beechland Heights

Figure 3.4 summarizes the discussion of the culture-learning process and points up its complexity in multicultural societies like the United States, Canada, Australia, and England. Although the sources of cultural identity are the same for all societies, each society–indeed, each community–varies considerably in the number and character of its socializing agents. Thus, in a relatively simple society like the Maasai of Kenya, the sources of cultural identity shown in Figure 3.4 will be transmitted through very few socializing agents, most notably the family and the members of other families in the community. Because these families have nearly every aspect of life in common, there is likely to be little conflict in the way the various attributes of culture (e.g., age, sexuality, social status) are transmitted to the individual in such a society. The same, by the way, can be said of small towns and villages anywhere in the world.

Figure 3.4
The Culture-Learning Process

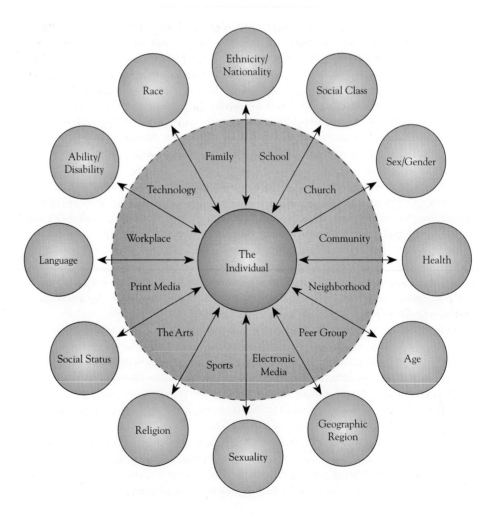

In complex societies like the United States and many other industrialized nations, however, most individuals interact daily with a vast array of socializing agents, each of which puts a slightly different spin on each of the cultural attributes. For example, your place of worship is likely to have a significantly different view of sexuality than your peer group or your favorite television program. Do you think, for instance, that in Beechland Heights, Dinorah Rodriguez finds a discrepancy between the teachings of her Catholic upbringing and the sexual ideas she views on music videos or television's sitcoms or soap operas? This daily interaction with a variety of socializing agents, each of which may have a unique interpretation of cultural attributes, means that individuals are bombarded with a variety of conflicting cultural messages.

Furthermore, individuals are not simply passive recipients of incoming messages. Once a message is received, each individual interprets and acts (or not) on its content according to his or her own personality and prior experiences. This interactive aspect of culture learning is depicted in Figure 3.4 by the directional arrows that connect the individual to various socializing agents and through them to the universal cultural attributes. In short, culture learning is a two-way process in which individuals are both forming and being formed by incoming cultural messages. And in many ways, no two individuals construct their world in the same manner.

Perhaps another example would be helpful. Gollnick and Chinn (2002) describe two hypothetical women who live in Chicago and who are both 30 years old, white, middle class, Polish American, and Catholic. One woman identifies very strongly with her Polish American heritage and her church in the context of living in Chicago, which has a large Polish American population. She does not identify very strongly with her age group, her class status, or her gender. The other woman defines herself as a feminist, is equally interested in her urban life, and is conscious of her age but does not pay too much attention to her ethnic background, her religion, or her social class. The significance of these patterns lies not in each woman's self-definition but in the attitudes, values, knowledge, and behavior that such definition entails.

The first woman may well spend more time with family than with nonrelated friends, may be a member of a right-to-life group, might choose wine rather than Perrier, may be knowledgeable about and participate in Polish ethnic organizations, and is likely to understand, if not speak, Polish.

The second woman may find her most intimate companions among women's groups, be pro-choice in her stand on abortion, choose to live in the city despite the possibility of living in a small town or the country, and–if she does not have children–hear her biological clock ticking.

This example illustrates how individuals operating in relatively similar settings with relatively similar environmental demands and socializing agents can develop distinctly different cultures. Perhaps you can begin to imagine how different groups and individuals operating in different settings with differing environmental demands and using different sets of socializing agents can develop distinctly different cultures. Figure 3.4 can help you recognize the multitude of factors that enter into the cultural identity equation.

In addition, consider that each of the two outer circles in Figure 3.4 can spin, so that every cultural attribute can be filtered differently by each of the socializing agents, which might combine differently with a variety of personality types. For instance, a passive-reflective individual would interact with the many incoming cultural messages differently than a volatile, nonreflective person might. You can begin to see how complex culture learning can be; how variable individuals can be in the manner in which they receive, process, and output the various influences they encounter; and how these messages can be transformed into differing behavior and belief patterns. Although you might think that in reality an infinite number of cultural formations is possible, the three parts in Figure 3.4 can be used with a little practice as a diagnostic tool for analyzing any multicultural or intercultural situation.

Despite this enormous potential for variation among individuals and within groups, similarities, or generalizations, can be made about groups of people, and these generalizations are referred to throughout this book. People have a tendency to use information that may or may not be reflective of all individuals within a given group. We must always be cautious when using culture-specific information to discuss whole groups because there will always be individuals who do not fit. Individual differences between two people who belong to the same group may be greater than between two people who belong to different groups.

Generalizations differ from stereotypes about people, and this point must be kept in mind. **Generalizations** refer to the tendency of a majority of people in a cultural group to hold certain values and beliefs and to engage in certain patterns of behavior. Thus this information can be supported by research and can be applied to a large percentage of a population or group. Stereotypes refer to the application of a generalization to *every* person in that group. Thus unsupported information blurs specific knowledge about other individuals. Such stereotypes would, for instance, say that Steven Wong *must* get very good grades because he is Chinese and male, and Shameka Collins *ought* to be more interested in a secretarial job because she is African American and female. Clearly, such stereotypes are in error, as life in Beechland Heights demonstrates.

Activity 30:
**Ethnic Literacy Test:
A Cultural Perspective
Differentiating
Stereotypes from
Generalizations**

Variations in Cultural Attributes, Socializing Agents, and Cultural Learners

Building a positive attitude toward differences requires a more sophisticated way of looking at diversity. Much of the educational research on individual differences related to culture rests on three assumptions. First, it is assumed that there is a standard or ideal against which difference can be seen, measured, or understood. In American society, people who are white, middle class, Protestant, English-speaking, healthy, physically and mentally typical, heterosexual, and male are said to make up the dominant cultural group. This "ideal" is, of course, a stereotype, much like the stereotypes of other cultural groups. It is important to note, however, that in the United States this particular stereotype refers to people who are socially privileged by virtue of birth characteristics over which they have little or no control (Howard, 1993; McIntosh, 1992). They are also educationally privileged in that their preschool socialization tends to prepare them for schooling, which is based on middle-class attitudes and values. One unfortunate consequence of belonging to this model group is that its members don't have to think of themselves as just one of many groups, each with its particular pattern of characteristics. Because they are the model group, they fit into perceived societal norms and thus do not have to think about their cultural patterns much at all (see the discussion of "white privilege" in Chapter 6). It also must be recognized that many of the nation's institutions have been built with this stereotypical model group as their foundation–the very framework that is in conflict with an increasing number of Americans–and we must work to change this infrastructure.

The second assumption is that any deviation from this normative group is the very definition of difference. If a person speaks only Spanish rather than English or is Asian rather than European American; Jewish rather than Protestant; female rather than male; homosexual rather than heterosexual; working class rather than middle class; chronically ill or with a physical, emotional, or mental disability rather than healthy or typical, that person is likely to be perceived as different, and this difference is seen as a deficit to be overcome.

Finally, research on difference assumes that studies of large groups of children with certain characteristics will tell us a great deal about all children who possess some or most of these characteristics. This assumption has at least two serious problems, however. One is that while most research looks at only one characteristic at a time (e.g., gender or social class), no one ever belongs to just one group. Every individual simultaneously belongs to a number of groups: gender, social class, ethnic, and so forth. What these "single-characteristic" studies look for are central tendencies, ways in which each particular group of children is the same. This tendency to focus on one narrow point may be problematic and may encourage stereotypes. In and of themselves, such stereotypes are oversimplifications that tend to ignore the diversity of behavior differences that exist within a group.

While this single-characteristic research has taught us much, it does not enable us to focus on differences within groups, only on differences between groups. Furthermore, it compares groups according to only one characteristic. Thus it does not help us understand how various characteristics (gender, social class, ethnicity, disability, etc.) combine with one another to form individual personalities and learning styles. For example, to be a deaf American who uses American Sign Language with other deaf people but uses English in interacting with hearing persons, as Humphries (1993) noted, is "to be bicultural and bilingual. This is just for starters. To be a deaf sign language user *and* African American, Hispanic, Asian/Pacific Islander, or American Indian in the United States is to be multicultural" (p. 15).

The second serious problem is that such research is most often statistical and tends to be interpreted by practitioners (and the public) in more global terms than its results warrant. If, for example, 65% of a given group of girls are found to be less successful at math than a comparable group of boys, the tendency is to believe that *all* girls are less successful at math. Although this generalization is not warranted by the research, it tends to become "true" in the minds of many people and thus to influence their behavior toward girls. Similarly, educators' attitudes and practices regarding students with disabilities have too often been based on broad labels or classifications such as *mental retardation, learning disability,* and *behavior disorder,* all of which obscure wide individual differences.

This book tries to avoid this problem of group stereotyping by looking at the universal connections between culture and learning. These connections are universal in the sense that they seem to apply to all people no matter what their various group affiliations. Figure 3.2 illustrates the sources of cultural knowledge that, when mixed together, form the cultural identity of *all* groups and individuals. These attributes are, for the most part, societal designations that have little meaning for the individual except as experienced through various socializing agents such as the family, house of worship, neighborhood, and peer group. In other words, individuals acquire a cultural identity within the larger society through their experiences with a variety of daily socializing agents.

What teachers must understand is that cultural-learning patterns vary considerably both between and within various cultural groups. Subsequent chapters describe in more detail some of the ways in which differences in cultural learning may lead to misunderstanding and conflict in schools and classrooms. This book also shows how these same differences can be used as a positive resource in learning-community classrooms. For now, play with the model in Figure 3.4. Ask yourself what the universal attributes mean to you in view of your own life experiences and which socializing agents have accounted for your understanding of them. Do the same for others who are close to you such as family members and friends.

This book will ask these same questions about students, teachers, parents, and school administrators. With the help of the stories incorporated in this book for illustrative purposes and the cases presented for analysis, you will gradually become a sensitive and skillful teacher of *all* children, not just those whose cultural background matches your own. For, as you have seen in Beechland Heights, although a person may *seem* to be quite different from you by virtue of membership in a different race or class or religion, that person may also share some important cultural aspects with you. And even when an individual *seems* to have many cultural aspects in common with you, they may in fact be quite different in some important ways.

Critical Incident

Definitely College Material

Steven Wong is the child of a rather well-to-do professional family. Compared to many students in his community, he is well traveled, having had the opportunity to visit China as well as other countries throughout Asia in order to maintain family and cultural connections. He has also had exposure to many different opportunities as he was growing up. To his parents' dismay, Steven is not excited about attending college, sometimes saying he would rather study the martial arts as a professional and at other times saying he would like to leave the area, perhaps move out west, and "find" himself.

• How might you explain Steven's apparent ambivalence toward college?

• How would you explain the fact that at times he wishes to pursue the martial arts and at other times he is seemingly uncommitted to anything?

• What factors in his school and community might contribute to his confusion? If he were to come to you, a teacher, asking for guidance, how would you advise him?

Critical Incident

Who, Exactly, Am I?

Dinorah Rodriguez is a first-generation immigrant to the United States; her parents are recent immigrants. Dinorah's father works in a local factory and has learned to speak English rather well. Her mother, however, has never worked outside the home and, as a result, has not had as strong a reason to learn English. Thus, at Dinorah's home, more Spanish is spoken than English, most meals reflect the family's Mexican tradition, and most interactions are restricted to family or others from the Latino community. Dinorah feels as if she is under great pressure, caught between two worlds, torn between the expectations and demands of her own family and culture and those of her American classmates. She is embarrassed to have friends over to her house and has always been uncomfortable when her parents attend school functions as well as parent-teacher conferences.

- What cultural factors can you identify that are immediately responsible for her conflicts?
- If Dinorah came to you, her teacher, asking for advice, what would you focus your attention on?
- If you were Dinorah, what would you want from your friends? From your teachers? From your parents?

Critical Incident

What's Wrong With a Golf Scholarship

Michael Williams, who comes from a working-class family and was raised by his grandparents and mother, is planning to go to college, although he does not have a particular major in mind. He is, however, pretty certain that he would like to continue with his golf and hopes to obtain a college scholarship through the sport. Many people in his community would have expected him to play basketball rather than golf.

- To what would you attribute this?
- To what would you attribute his love of golf?
- What obstacles might Michael encounter as he pursues his goals?
- If he came to you, his teacher, troubled because many people did not seem to support his wishes, what advice might you give him?

Critical Incident

Am I Black or White?

Shameka Collins lives a life many people could not imagine. Being biracial in American society has presented for her both numerous opportunities and many challenges. Many doors were open to her, especially when she was young, but since her father began working away from home, she feels as though things have changed.

Shameka identifies herself as African American now, not because of what she thinks but because of what everybody else thinks. It's just become easier, she says. In seventh and eighth grades, soon after her father left, Shameka saw a counselor on a regular basis. She told her counselor that sometimes she doesn't feel like a black person because in many ways she was raised white. When she was younger, she would tell the counselor, she used to wish that she was just one race, because then she could say that's what she was and it was less confusing for people. But that wish created a dilemma for her. She felt that if she just said she was black, then she was denying her white side. And if she said she was white, she was denying the other side.

- How might you help Shameka understand her internal conflicts?
- If you were Shameka's classroom teacher, what might you do to make things easier in the classroom for her, or others like her?

Critical Incident

Where Do I Fit In?

Growing up in Beechland Heights, Jacob Goldsmith knew there were people from a variety of backgrounds. But because he attended the Jewish day school until eighth grade, he spent most of his time with other Jewish children from the local communities. It was, unexpectedly, quite an adjustment when he moved to the local high school, where he suddenly found himself a minority and with many other young people whom he did not know. He found it especially difficult in ninth grade, his first year in the school, around the winter holidays when most of his classmates were busy preparing for Christmas. Jacob was reluctant to bring many peers home because his home was not extensively decorated for the holidays–his family had a small menorah on the dining room table. He was uncomfortable going to holiday parties, especially ones that had a gift exchange. And he was surprised and a bit embarrassed that, on occasion, he wished his family could have a Christmas tree like everyone else. He often wondered why his parents just didn't move to another part of the state where there were more Jews.

- If you were Jacob's teacher, how would you help him to understand his situation? What would you suggest he do?
- What other children do you think might be having similar experiences as Jacob? If you were on a school diversity committee, what would you suggest the school consider doing to better understand the experiences students like Jacob were having?

Summary

All people, regardless of the culture in which they were raised, share certain common experiences. This chapter presented the dynamics of culture and the culture-learning process that all people, students as well as teachers, experience and bring with them to the school context. Of particular interest to educators are the primary and secondary socialization processes and the 12 sources of cultural knowledge that represent the diversity of knowledge and experiences to which people are exposed. Critical to educators concerned with improving people's skills in intercultural understanding and communication is the recognition that some of the results of the socialization process present barriers to cross-cultural interactions. Effective multicultural education understands and addresses such issues as critical process as well as content.

Chapter Review

Go to the Online Learning Center at www.mhhe.com/cushner7e to review important content from the chapter, practice with key terms, take a chapter quiz, and find the Web links listed in this chapter.

Key Terms

ability/disability 82	generalizations 98	race 80
age 84	geographic location/	racism 80
categorization 93	region 84	religion/spirituality 83
culture 69	health 81	sex/gender 80
culture-general	in-context learning 78	sexuality 84
approaches 77	language 85	social class 82
culture-specific	microculture 71	social status 85
approaches 77	objective culture 74	socialization 88
enculturate 75	out-of-context	stereotypes 94
ethnic group 71	learning 78	subculture 70
ethnicity/nationality 83	people of color 72	subjective culture 75
ethnocentrism 92	perception 93	

Active Exercise

Additional Active Exercises are available online at www.mhhe.com/cushner7e.

The Nature of Culture and Culture Learning

Purpose: To identify qualities that characterize the concept of culture.
Instructions: Read and review the following material. Respond accordingly in the space provided using examples from your own life.

The process by which people come to believe that there is a "right" way to think, express themselves, and act–in other words, how people learn their culture–is called **socialization.** It is the process by which individuals learn what is required of them in order to be successful members of a given group, whatever that group may be. Socialization is such a potent process that people are hardly aware that other realities can exist. This results in the presence of **ethnocentrism,** the tendency people have to judge others from their own culture's perspective, believing theirs to be the "right" or "correct" way to perceive and act within the world.

Most people in today's industrialized societies can be considered to be multicultural because they have been socialized by a number of different individuals or groups that influence their behavior and thought patterns (e.g., gender, nationality, ethnicity, social class, religion, and so forth). At this point, it may be helpful to look at how culture, in the broadest sense, influences people's behavior.

Brislin (2000) and Cushner and Brislin (1996) offer a discussion of features that are helpful in understanding culture's influence on behavior and that can be applied to the multiple influences suggested previously. This list is summarized below. You should consider each, and then apply it to your own lives and experiences with the various groups with which you interact. First, individually identify examples from your own past that reflect *each* of the aspects of culture. Then share your responses in small groups. Be ready to share an example of each aspect with the larger group.

1. Culture usually refers to something that is made by human beings rather than something that occurs in nature. Thus, sand along a beach may be a natural occurrence, but the condominiums along the beachfront are not.

    My example:

2. Culture concerns itself with people's assumptions about life that are often unspoken or hidden from consciousness. Thus, most Americans, when putting a hand out to greet someone new, assume they will do likewise and then can shake hands. This may not be the case when meeting someone from Japan.

    My example of an aspect of my culture that I believe is "hidden" or a "secret":

3. Culture is a collective creation that most members of the group practice. In the United States, as well as many other countries, it is common for people to unconsciously walk on the right side of a hallway or sidewalk. In other countries, such as Britain, Australia, or New Zealand, it is common for people to walk on the left side of hallways and sidewalks.

    My example of something most people from my cultural group practice that might be different from another group:

4. Clear childhood experiences that individuals can identify exist that help to develop and teach particular values and practices. For instance, the American value of individualism is often introduced to young people through early jobs they may have had (paper routes, babysitting, etc.).

    My example of something I did in my childhood that teaches a cultural value or practice:

5. Because culture is often a secret and most people do not share a common vocabulary and understanding, people are often unable to comfortably discuss cross-cultural problems with others. Cultural differences, thus, become most evident in well-meaning clashes.

    My example of a culture clash that occurred because people did not understand the differing cultural perspectives that were operating at the time:

6. Culture allows people to fill in the blanks so they do not have to repeat the rules for every action to other members of the group. Thus, when someone is invited to a happy hour after work, it is clear to most people that they should expect to spend no more than a couple of hours at the bar or pub, and not plan to make a night of it.

   My example of a common behavior that seems mostly automatic and commonly understood:

7. People experience strong emotional reactions when their cultural values are violated or when a culture's expected behaviors are ignored. Thus, recent rulings in France that student's heads must remain uncovered in school has drawn strong criticism from the Islamic community.

   My example of a strong emotional response I have observed when people's cultures clash:

8. When changes in cultural values are contemplated, like legalizing same-sex marriages or outlawing the right of citizens to carry handguns, the reaction that "this will be a difficult uphill battle" is likely.

   My example of a major cultural change that is or was difficult for people to make:

Reflective Questions

1. Look back at Webb and Sherman's definition of culture on page 72. Compare two different cultures or ethnic groups that you are familiar with in terms of the categories to which they refer. What categories are similar and which ones are different? How would you explain the differences and similarities?

2. Differentiate between objective culture and subjective culture. Can you provide two examples of each from the cultures or ethnic groups you identified in the first question?

3. Consider the 12 sources of knowledge described in the chapter. Complete an inventory on yourself. How might your inventory differ from one of your parents? Compare your inventory to that of a classmate. How are they similar? Different? How would you explain some of the differences?

4. How does the way your parents or community socialized you to understand your social class differ from the way the popular media does? How about your understanding of your gender? How about your understanding of sexual relations?

References

Ah, but the mystery. (2000). *Akron Beacon Journal,* p. A12.
Banks, J. A. (Ed.)(1989). Multicultural education: Characteristics and goals. *Multicultural education: Issues and perspectives* (pp. 3–32). Boston: Allyn & Bacon.

Beardsley, E. (1977). Traits and genderization. In M. Vetterling-Braggin, F. A. Elliston, & J. English (Eds.), *Feminism and philosophy* (pp. 117–123). Totowa, NJ: Littlefield.

Bellah, R. N., Madsen, R., Sullivan, W. M., Swidler, A., & Tipton, S. M. (1985). *Habits of the heart: Individualism and commitment in American life.* New York: Harper & Row.

Bennett, C. L. (1990). *Comprehensive multicultural education: Theory and practice.* Boston: Allyn & Bacon.

Berger, P. L., & Berger, B. (1972). *Sociology: A biographical approach.* New York: Basic Books.

Blaisdell, B. (2000). *Great speeches by Native Americans.* New York: Dover.

Brislin, R. (1993). *Understanding culture's influence on behavior.* Fort Worth, TX: Harcourt Brace Jovanovich.

Brislin, R. (2000). *Understanding culture's influence on behavior* (2nd ed.). Fort Worth, TX: Harcourt Brace Jovanovich.

Bullivant, B. M. (1993). Culture: Its nature and meaning for educators. In J. A. Banks (Ed.), *Multicultural education: Issues and perspectives* (2nd ed., pp. 29–47). Boston: Allyn & Bacon.

Chomsky, N. (1966). *Cartesian linguistics.* New York: Harper & Row.

Coon, C. (2000). *Culture wars and the global village: A diplomat's perspective.* Amherst, NY: Prometheus.

Cortes, C. (2000). *The children are watching: How the media teach about diversity.* New York: Teachers College Press.

Cottrell, R. J. (1990). America the multicultural. *American Educator, 14*(4), 18–21.

Cushner, K. (1998). Intercultural education from an international perspective: An introduction. In K. Cushner (Ed.), *International perspectives on intercultural education* (pp. 1–14). Mahwah, NJ: Lawrence Erlbaum.

Cushner, K., & Brislin, R. (1996). *Intercultural interactions: A practical guide.* Thousand Oaks, CA: Sage.

Dewey, J. (1966). *Democracy and education.* New York: Free Press. (Original work published 1916)

Friedman, I. (1984). *How my parents learned to eat.* Boston: Houghton Mifflin.

Giroux, H., & Simon, R. (1989). *Popular culture: Schooling and everyday life.* Granby, MA: Bergin & Garvey.

Gollnick, D. M., & Chinn, P. C. (2002). *Multicultural education in a pluralistic society* (6th ed.). Upper Saddle River, NJ: Merrill/Prentice Hall.

Herek, G. M. (1986). On heterosexual masculinity: Some physical consequences of the social construction of gender and sexuality. *American Behavioral Scientist, 29*(5), 570.

Hofstede, G. (2001). *Culture's consequences: Comparing values, behaviors, institutions and organizations across nations* (2nd ed.). Thousand Oaks, CA: Sage.

Howard, G. R. (1993). Whites in multicultural education: Rethinking our role. *Phi Delta Kappan, 75*(1), 36–41.

Humphries, T. (1993). Deaf culture and cultures. In K. M. Christensen & G. L. Delgado (Eds.), *Multicultural issues in deafness* (pp. 3–16). White Plains, NY: Longman.

Huxley, F. (1957). *Affable savages.* New York: Viking Press.

LeVay, S., & Hamer, D. H. (1994). Evidence for a biological influence in male homosexuality. *Scientific American, 270,* 44–49.

McIntosh, P. (1992, January–February). White privilege. *Creation Spirituality,* pp. 33–35, 53.

Pearce, R. H. (1965). *The savages of America: A study of the Indian and the idea of civilization.* Baltimore: Johns Hopkins University Press.

Rosenstiel, T. B. (1989, August 17). Viewers found to confuse TV entertainment with news. *Los Angeles Times,* p. A1.

Sapir, E. (1949). *Culture, language, and personality.* Berkeley: University of California Press.

Sheehy, G. (1994). *New passages: Mapping your life across time.* New York: Ballentine Books.

Triandis, H. (1972). *The analysis of subjective culture.* New York: Wiley-Interscience.

Vygotsky, L. S. (1962). *Thought and language.* Cambridge, MA: MIT Press.

Warren, D. M. (1873). *An elementary treatise on physical geography.* Philadelphia: Cowperthwait.

Webb, R. B., & Sherman, R. R. (1989). *Schooling and society* (2nd ed.). New York: Macmillan.

Whorf, B. L. (1968). Science and linguistics. In Alan Dundes (Ed.), *Everyman his own way: Readings in cultural anthropology.* Englewood Cliffs, NJ: Prentice Hall.

Yetman, N. R. (Ed.). (1991). *Majority and minority: The dynamics of race and ethnicity in American life* (5th ed.). Boston: Allyn & Bacon.

Zakaria, F. (2008). *The post-American world.* New York: W.W. Norton, p. 1.

Zelizer, V. A. (1985). *Pricing the priceless child: The changing social value of children.* New York: Basic Books.

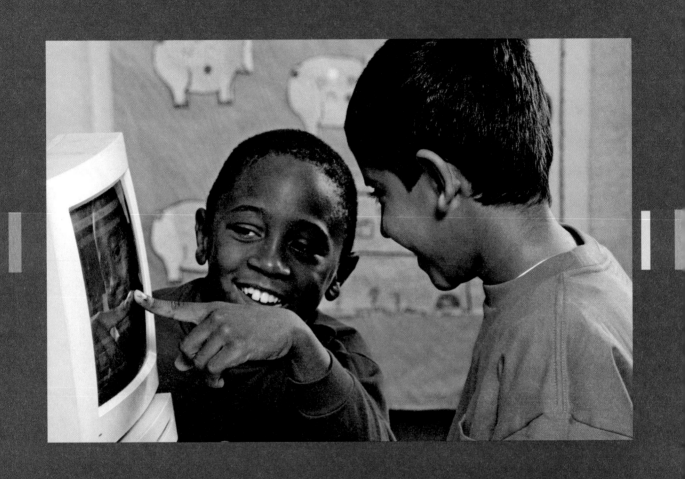

Chapter

4

Classrooms and Schools as Cultural Crossroads

Focus Questions

1. How might the cultures of students and teachers be similar or different? How might they be in support of one another? In conflict with one another?

2. What cultural characteristics might people who appear to be different from one another share? How can teachers begin to understand the culturally determined traits and behaviors of students and families?

3. How might teachers become better prepared for the cross-cultural differences they are certain to encounter among students? How can they begin to help their students understand and appreciate these differences, thus preparing them better for a global society?

❝ It is often hard to learn from people who are just like you. Too much is taken for granted. Homogeneity is fine in a bottle of milk, but in the classroom it diminishes the curiosity that ignites discovery. ❞

VIVIAN GYSSIN PALEY

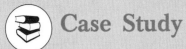

Case Study

Melinda's Induction Year Dilemma

Melinda had just completed a degree in science education at a large northern university and was excited about the prospects of teaching in one of the area high schools. All through her teacher preparation she had been encouraged to pursue the sciences as an area of specialization. She had often heard about the shortage of science teachers, especially women in the sciences, and thought she might have an edge in terms of employment as well as be a model for other young girls. Melinda felt confident that she would obtain a position in a high school not too far from where she had grown up and gone to school. She had held this dream ever since her own high school years.

When Melinda finally graduated, however, the employment situation in the area close to her home had changed. Many of the schools had fallen on difficult financial times, and in most districts, school levies had failed year after year. When school districts from the South came to recruit teachers at her university, Melinda found herself seriously considering the possibility of relocating. After all, she did want to teach, and she felt well prepared for any classroom situation.

When offered a position at Wake Central High School, Melinda gladly accepted and eagerly made plans to move to North Carolina. Wake Central High is an urban school of approximately 2,200 students in grades 9 through 12. Approximately 25 percent of the students are black, 6 percent Latino representing Mexico as well as a number of different nations throughout Central and South America, 5 percent Asian descent, 60 percent are European American, and about 4 percent represent other parts of the world. A majority of students come from families at or below the poverty level. The school has a large vocational program in which more than half the juniors and seniors are enrolled. Approximately 20 percent of the faculty is a mix of Latino and African American; the rest are European American.

Wake Central High has an aging faculty, with an average age of 46. Last year the principal, Mr. Henderson, was unable to hire any teachers of color. This year he was able to attract one new Latino and two new African American faculty members among the new teachers. Melinda was one of three European Americans hired in the same year. She was excited about her first teaching situation and confident that she would be successful. She had, after all, taken a course in multicultural education in her undergraduate teacher education program, and at least knew some of the basic concepts and theories.

A few months after the start of the school year, Melinda knew that she was confronting a reality far different from the one she had origianlly imagined. She felt unprepared for the student diversity that she faced each and every day, and she had no idea how to help students address what she felt were basic educational needs. She was unaccustomed to the variety of languages

Schools, in particular, are cultural crossroads in a society where distinct but overlapping student, teacher, parent, community, and school cultures intersect. This chapter examines what occurs when people from different cultures come together, as they increasingly do in globally oriented pluralistic societies. We then take an in-depth look at a culture-general model for understanding intercultural interactions. We introduce an intercultural perspective, which draws from the work of cross-cultural psychologists and trainers who, more than any other group of scholars and practitioners, have been developing practical strategies to help people understand and navigate the oftentimes tricky waters of intercultural interaction. Finally, we present this model in action and provide opportunities for you to apply this model to the analysis of some common cross-cultural situations found in school settings.

and dialects spoken by students, had little understanding of what went on in students' lives outside school, and struggled daily to present class lessons that motivated and involved students. And to top everything off, Melinda found herself in the middle of significant racial strife.

It seems that in January of the previous year, Mr. Henderson had met with the African American teachers at their request. They had many concerns, ranging from insufficient minority representation on the teaching and coaching staffs to the way white teachers were interacting with many of the African American and other students of color. They felt that most white teachers did not appreciate the need for the proposed Martin Luther King recognition activities; they were disappointed at the lack of white response to a request for donations to the United Negro College Fund; and they felt a negative response to Black History Month activities and other efforts to make the curriculum more culturally relevant.

As a result of this meeting, a Human Relations Committee was formed. This volunteer group planned and organized a two-day race relations institute. The results of the workshop were disastrous. Instead of improving race relations in the school, the situation became worse. A group of white teachers sent around a list of possible themes for the coming school year that were perceived as racist by the African American teachers. A group of concerned black teachers and parents sent letters to community leaders and higher-level administrators voicing their concern. Once parents of the Latino students became aware of the situation, they started demanding equal attention to address the needs of their children, many of whom became increasingly alienated from school-related activities. Students formed a group they called "Students Against Racism" as a means to express their concerns and frustrations.

In March of last year, Mr. Henderson had met with the equal opportunity officer in the district and with a racially mixed group of teachers. While concerns were aired, none of the problems were solved. A discussion was begun, but as Mr. Henderson puts it, "We have a long way to go. We definitely have some white teachers who are insensitive to the needs of others, as well as some teachers of color who perceive the white teachers as racist. I'm not quite sure how to begin addressing the students' needs, except to say that we will continue to bring the various parties together to address whatever needs arise. I only hope people will stay with me for the long haul."

Melinda was quite uncomfortable attending faculty meetings, and the spin-off was affecting her classroom interactions. She was frustrated, unsure of what was really going on, and uncertain if she could remain in such an environment. She began to seriously question how anyone could teach in such a stressful situation, and if she should just go back home where she at least understood the lay of the land.

Schools and Classrooms: Where Cultures Intersect

Within the important limitations of economic circumstance, most people choose the neighborhoods they live in, the places they work and shop, and where they spend their leisure time. In schools, however, as nowhere else in American society, people of many different backgrounds are forced to come together in close quarters for significant periods of time. In this section we first examine the various cultures (student, teacher, parent, and school) that come together in the context of the school. Second, we examine the role of the teacher as a cultural mediator who is responsible for developing a cooperative learning community within this potentially chaotic setting.

The Students of "Generation Y"

Student Culture

Students make up by far the largest percentage of people in a school community. Roughly 56 million students were enrolled in public schools in the year 2009, with an additional 7 million attending private institutions (NCES, 2009). Perhaps more than most social groups, as discussed in Chapter 1, students represent and exhibit the greatest diversity in American society. Not only do students reflect the cultural identities of their families (ethnicity, religion, social class, etc.), they also define themselves by creating their own particular in-school groups.

It is a cultural universal that all people categorize others into one of two major divisions: those with whom they identify and wish to spend their time (called ingroups), and those with whom they may interact in the workplace or hallways yet keep a respectable distance from (known as outgroups). Ingroup formation in school can be based on many different criteria, from the more potent cultural identities already discussed (e.g., ethnicity, race, gender) to the relatively fluid but no less important unifying features of academic groups (e.g., biology club, French club), special interest or skill groups (e.g., choir, football), or groups that are, from the point of view of most adults, less desirable but nonetheless purposeful, such as gangs. Stop for a moment and think of the many varied student cultures that can be found in schools, some to which you belonged and some which you may have even shunned. Typically, individual students gain a certain school identity from participation in these groups. These microcultures within the school operate in ways similar to the macroculture outside it. Individuals learn appropriate rules of interaction, modes of communication, expression of values, and so forth. And as with larger groups such as nation-states, membership in these in-school microcultures (gangs, chess club, choir) often brings exclusion from other microcultures (other gangs, sports teams, band).

Teacher Culture

Teachers make up the other dominant social group within the school community, with more than 3 million teaching in public schools and another 500,000 in private institutions (NCES, 2009). But unlike the diversity found within the student population, teachers are a relatively homogeneous group. Indeed, a disturbing reality, given the increasing diversity of students in public schools, is the relative cultural homogeneity of the teaching force. In the United States, about 85% of the teaching force are European American and three fourths are female. Despite recent efforts to recruit underrepresented groups into the teaching profession, it is projected that well into this century the majority of new teachers will continue to be female and white. This statistic is not surprising. Teachers in the United States have always been mostly female and white, at least since the early part of the 19th century. However, this statistic raises interesting issues about the cultural and economic backgrounds of teachers in contrast to that of students.

The fact that a large proportion of our teachers are female is related to the power structure of schools. Teachers have a good deal of authority in their classrooms, but it is not true that they have much authority in the schools. For example, teachers are just beginning to have something to say about school policy or about the curriculum they are expected to teach. Reasons for this lack of authority may vary, but an important one has to do with the way in which large numbers of women

Women in Teaching

entered the teaching profession in the 1830s and 1840s. Prior to that time, the person behind the schoolroom desk was a schoolmaster, a man. However, after about 1830, the growth of industry began providing more and more lucrative jobs for men, leaving teaching vacancies in the classroom. At the same time, the common school movement was evolving across the United States, opening up additional teaching positions. Conveniently, it was determined that women, who were "natural mothers" and therefore possessed the knowledge, skills, and talents needed to deal with young children, must also be "natural teachers." The elementary school was projected as an extension of the home and the teacher an extension of the mother. The fact that women would work for about one third the wages paid to male teachers was also a significant factor in their employment in American schools.

Given the history of their entry into the profession, female teachers have never had the status that male teachers once had. Unfortunately for all teachers, the low status of women teachers has become associated with teachers more generally. Administrators, who have greater authority, higher pay, and higher status, still tend to be mostly European American men. Thus, in our society, schools have become organized in such a way that leadership and policy are very often the exclusive province of white, male administrators.

Parent Culture

It is increasingly recognized that parents play a critical role in the academic success of their own children as well as in building a sense of community within the school. Yet it may sometimes be difficult to encourage all families to be active participants in the classroom. New immigrant and refugee families may come from cultures where the status of the school was such that parents had little say, or were actively discouraged from contributing and participating in school life, leaving all decisions and actions to the "professionals" in charge. Language facility may be another barrier that keeps many parents from contributing fully to school life. Sometimes socioeconomic  and perceived status differences may discourage parents from feeling welcomed in the school. Effective teachers and other school officials seek ways to invite and otherwise encourage participation from a wide range of families who may not have much direct exposure and experience in schools. This may include such things as meeting in various community centers, sending communications home to families in multiple languages, employing bilingual teachers and other staff, and having translators available for parent-teacher conferences.

School Culture

Both schools and the teachers who inhabit them are, to a large extent, culture-bound, and the culture most are bound to is the dominant culture of European American, middle-class society. This, however, is only one of the many culture groups in the United States. One purpose of public schooling has always been to transmit the cultural beliefs, values, and knowledge affiliated with the dominant group to those in the next generation. The danger, of course, is the ethnocentric tendency of most people, teachers included, to believe that their own cultural tradition represents the "best" way. Too often, the perception of both power and virtue combine to lessen the chance that white, middle-class teachers will make a real effort to understand the cultural differences that direct the lives of many of their students. At best, many of these teachers are predisposed to regard diversity as interesting; at worst, they are likely to regard it as a deficit. Teachers seldom come to their classes with the notion that diversity is an exciting and enriching phenomenon. Sara Lawrence Lightfoot (1989), who has committed her professional life to understanding and assisting with issues of diversity in schools, describes many good teachers as wishing that the diversity they see in September will somehow fade away as the class becomes a group.

Teachers as Cultural Mediators

The cultural interplay between teachers, students, parents, and their school produces a context within which significant culture learning can occur. In a sense, teachers must become cultural mediators in their classrooms and must walk both sides of a double-edged sword. Teachers must become more knowledgeable about the role of culture in teaching and learning while becoming better able to address the educational needs of students and families from a variety of backgrounds. At the same time, teachers must turn this knowledge and skill into content that actively engages students in learning about and more effectively accommodating cultural differences. Students need to learn how culture is formed and how to understand and handle the many intercultural interactions they are certain to encounter.

Throughout this process, it is imperative that teachers and students understand that a certain amount of adjustment and discomfort may occur. It is well to remember that when we as individuals are confronted by someone who looks, behaves, or thinks differently from ourselves, we suddenly become aware that our way of doing things may not be the only one. Such a confrontation often affects us at an emotional level—we may feel anxiety, uncertainty, and discomfort. Lacking a vocabulary to describe most cross-cultural differences and wishing to avoid discomfort, people may choose to avoid further interaction with those who are different from them. Such avoidance behavior perpetuates the cycle of discomfort, mistrust, and ignorance and confounds our efforts to improve intergroup relations.

These same feelings often characterize teachers whose students are different from them and perhaps different, as well, from the value and behavior norms of the school. From the school's point of view, such students are often perceived as having deficits that need to be overcome through some type of remedial action. Sadly, such actions are often punitive to students, involving exclusionary practices such as tracking and negative labeling (e.g., at-risk students, learning disabled). Because most of us do not have a wide variety of experience with cultural patterns other than our own, deliberate instruction in culture, including acquiring a vocabulary in order to talk about its patterns, its substance, and its behavioral results, is one way to create a dialogue concerning differences. Such strategies help us to truly understand ourselves and others.

Cross-Cultural Adaptation

It would be easy for teachers to give in to discouragement and try to find a school where the students were like them. The reality, however, is that such schools rarely exist in today's world. Teachers will have to adjust to the fact that they will continue to find themselves in significantly diverse settings.

Early studies of cross-cultural experiences suggested an often predictable pattern of adjustment when one interacts with people different from oneself. Studies of international travelers, for instance, led cross-cultural psychologists and trainers to identify a number of phases people experience during their adjustment to an intercultural setting (Lysgaard, 1955; Oberg, 1960; Trifonovitch, 1977). These early models, although brought into question in recent years, present a visual representation that plots people's experiences on a graph, with emotional experiences along the vertical axis and time across the horizontal axis. The resulting image thus appears as a U, hence this process of adjustment to living and working in another culture is often referred to as the U-curve hypothesis (Figure 4.1).

These early studies suggested that, at least initially, most people are intrigued and perhaps even enraptured by the prospect of a new intercultural experience. They have some preconceived ideas of what the new culture will be like and how they might integrate into the new setting. In some cases, they do not initially perceive that the experience will be much different from experiences they have had in the past. Often they are excited at the idea of moving to a new place, of "starting a new life," as Melinda was in the case study. In this stage, individuals enter what has been appropriately termed the honeymoon phase, where things are new and fresh; there are new people to meet, new ways of interacting, new foods to eat, new ideas to consider—nothing could be better!

After some time, however, when people begin to get a sense that what looks different really is different and that those differences are important, the constant demand to adjust to new stimuli and to function well in a new setting may become too difficult to accept. Most people react to the stress by entering a state

Activity 11:
Adjustment to Change

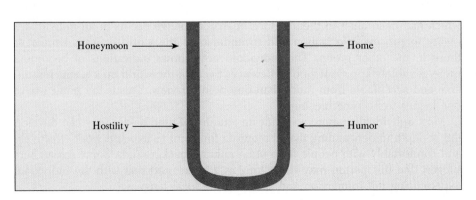

Figure 4.1
U-Curve Hypothesis

of hostility and begin to move down the left side of the U. In this phase, people generally attempt to cope with three problems: (1) other people's behavior does not make sense to them; (2) their own behavior does not produce the expected results; and (3) there is so much that is new in the environment that they have no ready-made answers to the questions that may arise.

There are many examples of similar adjustment curves in the psychological literature (e.g., newlyweds, retirees). Beginning teachers and new students moving into the culture of a particular school face a double challenge. Teachers new to the profession must simultaneously adapt to the culture of the surrounding community and to that of the teaching profession, which, of course, has a culture of its own. In the school context, new teachers must integrate themselves into the norms and attitudes of both a well-established teaching staff and their students, who bring with them the norms of their own communities. During the hostility phase, new teachers, like new arrivals in any new culture, may become so frustrated by their inability to make sense of their new world that they begin to react in an aggressive and perhaps hostile manner. At the same time, new students must also adjust not only to the school culture, which may be very different from their home and neighborhood cultures, but also to the behavioral and academic expectations of schooling and to the many possible student microcultures within the school. During the hostility phase, students can become so frustrated that they may give up, act up, or drop out.

At this point the individual must make a critical choice: remain, and learn how to function effectively within the new setting; or allow the frustrations to build, and eventually retreat from the unpleasant situation. In this phase, those individuals most likely to succeed in their new setting begin to confront their new cultural environment. They learn to cope with embarrassment, disappointment, frustration, anxiety, and identity problems at first, and then begin the process of culture learning by focusing on the subjective culture of the new environment.

Once this culture-learning stage begins, people typically begin to emerge from this reactive, hostile phase and enter the third phase, up the right side of the U. Often referred to as the humor phase, this phase is a positive step toward the reshaping of cultural identity. People who reach the humor phase begin to understand more of the new culture and can begin to laugh at some of their earlier misconceptions and mistakes.

Finally, people who succeed in altering their own cultural identities to include the new experiences climb the final leg of the U and enter the phase called home. In this phase, individuals are able to interpret the world and interact with others both from their own perspective as well as from the perspective of that which had been alien to them before. A major change occurs in an individual's ability to process information and to understand the world in ways similar to those in the other group. The individual now shows indications of becoming more genuinely appreciative of differences because the world now seems reasonable and acceptable from more than one point of view. This is the point where one begins to become bicultural.

Most individuals require a significant amount of time before they can develop the in-depth understanding that is required for them to live and work effectively and comfortably with people from other cultural backgrounds. Some researchers suggest that this period may be as long as 2 years—and that with the individual experiencing full immersion and speaking the local language.

A related experience is often encountered by bilingual learners whose primary language is not English. Such children often encounter two levels of linguistic adjustment (Cummins, 1979). On one level, children may acquire Basic Interpersonal Communication Skills (BICS) relatively quickly and within 2 or 3 years appear to be quite fluent—on a surface, or objective, level. That is, non-English speakers may quickly be able to communicate effectively with other children on the playground, during their free time, and during informal interactions in the classroom. Yet when these children are given standardized tests of educational achievement, they do not do as well—a secondary, deeper level of linguistic competence is at play. That is, students may need between 5 and 7 years to attain Cognitive Academic Language Proficiency (CALP)—the level of linguistic competence in a second language that is typically required in schools. Clearly, if acquiring a cultural identity through primary socialization requires full immersion in a culture over a long period of time, it stands to reason that reshaping a cultural outlook as a result of secondary socialization will also take considerable time.

In Chapter 3, Figure 3.4 provided a visual overview of how the various sources of cultural identity are acquired by individuals through interaction with the many socializing agents they encounter. Although the sources of cultural identity (e.g., race, language, sexuality) are universal and appear in all societies, the socializing agents (family, school, media, and so forth) that transmit them vary considerably from one society to another. In most industrialized societies, a wide variety of socializing agents bombard people daily, often with contradictory messages. In agriculturally oriented societies, on the other hand, a few primary socializing agents (e.g., family and gender group) may share the bulk of the culture-transmission process. The result is that individuals with different cultural patterns develop very different worldviews.

Acculturation and Identity

Extended intercultural contact can have a significant impact on individuals as well as groups. **Acculturation** refers to the changes that take place as a result of continuous firsthand contact between individuals of different cultures (Berry, 1990, 2004; Redfield, Linton, & Herskovits, 1936). Such contact not only produces changes in people's attitudes, values, and behaviors, but may also significantly affect their cultural identity. Historical as well as present-day experiences of different groups may determine, to a great extent, the outcome. For instance, immigrants and refugees who enter a new culture with long-standing, distinctive cultural norms may have very different experiences from members of established ethnic minority groups (Ward, Bochner, & Furnam, 2001). Newcomers, for example, may have come from relatively homogeneous countries such as Japan, where cultural identity is rarely challenged, and may have had no experiences with the new host culture. Under such conditions, the pressures for cultural change are often intense, immediate, and enduring. For successive generations, the pressures may take on a different form as the groups evolve into established ethnic communities.

John Berry (1990) addressed two issues that are at play when differentiating among acculturating groups. Comparing the degree of mobility and the degree of choice (or voluntariness of contact), he identified four distinct groups of interest to educators: (1) those people with a high degree of mobility and who

Figure 4.2
Acculturating Group
Types

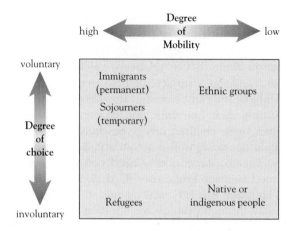

Definition of Terms

voluntarily made the contact are referred to as **immigrants** (relatively perma-nent) or **sojourners** (temporary visitors); (2) those with a high degree of mobil-ity but little or no choice related to their contact are considered **refugees;** (3) those with a low degree of mobility but a high degree of voluntary contact with others are known as **ethnic groups;** and (4) those with a low degree of mobility and a low degree of voluntary contact reflect the native people, or **indigenous people,** of a nation (Figure 4.2). Members of each of these groups can have distinct needs and experiences within the school community.

People also differ in the degree to which they wish to retain or are willing to change their cultural identity. Here, people's acculturation attitude can be determined by their responses to two distinct questions: "Is it of value to me to maintain my own cultural identity and characteristics?" and "Is it of value to me to maintain relationships with other groups?" As shown in Figure 4.3, four distinct outcomes are possible in response to these questions. In **integration,** people maintain relationships with other groups while at the same time main-taining their own cultural identity and characteristics. Such people retain their own unique cultural identity while working fairly well within a mainstream culture. They can, in a sense, walk in two worlds and are well on the way to being bicultural. American Jews are often cited as an example of a well-integrated group in U.S. society; there are many well-established Jewish agencies,

Figure 4.3
Acculturation Strategies
of Ethnocultural Groups

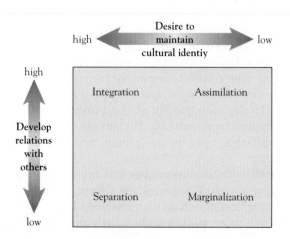

educational offerings, and community organizations that people can interact with while they maintain relatively positive interactions and involvement within the mainstream.

In **assimilation,** people maintain relationships with other groups but generally do not consider it of value to maintain their own cultural identity. An assimilation decision that is freely chosen is often referred to as the "melting pot." However, when assimilation is forced, a situation more akin to a pressure cooker might develop. Although American society has often been referred to as a melting pot, some people contend that significant social and cultural barriers prevent many people from achieving assimilation and that many people simply do not wish to give up their heritage in favor of a mainstream culture. The pot, some would say, never melted.

In situations where people value their own cultural identity but do not value relationships with other groups, two possible outcomes exist. When the situation is by choice for both groups, it is referred to as **separation.** When such a scenario is forced on one group by another, more dominant group, the situation is called **segregation,** as was prominent in the American South in the first half of the 20th century or under apartheid in South Africa until 1994.

Finally, a unique situation occurs when people do not value their own identity nor do they value relationships with other groups. In such a scenario, **marginalization** may occur, and individuals may experience extreme cases of ethnocide or deculturation.

Members of each of these four groups have distinct needs, experiences, and expectations of the school community. It is possible to observe each of the four acculturation attitudes within a given family unit. Imagine a family of four from a small village in Guatemala who recently immigrated to the United States. The father may lean toward integration for job prospects. He may work hard to learn English so he can fit in at work yet may still remain quite active with local Guatemalan/Latino community affairs. The mother, unable to enter the host society, may work hard to retain her Spanish language and her local social interactions. She then becomes a separatist. Hearing the Spanish language at home and eating Guatemalan food all the time may bother the teenage daughter. She may prefer assimilation, so she works hard to speak only English and to blend in through school activities. The brother, on the other hand, may not want to accept his Guatemalan heritage but may be rejected by his classmates. He may retreat and thus become marginalized.

Themes From Cross-Cultural Psychology

The fields of cross-cultural psychology and intercultural training offers teachers the following set of themes or principles that can be used to study cross-cultural interactions in the classroom (Pederson, 1988).

1. *People tend to communicate their cultural identity to others in the broadest possible terms.* For instance, on meeting someone for the first time, you may communicate many different things about yourself—your age, nationality, ethnic group, religious affiliation, where you grew up, and the nature of your family. At other times you may describe your status at work or in the community, your health, your social class, or the way you have come

Activity and
Reading 5:
**Understanding
Cultural Complexity**

to understand your gender. Each of these sources of cultural identity carries with it associated rules for behavior. When offering such information to new acquaintances, we give them cultural clues regarding what to expect from us and how to interact with us. Multiple "cultures" influence us at various times, so every one of us may be considered multicultural.

2. *Because we are all multicultural, our cultural identity is dynamic and always changing.* As our environmental circumstances and group associations change, we adapt our cultural identity and behavior accordingly. For example, in certain circumstances our gender-related knowledge and beliefs may be predominant; at another time our religious beliefs may stand out; and at still another, our ethnicity may be most important. Thus, our multicultural nature leads to behavior variations that are sometimes difficult to understand and appreciate.

3. *Although culture is complex and variable, it is nevertheless patterned.* Culture helps individuals make sense of their world and thereby to develop routinized behavioral patterns to fit different environments. Common phrases such as the "culture of the organization," the "culture of the community," or the "culture of the society" refer to the fact that culture is not simply patterned for an individual but also for a setting, a community, or a society as a whole. When viewed from the outside, these patterns can appear quite complicated and difficult to understand. Yet each of us moves quite easily among the cultural patterns with which we are familiar. When confronted by someone whose behavior is *not* familiar, it is the responsibility of the outsider to listen, to observe, and to inquire closely enough so that the patterns of that person (or social group or society) become evident and understandable. To do so decreases the possibility of misunderstanding and conflict and increases the possibility of new and useful understanding and appreciation.

4. *Interactions with other cultures can be viewed as a resource for understanding.* In this case, complexity can be an asset. The more knowledge and experience we have with other groups, the more sophisticated we can be in our interpretation of events. The more complex our thinking is, then, the more lenses or insights we can bring to help understand a given situation. Culturally different encounters help prepare us to deal more effectively with the complexity that is increasingly a part of our lives. In short, the number of cultural variables we learn to accommodate will determine our ability to navigate within a fast-moving, ever-changing society.

5. *Behavior should be judged in relation to its context.* Observable behavior cannot be understood apart from the context in which it occurs. Seen outside its context, another's "different" behavior can, at best, seem meaningless and, at worst, be profoundly misinterpreted. Contextual inquiry enables us to be more accurate in our judgments of others. Consider this real-life example of an 11-year-old boy who would become rowdy and disruptive in the classroom every day about 2:00 in the afternoon. Inevitably, the teacher sent the child to the office, where he was promptly sent home. Defined in terms of the middle-class cultural context of the school, this child was definitely a troubled child, and he was so labeled by nearly all the adults in the building. Eventually, however, an astute counselor recognized a pattern and did some inquiry. It turned out that the mother's

boyfriend would come home every day about 2:45, often quite drunk and abusive. In his rage, the boyfriend frequently abused the mother. The boy, quite accurately understanding the cultural pattern of the school, figured out that his misbehavior would result in his being sent home and that if he was sent home by 2:30, he would arrive before the boyfriend did and thus be able to protect his mother. Suddenly this so-called troubled boy's behavior makes sense, and he becomes something of a hero because he had found a way to protect his vulnerable mother. Without full knowledge of the context, behavior is often meaningless or badly misinterpreted. Culture provides the context from which to view others.

6. *Persons holding a intercultural perspective continually strive to find common ground between individuals.* In a sense, we must strive to be bifocal. That is, we must be able to see the similarities among people as well as their differences. While it is the differences that tend to stand out and separate people, it is precisely in our similarities where common ground, or a common meeting point, can be found. An intercultural perspective permits disagreement without anyone necessarily being accused of being wrong. If culture in all its complexity is understood as an individual's attempt to navigate the river of life, then cultural differences can be understood simply as pragmatic acts of navigation and judged accordingly. In this view, cultural differences become tolerable and the "we-they" or "us-them" debate is avoided. There are no winners and losers. We are all in this together. Either we all win—or we all lose.

A Model of Cross-Cultural Interaction

For years researchers from cross-cultural psychology have searched for methods that could be used to analyze, understand, and improve intercultural interactions. Cushner and Brislin (1996) developed a framework for understanding the dynamics of any intercultural encounter between individuals with different cultural patterns. The approach is grounded in the recognition that people have similar reactions to their intercultural encounters regardless of the setting or the person they are interacting with, regardless of the role they adopt, and regardless of their own cultural background. Research suggests that because these phases are experienced universally, they can serve as the basis of an analytical model that anyone participating in an unfamiliar cross-cultural encounter can use as a tool for assessing or sizing up the situation (Figure 4.4). Although most people assess informally, using whatever bits and pieces of relevant experience they may have, a general assessment model provides a more systematic and effective means of assessment.

Cross-Cultural Communication

Figure 4.4

Stages of Intercultural Encounters

Because this model is deliberately general, its usefulness lies in its adaptability to any intercultural encounter. It captures the experience of cultural differences from a variety of perspectives (emotional, informational, and developmental), and it offers frameworks within which specific problem situations can be addressed. However, it does not go beyond its diagnostic purpose. That is, the model does not offer prescriptive courses of action for dealing with difference. Such approaches are not only impossible, they are unethical given the complex realities of today's classroom. It is the individual student or teacher, empowered with cross-cultural knowledge, who must inquire into the causes and then propose solutions to the specific problems and issues that arise. The discussion that follows provides an examination of each stage in the culture-general framework and describes each of the 18 themes encompassed by this model. The critical incidents, or scenarios, found later in the chapter will give you an opportunity to apply this framework.

Stage 1: Understanding Emotional Responses in Intercultural Interaction

In any intercultural encounter, people's emotions are quickly aroused when they meet with unpredictable behavior on the part of others or when their own behavior does not bring about an expected response. The nature and strength of these emotional reactions quite often surprise the people involved, especially in the case of students who do not anticipate the differences between their own cultural patterns and those of the school. Strong emotions can also be experienced by teachers, like Melinda in the case study, who find themselves in a school or classroom context that is significantly different from what they expect. Recognizing and accommodating the strong emotional responses that people are certain to have when they become involved in intercultural interactions is critical to successfully negotiating those interactions. Figure 4.5 identifies the emotional responses most commonly experienced by persons confronting an unfamiliar culture. A brief description of these responses follows.

Figure 4.5
Emotional Responses in
Intercultural Interaction

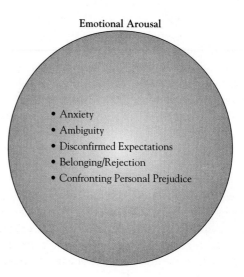

Emotional Arousal

- Anxiety
- Ambiguity
- Disconfirmed Expectations
- Belonging/Rejection
- Confronting Personal Prejudice

Anxiety

As individuals encounter unexpected or unfamiliar behavior on the part of others, they are likely to become anxious about whether their own behavior is appropriate. Children and teachers in new schools, individuals in new jobs, and families in new communities will all experience some degree of anxiety as they attempt to modify their own behavior to fit new circumstances. Such feelings may be powerful, while their cause, if it is due to cultural differences, may be unaltered. Feelings of anxiety may result in a strong desire to avoid the situation altogether, and individuals sometimes go to great lengths to do so, all the while rationalizing their avoidance behavior on other grounds.

Activity and Reading 12: **A Culture-General Framework for Understanding Intercultural Interactions**

Ambiguity

When interacting with those who are culturally different, people may often receive messages that are not quite clear—yet they must make decisions and somehow produce appropriate behavior. Most people, when faced with an ambiguous situation, try to resolve it by applying culturally familiar criteria. For example, it is quite common, when giving instruction to individuals who are just beginning to speak English, to ask them if they understand what has just been said. In an attempt not to seem ignorant or impolite, people will often respond in the affirmative, but then act in ways that suggest they do not fully understand. Because the new intercultural situation may not fit familiar criteria, this strategy is often ineffective.

The uncertainty of ambiguous situations may be the most critical element in the development of anxiety and is one of the more important factors in intercultural misunderstandings. People who are effective at working across cultures are known to have a high tolerance for ambiguity. That is, in situations where they do not have full understanding of what is going on, they can tolerate a certain degree of uncertainty and discomfort, are skilled at asking appropriate questions, and are able to modify their behavior accordingly.

Disconfirmed Expectations

Individuals may become upset or uncomfortable not because of the specific circumstances they encounter but because the situation differs from what they expected. Despite the recognition that differences are all around, people have a tendency to expect others to think and behave in ways similar to themselves. Thus, when involved in intercultural interactions, most people are surprised and disconcerted when others do not respond in expected ways. For example, a child may consistently look at the floor when being spoken to by an adult rather than looking the adult in the eye. This reaction sets up a cycle in which unexpected behavior is attributed both negatively and inaccurately according to preconceived notions of what is right, or correct (this student isn't paying attention and is disrespectful). Further actions, such as the student being scolded for showing disrespect based on such negative or inaccurate attributions, also do not produce the intended result (the student continues to look at the floor). This situation is often very upsetting for all parties involved. For another example, teachers, especially new ones, want to succeed and do well in their classrooms. If the reality of the classroom does not meet the new teacher's expectation, significant

discomfort may result. Think back to Melinda's initial expectations of her move to North Carolina and the reality she ultimately encountered.

Belonging/Rejection

People have the need to fill a social niche, to feel that they belong and are at home in the social milieu in which they find themselves. When they are immersed in an intercultural situation, this sense of belonging may be difficult to achieve because they do not know the rules of behavior in the new situation. Instead, people may feel rejected as outsiders, and when this sense of rejection is strong enough, they may become alienated from the situation altogether. Students, for example, who feel alienated from the classroom or school are more likely to become discipline problems and have difficulty paying attention to classroom work. Similarly, teachers who work with youngsters very different from themselves may feel alienated from their students and their students' families and may respond with undue exercise of power or with burnout.

Confronting Personal Prejudices

Finally, a person involved in intercultural interactions may be forced to acknowledge that previously held beliefs about a certain group of people or certain kinds of behaviors may be inaccurate, inappropriate, or without foundation. Such a revelation may result in embarrassment or shame. It may also require a basic change in attitude and behavior toward others. For instance, it is not uncommon for young college students who grew up hearing from parents or other adults that certain groups of people were lazy or unintelligent to suddenly confront contradictory evidence when they encounter people from that group in their dormitories, classrooms, or the workplace. People confronting personal prejudices must decide to question their earlier beliefs and change their subsequent behavior, or maintain those beliefs even in light of their new information. Since change is difficult even in the best of circumstances, people often continue to harbor their prejudices even when faced with contradictory evidence. Making the cognitive shift can be very demanding, but it is essential. Teachers may have a difficult time working with others in this regard.

Stage 2: Understanding the Cultural Basis of Unfamiliar Behavior

In addition to accommodating their feelings, the parties in an intercultural encounter need to understand the impact of the particular cultural influences that have shaped one another's knowledge about the world. Individuals typically try to understand another person's behavior according to their own cultural knowledge base. Put another way, since most people do not have extensive experiences with people who think and act differently from them, they tend to interpret another's behavior in terms of their own cultural frames of reference. This tendency is the basis of ethnocentrism. In brief, people see what they expect to see, and with incomplete information or inaccurate knowledge, they may make inappropriate judgments about a given situation.

Consider the student referred to earlier who consistently looked at the floor when being spoken to by an adult. *Some* children from certain ethnic groups (e.g., some Mexican Americans, African Americans, or South Pacific Islanders) *may* be taught to demonstrate respect for elders or persons in authority by avoiding eye contact. Hence, a child who is being spoken to by an adult would avoid gazing in that person's eyes. On the other hand, *most* European American children (who become the majority of teachers) are socialized to look a person of authority directly in the eye. Imagine the outcome of an interaction involving a Mexican American, African American, or South Pacific Island child being addressed by a European American teacher. The child, as she or he may have been taught, looks away from the gaze of the teacher, thereby demonstrating respect. The teacher, expecting eye contact as a sign of respect, may interpret the child's behavior as "He is not listening to me" or "He does not respect me." This incorrect judgment may result in a reprimand, in response to which the child attempts to show respect by continuing to look away. Without understanding the cultural basis for this behavior, future interactions between this particular teacher and student may be in serious jeopardy.

The individual skilled in intercultural encounters learns to suspend judgment and seek alternative explanations of unexpected behavior rather than to simply interpret such behavior according to his or her own cultural framework. The question "Why is this behavior occurring?" precedes the question "What is the matter with this child?"

There are many aspects of cultural knowledge, each of which reaches the individual through a network of socializing agents (see Chapter 3). Regardless of the complexity of this socialization process, the resulting knowledge base

Figure 4.6
Analyzing Unfamiliar
Behavior

- Communication and Language
- Values
- Rituals
- Situational Behavior
- Roles
- Social Status
- Time and Space Orientation
- Relationship to the Group

functions to give us satisfactory explanations of our world and to tell us how best to interact with the people around us. Within this cultural knowledge base, however, the following kinds of knowledge are likely to differ across cultural patterns (Figure 4.6).

Communication and Language Use

Communication differences are among the most obvious issues that must be confronted when crossing cultural boundaries. Language issues exist whether the languages involved are completely different (e.g., Japanese, Kiswahili, English, American Sign Language), are similar in root but not in evolution (e.g., French, Italian, Spanish), or are variations or dialects of the same language (e.g., French, French-Canadian, English, Ebonics). In any case, it is not always easy to learn a second or third language, although it is increasingly becoming a necessity. In addition, nonverbal communication customs such as facial expressions, gestures, and so forth also differ across cultural patterns, so that what a particular gesture means to one person may be very different from what it means to someone with another cultural pattern. The familiar head nod up and down that means "yes" to you may indicate "no" in Greece, for instance.

Values

The development of internalized values is one of the chief socialization goals in all societies. Values provide social cohesion among group members and are often codified into laws or rules for living; for example, the Ten Commandments for Christians and Jews, the five pillars of Islam, or the Hippocratic Oath for doctors. The range of possible values with respect to any particular issue is usually wide, deeply held, and often difficult to change. For example, in the dominant culture of the United States, belief in progress is highly valued and seemingly religious in character. A teacher holding that value may have a very difficult time interacting with parents who seem not to value their daughter's academic potential. The young woman's parents may believe that she should assume the traditional role of wife and mother after high school rather than seek a college education.

The teacher, on the other hand, may believe that the young woman should "look to the future" in another way, "change with the times," and "make progress" for herself. These differences are not small and can be the cause of tremendous tension.

Rituals and Superstitions

All social groups develop rituals that help members meet the demands of everyday life. Such rituals vary in significance from rubbing a rabbit's foot before a stressful event to the intricate format of an organized religious service. The difficulty, however, is that the rituals of one social group may be viewed as silly or superstitious by members of other social groups. Increasingly, children from a wide variety of religious and cultural backgrounds bring to school behaviors that are often misunderstood and labeled "superstition." Traditional Native American spirituality, for example, often includes rituals involving the personification of natural objects such as trees, rocks, and animals. People who have been brought up with a scientific and technological mindset usually view such personification as superstition.

Situational Behavior

Knowing how to behave appropriately in a variety of settings and situations is important to all people. The rules for behavior at home, school, work, sporting events, and so forth are internalized at an early age and, of course, vary with the given context. Such rules can be easily broken by an individual who has internalized a different set of rules for the same setting or situation. A child, for example, who has learned that learning is best accomplished by quiet and intense observation is likely to run afoul of a teacher who believes that learning is best accomplished by active participation with others in class.

Roles

Knowledge of appropriate role behavior, like that of situational behavior, may vary from role to role and group to group. How an individual behaves as a mother or father, for example, may be different from how that person behaves as a teacher. Similarly, the role of mother, father, or teacher may vary among sociocultural groups. Furthermore, role patterns change over time. For example, middle-class mothers now are increasingly also working mothers, which necessitates considerable alterations in the role of mother. Indeed, this change in middle-class motherhood brings it into closer correspondence with the pattern that has long been established by working-class mothers.

Social Status

All social groups make distinctions based on various markers of high and low status. Both social class and social status are the result of stratification systems whose role assignments may vary considerably from group to group. The role of the aunt in the African American community, for example, has a much higher status than it does in middle-class, European American society. Often the aunt of an African American child bears considerable responsibility for the well-being of that child. Middle-class, European American teachers who are unaware of this status and relationship may, when confronted by a proactive aunt, believe that the child's mother is somehow shirking her responsibilities.

Time and Space

Differences in conceptions of time and space may also vary among social groups. In addition to differences in the divisions of time (e.g., a week, a crop harvest), groups vary in the degree to which time is valued. It is common for many European Americans, for example, to value punctuality because it is seen as an expression of respect. Because time is so highly valued, such people pay much attention to its use–time is seen as money, something to be spent or saved, or in some circumstances, to be wasted. Measures of time and their value may be much more elastic in some less-industrialized societies where work is less synchronized. Similarly, the ease and comfort of a person's position in space vis-à-vis other people may vary. How close one person stands to another when speaking and the degree to which people should stand face-to-face with another are both subject to cultural variation.

Relationship to the Group Versus the Individual

All people sometimes act according to their individual interests and sometimes according to their group allegiances. The relative emphasis on group versus individual orientation varies from group to group and may significantly affect the choices a person makes. In the dominant culture of the United States, for instance, individualism is highly valued. Schools have traditionally reinforced this value through emphasis on "doing one's own work," the ability to "work independently," and the recognition of "individual responsibility." However,

other social groups, such as the Japanese or some American ethnic groups, place much greater emphasis on group behavior, group solidarity, and group helpfulness and well-being. These social groups often consider it wrong to stand out, to be independent, to "rise above" the group. In a major study comparing national cultures on this dimension, the United States, Australia, and Great Britain stood out among the top nations on individualism (Hofstede, 1983). Guatemala, Ecuador, Panama, Indonesia, and Taiwan ranked among the highest on collectivism.

Stage 3: Making Adjustments and Reshaping Cultural Identity

Finally, as a result of prolonged intercultural interaction, individuals may experience personal change. That is, people may alter the way they perceive others and themselves, as well as how they process those perceptions. Typically, for example, individuals who have had significant intercultural experiences become more complex thinkers. This accomplishment is, of course, one of the central goals of multicultural education because it enables people to handle more culturally complex stimuli, to be more accurate in their interpretations of others' behavior, and thus to deal more effectively with the differences they encounter. As individuals continue to have intercultural experiences, they become less culture-bound and more understanding of how others perceive the world. Such individuals can now see from another's point of view; they are more complex thinkers and can handle a greater variety of diverse information. They are also less likely to make inaccurate judgments or attributions because they are more likely to inquire into puzzling beliefs and behavior, thereby improving their understanding.

Think back to the gaze-avoidance behavior in the interaction between the European American teacher and the Mexican American, African American, or South Pacific Island child. The interculturally knowledgeable teacher understands the meaning that underlies the child's gaze-avoidance and more accurately judges the child to be listening and demonstrating respect. Although even people who have considerable intercultural experience may have limited knowledge of the content of a particular cultural knowledge base, they do know that all people process information in similar ways, and they are willing to investigate the outcomes of such processes. Several important ways of processing information are listed in Figure 4.7, each of which can be investigated by the participants in intercultural exchanges.

Categorization

Because people cannot attend to all the information presented to them, they create categories for organizing and responding to similar bits of information. Cultural stereotypes, for example, are categories usually associated with particular groups of people. People involved in intercultural interactions often categorize one another quickly according to whatever category systems they have learned. Examples of this kind of categorization might be old/young, rich/poor, native/foreigner, and typical/disabled. The context within which people categorize each other also influences the categorization process. Recall the earlier example of the

Figure 4.7
Ways of Processing
Information

- Categorization
- Differentiation
- Attribution
- Ingroup/Outgroup
- Learning Style

boy who was sent home from school before the end of each day. From one perspective, the boy was categorized as a troublemaker. Once the context of the situation was better understood, the boy was seen as a hero, doing whatever he could to help protect his mother. Of particular importance is the fact that category systems and their meanings not only differ from group to group but also are rarely neutral in value. Thus, "placing" another person in a particular category may also "place" that person in a more or less valued position (e.g., many people place being learning disabled in a less valued position than not to be learning disabled).

Differentiation

Information related to highly meaningful categories becomes more refined or differentiated. As a result, new categories may be formed. Such refinement or differentiation is usually shared only among people who have had many experiences in common (e.g., doctors) and thus may be unknown even to those whose background, apart from occupation, is similar. A good example of this process is the way in which people in Asia might differentiate rice. Because it is an extremely important part of their diet and thus their way of life, rice can be referred to by many different terms and can have many different uses. For most European Americans, rice is not as important, and thus fewer references are made to it. A school-based example of differentiation might be found in the manner in which students in a particular high school differentiate their peers into groups such as brains, nerds, jocks, and so on. Although a similar type of differentiation may occur in most high schools, the particular categories and their meaning may differ considerably from one school to the next.

Ingroups and Outgroups

People the world over divide others into those with whom they are comfortable and can discuss their concerns (ingroups) and those who are kept at a distance (outgroups). Based on initial categorization and differentiation as well as on continuing interaction, individuals may identify one another as potential members of their own ingroup or as members of an outgroup. People entering new cultural situations must recognize that they will often be considered members of an outgroup, will not share certain ingroup behavior and communication, and thus will be kept from participating in certain ingroup activities. A really good, if somewhat mundane, example of this process is the situation experienced by a substitute teacher who is, by definition, an outsider in the culture of the classroom and school.

Learning Style

Sometimes called cognitive style, learning style refers to a person's preferred method of learning. Learning styles are partly the result of strengths and weaknesses in sensory perception (one's hearing may be more acute than one's vision, for example). However, cultural patterning may teach a child to attend to certain kinds of stimuli rather than others, as when children from collectivist societies learn better in cooperative groups. How (and what) an individual perceives, the categories into which that person places sensory stimuli, and whether that person prefers to learn through observation, listening, or action can all be based on cultural patterns. For example, some Native Hawaiian or Native American children, as they are growing up, learn from a variety of individuals, both adults and other children. Such children may also participate more in group learning; that is, they may learn and practice a skill with other children, not necessarily on their own. These children's preferred learning style (the way in which they have learned how to learn) may be more group oriented than the learning style of the majority of their European American counterparts, who have a tendency to learn how to learn in a more individualistic manner. Such children may not achieve as well in a more traditionally oriented classroom as they might in a cooperative learning situation.

Attribution

People not only perceive others according to familiar categories, they also make judgments about others based on the behavior they observe and its meaning in their own social milieu. They judge others, for example, as competent or incompetent, educated or naive, well-intentioned or ill-intentioned. Psychologists call these judgments *attributions* and tell us that within about 7 seconds of meeting someone new, initial judgments are made. These initial "sizing-up" judgments, once made, are usually quite resistant to change. Human judgments, however, are fallible, and certain judgment errors occur repeatedly in human thought. One of these, called the fundamental attribution error (Ross, 1977), describes the tendency people have to judge others on different sets of criteria than they apply to themselves, particularly with respect to shortcomings. Thus, if I fail at a given task, I am more likely to look to the situation for an explanation–it was too hot, someone else was unfair to me, the task was too hard. If I observe someone else fail at a task, I am more likely to explain the failure in terms of the other person's traits–she is lazy, he is stupid, she is uncaring. This tendency is even more prevalent when individuals with different cultural patterns interact because there is likely to be unfamiliar behavior in such situations. Given the speed with which people make judgments and the probable lack of intercultural understanding, attribution errors abound in intercultural situations. Couple this with the tendency people have to form categories (and thus, sometimes, negative stereotypes about people) and you can quite easily see how a very detrimental, complex situation can evolve.

Applying the Culture-General Model

At this point, you may appreciate the potential of the culture-general model but not know how it can be applied in your daily interactions. The main value of such a model is that it allows people to build a common, culture-related vocabulary that can be used to analyze intercultural interactions in a variety of contexts. That is, it provides a tool whereby people can more accurately judge the nature of the interactions in which they are reading about, witnessing, or participating. The following discussion of Mexican Americans is paraphrased from Farris and Cooper's book, *Elementary Social Studies: A Whole Language Approach* (1994). In the discussion, specific themes of the culture-general model are designated in italics. Following this discussion are a few cases for you to analyze.

Although tremendous diversity exists within the Mexican American culture, some generalities about the traditional Mexican American experience can be made. To begin with, there is strong identification with the family, the community, and the ethnic group at large (*belonging; relation to the group; ingroups and outgroups*). The individual achievement readily encouraged in many European American children is not stressed. Rather, achievement for the child means achievement for the family (*status; relation to the group; roles*). Parental involvement in the education of Mexican American children is important for the children's success. Because parents provide a positive support system, every attempt should be made to inform parents of their child's progress. Sending work home as well as accepting items from the home in school helps strengthen the necessary home-school relationship (*belonging; roles; values; learning styles*).

Mexican American culture typically encourages cooperation rather than the competition that is more frequent in European American culture. As a result, many Mexican American children may find the typical reward structure of schools confusing and frustrating. Teachers may find greater success when motivation is applied to a group activity rather than for personal gain such as a letter grade (*relation to the group; learning styles*).

Mexican Americans also tend to be sensitive to the emotional needs of others. Strong interpersonal relationships should be expected. As such, teachers should encourage children to help one another (*belonging; learning styles; relation to the group*). Mexican American children are also more likely to use both verbal and nonverbal means to elicit a teacher's attention. This may explain their reluctance to ask a teacher for help or to pose a question; their actual request may have been nonverbal (*communication and language use; attribution*).

The Mexican American humanistic orientation extends well beyond the nuclear family. Extended family actively includes primos, or cousins with the same last name but no blood relationship; tocayos, or namesakes, those with the same first name; cuñados, or brothers-in-law; cuñadas, or sisters-in-law; and the very important padrinos, or godparents, ahijados, or godchildren, and compadres, or natural parents to the godparents. All these individuals (and others) may play significant roles throughout the individual's life (*roles; ingroups and out-groups; relation to the group; belonging, categorization*).

In such an extended family, status and role relationships are rigidly defined. Younger children defer to older children, and females often defer to males. Respect for parents is expected, regardless of one's age. Sexual roles are well defined, with females having responsibility for the condition of the home and the raising of children. Males, having higher status, are primarily the wage earn-ers (*roles; class and status; categorization*). There is also a strong obligation to the family. Teachers should keep these roles and obligations in mind when hearing that students have responsibilities such as caring for younger children after school or working in the family business (*values; relation to the group; roles*).

Finally, among Mexican American families there exists a strong orientation and identification with Mexican Catholic ideology. This powerful force reinforces their value system, many of their daily actions, and their respect for parents, family, and tradition (*rituals and superstitions; values; belonging*).

Identifying Commonalities Among Groups

In the brief example about Mexican American culture, at least 11 cultural-general themes were evident; perhaps you have identified others. Used in this manner, the cultural-general model can help both students and teachers find common-alities among the cultural differences they encounter. For example, some aspects of the Mexican American experience are similar to those in other ethnic experi-ences, and some are different. Some may be similar to your own experience, and others will be different.

Viewed in the broadest terms possible, the goal of this model goes beyond simply negotiating intercultural interactions or adapting one's teaching to accom-modate culturally diverse learning styles. Its search for commonalities among people of all cultures offers the possibility that all individuals in a pluralistic society will feel sufficiently similar that they can confront differences without going through the hostility stage shown in Figure 4.1. In short, awareness of similarities—kinship feelings, for example—can motivate people to learn about and appreciate differences. This model offers a way to go beyond tolerance, which often means "letting people alone," to begin to build a truly intercultural society.

Identifying Differences Within a Group

The Mexican American discussion presented in this chapter has at least two dimensions in which the cultural-general model is useful: (1) in building a com-mon vocabulary around differences, and (2) in using those concepts to analyze culture-specific information. The information about traditional Mexican Ameri-can culture provided an example of using the model across ethnic/nationality boundaries—differences that are most commonly thought of as cultural differences—and of looking for commonalities among specific cultural ideas and practices. A third dimension of difference is also made more visible through the use of the culture-general model, and that is in identifying and analyzing differences within a specific cultural group. Such differences as, for example, social class, geo-graphical location, sexual orientation, or religion are not always easy to "see" but may in fact be important differences in the way individuals perceive the world, interact with one another, and approach learning.

Questions raised by a consideration of these kinds of differences can lead to inquiry about, for instance, whether particular Mexican American children are Catholic, whether particular Mexican American children have learned to operate in a cooperative manner, or whether particular Mexican American children identify strongly with their extended families. Research has shown, for example, that some of these cultural attributes may diminish in successive generations of Mexican American families. Indeed, to automatically assume that such characteristics will occur in all children and adults of Mexican American descent is unwisely to stereotype all individuals who "belong" to a particular ethnic group, and to run a grave risk of misinterpreting observable behavior.

Critical Incidents at Wake Central High

**Activity 13:
Critical Incident
Review**

The next step in understanding the culture-general model is to apply it in the analysis of some school-based intercultural encounters. Only by doing so is it possible to understand the degree to which culture influences teaching and learning in schools. This section examines the kinds of incidents that might occur in the fictitious Wake Central High School described in this chapter's case study. You should realize, however, that the incidents reported here could easily occur in most schools in the United States.

Go back to the Case Study and take a close look at Melinda's induction year. Stop at this point and consider some of the culture-general themes that may be at play. It seems obvious that this situation is highly charged and emotional for many of the people involved. To begin with, Melinda must reconcile the reality of this situation with her early expectations. Thus, Melinda is clearly experiencing a case of disconfirmed expectations. Melinda must begin to understand the real situation and adjust her behavior according to what is, rather than to what she expected.

Melinda is also faced with a considerable amount of ambiguity in her new situation. Although she is enthusiastic about the challenge of an urban teaching experience, she is quite unprepared for its specific dimensions. Such a situation promises to elicit a high degree of uncertainty or ambiguity. Melinda is aware that certain actions are expected, but unsure of what those actions are or how to begin to learn them. At another level, Melinda is certainly experiencing a high degree of anxiety as she strives to integrate into the faculty of the school. Such ambiguity and anxiety, though common, must eventually be negotiated if Melinda is to be effective in her new setting. As Melinda begins to build closer relationships with other teachers and gain a better understanding of her students, her emotions will come under control and she can begin to feel as if she belongs in this setting.

Melinda's situation represents only one of many ambiguous situations that might arise in such a diverse setting as Wake Central High. The Critical Incidents describe some other situations that could conceivably occur. Read each incident and consider responses to the questions that follow, or discuss these in small groups. You will find some discussion at the end of the Critical Incidents section.

Critical Incident

Andre's Role Dilemma

Andre is a 23-year-old, first-year social studies teacher hired at the same time as Melinda. African American and from a middle-class background, Andre has always prided himself on knowing a lot about people at all socioeconomic levels and from many different ethnic groups. Andre began the year with the intent of relating especially well to the African American students. He intends to show them that he is really one of them and understands their needs.

While walking down the hall on his first day in school, Andre sees a group of young African American males standing near a wall of lockers. They are wearing typical casual clothes–low-slung pants, T-shirts, and sneakers. Andre is dressed in slacks, shirt, tie, and sport coat. Andre greets the group with a hearty "What's happening, bro?" The students look at him and continue with their own conversation. Andre tries to strike up a conversation by asking about any good rap groups in the school, saying that he has done some "bad rappin'" himself. The boys eye him up and down, then slowly move on down the hall. Andre is puzzled, thinking that they would respond to his approach and would see him as a "brother."

The next day, Andre sees the same group again and begins to approach them. Seeing him coming, one of the group steps forward and quite sarcastically says, "Hey, bro! You be down in Room 104 (the teachers' lounge), not in my face!" Then the group walks away. Andre does not understand the group's obvious hostility and rejection.

• Why do you think the students rejected Andre's attempts to be friendly?

• What culture-general themes do you see operating in this scenario?

Critical Incident

Rosita's Alientation Problem

Rosita Gomez had been in the United States for 2 months, arriving as an orphan from El Salvador, and sponsored by a European American, middle-class family. Before her arrival, her American parents went to Wake Central High School and provided the administrators and faculty with information about her situation. To make her adjustment easier, a number of teachers organized a group of students to act as sponsors for Rosita. The students were to teach her about the school and community and help her with transition problems as well as to offer friendship.

During these 2 months, the appointed students have indeed helped Rosita in school and have been friendly to her. They have encouraged her to become involved in student council and to attend after-school extra-help sessions whenever needed. Rosita, though, is often left out of students' social activities such as parties, group movie dates, and volleyball games, and she thinks she is being treated as an outcast. She feels lonely and afraid and complains to her American parents and school counselor about her feelings. Her complaints confuse the other students and teachers very much because they have tried hard to make Rosita feel at home.

• How might you explain this situation?

• What culture-general themes do you see operating here?

Critical Incident

Joao's Identity Crisis

Joao is a teenager from Providence, Rhode Island, who has been sent to live for 2 years with his aunt and uncle in North Carolina. This is the first time that Joao has been away from his immediate family, who immigrated from Portugal when he was a child. His family is strongly united and feels a deep pride in their Portuguese heritage. Joao had heard that Wake Central has a reputation as a place where students from different backgrounds get along well together, so he has not been worrying about being the only Portuguese in the student body. He has looked forward to attending his new school.

During Joao's first week in school, he discovered that several members of the faculty viewed him as belonging to a group of students who spoke Spanish. A few teachers greeted him in Spanish, and one suggested that he join a club for mainly Central American students. Joao was surprised and resentful that these teachers just assumed he was Hispanic. During his second week, a teacher gave him a notice to take home to his uncle, and it, too, was in Spanish. Joao startled the teacher by breaking into tears and loudly protesting, "Please try to remember— I'm Portuguese!"

- How would you explain Joao's reaction?
- What culture-general themes may be operating here—from all perspectives?

Critical Incident

Rema's Classroom Concerns

Rema is a 16-year-old girl from Lebanon who came to the United States just one year ago. Although she still has some difficulties in speaking and writing English, her language skills are sufficient for her to be academically successful in Wake Central High. Midway through the 11th grade, Rema was achieving B's and C's in all her classes, including Andre's social studies class.

Actually, social studies is Rema's favorite subject, and Andre continually remarks to others on the breadth and depth of her reading. Rema reads voraciously and does not limit herself to that which is studied in class. She keeps up on international news and reads literature in two languages.

Andre is concerned, however, about Rema's test scores. When the class takes a multiple-choice, true-false, or fill-in-the-blank test, Rema's grades are usually among the highest. When the class is assigned an interpretive essay, however, Rema's grade is always much lower. Andre has said many times, "Rema just never really gets to the point; she tries to talk about everything at once." Despite repeated efforts to remedy this writing problem, Rema continues to write confusing analyses.

- How might you best explain this situation?
- What culture-general concepts do you see in this situation?

Lack of Communication With Kaye

Issues of communication affect dialogue among teachers as well. Kaye Stoddard is in the middle of her first year as assistant principal at Wake Central High. She is an energetic person who seeks out staff input concerning school policies and curriculum. She encourages staff participation through periodic surveys and group discussions at staff meetings. Lately, however, Kaye has been disturbed about the dearth of input she is receiving from the two Latino teachers. She is particularly interested in their ideas because so many of the school's students are Latino. Although she has solicited feedback through weekly questionnaires in each teacher's mailbox, most of her replies come from the European American teachers.

• How might this situation be explained?
• What culture-general concepts may be at play?

Discussion of Critical Incidents

Andre's Role Dilemma

There are many possible explanations for Andre's situation. First, the group may feel that Andre's clothes are too different. They can't relate to this different-looking adult (*outgroup, categorization*). Second, Andre's use of Ebonics or Black English may be incorrect to this particular time and place and thus may label him in their eyes as a "phony"–someone who can't be trusted (*communication; outgroup*). Third, it is possible that Andre came on too hard to these particular students and that he was seen as pushy and was rejected because of it (*role; situational behavior*).

Using the culture-general framework to analyze the situation suggests another possible explanation. The group may not accept Andre because they see him as an outsider regardless of his race or his language. Andre is still a teacher in the eyes of these students (*role; status*) and one that they do not yet know. Andre has been categorized by the students in a different way than he would categorize himself; that is, as an outgroup member rather than as the ingroup member he expected to be (*categorization*).

It is important to differentiate the particular criteria that others use to form categories and thus the meaning attributed to those groups. Although Andre may have been fairly close to their age and talked their talk, he is still seen as an adult teacher, an authority figure who may not be trusted, at least at the outset. As a teacher, he should not expect to be included as one of their group. Their response told him that he should be in Room 104, that he is a teacher and should act like one. New teachers are usually eager to be accepted by students. This desire is normal, especially because teachers may not be far removed from the lives and concerns of high school students themselves. Given time, Andre can establish the rapport he wants, but he must do so in his role as a teacher.

Rosita's Alienation Problem

It is possible that Rosita, having had a major transition in her life recently, is magnifying the situation. Perhaps the circumstances are such that she is experiencing what is commonly referred to as culture shock. However, culture shock is a very generalized term that refers to an overall reaction to a complex series of events; the term isn't very useful when analyzing specific situations. There is something more specific going on here.

It is also possible that the students do not really like Rosita and are trying to have as little to do with her as possible. The appointed students may feel put upon by their teachers and are thus taking it out on Rosita. However, the students are having what appears to be extensive contact with Rosita in school. If they did not like her, they would probably forgo school contact as well.

Viewed through the culture-general model, it is possible that Rosita's predicament can be understood in terms of *ingroup and outgroup* behavior. In every culture there exist ingroups, people who are comfortable with one another, share similar values and casual language, and seek each other's company. Ingroups allow people to share their concerns, laugh and joke about problems as a way to reduce tensions, and generally just let their hair down. The students in this situation represent such an ingroup. Rosita has left her own ingroup behind in El Salvador and needs to reestablish herself as part of a new ingroup. The students, however, do not see Rosita as being part of their ingroup, at least not yet. She would not understand most of their jokes, does not share their intimate and extensive knowledge of other students and teachers, and could not enter into their conversation easily. The students thus do not invite Rosita to share in their social activities. Not belonging to an ingroup, Rosita feels like an outcast (*belonging*) and is missing the support system so needed during her difficult transition to a new culture.

Joao's Identity Crisis

Many different issues may be at play in Joao's situation. First, Joao might have felt some dislocation at being sent to live with his aunt and uncle in the first place. His sense of unity with his family in Providence was very strong, and it is reasonable to suppose that he missed them very much (*belonging*). Second, in Providence Joao had been attending schools where many other students were native Portuguese. The idea of going to school with students from other ethnic and cultural groups—but not Portuguese—although initially interesting, might also have been somewhat frightening (*ingroup and outgroups*). It is also possible that Joao's parents had kept him under such tight discipline that he never learned much self-discipline. Thus, his first experience of living away from home may have been so demanding that he was unable to control himself.

At another level, Joao was obviously upset about being identified as a member of a cultural group other than his own (*categorization; values*). Proud to be a native Portuguese and having shared this pride with other Portuguese students back in Providence, he couldn't adjust to being viewed as a Spanish speaker from Mexico or Central America. In addition, he was used to teachers who recognized the Portuguese language and culture, and he was perhaps shocked to find teachers who did not (*disconfirmed expectations*).

The teachers meant to be helpful to Joao, of course. They no doubt thought he came from one of the Spanish-speaking countries because they needed to quickly fit him into one of the ethnic and cultural categories already familiar to them. Because the Portuguese language is similar enough to Spanish that Joao could understand the teachers when they addressed him in Spanish, they found it convenient to *categorize* him with the other Spanish-speaking students.

Rema's Classroom Concerns

There are many ways to explain Rema's writing performance. It is possible that she lacks the basic writing skills and vocabulary necessary to write lengthy compositions of this kind. However, her overall academic performance indicates that she is competent in English vocabulary and writing. Her problems with written expression are probably not due to technical deficiencies.

It is also possible that Rema has misunderstood or misinterpreted the main elements of the work she is studying. But having read works of equal breadth and depth on her own, it is unlikely that Rema is unable to analyze and appreciate what she is reading.

Alternatively, Rema may not be able to think clearly under the pressure of tests. However, she doesn't seem to exhibit this problem in objective tests; she shows no particular "test anxiety." So Rema's problem seems to lie elsewhere.

Analyzed from the standpoint of cultural differences, however, it is possible that Middle Eastern and North American preferred *learning modes, cognitive styles, and communication patterns* are very different. In many cultures, communication is accomplished through associations. Everything that is associated with an idea is considered relevant when thinking about or communicating a concept. Such communication may seem highly indirect to a European American, who typically gets right to the point and reasons in a systematic, step-by-step fashion. In contrast, a Middle Easterner may make many loops while communicating a particular point. In short, when viewed in terms of her native culture, Rema's highly associative compositions demonstrate both her knowledge of the subject and her overall intellectual ability. Once Rema and her teacher are aware of these culturally different writing styles, they can take some practical steps to improve the situation.

Lack of Communication With Kaye

One simple explanation for Kaye's dilemma might be that the Latino teachers do not want to interact with Kaye because she is not Hispanic. However, there is no justification for this explanation. The entire school population is mixed, thereby making it difficult for the Latino teachers to limit their interactions with non-Latinos. Also, there is no indication that Kaye feels that she is the target of hostility.

It is also possible that the European American teachers dominate the Latino teachers, giving them little chance to express their opinions. Again, however, there is no indication that domination is the problem. Nor is there any indication that the Latino teachers are indifferent concerning the subjects Kaye includes in the surveys and meetings. Like other professionals, most teachers have strong opinions about many issues in their workplace.

A more probable explanation can be found in culturally different *communication* styles. Kaye has taken an impersonal approach to eliciting opinions, whereas the Latino teachers may favor a more personalized approach. Latino culture strongly emphasizes the affective side of interpersonal relationships. Personalized contact is thus very important to many Latino teachers. Although Kaye is genuinely interested in the opinions of all her teachers, she has approached them impersonally through her written surveys and large-group staff meetings. The Latino teachers might respond more easily if approached individually or addressed personally at a meeting. At the same time, many Latinos feel strong affiliation with the group (*relationship to the group; individualism versus collectivism*), and the Latino teachers might respond even more enthusiastically if they were asked for their ideas and opinions together in a small group.

Each of these Critical Incidents has explored several of the many possible cultural issues always at work in diverse settings like Wake Central High School. They illustrate ways in which classrooms and schools function as cultural crossroads, as places where people with infinite variations of cultural knowledge, beliefs, values, and skills meet and are forced to interact. In this chapter we have presented a culture-general model that offers a language and concepts that provide a common framework for all such interactions, no matter what their variation. Perhaps you would like to analyze experiences you have had that might be understood in light of the culture-general model. See if you can think of some.

Part 2 of this book presents longer Case Studies in which teachers, students, administrators, parents, and others also experience various cross-cultural interactions in the context of evolving ideas of good practice in schools. Remember as you read on that there is never any "one best answer" to the issues that arise. Indeed, an understanding of the complexities of cultural diversity suggests that in many instances the idea of a single "best solution" is not only impossible but is also inimical to a culturally pluralistic environment. In short, teachers must learn to feel comfortable with, appreciate the possibilities of, and negotiate effectively in ambiguous situations.

Summary

In no other social setting in society does such a diverse gathering of people come together for a prolonged period of time than in the school. Thus, the potential for a wide range of intercultural interactions between students and teachers is great. This chapter introduced the 18-theme culture-general framework for understanding intercultural interactions between people, regardless of their cultural backgrounds, who they are interacting with, or the roles that they adopt. Such a framework provides an opportunity for people to better understand their emotional reactions to intercultural situations, the knowledge base that people bring with them as a result of being socialized within any given culture, and the manner in which people's cultural identity may be reformed. Such a framework also provides a vocabulary and categories with which people can discuss cross-cultural issues with others.

Chapter Review

Go to the Online Learning Center at www.mhhe.com/cushner7e to review important content from the chapter, practice with key terms, take a chapter quiz, and find the Web links listed in this chapter.

Key Terms

acculturation 117
assimilation 119
ethnic groups 118
immigrants 118

indigenous people 118
integration 118
marginalization 119
refugees 118

segregation 119
separation 119
sojourners 118

Active Exercise

Additional Active Exercises are available online at www.mhhe.com/cushner7e.

Observing Cultural Differences

Purpose: To apply the 18-theme culture-general framework to casual observations made during interactions with others.

Instructions: Make extended observations of yourself as well as others over the course of about a week. The focus of your observations should be on potential misunderstanding or miscommunication between people of different cultural backgrounds (remember that we define culture rather broadly). Record your observations as precisely as possible, identifying any and all of the culture-general themes that you believe apply. Finally, propose alternative explanations or attributions for the behavior you have observed from two (or more) perspectives. Use the following as a guide, but do not necessarily limit yourself to the space provided. You should make *at least* five different relevant observations. Make additional copies of this form if needed.

Example

Interaction as I Observed It	Cultural-General Theme(s)	Possible Attributions
Two girls, one Mexican and the other European American, discuss plans of what they will do Friday night. Mexican girl insists upon asking her parents' permission before making commitment to her friend.	Family roles Individualism vs. Collectivism	Collectivist orientation (tendency for Mexican). May require approval from others before taking action, whereas European American (individualistic tendency) is more comfortable making her own plans.

Observation 1

Interaction as I Observed It	Cultural-General Theme(s)	Possible Attributions

Observation 2

Interaction as I Observed It	Cultural-General Theme(s)	Possible Attributions

Observation 3

Interaction as I Observed It	Cultural-General Theme(s)	Possible Attributions

Reflective Questions

1. Reflect on the 18-theme culture-general themes introduced in this chapter. These themes are meant to identify issues that people are likely to encounter when interacting with people different from them. Using the following sentence as a starting point, fill in the blank with each of the 18 themes and answer the questions accordingly.

    "Can you think of a time when _____ was evident in your life or in interactions with others? How might this have interfered with your ability to function effectively? When might it be an asset to you?"

2. Interview a student or a family who has come from another country. What experiences can they recall about their cultural adjustment to a new land? What have you learned from them about their experience that would assist you as a teacher?

3. Reflect on the acculturation groups discussed in the chapter. What are some needs that would be similar and different among students who were immigrants, refugees, minority group members, members of an indigenous group, or short-term sojourners (such as year-abroad foreign exchange students)?

4. Locate a newspaper article that discusses a cultural conflict in a school or community. How can you apply the 18-theme cultural-general framework to better understand the dynamics at play?

References

Berry, J. (1990). Psychology of acculturation: Understanding individuals moving between cultures. In R. Brislin (Ed.), *Applied cross-cultural psychology* (pp. 232–253). Newbury Park, CA: Sage.

Berry, J. (2004). Fundamental psychological processes in intercultural relations. In D. Landis, J. Bennett, & M. Bennett (Eds.), *Handbook of intercultural training* (3rd ed.). Thousand Oaks, CA: Sage.

Cummins, J. (1979). Cognitive/academic language proficiency, linguistic interdependence, the optimum age question and some other matters. *Working Papers on Bilingualism.* No. *19*, 121–129.

Cushner, K., & Brislin, R. (1996). *Intercultural interactions: A practical guide* (2nd ed.). Thousand Oaks, CA: Sage.

Farris, P. J., & Cooper, S. M. (1994). *Elementary social studies: A whole language approach.* Madison, WI: Brown & Benchmark.

Hofstede, G. (1983). Dimension of national cultures in fifty countries and three regions. In J. Deregowski, S. Dzuirawiec, & R. C. Annis (Eds.), *Expiscations in cross-cultural psychology* (pp. 335–355). Lisse, The Netherlands: Swets & Zeitlinger.

Lightfoot, S. L. (1989). Interview with Bill Moyers. *The World of Ideas* [Television series]. American Broadcasting Corporation.

Lysgaard, S. (1955). Adjustment in a foreign society: Norwegian Fulbright grantees visiting the United States. *International Sociol Science Bulletin,* 7, 45–51.

National Center for Educational Statistics. (2009). *Digest of educational statistics.* Retrieved December 21, 2009, from http://nces.ed.gov/programs/digest/ d08/tables/dt08_001.asp

Oberg, K. (1960). Culture shock: Adjustments to new cultural environments. *Practical Anthropology, 7,* 177–182.

Pedersen, P. (1988). *A handbook for developing multicultural awareness.* Alexandria, VA: American Association for Counseling and Development.

Redfield, R., Linton, R., & Herskovits, M. J. (1936). Memorandum for the study of acculturation. *American Anthropologist, 38,* 149–152.

Ross, L. (1977). The intuitive psychologist and his shortcomings: Distortions in the attribution process. In L. Berkowitz (Ed.), *Advances in experimental social psychology* (Vol. 10). New York: Academic Press.

Trifonovitch, G. (1977). Culture learning–culture teaching. *Educational Perspectives, 16*(4), 18–22.

Ward, C., Bochner, S., & Furnam, A. (2001). *The psychology of culture shock.* East Sussex, England: Routledge.

Chapter

5

Intercultural Development
Considering the Growth of Self and Others

Focus Questions

1. Have you ever said to yourself something like, "I certainly wouldn't have thought that way a few years (or months) ago. I've changed and see things much differently than before"? As a teacher, you expect students to learn, to grow, and to change as a result of certain experiences or encounters. What benchmarks might you use to determine if your students are becoming more sophisticated in their understanding and analysis of culture and intercultural effectiveness? What benchmarks might you use to determine if you are becoming more sophisticated in your understanding and analysis of culture and intercultural effectiveness?

2. What differences can you identify in people who are more ethnorelative or intercultural in their orientation in comparison to those who exhibit more ethnocentric or monocultural behaviors?

3. How might you design experiences that move students from an ethnocentric orientation to one that is more ethnorelative?

" One of the higher callings for young people in the coming century will be working to increase intercultural understanding. Such people will be the missionaries of the age, spreading light among groups . . . by giving them a modern vision of the new global community. "

CARL COON

This book not only helps you develop an understanding of how individuals are socialized into their immediate social and individual identity groups (i.e., family, ethnic group), it also addresses your subsequent ability to accept and interact effectively with other people. In this chapter we look at what it means to develop greater awareness and sensitivity to your own culture as well as the cultures of other people. We begin by presenting some general models of ethnic and racial identity and end by looking closely at the developmental model of intercultural sensitivity as a means to become interculturally competent.

The following Case Study presents multiple perspectives and viewpoints on issues related to culture and intercultural interaction in a school and community. As you read the Case Study, try to identify the variety of points of view. The Critical Incidents at the end of the chapter will bring you back to the Case Study as you explore the development of intercultural sensitivity.

Developmental Models of Ethnic and Racial Identity

You have not always been the same physically, cognitively, emotionally, or experientially. What does it mean to develop, to change over time, to see and interact in the world from a new and different perspective? Developmental models of all kinds propose a hierarchical scheme whereby an individual progresses from one level to the next, usually as a result of direct experience and maturation. Numerous developmental or stage models have been proposed over the years that have relevance to educators, including Erikson's (1968) concept of psychosocial identity formation, Kohlberg's (1969) stages of moral development, and Piaget's (1971) stages of cognitive development. Models related to the study of culture and intercultural education have only recently emerged. The earliest can be traced to the various ethnic identity models proposed after the height of the civil rights movement.

Developmental Psychologists

Ethnic identity theory refers to defining for oneself the personal and social meaning of belonging to one particular ethnic group (Grant & Ladson-Billings, 1997). Often used interchangeably, but nevertheless qualitatively different, is the concept of **racial identity.** Race, as has previously been stated, is sometimes socially defined on the basis of physical criteria (e.g., skin color, facial features), whereas an ethnic group is socially defined on the basis of cultural criteria (e.g., customs, shared history, shared language). You may identify as a member of an ethnic group but not think of yourself in racial terms. The opposite can also be true.

A variety of racial identity models have been proposed, most of them influenced by the black consciousness movement. Cross (1991) proposed a five-stage model that described a process of moving from low racial consciousness, through a period of active examination of what it means to be Black, and finally to internalize a positive Black identity. These five stages are pre-encounter, encounter, immersion-emersion, immersion, and internalization. Spring (2004) adapted this culture-specific model to other groups, including other dominated cultures, as well as to immigrant groups in general. Following is a summary of Spring's adaptation.

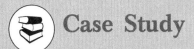

Case Study

Dissent at Maplewood School

Sue Murray (fifth-grade math and science team teacher): It didn't begin with Mr. Jameson's letter to the editor in the local paper late in February, but that was when it did gain momentum and draw an increasing number of people into the issue. And now, just 2 months from the end of the school year, all kinds of people are angry and hurt, many are confused, teachers are getting anxious, and the students don't know what to think. Mr. Goodwin, the principal, seems to be doing all that he can to bring the various parties together, and as I understand it, they are making considerable progress. Let's see if I can piece together all that has happened. I'll begin with the letter I just referred to. Then there are a few other letters to the editor that show the range of responses.

Dear Daily Record Editor,

As a taxpayer and citizen of this fine city, I resent what I see going on in the schools. As I know them, schools are meant to prepare young people for the future. If students are to go to college, then they should have the prerequisite courses they need to succeed. If they are to learn a trade, then the school is to provide them with the skills they will need to do their job. A student who is undecided on what the future will hold should be given an opportunity to try many different things. This is all well and good, and is as it should be. It is the way schools have operated since I went to them many years ago.

But since when have the schools become responsible for addressing all the demands of any group that comes along and claims they have been mistreated or ignored in society? I do not think the schools should be teaching multicultural education. What is it anyway? No one has shown me a book on multicultural education that students study from. It's not a part of the state proficiency test. It's not tested on the SAT. We used to have good schools here that worked for everyone. Now they don't seem to be working at all. Why should teachers and students spend all their time holding debates, doing plays, having so-called cultural festivals and potluck dinners, and paying good money to invite some cultural dance group in to perform for kids? Let's get it straight, schools have a responsibility to prepare people for life, not to teach everyone about other groups' problems. With so many different people now living in America, there would be no more room in the school day if that were all teachers taught. Besides, aren't we all supposed to be Americans anyway? If people don't like the way things are, they should go back to where they've come from. After all, they came to America—they should do it the American way!

But perhaps it is not all the teachers' fault. Perhaps there is a lack of leadership in the schools—from the administrators to the board of education. And while I cannot stop paying my taxes, I can vote "NO" for the next school levy and vote to replace the current members of the board. I think many others would agree with me and follow my lead.

John Jameson, a disgruntled citizen
February 27

Editor, Daily Record,

I am writing in reference to Mr. Jameson's letter about issues in the schools. I agree. It's time we take a stand and stop pandering to every group that comes along. My son returned from fighting in Iraq and has been out of work for six months now, and he can't seem to get a job because of such things as affirmative action and job-outsourcing. Yet I see many other people working in jobs that could go to real Americans who support our country in very real ways. I've traveled to other countries and each time I do I am reminded about how much better we have it here in America. I think the schools are part of the problem, and they'd better shape up soon.

Rebecca Reynolds
March 5

(continued)

To the Editor of the Daily Record,

I wish to disagree with the letters written by Mr. Jameson and Ms. Reynolds who complained about the schools addressing multicultural education. As someone who works in the business community, I know how fast the world is changing—much faster than many people in this city seem to be—and our children must be prepared for these changes. School may be the only place where children can learn about other people—about other cultures, about how different people think and act, and about how to learn to get along with those who are different. Most parents are too busy or not experienced enough to tackle such a difficult task; therefore, we need the schools to do this for us. After all, it is in the school, like nowhere else in society, that children of different backgrounds come together for long periods of time. What better place is there for children to learn about diversity? I am in full support of our schools doing all they can to address diversity, and I hope others in this community come forward with their support as well.

Joyce Maples
March 8

Sue Murray: As I already said, it wasn't the letters to the editor that started everything, but they do give you a sense of the variety of people's reactions. Ever since the start of the school year tensions have continued to mount. It seems as if no one is happy with the way things are, and I don't understand why. I was excited to begin teaching in the fifth-grade team after teaching for 5 years in a fourth-grade self-contained classroom. But with all the developmental changes the children are going through and all the ethnic and racial tensions that have emerged, I don't know if I can take another year. We have parents who are angry that we are not addressing what they think are critical issues. We have had a number of parent meetings involving all the teachers as well as the principal where we attempted to discuss their concerns, but nothing seemed to help. And many parents and other local citizens have been showing up at school board meetings to voice their concerns.

I think the problems began back in October at the school Halloween party. We have been concerned about violence in general and the increase in the number of violent movies that influence many of the children's choices of costume. Rather than have children dress in whatever costume they might if they went out trick-or-treating, we encouraged them to come dressed as some historical, political, or social figure. I was really surprised when two boys, Tom and Daniel, came dressed as Native Americans and three others, Keenan, James, and Troy, came dressed as sports mascots—one as a Cleveland Indian, one as a Washington Redskin, and one as an Atlanta Brave. What a social commentary they were making, and quite sophisticated, I might add, for a group of young middle school students. They had placards that challenged people's stereotypes: some demanded changing the team logos and some argued to maintain them out of tradition. Even the imbalance of power was evident in the three-to-two mix they presented. Many of the children were oblivious to the messages these students were trying to make, but not all. Some, in fact, were quite taken by their statement. Their presence even caused a stir among some of the parents who came to observe the annual Halloween march around the school. Mrs. Marks, the president of the PTO, took a photo of them for the school newspaper. The paper was printed just before Thanksgiving. I think it was this incident, in combination with some of the Thanksgiving plays and classroom activities, that really set things off. Some parents of the younger children in the school started complaining that putting on a traditional Thanksgiving play was perpetuating stereotypes. I do agree with them on that account. It was soon after we came back to school after the winter break that I really began to be bothered by all this attention to diversity. Some of the African American parents started complaining that not enough was being done to present their culture and that we shouldn't be doing things only during February for Black History Month. The PTO was asked to form a multicultural committee, and aside from Mrs. Marks, it seemed that there were mostly minority parents involved.

And then, what really got me was when Mr. Goodwin, the principal, called me in to his office. He said one of the African American parents complained that I wasn't a good teacher. The father said that his son wasn't learning from me and that I was treating some of the kids differently. I don't treat any of my students any differently. And I really think the parents would accuse me of playing favorites if I did start doing things differently for different groups. After all, we all want the kids to learn what's best for them. And we've been pretty good about being able to make that happen in this school—for everybody. I think the diversity is an asset for us. The more differences we have here, the better. More difference equals more creative ideas in the classroom, and I certainly wouldn't want all the kids to be the same around here. It's bad enough that most of the teachers are pretty much the same. If everyone were the same, it would be boring. The more cultures people can know about, the better off we'd all be. I have my master's degree with a specialty in math, and I'm pretty good at science. I'm a good teacher. I can't help it if some of the kids don't catch on as quickly as the others. I work hard at what I do, and I resent being accused of playing favorites or not treating all kids the same. Some of these parents should try to teach a room full of kids who are overloading on hormones. It's not easy work, you know.

I asked Mr. Goodwin to let me know which of the parents complained, but he wouldn't tell me. I told him that I'd rather meet personally with the parents to discuss the issue instead of them hiding behind the principal. He said he was arranging a parents' meeting soon and that would be the time for people to discuss their feelings. He said he was considering bringing in a facilitator to help keep the discussion in a positive light.

I wonder how my teaching team feels?

Pre-Encounter

Individuals in the pre-encounter stage typically exhibit a certain amount of self-hatred, often buying into the negative stereotypes perpetuated by the mainstream society through television, radio, newspapers, and conversation. These negative stereotypes, then, are often internalized and become a part of the person's ethnic identity. Individuals at this level begin to see themselves as lazy, stupid, sloppy, thieving—whatever the prevailing stereotype happens to be. Once these feelings are internalized, young people at this level might speak of their entire group as lazy or stupid. A self-fulfilling prophecy takes over, and these individuals identify themselves as probable failures in school—and ultimately fail.

Young children are especially prone to the messages given by others. Immigrant children may face problems similar to those of other dominated groups as they become victims of negative stereotyping because of their different speech patterns, mannerisms, or dress. The Asian American stereotype of the "model" student, although seemingly positive, may also imply passivity and obedience. Asian adults, then, may suffer from being typecast as submissive and meek. And don't think that European Americans are exempt from having to confront negative stereotypes. A number of ethnic American groups (Polish Americans, German Americans, Jewish Americans, Italian Americans, etc.) have organized to combat the many negative images often perpetuated about them.

Encounter

In this stage, individuals confront an incident that forces them to question the negative stereotypes that have become part of their ethnic identity. Numerous incidents in recent years have caused many people to reevaluate their pre-encounter identity. Reactions to highly publicized incidents of

racial profiling by many law enforcement agencies, or incidents of racism in education have led many people to rethink their ethnic identity. At this stage, people begin to see self-hatred as a product of negative stereotypes and see themselves as part of a larger group experiencing similar social barriers. People begin to ask themselves, "Why do I think this way about myself and my people?"

Immersion-Emersion

In this in-between stage, people begin to rid themselves of their ethnic self-hatred, to rediscover their traditional culture, and to take on a new ethnic identity. People may adopt the symbols of their people, such as wearing the traditional clothing of their group, adopting new hairstyles that reflect their group, learning to make the traditional foods, and so forth. African Americans, for instance, may wear a dashiki, Italian Americans may purchase pasta machines, Muslim Americans might wear a kufi, and Jewish Americans may don a kippa.

Immersion

This stage is represented by a complete immersion in a person's ethnic culture. Mexican Americans may join organizations focused on Chicano issues; Puerto Ricans may get involved in discussions about independence versus statehood; Native Americans may join active American Indian movements; people seek out the literature and music of their culture; and so forth. This stage represents a highly ethnocentric orientation, and people may adopt a "holier-than-thou" attitude. People may also adopt a somewhat militant stance, challenging existing social and institutional practices. Mexican American students in some public schools in Los Angeles, for instance, went on strike a few years ago, demanding that Chicano foods be served in cafeterias.

People's immersion in their ethnic culture changes their perspective on events. People may begin seeing the importance of their people's contributions to the greater society, such as the influence of Italian art and thought to Western art and literature, or West African contributions to the sciences and art. People begin to read various accounts of history from multiple perspectives, pointing out that most of what children learn in school has been told from a Eurocentric point of view.

Internalization

At this stage, individuals come to terms with living within the culture of the United States (or other mainstream society) while maintaining a relationship with their ethnic culture. People become fully bicultural or multicultural and adopt a view of the mainstream culture that is both accepting and critical. They can identify with certain aspects of the dominant society (material abundance, perhaps) while rejecting other aspects (racism, for instance). African Americans may say, "Some whites are racist, but not all. Whether I like everything or not, I have grown up here and it is my home too. Things can improve if we keep on working toward that goal." Anger becomes focused on certain aspects of society—combating discrimination in schools or racist impressions in textbooks, for instance.

Like Spring, Banks (1988) looked at the emerging stages of ethnic development of individuals within a particular group and proposed a similar six-stage model. The first three stages—ethnic psychological captivity, ethnic encapsulation, and ethnic identity clarification—are similar to those of Cross (1991). The latter three stages speak more readily to a global society.

Banks's stage 4, called biethnicity, refers to individuals who have both a strong sense of their own ethnic identity and a healthy understanding and respect for others. Individuals at this stage participate equally as well and as comfortably in two different groups—their home ethnic group and that of at least one other, usually that of the mainstream. They have become bicultural. American Jews are often thought to be in this stage because they function effectively in numerous Jewish organizations while at the same time interacting in the greater society with relative ease. Similarly, many African Americans (or any other group for that matter) are able to move with ease and respect between their own community culture and that of the mainstream. This stage reflects people who are successfully integrating, not assimilating, as referred to in the discussion on acculturation in Chapter 3.

Stage 5 in Banks's model, multiethnicity, represents the idealized goal for citizenship identity within such ethnically pluralistic nations as the United States, Canada, or Australia. Individuals at this stage have an understanding and appreciation of many groups, are able to function somewhat effectively within a variety of ethnic or cultural communities, and maintain an allegiance to the nation-state and its idealized values.

Finally, at stage 6, globalism and global competency, individuals reflect positive ethnic, national, and global identities while demonstrating the knowledge, attitudes, skills, and abilities required to function effectively in ethnic cultures from a variety of contexts. They have, as Banks (1988) suggests, internalized the ethical values and principles thought to be universal for all of humankind, and have developed the skills, abilities, and commitments that are required to act on these levels.

Cross (1991) suggested that internalized identity serves three main functions. One, by providing a sense of psychological security, it protects people from the insults that may come from other groups. Two, it provides people with a sense of belonging to a larger cultural group. And three, it provides a foundation for dealing with people from other cultures.

The next section looks at recent conceptions related to the development of intercultural competence and considers how these are fundamental to our efforts to deliver an education that addresses the goals of diversity.

Intercultural Competence

Just what does it mean to have an intercultural mind-set? What are the attitudes and behaviors of people who are not only comfortable but effective working across cultures? How would you recognize such an orientation in teachers and students? In yourself? How can we assist people to develop such an orientation?

Early studies in intercultural competence attempted to identify the specific behaviors that were evident in individuals who were effective at living and working across cultures. Such studies suggested that interculturally effective people have three

Activity 2:
**Inventory of Cross-
Cultural Sensitivity**

qualities in common: (1) they are able to manage the psychological stress that accompanies most intercultural interactions; (2) they are able to communicate effectively across cultures–verbally as well as nonverbally; and (3) they are. able to develop and maintain new and essential interpersonal relationships (Brislin & Yoshida, 1994). Other conceptualizations of intercultural effectiveness and sensitivity consider the interplay between the cognitive, affective, and behavioral domains (Bennett, 1993).

People with an intercultural mind-set, for instance, move from an avoidance or a tolerance of difference to a respect and appreciation of difference. They move from an unconscious ethnocentrism to a more conscious awareness of their own and others' cultures. And instead of being conscious of what not to do to avoid racism, sexism, and other prejudices, they understand what to do to create respectful, productive intercultural relationships. Interculturally effective people are proactive in nature and seek out diverse perspectives and contributions when making decisions and taking actions.

In learning to manage effectively across cultures, people should strive to develop a number of skills. They should respond to others in a nonjudgmental manner; attempt to propose more than one cultural interpretation for behavior (in other words, generate multiple attributions and check them out); learn to mediate conflicts and solve problems in culturally appropriate and effective ways; motivate others in the context of their cultural values; promote effective intercultural interaction through mutual adaptation to style differences; respect cultural differences through the analysis of strengths and limits of different perspectives, skills, and knowledge; model culturally sensitive behaviors and attitudes; seek out new learning about cultural differences; and institutionalize an intercultural perspective in their personal and professional practice. Ultimately, intercultural competence refers to the maintenance of a vision that stresses the dignity of all cultures and the productivity of pluralism, to the development of a mind-set that recognizes ethnocentrism and seeks the value of difference, and to the adoption of a skill set that employs intercultural communication in effective and ethical ways.

Interculturally competent individuals are able to solve problems and take appropriate risks, shift their frame of reference as required, recognize and respond appropriately to cultural differences, listen empathically, perceive others accurately, maintain a nonjudgmental approach to communication, and gather appropriate information about another culture. In real life outside the classroom as well as within, such skills are critical when people engage in decision making, negotiation, or problem solving across cultures; when subordinates and authority figures from different backgrounds interact extensively; or when individuals or families make major transitions. The school and classroom provide an ideal context in which to practice and develop these skills.

Intercultural competence may be as much a tool for survival in today's world as is the development of literacy, mathematics, and technological skill. Educators today must strive to fully integrate an intercultural education and perspective while carrying on with the traditional educational needs of communities and nations. Yet these are not easy issues to adequately address. Intercultural education and training is a delicate and difficult endeavor that must be approached with the greatest of sensitivity. Bennett (1993) pointed out that intercultural interactions among human populations have typically been accompanied by violence and aggression:

> Intercultural sensitivity is not natural. It is not part of our primate past, nor has it characterized most of human history. Cross-cultural contact usually has been accompanied by bloodshed, oppression, or genocide. Education and training in intercultural communication [and we might say intercultural education] is an approach to changing our "natural" behavior. With the concepts and skills developed in this field, we ask learners to transcend traditional ethnocentrism and to explore new relationships across cultural boundaries. This attempt at change must be approached with the greatest possible care. (p. 21)

In addition to the intense reactions identified by Bennett, evidence for the unnaturalness of intercultural contact can be seen in people's everyday behaviors. Many people, including those who do not harbor intense prejudices, admit that interactions with culturally different others tend to be more anxiety provoking than are interactions with very similar people (Cushner & Brislin, 1996). For a smaller number of people, this anxiety leads to a strong preference for interactions with similar others (a small ingroup) and an active avoidance of intercultural interactions. Such people, however, will not fare well in today's world, where intercultural interaction is increasingly commonplace.

Intercultural Competence

Developing Intercultural Sensitivity

So how do people develop intercultural sensitivity? Of great concern is the relative lack of information most teachers and teacher educators have about intercultural development and sensitivity. Just what is meant by this concept? How do we know when we "have it"? What are the benchmarks that teachers should strive for with their students? If we are to aid people's intercultural development, where do we begin to understand how people move from an ethnocentric perspective to one that is more ethnorelative in orientation? These are all legitimate questions and issues to consider.

While no single study can be cited that lists all of the essential qualities of intercultural competence, researchers and practitioners in such fields as intercultural communication and training have something concrete to offer teachers and teacher educators when it comes to understanding how people become interculturally competent. Deardorff's Pyramid Model of Intercultural Competence (2006) identifies the need for individuals to exhibit certain motivational attitudes—such as respect, openness, and curiosity—that subsequently lead to the acquisition of knowledge, comprehension, and skill (see Figure 5.1).

Bennett's (1993) developmental model of intercultural sensitivity (DMIS), provides a framework for understanding individual development and awareness along a continuum from highly ethnocentric to highly ethnorelative, and this framework can help us better understand some of the dynamics that might occur in stages 5 and 6 in Banks's model of ethnic identity development.

Figure 5.1

Pyramid Model of
Intercultural Competence
(Deardorff, 2006)

Desired External Outcome:
Behaving and communicating effectively and appropriately (based on one's intercultural knowledge, skills and attitudes) to achieve one's goals to some degree.

Desired Internal Outcome:

Adaptability (to different communication styles, behaviors and cultural contexts)
Flexibility (behavioral and cognitive)
Ethnorelative view, Empathy

Knowledge and Comprehension:

Cultural Self-Awareness
Deep understanding of culture
Culture-specific information
Sociolinguistic Awareness

Skills:

Listening, observing, interpreting, analysis, evaluate, relate

Requisite Attitudes of:

Respect – valuing other cultures
Openness – to people from other cultures; withholding judgment
Curiosity – tolerating ambiguity and uncertainty

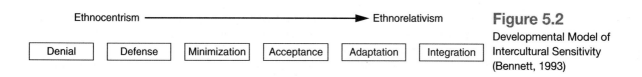

In explaining the DMIS, Bennett notes that an increase in cultural awareness is accompanied by improved cognitive sophistication. Specifically, as people's ability to understand difference increases, so does their ability to negotiate a variety of worldviews. As a six-stage model that describes the experience of cultural difference, the DMIS is linear to the extent that it allows us to address the question, "So, what do we do next?" Such a model provides a valuable tool to educators of both young people and adults as they struggle to achieve greater cross-cultural sensitivity.

The developmental model of intercultural sensitivity is based in grounded theory from the observations of thousands of subjects who appeared to develop in similar ways. Three stages lie on the ethnocentric side of the continuum, and three stages reflect increasingly ethnorelative perspectives and skills. The DMIS is a constructivist model, which helps us to better understand the complex phenomena of culture and intercultural experience, and it explores the "experience, or complexity, of difference." There is a strong affective dimension at most levels, especially in the early stages. As people move through the stages, their worldview becomes increasingly complex. On the ethnocentric side, an individual may be at denial, defense, or minimization. On the ethnorelative side, an individual may be at acceptance, adaptability, or integration (see Figure 5.2).

Ethnocentric Stages of the DMIS

Denial

Denial refers to the inability to see cultural differences and is reflective of individuals who isolate or separate themselves in homogenous groups. Individuals at this stage tend to ignore the reality of diversity and are often characterized by well-meant, but ignorant, stereotyping and superficial statements of tolerance. At this stage, an individual's understanding of difference is minimal. Cultural difference, if it is considered, is sometimes attributed to a deficiency in intelligence or personality. There is a tendency to dehumanize outsiders, viewing them as simple, undifferentiated aspects or objects of their environment, thus making them easy targets for discrimination, exploitation, or conquest.

At a societal level the denial stage can be exemplified by separatists, such as under apartheid in South Africa or segregation in the southern United States. Such people may have a very complex experience and many categories for dealing with their own reality, but they have limited, if any, experience and few categories for dealing with cultural difference. When experiencing difference, people in this stage tend to organize others in terms of already existing categories, seeing others and the world as subversions of themselves and their own world. People in this stage overemphasize familiar categories; just not seeing the differences. If they are Americans in Paris, for instance, they have an "American" experience, and say things like, "Paris is like the United States–cars, tall buildings, McDonald's." If thinking about immigrants, a person in denial sees major issues rather simplistically. Because they have the category of language differ-ences (a general understanding), but not of assimilation or adjustment (a specific and more complex issue), they may support language development programs as a means to deal with the problem. While such efforts may be helpful on the surface, they tend to ignore other, more fundamental aspects of the groups' problems (such as racism and discrimination).

Bennett calls this stage the "stupid questions syndrome," suggesting that people in denial tend to have a few, say, perhaps four, ideas or pieces of stereotypic knowledge about a given country or culture. Consider Africa, the only continent that many people refer to as a country. The stereotypic knowledge many European Americans have about Africa might include wild animals, poverty, illness, and jungle. Everything about Africa, then, is thought of in terms of these four ideas. When an individual at this stage meets an African, all these images come to the forefront. Such a person may think or ask, "So, when you leave your hut in the morning, aren't you afraid the wild animals from the jungle will attack you?"

Stop for a moment and think about the categories many people around the world might have of Americans. Do they tend to see Americans as overweight (lovers of fast food), lazy, rich, and all driving big cars? If so, a person from overseas who is in the denial stage, when meeting an American, might ask, "So, when you leave your big house in the morning, do you get in your big car and drive to McDonald's for your big breakfast?" They are bringing forth all their stereotypic information in their judgment of an American. Is this a true and accurate characterization of American people? Of course not. Nor is it a true and accurate characterization of people on the African continent.

Outside of one's own context, things are rather fuzzy. People in denial see others as living in a different reality and, without having much knowledge of those people, may say such things as:

"Live and let live! That's what I say. Mixing just causes trouble."

"Business is just business the world over."

"As long as they all speak English, there will be no problem."

"Technology doesn't care about culture."

"They were born here, so they should know how to do it the American way."

"With my experience, I can be successful in any culture without any special effort."

"I never experience culture shock."

Denial has profound consequences, and when people at this stage are brought together with others, unpleasant things can sometimes occur. Because such peo-ple have many categories for dealing with their own culture, but few, if any, for dealing with other cultures, they may have only one single category for foreigners—"people of culture." The title of a book on the Cambodian war expe-rience, *To Destroy You Is No Loss: The Odyssey of a Cambodian Family* (Criddle, 1996), captures an extreme sentiment of someone in this stage. An orientation such as this can lead to atrocities like the Holocaust, the wave of sectarian violence recently experienced in Iraq, or the "ethnic cleansing" recently witnessed in Darfur. People begin to believe that other people do not have feelings like they have, and they then treat those people as less than human.

Children in this stage are socialized that theirs is *the* view of the world, instead of learning that theirs is *one* view of the world. Although the thinking of people at this stage isn't necessarily evil, it is ignorant, and their behavior can become evil. Individuals at this stage are not capable of thinking about difference and must discover commonalties among people before they can progress to more sophisticated levels. Moving individuals from this stage to the next involves helping them to develop better skills of category discrimination and to become more sophisticated in their thinking and more complex in their cognitive processing.

Defense

Defense is the next stage of the developmental model of intercultural sensitivity. Movement into this stage is driven by the inadequacies of the existing rudimentary categories. This stage is characterized by a recognition of cultural difference coupled with negative evaluations of those whose culture is different from one's own. The greater the cultural difference observed, the more negative the accompanying evaluation. Strong dualistic us–them thinking is common in this stage and is often accompanied by overt negative stereotyping. When forced into contact with others, individuals in this stage often become defensive. They tend to reflect a feeling that "we're all becoming the same" or "the world is really all becoming American." People at this stage prefer to separate themselves from others because they don't have categories for dealing with difference. Although people at this stage are beginning to develop a more differentiated view of others, they tend to have a "hardening of the categories" and a narrow focus on a small, typically elite sample of a society. Such people defend their way as the one best way.

Three areas of defense are typically found: denigration or derogation, superiority, and sometimes reversal. Denigration or derogation refers to belittling or actively discriminating against another person. Superiority assumes extreme ethnocentrism to the point where one looks down on another. Reversal refers to changing sides or evaluating one's own culture as inferior to another. In an intercultural context, reversal is often referred to as "going native" and is evident when people return home from an overseas experience, identifying more with their host culture and criticizing their own. Individuals who exhibit reversal tendencies may avoid contact with fellow citizens and associate solely with host nationals. In the racial identity models discussed earlier in this chapter, such behavior might reflect the pre-encounter stage.

Defense protects an individual's own worldview of the possibilities of other realities. No longer hidden away, other (meaning different) people suddenly become a force that must be reckoned with. Individuals at this stage tend to develop a polarized worldview. They put up a fence and raise their own flag, so to speak, and keep others at a distance. Such a scenario results in an us–them situation and may lead to the formation of militia groups or gangs. Both sides, the dominant group as well as the minority group, act to protect their own position. In reversal, nothing changes in one's worldview; one just changes sides and acquires the prejudices of the other group.

People in the defense stage may make statements such as the following:

"Genetically, they just don't have the capability to understand these things."

"The only way I can live around them is to spend most of my time at the expatriate (or country) club."

"We invented this stuff, and we're really the only ones who can make it work."

"This company was built on our values, so our opinions are the most important."

"These are American schools, and they've worked really well for us. Others should just learn to do it our way."

"I am so embarrassed by my fellow citizens that I spend all my time with the locals." (This statement is an example of reversal.)

"Women are naturally passive, so they wouldn't fit at this level."

"Asians are not assertive, hence they are poor leaders."

It's not uncommon for people to be in the defense stage, but they must be encouraged to move on. Because defense is a heavy affective state, people need to be supported in this stage. Developmental tasks require supporting people affectively while stressing the commonalities among people. People moving from this stage begin to say such things as "We're all in this together" and "We all came in different boats–but we're now in this one together." A good place to begin when considering how to move people from this stage is to point out such differences as learning style (using learning style inventories) and communication patterns that demonstrate that all individuals and groups have differences. The 18-theme culture-general model also works well here.

Minimization

Minimization, the last stage still on the ethnocentric side of the continuum, is entered with the discovery of commonality. People begin to recognize and accept superficial cultural differences such as eating customs, money, and so forth at this stage (the tip of the iceberg in Figure 3.1), yet continue to hold the belief that all human beings are essentially the same. The emphasis at this stage is on the similarity of people and the commonality of basic values, with the tendency to define the basis of commonality in ethnocentric terms (i.e., "since everyone is essentially the same, they're really pretty much like me"). This perceived commonality could exist around physical universalism ("We are all the same–we all eat, sleep, breathe, bleed red, and die"; "We are all people of color after all") or around spiritual universalism ("Deep down we are all children of the same God, whether we know it or not").

Minimization is a very profound stage. There is evidence to suggest that most teachers, for instance, are at this stage–and they are pleased to be here because they have transcended defense (Mahon, 2003). It is difficult to move people from this stage because they think they are doing okay. This stage, for instance, can become official institutional policy, which can be problematic as people tend to be "nice but color blind." Individuals at the minimization stage see people as basically the same, with little recognition of the differences that in fact do exist. People at this stage tend not to make reference to physical characteristics (race, for instance), believing that such traits are not important as long as they just treat all people the same. In minimization, people ignore the influence of culture and lived experience that may be quite different among people, believing that all people have the same needs–but in reality they don't.

In this stage an ethnocentric assumption exists that everyone should share the same reality–usually *my* own. People say and believe such things as, "If everyone knew of my religion, they'd all want to follow it." In schools, people might say, "They came to this country, so they know we must have the best education system." At the corporate level, people may say, "We should introduce shopping malls everywhere because they work so well," or "We couldn't survive without computers." Internationally you might hear people say, "Australia is just like the United States, only 20 years behind." But you must keep in mind, as is becoming increasingly clear on the global scale, that everyone in the world does not aspire to be American.

At the minimization stage people may say things like the following:

"The key to getting along in any culture is to just be yourself–authentic and honest."

"Customs differ, of course, but when you really get to know them they're pretty much like us."

"I have this intuitive sense of other people, no matter what their culture."

"Technology is bringing cultural uniformity to the underdeveloped world."

"No matter what their culture, people are pretty much motivated by the same things."

"If people are really honest with themselves, they'd recognize that some values are universal."

"It's a small world after all."

"I don't see any difference–race, gender, or culture. We're all just people."

The developmental task to move people out of this stage is cultural self-awareness. Pointing out aspects of an individual's own culture and showing how it might differ from another person's is a good place to begin. However, resistance among people might develop around such things as strongly held values. Cultural awareness does not mean that people must like and accept everything; it is not a case of "anything goes." People can maintain a sense of morality about them by contextualizing another's behavior and beliefs. Take nudity, for example. Is it appropriate to take off your clothes? Well, it matters–the context is critical. In certain circumstances it is appropriate to take off your clothes (as in the shower), but in other situations (out in public), perhaps not. The context is the key to legitimizing the behavior. Culture, thus, becomes the context from which to explore another's values. Once the context is set and understood, then individuals can decide how they will behave.

Once cultural awareness is achieved, the person can move from minimization to acceptance. Although minimization is the most advanced stage of the ethnocentric side of the DMIS continuum, people at this stage often negate the importance and value of cultural difference and tend to believe that "people are all alike," meaning that "everyone is just like me." Individuals at the minimization stage tend to see people as basically the same and make little recognition of the differences that are significant, that continue to divide people, and that underlie most intercultural interactions.

Bennett asserts that a paradigmatic shift in thinking must occur for an individual to move from the ethnocentric stages of the continuum into the ethnorelative side. Movement into the ethnorelative stages represents a significant change in one's view of difference, from something to be avoided to something that is sought out. Individuals in the ethnorelative stage search for ways to adapt to difference and begin to recognize that people live in culturally different contexts. The notion of context is not understood in ethnocentric stages.

Ethnorelative Stages of the DMIS

Acceptance

Acceptance of difference is the first stage on the ethnorelative side of the continuum. This stage represents an individual's ability to recognize and appreciate cultural difference in terms of both people's values and their behavior. Acceptance of cultural differences is seen as understanding that there are viable alternative solutions to the way people organize their existence and experience. At this stage, the individual is beginning to demonstrate the ability to interpret phenomena within a cultural context and to analyze complex interactions in culture-contrast terms. Categories of difference are consciously expanded and elaborated, with people understanding that others are "Not good or bad, just different." Later, the individual can see those beliefs, values, and other general patterns of assigning "goodness" and "badness" to ways of being in the world that exist in a variety of cultural contexts. People in this stage also begin to seek out cultural difference.

Acceptance of another's difference does not necessarily mean agreement nor necessarily, how to adopt to those differences. People may have respect and value for cultural differences, but not necessarily agree with all they see. It is here that people begin to discriminate–they have "taste." People do have individual tastes and preferences, and not all cultures or cultural practices will be liked or valued by all people (the cultural belief that the role of all women should

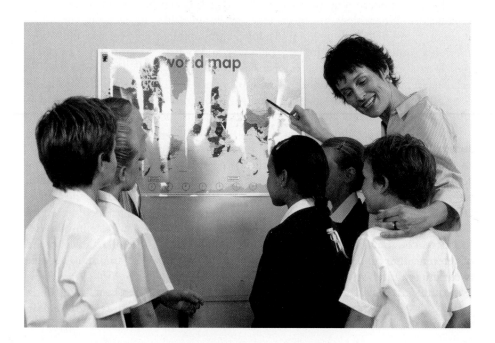

focus on home and family, for instance, is not universally accepted). The more sophisticated knowledge you possess in a category, the more personal preference you can bring (as a wine connoisseur is able to do). This behavior is not ethnocentric as long as you assume that the other is equally complex and acceptable within a given context. Even though people find that they may not necessarily agree with all they see practiced within another culture, they can, at least, understand what they witness. Teachers at this stage, for instance, might understand that family or other collective influences may be greater for a Latino or Asian child than for an Anglo counterpart, and this understanding may temper their expectation that students make their own independent choices on major life decisions. They may then seek out ways to work more closely with a student's family.

People in this stage may say things like the following:

"The more difference the better—more difference results in more creative ideas."

"You certainly wouldn't want to be around the same kind of people all the time—the ideas get stale, and besides, it's boring."

"I always try to study about a new culture before I go there or interact with the people."

"The more cultures you know about, the better comparisons you can make."

"Sometimes it's confusing, knowing that values are different in various cultures and wanting to be respectful, but still wanting to maintain my own core values."

"I know that my African American students and their families, and I, a European American man, have had very different life experiences, but we're working together as a learning community."

"Our new student is from Mexico. Where can I learn about Mexican culture so I can be more effective in the classroom?"

But acceptance alone is not sufficient to drive effectiveness with another culture. It is necessary to develop new skills to be more effective teachers or businesspeople.

Adaptation

Adaptation is the stage during which people begin to see cultural categories as more flexible and become more competent in their ability to communicate across cultures. Individuals are able to use empathy effectively, shift frames of reference, and are better able to understand others and be understood across cultural boundaries.

Movement into this stage from the previous one is driven by a need for action (better teaching, more profit) and cognitive empathy—the ability to change frames of reference. A significant amount of groundwork must be laid before a shift can occur and people are ready to learn new skills. The greater the cultural gap, the more difficult it will be to make the shift. The individual begins to experience reality in a more "other" way and can understand and feel about the world as the other would.

International Perspective: What's Happening Elsewhere in the World?

Addressing Cultural Diversity in the German Classroom

Juliana Roth
Institute of Intercultural Communication, Munich University

Cultural Diversity in German Society

Ethnic diversity is a relatively new phenomenon to German society. Well into the 1950s most Germans lived in predominantly homogeneous cultural environments, travel abroad was regarded as exotic, and visitors from foreign countries were rare. Foreign languages and lifestyles were not a part of everyday life of the majority of people, restricted primarily to those of the educated middle class and valued mostly as aesthetic and literary phenomena, with little relevance for everyday reality.

The situation began to change in the 1960s when Germany, together with several other European countries, began to recruit workers from southern and southeastern Europe. Waves of predominantly male migrants from Italy, Spain, Greece, Yugoslavia, and Turkey received contracts to work in the factories of the then booming industrial centers. In the course of the German *Wirtschaftswunder* (economic miracle) the need for the manpower of the "guest workers" allowed them to stay on beyond their initial contracts and to be granted permanent residency. By the late 1970s, the "guests" had turned into residents, had founded families, and were beginning to settle their lives in their new environment. In accordance with German immigration law, migrants could be granted permanent work and residence permits without being naturalized as German citizens. These developments resulted in a significant shift in the public opinion on work migration, especially when the majority population realized that the "guests" were going to stay for good in their midst. A familiar German quotation from that time was *Wir riefen Gastarbeiter und es kamen Menschen* ("We called in guest workers and there came human beings").

Today, more people with backgrounds different from the dominant culture live in Germany than ever before in history. The result is a dramatic increase in the diversity within the nation's classrooms—and in the pressure on the (predominantly mainstream) teachers, few of whom are trained to work in multicultural settings. Intercultural education in Germany is thus considered a new and demanding topic within the field of education.

The nationalities previously mentioned still represent the major migrant groups in Germany, the Turkish community being by far the largest among them. A substantial number of these migrants have, in the meantime, received German citizenship, while others have kept the citizenship of their country of origin and continue to reside in Germany on the basis of permanent resident and work permits. Furthermore, there is a sizable group of ethnic Germans and Jews from Russia, most of whom are Russian-speaking; who are granted German citizenship status on the basis of specific legal provisions concerning the repatriation of the descendants of ethnic Germans and the compensations for Jews. There are also some smaller, but growing, groups of recent political and war refugees from Africa, Afghanistan, Iraq, and so forth who are granted permanent resident rights in special circumstances. Other sources of cultural diversity are the rapidly increasing binational marriages as well as the growing mobility of the workforce, both within the European Union and globally.

The focus on the legal status of migrants is not accidental. Many legal regulations in the German educational system are rooted in the distinction between citizens and noncitizens, which results in a variety of problems in the growing number of culturally diverse schools. This distinction adds to the traditional differentiation between locals (German born) and migrants (non-German born), creating additional and complex occasions for discrimination and conflict. Immigration policy and bureaucracy differentiate sharply between "those who have always been here" and newcomers. This distinction is carried into the following generations, and in some segments of society persists even after migrants have received German citizenship. Thus one can speak of an institutionalization of "otherness"—a phenomenon with important consequences for all educational contexts.

Approaches to Intercultural Education

The term "intercultural education" and the concepts related to it were first introduced in Germany in 1974. By that time, the impact of migration had already become visible in kindergartens and schools that were increasingly attended by the children of the first generation of guest workers. The fact that work migration to Germany was then equivalent to migration from the (then) poorer regions of Europe to the rich countries in the north and west of the continent had a decisive influence on the main paradigms of the new field of intercultural pedagogy and explains its deficit-oriented approach. Due to the language deficiencies, cultural differences, and the low social and lesser legal status of the migrants, pedagogical work in multicultural settings was closely associated with work with disadvantaged social groups. The view of migrant children as being deficient (lesser or no command of the German language, cultural differences, etc.) automatically assigned the local (German born) children a higher status and defined the relationship between both groups as uneven or asymmetrical, in favor of the members of the majority population.

This explains why until today the central question of intercultural pedagogy in Germany revolves around the majority–minority issue: How can the members of majority and minority groups be guided toward responsible and rational interaction? The two major dimensions of this question relate to (a) the unequal distribution of power between the majority population and the minority groups and (b) the definition of cultural difference. For historical and political reasons, the majority–minority distinction is considered basic and unquestionable in German society (as in most other European societies). Most European nations derive their identity from a shared history, language, and culture, a fact that explains the automatic exclusion of every person of a different origin. Heritage thus represents the main criterion for belonging to the community of locals, overriding residence and citizenship as other possible criteria. In societies with such a paradigm of an ingrained division between native locals and foreign migrants, but with a factual cultural diversity, rational debate and negotiation appear as the only possible way of managing the uneven distribution of power.

Even more problematic is the positioning of differences between the majority and minority groups. For the definition of its identity, any group relies on the perceptions of its members of themselves and of the members of other groups, and thereby focuses on those features that distinguish them from the other groups, that is, that constitute the group's "culture." The automatic attribution of all group differences to culture and the use of culture as an explanatory variable for any behavior, however, are viewed very critically by German researchers in intercultural education. They are fully aware of the risks of the integration of the concept of culture into the foundations of pedagogical theory. In view of the stated goal of intercultural education—namely, to bring students from different cultures together—emphasizing culturally based differences can mean enhancing their divisive power and giving way to discriminatory actions. A rational and responsible management of cultural differences in the classroom is thus seen as a possible way out of this dilemma.

Intercultural Theory and Classroom Practice

There are several important features of the field of intercultural education in Germany. There is a discrepancy between the availability of theoretical knowledge and its application to educational practice. Since the first efforts in the 1970s to address cultural diversity in the classroom, then under the name of *Ausländerpädagogik* (foreigners' pedagogy) and primarily geared at teaching German language proficiency, there has been a continuous development of research paradigms and of a substantial body of theories. The development

is marked by a very critical discussion of the notion of culture and the ways it should enter multicultural pedagogical concepts. The development of theories followed the general lines of political and social models for coexistence in culturally diverse societies whose goals have always been very high. The current integration model requires all social groups to engage in a process of reciprocal adaptation based on mutually negotiated ideas, values, and meanings. It goes without saying that the translation of this ideal into the social reality of unequal power distribution and factual majority–minority distinctions is bound to be a very challenging endeavor.

Contrary to the elaboration of intercultural pedagogical theory, there have been few attempts to introduce this knowledge into academic curricula or the instruction of students in education. There is still little effort to prepare future teachers for their work in culturally mixed environments and to develop their practical skills for this task. The high theoretical and moral demands of the conceptual frameworks have indeed made it difficult to operationalize the notion of culture and to address practical pedagogical issues.

With constantly increasing migration and growing problems of integration, however, teachers are under pressure to acquire skills and knowledge that enable them to deal with the cultural diversity in their classrooms on an everyday basis. Because researchers and theoreticians seem reluctant to provide practical knowledge and guidance toward feasible intercultural instruction, teachers are looking for new ways to make up for this deficit.

To meet these needs, a very dynamic field of intercultural education has developed in recent years in the realm of further and continuing education. Many nonacademic educational institutions offer a variety of program formats including workshops with practical, hands-on instruction for interested teachers of all school levels. They are part of the well-developed and institutionalized German system of continuing education that provides extended and qualified education parallel to one's professional career.

Intercultural education as a topic of continuing education has meanwhile developed its own tradition that relates only marginally to the complex discussions on the issues of culture and integration in intercultural pedagogy. It is centered around practical needs: main topics usually address knowledge about possible cultural variations in communication, learning and teaching styles, social relations, motivation, and how to apply this knowledge to real-life interactions in the classroom. The criticism of these formats of intercultural education usually concerns their insufficient rootedness in intercultural theory, and in fact they often avoid more intense theorizing for lack of time and demands

(continued)

on efficiency. Other critics emphasize the relevance of the specific German social and political environment of migration and integration and the institutional characteristics of the classroom context in view of the fact that educators tend to rely on concepts and contents taken from popular textbooks, most of which implicitly depart from the American paradigms of multiculturalism.

Intercultural education in Germany does not yet have a clear profile, nor has it become an established component of everyday classroom teaching practice nor in the training of future teachers. A special feature of intercultural education in Germany is its strong presence in programs for further education whose popularity is very much on the rise, aimed at the practical support of active teachers. The cultural diversity of Europe's population and workforce as well as global mobility will undoubtedly continue to grow, and so will the demand for interculturally qualified professionals. These future practical needs will call for new, clear, and feasible solutions for cultural problems in the classroom and for the education of German teachers to more effectively address them.

Two forms of adaptation exist: cultural adaptation and behavioral adaptation. Cultural adaptation refers to the ability to consciously shift perspective into alternative cultural worldview elements and to use multiple cultural frames of reference in evaluating phenomena. Behavioral adaptation refers to the internalization of more than one complete worldview, enabling people to shift into different frames without much conscious effort and then act in culturally appropriate ways. It is at this stage that we say that people are becoming bicultural or multicultural. A teacher at this stage, for instance, would be able to modify his or her responses to and expectations of students from lower versus middle socioeconomic groups as necessary when it comes to students' ability to participate in after-school extracurricular activities. Fellow students may understand that the needs of refugee students are quite distinct from those of international exchange students—even though they may both be from abroad—and will, in turn, respond differently to them.

But at this stage people are not simply acquiring skills. Nor are they simply regurgitating lists of dos and don'ts; this type of reaction creates emulation, not empathy. Knowledge and behavior here are linked by conscious intention, with category boundaries becoming more flexible and permeable, and intentional perspective taking and empathy being evident.

In the adaptation stage, people may say things like the following:

"To really help this student learn, I'm going to have to change my approach."

"I know they're really trying hard to adapt to my style, so it's only fair and right that I try to meet them halfway."

"I interact with my male and female colleagues somewhat differently to account for differences in the way respect is communicated."

"I can maintain my values and also behave in culturally appropriate ways."

"To solve this dispute, I need to change my behavior to account for the differences in status between me and my Arab customer."

"I interact with my Latino families from Central and South America differently to account for differences in the way respect and authority are communicated."

Integration

Integration is the final stage of the developmental model of intercultural sensitivity. Although it is rarely achieved, it reflects those individuals who have multiple frames of reference and can identify and move freely within more than one cultural group. Integration refers to the internalization of bicultural or multicultural frames of reference, with individuals at this level being able to mediate between multiple groups. They tend to maintain a definition of self-identity that is marginal to any particular culture and to see themselves as "in process," characterized by acceptance of an identity that is not based in any one culture. People at this level are able to facilitate constructive contact between cultures and tend to become cultural mediators or cultural bridges. This level is a rare and difficult one for people to achieve, and it is difficult to measure.

People at this stage may say such things as the following:

"Sometimes I don't feel like I fit anywhere."

"Everywhere is home, if you know enough about how things work there."

"I feel most comfortable when I'm bridging differences between the cultures I know."

"Whatever the situation, I can usually look at it from a variety of cultural points of view."

Understanding that intercultural development is an evolutionary and not a revolutionary process should greatly influence the manner in which we educate both children and teacher education students. Intercultural competence is not achieved in one course or one single experience. Rather, it comes about after recognizing where one is on the developmental continuum, and then engaging in systematic, oftentimes repetitious, and well-planned exposure to intercultural interactions that are designed to nudge one to increasingly complex levels. Think back to the discussion of adjustment in Chapter 4 that emphasized the rather long time required before individuals become fully adjusted to another cultural setting—and that came after full immersion in a new place. Moving too quickly along the continuum is akin to the scuba diver plunging immediately to a depth of 100 feet without taking the requisite time to equalize pressure and accommodate to the new environment—the shock can just be too great for the body to accept. Alternatively, gradual movement or immersion enables the diver to adjust to the changing circumstances and thus to function more effectively in the new environment. So, too, should it be with intercultural development. Understanding and integrating what we know about intercultural development and sensitivity into the education of young people and teachers will result in a more culturally effective and culturally competent citizenry.

Critical Incidents at Maplewood

The Case Study introduced at the beginning of the chapter ended with Sue Murray asking, "I wonder how my teaching team feels?" This chapter's Critical Incidents are perspectives from other teachers in Maplewood School. At the end of each, you will be asked to categorize the teacher's orientation according to the DMIS.

Critical Incident

I'm in "seventh heaven," you could say. I came into the teaching field after spending 2 years as a Peace Corps volunteer teaching English in Kenya. It was the best 2 years of my life. I learned to speak Kiswahili fairly well and had a chance to teach in both a secondary school and a local teachers' college. I spent weekends working with younger children in the village in which I lived. We did general maintenance around the village, started all kinds of community action projects such as building a public shower, and organized a variety of community artists to showcase the local culture.

That experience changed my life. I grew up in a community not far from where I now teach. In many ways it was quite similar to Maplewood–there were few minorities, although that has changed somewhat over time. I didn't have too many friends who were different from me–we were all pretty much the same. Not much diversity, they'd say now, although that wasn't a term we used back then. We were all just "normal," I guess you'd say.

I became interested in the Peace Corps after many years of learning about different people in general. As a little kid I remember looking at *National Geographic* magazine at my uncle's house. He was a geologist and taught at a local community college. I was interested in the pictures–the different ways people dressed, or didn't dress. I was also quite intrigued by the various ways people decorated themselves– from their jewelry to tattoos and body painting to body piercing. I guess even kids in this country today, when you think about how they pierce or tattoo their bodies, have much in common with some of the people I would read about then. But most kids probably wouldn't see the similarity.

In high school, I was active in the Exchange Student Club. I could never afford to be an exchange student myself, but I was always interested in other people. Then, I had one teacher, Mr. Philips, my 11th-grade English teacher, who had spent 2 years in Thailand as a Peace Corps volunteer. I was really intrigued by him and his experience. It was then that I began thinking about doing that myself. I applied during my student teaching semester and was accepted to the program in Kenya.

What an eye-opener that 2-year experience was for me. I changed more in that time than I ever could have imagined. I'm sure the experience had more of an influence on me than I had on those in my village, who I became really attached to, by the way. I'm now trying to arrange to have a more formal link between the village school and our school, but I haven't yet been able to raise enough money to do anything substantial.

I would like all of my students to have experiences like those that I had. But you know, it's hard to do. When I returned from Kenya, most of my family and friends weren't very interested in hearing about my experiences–they wanted me to just fit right back into how I used to be and the way they were. But I couldn't. I had changed too much. Many of the things they were interested in seemed rather unimportant to me. This created some friction between my friends and me for a while. The Peace Corps tried to warn us about this problem when we returned. They said we would experience a reverse culture shock, that coming back home would be difficult because we had changed so much and most others at home had not. Boy, were they right! I keep in closer contact with many of my old Peace Corps friends now than I do my older friends from home.

Perhaps here in the school I can do something that can make a difference in the way young people view others. That's why I'm kind of glad all this discussion about diversity is happening now. I think it's a wake-up call that, if we're not prepared for it, will bring all kinds of trouble. There is a place for us as teachers to work with young people on these issues. Not only can I share some of my experiences, but perhaps I can create experiences for the students themselves that will help to introduce them to others in their world in a more personal and substantial way. I think it's critically important that people learn how to view the world from more than one perspective, and I hope to be able to develop this ability in my students. They have to begin to understand the plight of the world's indigenous peoples, understand the experiences of the African American and Native American in this country, and show greater concern for the environment. And teaching is a great vehicle from which to do this. I'm beginning to feel most comfortable when I'm helping people see the world around them from another perspective–kind of as a bridge builder. I can now look at most situations from at least two cultures' points of view. I think young people today need this mind-set as well.

- Where on the continuum of the DMIS would you place John?
- What kinds of activities might John do with his current students that would build on his experiences in Kenya?

Critical Incident

Fran Violet, Fifth-Grade Language Arts Teacher

I'm really getting tired of all the commotion, although I won't come out and say it to too many people. I feel like an outsider at some of the teachers' meetings we've had. There seem to be two camps developing among the staff. There are those who are in favor of making changes to address the so-called needs of other groups, and others, like myself, who are rather quiet and in the background continuing to do a good job, or so we believe, just teaching kids.

I've been teaching in the district for 25 years now and have seen all kinds of educational fads come and go. I'm pretty sure this attention to culture will just do the same. After all, we only have so much time in the day to teach all that we are supposed to teach. And there's such an emphasis today on competency tests, which don't even measure multicultural education. It's probably only a matter of time until all the hoopla dies down. It even angers me when I think that I've had to attend after-school workshops on multicultural education. They really didn't teach me anything I could use. They were more of a gripe session presented by some people who had a bunch of complaints to make. Then they handed us a list of multicultural books we should have the kids read. Come on. Give me a break. Do they really expect me to become motivated by that?

And the kids! I've seen quite a few changes since I began teaching here. That's what I think the problem is. It's not about culture. Yes, it's true that there are more minority children in the school now than there were a number of years ago. But the problem, as I see it, is about kids and their families. It doesn't matter what a child's cultural background is. I look at kids pretty much the same. Sure there are some differences, like some just pick things up quicker than others do. Some are better in certain subjects than others. Some are better in sports or art or music.

But all in all, kids are basically the same. I want them all to succeed in school, and I do my best to teach them all. While people's cultures may differ, once you get down to it, kids are kids, and all people are pretty much the same. All people, after all, have the same basic needs. I have a general sense of other people; no matter what culture they are from, I can usually read them pretty well. If kids don't have a solid, stable family, then that's where there's going to be trouble. There has been such an increase in the number of children coming from broken families. Why, one year I had 20 out of 28 kids who came from some sort of rearranged family. If you ask me, that's where the problem lies.

- Where on the continuum of the DMIS would you place Fran?
- What suggestions might you make to Fran to help her advance along the DMIS continuum?

Critical Incident

Steven Goodwin, Principal

Ever since I became principal of this school 6 years ago, I have been on a continuous learning curve. I had no preparation in college for issues of diversity. It wasn't even talked about when I first went to school 25 years ago. It's kind of been "trial by fire," you might say. As our community changed and as I became more involved in school administration, I suddenly had so many new things to which I had to adjust. I had training to be a school principal at a nearby university, but most of that training focused on leadership, finances, and management from a dominant-culture perspective. My professors were from, I guess you would say, the "old school," where everything was supposed to fit one particular orientation. But I quickly learned that things are different in the real world. Ever since our community demographics began to change and people began moving from the city to our suburb, the rules have never quite been the same. And I think I'm beginning to understand it quite well—although it still requires a lot of work on my part. And I'm not sure I always get it right.

Take this recent dispute, for instance. This community has always supported the local sports teams. Even our high school mascot is an Indian, and no one had questioned it since it became part of our culture some 60 years ago. That is, until this year. And I'm beginning to understand the other side of the coin now. I guess the more time I spend with people from other groups and learn about their cultures, the more I begin to understand their point of view, their language, and their way of interacting. For so many years, all people have been forced to adapt to one mainstream point of view—like it or not! And I guess for the most part, at least for so many years, people tried pretty hard to adapt. Some might say they were forced to adapt. For many years we called it the "melting pot"; all people were to become like the majority culture. For some it worked. As I understand it, and it makes sense to me, it was fairly easy for most European immigrants to fit into the mainstream culture in the early part of the 1900s. Most of these immigrants came from similar language backgrounds—at least they were all European—and shared relatively similar ways of life. Once they learned the English language, their physical features allowed them to pretty much fit right into the mainstream. And then their foods became part of the national diet, like Italian, Polish or German influences.

Many other immigrants, however, had quite different experiences. African Americans were forced or involuntary immigrants, never wanting to be here in the first place. And today, most immigrants come from countries whose languages, ethnicity, skin color, and general way of life are significantly different–not only from the mainstream but from one another as well. This alone makes it very difficult for people to "just fit right in."

I guess I look at it this way. So many people have been struggling to adapt to our way of life for so long that it's only fair that we now try to make some changes. I guess for me that means that so many people in the schools have been trying hard to adapt to my style that it's only fair that I try to meet them halfway. To solve some of the problems we face in our school and community, I'm going to have to change my approach. I'm beginning to understand that I can maintain my own culture's values, but at the same time I can learn to behave in ways that are appropriate for another culture. Now it's getting easier for me to say that about my behavior. But I recognize that for many others in the school community, including parents as well as some of the teachers, the situation is not so clear. Many of them are threatened and are not sure how to make the changes. I'm working real hard, in addition to all the other things I have to stay on top of, to encourage this school community to face these issues and address them in positive ways. I also recognize that I will have to continue to be a role model for others to demonstrate how this diversity can be accomplished. I constantly try to learn about other people and account for cultural differences in my interactions with them and to help our school community do the same.

- Where on the continuum of the DMIS would you place Steven?
- What are some things Steven might do to encourage development among his school community, especially among the more resistant teachers and families?

Summary

Fundamental to effective multicultural education is an understanding of the manner in which people develop their racial and/or ethnic identity and, in particular, intercultural development–how they develop their ability to understand and interact more effectively with people different from themselves. The developmental model of intercultural sensitivity (DMIS) was introduced as one means to understand how people can grow from being ethnocentric to becoming more ethnorelative in their orientation.

Chapter Review

Go to the Online Learning Center at www.mhhe.com/cushner7e to review important content from the chapter, practice with key terms, take a chapter quiz, and find the Web links listed in this chapter.

Key Terms

acceptance 160	denial 155	minimization 158
adaptation 161	ethnic identity 146	racial identity 146
defense 157	integration 165	racial profiling 150

Active Exercise

Additional Active Exercises are available online at www.mhhe.com/cushner7e.

Learning About Others

Purpose: To learn about cultural differences by interviewing someone from a different culture or ethnic group while applying concepts from the culture-general framework.

Instructions: Find someone from a culture different from your own to interview (preferably someone outside your immediate and known peer group). Try to choose someone you think will have different attitudes, opinions, and experiences than you have. Choose some questions from the list that follows, or develop some of your own. Before you interview the person, answer the questions for yourself. For each of the questions, follow up with "Why?" in order to explore underlying values. Take notes of the responses. Discuss the questions and the "why" with the other person until you have found at least five major areas where there are clear differences between your answer and the other person's. Also be sure to identify five major areas where you are in agreement with one another. Prepare a short paper or presentation that summarizes your findings.

a. What people in your life are the most important to obey? Why?

b. Who makes final decisions in your life at home and school? Why?

c. Who do you think determines your fate–the individual, the family, or God? Why?

d. Whom should you respect? How do you show respect? Why?

e. Who should help determine your identity? Why?

f. What does it mean to be successful in life? Why?

g. Whom should you trust? Why?

h. What are the signs of success? Why?

i. What provides "security" in your life? Why?

j. Who should your friends be? Who decides? Why?

k. Where, and with whom, should you live? Why?

l. Whom should you marry? At about what age? Who decides? Why?

m. What is expected of children when they are young? Why?

n. What should you depend on others for? Why?

o. When should you be self-sufficient, if ever? Why?

p. What should you expose to others, and what should be kept private? Why?

q. How should you plan for your future? Why?

r. What should be remembered from your heritage? Why?

s. What was better when you were younger or during your parents' youth? Why?

t. What do you wish for your children that you could not have? Why?

1. What did you learn about the other person that is significantly different from you? How might this knowledge affect the interviewee as a learner? You as a teacher?

2. What did you learn about the other person that is similar to you? Were you surprised by this? How might this knowledge affect you as a teacher?

Reflective Questions

1. Return to the case study introduced at the beginning of the chapter. Where on the continuum of the DMIS would you place each of the individuals: Sue Murray, John Jameson, Rebecca Reynolds, and Joyce Maples? Justify your decisions.

2. Draft a brief response to each of the three who wrote letters to the editor: John Jameson, Rebecca Reynolds, and Joyce Maples. As a teacher, what would you emphasize in your response?

3. Where on the DMIS would you place yourself? What criteria are you using to make your judgment?

4. Early in the chapter it was stated that although you may identify as a member of an ethnic group but not think of yourself in racial terms, the opposite can also be true. Can you provide examples from each perspective?

5. Differentiate race from ethnicity, and provide clear examples from each category. Then, provide one or two examples where there might be confusion between these terms.

References

Banks, J. (1988). *Multiethnic education: Theory and practice* (2nd ed.). Newton, MA: Allyn & Bacon.

Bennett, M. J. (1993). Towards ethnorelativism: A developmental model of intercultural sensitivity. In M. Paige (Ed.), *Cross-cultural orientation* (pp. 27–69). Lanham, MD: University Press of America.

Brislin, R., & Yoshida, T. (1994). *Intercultural communication training: An introduction.* Thousand Oaks, CA: Sage.

Criddle, J. (1996). *To destroy you is no loss: The odyssey of a Cambodian family.* Providence, UT: East/West Bridge Publishing House.

Cross, W. E. (1991). *Shades of black: Diversity in African-American identity.* Philadelphia: Temple University Press.

Cushner, K., & Brislin, R. (1996). *Intercultural interactions: A practical guide* (2nd ed.). Thousand Oaks, CA: Sage.

Deardorff, D. (2006). Identification and assessment of intercultural competence as a student outcome of internationalization. *Journal of Studies in International Education, 10*(3), 241–266.

Erikson, E. H. (1968). *Identity, youth, and crisis.* New York: Norton.

Grant, C., & Ladson-Billings, G. (1997). *Dictionary of multicultural education.* Phoenix, AZ: Oryx.

Kohlberg, L. (1969). *Stages in the development of moral thought and action.* New York: Holt, Rinehart & Winston.

Mahon, J. (2003). *The intercultural sensitivity of practicing teachers: Life history perspectives.* Unpublished dissertation, Kent State University, Kent, Ohio.

Piaget, J. (1971). The theory of stages in cognitive development. In D. Green (Ed.), *Measurement and Piaget.* New York: McGraw-Hill.

Spring, J. (2004). *The intersection of cultures: Multicultural education in the United States and the global economy* (3rd ed.). Boston: McGraw-Hill.

Multicultural Teaching in Action

Creating Classrooms That Address Race and Ethnicity

Focus Questions

1. Do you believe all people are prejudiced? If so, in what ways do you display prejudice?

2. Did you hear messages about certain groups of people as you grew up that you no longer support? How did you come to change your beliefs or point of view?

3. How are factors of racism and prejudice evident in schools?

4. What behaviors are effective when dealing with people who hold extreme prejudices? What actions might teachers take to reduce prejudice in their students?

❝ Prejudice is a great time saver. You can form opinions without having to get the facts. ❞

E. B. WHITE

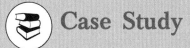

Case Study

The Chameleon

The school board meetings were generally not as heated as they were that night in October when the issue of bilingual education was brought up for discussion. More than 600 residents showed up for the meeting; so many that a new location had to be found and six police officers had been called into the auditorium as a precautionary measure. What had started a couple of weeks earlier when a few students accused some teachers and administrators of prejudice and discrimination had now developed into a districtwide debate about the purpose and success of multicultural education. The current state of affairs had certainly come a long way from the initial problem, which developed when a few Mexican American and Vietnamese students had not been chosen for the cheerleading squad. Some people were saying, in no uncertain terms, that students who were just learning to speak English could not be understood well enough to be on the cheerleading squad. One of the adults in the community was overheard to say, "If small groups of individuals had a difficult time understanding these particular students, how could a crowd of already screaming sports fans?" Over the past 2 weeks, majority students throughout the school began repeating these arguments. There had even been some fights between a group of Spanish-speaking boys and a group of African American football players.

Jane Myers, who has been teaching in this school for 7 years, had never experienced such heated debate and outright antagonism before. And to top it off, the administration seemed to be dragging its feet and not quite sure how to address the issue.

Ms. Myers located the phone number of a presenter she had seen a year earlier and arranged a time for him to come to the school and meet with the junior and senior classes. She knew that something rather dramatic, but real, had to be done to get people talking with one another. John Gray could certainly facilitate that!

John Gray arrived on the planned day with plenty of time to have a cup of coffee, meet the principal, and arrange the auditorium for his needs. He had agreed to do the program, but only if persons in positions of authority would also attend; this group included Mr. Johnson, the principal; the two assistant principals; and even two of the school board members.

Ms. Myers welcomed the more than 500 students once they settled into their seats in the auditorium. "This morning we have a speaker who will use a teaching approach known as psychodrama to help us explore issues related to prejudice and racism. Mr. John Gray is a former personnel manager with a major Fortune 500 company and holds an MBA from Harvard University. Please join me in welcoming him to our school."

John Gray approached the stage as the students applauded. He was quite distinguished looking, really the picture of a rather successful, polite, white business executive. He stood more than 6 feet tall and wore a gray business suit, white shirt, and red tie. His hair was straight and graying, and he had rather angular and prominent facial features.

He began in a pleasant manner, smiling and stating that he had not come with any kind of prepared speech. He would, instead, just share some ideas with the students and allow for some open discussion. But he did make some rather pointed comments. "I'll begin this morning by saying that if you are silent with me, I will be making three assumptions about you and the silence. One, if you are silent, that tells me that you understand everything I am saying. Two, silence tells me that you agree with whatever I am saying. And three, silence tells me that you support what I am saying. Is this clear?" He paused.

"The only way I'll know anything different is if you break the silence. You see, silence, to me, is very critical. Silence suggests inaction, and the inaction, in a sense, becomes a form of action." He waited again and took in the audience's silence. "So, you all just sent me the message that you understood what I just said, that you agreed with what I said, and you supported me by your silence."

There was some light laughter and apparent nervousness among the audience. A crucial contract had just been entered into with the group.

"Like any good teacher," Gray began, "I use three instructional approaches. You might think of these in terms of how you learn to do complex things, let's say learning to ride a bike. When

I use the lecture method, I tell you about riding. Now this approach may transfer a significant amount of useful information, but it does not provide you with the opportunity to practice the appropriate actions. Would you learn how to ride the bike? Probably not! The second approach I call the 'show-me' approach. I can demonstrate for you how to ride a bike. This approach may enable you to see what is expected, but once again, it probably will not result in you learning how to ride. There just is no opportunity to practice the skill. Now the third approach I call the 'involve-me' approach. Once you are involved, you really do begin to learn."

Gray went on to introduce the concept of prejudice and gave example after example of how people's preferences, or prejudices, can become problematic if they are extended and expected from all people. Whereas, he said, he had a prejudice toward apple pie, but he did not think that all people should have only apple pie. At the same time, other people had no right to tell him what flavor pie to consume. But if Mr. Johnson, as the principal, went around and told all the students that they could eat only apple pie in school or they would be punished, then Mr. Johnson would be combining his prejudice with his power and discriminating against a certain group of people—cherry pie eaters, for instance. Then, Gray said, we get into a thing called 'pie-ism.' That, he explained, was when people and institutions, like schools, got into conflict, and then the silence had to be broken.

Gray posed a question to students. "How many of you think you are prejudiced?" Only a few hands went up. "Well, I for one think you are all prejudiced and that you are ignoring the reality in yourself. I think it's important that we all recognize that we have certain information about other people that we have been taught that may not be accurate, but yet we continue to support."

There was silence in the room.

"So, if I go by the silence, you are all agreeing with me. See, you are all prejudiced, you just weren't willing to admit it earlier."

Suddenly a hand went up from the middle of the auditorium. Gray called on the student, and he rose to speak.

"I don't think you can get away with calling me prejudiced," said the student. "I have many black and Hispanic friends, and I'm not alone. Many others in this school have friends from different backgrounds."

"Oh, I know where you are coming from," replied Gray. "You're just showing off in front of your friends to let them know how liberal you are. You can't fool most of us—we know your kind."

The student sat down quietly. Others in the room began to fidget in their seats. A female student then jumped up to defend the boy.

"How can you say that about him, you don't even know him? I think you're being prejudiced!" she challenged.

"You may be partially correct," replied Gray, "but I also know where you're coming from. Tell me," he asked, "are you Jewish?"

"No, I am not," she answered. "And why is that important?"

"Because I am a Christian; a good Christian; and I think if Jews want to believe in a God other than Jesus Christ, they should go back to Israel where they belong."

The students grew restless and agitated.

"How can you say such a thing? What does that have to do with anything?" another girl blurted out.

"What, may I ask, do you want to be when you grow up?" asked Gray.

"A politician," she replied.

"Oh, I don't think I'd spend my time doing that if I were you," he quickly responded. "Women can never really hold positions of authority and power because they are generally much more emotional than men. And there are many studies that prove that. In fact, a recent research study undertaken at the University of California at Berkeley—you know of it, I assume—stated that without a doubt women are more prone to tears and cry more when under pressure. No one can be a successful leader when their emotions get in the way, and

(continued)

women have that problem all the time—just look at how you are acting with me. Now you wouldn't want a leader to behave like this, would you? And I know that some of you in the audience will differ with me, but that's all right. That's your choice."

A few members of the audience laughed. Two students who were close to the back got up to walk out, and Mr. Johnson approached them and quietly asked them to return to their seats.

"You know what really bothers me?" Gray continued without seeming to miss a beat, "is that affirmative action order. That order told me that I had to hire a certain number of minorities and women in my organization, and I resented that. I didn't like being forced into anything, especially having to hire people who could not do the job."

An African American male student jumped in. "What do you mean by people who couldn't do the job?"

"Well, you know," replied Gray. "Your people have trouble passing certain competency tests. Take teacher tests, for instance. Your people just can't pass those tests at the same rate that white teachers do. And you want to be teachers and teach my children? I think there's something terribly wrong with affirmative action. It's getting to the point where my children had to have a card saying they were minority or female before they could be considered for a job. That's just not right."

The students were silent.

"So I felt that I had to break the silence and fight back. I thought that if I could reach young people like yourselves in schools—because you are our future—I want to encourage you to speak out. Young man, may I ask you where you are from?"

"I'm from Africa. Nigeria to be exact. I was not born as an African American, although my family is working on getting our American citizenship."

"Well, let me suggest something to you. You're in a good school. When you learn to speak like a good American, then I can look to you as a good American who can understand what I'm trying to say. Why don't you solve the problems that you have in Africa before coming here and getting so upset with me? I see why your school is having such a debate about bilingual education. How many of you speak English as your first language, might I ask?"

The students—boy and girls, whites and blacks, Latinos and Asians—as well as teachers and administrators sat silently as most of the hands went up.

"And what is this school doing to promote diversity?" Gray asked.

Mr. Johnson jumped in. "Mr. Gray, I did promise you academic freedom. But please try to keep your comments from being personal in nature. Students, if you have questions to ask of Mr. Gray, you can do that now. You don't have to wait for a question-and-answer period, but do ask one at a time."

"Well, I think that as a group you're showing disrespect for me," Gray continued, directing his comments toward Mr. Johnson. "Maybe I'm wasting my time with you. I really resent the way I've been treated. I don't know if you planted people in the audience to attack me, but I resent the laughter I've heard as well as some of the putdowns from those of you who may have a view that differs from mine. I've got better things to do than to stay here with you. No wonder you're having all these troubles about bilingual education in your school. I really resent the way I've been treated."

And with that, John Gray picked up his materials and walked off the stage. The students applauded as he left.

After Gray left the stage, Mr. Johnson approached the microphone. "I guess the lecture is over, and by the sounds of it, there are many people who have many things they'd like to say. I suggest we go back to our homeroom classes for a while and discuss what we have all just experienced. Then we can all come back together and meet here in the auditorium right after lunch."

Note This case study concludes with some very important additional information contained in the critical incidents at the end of the chapter. It is based on the video program *Chameleon* by John Gray and Associates; and on a section from the book *A Country of Strangers: Blacks and Whites in America,* by David K. Shipler (New York: Vintage Books, 1997).

Lay Versus Scientific Understanding of Race and Ethnicity

This chapter's Case Study vividly illustrates issues of racism and prejudice in action. It also provides a context in which to apply some of the 18 culture-general themes introduced in Chapter 4. For instance, what attributions do you think the students were making about John Gray? What judgments were you making about John Gray as you read the Case Study? How would you react in the presence of someone like him?

Pedagogies: Old and New

Teachers and school administrators who understand the deep-seated influence that race and ethnicity play in people's lives do not shy away from confronting these issues. On the contrary, they understand the historical significance and current state of affairs that this sensitive and controversial experience assumes in people's lives, and they believe they have an obligation to address these issues in their teaching. Such teachers understand the role that race plays, both in the lives of individuals and in society at large. Such teachers, especially those working primarily with children from the majority culture, understand that their students may be quite unaware of the impact that race can have on others' as well as their own lives. These teachers provide significant guidance, support, and structure to classroom and school environments that encourage new interactions and opportunities to openly discuss and learn about race and ethnicity. And increasingly, there are a number of school programs and curriculum guides that have proven effective at improving relations between individuals and groups (see Stephan & Vogt, 2004, for a review of many of these).

Roles: Old and New

In classrooms that actively address issues related to race and ethnicity, teachers understand their role as active agents of change and they are not afraid to openly discuss race and racism, thus making it an important topic for conversation. They reach out to individuals as well as to community organizations that represent various ethnic and racial groups' perspectives and experiences. Such an approach provides for authentic voices while building necessary bridges between young people and the community. Not only are children exposed to alternative perspectives, they also interact with community representatives who are actively working to change the status quo. Such activity models for young people the desired outcomes of an effective multicultural curriculum, principally the skills and attitudes needed to become proactive agents of change. And these approaches get young people engaged in change efforts that affect their own school.

Place of Content Knowledge: Old and New

In recent years, race, like ethnicity, has been viewed less as a biological reality and more as a cultural construct, both of which are functions of the categorization process (Kottack & Kozaitis, 1999). Americans categorize things in numerous ways, and the use of the term *race* is no exception. People may categorize themselves, or be categorized by others, according to such factors as language, religion, geography, history, ancestry, or physical traits. Think back to the range of socializing agents discussed in Chapter 3. When people assume that an ethnic group has a biological basis, they are referring to that group as a race. But there is increasing evidence that race has no biological basis. For instance, Hispanics or Latinos, referred to by some people as the Hispanic race, are quite a diverse group, with members tracing their heritage from Central and Latin America, the Caribbean, and Spain. Hispanics, or Latinos, are an example of a linguistically based ethnic group (Spanish speaking), not a biologically based race. Thus, not only is the term *race* used rather loosely, but it is also often used incorrectly.

The concept of race is intended to reflect the shared genetic material, or **genotype,** within a group of people. Most people, however, scholars included, tend to use **phenotype** traits, visible traits such as skin color, to classify people according to a given race. There are many problems with using the phenotypic approach to race. For one, cultures vary in the importance given to a particular trait, and there is no agreement on which phenotypic characteristics should be emphasized. Skin color, the most apparent difference to early scientists, thus became the criterion most often used. Arbitrary cultural value was attached to skin color, which subsequently became the basis for discrimination.

It is not uncommon to still find textbooks that present the three great races as distinct from one another—white, black, and yellow. This rather simplistic and inaccurate categorization scheme used race as a power mechanism by keeping white European colonizers separate from their Asian and African subjects. Attempts to make these groupings sound more scientific—by using such terms as *Caucasoid, Mongoloid,* and *Negroid*—cloud the reality that white people are really various shades of pink, beige, or tan, black people are various shades of brown, and so-called yellow people are really various shades of tan or beige. Another problem with such a categorization occurs with such groups as Polynesians, Native Americans, and Australian Aborigines. And then there is the phenomenon of racial mixing, accelerated by European expansion, that occurred on a global scale as people, labor, and goods were increasingly exchanged between nation-states. No such clear-cut categorization of people based on skin color is sound.

Race as a cultural construct, however, is quite alive. But again, cultures vary in the manner in which race is construed. In the United States racial identity is acquired at birth as an ascribed status, not based on simple biology or ancestry. Consider the child of a racially mixed couple involving one African American and one European American parent. It is obvious that half the child's genetic material comes from each parent. However, American culture classifies the child as black, although it makes just as much sense to classify the child as white. In such a case, heredity is being overlooked. And to confound the situation even more, racial categorization can vary from state to state. For instance, in some states, any person known to have any African American blood in his or her heritage will be classified as black. Such a situation is referred to as **hypodescent** (where *hypo* means "lower") because it automatically places the child in the minority group (Kottack & Kozaitis, 1999).

A case from Louisiana vividly illustrates the role that the government can play in legalizing or inventing racial classification. Susie Guillory Phipps, a light-skinned woman with European facial features and straight black hair, discovered that she was black only when she was an adult. When she ordered a copy of her birth certificate, she found that her race was listed as "colored." She had, however, been brought up white and was twice married to white men. Phipps challenged a 1970 Louisiana law that classified as legally black anyone with at least one–thirty-second "Negro blood." The state insisted that her racial classification was correct even though the state's lawyer admitted that Phipps looked like a white person (Yetman, 1991).

Assessment: Old and New

Assessment across cultural, racial, and ethnic boundaries has historically been a sensitive issue. The traditional cross-cultural research literature is filled with numerous studies that report the unfortunate but common practice of taking an assessment instrument developed and normed on one culture and using it with little or no modification in another cultural setting. Such use more often than not results in inaccurate judgments of people because (1) certain concepts that are important in one culture may be missed by some assessment instruments; (2) procedures developed in one country or culture may not be appropriate; or (3) it may be assumed that all people share in certain experiences that are not, in fact, universally practiced. Assessment that is sensitive to the role of race, ethnicity, and culture considers the sociocultural context of the learner and the learner's family as well as that of the examiner, and addresses such issues as biases, stereotypes, and prior experience as well as the selection of appropriate testing instruments or interview procedures. Awareness of such issues enhances the possibility of more relevant and culturally sensitive assessments. In addition, issues related to language and its complexities must also be considered when selecting and conducting assessments. The teacher who is sensitive to racial and ethnic concerns also struggles to understand that people display strengths and talents in many different ways.

Bias in Testing

Understanding Prejudice and Racism

Discussions of categorization and stereotyping (see Chapter 4) inevitably lead into a discussion of issues surrounding prejudice and discrimination. People have a tendency to surround themselves with others who provide social acceptance and help in time of need. As a result, people spend a considerable amount of time and energy learning the norms of the groups to which they wish to belong. One consequence of this is that individuals begin to think that the familiar behaviors of their group are good and natural and that those of others are less good and less natural. Recall that *ethnocentrism* refers to the tendency people have to make judgments based on their own standards and to apply those standards to others. When people make nonreflective judgments about others, these judgments are called *prejudicial*. The word **prejudice** implies a lack of thought or care in making a judgment (or attribution); prejudicial responses are quick, narrow in scope, and based, oftentimes, on negative emotions rather than accurate information. Prejudice appears to be a cultural universal; that is, people around the world tend to behave in similar ways toward certain other groups.

Although racial and ethnic prejudice can be expressed in both positive and negative ways, in the United States it has primarily negative connotations.

Prejudice is often defined as a dislike based on a faulty and inflexible generalization that can be directed toward a group as a whole or toward an individual simply because she or he is a member of that group (Allport, 1979). The fact that prejudicial beliefs are rooted in inflexible generalizations means that educators will meet with great resistance to their efforts at change.

The Functions of Prejudice

It is easy to judge others' prejudices (and even our own) rather harshly, but it is equally important to understand that if prejudice did not have a psychological function it would quickly disappear. Just as fear encourages people to prepare for danger and pain makes people aware of some problem, prejudice also serves an adaptive purpose.

Among the early researchers studying prejudice, Katz (1960) suggested that prejudice serves at least four functions: adjustment function, ego-defensive function, value expressive function, and knowledge function.

Adjustment Function

People need to adjust to the complex world in which they live, and if holding certain prejudicial attitudes aids that adjustment, they will be maintained. For instance, a teacher who believes that members of certain minority groups or people with disabilities are incapable of achieving at a high level then has an excuse for not finding alternative methods of reaching them. This attitude reduces the work-related responsibilities of the teacher, making life a bit easier for the teacher. However, it obviously prevents these students from achieving their full potential.

Ego-Defensive Function

People may hold certain prejudicial attitudes to protect their own self-concept. If less successful students want to think of themselves as on equal terms with higher achieving students, they may be inclined to view the comparison group as cheaters. Holding this attitude protects the self-image of these individuals without any painful self-examination of the reasons for their own lack of success. The ego-defensive function also protects a positive view of one's ingroup. Rejection of others then becomes a way of legitimizing one's own viewpoint as well as a way of avoiding the possibility that others may have an equally legitimate point of view. This is similar to the level of "defense" on the developmental model of intercultural sensitivity (Bennett, 1993) discussed in Chapter 5.

Value-Expressive Function

People use prejudicial attitudes to demonstrate their own self-image to others. If people believe they are custodians of the truth about the role of education, for instance, or that the god of their religion is the one true god, then other groups must be incorrect in their thinking. If one's group has attained success through the use of highly valued technology, then those who do not have this technology must be backward. The value-expressive function presents a certain image to the world whereas the ego-defensive function protects that image by blaming others when things go wrong.

Knowledge Function

Some prejudicial attitudes make the stereotypical knowledge of one's ingroup the basis of one's personal judgments and actions. Our interactions with others, for instance, may be directly dependent upon the internal images and messages we carry in our minds. Thus, if a teacher believes that a certain group of people are inferior or have inherent deficiencies, that teacher's interaction with students will reflect his or her beliefs. Holding these attitudes allows individuals to make quick (usually negative) decisions when faced with choices involving individuals from the outgroup. There is often a close relationship between the knowledge and adjustment functions. The former has to do with the information that one's ingroup believes is important, the latter with how people use that information in making decisions.

Such behaviors may have a profound impact on the relationships and interactions children have with their teachers, significantly impacting educational achievement. Interviews of Maori children in New Zealand, for instance, report time and again that negative, deficient beliefs and behaviors on the part of teachers were central to developing negative relations and avoidance behavior of students (Bishop and Berryman, 2006).

Prejudice Formation: The Components of Prejudice

Three components of prejudice are generally identified: cognitive, affective, and behavioral. The *cognitive component* refers to the need people have to simplify the world around them, considered as the process of categorization discussed in Chapter 4. Recall that stereotypes are merely categories of people, and narrowly constructed categories may result in negative stereotypes. The *affective component* refers to the feelings that accompany a person's thoughts about members of a particular group. The affect attached to any statement can, of course, be positive or negative. This is the component most often thought of when people think of prejudice. The *behavioral component* is the discriminatory behavior that people who harbor prejudices are capable of directing toward others, especially when the same person possesses both prejudice and power. Power differentials are often evident between differing racial and ethnic individuals and groups.

Educators can work with each of these components in different ways. In Chapter 4 we learned that the categorization process is a cultural universal that helps all people simplify the multitude of stimuli they confront each day. As educators, we must recognize this fact, make a point of informing others about it, and work to broaden our students' (and our own) categories. One long-term goal of both multicultural and global education is for individuals to become broader, more complex thinkers. That is, as educators we should strive to help people develop the ability to perceive and evaluate situations from a number of perspectives, not just their comfortable, native orientation. In addition to this cognitive dimension, the affective and behavioral components are also under the control of educators. Strategies and programs that have successfully reduced negative affect and behavior toward others will be discussed in the following sections.

How Children Learn Prejudice

We have known since the 1940s that children seem to be aware of their own racial or ethnic background from about age 3 or 4, and tend to have prowhite/antiblack bias as well (Augoustinos & Rosewarne, 2001; Clark & Clark, 1947; Katz, 1983). It is in the early childhood and elementary school years that children's attitudes toward members of other groups are being formed and crystallized. Thus, a critical role of schooling should be to provide positive experiences that cause children to rethink their beliefs about group differences. On their own, children are unlikely to engage in reevaluation.

The literature on prejudice formation in children identifies a number of ways in which children may learn to be prejudiced: observation, group membership, the media, and religious fundamentalism (Byrnes, 1988; Hofheimer-Bettman & Friedman, 2004; Ponterotto & Pedersen, 1993).

Observation and Passive Learning

Children learn negative prejudice by observing the behavior of others, particularly respected elders. If those who surround a child display racist, sexist, homophobic, anti-Semitic, or other negative attitudes, children may be inclined to follow suit. Although children often learn much unconsciously from the subtle messages given by others, some learn prejudice from more blatant efforts by parents and community. This learning typically occurs unconsciously and early in one's life, thus making the unlearning of such beliefs a tremendous challenge.

In a similar manner, school also plays a powerful role in the lives of children. Aspects of school culture can inadvertently promote and reinforce negative racial prejudice by having relatively homogeneous administrators, staff, and student body; a curriculum that emphasizes the perspectives and experiences of the dominant culture; and a learning environment that stresses one value system.

Group Membership

Children, like other individuals, want to feel that they belong to a group. If the group that the child identifies with excludes or devalues certain others, the child is likely to adopt that behavior and those attitudes. Thus children may learn prejudice simply as a survival technique, as a way to fit into a group. Some children, for instance, are actively prepared from a very early age for adult roles in various religious cults or in secular organizations like the Ku Klux Klan.

The Media

Exposure to media is another way in which children learn prejudice. Although the media may not actively teach prejudice, it sometimes reinforces stereotypes or in some cases introduces stereotypes where they may not already exist. Portraying minority group members in stereotypic or negative roles, or being invisible, especially in positions of leadership and authority, are examples of how media influence children's thinking. Cowboy and Indian films, for instance, have had a significant impact on children's views of Native Americans (Cortes, 2000).

Both electronic and print media, through children's stories, often equate beauty with goodness and ugliness with evil. The symbolic association with evil of physical disabilities such as hunchbacks, peg legs, eye patches, and hooked arms have been shown to encourage a negative attitude toward disabilities (Bicklin & Bailey, 1981).

Religious Fundamentalism

The more orthodox or fundamental a person's religious beliefs are, the greater the prejudice toward other religious and cultural groups is likely to be. People's strict adherence to certain religious practices may actively encourage them to believe that all other doctrines, as well as the individuals who believe in them, are at best "wrong" and at worst dangerous.

Extreme Cases of Prejudice

Racism

The term *racism,* as already discussed, refers to the transformation of negative race or ethnic prejudice through the use of power and directed toward individuals or groups thought of as inferior. Although overt racism, as displayed by John Gray in the case study, seems to have declined over the years, more subtle forms continue to thrive (Ponterotto & Pedersen, 1993). It is important to understand that both individuals and institutions can display racism. *Individual racism* is evident when a person who harbors negative prejudice discriminates against another individual. *Institutional racism* reflects intentional or unintentional institutional policies that unfairly restrict the opportunities of specific groups. Policies or practices that make it difficult for certain groups to participate in certain activities, for example, by charging fees for services that are out of the range of some groups, are examples of institutional racism.

Hate Groups

The *Dictionary of Multicultural Education* defines hate groups as any organized body that denigrates select groups of people based on their ethnicity, race, or sexual orientation or that advocates the use of violence against such groups or their members for purposes of scapegoating (Grant & Ladson-Billings, 1997). The term, as used in the United States, is generally applied to white supremacist groups such as the Ku Klux Klan, the White Aryan Resistance, and the Church of Jesus Christ Christians/Aryan Nations. Local chapters of hate groups tend to target racial or ethnic minorities in their immediate area, but all of the groups are antiblack and anti-Semitic.

Hate Groups

It is difficult to obtain accurate figures on the number of hate groups or individual membership in such groups, but estimates suggest that more than 900 groups, representing some 20,000 to 200,000 members, existed in the United States alone in 2008, an increase attributed to Barak Obama's White House win (SPLC, 2008). Some of these groups limit their activities to producing and distributing literature, actions that would be most typically observed in schools; others are known to commit acts of violence, including vandalism, intimidation, assault, and murder.

Privilege: The Invisible
Knapsack

White Privilege Peggy McIntosh

People can in many ways unknowingly contribute to the existence of prejudice. A particular situation, referred to as *white privilege,* exists when white people, who may have been taught that racism is something that puts others at a disadvantage, are not taught to see the corresponding advantage that their color brings to them.

Peggy McIntosh (1992) referred to white privilege as "an invisible package of unlearned assets that I can count on cashing in each day, but about which I was meant to remain oblivious. White privilege is like an invisible weightless knapsack of special provisions, maps, passports, codebooks, visas, clothes, tools, and blank checks" (p. 33).

White privilege, like its counterpart male privilege, remains largely unconscious for most perpetrators and may lead to white racism (Sleeter, 1994). This may be due to a number of factors such as that whites have traditionally been in the majority, have accumulated greater power and wealth on the backs of others, and control much of the nation's resources and media, making it possible to insulate themselves from the plight and rage of others. And as Sleeter (1994) contends, this is perpetuated by having tacit agreement among whites to continue to reap the benefits of the past, and not to talk about it except in ways that continue to present current race relations as legitimate. In addition, at the individual level, people generally do not recognize their own behavior and how it may oppress others. Rather, people typically attribute success and status to personal traits rather than situational factors (recall the fundamental attribution error discussed in Chapter 4), believing that they have "earned" or otherwise are worthy of what they have acquired.

McIntosh identifies numerous instances where whites in general are at an advantage over people of color. For instance, most whites can arrange to be in the company of people of their own race most of the time, can find a home in an area they can afford and in which they would want to live, can go shopping alone most of the time without being followed or harassed, will find examples of their own race as the foundation of the school curriculum, and will not be asked to represent their entire race whenever the issue of race or ethnicity is broached. In what ways can you see that you or others around you may have been privileged?

Racial Profiling

Although there is no single, universally accepted definition of racial profiling, it generally refers to the law enforcement practice of targeting someone for investigation while passing through some public space (public highways, airports, etc.) where the reason for the stop is a statistical profile of the detainee's race, ethnicity, or national origin (especially prevalent in times of national crises and war). In such instances, race may be used to determine which drivers to stop for minor traffic violations (sometimes referred to as "driving while black"), which motorists or pedestrians to search for contraband, and more recently, which travelers to single out for more extensive security clearance before boarding an airplane.

Racial profiling has increased in frequency in the United States in recent years, both for traditional domestic groups, such as African Americans, and among more recent immigrants, such as Arab Americans. Despite the civil rights victories of 30 years ago, official racial prejudice is still reflected throughout law enforcement practices as well as the criminal justice system. Although some observers claim that racial profiling doesn't exist, there is an abundance of stories and statistics that document the practice.

Strategies for Prejudice Reduction

It is in schools, perhaps more than in any other social setting, where people have intimate and regular interactions with a wide diversity of people. But it is not safe to assume that just because people are in close proximity to those different from themselves that positive outcomes and cross-group friendships necessarily develop. Close analysis of many school desegregation studies has demonstrated some rather surprising and counterintuitive effects. For one, greater diversity does not necessarily lead to an increase in cross-racial friendships, either in the short term nor long term. The opposite, in fact, can be the case. Moody (2001), for instance, found that the more diverse the school, the greater the tendency of students to self-segregate into ingroups based on race and ethnicity.

Some of this may be attributed to a U. S. emphasis on individuality as opposed to a collective orientation (Bronson and Merryman, 2009). Americans, in general, define their ingroup preferences according to their individual likes and dislikes. Thus, individuals learn to see differences and then form subgroups based on their individual likes and similarity to others (e.g., they join organized sport and recreation groups with others like themselves). Although singular, individual identity is a long-term goal for many U.S. citizens, it is ultimately achieved by joining many distinct subgroups—especially in the high school years. On the contrary, in a highly collectivist culture like Japan that values and seeks social harmony over individualism, young people are discouraged from seeking individual preferences. In a rather ironic way, it seems that the more the culture emphasizes individuality, the greater tendency to form subgroups we are likely to see in school as young people search to find their own identity.

It is thus essential that educators at all levels take the opportunity to become proactive in understanding and improving intergroup relations. This should take place on two levels—through teacher (and parent) talk as well as through formal curriculum efforts.

Parent and Teacher Talk

In their book, *Nurture Shock: New Thinking about Children,* Bronson and Merryman (2009) point out some other surprising research that challenges the assumptions many parents and educators have made about behavior and its impact on racial attitudes of young people. Many parents and teachers, for instance, assume that children will only see and be interested in race when it is pointed out to them, and thus go to great lengths to ignore the concept. A number of studies report a high percentage of parents who are uncomfortable talking about the topic of race in any meaningful manner. A 2007 study of 17,000 families with children in kindergarten (Brown et al., 2007), for instance, reported that 75% of European American parents and 45% of African American parents never, or almost never, discussed issues of race with their children. But racial differences, as gender, *are* evident to children. If the topic is not discussed openly and intelligently, children are then left to their own devices to make meaning,

or to the influence of others (e.g., peers, the media), that may result in misinformation, or worse, racist notions. As discussed above, U.S. children and young people rather spontaneously develop ingroup preferences, often based on similarity of appearance such as skin color (Bigler, 1999). This preference then extends to a belief that those who look like me are similar in other aspects as well—and the things I do not like belong to those who look dissimilar.

Teachers and parents may assume they are creating a color-blind environment for children when they avoid discussing issues of difference related to race (or other categories for that matter). Recall the concept of minimization discussed in Chapter 5. People find this a comfortable place to be, saying such things as, "I don't see differences, I just see children," or, "I treat everyone alike." It is, thus, essential that parents and teachers not only develop a knowledge base about issues related to race and racism, but a comfort level as well so they can lead or enter such conversations on a regular basis with ease.

**Prejudice and
Prejudice Reduction**

Curriculum Transformation

Critical to reducing prejudice and establishing an interculturally sensitive classroom is the teacher's understanding of, and ability to integrate, intercultural awareness and prejudice reduction activities into the curriculum. We are fortunate that the educational research literature supports our efforts to reduce prejudice. Indeed, there is some indication that if we are proactive and mindful, we may even be able to decrease the likelihood that prejudiced attitudes will develop (Byrnes, 1988).

Educational strategies that have demonstrated the ability to reduce prejudice generally fall into four categories: (1) improving social contact and intergroup relations, (2) increasing cognitive sophistication, (3) improving self-esteem, and (4) increasing empathy and understanding of other groups. These categories all have curricular implications, which are discussed in the following sections.

1. Improving Social Contact and Intergroup Relations

From a programmatic standpoint, the most promising of all change efforts stems from the work of researchers interested in intergroup interaction. Allport (1954), in proposing the contact hypothesis, suggested that one way to reduce negative prejudice is to bring representatives of different groups into close contact with one another. Sometimes this method proves helpful, but not always; occasionally, negative prejudice is reinforced or, in fact, formed where it did not previously exist.

A different hypothesis suggests that it is the conditions under which groups come together that are critical. Certain characteristics of the contact situation are required to ensure positive outcomes. Considerable efforts under many different circumstances (bilingual classrooms, integrated housing and schools, summer camp programs) have led to recommendations concerning the best conditions under which social contact can be improved. These conditions relate to equal status, superordinate goals, encouragement, and personal familiarity.

Equal Status Contact

Amir (1969), working in integrated school settings in Israel, found that if individuals coming together perceive that they have equal status, or equal access to any rewards available, conditions are set for improved relations. In Switzerland, for instance, French, German, and Italian are all recognized as official languages of the country, with all documents made available in all three languages. Speakers of diverse languages, therefore, are all appreciated, well informed, and provided with the tools that enable them to participate in the society at large. This seems to be completely the opposite of the current movement under way in many states in the United States to make English the official language, even though this country boasts the fifth largest Spanish-speaking population in the world.

In the school context, equal access to rewards can be understood to mean equal access to knowledge, grades, or extracurricular offerings. For all students to have equal access to knowledge and grades, culturally relevant and responsive teaching through appropriate curricula and instructional strategies must be employed (Gay, 2000; Ladson-Billings, 1995). Culturally relevant or responsive teaching reflects a wide range of practices that places culture at the core of teaching and learning. This involves many of the elements explored throughout this book, including such things as acknowledging the cultural heritage of various ethnic groups; building bridges between home, community, and school; employing a range of instructional strategies that are responsive to varying student learning styles; and integrating diverse content and resources into all subject areas.

Enabling all students to gain all the benefits schools have to offer includes encouraging their participation in extracurricular offerings, which may not occur in the "natural" course of events. Social class status, for instance, has a significant impact on the kinds of school experiences in which a child may participate. Children from lower socioeconomic groups tend to participate in fewer after-school activities than do their middle-class counterparts, and thus may not reap the potential benefits of such participation. For example, the development of skills related to group and team thinking and acting that have been shown to be associated with successful managerial or other higher level employment are often learned through extracurricular activities rather than in formal classrooms (Brislin, 1993). Likewise, developing the ability to engage in a wide array of interpersonal interactions is greatly enhanced through participation in the non-formal side of the curriculum. Legislation regarding equal rights for disabled persons is also intended to bring equal access to children with disabilities, as is Title IX of the Education Amendment that is designed to eliminate discrimination based on gender.

Superordinate Goals

Achieving equal status contact in and of itself, however, is not sufficient. Individuals who come together and work toward achieving some superordinate goal or common task that could not be satisfied without the participation of all involved are more likely to learn to get along. This concept stems from the work of Sherif (1958), who found that although it was relatively easy to create hostility and aggression between two groups of boys at summer camp, it was far more difficult to bring them back together again as one larger, cooperative group. He was finally able to bring both groups back together by staging an incident in which a bus got stuck in the mud while on the way to a camp outing. For the bus to continue on its way, and for the young people to continue on to their outing, they all had to work together to push the bus back onto the road. This superordinate goal, which could not have been achieved without everyone's participation, required all the campers to work together for overall success.

In the school context, superordinate goals are readily available in the form of team sports, drama productions, and music performances and through cooperative learning activities that can be easily integrated in the classroom setting. When students with disabilities participate in the mainstream of school life (extracurricular as well as academic activities), such co-participation with nondisabled peers in pursuit of common goals is possible. Similarly, students who have opportunities to work with others across racial and ethnic boundaries in activities like sports, plays, and concerts tend to develop more positive attitudes toward one another. Educators who work in schools that are more homogenous will need to put more effort and imagination into planning activities that involve diverse groups. Such activities may teach students to "see" invisible differences, such as differences in learning style, differences in religious attitudes, or differences in knowledge and perceptions related to gender roles. Activities might also involve cooperative efforts with other communities and schools or efforts to encourage the implementation of international exchange student programs on a regular basis. Educators could encourage integrated activities between students with disabilities and without disabilities, across traditional age barriers, between high school and elementary school students, or between older people in the community and students of all ages.

Encouragement of Intergroup Interaction

To be effective, efforts to reduce prejudice must be seen as important at all levels of the school–from the classroom to the lunchroom to central administration. Such efforts cannot be seen entirely as the whim or "cause" of an individual teacher or particular group. Teachers, school administrators, and as many other adults as possible must actively encourage and show support for such efforts. Do not interpret this caveat, however, to mean that an individual teacher cannot initiate such changes. Innumerable teachers acting independently or with a small group of colleagues have demonstrated that the initial efforts of a single individual can have broad effects, especially in curricular decisions. Although the school system controls much of a teacher's ability to make significant and permanent change partly in the way it controls available resources, it by no means controls everything. Indeed, many, if not most, school systems today are eager and willing to support a teacher who is trying something new in the way of curricular revision. Careful documentation of the revision process and its results are needed to institutionalize the changes that are effective and to refine the teacher's initial work.

Personal Familiarity

A high acquaintance potential must exist during intergroup contact situations, encouraging close contact between individuals in a given situation. In other words, people must have the opportunity to get to know the "other" person in ways that render the stereotypic image clearly inappropriate. It is very difficult, for instance, for a student to believe that all people on welfare are lazy when that student knows firsthand that Susan and her mother are both working as much as they are allowed to within the welfare rules and that if Susan's mother took an available job that did not include health benefits, she would lose the health card she is using to treat Susan's chronic asthma.

Informal activity, perhaps even structured into the day or on weekends, must occur. Students can be placed in different heterogeneous groups for a variety of purposes, or they can be encouraged (or required) to participate in mixed team sports–any situation that will enable them to get to know others on a personal basis.

Some Cautions in Applying the Contact Hypothesis

Although application of the contact hypothesis generally proves beneficial, applying it in the real world of school settings has always been problematic due to a variety of factors. Many schools, for example, are relatively monocultural and appear to be homogeneous, providing little opportunity for intergroup contact to occur. In such situations it might be best to stress the diversity that is evident within a group, such as socioeconomic, religious, or gender differences.

But even when cultural, ethnic, racial, and socioeconomic diversity is evident in the school, other factors often mediate against regular, meaningful intergroup interaction. Problematic issues of applying the contact hypothesis in schools may center on the criterion of equal status contact. Although equal status contact provides much of the foundational structure that underlies many group activities in the classroom, including cooperative learning strategies, it may be difficult to bring this about in the somewhat artificial setting of the school primarily because groups do not have equal status outside the school. Students do not leave their social status at home when they come to school. Social contact efforts, therefore, may lead to increased stereotyping among groups.

Some schools continue to experience patterns of racial and ethnic segregation, often as a result of segregated housing patterns, which reduces the possibility of intergroup contact, certainly out of school. And in many instances, integrated schools may end up resegregating themselves through the practice of ability or achievement tracking. Grouping students by academic ability has long been, and continues to be, practiced in many schools and may result in the unintended segregation of students by ethnicity or race (Stephan, 1999). Tracking, or segregation by group, may relegate a disproportionate number of low-income students and students of color to lower-tracked classes in which they receive inferior education, thus perpetuating the problem. Tracking can occur for a variety of reasons and in many different contexts, not only by achievement nor only in the classroom; tracking also may occur as a result of participation in extracurricular activities, on the playground, or in the lunchroom.

Schools, too, may be segregated simply by the neighborhoods that they serve. Another problem with the equal status concept is that it may not generalize beyond the immediate context in which an intervention occurs. That is, while intergroup relations may appear to improve among individuals who come into contact in the school setting, such attitude change may not transfer to other contexts. Equal status between two groups may not generalize to other outgroups or when status is not equal, as in a community context.

Community level factors may also play a role. Blau, Lamb, Stearns, and Pellerin (2001) looked at the relationship between equal-status contact in neighborhoods and subsequent achievement in school. They found that all students, regardless of their race, achieved at lower levels in their social studies courses when they lived in homogeneous communities in which race and socioeconomic status were closely related. That is, neighborhoods that were homogeneous with regard to race and class did not provide a favorable context for the challenges of learning about key social science concepts such as social differentiation.

2. Increasing Cognitive Sophistication

Strategies designed to increase cognitive sophistication or complexity have been shown to have a positive impact on prejudice reduction (Hofheimer-Bettmann & Friedman, 2004). Cognitive complexity refers to the degree to which an individual differentiates or makes distinctions between discrete aspects of an event, and/or makes connections or relationships among these elements. Persons high in cognitive complexity are able to analyze or differentiate a situation into many constituent elements, and then explore connections and potential relationships among those elements. Complex people tend to be more open to new information and to form more accurate impressions of others than less complex persons. People of high complexity are attracted to a broader variety of people, are more flexible in their thinking, use fewer stereotypes, tend to search for more information when faced with a decision, tend to be more creative, and are less influenced by the persuasive communication of others (Streufert & Swezey, 1986).

A considerable amount of research points to the fact that individuals who think in narrow terms are more likely to have a high degree of prejudice. Strategies that are designed to help individuals avoid stereotypes and overgeneralizations and become aware of the biases in their thinking and behavior do help them become less prejudiced. This research suggests that we will see positive change

Activity 31:
Determining Bias in Textbooks

in this dimension when we focus our teaching efforts on improving students' critical thinking skills. Thinking in a critical manner is antithetical to prejudicial thinking. Rather than reacting quickly because of an emotional response, students must search for and examine the reasons or motivations behind their thoughts and actions. People who think critically tend to question, analyze, and suspend judgment until all available information is collected and examined.

Teachers should work hard to create the kind of classroom environment that encourages critical thought. In such classrooms, students feel respected and have a certain degree of trust. Students cannot function at higher levels of cognitive activity when their anxiety level is high. Feelings of safety and trust are thus a corollary of student risk taking. Recall the role that the culture-general themes of anxiety, belonging, and status play in people's sense of emotional stability.

The classroom should also reflect, as Lipman (1980) stated, a "community of inquiry," or as described later in this book, a "learning community." Such an environment is characterized by questions of all kinds—those for which there are "right" answers and those that have more than one right answer. Indeed, some educators feel that to prepare students for the real world outside school, teachers' questions must force students to consider all sides of the problem, some of which may, in fact, be conflicting.

A balance should be maintained between teacher talk and student talk. Students must believe that their ideas are important and that what they have to say is critical. It is through discussion with others and through the sharing of ideas and problems that critical thinking develops. Within the context of a safe, open classroom discussion, all students should be allowed to participate and to feel that their participation was successful. Students should be taught to think about their thinking and should be able to justify their reasoning with evidence. An emphasis should be on *metacognition,* or becoming aware of how one has come to a decision. Students who are aware of how they arrive at defensible positions are on their way to becoming independent, self-regulated learners.

To think critically means to think broadly, to take all sides of a problem into account, and to weigh the resulting evidence. In short, to think critically is to avoid simplistic approaches. Too often, students are encouraged to "learn what is in the book," which frequently means to avoid "thinking" altogether. Teachers who create an environment in which risk taking is encouraged, in which cooperation in problem solving is stressed, and in which mistakes are not perceived as sins or personal faults are more likely to engender achievement in students. In such classrooms, an emphasis on thinking skills is not seen as an addition to an already overcrowded school day. It does not require a special course or time of day. Rather, critical thinking is a goal that permeates each and every lesson and all teacher–student contact.

3. Improving Self-Confidence and Self-Acceptance

Pettigrew (1981) established a clear inverse relationship between the degree of prejudice a person harbors and the individual's sense of self-worth. That is, the more confident a person is in his or her own sense of identity and competence, the lower is that person's degree of prejudice, and vice versa. Although the relationship is not necessarily cause and effect, there are strong indications that self-acceptance is critical to mental, physical, and emotional health. Children with high self-esteem tend to be open and respectful of other people and maintain their sense of self without having to denigrate others.

Classroom activities designed to increase self-confidence also tend to bring about a decrease in levels of prejudice. Children can develop confidence in themselves when they are in educational environments in which they feel secure and accepted, in which their participation is valued, and in which they know the boundaries or limits. Involving children in lessons in which they can see themselves or their culture reflected in a variety of ways helps to create a solid sense of self as well as a classroom that is respectful and understanding of others. Creating such environments should be of prime concern to educators.

4. Increasing Empathy for and Understanding of Others

Although prejudice reduction is enhanced through social contact, cognitive sophistication, and an increase of self-esteem, long-term gains require educational activity that actively engages the emotions. Activities designed to help students see the world from another's perspective and thus develop **empathy,** or an understanding of the thoughts and feelings of another, are effective in reducing prejudice and improving intergroup relations (Garcia, Powell, & Sanchez, 1990). Classroom dramatizations and skits, reading narratives from another's perspective, and simulations are excellent tools for helping children become sensitive to others who act or look different.

Shaver and Curtis (1981), for example, offered a simulation to help children understand what it is like for those with speech difficulties. They suggested students put something in their mouths (such as a small clean rubber ball or dental cotton–something large enough that it won't be swallowed) and then make a telephone call to a store and ask for information. Students can then discuss how it feels to be unable to communicate effectively.

The classic cross-cultural simulation Bafa Bafa, or the children's version Rafa Rafa, provides an excellent way for students to gain an understanding of what it is like to move into another cultural group (Shirts, 1977). In this experience, individuals learn "proper" behavior associated with the creation of two distinct cultural groups. After some time, members of each group have the opportunity to interact with one another. They very quickly experience feelings of anxiety, rejection, apprehension, and confusion—those feelings often referred to collectively as culture shock. Most individuals who have made a significant transition from one country or culture to another encounter such feelings. This simulation allows students (and teachers or parents) to explore the feelings and experiences of immigrant, migrant, or refugee students; international exchange students; students in newly desegregated schools; newly mainstreamed children with disabilities; or just about anybody cast in the role of "new kid on the block."

Students may also write stories or act out plays and dramatizations of situations that characterize acts of prejudice and discrimination. In this manner, students "step into the shoes" of another, thereby gaining an insider's perspective of what it is like to be discriminated against.

Comprehensive Programs That Improve Intergroup Relations

In addition to the efforts that individual classroom teachers and large-group activities can make (e.g., team sports, school plays), a number of educational programs have been developed that demonstrate a positive effect on students' attitudes, values, and behaviors (Stephan & Vogt, 2004). Brief descriptions of successful programs designed for K–12 children are presented next.

Antibias Education for Young Children

In 1989 the National Association for the Education of Young Children (NAEYC) published *Anti-Bias Curriculum: Tools for Empowering Young Children*. This approach aims to help children develop the knowledge and skills they will need to work together in diverse, inclusive schools and communities. The four interacting goals of culturally relevant antibias education for young children are (1) nurturing every child's construction of knowledge, confident self-identity, and group identity; (2) promoting each child's comfortable, empathetic interaction with people from diverse backgrounds; (3) fostering each child's critical thinking about bias; and (4) cultivating each child's ability to stand up for her- or himself and for others in the face of bias (Derman-Sparks, 2004). The antibias approach is under development and influencing practice currently in a number of countries.

Cooperative Learning

Cooperative learning strategies refer to a set of approaches that modify standard academic topics in such a way that the materials are learned in small, oftentimes interethnic, cooperative learning groups. Applying the criteria discussed in the section titled Improving Social Contact and Intergroup Relations, students work with one another in cooperative groups in pursuit of the common goal of achieving the objectives of the lesson at hand. Eight different cooperative approaches have been studied, with a considerable amount of research demonstrating that when the conditions outlined by Allport (1954) are met in the classroom, students are more likely to have friends across racial and ethnic groups than they would when compared to students in the traditional classroom (Cooper & Slavin, 2004).

A World of Difference

The Anti-Defamation League's *A World of Difference* program is one of the largest and best-established efforts developed for schools to address issues of prejudice and racism. Teachers receive training in the use of specially designed curriculum materials that not only sensitize students to the existence of prejudice, bigotry, and discrimination but help them develop the skills needed to respond effectively to others. The instructional approach through the program is highly interactive, with an emphasis on students' everyday concerns related to issues of identity, the prevalence of bias, examining instances of exclusion in their own schools, and ways of developing more positive intergroup relations (Hofheimer-Bettman & Friedman, 2004).

Facing History and Ourselves

This program examines contemporary issues of prejudice, racism, and anti-Semitism by examining the unique circumstances surrounding Nazi Germany and the Holocaust and other examples of genocide. The program emphasizes the development of critical thinking skills while concerning itself with the moral issues of justice, human rights, and concern for the welfare of others. Students develop skills in the use of inquiry, analysis, and interpretation by examining the rise of power of the Nazis and the events that led up to the Holocaust and relating it to current events in their own schools and communities. Issues related to group identity are emphasized as students learn about hatred, stereotyping, scapegoating, ethnocentrism, power, and obedience (Tollefson, Barr, & Strom, 2004).

Critical Incidents

The Case Study introduced at the beginning of the chapter ended with John Gray leaving the school assembly and Mr. Johnson sending students back to their homeroom classes for some discussion of what had just occurred. This chapter's Critical Incidents extend the encounter and raises a series of questions for you to consider.

Critical Incident

Do You Know Anyone Else Like John Gray?

There was much discussion among the students as they went back to their classes. When Jane's group reconvened in the classroom, it took her a few minutes to calm them down.

"Was he for real?" one of them asked.

"How could he be? Someone would kill him on the street if he went around talking like that to everyone!" another replied.

Jane jumped in. "How many of you know someone like John Gray?" she asked. The room quieted down. About six hands went up.

"So," Jane continued, "it seems that some of you know someone pretty similar to Mr. Gray. Who might that person be?"

International Perspective: What's Happening Elsewhere in the World?

Diversity Issues in South African Schools

Jean Baxen and Gerald Wangenge-Ouma
University of Cape Town

Teacher education programs generally have not been successful in influencing pre-service teachers' belief systems (Brindley & Laframboise, 2002), and South Africa is no exception. It has been well documented that prospective teachers, by and large, enter teacher education programs with their own ideas of what "good" teaching is that are based on their own experiences (Brindly & Laframboise, 2002). Although, in general, this might be the nature of teacher education programs, in South Africa these practices have been deeply rooted in separatist education policies[1] and the concomitant practices operative in education institutions during the Apartheid regime. The homogeneity of educational institutions prior to the new democracy of 1994 diminished tensions with regard to race, religion, ethnicity, identity, and interest.

Prior to 1994, teacher education institutions, in particular, seemed unable (or unwilling) to provide contexts in which prospective teachers could discuss, examine, or confront the complex subject of diversity in ways that would help them deal with such challenges as and when they arose in the school environment. Teachers were trained within racially and linguistically homogenous tertiary institutions in which they were not expected to question or challenge the status quo, let alone question the content of the curricula offered to them or

by them at schools. The traditional pedagogical methodologies (primarily Fundamental Pedagogics[2]) advocated and privileged within training institutions encouraged teachers to develop noncritical, complying citizens who would know their place in society.

But understanding how teachers engage with diversity in schools extends beyond merely laying the "blame," so to speak, at the feet of institutions (schools and institutions of higher learning) and concomitant institutional cultures. Teachers' perceptions, experiences, and pedagogical practices are deeply embedded in past and present histories and practices that extend beyond institutions to a political, social, and economic system that entrenched white hegemony and black subordination. This past has and continues to affect the educational landscape, with schools acting as sites of contestation in the discursive space in which students and teachers are continually negotiating and renegotiating ways of being.

Schooling in South Africa Prior to 1994

Prior to the negotiated political settlement of 1994, which ushered in a democratic dispensation, education in South Africa was managed by 18 racially and ethnically divided education departments (Carim & Soudien, 1999). Schools were set aside for the exclusive use of different "races" and ethnic groups: Africans,[3] Indians, Coloureds, and Whites.

197

This categorisation of schools limited interracial, ethnic, and cultural interactions and, to a large extent, diversity in schools.

The racial and ethnic classification of South African schools remained in place until 1990 when a new policy that allowed schools to enroll learners from outside their racial and ethnic classification was introduced (Carim & Soudien, 1999). The new policy transformed South African schools from monocultural spaces to multicultural, multiethnic, and multiracial spaces. This pattern is most distinct in many formerly white schools in which the demographic profile of the student population has changed to include a more diverse racial population. However, even though the open admissions policy has been in place since 1990, many pockets of exclusivity, especially race-related, are still present in South Africa. For instance, one is unlikely to find white learners in schools in poor black neighborhoods just like it would be unlikely to find many black learners in high-cost, white-dominated schools (Vally & Dalamba, 1999).

This notwithstanding, and for the most part, the pattern emerging in the "new South Africa" is one that is class and/or socially and economically rather than racially determined. It presents challenges that cannot always be named for what they are because sometimes they are presented in subtle or even covert ways. What follows is discussion of some diversity issues and challenges identified by education students of the University of Cape Town during teaching practicums in 2006 and 2007. The issues are those identified as present in both primary and secondary schools.

Diversity Issues Affecting Schools in South Africa Today

Issues of diversity in South African schools are multifaceted. They encompass racial, linguistic, class, gender, religious, physical, and other differences (Hemson, 2006). The degree to which these issues manifest varies from school to school. In some schools certain diversity issues, for example, racism, manifest in subtle ways; in other instances, these are overt and easily recognizable.

Racial Diversity

South Africa is a racially diverse country with a history of institutionalized racism, or apartheid. The apartheid regime classified South Africans into four races: White, Indian, Coloured, and Africans. Consistent with apartheid's philosophy of separateness, the four races were not allowed to live together in the same neighborhoods, attend the same schools, or even intermarry. Falling in love across racial lines was taboo with incarceration as likely punishment.

This racial separateness is still alive in South Africa today, especially in schools. Although in several schools almost all the four races are proportionally represented, in many schools racial

representation is skewed. In many high-cost schools, previously set aside for whites only, many of the learners are white with a few Africans, Coloureds, and Indians. Previously white state schools find themselves accepting more children of colour. However, it is not uncommon for such schools to lose their white population to private institutions. Although a few white learners are found in some schools with a majority of nonwhite learners, this is rare. Poor schools in black and coloured neighbourhoods will likely have only black learners. In many of these schools, the only whites present would be a few teachers, if at all.

Racial minorities often feel "othered" and marginalized. The students on teaching practicum noted several manifestations of this marginalization, both in the classroom and outside, during school assemblies, during break and lunch times. In the classroom the main ways in which this othering happened was by the teachers showing more interest in, and concern for, learners of the dominant race (often the teacher's race) and treating learners of the minority races as strangers or even nonexistent in the classroom. Another manifestation of othering observed in the classroom was during group work. In some cases, learners of the dominant race would consciously avoid being in the same group as learners from the minority races. Both overt and subtle incidences of racism between learners, teachers, and teachers and pupils have been reported in many South African schools (Vally & Dalamba, 1999), including derogatory and racial name-calling and indifference toward teachers and learners of a different race.

Linguistic Diversity

There are 11 official[4] and many unofficial languages spoken in South Africa. Other than the many indigenous languages, the influx of immigrants and refugees has introduced many other languages in the country. According to the constitution of South Africa, learners have a right to be taught in an official language or languages of their choice. However, the languages that are widely spoken in a particular province are usually taken as the "official" languages in that particular area, and thus inadvertently become the languages of instruction in schools. For example, in the Western Cape, one of the country's nine provinces, the languages of instruction (which are also the official languages in the province) are Afrikaans, English, and IsiXhosa. The language of instruction varies from school to school. Some schools are dual medium, in most cases English and one of the other languages. Language is, therefore, a very complex diversity issue in many South African schools.

Linguistic diversity is a challenge in several ways. In cases where the school's language of instruction is not a learner's first or home language, effective learning for such learners is usually impaired. This is the challenge facing many black learners from poor families who attend English and Afrikaans-medium schools. Many of these learners have an African language as their home language and their mastery of English, but especially Afrikaans, is poor. Reports by teaching practicum students suggest that because of the language barrier these learners tend to perform poorly at school. The language problem also "silenced" learners with regard to participation in classroom discussions and related activities.

Given the intricate relationship between language and race in South Africa, the language problem has, to some extent, inhibited interracial interactions in schools. Tang (2007) reports a case in a school in the Western Cape where white and coloured learners found it difficult to interact with African learners because the African learners always communicated in IsiXhosa, which excluded non-IsiXhosa speakers. Tang (2007) also reported that the African learners in the school found it difficult to interact with their white and coloured colleagues who always communicated in English and/or Afrikaans. The language problem, Tang (2007) reported, encouraged the formation of racial groupings or cliques. It encouraged "othering" between the various language speakers.

Religious Diversity

Many South Africans are religious, and they belong to different faiths, with Christianity and Islam being dominant. Generally, religious diversity is accommodated in South African public schools. The official policy regarding religious practices in South African schools is that schools can conduct religious observances provided these occurred on a free, voluntary, and equitable basis. In some schools certain religions are dominant and their practices are regularly observed. For example, in schools where Christianity was the dominant religion, it was not uncommon for the school day to start with a Christian prayer, a reading from the Bible, and the singing of a hymn. Similarly, some schools with a predominant Muslim population always broke early on Fridays for learners and

teachers to attend mosque. Some schools gave learners and teachers who belonged to a different religion from the dominant one at school the option of staying away from observances. In other schools, all religions were treated equally, with opportunities for learners to not only practice their religions openly, but for others to learn about the religions of the world. In such schools, texts from various religions are usually read at every observance, for example, assembly.

Conclusion

This discussion of diversity issues in South African schools is by no means exhaustive or critical. It does not highlight the complex ways in which students and teachers navigate their way around these issues. It has provided a simple historical account that attempts to contextualize diversity issues in South African schools and highlight a few issues, among a host of others.

Notes

[1] Coloured Persons Education Act, 1963; Education and Training Act, 1979; Private Schools Act House of Assembly, 1986; and Education Affairs Act, 1988.
[2] Fundamental Pedagogics is a locally (South African) developed approach to teaching and learning, which is embedded in Dutch phenomenological philosophy. It is based on suppositions of supremacy and authoritarianism. It is an approach to education that privileges the teacher as the knowing adult who is responsible for preparing the child for adulthood. What is of consequence here is the unquestioning mode of delivery purported by this approach.
[3] This racial group was further categorised into nine ethnic groups that included Tswana, Xhosa, and Zulu, Venda, Sotho, and so on.
[4] These are Afrikaans, English, IsiXhosa, IsiZulu, IsiNdebele, SiSwati, Nothern Sotho, Sesotho, Setswana, Tshivenda, and Xitsonga.

"My uncle Pete's a lot like him," a boy offered from the back of the room. "Whenever we're together at family gatherings he just rants and raves about 'those people' this and 'those people' that. He really seems to resent it when someone from another race appears to do well. He once moved out of a neighborhood that was becoming integrated. He gets so loud and forceful at times that we all just want to leave . . . but we can't . . . he's a close relative, you know. Boy, it really bothers me."

Sue picked up from across the room. "My sister has changed quite a lot since she got married a few years ago. I don't ever recall her being prejudiced at home. I'm not, and my parents don't seem to be. But ever since she married George she's become quite racist. I don't understand it. She has a college education, but her husband doesn't. She just seems to have adopted whatever he thinks. I've gotten into a few arguments with her, but not when her husband is around. I'm kind of afraid to speak up when he's in the room."

"What are you most afraid of, Sue?" asked Ms. Myers.

"Well," Sue continued, "he's quite loud when he gets upset. I've seen him insult other people, and I'm just afraid I couldn't take his tirade. And besides, I don't want to upset my sister, so I just keep quiet. I don't know if that's the best thing to do."

"Sometimes my father gets like him," Samantha added. "I've fought with him a few times when I've heard him say some rather negative things about people, especially about some of my friends at school. He gets quite upset with me when I challenge him, but it really bothers me that he can be so close-minded—and insult my friends at the same time!"

- Does John Gray remind you of anyone you know?
- When you are with this person, what feelings does it generate in you?
- What do you do when you have those feelings?
- How do you interact with this individual? Is this an effective strategy to employ?

Critical Incident

Reflections From John Gray

After the classroom discussions the students gathered back in the auditorium. As they settled into their chairs, Mr. Johnson walked onto the stage, took the microphone, and reported that there had been some very lively discussions in each of the homerooms. Mr. Johnson went on to report that he had been able to convince Mr. Gray not to leave because he thought it would be good to have Mr. Gray join them as they talked about their experiences and their various discussions.

There was quite a bit of talking and movement among the students when Gray returned to the stage. He took the microphone from Mr. Johnson and sat on a stool on the right side of the stage.

"I'm glad Mr. Johnson talked me into staying," Gray opened. "I understand you had quite lively discussions in your homerooms. That's good, because it is only after we begin talking about some of these issues that we will ever be able to solve them. In this case you were breaking the silence, and I applaud you for that. I'd like to talk with you now about your reactions to me. I wonder if any of you have any questions for me now?"

There was nervous commotion throughout the room until one student stood up.

"Are you for real? How would you deal with a person like yourself?" he asked.

"That's a very good question," replied Gray. "Let me tell you a few things about me, and then we can look at a few things about you. Would that be all right with you? And, by the way, what differences do you notice about me now?"

"Well, for one thing," a student replied, "You seem much more relaxed. You are not confronting us; you are sitting, and you seem to be listening to what we are saying."

"How do you know I am listening?" asked Gray.

"Well, for one, you are responding to what I just said. You asked me a question and waited for my response."

"Yes, I will admit that sometimes I get to the point that I do not listen nor respond to the things you might say to me. But when I am doing that, I must tell you, I am not acting. I am not role-playing with you. What I am doing is what I call 'role-taking,' and let me define that. I did not memorize a script and come in here to play the role of a bigot. That's what happens in role-playing. But I was role-taking here with you this morning. I was sharing with you many messages that I heard when I was growing up—perhaps some of the messages you, too, have heard while you were growing up and perhaps still hear today. Maybe some of you shared that in your group discussions. Now while I may have heard those messages when I was younger, I do not support them today. But I do hear them in my head every now and then. I have to stop and remind myself that those are old messages, often prejudices, and I do not believe them anymore. They are like tapes that suddenly turn on in my mind when I'm in certain situations. But now that I am aware of them and now that I have more sophisticated knowledge and experience today, I know how to turn them off. So, in role-taking I was sharing messages that I grew up hearing and I was playing them all back for you. Do you recall what was said to you at the beginning of the session? You were told that you would participate in a psychodrama that would illustrate racism and prejudice in action. How many of you heard that? While you were told up front what was to happen, most of you were still personally drawn into the experience."

"I was also searching for your buttons with the hope that you would begin to feel what it might be like to be discriminated against for no other reason except being placed in a category based on some outward characteristic. That's in part what a prejudice is—it's making judgments about an individual based on some preconceived knowledge you may have about a group, even if that knowledge is incomplete or wrong. And, by the way, I apologize if I forgot 'your group.' Perhaps I neglected to talk about gays or the elderly or overweight people. All of us belong to a variety of groups that can be stereotyped and discriminated against. And that statement I made about research and women in leadership? That was not accurate. You have to be careful about how messages are presented. Sometimes they may sound quite authoritative, yet may not be truthful."

"What I'd like to do now is give you some feedback on how I saw you dealing with me so that when you are in a similar situation you can better evaluate what it is you would like to do. Is that all right?"

Many students signaled that that would be useful information.

- Reflect on the interaction between John Gray and the students. What kinds of reactions and responses did the students have to John Gray?

- What are some possible consequences when people respond in such situations with laughter or silence?

Critical Incident

John Gray Shares an Important Part of Himself

John Gray reflected upon the encounter in the auditorium and offered to give some feedback to the students.

"One thing I recall," Gray continued, "was hearing quite a lot of laughter in the group. I remember in one group asking a man why he was laughing.

He replied that he was laughing to prevent himself from coming up on stage and carrying me out the door—and that I better hope he kept on laughing. But consider the consequences of laughter in such a situation. Think of a young child, perhaps a brother or sister or niece or nephew. And think of when someone might laugh when they hear an ethnic joke or when they are watching a show on television like the Archie Bunker *All in the Family* show. Is it possible that through the laughter we create stereotypes that may not have existed before? The child, seeing people laugh at ethnic jokes, may think, 'I like to see people laugh. Telling that joke makes people laugh.' Then he or she goes into the class-room and tells that ethnic joke and begins the whole process over again. So, it's important to think about the consequences of laughter and the role we play."

"So, what can people do in a situation like this?" one student asked.

"I think it's important that we take a stand, tell others that we do not appre-ciate or support the telling of ethnic jokes, so others hear an alternative voice," said Gray. "You may not be the most popular person at the moment, but I can guarantee you that someone in the group will appreciate your sensitivity and your efforts."

"Now, related to this, let's talk about silence. Many of you were silent this morning. You may not have agreed with everything I was saying, and some of you may have actually agreed with some things you heard, but very few of you made your feelings known. Oh, you may have nudged someone sitting next to you and said something like, 'he can't be real.' But let me remind you that I am real. There are people all around you, people who, while they may not be as vocal as me, believe and act in such a manner in their neighborhoods and homes."

"But let's think about the consequences of silence. I think about Hitler. He got into power because people around him were silent and didn't challenge him. When you are silent, you are giving tacit approval of the messages you hear around you. So, my challenge to you is to break the silence. When you see an act that you know is wrong, or when you hear someone say something that you know is damaging, make yourself known. Even by simply standing up and stat-ing something like, 'You know that statement you just made, I disagree with you and think it is wrong.' You will do wonders at drawing the attention away from the bigot and will make those around you know that there is at least an alterna-tive point of view. Your simple comments can go quite far at making change."

It was becoming obvious that the students had spent quite a bit of time talk-ing about these difficult topics throughout the day. Gray sensed that it was time to bring the day to a close. The students had had quite an experience. Little did they know that they were about to be challenged once again.

"I know it's been a long day for us all, and I believe we've learned quite a lot. And if you think about it, you did most of the teaching here today. I think I spent less than an hour with you this morning, yet you have been engaged in this topic for most of the day."

"There is another part of myself that I have a need to share with you," he went on. "Sit back for a moment and think about me now. What images come to your mind? What judgments do you make about me now?" He paused a minute or two.

"Let me share something else with you. For over 20 years I have been using my physical appearance to illustrate the myth of race and the impact of color. Perhaps by sharing a little bit about myself I can make people stop to think about the judgments they make about others, as well as about the myth of race and the impact of color. You see, under the definition of race in this country, I would like you to know that I am black, or African American, my parents are black, both sets of my grandparents were black, I am married to a woman who is black, and I have five children of various shades."

There was silence and disbelief around the room. Students and teachers were looking back and forth at one another and at Gray, who still, by anyone's determination, looked as European American as could be. Then he showed some slides on the screen. One was of his family, showing the range of colors that were represented. Then there was one of his parents—obviously black, but light-skinned, with Gray, appearing white, among them.

"For many of you, your heads will be spinning right now. But I want you to know that what you see may not always be what you get. I am for real, and my experiences are real. Many of you may be confused because none of the visual cues about my ethnic identity are evident. Your judgments are now in question. I ask you to question all the judgments that people are so quick to make. And perhaps in your classes tomorrow you can further discuss issues related to color, race, and racism. I'd be interested in knowing what you do as a school and as individuals around these issues as the year progresses."

And with that, John Gray left the school.

- What do you think John Gray means when he asks the students to reflect upon the "myth of race and the impact of color"?
- How does skin color influence people's judgments or attributions?
- Can you recall a time when you or someone you know made a judgment that was premature and the reality turned out to be different from what was expected? What were the consequences of the quick judgment?
- What suggestions might you offer to others that will help them to avoid the temptation to make quick judgments or attributions?

Summary

Prejudice and racism have both been rampant in many forms throughout American society. In this chapter we provided an overview of issues related to prejudice and racism, beginning with a historical perspective and then tracing some of the major developments in efforts designed to address its occurrence in society. We then explored the concept of prejudice, prejudice formation, and prejudice reduction, emphasizing that various actions taken by teachers, schools, and communities can go a long way toward reducing, and in some instances preventing, its occurrence.

Chapter Review

Go to the Online Learning Center at www.mhhe.com/cushner7e to review important content from the chapter, practice with key terms, take a chapter quiz, and find the Web links listed in this chapter.

Key Terms

empathy 194   hypodescent 180   prejudice 181
genotype 180   phenotype 180

Active Exercise

Additional Active Exercises are available online at www.mhhe.com/cushner7e.

What Does It Feel Like to Be Excluded?

Purpose: To develop empathy by imagining what it might be like to be excluded or discriminated against, and to propose possible responses.

Instructions: Developing an understanding of the experience of others in a pluralistic society is critical if teachers and students are to develop a fuller knowledge of culture and its various forms. One way to develop such a skill is to listen to the voices of individuals who have felt excluded from the mainstream for one reason or another—perhaps due to overt racism; subtle, institutional racism; general ignorance; subtle pressure; or genuine dislike. Read the following quotes and try to identify one or two feelings associated with them. Then, consider what you as a teacher might say and do in response (adapted from an exercise developed by Beth Swadener).

Low-income mother: "My son understands that we have no money the last week of each month, and yet he was pressured by his teacher to have a new workbook by the next class. When we could not afford it that week, he was made to sit out of class. The teacher said, "Everyone else remembered to get their book, why not you?"

As the mother, I feel _____

_____

_____.

As a teacher, I might _____

_____

_____.

Jewish parent: "Last year our daughter asked me, 'Could we have a Christmas tree and just not use it?'"

As the parent, I feel _____

_____

_____.

As a teacher, I might _____

_____

_____.

Chinese parent: "My daughter asked me, 'Can I have blonde hair? It's better to be blonde.'"

As the parent, I feel _____

_____

_____.

As a teacher, I might _____

_____

_____.

Native American parent: "The schools continue to miseducate my son. The images he has of native people are limited, and there is virtually no relevant Native American history taught in his school."

As the parent, I feel _____

_____

_____.

As a teacher, I might _____

_____

_____.

Islamic parent: "My child's school has many Christian-based activities and has never even recognized that some of the students are not Christian."

As the parent, I feel _____

_____

_____.

As a teacher, I might _____

_____

_____.

Single parent: "I feel that all my son's behavior at school is blamed on the fact that I'm a single parent, and that many judgments about our family are made based on no other evidence than our 'single parent family' status."

As the parent, I feel _____

_____

_____.

As a teacher, I might _____

_____

_____.

Vietnamese parent: (translated from Vietnamese) "My children speak and read better English than I do. It is so hard when lots of letters and information come home from school in English. I also feel that my children are losing respect for their parents and the elders in this country."

As the parent, I feel _____

_____

_____.

As a teacher, I might _____

_____

_____.

Extend this activity by collecting some of your own quotes from statements by children, parents, and other community members that represent diverse groups and who have felt excluded. Record three of your own examples.

Classroom Activities

1. Review sample elementary textbooks from various content areas (social studies, science, etc.) and across grade levels. In what topic areas would you find it easiest to integrate concepts related to race, ethnicity, and prejudice? How might you do this in a 3rd grade classroom? A 6th grade classroom?

2. It is very common in elementary schools to reserve part of each day or week to current events. Review a week's worth of newspapers from your local area. Identify two to three news events or other items from the paper that would lend themselves to discussion of race and prejudice for children in grade three or four. How might you integrate this into your classroom?

3. Recall the surprising finding that greater diversity in a school does not necessarily on its own lead to an increase in cross-racial friendships. What are some suggestions that you might offer a local high school that would increase the likelihood that more meaningful cross-racial relationships might develop among students?

4. It is important to help young people understand the power and pervasiveness of stereotypes, both of those they hold of others as well as how others may stereotype them. Propose a lesson you might develop for high school students that helps them explore how the stereotypes they hold may influence their actions in a negative way. How can you help them understand the stereotypes those outside of their own country may hold of them, and to explore their validity?

Reflective Questions

1. What are some ways in which Jane and the other teachers could continue to educate themselves about new methods related to prejudice reduction while simultaneously keeping up with student needs and school requirements, especially when time is such a problem?

2. Not every teacher and administrator in the school appreciates the direction Jane and some others are taking toward antiracist education. How might Jane continue to broaden her students' perspectives in the face of criticism from her colleagues?

3. What experiences have you had in educational institutions that were effective at developing positive intergroup relations? What aspects of the contact hypothesis were evident?

4. If a close friend or family member were to make a prejudiced comment or tell an ethnic joke, would you protest? Why or why not? What about if it was a stranger who said the same thing?

References

Allport, G. (1954). *The nature of prejudice*. Reading, MA: Addison-Wesley.

Allport, G. (1979). *The nature of prejudice* (25th anniv. ed.). Reading, MA: Addison-Wesley.

Amir, Y. (1969). Contact hypothesis in ethnic relations. *Psychological Bulletin, 71*(5), 319–343.

Augoustinos, M., & Rosewarne, D. L. (2001). Stereotype knowledge and prejudice in children. *British Journal of Developmental Psychology, 19,* 143–156.

Bennett, M. J. (1993). Towards ethnorelativism: A developmental model of intercultural sensitivity. In M. Paige (Ed.), *Cross-cultural orientation* (pp. 27–69). Lanham, MD: University Press of America.

Bicklin, D., & Bailey, L. (1981). *Rudely stamp'd: Imaginal disability and prejudice*. Washington, DC: University Press of America.

Bigler, R. (1999). The use of multicultural curricula and materials to counter racism in children. *Journal of Social Issues, 55*(4), 687–704.

Bishop, R., & Berryman, M. (2006). *Culture speaks: Cultural relationships and classroom learning*. Wellington, New Zealand: Huia Publishers.

Blau, J., Lamb, U., Stearns, E., & Pellerin, C. (2001). Cosmopolitan environments and adolescents' gains in social studies. *Sociology of Education, 74,* 121–138.

Brindley, R., & Laframboise, K. L. (2002, May). The need to do more: Promoting multiple perspectives in pre-service teacher education through children's literature. *Teaching and Teacher Education, 18*(4), 405–420.

Brislin, R. (1993). *Understanding culture's influence on behavior*. Fort Worth, TX: Harcourt Brace Jovanovich.

Bronson, P., & Merryman, A. (2009). *Nurture shock: New thinking about children*. New York: Hachette Book Group.

Brown, T. N., Tanner-Smith, E., Lesane-Brown, C. L., & Ezell, M. E. (2007). Child, parent, situational correlates of family ethnic/race socialization. *Journal of Marriage and Family, 69*(1), 14–25.

Byrnes, D. A. (1988). Children and prejudice. *Social Education, 52*(4), 267–271.

Carim, N., & Soudien, C. (1999). Critical anti-racism in South Africa. In S. May (Ed.), *Critical multiculturalism: Rethinking multicultural and antiracist education* (pp. 153–171). London: Routledge Falmer.

Clark, K., & Clark, M. (1947). Racial identification and preference in Negro children. In T. M. Newcomb & E. L. Hartley (Eds.), *Readings in social psychology.* New York: Holt, Rinehart & Winston.

Cooper, R., & Slavin, R. E. (2004). Cooperative learning: An instructional strategy to improve intergroup relations. In W. G. Stephan & W. P. Vogt (Eds.), *Education programs for improving intergroup relations: Theory, research and practice* (pp. 55–70). New York: Teachers College Press.

Cortes, C. (2000). *The children are watching: How the media teach about diversity.* New York: Teachers College Press.

Derman-Sparks, L. (2004). Culturally relevant anti-bias education with young children. In W. G. Stephan & W. P. Vogt (Eds.), *Education programs for improving intergroup relations: Theory, research and practice* (pp. 19–36). New York: Teachers College Press.

Garcia, J., Powell, R., & Sanchez, T. (1990, April). Multicultural textbooks: How to use them more effectively in the classroom. Paper presented at the annual meeting of the American Educational Research Association, Boston. (ERIC Document Reproduction Service No. ED320262)

Gay, G. (2000). *Culturally responsive teaching: Theory, research and practice.* New York: Teachers College Press.

Grant, C., & Ladson-Billings, G. (1997). *Dictionary of multicultural education.* Phoenix, AZ: Oryx Press.

Hemson, C. (2006) *Teacher education and the challenge of diversity in South Africa.* Cape Town, South Africa: Human Sciences Research Council.

Hofheimer-Bettman, E., & Friedman, L. J. (2004). The Anti-Defamation League's A World of Difference Institute. In W. G. Stephan & W. P. Vogt (Eds.), *Education programs for improving intergroup relations: Theory, research and practice* (pp. 75–94). New York: Teachers College Press.

Katz, D. (1960). The functional approach to the study of attitudes. *Public Opinion Quarterly, 24,* 164–204.

Katz, P. A. (1983). Developmental foundations of gender and racial attitudes. In R. H. Leahy (Ed.), *The child's construction of social inequality* (pp. 41–78). New York: Academic Press.

Kottack, C. P., & Kozaitis, K. A. (1999). *On being different: Diversity and multiculturalism in the North American mainstream.* Boston: McGraw-Hill.

Ladson-Billings, G. (1995). But that's just good teaching! The case for culturally relevant pedagogy. *Theory into Practice, 34*(3), 159–165.

Lipman, M. (1980). *Philosophy in the classroom.* Philadelphia: Temple University Press.

McIntosh, P. (1992, January–February). White privilege: Unpacking the invisible knapsack. *Creation Spirituality, 33–35,* 53.

Moody, J. (2001). Race, school integration, and friendship segregation in America. *American Journal of Sociology, 107*(3), 679–716.

National Association for the Education of Young Children. (1989). *Anti-bias curriculum: Tools for empowering young children.* Washington, DC: Author.

Pettigrew, T. F. (1981). The mental health impact. In B. P. Bowser & R. G. Hunt (Eds.), *Impacts of racism on white Americans* (pp. 97–118). Beverly Hills, CA: Sage.

Ponterotto, J. G., & Pedersen, P. B. (1993). *Preventing prejudice: A guide for counselors and educators.* Newbury Park, CA: Sage.

Shaver, J. P., & Curtis, C. K. (1981). *Handicapism and equal opportunity: Teaching about the disabled in social studies*. Reston, VA: Council for Exceptional Children.

Sherif, M. (1958). Superordinate goals in the reduction of intergroup tension. *American Journal of Sociology, 63*(4), 349–356.

Shirts, R. G. (1977). *BAFA BAFA: A cross-cultural simulation*. Del Mar, CA: SIMILE II.

Sleeter, C. (1994). White racism. *Multicultural education,* Spring.

Southern Poverty Law Center (2008). Accessed February 24, 2010 at: http://www.splcenter.org/get-informed/hate-map.

Stephan, W. G. (1999). *Reducing prejudice and stereotyping in schools*. New York: Teachers College Press.

Stephan, W. G., & Vogt, W. P. (2004). *Education programs for improving intergroup relations: Theory, research and practice*. New York: Teachers College Press.

Streufert, S., & Swezey, R. W. (1986). *Complexity, managers, and organizations*. New York: Academic Press.

Tang, C. (2007). *Diversity in education assignment*. Unpublished manuscript, School of Education, University of Cape Town.

Tollefson, T., Barr, D. J., & Strom, M. S. (2004). Facing history and ourselves. In W. G. Stephan & W. P. Vogt (Eds.), *Education programs for improving intergroup relations: Theory, research and practice* (pp. 95–110). New York: Teachers College Press.

Vally, S., & Dalamba, Y. (1999). Racism, 'Racial integration' and desegregation in South African public secondary schools. *A report on a study by the South African Human Rights Commission*. Unpublished Report.

Yetman, N. (1991). *Majority and minority: The dynamics of race and ethnicity in American life* (5th ed.). Boston: Allyn & Bacon.

Chapter

7

The Classroom as a Global Community

Nationality and Region

Focus Questions

1. What does it mean to be an internationally competent individual? How does this develop in people, and how can teachers facilitate this development?

2. What does it mean to be a globally connected society? What are some powerful concepts that underlie an international or global perspective?

3. How have recent conflicts and the interdependence of nations altered what we do in schools?

4. What are some practical strategies that can be used to prepare students to better understand and interact with others around the world so they might prevent or solve problems that are global in nature?

" We are living in a new age which itself is defined by the fact that challenges we face do not respect any conventional boundaries. They don't respect geographical boundaries and they don't respect old definitions. "

RICHARD F. CELESTE

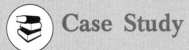

Case Study

A Global Classroom

It was 8 o'clock on a Tuesday morning in early February as Jerome Becker rushed into the front office with good news. Yesterday's mail had brought the package his class had been anxiously awaiting—a completed story from a school in southern India. Now he would be able to share its contents with the class. Jerome was eager to tell his principal, Mrs. Lewis, because she had seemed so certain that this project would fail and that the children would be let down. Well, this time it hadn't, and Jerome was delighted.

Jerome's first year as a teacher had started with great difficulties. Within 2 weeks of the start of the school year the entire school watched in horror as the World Trade Center and Pentagon were attacked by terrorists. Thousands of innocent lives were lost before everyone's eyes. For the first time, Americans watched helplessly as their world of predictability and security was transformed to a new degree of uncertainty and horror. The very strengths of the United States— the openness, trust, and freedoms that people had come to expect—suddenly became its greatest weaknesses and were replaced with fear, paranoia, and uncertainty. People responded to the tragedy with anger, resentment, fear, and mistrust. In many respects, things hadn't changed much in subsequent years: global conflicts arise with increasing frequency, suspicion and anxiety of others is still rather common, and the nation continues to be engaged in war efforts.

The past summer, children in the district had been in an increasing number of confrontations with one another in the malls, on playgrounds, even on recreation department ball fields. Vandalism and fighting, which had been relatively uncommon in this community of 60,000 just outside of Grand Rapids, Michigan, suddenly were occurring with far greater frequency. The troubles that people had read about in other major cities no longer seemed to pass by this relatively peaceful community; they had become an increasing part of the local scene. The problems didn't end with the summer; they came right into the classroom in full force with the new sixth-grade class—name-calling, fighting, and threats of gangs.

Tensions seemed especially strong between the African American, Arab American, and European American students when a number of soldiers from the region were killed in one particular incident in Iraq. This situation worried Jerome even more. His students, like many other Americans, found it increasingly difficult to differentiate between many in the Arab communities who had lived in and around the state for years and had become trusted community members and the terrorists that seemed to be portrayed in the daily news. Arabs and Muslims became the targets of increasing hatred, prejudice, and discrimination in the community, and the hatred was finding its way into the classroom almost on a daily basis. Jerome saw that now was obviously an opportune time to address these critical issues in a very real manner, but he was unsure of how to do this in the most effective way. There were few books available to guide him through such a process, and he just was not certain where, and how, to begin.

Jerome decided that he had to attempt something—it was time to alter the course of events in his classroom. He had taken some workshops in multicultural education, global education, and cooperative learning over the past few summers and was eager to try some of the strategies he had studied. He was also beginning to integrate various parts of his elementary curriculum; he saw several opportunities to link language arts, social studies, and the arts. He was even willing to try to integrate other areas of the curriculum while exploring how he might add a global perspective. After all, he had nothing to lose and everything to gain in his attempts to bring some peace to the class and to help his students live more peacefully with one another.

Because several of his students were first-generation children whose parents had recently immigrated to the United States, Jerome decided that working to develop an international perspective might provide them with concepts and activities that would cut across the various ethnicities and nationalities in his class. An international approach could also help his students better understand the circumstances faced by many of the Muslims and Arabs, not only in the local community but in other parts of the world as well.

With this goal in mind, Jerome began with a unit on immigration that he hoped would develop empathy in his students for newcomers to this country. He also hoped this sense of empathy would be applied to the relatives and ancestors of students with deep roots in the

United States. An activity on immigration might also serve to bring the group together as they explored both the similarities and differences in their backgrounds. He asked his students to go home and interview family members about their own or their ancestors' experiences coming to this country, asking them to inquire specifically about the following topics:

1. From what country did your ancestors come?
2. When did they leave their country of birth?
3. Why did they leave that place?
4. What was their experience when they first came to this country? Do people remember any hardships? Were any stereotypes and prejudice directed at them?
5. Where did they first arrive in this country?
6. How did they come to live in Michigan? When did they come here, and why?
7. Are there any traditions from the home country that are still practiced?
8. What makes our people unique in this country today?

Activity 8:
Family Tree: Tracing One's Roots and Family History

A week later, Jerome had students come to the front of the room, share their stories, and locate their family's place of origin on the world map. He gave them each a piece of yarn, and as they located their country of origin, he asked them to attach it to the map at that country and extend the yarn to Grand Rapids. He was surprised by the results of this exercise.

The discussion that followed the presentations was enlightening for both Jerome and his students. He was not surprised to see many of the students stand up and talk about their family history with a sense of pride. For many of them, this was the first time anyone had asked them about their ancestry. It seemed to Jerome that this was also the first time that the students had listened intently to one another's stories. There seemed to be a real sense of contribution for most of the students. They were especially interested in Guy's and Hannah's stories. Some of Guy's ancestors had arrived in the country in the 1600s. He shared stories of people jumping ship off the New England coast and ending up in Vermont. Hannah shared stories of her grandparents' escape from Hitler's armies and how lucky most of her family had been to get out of Germany alive before the Holocaust had really taken hold. She did know, however, that two of her relatives had perished in the Holocaust.

What surprised Jerome, however, was the difficulty that some students had with the exercise, especially Steve and Ahmed. At first, Steve avoided participating in the exercise by offering the excuse that he had left his notes at home. The next day, when urged again to participate, Steve stood in front of the class and mumbled something like, "I'm adopted and I don't know anything about my parents." There was complete silence. An awkward moment or two followed, until Jerome quietly said, "My father was adopted too, and he didn't know much about his background either. His adopted family helped him learn about their Polish background, and he grew up in that tradition. Perhaps there are some traditions that your adopted family follow that you can take for your own. What background is your adopted family?"

Steve began to relax when he replied, "Well, I guess they're all German. I mean, my grand-parents speak a little German when they visit, and my parents make it a point to go to the Oktoberfest every year. My father really likes it when he has his German beer. They're even talking about visiting Germany in the next couple of years and plan on taking me and my sister. I guess I'm really German, but I'm not sure what it means to be German. I feel very much American, if you know what I mean."

Jerome asked how many others felt more "American" than affiliated with their ethnic ancestry. Almost all the students raised their hands. "Well," said Jerome, "it is good that we all feel American, because we are, but I want you to think about what being American means." He let the matter drop there for a time.

Ahmed's response to the exercise, however, was not as easy for Jerome to handle, but it was exactly what he knew had to occur. Jerome knew that Ahmed's family had been under a

(continued)

lot of stress since the attacks. Ahmed's father had a habit of keeping him at home on occasion, especially when confrontations in the Middle East were escalating, and had asked Jerome to be especially sensitive to the actions and words of others. Jerome replied that he would and that he, too, was concerned. Ahmed stood up and, with a certain uneasiness and a few tears, stated, "I'm from Jordan, my father's a doctor, and he came here to study and practice medicine. Every once in a while, people accuse me of being a terrorist and responsible for many of the problems they face. We have nothing to do with the problems in the world. We, too, cry at our home when attacks occur and people are injured or killed by war. We prayed at the mosque, both for peace and the safety of all of us in America. We're not the enemy. We love this country too, but sometimes no one seems to care what I think. Why do we get blamed all the time?"

Jerome, taken aback by Ahmed's strong emotional outburst, wasn't quite sure what to say and was feeling a bit uncertain about, and perhaps threatened by, Ahmed's comments. After taking a deep breath and pondering the situation for a moment, he could sense the anger and fear that must be felt by those everywhere who have been subjected to prejudice and stereotypes, especially during times of war and national conflict. A similar situation occurred in the United States just after Pearl Harbor was bombed by the Japanese. Except then, almost immediately, Japanese Americans were rounded up and placed in internment camps out of fear that they were the enemy. Although such extreme behavior was not happening this time, and although the president of the United States along with many other civic leaders continuously urged understanding and compassion toward our Arab American and Muslim citizens, the apprehensions, tensions, and mistrust could still be felt.

Jerome spoke with the class as they all reflected on the experiences they had had in recent years. Most members of the class agreed that they weren't angry with Arabs in general, but Jerome knew there was still quite a lot of work to do to help his students understand and feel more comfortable with Ahmed. Perhaps Ahmed's parents would be willing to come to class and share information about their heritage and culture. Such presentations might help to build some bridges of understanding and trust, at least within the classroom and school community.

With that, Jerome returned to his desk, feeling that he was at least taking the first steps toward opening up some lines of communication between himself, his students, and their families. In a larger group discussion of their ancestors, students were asked to identify generalizations in people's presentations and to pose hypotheses to explain what they observed. Peter noticed that most people seemed to come to the United States for better job opportunities, or for more money, as he put it, both in the past and today. A few people came for religious freedoms. Jeremy used this point as an opportunity to discuss religious freedom today for Muslims in America. Kathy noticed that everyone, except for one of David's relatives, came from somewhere else. When encouraged, she went on to suggest that almost everyone was an immigrant at least once in his or her past. Mark, an African American child in the class, reminded everyone that his ancestors didn't come here by choice and perhaps that explained many of the differences that exist between African Americans and other groups. Jerome took this opportunity to discuss with the class the differences between voluntary and involuntary immigration.

Jerome then began to probe into students' feelings about the immigrants they read about in recent news. Most were familiar with stories of Haitian refugees, the situation in Cuba, and the constant debate about Mexicans crossing the border into the United States. A few were aware of immigrant and refugee groups from Southeast Asia and the fact that many whites had left Zimbabwe and were now leaving South Africa. Jerome was hoping that a discussion about the plight of today's refugees and immigrant groups would enable students to identify with their situation and to compare it to that of their own ancestors. A few were able to make this leap, but most only nodded in half-hearted agreement. Jerome was content that perhaps he planted a few seeds for future discussion and activity, which he promised himself he would develop. He ended the discussion by asking the students to read the following parable.

Once there were three men who had never seen oranges. They had heard many wonderful things about the fruit and wanted very much to have some. The first man set out with excitement. He traveled for many days and began to worry that he would get lost. The farther he went, the more he worried. Finally, he sat under a tree, deep in thought. "No silly fruit is this important," he decided. He got up and turned toward home.

The second man was a very bold fellow. He rushed off, dreaming about oranges as he traveled, and ended up at the same tree. Round orange fruits were all over the ground and in the branches. Thrilled with his success, he grabbed one of the fruits off the ground and bit into it. It was rotten and bitter. "Ugh! What a stupid fruit," he said, and returned home empty-handed.

The third man did research before he left home. He also asked questions of people he met as he traveled. Lo and behold, he found the same tree full of oranges. He examined many oranges and chose one that was not too hard, nor too soft. It was juicy and delicious. He took some seeds home, planted them, and eventually became a famous grower of fruit.

Jerome asked his students to think overnight about the possible meanings of the story. Tomorrow they would begin a writing assignment using this parable to link some of the issues that had been raised in their discussion.

Two months later, the classroom was alive with activity. Ahmed's parents had already been in to share part of their family traditions, as had the parents of three other children. The fact that the sixth-grade social studies curriculum looks at world cultures made this project comparatively easy. It was also easy to integrate a number of books on various cultures into the language arts program. Jerome's focus was always on prejudice, discrimination, and how people might overcome the differences that existed between one another. The students had already read such books as *The Diary of Anne Frank* and had viewed and discussed a number of films. They were to read a few more books by the winter holiday. Jerome also had started a Friday afternoon intercultural forum in which students participated in a variety of activities designed to enhance their regular courses while expanding their horizons, always with an eye on how relations with Arab and Muslim students could be enhanced.

One particular activity engaged the students so much that it expanded into the whole language arts program and involved all the students in the class. It was the end result of this activity that Jerome had been so excited to share with Mrs. Lewis, the principal. Jerome had read about a particular project, a partnership story project that was designed to integrate language arts, social studies, and cooperative learning (Cushner, 1992). Through small group activity, students in one country organize a story, decide on a topic or problem, identify the main characters as well as a setting, and write the first half of the story. This first half of the story is mailed to children in another country who are asked to complete the story and translate it into their own language. When completed, the classrooms have an internationally developed product translated in two languages. The story can also be co-illustrated. In addition to collaborating on the story, classrooms can exchange a variety of artifacts, photos, letters, and so forth.

Jerome had written to a relative of one of his students who worked in a school in Madurai, India. She was interested in the story-writing project and was willing to collaborate if Jerome's class would agree to begin the project. The class broke up into three groups, each writing the beginning of a story. Because they had been studying the environmental crisis in social studies, Jerome asked them to build their story line around this topic. Each group started a story. One was an adventure story involving a school of fish in a polluted lake. Another was a mystery involving a missing mineral. The third focused on abuses of the world's wildlife. Then they mailed all three unfinished stories to the Indian sixth-grade class.

The students were very excited that morning when Jerome told them that the completed stories had been returned. It had been 6 weeks since the class mailed their story beginnings to India. Rather than just share the endings that had come back, Jerome decided to turn the activity into a real culture-learning experience by rereading his own students' unfinished stories and then asking them to imagine how they thought the Indian students would complete each story. After Jerome finished reading the first half of each story to his class, he showed them the beautifully written Tamil script and the pictures that the Indian class had used to complete the stories. You can read the completed story, and the results of their cultural inquiry, at the end of the chapter.

215

Education in a Global Society

It is the purpose of schools to prepare students for life in the larger societies in which they live. In a democratic society this responsibility means preparing students not only to know about democracy but also to be able to put it into practice. In a globally interdependent world, this responsibility means preparing students for a future in which they will come into increasing contact with people different from themselves. It means a reality in which an increasing number of American firms have offices in overseas locations and, similarly, an increasing number of international firms have offices within the United States. It means political boundaries that are constantly shifting and rapidly changing, thus creating opportunities and challenges not imagined in recent decades. Moreover, it is no longer necessary to leave one's own community to come into regular contact with people from other nations or to be significantly influenced by the actions of others from far away.

However, compared to young people in other nations, American students typically score low in terms of knowledge of and interest in international affairs (Lutkus, Weiss, Campbell, Mazzeo, & Lazer, 1999; Niemi & Junn, 1998). Avery and Hann (2004) summarized the amount of exposure American students report having related to international politics. For example, only 49% of students reported studying other countries' governments in the past year; 43% reported having studied about international organizations; students were more likely to talk about U.S. government affairs than international politics; only 53% of U.S. students reported that they "sometimes" or "often" read articles in newspapers about what is happening in other countries; and students born in the United States are less likely to read international news than those who were born outside the United States.

As a result, educators are beginning to seek out concepts, skills, and strategies that will help students understand what is happening in other parts of the world so they can function more effectively in a globally interdependent world. A central focus of this effort is to develop an understanding of globalization and to attain an education that is international and intercultural in scope.

What Is Globalization?

**Thomas Friedman
and *The Lexus and
the Olive Tree***

Globalization, referring to an increase in the scope and magnitude of human contact with its subsequent escalation of interaction and interdependence, seems to be the defining concept at the beginning of the 21st century. In his recent book, *The World Is Flat*, Thomas Friedman (2006) traced the start of this phenomenon back to the time when Columbus traversed the globe more than 500 years ago. As Friedman and others have pointed out, recent advances in communication and transportation technologies have resulted in a rapidly shrinking world, which has increased and sometimes forced contact among people from diverse cultures.

Living in the "flat" world that Freidman depicts poses many challenges that transcend cultural, ethnic, and national boundaries. We increasingly find ourselves in a world characterized by an interconnectedness in our economic, environmental, political, and social systems that brings about increasingly complex intercultural interactions, conflicts, and change. The world comes closer together

through global terrorism, diseases such as AIDS and worries about an avian or H1N1 flu pandemic, struggles for peace, drug trafficking, the threat of environmental decay, and the interdependence of our economic systems. The distinctions between what is local and what is global have been blurred, and many people find it difficult to comprehend the new scenario in which they find themselves. Life in the 21st century requires that those who are striving to work together in various endeavors around the globe develop understanding of and sensitivity to the views of others as well as a sense of connectedness that taps into common values and goals. In today's world, global citizens must be able to communicate and collaborate with those whose attitudes, values, knowledge, and ways of doing things differ significantly from their own. Building bridges across cultural boundaries requires a high degree of flexibility, a tolerance for ambiguity, and an understanding of the role culture plays in shaping thinking and behavior. Because these traits are not necessarily innate and consequently need to be developed, education can and must play a key role in facilitating the bridge-building process. How can we begin to understand the phenomenon of globalization, and how does it affect teaching and learning? In an earlier book, Friedman (2000) provided one of the clearest descriptions of globalization and its impact on society, and we discuss this in the following section.

Globalization

Characteristics of Globalization

Globalization replaced the Cold War in the late 1990s, and with it came many distinct changes in the way in which people around the world interact with one another and their immediate, as well as distant, environment. Friedman used the Lexus and the olive tree as symbols to differentiate the two extremes. He said,

> the Lexus and the olive tree were actually pretty good symbols of this post–Cold War era: half the world seemed to be emerging from the Cold War intent on building a better Lexus, dedicated to modernizing, streamlining, and privatizing their economics in order to thrive in the system of globalization. And half of the world—sometimes half the same country, sometimes half the same person—was still caught up in the fight over who owns which olive tree. (p. 5)

Whereas the Lexus characterizes everything that is modern, fast-paced, and dynamic, the olive tree represents everything that keeps people rooted to a particular location, idea, or way of life, with many seeing the conflict as between fundamental religions and societies and the more progressive West as the epitome.

Globalization is characterized by integration; the world has become an increasingly interwoven place, and a person's opportunities are determined by the connections that person has with others. Another feature of globalization can be summarized in a single word–the Web. We have gone from a Cold War system built around division and walls with one of two superpowers in charge to a system built around integration and webs. During the Cold War we knew that at least two people were in control of events. In the globalization system we reach for the Internet, which is a symbol that we are all increasingly connected and nobody is quite in charge–unlike the Cold War.

Globalization is a dynamic, ongoing process. It is the inexorable integration of markets, nation-states, and technologies to a degree never witnessed before, with a powerful backlash from those brutalized or left behind by the new system. Globalization has its own dominant culture that tends to create a homogenizing set of circumstances. In previous eras this sort of cultural homogenization happened on a regional scale–the Romanization of western Europe or the Islamification of Central Asia, North Africa, and the Middle East by Arabs. Today, globalization has tended to involve the spread, for better or for worse, of Americanization and commercialization–from Big Macs to iMacs to Mickey Mouse. Whereas the Cold War was a world of friends and enemies, the globalization world tends to turn all friends and enemies into competitors.

The Cold War system of power was built around nation-states. Today, the globalization system is built around three balances that overlap and affect one another: (1) the traditional balance of power is now in the hands of one nation, the United States, which is the sole and dominant superpower and has tremendous influence over much of what happens in many nations around the world (although China and India are fast becoming increasingly important); (2) there exists a balance between nation-states and global markets, made up of millions of investors around the world who Friedman refers to as the "electronic herd," able to, with the click of a mouse, influence financial markets around the world; and (3) there exists the sensitive balance between individuals and nation-states. Because globalization has brought down many of the dividing walls and because it simultaneously wired the world into networks, the individual suddenly has more power to influence both markets and nation-states than at any time in world history. As a result, in addition to superpowers and supermarkets, we now have super-empowered individuals, some of whom are quite angry and powerful. In the late 1990s, before the attack on the World Trade Center and the Pentagon, Osama bin Laden declared war on the United States. In response, the U.S. Air Force retaliated with a cruise missile attack on him. Seventy-five cruise missiles that cost $1 million apiece were fired at one person! This action was an example of a superpower against a super-empowered individual. And, at least as of this writing, he has not been stopped.

Teaching With a Global Purpose

How can educators begin to respond to such changes in the social order, begin to understand the current state of affairs, and still empower their students with the knowledge and skills to be more effective with their international counterparts? The fact is that Americans (and others) are increasingly engaged with other people, thus demanding greater cross-cultural sensitivity, understanding, and a recognition of the shared values and challenges as well as differences among populations. We must begin asking ourselves questions such as these:

- When is the best time to begin addressing an international perspective?
- How do we learn about one another in ways that span boundaries and enlarge our understandings?
- How do we accomplish this learning in a way that respects the sacred while promoting the secular?
- How do we interact with others in a socially responsible way so as not to exploit but to grasp the essence of other peoples and their important contributions to a clearly global society?

The lack of barriers and walls that globalization brings presents its own set of new challenges. The concept of learning communities is discussed in other chapters, but those contexts are concerned mostly with integrating domestic diversity. This chapter discusses learning communities that are true global communities in which members are committed to thinking, growing, and inquiring with people who cross cultural as well as national boundaries. We are thus faced with new and significant challenges. For instance, how can we build the trust and intimacy that is essential to community with those who live in distant countries? Technology may be one tool that empowers us to reach further into the world, but we must be careful that we do not neglect the work that is needed to develop and maintain true interpersonal relationships and community. This issue is of grave concern because we may have a tendency to look to people in other countries as new customers or competitors and, thus, may interact with them at only a surface level. We may impose our own standards, for our own good, on other people and thereby neglect the impact our presence might have on them. We are then surprised when they resent our presence.

Education for a Global Perspective

A number of professional educational associations have addressed issues related to global and international education over the years. The National Council for

The National Council for the Social Studies

the Social Studies defines a global perspective as the development of the knowledge, skills, and attitudes needed to live effectively in a world possessing limited natural resources and characterized by ethnic diversity, cultural pluralism, and increasing interdependence. Teaching toward a **global perspective** emphasizes the following ideas:

1. The human experience is an increasingly global phenomenon in which people are constantly being influenced by transnational, cross-cultural, and multicultural and multiethnic interaction.

2. The goods we buy, the work we do, the cross-cultural links we have in our own communities and outside them, and increased worldwide communication capabilities all contribute to an imperative that responsible citizens understand global and international issues.

3. There is a wide variety of actors on the world stage, including states, multinational corporations, and numerous voluntary nongovernmental organizations, as well as individuals.

4. Humankind is highly interdependent with the state of the global environment.

5. Citizen participation is critical at both local and international levels.

Education for a global perspective helps individuals better comprehend their own condition in the community and world and make more accurate and effective judgments about other people and about common issues. It emphasizes the study of nations, cultures, and civilizations, including our own pluralistic society, and focuses on understanding how these are interconnected, how they change, how one has influenced another, and what each individual's roles and responsibilities are in such a world. An education with a global perspective provides the individual with a realistic, balanced perspective on world issues and an awareness of how enlightened self-interest includes concerns about people elsewhere in the world. The catchphrase "Think Globally, Act Locally" has served the field of social studies education well. Making global concerns concrete, immediate, and meaningful to students is difficult yet critical.

How Do We Achieve the Cognitive Demands Required for a Global Mind-Set?

The process of international socialization lies at the intersection of cognitive, affective, and behavioral processes. It does not, however, come automatically with cognitive development or physical maturity. Rather, like many developmental processes, certain experiences at critical times seem essential to alter attitude and knowledge formation in this domain. Some characteristics of intellectual development, for instance, may prohibit an international perspective from emerging until an individual has reached a certain age or stage of development. Thus, critical periods may exist for the international socialization of young people, thus becoming bookmarks for educators.

Educators make frequent reference to Piaget's stage theory of development to ground their understanding and explanation of developmental opportunities of young learners. Piaget proposed four stages of cognitive development: the sensorimotor period from birth to 2 years of age; the preoperational period from 2 to 7 years of age; concrete operations from age 8 to 12; and formal operations beginning at around age 12. The preoperational and concrete operations periods are of most interest with regard to the international socialization of young people.

Characteristic of the preoperational period is that children begin to internalize mental representations of the world around them. Until this ability is perfected, children do not seem capable of taking the perspective of another and are said to be egocentric, with the world being viewed as if the child was the center of the reality. A child at this stage is generally incapable of cooperative play (Bybee & Sund, 1982), providing evidence of this egocentricity. Rather, two tend to play independently, with little or no concern for the actions of others.

There is a gradual shift away from cognitive egocentrism as children progress to concrete operations in the middle childhood years. Children at the age of 7 or 8 are able to correctly identify the right and left hand of a person standing opposite them. This partial relativism becomes a more true relativism around age 10 or 11, when children can correctly identify that an object in the middle can be both on the right and left of something. Flavell, Botkin, and Fry (1968) applied this in their work on perceptual role-taking ability by demonstrating that children in this age period have an increased ability to communicate with others by comprehending the perspective of the listener. They thus begin to understand that others may have a viewpoint that is different from their own.

Related to this is a process Piaget termed perceptual or cognitive centration, referring to the tendency children have of being so overwhelmed by one aspect of a visual experience that they are unable to attend to other aspects of a situation. This helps to explain why young children often are unable to acknowledge conflicting or contradictory points of view on social issues, often seeing things as black or white, right or wrong. As children progress from the preoperational stage to concrete operations, they begin the process of decentering, especially if provided guidance and practice, and can accommodate shades of gray and alternative points of view. Selman and Schultz (1990) report that between 9 and 15 years of age children acquire the skill of third-person perspective taking.

Children's thought processes, too, shift from being static to dynamic. That is, the preoperational child is generally unable to conceive of change upon an object—what is perceived is assumed to have always been, and unlikely to change. As the child progresses to the next stage, the world is seen as more dynamic and changeable. In addition, as children become older, they become increasingly capable of demonstrating concern for the needs of others in the community at large. This may help to explain the shift from a present, concrete orientation to a more future, abstract, and general orientation noted by Adelson and O'Neill (1966) in their study of the growth of political ideas in early adolescents.

In support of using developmental theory to explain international socialization, studies indicate that political understanding and learning are initiated at a relatively early age as children begin to interact with authority roles, make decisions, and deal with interpersonal and intergroup cooperation and conflict. The types of experience encountered affect subsequent attitudes regarding national and international identity and perception. Remy, Nathan, Becker, and Torney (1975) concluded that children in the intermediate grades (grades 4 to 8) have a sense of their national identity and are beginning to develop attitudes, values, and beliefs of their own nation and others as international beings and actors, as well as gaining knowledge about such issues as war and peace.

The middle childhood years (ages 8 to 12) may represent the critical period in the development of an international or intercultural perspective in children, especially considering the existence of attitude flexibility that is later followed by attitude rigidity. This age seems to be characterized by rapid cognitive development, especially related to the area of perspective and role-taking ability, low rejection of groups, high attitude flexibility, development of more differentiated intergroup perceptions, and is a time when one is beginning to be able to perceive another's point of view. For those of us concerned with the role of experience in the attainment of intercultural sensitivity, this represents an ideal time to begin traveling with young people and having them participate in international summer camps. Educational efforts to develop an international and intercultural perspective should, therefore, begin during these years.

Is Technology Facilitating a Global Mind-set?

An interesting intercultural conundrum has emerged related to our understanding of intercultural competence, teachers, and young people that offers evidence that positive change is underway. Recall that in Chapter 5 we discussed intercultural competence and the use of the Intercultural Development Inventory, or IDI, as a tool to assess intercultural sensitivity among various populations (Hammer and Bennett, 1998). Studies looking at the intercultural sensitivity of teachers repeatedly show the majority to be on the ethnocentric side of the continuum. Mahon's 2003 study found that of 155 teachers in the Midwest, all were at Minimization or below (Mahon, 2003; 2006). A more recent study by Mahon (2009) among 88 teachers in the Western states found 84% to be in Minimization or below. Grossman & Yuen (2006) reported that of 107 teachers in Hong Kong, 98% were in Minimization or below. And Pappamihiel's 2004 study of early childhood education students, although not using the IDI but based on the DMIS, reported that even after taking two multicultural education courses, few of the 28 preservice teachers surveyed would differentiate behavior w/ESL children, giving them all hugs and smiles as the essential expression of caring, placing them clearly in Minimization or below (Pappamihiel, 2004).

Two studies looking at the intercultural sensitivity of young people show some surprisingly unexpected results. Pederson (1998) used a modified version of the IDI with 145 12-year-old seventh graders, and found 35% in high Minimization and 35% in Acceptance. And among 336 high school students in an international school in Southeast Asia, Straffon (2003) found 71% to be in Acceptance and 26% in Cognitive Adaptation, with only 3% on the ethnocentric side. Both of these studies showed that the greater the amount of exposure to difference (city versus suburban and rural schools in the Pedersen study and the amount of time in international schools in the Straffon study), the higher the level of intercultural sensitivity.

Herein lies the conundrum: the majority of teachers—those we make responsible for advancing the knowledge, skill, and attitude of young people—appear to be stuck on the ethnocentric side of the continuum, while their students show evidence of being more sophisticated in terms of intercultural development. How might this be explained? It is possible that we do not have sufficient tools to assess intercultural sensitivity in young people. It is also conceivable that any intercultural sophistication people may acquire when they are young diminishes as they age and are socialized into adulthood. It's also possible that something else is going on—perhaps even a confluence of powerful and fundamental changes in both society in general as well as within the field of education more specifically, all with intercultural overtones, that are converging at this time that may accelerate the rate and frequency at which young people are exposed to new experience, new people, and new ideas. And this is especially important when viewed in terms of the developmental readiness of acquiring an intercultural perspective.

The United States currently has about 4.5 million K-12 teachers (U. S. Census Bureau, 2004), more than half of whom are baby boomers. The experiences of children growing up, interacting and learning about the world today, are significantly different from the experiences of most teachers. Although we have no data on the intercultural sensitivity of people in earlier generations, recall the conundrum: young people appear to be more culturally sensitive than those in older generations. A multitude of factors may be coming together suggesting that the seeds of change may be sown and that we may be on the verge of something we have not witnessed in the past. This confluence of factors includes:

- an increase in the number of children attending school worldwide;
- an increase in overall exposure of young people to cultural diversity through increased movement of people across national borders as tourists, immigrants, and refugees and greater global media exposure;
- a concerted effort in schools to provide more culturally relevant content, including increased attention to second language learning;
- greater understanding and attention to intercultural concepts as they relate to the instructional process itself; and
- a growing desire on the part of young people to travel and study outside their home countries.

Perhaps the shift in intercultural competence is beginning to take place as a result of the increased integration and ubiquitous nature of digital technologies in schools around the world. Millennials, the most technologically savvy generational group so far, are more proficient with technology than most of their teachers and parents. In 2004, 85 percent of students in this generational group in the United States owned or had regular access to at least one computer; 72 percent checked e-mail daily; and 26 percent used instant messaging (Kruse, 2004). This certainly has increased in recent years with social networking sites such as Facebook now boasting more than 300 million regular users, and more and more mobile phones, text-messaging, and Twitter in use. Technology is also much more pervasive, and Internet penetration rates are increasing worldwide—especially in Africa where it has increased 1,359%; the Middle East where it has increased 1,360%; and in Latin America where it has increased 873% since 2000 (Miniwatts Marketing, 2009).

International linkages in education have existed at least since the 1920s when a number of global learning networks began in Europe and the United States. Such efforts made use of available technologies and modes of communication that enabled classrooms to exchange cultural artifacts such as letters, photos, and flowers from their local area with children in other parts of the world. Today's technology makes it increasingly easy to bring children into more frequent and regular interaction with one another—and oftentimes in very meaningful ways.

A number of engaging Internet-based school linkage initiatives exist and they will be reviewed at the end of this chapter. Suffice it to say for now that there is a flurry of activity and a world of opportunity that is just beginning to unfold for children around the world that may explain the intercultural conundrum presented earlier.

Curriculum Transformation: The International Perspective

The integration of a global perspective across the curriculum was made practical by Robert Hanvey's 1978 paper, "An Attainable Global Perspective." In this work, Hanvey identified five elements of a global perspective that can be transformed into teachable skills and perspectives that cut across academic disciplines and grade levels. Each of these elements is examined in the discussion that follows.

Perspective Consciousness

Perspective consciousness refers to a person's awareness that he or she has a view of the world that is not universally shared, that this view is shaped by unconscious as well as conscious influences, and that others may have profoundly different views. This dimension especially differentiates opinion from perspective. Opinion refers to the surface layer of a person's thoughts. It is the tip of the iceberg, so to speak, showing only a small portion of its totality. Underneath the surface lie the generally hidden, unexamined assumptions and judgments people make about life, about others, and about right and wrong (think back to the iceberg analogy of culture in Chapter 3). The assumption that human dominance over nature is both attainable and desirable is an example of a perspective that lies deep in many Western minds. It was not until this traditionally unexamined assumption surfaced that many philosophical choices that previously had escaped our attention were raised. As a result, debate involving our relationship with the environment ensued and stimulated considerable thought, activity, and discussion. Today, we struggle to understand our role in both the cause and correction of global warming. Similarly, the feminist movement raised the consciousness of women and men regarding the role of women in society. In the process, deep layers of chauvinism inherent in much of our thinking about male and female roles were revealed. Likewise, concerned parents, addressing the unmet needs of their exceptional children, pointed out how the educational system (and society in general) discriminated against a large segment of society, and as a result, were the cause behind many of the current practices related to exceptionality.

Children can develop perspective consciousness in a number of ways. Social studies curricula, for example, can help students examine their own culture's behavior from another point of view. Ethnocentrism suggests that most individuals have a tendency to overemphasize their own culture's accomplishments and point of view. Children can be encouraged to question their own cultural perspectives and to consider how others might view them. When studying people in other parts of the world, for instance, students can be asked to explore why most people prefer to live in their native habitats despite what may appear to be rather difficult conditions. Why, children in your classrooms might ask, would anyone want to live in the Arctic, where people have to contend with extremes in temperature and have to hunt for their food? Or why would the Mundurucu people of the Amazon River in South America want to live where the temperature is extremely hot year-round; where there are poisonous animals and annoying insects to contend with; and where the food staple, the poisonous manioc, has to be boiled and pounded over hot fires in the sweltering heat just to make it eatable? Likewise, children growing up in those regions of the world might ask the same of our young students: how can anyone live in an environment where the air is polluted, where the water is trapped in pipes and treated with chemicals, and where food is not freshly hunted and prepared but is packaged and loaded with preservatives so its shelf life can be extended? It can be quite enlightening and engaging to help students see how strange their own behavior looks to others as others' might appear to them.

Children can also develop perspective consciousness by reading some of the numerous books that have been written either from another's perspective or from an insider's point of view. Children's books such as *The True Story of the Three Little Pigs as Told by A. Wolf,* (Scieszka, 1989) or, *The Wolf's Story: What Really Happened to Little Red Riding Head* (Forward, 2005) for instance are good ways to help children see that other points of view exist around most topics. In addition, teachers can use common optical illusions to help children see how the same image can appear differently when viewed from alternate perspectives. Even young children can recognize that others may interpret events in quite different ways, making comments such as, "He says I'm not big enough to play."

State of the Planet Awareness

The awareness of prevailing world conditions and trends includes such aspects as population growth and migration; economic conditions; resources and the physical environment; political developments; advancements in science and technology, law, and health; and various forms of conflicts. Most people, even from highly mobile societies like the United States, spend the majority of their time in their local area. However, developments in communication technology have brought the world, if not into most people's homes, certainly within most people's reach. Extensive global media coverage via television news is making its impact felt at the diplomatic and war tables as well.

The liberal weekly *Die Zeit* of Hamburg, Germany, relates two incidents that capture the extent of the impact made by the aggressive CNN news broadcasting team relatively early in its existence:

> In the summer of 1989, when the U.S. government was searching for a response to threats that hostages in Lebanon would be killed, a White House advisor was asked where President George Bush was spending the day. "He is in his office, watching CNN," the advisor said. "CNN is interviewing Middle East experts; maybe one of them will have an idea that the president can use." And when the Americans marched into Panama in December, 1989, Soviet leader Mikhail Gorbachev made use of the medium. CNN's Moscow correspondent was called to the Kremlin in the middle of the night. There, a press aide read a condemnation of the invasion for the camera. The official note to the U.S. ambassador was not delivered until hours later. The Kremlin's excuse was that it was counting on Washington getting the Kremlin's reaction immediately via CNN. (CNN, 1990, p. 34)

Another illustration of the media's educational role can be seen in its coverage of the first Gulf War in the winter of 1991. The U.S. military, knowing that Iraq was watching coverage of the war on CNN, actually planned their movements differently from those they were reporting to the American public so as to confuse the enemy. Thus, while the media makes **state of the planet awareness** a possibility as never before, it also makes the spread of misinformation easier and faster than ever before. Also, if we are not careful, we may find it very easy to believe that the real world consists only of televised images according to CNN. Or recall the story line in the successful film *Wag the Dog,* which portrays a media-produced war created to divert public attention from unethical presidential behavior.

General public awareness of the state of the planet must become a priority. Children must be taught to reflect on national and world conditions and to ask questions that go beyond the obvious. For example, they should be aware that despite all of the United Nation's accomplishments, conditions for most of the world's people show serious deterioration (Childers & Urquhart, 1994; UNHCR, 2008; HAMER, 2007). For instance:

1. The world's population has grown more in the last 50 years than in the past 4 million years and is the single biggest threat to our planet and its resources. By the year 2050 there will be 4 billion more mouths to feed. This number alone is equal to what the total world population was in 1975.

2. Four hundred million people are unemployed in the "south" (the preferred term for those countries once referred to as undeveloped or third world). Forty million new jobs are needed each year just to maintain the present

world condition. Under present north-south imbalances, there is not the remotest chance that these jobs will materialize.

3. Over 1 billion people live in poverty today, 40% more than in 1980. In 1960, the wealthiest one fifth of the world's population were 30 times richer than the poorest one fifth. Today, the wealthiest one fifth of the world's population are 60 times richer than the poorest one fifth. Viewed from the perspective of a single country, such conditions represent the classic condition for a massive and violent revolution.

4. Television, radio, film, and the Internet has spread to the poor countries knowledge of the affluent lifestyles of the minority in the north and of some southern elites, permitting angry comparisons with the desperate poverty of the vast majority in the south.

5. In 1951, when the United Nations High Commission on Refugees (UNHCR) was founded, there were some 1.5 million legally classified refugees worldwide. Today, there are more than 20 million refugees worldwide. A further 24 million people have been displaced within their own countries due to ecological, economic, and political upheaval.

6. World grain production per capita has shrunk by half since 1950. In Africa, grain production has dropped 28% since 1967 due to the effects of drought, desertification, erosion, and population growth. Every day, more than 16,000 children die from hunger-related causes. This is one child every 5 seconds.

7. The rate of environmental deterioration continues unabated despite the best intentions of the activists and policymakers. The problems posed by global warming, ecosystem destruction, and ozone depletion demand urgent attention. Currently, 1 in 5 people in the world survive on less water per day than is used to flush a toilet.

8. On a global basis, only $1.90 is spent, per person per year, on the United Nations. This figure compares to $150 spent per person worldwide on weapons.

Activity 23:
The Plight of Women on a Global Scale

Most people do not know that within the United States, 43 million Americans are considered disabled or handicapped. Nor do most people know how many Americans go hungry or are homeless, or how many children are born addicted to cocaine or suffer from AIDS-related complications. Students must be actively encouraged to expand their knowledge base, to review international news sources, and to inquire into the knowledge and perspective of international visitors. Such actions, incidentally, would also help students develop the first dimension of global education, perspective consciousness.

Understanding one's place relative to others in a global society is critical. If the world population were reduced to 100 people while maintaining existing human ratios, there would be 60 Asians, 12 Europeans, 13 from North and South America, and 14 Africans; 49 would be female and 51 male; 82 would be nonwhite and 18 would be white; 67 would be non-Christian and 33 Christian; 89 would be heterosexual and 11 would be gay or lesbian; 32% of the entire world's wealth would be in the hands of only 5 people and all 5 would be citizens of the United States; 80 would live in substandard housing; 67 would be unable to read; 50 would suffer from malnutrition; and only 1 would have a college education and 1 would own a computer (Family Care Foundation, 2008).

Cross-Cultural Awareness

The cross-cultural dimension of global education includes an awareness of social and cultural diversity around the world and at least a beginning awareness of how one's own culture and society might be viewed from other vantage points. Hanvey suggests that this dimension may be the most difficult to attain because people typically do not have the time or expertise needed to truly understand those who are different from themselves. We also know that understanding about others does not necessarily follow from simple contact. Lengthy, structured, and intimate contact under certain conditions is required to gain an insider's understanding of those in another culture (see Chapter 6 for a more in-depth discussion of intergroup relations).

How can schooling best develop **cross-cultural awareness** in young people? To define what schools might reasonably hope to accomplish in this direction, it may be helpful to recall the iceberg model of culture as you consider four levels of cross-cultural awareness posited by Hanvey.

The first level involves awareness of superficial or extremely visible cultural traits, the kind that often become the basis for stereotypes: skin color, dress, language patterns, ceremonies, and so on. Much of this information is obtained through textbooks, television, and tourism. At this level, the individual outside a given culture typically interprets observed actions of others as exotic, or worse, bizarre. This level is most like the denial and defense stages of the DMIS discussed in Chapter 5.

The second level involves awareness of significant but more subtle cultural traits that contrast markedly with one's own. Such information is often gained as a result of culture conflict situations and is often interpreted as unbelievable. The reaction here, however, is more on an emotional level. Interactions are considered frustrating, irrational, and against "common sense," similar to those encountered at the DMIS stage of defense.

The third level also includes an awareness of significant and subtle cultural traits that contrast markedly with one's own. However, this level is characterized by more intellectual emphasis and analysis. Others' behavior is better understood and seen as more like one's own. This level might be likened to the minimization stage on the DMIS.

The fourth level involves awareness of how another culture feels from the perspective of an insider. People attain this perspective through cultural immersion: that is, from living the culture. Information is perceived as believable not simply because it is understood at the cognitive level but because of its familiarity at the subjective or affective level. This level might be likened to reaching the state called "home" on the U-curve or the DMIS stages of acceptance, adaptation, and integration.

Effective culture learning is more of an affective and behavioral process than a cognitive process. A person truly learns about another culture by living it, not by being told about it. Development of intercultural competence may be, as Hanvey and others have noted, the most difficult, yet the most critical, of the five dimensions to achieve. However, strategies do exist that can assist people on their way to becoming interculturally competent. The culture-general framework used throughout this text, for instance, can have a significant impact on cognition, affect, and behavior in cross-cultural settings (Cushner & Brislin,

1996). It is a cognitive tool that engages the emotions and may be just the tool for the school context.

Knowledge of Global Dynamics or World Systems

Attaining this fourth dimension of a global perspective, knowledge of global dynamics or world systems, requires a modest understanding of how world eco-systems operate. Educators can stress the interconnectedness of things by asking students to consider the impact one particular decision or action will have on another. The following examples illustrate interconnectedness.

The Importance of Systems Thinking

In southeastern Australia, the fluctuation of various fish populations in area river basins was found to be caused by an increase in estrogen in the water. Following an extensive investigation, it was determined that this hormone found its way into area waterways by being flushed out in toilet wastewater. Women using birth control pills eliminated higher-than-usual levels of estrogen in their urine. This increase of estrogen in the wastewater directly affected the behavior of fish downstream! This is a good example of an unanticipated, unintended outcome. And, we are now learning that fish caught in many U.S. waters contain pharmaceutical residues, including medicines to treat high blood pressure, bi-polar disorder, and depression.

Now consider an example of the vulnerability of ecological systems to changes in distant parts of the world. The recent increase in mosquito populations across the United States can be directly tied to our tremendous appetite for inexpensive fast-food hamburgers. Stop for a moment and consider some of your own hypo-theses to explain this phenomenon. What have you proposed as the cause? Not so surprisingly, many people know that an increasing proportion of the meat we eat comes from cattle raised on land that was once rain forest in Central and South America. But most would still not see the connection. We have come to understand that these rain forests provide the winter nesting sites for many of the northern hemisphere's migrating bird populations. As an increasing percent-age of the rain forest is destroyed, so too are the winter nesting sites for these birds, resulting in a greater than normal death rate for the species. The decline in bird population has resulted in fewer songbirds returning north each year, and consequently, an increase in the mosquito population that forms a major part of the birds' diet. This is a vivid example of the impact that individual choice, in this case eating habits, can have. The global educator's catch-phrase, "Think Globally, Act Locally" again becomes paramount.

When a new element is introduced into any system, it has unanticipated effects. Hanvey suggests that there are no side effects, only surprise effects. Thus, when we intervene in any system, we should be prepared for some surprising consequences. Think of a spider's web. Although the web is composed of mul-tiple strands, when one is touched in even the slightest manner, it vibrates and affects the entire web. We confront numerous other examples of this principle in action almost every day. Global warming caused by the carbon dioxide buildup in the atmosphere, depletion of the ozone layer, the greenhouse effect, the poisoning of groundwater, and the weakening of the eagle's egg as a result of DDT moving up the food chain are all examples of these surprise conse-quences, which we are now trying to correct. We must learn, as Hanvey suggests, to look for the "concealed wiring," the hidden functions of elements in a system.

Awareness of Human Choice

Hanvey's fifth dimension, awareness of human choices, represents the final critical step in attaining a global perspective. The problems of choice that confront individuals, nations, and the human species as they increase their knowledge of the global system are addressed in this dimension. Until recently, people were generally unaware of the unanticipated outcomes and long-term consequences of their

actions. This is no longer the case as a global consciousness or cognition is emerging. People now must consider the implications of an expanded knowledge and communication base. Negligence, or even making an unwise choice out of ignorance, may set the stage for countless problems at some future time.

Fortunately, we know a great deal more than we used to, and choices do exist. Consider the use of chlorofluorocarbons (CFCs) and the growing problem of ozone depletion. We have two choices: we can continue to use CFCs because at the present time they make refrigeration and propellants possible, or we can stop using them because of their effect on the environment, while actively seeking a replacement product. The simple substitution of pump spray mechanisms for propellant sprays on a variety of

products is a good example of a successful alternative. It is awareness of the problem, however, that often makes the difference in the success of alternatives.

Children can make remarkable strides toward realizing their power and ability to bring about change. Many years ago, Israeli elementary schoolchildren went on a campaign to protect some of their nation's threatened wildflower populations. They raised the awareness of adults to such an extent that the adults stopped indiscriminately picking the flowers. Many of the threatened flowers have since been removed from the endangered species lists.

Likewise, a number of years ago one of the authors of this text initiated a school exchange program between fifth- and sixth-grade children in northeast Ohio and schoolchildren in the Yucatán peninsula of Mexico and in Belize. Seventeen children went on the first trip from Ohio to Belize. One gesture of appreciation the Ohio children made to their host community was to present the village school with a world atlas signed by everyone at the visitors' school. The gift seemed to be the first book the Belize school actually owned. This discovery made such an impression on the students from Ohio that on their return home they decided to do something about the situation. All the fifth- and sixth-grade students in the school became involved in operating an after-school snack bar, collecting usable books from the community, and packaging them for shipment overseas. With the proceeds from their snack bar and their collection efforts, students were able to send more than 500 books to their peers in this small village in Belize. Needless to say, the children felt tremendous pride, realizing that they, personally, could have such an impact on individuals so far away. This lesson was one that no textbook could teach them and that they will never forget.

What, Specifically, Should Students Study?

The American Forum for Global Education (AFGE, 2004), one of the nation's first eduational organizations devoted to helping educators understand how best to develop a global understanding in their students, identified three major areas on which a global education curriculum should focus: global issues, problems, and challenges; culture and world areas; and the United States and the world. Within these three larger themes, 10 specific topics of study are recommended:

1. Conflict and its control, including terrorism and national security
2. Economic systems and international trade
3. Global belief systems, including the study of differing philosophies and religions
4. Human rights and social justice, including gender equity issues as well as health, education, and food security
5. Management of the planet's resources, including the study of energy and environmental degradation
6. Political systems, including a study of the United Nations, negotiations and treaties, and nongovernmental organizations
7. Population, including population control and immigration and emigration concerns
8. Human commonality and diversity through the study of race and ethnicity, thus working to reduce prejudice and ethnocentrism
9. The technocratic revolution, looking at the increasing roles that science, technology, and communication play in people's lives
10. Sustainable development, including studies of urban growth and the disparities that exist between countries of the north and those in the south

Characteristics of a Global Classroom

Most schooling is an ethnocentric activity, with most national systems of schooling addressing the needs of the nation they serve and transmitting the "proper" attitudes and beliefs thought to be necessary to maintain the society. Long-term goals in most schools, however, reflect some of the ideals of a global perspective. If you were to closely examine the philosophical goal statements of most schools, you would find statements such as these: to appreciate people from other cultures; to develop sensitivity to the needs of people different from themselves; to increase knowledge about people around the world.

The philosophical stage has been partially set, but the methods for implementing such goal statements have created a problem. Schools in the United States, as well as most parts of the world, typically present curricular experiences through a predominantly cognitive approach and from a rather narrow ethnocentric point of view. In addition, until recently, curriculum development efforts have had little input or interaction from people of different backgrounds. Such assumptions and practices are presently being called into question. To build true professional global communities in which teachers and students can begin to collaborate in real-world problem solving, we will need to help students learn firsthand about cultures of other countries, share what they are learning locally and globally with others, collaborate on common projects across national boundaries wherever possible, study and live in other countries with students from those countries, welcome global career opportunities, and develop capacities for success in a global village. But how can these goals be achieved?

Broadly speaking, a globally competent student has knowledge and genuine curiosity about the state of the world that includes an understanding of the historical experiences of other people, their cultural practices, environmental and economic concerns; sufficient cross-cultural skills that enable her or him to communicate effectively with people from other countries and cultures; and a commitment to inclusive ethical citizenship and social action. Teachers, too, must exhibit similar knowledge, skills, and dispositions if they are to effectively guide their students toward global competence. Teachers should know the international dimensions of their subject matter; have the pedagogical skills to assist their students to analyze primary sources from other nations; and a willingness to guide students to become responsible global citizens.

In a classroom with a global perspective, global education is not merely an add-on to an already overcrowded curriculum. Rather, relevant concepts and activities that develop a global perspective are woven throughout the curriculum. Most important, global classrooms seek to help students develop such critical cognitive skills and attitudes as empathy, interconnectedness, perspective taking, cross-cultural understanding, action orientation, and prejudice reduction. In such classrooms, students are active in building connections with others. They may have pen pals, or e-pals, with children in other parts of the world. In addition to communicating through writing with others and thus developing their language skills, students may be sharing audiotapes, videotapes, photographs, classroom materials, and other artifacts that reflect their own and each other's cultures. Children may read books about people's lives in other communities, which helps develop a global perspective while simultaneously achieving the goals and objectives of a language arts curriculum. Students may work on collaborative writing projects with peers in other countries, as Jerome's class was doing with students in India. In short, students go about developing their language arts and other skills with other people in mind.

Pedagogies: Old and New

All the pedagogical techniques discussed in this book also apply to the global classroom. Indeed, the use of developmentally appropriate practice, collaborative and cooperative groups, and student involvement in planning takes on a new and richer dimension when placed in the context of an international perspective. However, a global perspective can also be introduced in more traditionally oriented classrooms. What is important here is the notion of a broader perspective. In addition, students in global classrooms may use technology in creative ways. Classroom computers can be connected to networks that enable children to communicate on a regular basis with others from around the world. Joint activities may develop whereby classes in two or more countries collaborate in real time, on some global issue, as is being done in an increasing number of schools that use video teleconferencing technology to motivate young people in social studies and foreign language education (Roberts, 2007). Schools may also use digital technologies to link classes, enabling them to transfer artwork, poetry, essays, and other student work to other schools. Students can conduct conference calls with peers around the world while transmitting pictures of themselves, thus adding a highly personal dimension to the interaction. Rather than simulate a French café in a traditional French language class, some schools have had video teleconferences in French cafés, thus allowing students to see and interact directly with students overseas in a real-life setting. Or young people from around the world can come together via technology to discuss a global current event.

Linking Students Around the World

Although it is helpful to have such technology in global classrooms, much can be done without it. Students can, for example, make excellent use of maps, local and national newspapers, encyclopedias and other books, taped television programs, and United Nations materials. Educators do not need more advanced technology than the mail service to introduce students to pen pals around the world. When crises occur around the world, children's messages to others can have quite an impact. Rennebohm-Franz (1996) reports that the impact of a group of first-grade children sending letters of emotional support to children in Kobe, Japan, following the earthquake in 1995 helped both her students and those in Japan feel connected to one another. One child's drawing showed her family standing outside their house at night with the following message of hope and connectedness:

> I hope you get your houses built. This is a picture of me and my family looking out at the night. Maybe you see the same stars and moon we do. (p. 266)

The class received a message back from the teacher, stating:

> We began receiving your heartwarming messages from around the world.... We have posted the pictures, letters and messages in the classrooms and hallway bulletin boards of city schools that are serving as refugee centers. For those of us living among the aftermath of Kobe's quake, these messages have had an immeasurable heartwarming effect. They have given us an opportunity to realize that emotional support is just as important as material support and that we are all inhabitants of the same small planet. (p. 266)

Roles: Old and New

In global classrooms, local members of the international community are considered to be an integral part of the school. As events unfold around the world, representatives from the various communities are invited into classrooms to share their experience and perspectives. These presentations may occur at regular times in certain classes (e.g., social studies, language arts) or during regular school assemblies devoted to world events. Such involvement serves to break down some of the personal barriers that tend to develop between people. Not only are students introduced to different perspectives, they are also introduced to various cultures and languages firsthand. Such activities add a personal element to the content under study that a textbook cannot while serving to build bridges of understanding in the local community. Thus, when a natural disaster occurs somewhere in the world or when a conflict breaks out, children can associate it with real people; it is no longer an abstract event unfolding in some far-off, abstract corner of the world. Finally, having adults from other parts of the world serve as teachers helps students understand that teaching and learning can occur in a variety of ways.

Place of Content Knowledge: Old and New

Globally oriented classrooms, like collaborative classrooms, integrate subject matter from various academic disciplines. Often these integrated curricula are jointly developed by educators from many countries. This collaboration, of course, helps ensure the accuracy of the content being studied. For example, the Pacific Circle Consortium developed educational materials that integrate the perspectives and contributions of educators from the United States, Canada, Australia, New Zealand, and Japan as well as some Pacific Island nations. One of their products, *The Ocean Project,* used the Pacific Ocean as a curriculum vehicle for students located in countries on the Pacific Rim. Two such projects have been developed. One provides fifth- and sixth-grade students in two different countries with an integrated look at the culture, environment, economics, and cultural interaction of the other group's region. At the beginning of the unit, each group of students studies local conditions (environment, culture, economics, etc.). Next, a simulated transoceanic voyage brings the students to the other country, where they study similar concepts in that location. Students in Honolulu, Hawaii, and Hiroshima, Japan, for instance, thus learn about one another's way of life and local environment. A similarly developed unit for upper secondary school students looks at the use of the world's oceans, treaties, and international law. An international project on Antarctica has also been developed. Additional collaborative projects that can engage your students are discussed later in the chapter.

Assessment: Old and New

Assessment in global classrooms may generally be described as global and comprehensive as well. That is, because of the wide variety of activities and the emphasis on cross-disciplinary or interdisciplinary studies, global classrooms can easily use both traditional and alternative forms of assessment. If technology is used in global classrooms to stimulate curricular activities, it can also be used in evaluation. Everything from computer-generated assessments in which students receive immediate feedback to the production of videos, PowerPoint presentations, Webquests, and other technology-based activities can be assessed for how they demonstrate what students know and can do. Increasingly, the assessment of many internationally collaborative activities has proven to have a significant impact on knowledge attainment. The central point to remember in the assessment of global classrooms, as well as of other kinds of classrooms described in this book, is that when a wide variety of activities enhances the curriculum, they can be evaluated in a wide variety of ways.

Teaching the Global Perspective

Development of a global perspective should be integrated throughout the school curriculum, not just in the social studies. Although large-scale infusion is desirable, an international perspective can be integrated into the curriculum by individual teachers offering international focus courses, by internationalizing instructional methods and materials, by encouraging international travel as an important part of one's education, and by internationalizing the disciplines.

International focus courses exist in such areas as anthropology, regional history, geography, global or world studies, foreign language study, art and music, world religions, ethnic group studies, and international business. Such courses seem most appropriate at the middle and secondary level and quite readily emerge from the disciplines themselves.

Internationalizing instructional methods and materials might emphasize intercultural interaction in the classroom using the special experiences of immigrant and international students as resources. Teachers should employ culturally appropriate instructional and assessment strategies, and textbooks should be reviewed for balance. Partnership programs with other schools and countries, such as those with the schools in India and Belize referred to earlier, can also be developed.

Teaching the Global Perspective

Well-developed international travel experiences can also be an integral part of many classes, from eco-tourist ventures in Central American rain-forest regions to language experience or arts opportunities in foreign countries. Such programs, if designed to go beyond the typical tourist experience and into the local culture, can provide that experiential dimension that is so critical to effective culture learning (Cushner, 2004).

Internationalizing the disciplines involves infusing key elements of a global perspective across the entire curriculum. There are numerous ways this infusion can be accomplished at all levels and in all content areas. For instance, in reading and language arts, students might study how non-American and non-British writers use the English language. World literature courses should strive to include numerous examples from a non-Western origin. And literature should be integrated with the social sciences as a way to introduce multiple perspectives on abstract concepts. Children's literature can also be used to present concepts of interest in international education. Classic Dr. Seuss books, such as *The Lorax* and *The Butter Battle Book*, can be used in a study of the environment and the nuclear arms race, respectively. Students might also analyze the portrayal of minorities and internationals in basal textbooks.

In science education, teachers might help students observe and understand the natural world and study the problems created as a result of increased technology and innovation. Students should be encouraged to ask questions about global warming, about water shortages, or about growing threats of extinction. Then, students should be encouraged to propose solutions to many of these problems, solutions that require knowledge and input from diverse peoples and cultures, all of whom "own" the problems and will ultimately have to come together to solve them. Although technology may be universal, as proposed for possible solutions to problems, its application is quite specific. The study of what constitutes "appropriate" technology in a given situation demands sensitivity to such aspects as local environment, culture, history, and language. The topic of unplanned change can be introduced through the study of biology and evolution.

Inequities of energy consumption across the planet can be explored. Finally, the global nature of such systems as the water cycle, the mineral cycle, and the energy cycle can be studied.

In foreign language education, cultural studies can be expanded beyond the mother country to include colonized people as well as immigrant and refugee populations. The role of translators in world diplomacy can be studied. Foreign languages can be taught through folk songs, and English as a Second Language or English as a Foreign Language can be introduced to foreign language teachers and students.

Mathematics education should stress the metric system. The United States is the only nation in the world not actively using metrics. Math concepts can be illustrated through problems that simultaneously teach about world trends and global issues. Traditional numeration systems from other cultures can be studied. The mathematics and possible computer application of Islamic art can be analyzed. Likewise, the impact of women on the development of mathematics (as well as other topics) can be introduced.

Finally, history and the social studies should look at various perspectives on similar issues. The American Revolution, for instance, certainly looked different through British eyes. Studying other nation's textbooks, maps, or discussing current events with international students can go far in helping students develop perspective consciousness. Issues of population growth, personal family migration, history, and cultural diffusion can become the focus of historical inquiry, as can the interaction between geography, culture, and the environment.

The bottom line is that students should be encouraged to ask difficult questions and to explore possible reasons and solutions from a variety of points of view. Why, for instance, does one fifth of the world's population (in the north or developed countries) use two thirds of the world's natural resources, and what might be done to counterbalance this? What does it really mean to be an over-populated nation when an individual in the north has the same impact on the earth in terms of pollution and utilization of resources as 24 or 25 individuals in the south? And why should soybeans, for instance, be exported from Brazil to feed cattle in the Western nations, to the detriment of the small farmers in South America and the benefit of wealthy corporations in North America? These questions are difficult to explore, but are ultimately ones that have to be addressed if the people of the world are ever to live in true balance.

Studying the Global Environment

Programs That Link Schools

In addition to the many global education activities and projects in which individual schools and classrooms can participate, a number of projects and networks have been formed that are designed to better inform and connect schools around the world. Following are summaries of a few of these programs in which students from around the world may participate.

Associated Schools Project Network of UNESCO

The Associated Schools Project Network (ASPnet), boasting the largest international program for schools in the world, provides a network for more than 7,900 schools from 176 nations to engage in a variety of collaborative activities (www.unesco.org/education/asp). The Baltic Sea Project, for example, begun in 1998, works with

200 schools in nine countries that border the Baltic Sea, raising awareness of environmental issues in the region while helping students understand the science, social, and cultural aspects of human interdependence. Other projects include Breaking the Silence–The Transatlantic Slave Trade Educational Project (TST), World Heritage Education Project, the Educational Toolkit on Dolphins, an online 24-hour student conference on globalization, a UNESCO antiracism campaign, and the innovative Mondialogo Intercultural Dialogue and Exchange initiative.

Bridges to Understanding

Bridges to Understanding (www.bridgesweb.org) uses digital technology and the art of storytelling to empower and unite youth worldwide, enhance cross-cultural understanding, and build global citizenship.

ePals

ePals (www.epals.org) is a global community that has linked more than 8 million students and teachers in 120,000 classrooms in more than 200 countries and territories through a number of electronic exchange programs.

GLOBE

GLOBE (Global Learning and Observations to Benefit the Environment, www.globe.gov) is a worldwide hands-on, primary and secondary school-based science and education program. GLOBE's vision promotes and supports students, teachers, and scientists to collaborate on inquiry-based investigations of the environment and the Earth system, working in close partnership with NASA and NSF Earth System Science Projects (ESSPs) in study and research about the dynamics of Earth's environment. Started on Earth Day 1995, today the international GLOBE network has grown to include representatives from 111 participating countries and 140 U.S. partners coordinating GLOBE activities that are integrated into their local and regional communities. Due to their efforts, there are more than 50,000 GLOBE-trained teachers representing over 20,000 schools around the world. GLOBE students have contributed more than 20 million measurements to the GLOBE database for use in their inquiry-based science projects.

LinkTV

LinkTV (www.linktv.org) is the first television channel and website dedicated to providing global perspectives on news, events, and culture, connecting viewers with people and organizations in the forefront of social change and the cultures of an increasingly global community. YouthNoise.org, a component of Link's Engagement division, is composed of 158,000 registered users from all 50 states and 176 countries, creating a virtual meeting place for the next generation of global social activists.

Peace Corps World Wise Schools

Peace Corps World Wise Schools (http://www.peacecorps.gov/wws/) has assisted more than 3 million U.S. students to communicate directly with Peace Corps volunteers all over the world, many who facilitate school linkage programs.

International Children's Digital Library

International Children's Digital Library (www.icdlbooks.org) is an online collection of books that represents outstanding historical and contemporary books from throughout the world. The ultimate goal is to have every culture and language represented so that every child can know and appreciate the riches of children's literature from the world community.

iEARN

iEARN (www.iearn.org) is the world's largest nonprofit global network that enables young people to use the Internet and other new technologies to engage in collaborative educational projects that both enhance learning and make a difference in the world. More than 20,000 schools representing more than 115 nations engage more than 1 million students each day in a variety of activities that work across national boundaries. While the use of technology is often the main focus, the fact that students engage across cultures makes this an ideal global education experience itself. In addition to the technology-based format, annual conferences enable teachers to meet face-to-face to exchange ideas and build relationships.

Global SchoolNet

Global SchoolNet (www.globalschoolnet.org) is a project that combines innovative teaching ideas with Web publishing, video conferencing, and other online tools to bridge geographic gaps, allowing young people around the world to learn together. Global SchoolNet is a growing international network of 70,000+ online educators who engage in online project-based learning activities. Since its inception, Global SchoolNet has reached more than a million students from 45,000 schools across 194 countries, and it welcomes new members at all times.

Global Classrooms

Global Classrooms (www.unausa.org/globalclassrooms) is an innovative United Nations–based educational program that engages public middle school and high school students in an exploration of current world issues through interactive simulations and curricular materials. Global Classrooms cultivates literacy and leadership as students explore important topics such as peacekeeping, sustainable development, and human rights.

During class simulations of the UN Security Council and other UN organizations, students tackle global concerns including poverty, refugee protection, and the environment as they role-play country, interest group, or nongovernmental organization positions. To bridge the gap in the Model UN community between experienced programs and traditionally underserved urban schools, UNA-USA has instituted Global Classrooms in American cities and in locations around the world. The objectives of the Global Classrooms program in these cities are to bring the benefits of international education and Model UN to public school students, diversify the Model UN community, and institutionalize international current affairs education in schools underrepresented in the Model UN community.

How Might This Look in Practice?

How might all these suggestions look in action? Let's go back to Jerome Becker's sixth-grade classroom and look closely at the Partnership Story activity his students were involved in and analyze what he was doing. Part One of the partnership story was written by Jerome's class, followed by the conclusion from the students in India (Part Two). Keep in mind that this activity was realized without the use of computer technologies, demonstrating that effective globally focused activities can link students even in rather remote parts of the world. Imagine the exchanges that can evolve in most classrooms today.

Part One (United States)

Once in a circus there was a tiger who would not perform because he was lonely. The circus owner sent his daughter, Maryetta, to the jungle to find a friend to perform with the lonely tiger. Maryetta's father gave her $1,000 to purchase a tiger. Her father told her to spend the money wisely.

The next day on a boat trip to the jungle, Maryetta met a trapper named Toby. Toby asked Maryetta why she was going to the jungle. Maryetta told him that she needed to purchase a tiger for her father's circus.

"What a coincidence," Toby remarked, all the while trying to figure out a way he might obtain Maryetta's money before the real trapper could reach her. "I am meeting a girl from a circus tomorrow."

"You are?" Maryetta asked, looking puzzled. "Do you know what circus she is from?"

"No," replied Toby, "but it must be yours. How many girls could there be going to the jungle tomorrow to buy a tiger?"

"I guess you're right. I'll meet you by the river at 10:00 tomorrow morning."

Toby wanted to get there before the real trapper did, so he said, "Why don't we meet at 9:00 and get an early start?"

They agreed to this and then went their own ways. The next day was a beautiful summer day, perfect for trapping tigers. Toby rented a boat and met Maryetta precisely at 9:00.

"I'll need to collect my fee of one hundred dollars each morning before we begin," Toby told Maryetta.

"I thought you told my father your fee was one hundred and fifty dollars per day," Maryetta said, wondering why he had lowered his fee.

"Oh, well, I guess I forgot what I said before. One hundred and fifty dollars it is then," said Toby.

"Alright, but I don't have a lot of money. Do you think we'll be trapping for a long time?"

"Probably only two or three days," Toby reassured.

"Well, then, let's get going!" exclaimed Maryetta.

At first, the boat trip down the river was pleasant. About noon, however, the boat struck a huge rock which punctured its side. Maryetta and Toby spent the rest of the day repairing the boat. As a result, they had to spend the night on the river bank.

During the night, Maryetta thought she heard voices. When she peeked out of her tent she saw Toby talking to a wolf. She couldn't believe her eyes or ears! Although she had been raised around the circus and always knew that animals were special, she had never talked to one! She listened intently.

"Go make friends with the tiger and bring him back here," Toby told the wolf.

"When do you want me to bring back that stupid tiger?" asked the wolf.

"Five days from now will be good. Then I will have enough money to buy the secrets I want from the old wizard."

"Okay, I'll see you then," said the wolf, and he crept away.

Maryetta silently closed the flap of her tent and slumped to the ground. Something was very, very wrong. How was she going to get back to the circus safely with the tiger and not let Toby know that she knew he was a fake?

The next morning Toby told Maryetta the boat was fixed. Toby then said, "I don't want to be rude, but where is my money?"

Maryetta answered, "I'll pay you later." She thought to herself, I have no intention of paying Toby.

Toby said, "I want my money now!"

Maryetta said that because the boat accident was not her fault she should not have to pay for the first day. Toby replied, "Well, it's not my fault either, and besides, we had an agreement."

They argued for a while, and Toby finally agreed that Maryetta could pay him later. He told her he would begin to look for the tiger today.

They boarded the boat together to begin the search for the tiger. Along the way they spotted a beautiful tiger being chased by a wolf.

Maryetta said, "Toby, I know you sent the wolf after the tiger and you better make sure the wolf doesn't harm him or you won't be paid!" They anchored the boat and went ashore.

Toby and Maryetta began to chase after the tiger and the wolf. Suddenly, Maryetta tripped over a vine and broke her leg. Toby came along, grabbed Maryetta's money, and ran off with it!

At this point Jerome stopped reading. He asked how many students remembered this half of the story. All hands were raised. He then asked them to write down a few sentences about how they thought the story would end. How do *you* think the story will end?

Of the 26 students in Jerome's class, 11 completed the story in a way that Maryetta's task is fulfilled. In these stories, Maryetta catches the tiger and takes it home, and it performs as desired in the circus. Three students resolved the story by creating a new character who saves Maryetta from her injury and from Toby. In 6 stories, the tiger frees Maryetta from her crisis, and in 3 of these stories, the tiger goes on to catch Toby. In 2 stories, Maryetta escapes, finds the wizard, and seeks revenge on Toby. In 1 case each, the wolf helps Maryetta first catch the tiger and then Toby; Toby steals the money from Maryetta and does not catch the tiger; Maryetta is cured in a hospital and becomes friends with Toby; and Toby spontaneously recognizes and reconciles his evil ways.

Jerome could sense the excitement of the students as they waited to hear how their Indian colleagues had completed the story. He sat on the edge of his desk and continued with the second half.

Part Two (India)

The wolf who was chasing the tiger stopped after hearing Maryetta's cries and ran toward her. He finally reached her. He felt sad when he saw the flow of blood from her leg.

"Don't be afraid. I shall help you," said the wolf.

The wolf then ran into the forest and brought rare herbs and placed them on her leg. At once, Maryetta felt relief from the pain and felt pleasant again. Maryetta looked at the wolf with love and gratitude.

The wolf asked Maryetta, "How did you fall?"

She explained everything to him. The wolf felt bad when he heard of Toby's treacherous deeds. The wolf told Maryetta that he would get the money from Toby.

Maryetta saw the birds, trees, and other creatures around her. Suddenly she didn't feel lonely any more. She felt happy that she was a part of an endless creation of nature. She felt the encouragement and nourishment given by the surrounding birds and trees.

Toby went straight to the old wizard with the money he robbed from Maryetta. After getting the money from Toby, the wizard taught him the mantras (magic phrases) that he could use to conquer the animals and humans. Toby then quickly left, greedy to make more money.

Then Toby saw a tiger running towards him in a frenzy. He tried to conquer the tiger with the mantras he had learned from the wizard. But the tiger pushed him down and tried to attack him. At that time, the tiger heard the voice of a wolf and he ran away.

The wolf and Maryetta saw Toby struggling for his life. The wolf did not like to help the treacherous Toby. He thought that this was the right punishment for his terrible deeds. But Maryetta was deeply moved by Toby's suffering. She felt sad that she did not have the money to admit him to a hospital.

Maryetta pleaded with the wolf to help Toby. The wolf halfheartedly ran and brought rare herbs. Maryetta made a bandage with the herbs for Toby's wounds. She also gave him some juice from the herbs. He then recovered and could breathe easy again.

Toby slowly came to consciousness and appreciated the gentle qualities of Maryetta and apologized to her. He revealed that he had given the money to the old wizard. He felt sorry that he was spoiled by his own greed.

In the meantime, the wolf went to the tiger. He asked the tiger, "Why did you try to kill Toby?"

The tiger angrily replied, "It is but natural that we are angry towards men who prevent us from living independently in the forest and who try to hunt us. Toby is trying to destroy us totally by violence, tricks, and mantras. For him, money is bad."

The wolf said, "Toby not only cheats the animals, but also the humans. For this greedy fellow, money is everything."

Toby was truly sad. He felt ashamed of himself and asked to be pardoned. Then the wolf, the tiger, Toby, and Maryetta danced together in joy in a circle.

Then Maryetta told the tiger, "In my father's circus there is a male tiger suffering without a companion. If you can come with me, he would be very happy."

Maryetta looked at the female tiger with love and affection. The female was moved to tears. She began to wonder if that male tiger was the one that had been taken away from her long ago. She agreed to go with Maryetta.

All four returned to the circus. The male tiger was happy to see the female tiger that he had been separated from so very long ago. Soon they were able to identify one another. What a pleasure it is when separated ones come together again!

Maryetta was very happy. She had learned to talk with the animals. Her love toward them grew many times over. She looked after the tigers with special care.

One day, Maryetta fell asleep while playing with the tigers. She listened to the conversations of the tigers as she woke up. She pretended as if she was sleeping and continued to listen to them.

The female tiger said, "Maryetta is a wonderful girl. But she does not realize the fact that the forest is our heaven. Even this golden cage is still a cage."

Maryetta was deeply moved. The next day Maryetta's father called her and said, "Maryetta, I have grown old. I am retiring from the circus as of today. Hereafter, you should run the circus."

Maryetta said, "I shall free those wonderful animals from this sorrowful, tortuous caged life, and I will go and live in the forest."

And that she did.

Jerome followed this reading with a discussion. To begin the discussion he asked each student to respond, in writing, to the following questions.

1.   In what ways is the ending different from what you expected?
2.   What surprised you as you heard the end of the story?
3.   What do you think you learned about Indian culture?
4.   What might reading this story tell you about American culture?

The discussion that followed was lively. Most of the children thought that good would prevail over evil. What seemed to surprise them, however, was that the bad characters changed for the good. On further probing, some of the children questioned whether human nature could be modified so quickly, as if through sudden insight or experience, and wondered if it might be possible with terrorists. Many students were also struck by the use of herbs and mantras in the story as well as the apparent reverence for nature and living things.

While the children were discussing what they thought they had learned about Indian culture, Karl suggested that Indians seem to care about nature in general and animals in particular. He also asked about the possibility of humans really talking to animals. He remembered watching a television show about how researchers were trying to communicate with dolphins, whales, and gorillas. Kathy seemed particularly moved by Maryetta's change of heart toward Toby and thought that Indians might care that other people are safe and peaceful. Kamal said he was learning about some of the ways African healers treated their patients and the fact that the Indians used herbs and mantras reminded him of this.

It was a bit more difficult, however, for the group to discuss what they might have learned about their own culture. With probing, Jerome was able to get something of a discussion going. Some students thought that both countries were alike in many ways. Others were surprised that, while most of the American students would let the characters in the story die, the Indian children seemed to have compassion for them.

The discussion of violence in the world in general as well as in American society, toward both people and animals, was the most lively. Finally, Maria pointed out that the way the story was completed showed that the Indian students believed that people's labels can change, whereas in the United States, she thought, a label might remain with a person for quite a long time. She was even bold enough to ask how many in the class still felt uncomfortable with Arabs and Muslims in the community. Jerome thought that Maria raised a good question, and he allowed it to develop into a whole class discussion about prejudice and racism in their classroom and in the community. At the end of the discussion, all of Jerome's students agreed with the Indian class that the two classrooms should continue a long-term friendship and an exchange of ideas, resources, and letters.

Perspectives on a Globally Oriented Curriculum

Reflect upon the Case Study at the beginning of the chapter. What Jerome attempted to do in the first part of the school year was to integrate into his curriculum three types of knowledge that will help his students evaluate their interpersonal experiences both inside and outside school. First, he integrated knowledge and understanding of prejudice formation and prejudice reduction. Second, he tapped into the growing body of knowledge related to the development of an international perspective. Third, he is applying cooperative learning strategies, thus providing students with necessary practice in developing the skills needed for collaborative living and working.

Jerome's classroom activities reflect a number of strategies related to global or intercultural education.

1. Jerome has demonstrated that it is possible to combine global education with the development of traditional curriculum skills in such areas as language arts, social studies, and art.

2. He has not shied away from real but sensitive issues such as prejudice and interpersonal conflict that greatly affect the lives of his students. Rather, he has acknowledged these issues as real problems that are worth confronting and analyzing. And he has done this in a subtle, creative manner that will set the stage for subsequent activity once everyone has a common foundation.

3. By integrating traditional content areas, the day is not broken into brief time slots during which content and curricular experiences are segregated from one another. Rather, classroom activities are designed to be meaningful and relate to the lives and experiences of the students. Through the partnership story, for example, students have an opportunity to develop their language arts skills while they learn valuable social studies concepts about culture, specific countries, and interpersonal interaction. At the same time, students work in cooperative groups and develop linkages with others around the world.

4. He has actively sought to reduce prejudice, not by simply telling students that it is wrong but by enabling them to learn, firsthand, about similarities and differences among at least two groups of people.

These examples represent just the beginning of what is possible in a globally oriented classroom.

Ethical Concerns

Clearly, there are a variety of ethical issues involved in developing a global classroom. Among them are the fair allocation of available resources (including computers and other technology), the need to consider families and communities when discussing global concerns, and perhaps most important, the need to balance advocacy with inquiry. Although it is tempting for educators to become advocates when discussing the world's problems, the role of schooling remains one of inquiry. Assessing students on the degree to which they are able to use the tools of inquiry, on the breadth and depth of their research, on their analytical skills, and on their creativity in proposing solutions is more appropriate than assessing them on the degree to which they subscribe to a particular point of view.

Similarly, there are ethical considerations involved in the length of time given to newer ideas such as global education. Its emphasis on attitude and behavior change may require educators to allocate large amounts of time to achieve even modest gains. Social psychologists have had a difficult time demonstrating that

International Perspective: What's Happening Elsewhere in the World?

Uniquely You

David Platt
Curtin University, Perth, Australia

The group of young people were sitting in a circle on plastic chairs that had been dragged under the protection of a small stand of Norfolk pines. The shade offered some respite on a searing mid-January Australian day, but there was no escaping the oppressive heat, hanging in the air even as the sun slowly began to settle lower in the sky.

"I have two older brothers and a younger sister." Abdi stood up, walked to the centre of the circle, and placed a bean on the growing pile in the bottom of the bowl. Five others stood, and their beans joined his. He tried again, "I am studying commerce with a double major in accounting and finance." Two more beans. He tried a third time, "Okay then, I can dunk a basketball," and then strode confidently to the bowl. Surely this was it. After a long pause Hassan stood, and with a sly smile added one of his beans. On the way back he playfully jabbed at Abdi. It would continue.

Abdi shifted in his seat, clearly wanting the focus to move from him to the next person in the circle. He looked uncomfortably at the ground and then raised his eyes back to the group, "I held my friend in my arms after he was shot. He died." No one moved. The joking and idle chatter that had carried on in the background stopped immediately. Abdi waited, and then stood. He walked to the centre of the circle and placed a bean in the bowl. Returning to his seat, he nudged the person next to him, "Your turn."

The activity was called *Uniquely You,* and on that hot January afternoon we were using it to break down some of the barriers that existed between a group of visiting American students and members of the local Somali Youth Association. We thought it would be a bit of fun for everyone, a chance for each person to be recognised and valued by the group for the things that made each of them different, unique. We thought that the activity would be a great way to further a deeper understanding of culture, of community, of difference and sameness. And it was. And more. Much more.

The group of Americans had come to Curtin University of Technology in Perth, Western Australia, in January of 2006 for a winter-term Human Rights course centred on issues relating to the treatment of refugees and new migrant communities. The students who came to Curtin were from a small liberal arts school in St Paul, Minnesota. The largest community of Somali people outside of Somalia is in Minneapolis, and these students worked with them in various ways almost every day. They had come to Perth to engage with members of the local Somali community because (after Minneapolis) the community in Perth is among the next largest in the world. A major focus of the course was to compare the different experiences of being a Somali refugee or migrant in Australia with those of the Somali people now living in the United States.

In January of 2006, Australians, much like Americans, were still struggling with understanding life in the post-September 11 world—a world further coloured in Australia by the Bali bombings of 2002 and 2005. Australia was firmly entrenched in the war in Iraq, and the political climate was charged with a sense of fear about the "types of people" who were being "let in" to the country. Five years earlier, the prime minister had managed to swing an election, in part, by rallying the country against the potential influx of illegal immigrants and "queue jumpers." Any person arriving in Australia without official status (e.g., asylum seekers) was subject to mandatory detention, and in December of 2005, Cronulla (a Sydney suburb) had erupted in racially and ethnically charged violence.

Against that backdrop, we strove to create an environment in which the young students from America could learn about refugees, migration, and human rights—not only by engaging in an academic experience but also through the development of relationships with the young women and men who had

significant, long-lasting behavior change follows from short-term attitude change efforts. Although it may be possible to demonstrate a change in attitude as a result of a short-term intervention (efforts at a summer camp program, for instance), there has been little evidence to demonstrate either that the attitude change persists or that it leads to a subsequent long-term change in behavior.

The converse may in fact be true, as seen in research concerning attitudes toward people with disabilities. An individual who has had little contact with persons with disabilities may initially react with discomfort or pity and be acutely aware of the disability. In one study, for example, teachers participating in an intensive 5-week summer training institute on teaching young children with disabilities initially demonstrated a negative change in attitude, as measured by the formed the Somali Youth Association of Western Australia. We believed that the issues could only be really understood if they were examined from the perspective of people whose experiences were fundamentally different than our own.

As part of the creation of that learning opportunity, Curtin University pledged to maintain an ongoing commitment to working with and for the Somali community. We did not want the experiences of that summer to be simply about creating an interesting learning environment for the young Americans here for a very short time. Instead, we envisioned it as the start of meaningful relationship with our neighbours. We knew that our partnership with the Somali community would only be authentic if the things we learned during that summer helped us to continue to shape the relationship—together.

We learned much from our Somali friends that summer. We learned about refugees and migration, about family and culture and community, about human rights. We learned about what it is like to be a young Muslim male living in a Western country in a world that is forever changed by the events and the aftermath of one day in September. We learned about the struggles of being a young Muslim woman, caught between the traditions of her heritage and the trappings of a consumer-driven culture. We learned what it is like to have been in Australia for so long that you consider yourself to be *Australian*—when everyone else still looks at you as foreign. We learned why there are too many Somali women heading households in Perth—they don't know where their men are, they might be dead. We learned that despite so many differences on the surface there were many more similarities. And we learned that we needed to continue learning.

As the American students began to pack their bags in preparation for the long trip back to the icy Midwestern winter, some of the older members of the Youth Association approached us and asked if we were serious about our commitment to working with them in the future. We said yes and asked what should come next.

"We need someone to help teach our children. Sometimes they struggle with their homework, and often we don't have the time or the language skills to really help them."

From that conversation was born a weekly on-campus tutoring program in which Curtin students spend about 2 hours working with Somali children and young people—helping with their homework. Again on a Saturday morning, other Curtin students venture to a local primary school to continue providing that support to the Somali community—to continue building the relationship.

While the *Homework Help* program provides Curtin students with a wonderful opportunity to hone their skills as teachers, the tutors are not just education majors. They are occupational therapy students, engineers, scientists, artists, designers, and even architects. They come to help, to share their skills and expertise with young people who need a bit of extra support, who embrace the personal attention and who begin to see that attending university is a real possibility. We maintain our commitment because we know that these outcomes are the things that the Somali community wants. They asked us to do this, and we are only too happy.

However, we do this for other reasons too. We do this because we know that our students will soon be asked to function as professionals in a rapidly globalising world. We know that, at the moment, in this world it is too easy to dismiss Islamic people as extremists. We know that it is easy to be afraid. We know that our perceptions of African migrants in our community are painted with one, very broad brush. We know that there are many among us who think that all Australians should "be just like me." We know that our students only learn to embrace change and celebrate difference if they are given opportunities to develop relationships with others.

So, we do what we can to globalise the learning experiences of our students so that they might pass on the message in their own spheres of influence. We do it because we believe that as future educators and engineers and accountants and therapists they will bring about change in our world. We do it because of 9/11, because of Bali, because of Somalia, because of Iraq, because of Cronulla, we do it because.

We do it because of Abdi.

Attitudes Toward Disabled Persons scale (Stahlman, Safford, Pisarchick, Miller, & Dyer, 1989). Positive attitudes, as defined by this scale, are those that regard a person with disabilities as essentially like everyone else, not as someone special. For many of the teachers in this study, this workshop was their first exposure to children with disabilities, and as a result, they had difficulty not being overly solicitous and eager to help. Later follow-up experiences with students with disabilities gradually led to more "normalized" attitudes.

Studies of classroom integration of children with disabilities generally have shown that mere exposure does not necessarily result in the formation of friendships. Teachers need to actively promote social interaction, model an accepting attitude toward all children, and design activities that enable children with and without disabilities to work together (Safford, 1989). Too often insufficient time is provided for these activities, and consequently, initial assessments are disappointing. For example, in one study involving preschool children, initial observation revealed that typical children seldom selected peers with disabilities in play situations, but repeated observations several weeks later showed significantly more acceptance (Dunlop, Stoneman, & Cantrell, 1980). This is consistent with the work done on the contact hypothesis discussed in Chapter 6.

Critical Incident

A Delayed Response

A couple of days after Jerome's class received the completion of their partnership story, Jerome overheard Lenny and Paul giggling and talking about how silly it seemed that people in India would use rare herbs as medicines. The boys thought it even more unusual that Indians would consider using mantras to control people and animals, and the two began referring to Indians in derogatory ways.

- Why do you think Lenny and Paul would, after 2 days, begin to ridicule the people they had spent time studying about?
- How would you handle the immediate situation?
- What might you do to prevent this reaction from happening?

Critical Incident

A Sensitive Assignment

When Jerome asked his students to trace their ancestry and present their findings to the class, he was taken aback by Kamal's response. Jerome knew that Kamal's family was, perhaps more than many African American families in the school, emphasizing their African heritage with their children. Kamal stood up and, with a certain anger in his words, stated, "I'm African, and I don't know my exact heritage. You see, you white folks took my people from their lands, mixed us up with all the other Africans you stole, and now lump us all together. My father tells me that African American people come from more than 15 different tribes in West Africa, and we don't even know which ones we belong to. That's why there's so much confusion in the world today. We've been stripped of our heritage."

Jerome was not quite sure how to respond to Kamal. If you were Jerome:

- What feelings might you be experiencing?
- How would you initially respond to Kamal?
- What advice would you offer to teachers who might do a similar exercise?

Summary

This chapter takes as its starting point the reality that we live in an intercon-nected, interdependent, global society and that it is the responsibility of teachers and schools to prepare students to live within it in a productive manner. Glo-balization has many meanings for many different people. In this chapter it means actively introducing students to people and ideas from around the world, helping students learn to think in terms of whole systems (economic, political, social), and acquainting students with global issues that are certain to have an impact on their lives. Globalization should help students participate with other students from all over the planet in thinking through hard questions involving not only intercultural competence but also the ability to span all kinds of social as well as geographical boundaries.

When people encounter situations that induce or require them to behave in new and different ways for an extended period of time, there is a real possibil-ity for long-term attitude and behavior change. If, for instance, school organiza-tional structures can be modified to encourage or require intergroup interaction over an extended period of time, the likelihood that everyone may learn to regard themselves as tolerant, understanding, and able to get along with people increases. Government legislation that provides mandates for altering organiza-tional structure on a national level is based on this idea. Official support and status for bilingualism in Canada or multilingualism in Switzerland are promising examples of this policy in action. Never believe, however, that mandates alone will do the job. What is required is persistent face-to-face activity and a good deal of trial and error!

Chapter Review

Go to the Online Learning Center at www.mhhe.com/cushner7e to review important content from the chapter, practice with key terms, take a chapter quiz, and find the Web links listed in this chapter.

Key Terms

cross-cultural
    awareness 228
globalization 216

global perspective 220
perspective
    consciousness 224

state of the planet
    awareness 226

Active Exercise

Additional Active Exercises are available online at www.mhhe.com/cushner7e.

Future's Window

Purpose: To project the needs of individuals and society in the years ahead, and to examine what this means for educators.

Instructions: In this activity you are to become a futurist and project into the future—both your own as well as that of the world. Divide a page into quadrants, with the top half representing your "Self" and the bottom half representing the "World." The left side of each half represents "5 years," and the right half represents "20 years" into the future. You are to make at least five entries in each quadrant; things you expect to have accomplished or to be dealing with in 5 years and in 20 years, and things you expect the world to be confronting, both in 5 as well as 20 years. Do not record what you wish will happen but what you predict will occur based on what you see happening today. Do this activity alone at first. If you are doing this in a group setting, after a short while, share your responses with others and compile a group list.

Self—5 years	Self—20 years
World—5 years	**World—20 years**

1. Look closely at what is on your list, or, if you have done this activity in a group, look closely at the compilation. What messages seem to jump out at you as you look closely at the response patterns? Do not be surprised if quick responses do not emerge. Take some time to analyze the similarities as well as the differences in the columns. What generalizations seem to emerge?

2. What questions do you have as a result of the generalizations you observed?

3. As people analyze their responses, it is not uncommon to say something like, "It seems as if things will be quite nice and easy for individuals, but there will still be problems in the world." This is a critical observation. If you have not already made this observation yourself, please consider it for a moment. Does such a statement hold true for your responses to the above task?

4. Let's assume that you can safely make the same observation and statement given the responses on your list. What is the responsibility one has to others? Why do you think it is that, in general, people project their own future to be fine even when the rest of the world continues to face problems and challenges?

5. Discuss your responses to the above with others in a group. Do not be surprised if there is much disagreement over people's responses.

6. Next, look closely at your projections for the world. What generalizations seem to stand out as you analyze this information?

7. Which of the following statements can you agree with given the projections you have made for the world? Check one.

The issues that the world will face seem quite pessimistic and insurmountable.

The issues that the world will face seem complex but generally will be resolved.

8. It is often said that each individual can and must do her or his own part to help improve the bigger picture. All of the problems the world will face, whether they are in fact solved or not, will require the coordinated efforts of many different people from many different career and cultural backgrounds who are able to work together. The problems of the world are such that they will be solved by the coordinated efforts of many different people and nations, or they will not be solved at all.

9. What is the role of education in helping people develop the ability to solve the problems that you believe the world will face?

10. What are some things you can do through your teaching that will help your students develop the awareness, knowledge, and skills necessary to collaborate with others whose ways of interacting and values may be quite different from their own?

Classroom Activities

1. A common activity in primary and middle school is to introduce students to the media and the world around them by having them report on current events from local newspapers and other sources. This activity extends the traditional current events activity, asking students to utilize the global media and report on a current event from multiple perspectives. Identify a current-event topic of global significance, such as an event that crosses national boundaries or an activity occurring in one nation that has direct impact elsewhere. Locate the same news story from *at least* three nations (at least one from a non–English-speaking nation). A few good places to find such sources include: www.inkdrop.net/dave/news.html; http://www.newspaperindex.com/; and http://www.allyoucanread.com/Top_100_Newspapers/

2. Children's literature is an exceptional way to introduce multiple perspectives to young people. Identify a topic of concern to children worldwide. Then, seek out children's books that address the topic or concept from multiple experiences. Develop an annotated bibliography of your recommendations and share it with others.

3. Film is another ideal way to introduce multiple perspectives and intercultural conflict to middle and secondary age students. A number of films have been produced that display people interacting in a variety of intercultural contexts—some humorous and others more serious in nature, but all providing visual examples of effective as well as ineffective

cross-cultural encounters. Some example of U.S. films addressing this include: *Mr. Baseball, Mosquito Coast, Moscow on the Hudson, Coming to America, Planet of the Apes,* and *Fiddler on the Roof.* Seek out additional films useful for this purpose. Foreign films also provide an exceptional opportunity to look closely into the lives of others. With this, you can do a comparative analysis by focusing on elements that reflect crosscultural similarities and differences in behavior, value, or belief.

4. Knowledge of global systems, as Hanvey proposed, is really about understanding global interconnectedness. High school students can research innovations in a range of contexts (e.g., science, technology, agriculture, medicine) and explore the "downstream" unanticipated impact of that innovation. The introduction of DDT, for example, while increasing crop yield many times over, had an unanticipated detrimental impact on other life forms once it entered the food chain. This was first noted in the late 1950s when spraying to control the beetles that carry Dutch elm disease resulted in early deaths of robins in Michigan and elsewhere. Researchers discovered that earthworms were accumulating the pesticide and that the robins eating them were being poisoned. Other birds later were impacted as well, including the eagle whose egg shells were weakened as a result of the chemical. What other systemic impacts can be identified?

Reflective Questions

The Case Study teacher, Jerome Becker, developed a number of activities and curricular redesigns that infused global awareness into his sixth-grade curriculum. Still, he is bothered by several aspects of his work.

1. How can he continue to educate himself about new methods of global education while simultaneously keeping up with student needs and school requirements? Time is definitely a problem.

2. He knows that the United States is a widely diverse country with many unsolved problems regarding race and ethnicity. How can he justify moving to a global perspective when the problems at home remain so critical?

3. Although he has been relatively successful in incorporating a global perspective into social studies, language arts, and some of the arts, how can he do the same with such seemingly culture-neutral subjects as mathematics and science?

4. He has found that many students do not relate at all to the idea of ethnicity. Rather, they think of themselves as Americans and have neither knowledge of nor emotional ties to their own ethnic roots. How can he encourage these students to appreciate and value ethnic and racial diversity without seeming to denigrate the American way of life?

5. Not every teacher and administrator in his school appreciates the direction Jerome is taking toward a global perspective. How can he continue to broaden his students' perspectives in the face of criticism from his colleagues?

References

Adelson, J., & O'Neill, R. P. (1966). Growth of political ideas in adolescents: The sense of community. *Journal of Personality and Social Psychology, 4,* 295–306.

American Forum for Global Education. (2004). Retrieved June 13, 2004, from http://www.globaled.org/

Avery, P. G., & Hann, C. L. (2004). Diversity and U.S. 14-year-olds' knowledge, attitudes, and experiences. In W. G. Stephan & W. P. Vogt (Eds.), *Education programs for improving intergroup relations: Theory, research and practice* (pp. 195–210). New York: Teachers College Press.

Bybee, R. W., & Sund, R. B. (1982). *Piaget for educators* (2nd ed.). Columbus, OH: Charles E. Merrill.

Childers, E., & Urquhart, B. (1994). *Renewing the United Nations system.* Geneva, Switzerland: United Nations.

CNN. (1990, December). Television for the global village. *World Press Review, 37*(12), 34.

Cushner, K. (1992). Creating cross-cultural understanding through internationally cooperative story writing. *Social Education, 56*(1), 43–46.

Cushner, K. (2004). *Beyond tourism: A practical guide to meaningful educational travel.* Lanham, MD: Scarecrow Education.

Cushner, K., & Brislin, R. (1996). *Intercultural interactions: A practical guide (2nd ed.).* Thousand Oaks, CA: Sage.

Dunlop, K., Stoneman, Z., & Cantrell, M. (1980). Social interaction of exceptional and other children in a mainstreamed preschool classroom. *Exceptional Children, 47*(2), 132–141.

Family Care Foundation. (2008). *If the world were a village of 100 people.* Retrieved from http://www.familycare.org/news/if_the_world.htm

Flavell, J., Botkin, P., & Fry, C. L. (1968). *The development of role taking and communication skills in children.* New York: Wiley.

Forward, T. (2005). *The wolf's story: What really happened to Little Red Riding Hood.* Somerville, MA: Candlewick Press.

Friedman, T. (2000). *The Lexus and the olive tree: Understanding globalization.* New York: Anchor Books.

Friedman, T. L. (2006). *The world is flat: A brief history of the 21st century.* New York: Farrar, Straus & Giroux.

Grossman, D., & Yuen, C. (2006). Beyond the rhetoric: A study of the intercultural sensitivity of Hong Kong secondary school teachers. *Pacific Asian Education, 18*(1), 70–87.

HAMER. (2007). *Ten shocking facts.* The Hawaii Association for Marine Education and Research, Inc. Retrieved April 10, 2007, from http://www.hamerhawaii.com/ten_shocking_facts_planet.htm

Hammer, M., and Bennett, M. (1998). *The Intercultural Development Inventory (IDI) Manual.* Portland, OR: Intercultural Communication Institute.

Hanvey, R. (1978). *An attainable global perspective.* New York: Center for Global Perspectives.

Hoopes, D. (1980). Intercultural education. *Phi Delta Kappa Fastback* (No. 144). Bloomington, IN: Phi Delta Kappa Educational Foundation.

Kruse, K. (2004). Buckle Up: Generation Y Is Here, Chief Learning Officer, Online publication, March 2004. Retrieved January 2007, from http://www.clomedia.com/conten/templates/clo_col_elearning.asp?articleid-410&zoneid=46

Lutkus, A. D., Weiss, A. R., Campbell, J. R., Mazzeo, J., & Lazer, S. (1999). *The NAEP civics report card for the nation.* Washington, DC: National Center for Education Statistics.

Mahon, J. (2003). Intercultural sensitivity development of practicing teachers. *Dissertation Abstracts International, 64*(7), 2353A (UMI No. 3097199).

Mahon, J. (2006). Under the invisibility cloak? Teacher understanding of cultural difference. *Intercultural Education, 17*(4), 391–407.

Mahon, J. (2009). Conflict style and cultural understanding among teachers in the western United States: Exploring relationships. *International Journal of Intercultural Relations, 33*(1), 46–56.

Miniwatts Marketing (2009). Internet World Stats Usage and Population Statistics. Retrieved October 16, 2009, from http://www.internetworldstats.com/stats.htm

Niemi, R., & Junn, J. (1998). *Civic education: What makes students learn.* New Haven, CT: Yale University Press.

Pappamihiel, E. (2004). Hugs and smiles: Demonstrating caring in a multicultural early childhood classroom. *Early Childhood Development and Care, 174*(6), 539–548.

Pederson, P. V. (1998). Intercultural sensitivity and the early adolescent. Doctoral dissertation, University of Minnesota. *Dissertation Abstracts International,* 9826849.

Remy, R. C., Nathan, J. A., Becker, J. M., & Torney, J. V. (1975). *International learning and international education in a global age.* National Council for the Social Studies, Bulletin 47, pp. 39–40.

Rennebohm-Franz, K. (1996). Toward a critical social consciousness in children: Multicultural peace education in a first grade classroom. *Theory into Practice, 35*(4), 265.

Roberts, L. (2007). *Harnessing information technology for international education.* Retrieved May 2, 2007, from http://internationaled.org/PDKroberts.htm

Safford, P. (1989). *Integrated teaching in early childhood.* White Plains, NY: Longman.

Scieszka, J. (1989). *The true story of the three little pigs as told by A. Wolf.* New York: Viking.

Selman, R., & Schultz, L. (1990). *Making a friend in youth: Developmental theory and pair therapy.* Chicago, IL: University of Chicago Press.

Stahlman, J., Safford, P., Pisarchick, S., Miller, C., & Dyer, D. (1989). Crossing the boundaries of early childhood special education personnel preparation: Creating a path for retraining. *Teacher Education and Special Education, 12*(1), 5–12.

Straffon, D. A. (2003). Assessing the intercultural sensitivity of high school students attending an international school. *International Journal of Intercultural Relations, 27,* 487–501.

UNHCR (United Nations High Commission on Refugees). (2008). Retrieved June 12, 2008, from http://www.unhcr.ch/cgi-bin/texis/vtx/home

U. S. Census Bureau (2004). Facts for Features. Retrieved November 4, 2009, from http://www.census.gov/Press-Release/www/releases/archives/facts_for_features_special_editions/001737.html

Developing Learning Communities

Language and Learning Style

Focus Questions

1. Do you remember learning to talk? If not, why not?

2. Think of occasions when you were speaking to someone and that person seemed not to understand what you meant. What do you think the reason was?

3. What is the difference between an accent and a dialect?

4. Have you ever been speaking to someone who was standing too close to you for your comfort? Why do you think you felt uncomfortable?

5. How do you learn best? If faced with the need to learn something new, what would you do (e.g., read about it, talk to someone about it, have someone show you)?

6. What do you think about bilingual education? Is it necessary for some children? Does it hamper English language learners?

" When we study human language, we are approaching what some might call the 'human essence,' the distinctive qualities of mind that are, so far as we know, unique to man and that are inseparable from any critical phase of human existence, personal or social. **"**

NOAM CHOMSKY

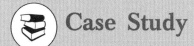

Case Study

Language and Learning Style in a Learning-Community Classroom

It is 4:00 on a Friday afternoon in mid-September, and Martina Chandler stands by the windows in her third-floor classroom watching the sun glinting off San Francisco Bay.[1] Typical of many high school classrooms, this one is a large rectangle, with a blackboard on one end, an electronic white board in the corner, windows along one side, and a variety of furniture and equipment, including five laptop computers for student use. Unlike many high school classrooms, however, the space in this room is organized for active work rather than for passive listening. Most of the furniture is adaptable to many uses: low, three-shelf bookcases on wheels can be moved around to create a variety of spaces; individual desks have been replaced by several round tables with moveable chairs that can accommodate four or five students at a time; individual carrels made of large boxes that fold up when not in use can be set up on small individual tables or on one long table so that students can work or study alone; learning center areas for various purposes can be created and re-created from a number of bright plastic "orange crates," also on wheels. Also in the room is a large, cushioned porch rocker inherited from Martina's grandmother. Even Ms. Chandler's desk is lightweight and movable when required by the classroom activities.

In addition, the walls are covered with maps, posters, and pictures from around the world. One striking poster has the Greek, Hebrew, Cyrillic, Spanish, Japanese, Arabic, French, and English alphabets side by side in bright colors. Another has a variety of drawings of students engaged in different styles of learning—reading, talking to one another, writing, building, singing, and dancing. Still another displays a language tree that shows the roots of the world's major languages.

Now that the last student of the day has left, Martina is thinking about the progress her students have made in the first 2 weeks of school. Although she has six classes, she is particularly interested in her 10th-grade English class, which has shown strong interest in setting class goals for the year and in deciding how they are going to achieve them. These students have caught the spirit of the learning-community classroom earlier than her other classes and seem to be enjoying themselves a great deal.

Unlike some teachers in her school, Ms. Chandler has chosen to teach heterogeneous classes. The 24 students in this particular class come from backgrounds that vary by family income, ethnic heritage and/or country of origin, religion, native language, past school achievement, and race. She views this variation as potentially enriching for herself and her students. It is very important to her that the class becomes a community of learners in which the sociocultural and linguistic backgrounds of all her students are known, appreciated, and used.

Prior to the beginning of school, Ms. Chandler began assembling her usual set of student files by looking up their official records in the school office. She recorded their full names, their birthdays, their parents' occupations, and any information available concerning their English language abilities as well as their abilities in languages other than English. From this information, she knew that this class was more linguistically diverse than others she had taught. Also, for the first time, she was going to have a deaf student and her interpreter in class. She was fairly certain that differences in the cultural and language backgrounds of these students would mean differences in their learning styles and personal interests.

The First Week: Exploring Names and Languages

Since beginning school 2 weeks ago, Ms. Chandler has devoted much of her classroom time to activities designed to help her students get to know one another and to begin forming a classroom community. At the end of the first class, she asked her students to talk with their parents about the origins of their first and middle names and what nationality their names represent. She also asked them to find out if their names had a special meaning in another language. "Tomorrow," she announced, "we will begin interviewing one another for the Class Bulletin Board."

When her students came to class the next day, Ms. Chandler used a technique she had read about to form the students into pairs. She had the students line up around the room according to their birthdays and then asked each student to be a partner to the student who had a birthday closest to him or her. When partnerships were established, she handed out the following list of questions for students to use in interviewing one another.

1. What is your name? What do you like or dislike about your name?

2. What do you know about how you got your name? Were you named after someone else? Who named you?

3. Are there members of your family who have the same name?

4. Do you have any friends who have the same name as you do?

5. Are there any famous people who have the same name as yours?

6. Are you at all like any of these people who have the same name as yours?

7. Does your name have any other meaning?

8. Was your name originally in another language? Was it spelled differently in that language? Does it have a special meaning in that language?

9. What does your family call you? Do you have a nickname?

10. What do you like to be called?

The class spent about 15 minutes interviewing one another. Then Martina asked them each to introduce their partner to the class by telling what they had learned. While each student was talking, she listened carefully and took notes. At the end of each introduction, Martina

(continued)

took a snapshot of each student and repeated the student's name. Class ended before they finished, and she told them they would complete the introductions the next day.

On Wednesday, after the introductions and picture taking were completed, the students were asked to hand in the notes on their question sheets. Then the class spent the rest of the period discussing the number of different languages, accents, and dialects represented in the class. One exercise that all the students liked was to pronounce aloud the following words:

greasy	here	car	bath	dog
get	aunt	because	idea	park
house	fit	Mary	were	right
fire	sorry	log	child	

The students were surprised to discover that, although everyone spoke at least some English, all of them also spoke dialects of some kind, some of which were regional and some of which were social in their origin. Anna and Mrs. Thomas (the deaf student and her interpreter) also participated by signing each of the words and talking about how the signs developed and how they might be used in sentences.

The students also considered English words that have been borrowed from other languages. Divided into groups of four and using one of the several dictionaries and other reference books in the room, students first tried to guess and then looked up the derivation of the following words:

algebra	Arabic
gingham	Malay
chocolate	Nahuatl (Native American)
khaki	Hindi
linen	Old English
safari	Arabic (through Swahili)
home	Old English
klutz	Yiddish
prairie	French
zombie	Congo
seersucker	Persian
skunk	Algonquian (Native American)
satin	Chinese
shampoo	Hindi
kimono	Japanese
piano	Italian
tycoon	Japanese
boondocks	Tagalog (Philippines)
smithereens	Irish
gorilla	West Africa (through Greek)

Ms. Chandler was pleased that the students had become so interested in the subject of "word borrowing" that they were determined to develop a Borrowing Dictionary to leave with

Martina for her other classes. By Friday of the first week, the pictures of all the students had been printed, and the class spent the period designing and putting together the Class Bulletin Board. Right in the middle of the pictures, they put a printed sheet that read as follows:

A Fable

In a house there was a cat, always ready to run after a mouse, but with no luck at all. One day, in the usual chase the mouse found its way into a little hole and the cat was left with no alternative than to wait hopefully outside.

A few moments later the mouse heard a dog barking and automatically came to the conclusion that if there was a dog in the house, the cat would have to go. So he came out only to fall into the cat's grasp.

"But where is the dog?" asked the trembling mouse.

"There isn't any dog—it was only me imitating a barking dog," explained the happy cat, and after a pause added, "My dear fellow, if you don't speak at least two languages, you can't get anywhere nowadays." (Tiedt & Tiedt, 1995, p. 168)

Over the weekend, Ms. Chandler looked at the notes she had made from the students' official files, the notes she had taken in class as the students were introducing one another, and the question sheets that the students had filled out. From these three sources, she developed a chart on the linguistic variability of the class (see Table 8.1).

Table 8.1 Tenth-Grade English Class: Linguistic Background/Language Proficiency

Name	Native Language/Dialect	Comments
Tran	Vietnamese	Recent immigrant; limited English but able to make himself understood if necessary; also speaks French; needs help with many words; clever use of gestures to get meaning across; no record of reading or writing scores.
Anna	ASL	Has a hearing deficiency; speaks English as a second language; speaks standard English reasonably well; prefers to sign; reading and writing scores good.
Peter	English	Second-generation Japanese American; has some Japanese but uses it only with his grandparents; reading and writing scores fairly high.
Tomas	Spanish/Mexican	Speaks English with a slight Spanish accent; reading scores moderate; writing scores fairly low.
Wei-Ping	Chinese/Mandarin	Speaks standard English well but very formally; does not use vernacular English; reading and writing scores high.
Grace	English	Monolingual in English; speaks standard English reasonably well but uses a good deal of slang; reading scores moderate; writing scores moderately low.
Joe	English	Monolingual in vernacular English; does not appear at all comfortable speaking in front of the class; reading and writing scores moderately low.
Rosita	Spanish/Mexican	Bilingual in Spanish and standard English; has a pronounced Mexican accent; reading and writing scores moderate.

(continued)

Table 8.1 *Continued*

Name	Native Language/Dialect	Comments
Ritchie	English	Bidialectal in black English and standard English; seems to be able to switch back and forth easily, depending on whom he's talking to and what he's talking about; reading and writing scores moderately high.
Natasha	Russian	Bilingual in Russian and standard English; speaks well in front of people; reading and writing scores high.
Steve	English	Monolingual in standard English; uses vernacular English mostly; lives with his father and grandmother, who are bilingual in Hungarian and English; reading scores moderate; writing scores moderately low.
Yoshi	English	Bilingual in English and Japanese; is second-generation Japanese and lives near his grandparents, with whom he speaks Japanese regularly; reading and writing scores moderate.
Maria	Spanish/Puerto Rican	Came to United States at age 5; fluent English speaker but still speaks some Spanish at home; reading scores moderately high; writing scores moderately low.
Kate	English	Monolingual in standard English; speaks easily and fluently in front of class; reading and writing scores high.
Dontae	English	Monodialectal in black English; recently moved here from South Los Angeles; has a lot of energy and speaks easily and quickly in his own dialect; reading and writing scores in standard English low.
Ricardo	Spanish	Bilingual in Spanish and vernacular English; speaks standard English with effort; reading and writing scores moderately low.
Hannah	English	Monolingual in vernacular English.
Komiko	English	Monolingual in standard English; third-generation Japanese American; parents do not speak Japanese and she has no one to learn it from; reading and writing scores moderate.
Abdul	Arabic/French	Trilingual in Arabic, French, and standard English; speaks standard English formally; reading and writing scores high.
Juanita	Spanish/Mexican	Bilingual in Spanish and English.
Tammy	English/ Appalachian	Monolingual in vernacular rural English; has a strong West Virginia "twang" accent; reading scores moderately high; writing scores low.
Jacques	French	Recent immigrant; speaks vernacular French, some vernacular black English, some standard English; reading and writing scores moderately low.
Elaine	English	Third-generation Japanese American; monolingual in standard English; uses considerable slang; reading scores moderate; writing scores moderately high.
Houa	Fulani/French	Trilingual in her ethnic-group language, French, and standard English; speaks somewhat less formally than other nonnative-born students; reading and writing scores moderately high.

The Second Week: Exploring Learning Styles and Family Stories

The second week, Ms. Chandler began class by asking students if they knew how they learned best. "They tell me that we're going to get software for the computers that will let us make podcasts. How many of you have used or even seen such software?" Two students raised their hands. "Okay," she said, "what would be the very first thing the rest of you would do to go about learning how to make a podcast?"

Students answered in different ways. Some said they would get a book on podcasting or on the particular software we were going to get, and start that way. Others said they would get someone who was familiar with podcasting to tell them about it first. Still others said there was no way they could learn without sitting down with the software and actually doing it. Steve and Joe said they would first look at the code in which the software was written.

Using this short discussion as an introduction, Martina divided the class into four groups, each sitting at its own table, and asked each group to look at and discuss the materials on learning style that she had placed on their tables. After each group had had a chance to discuss the materials and after a spokesperson at each table summarized their discussion for the rest of the class, Martina handed out a questionnaire she had designed to help students assess their own patterns of learning. She also pointed out additional books, articles, and materials in the classroom to which students could go for further information.

"I don't want you to think of this as some kind of intelligence test, or that you are 'stuck' with the main learning style you appear to have. All of us use many different approaches to learning all the time, and we are all quite able to learn new ones. The point of thinking about learning style is, first, that it is one more piece of the puzzle that is you and, second, that it will help explain to you why this class may be a bit different from others you have had. It's important to me that everyone in this room learns as much as possible. To do that, we'll always have a variety of ways of approaching knowledge and skills. I'll always encourage you to try out new approaches as well as to use ways that are familiar and comfortable for you. Okay?"

The students looked a bit skeptical, but they more or less willingly answered the questionnaire. The real discussion occurred when they compared their answers with others at their tables. It was still going on when the class was over.

For the rest of the week, Ms. Chandler and her students worked on family stories, building on some of the comments that had come out of the introductions exercise on the second day of class. Steve, for example, said that his grandmother always called him "Stefan," which is his name in Hungarian; Komiko commented that the only thing Japanese in her house were her family's names! Martina then introduced the notion of family stories as discussed by Elizabeth Stone (1989) in her book *Black Sheep and Kissing Cousins*.

Stone interviewed more than a hundred people from various backgrounds, regions of the country, and ages to see if there was a pattern to the influence that family stories had on the beliefs, values, and behavior of individuals. She concluded that family stories give us a sense of our past, of the norms and values held by the family, and perhaps most important, of the future that we might be able to expect by virtue of belonging to this particular family. She tells, for example, of one Irish family in which, because of too much drinking and a curiously morose temperament, many of the males committed suicide before the age of 50—a kind of "tragic O'Connor curse." A young African American, Stone writes, speaks proudly of his Creek Indian ancestors who burned all their corn as they were dispatched on the Trail of Tears so that their white oppressors couldn't benefit from their hard work—a story that describes a tradition of self-assertion and bravery in his family.

"Now, what I want you to do," Ms. Chandler said to her students, "is think about the stories about your family members that you've heard ever since you were little. Many of these stories may be about how your family came to the United States, or about how someone conquered terrible odds to achieve something, or about how your family regards love, courtship, and marriage. Some stories may be very short and some may be quite complex, but all

(continued)

of them usually teach you something about yourself as a member of your first 'culture.' Eventually, we're going to write these stories and share them with the rest of the class. Then, we're going to look at some common characteristics of your stories and some common characteristics of narratives in general. Tomorrow, friends of mine are coming in to tell some of their family stories, and then we'll start on our own."

Now it was Friday afternoon. The students had heard stories about family members escaping from Nazi Germany during the Holocaust, about a family in which one ancestor coined the word "robot," and about a family in which several generations of women had "fallen in love at first sight" and married because of it. Next week the students will begin their own stories and will help each other by offering critiques and suggestions.

"Maybe," she thought, "we'll have the podcasting software by then and can actually record them and put them on the class website!"

Case Analysis

The following list shows a number of strategies that Martina Chandler used both to create a learning-community classroom and to take advantage of various language backgrounds and learning styles so as to help her students explore and become more proficient in the use of standard English.

1. She organized her classroom furniture so that it could be altered by her and the students to fit a variety of activities.

2. In the first 2 weeks of school she helped students get to know one another through the introductions activity, the Class Bulletin Board, the learning-style discussions, and the family stories. Each of these activities is designed to increase understanding of commonalities and differences among members of the class.

3. She got to know students through the use of student files and her own charts.

4. She introduced other adults into the class as storytellers. She will continue to include family and community members as well as other school staff in her classroom.

5. She began the process of democratic experience by encouraging the students to develop their idea for a Borrowing Dictionary as a collaborative project.

6. She used a variety of teaching methods, including questioning, describing, collaborative learning, and the development of "voice," all of which coincide with her initial emphasis on names, individual language backgrounds, and family stories.

7. She used culturally based word exercises and learning style activities to put her students' similarities and differences at the center of the educational enterprise rather than at the margins. Given the linguistic diversity in this class, she set up situations in which such diversity can become a resource rather than a hindrance in the exploration and practice of standard English.

8. Finally, she did all of these things in the context of expanding students' awareness of language and, especially, improving their ability to use

standard English. In just 2 weeks Martina has provided a number of opportunities for oral and written expression that she can use to diagnose her students' language proficiency and then plan both the content and pedagogy for the class. The content of the English class—principally reading, writing, and speaking—is not only central to, but also enhanced by, the approaches and methods she employs.

Martina Chandler's impressive accomplishments during the first 2 weeks of school are just the tip of the iceberg of what she needs to know to accomplish the goals that she and her students set. In addition to the personal knowledge of one another that she and her students now share, Martina also needs three kinds of general language-related knowledge. First, she needs to understand the central role of the family in the acquisition and use of language. Second, she needs to understand how language functions as a communication tool and how it is possible to have different variations of that tool. Third, she needs to understand the relationships between language tools and parental culture and how this relationship influences learning style. We explore each of these dimensions of language in this chapter, but first it is necessary to look closely at what it means to develop a learning community.

Characteristics of a Learning Community

Education for democratic citizenship implies active participation in the life of the school and classroom community. What many school people are struggling with is the shift from simply adding these ideas to traditional classrooms to focusing on them as the basis for educational practice. In schools and classrooms where students and adults have succeeded in altering their focus, the look, feel, and sounds of a different kind of classroom life are easily discernible.

Learning Communities

First, learning-community schools and classrooms are organized for activity. Student work covers the walls of halls and classrooms. There may be an absence of "posted rules carefully outlining what one can or cannot do" (Wood, 1992, p. xviii). Arrangements of classroom furniture and equipment vary according to the work being done in them: easy chairs or sofas for reading and conversation, tables for assembling books and newspapers, tables and counters for scientific work, computer corners, and open spaces for gathering people together. There is a sense of "purposeful clutter in these schools and classrooms. They are places to do things in, not places to sit and watch" (pp. xiii–xiv).

Second, everyone present in the school participates in this activity-oriented environment. Young children are eager to show off the books they have written; older students are engaged in activities that range from interviewing older community members to completing a scientific inventory of nearby plants and animals. Parents and teachers are often found working together to develop and implement instructional goals (McCaleb, 1994). Principals, teachers, parents, and students often work collaboratively on joint projects such as publishing a newspaper or refurbishing the library. Because of all this ongoing activity, such schools and classrooms are rarely quiet, at least in the traditional sense of a school where adults talk and children listen. "Children are doing things, not just watching someone else. These are schools where learning is not a spectator sport" (Wood, 1992, p. xv).

Third, in learning-community schools and classrooms, there is a sense that everyone belongs to the community: students, teachers, parents, administrators, support staff, volunteers, and other members of the broader community outside the school. Relationships among all people are collaborative, and each individual perceives all others as both teachers and learners. In a learning community, each individual is valued: cultural and linguistic identity is affirmed by using what each person brings to school as starting points and building blocks (McCaleb, 1994, p. xii).

Rationale for Learning-Community Classrooms

Building communities of learners centers on a traditional goal for schools: that of preparing students to be citizens in a democracy. Although not a new idea, citizenship education is sometimes obscured by a seeming overemphasis on the preparation of students for the workplace. At the core of learning centers are two tenets: (1) the need to negotiate differences through sharing a common curriculum, and (2) the need for students to learn citizenship by practicing democracy. With respect to the need for a common curriculum, as long ago as 1915, John Dewey and his daughter argued against the separation of students into academic and vocational tracks:

> It is fatal for a democracy to permit the formation of fixed classes. Differences of wealth, the existence of large masses of unskilled laborers, contempt for work with the hands, inability to secure the training that enables one to forge ahead in life, all operate to produce classes, and to widen the gulf between them. Statesmen and legislation can do something to combat these evil forces. Wise philanthropy can do something. But the only fundamental agency for good is the public school system. . . .
>
> There must not be one system for the children of parents who have more leisure and another for the children of parents who are wage earners. The physical separation forced by such a scheme . . . brings about a division of mental and moral habits, ideals and outlook. . . . A division of the public school system into one part that pursues traditional academic methods, and another that deals with those who are to go into manual labor means a plan of social predestination totally foreign to the spirit of democracy.
>
> The democracy which proclaims equality of opportunity as its ideal requires an education in which learning and social application, ideas and practice, work and recognition of the meaning of what is done, are united from the beginning and for all. (as cited in Butts, 1978, pp. 222–223)

With respect to the need to practice democracy in order to learn democracy, Wood (1992) describes the requirements of the democratic life in the following terms:

> Fundamentally, democracy requires citizens who participate broadly in informed public decision-making with an eye toward the common good. Citizens must thus be literate, able not only to master the rudiments of reading, writing, and computing, but able to use these tools as ways of understanding the world and making their voices heard in it. We must also know how to find and evaluate information, how to sift through the items that bombard us daily, to sort the useful from the superfluous, and the clearly propagandistic from the approximate truths.
>
> Members of the republic must also have an ongoing sense of community, an obligation to the common good. Citizens should see themselves as members of a

community that makes their individuality possible, and they should value and nurture that community. Democracy also requires that we each have courage, that we believe our actions are important and valued, and that we have not only a right, but also an obligation to participate publicly. The democratic citizen is, in sum, the individual who has the intellectual skills and conviction necessary to participate publicly in making the many choices that confront us, in ways that will promote the common good. (p. xvii)

One way to provide a common curriculum in which all students practice the required skills of democratic participation is to create communities of learners in which all those involved–students, teachers, parents, administrators, counselors, nurses, and volunteers–actively participate in decisions regarding the educational process.

Pedagogies: Old and New

Much has been written lately about new ways of teaching that are presumed to benefit a wider variety of students. Included in these new ways of teaching are labels such as interactive learning, engaged learning, feminist pedagogy, inquiry learning, emancipatory curriculum, critical pedagogy, discovery learning, whole language, and collaborative learning. There are indeed some "new" aspects contained in these ideas, but in general they can all be grouped into the much more traditional category of good teaching. Moreover, most of them have been around for a long, long time.

Dialogue, for example, or what is sometimes known as interactive teaching and learning, is Plato's dialectic in contemporary dress. Discovery learning, or the use of teaching techniques that present students with questions and materials that impel students to active investigation, was the centerpiece of Abelard's teaching in the 12th century (Broudy & Palmer, 1965). Critical pedagogy, inquiry learning, feminist pedagogy, and collaborative learning all hearken back at least to John Amos Comenius in the 17th century. He believed that understanding was more important than rote learning, that demonstration was more effective than listening to experts, that education should follow the natural development of the student, that students should teach and learn from one another, and that both text material and learning activities should incorporate the student's own experience as a starting point.

What is relatively new in learning-community classrooms is not that such varied methods of instruction should exist, but that they should exist more or less simultaneously and be exercised by both children and adults. Their emphasis depends on the age of the student, the nature of the subject matter, and the kind of learning activities used. In a learning-community classroom there is plenty of room for all the old methods of dialogue: telling, demonstrating, modeling, and problem posing. In addition, several relatively new ideas about teaching are often incorporated in learning communities. One is that teaching strategies should attend to the development of "voice" among students. That is, teaching should encourage the expression of distinctive beliefs and experiences based on biological, sociocultural, and linguistic differences. In addition, because learning-community classrooms include parents and other community members as part of the classroom community, family or adult literacy may also be a pedagogical goal.

Roles: Old and New

As with pedagogy, traditional roles of adults and children in learning-community classrooms are not so much changed as they are expanded. Thus, the role of teacher as teller is expanded to teacher as guide, as coach, and sometimes as cheerleader! The role of teacher is also expanded to include other adults–parents, administrators, and community members who provide various types of specialized assistance to the regular classroom teacher. Similarly, the role of teacher is also extended to students, who serve as teachers and critics to one another. The role of learner, like that of teacher, is expanded in learning-community classrooms. Because everyone (teachers, students, administrators, parents, and community members) has unique experiences and specialized knowledge to share, it follows that everyone (adults included) will be a learner as well as a teacher.

Place of Content Knowledge: Old and New

In a learning-community classroom, the place and function of content knowledge also varies, although it is certainly no less important than in traditional classrooms. Thus mathematics, language, history, science, and the arts serve in dual capacities. Sometimes such knowledge is learned as an end in itself, which is the more traditional approach to content. At other times, content knowledge serves as a means to another end, such as solving a problem or constructing a new way of looking at the world, which is the newer approach to content learning. More often than not in learning-community classrooms, subject matter knowledge is

acquired in the service of other goals. For example, if students need to produce a newspaper, they must know how to use language in intelligible ways. If students are going to measure the amount of rainfall during a storm, they must know about fractions and forms of measurement. Conversely, in traditional classrooms, it is likely that such subjects as language and mathematics are taught as ends in themselves, with applications of that knowledge coming later (or maybe not at all). In learning-community classrooms, the project or activity often comes first, and the acquisition of knowledge and skills needed to accomplish the activity become necessary tools in the service of that activity. In this way, students come to appreciate the relevance of subject matter knowledge.

Assessment: Old and New

In traditional classrooms, assessment or evaluation of student achievement is largely accomplished through the practice of paper-and-pencil testing. Moreover, the results of such assessment are often used to separate (track) students into homogeneous groups, presumably for their own benefit. Standardized commercial tests indicate to administrators and the community how "well" or "poorly" an individual student or teacher or class or school is doing in relation to other students, teachers, classes, and schools.

In learning-community classrooms, such traditional paper-and-pencil forms of assessment are also used, especially in the now-almost-universal standards-based environment generated by the No Child Left Behind Act. However, in a learning-community classroom, these same tests are used for somewhat different purposes. For example, proficiency and unit tests are used for instructional feedback to individual students as well as for the purpose of grouping students or to provide interim or final grades. In addition, other forms of assessment including peer evaluation, portfolios, group tests, and self-evaluation are used. Teachers combine these various measures when judging what grade a student has earned.

At this point, you might be wondering how the ideas of a learning-community classroom are related to the issues of individual biological, psychological, sociocultural, and linguistic differences discussed in the earlier chapters of this book. As an example, look at the ways in which one important source of cultural identity–language–might play out in a particular learning-community classroom.

Perspectives on Language Acquisition

It is often said that language is what makes us human. Certainly, language is the primary means for socializing us into our families and our social groups and, through them, to acquiring our cultural identity.

Language and the Family

Berger and Berger (1972) refer to language as the first institution encountered by the individual. This conclusion may surprise you if you think of the family as being the first institution, the one that introduces us to language. Infants, however, can't know what a family is until they have acquired some form of language. Language objectifies, interprets, and justifies reality for the child, thus structuring the child's environment (pp. 68–69). It puts labels on roles (mommy, police offi-cer, teacher) and permits the child to extend those roles into the wider commu-nity. It also brings the meanings and values of the wider community onto the small stage of the immediate family. Consider the case of the father in the act of punishing the child:

> As he punishes, he talks. What is he talking about? Some of the talking may just be a way of giving vent to his own annoyance or anger. But, in most cases, much of the talking is a running commentary on the offending act and the punishment it so richly deserves. The talking interprets and justifies the punishment. Inevitably, it does this in a way that goes beyond the father's own immediate reactions. The punishment is put in the vast context of manners and morals; in the extreme case, even the divinity may be invoked as a penal authority. . . . The punishing father now represents this system. (pp. 69–70)

Institutional Aspects of Language in the Family

Language has several characteristics in common with other social institutions (Berger & Berger, 1972). First, language is external. It is experienced as "out there," in contrast to the individual's private thoughts or feelings (which, inci-dentally, are also structured by language and its meanings). Further, when an individual hears language spoken by another person, that person is speaking according to a particular language system that was created neither by the speaker nor the listener. It is external to them both.

Second, language has objectivity; that is, everyone who shares it agrees to accept the norms and conventions of its particular symbol system. Berger and Berger note that "the objectivity of one's first language is particularly powerful" (p. 72). They write:

> Jean Piaget, the Swiss psychologist, tells the story somewhere of a small child who was asked whether the sun could be called anything except "sun." "No," replied the child. How did he know this, the child was asked. The question puzzled him for a moment. Then he pointed to the sun and said, "Well, look at it." (p. 72)

Third, language has the power of moral authority to direct us. As children learn to speak their native language, they are usually excused small lapses in pronunciation and usage. As they grow up, however, inappropriate use of lan-guage may very well expose them to ridicule, shame, and guilt. Consider the child who speaks a language or dialect different from that of the school, the working-class college student who is expected to engage in polite conversation at a formal reception, and the adult who tries to speak in the rapidly changing vernacular of her teenage children. Not only are these individuals often misun-derstood, they are also often the objects of considerable disdain.

Finally, language is historical. It was there before we were born and will continue after we are gone. Its meanings were accumulated over a long period of time by myriad individuals now lost forever. Furthermore, language is a living, changing tool, with new words and meanings constantly being added, some for a few days, others for much longer. Some regard language as a "broad stream flowing through time" (p. 75). Berger and Berger write:

> An Austrian writer, Karl Kraus, has called language the house in which the human spirit lives. Language provides the lifelong context of our experience of others, of

self, of the world. Even when we imagine worlds beyond this one, we are constrained to put our intimations or hopes in terms of language. Language is the social institution above all others. It provides the most powerful hold that society has over us. (p. 75)

Given the power of language to shape us in many ways, it is well to keep in mind that it is not only our "own" language–formal or informal–that has such power. As Gonzalez (1974) notes,

There is no such thing linguistically speaking as a good language or a bad language, a superior language or an inferior language. Each language is appropriate for its time, place, and circumstances. All languages are complete in this respect. (p. 565)

Perspectives on Language Variation

A number of Martina Chandler's classroom activities are designed to show how language varies from one cultural group to another, as well as between individuals within the same group. Likewise, teachers and students sometimes speak different historical languages, but more often, they speak the same language in different ways. Moreover, teachers and students use both verbal and nonverbal means to communicate significant messages to one another.

Verbal Communication

Through an extensive process of evolution, humans have developed the ability to produce, receive, store, and manipulate a variety of symbolic sounds. Human beings, more than any other creature, depend on the production of sound in the form of verbal language as their primary means of communication.

Within any given language, however, vocabulary, pronunciation, syntax (grammatical structure), and semantics (the meaning of words) may differ widely. When Martina's students took turns saying words like greasy, fire, log, and aunt, they were clearly able to hear differences in pronunciation. Furthermore, the form in which language is conveyed may also differ, as, for example, in sign language where syntax is composed of a combination of specific movements of the fingers, hand, and arm as well as facial expressions. Most people are fascinated to watch this kind of speech, made public in recent years by signers who accompany performances on television or talks by public officials. Martina's students were also very interested in Anna's and Mrs. Thomas's use of sign in class. As Martina's students interviewed one another and then introduced their partners to the rest of the class, they were able to hear other variations in language, such as accents and dialects, as well.

Accents

An **accent** differs from the standard language only in the way words are pronounced, and it often results from pronunciation habits shared by people from a geographical region. People with a typical New England accent, for example, may pronounce the words *car, far,* and *bar* as if they were spelled caaa, faaa, and baaa. Similarly, people who have learned to speak English in Appalachia,

Accents and Dialects

the South, or the West may have significant differences in the way they pronounce the same words. People whose first language is not English may have difficulty pronouncing certain English words. Japanese speakers, for example, often have trouble with the letter *l,* and Russian speakers may have difficulty with the letters *w* and *v* as they are used in English words. Note that such speakers may be speaking quite proper standard English, but with an accent (Gollnick & Chinn, 2005). In Martina's classroom, Hannah and Tammy, who had both moved to California from West Virginia, had the softness and somewhat slurred accent of the West Virginia hills. Yoshi, who speaks both English and Japanese, can imitate his grandparents' Japanese accent as they speak English. Rosita speaks English with a pronounced Spanish accent.

Dialects

A **dialect** is a variation of some standard language form that includes differences in pronunciation, word usage, and syntax. Such differences may be based on ethnicity, religion, geographical region, social class, or age. Dialects differ not only in their origin but also in the specifics of their expression. Regional differences, for example, usually involve variations in the pronunciation of vowels (recall the example of people from New England). Similarly, Tammy and Hannah, as well as having Appalachian accents, speak a dialect of English sometimes referred to as **mountain English.** Social dialects, on the other hand, are most often distinguished from one another by variations in the pronunciation of consonants, particularly the *th* sound and the sound of the consonants *r* and *l.* Dontae, the young man from Los Angeles, exhibited this language pattern. Regional and social dialects and accents may vary together or be a combination from a number of sociocultural origins, depending on the life experiences of the speaker. Although a variety of dialects are spoken in the United States, the three most widely known are **black English** (or Ebonics), **rural English,** and **standard English.**

Ebonics (also called black English or African American language) is a dialect spoken primarily but not exclusively by urban African Americans. Although it is often associated with those who live in low-income communities, it is also spoken by African Americans from a variety of social classes and can serve, in part, as an expression of cultural identity. The influence of social class on Ebonics is seen mainly in the ability of black English speakers to switch back and forth between Ebonics and standard English. Dontae, who speaks Ebonics fluently, has difficulty switching to standard English and is not certain that he wants to do it. One explanation for the origin of Ebonics is that it is derived from Gullah, a Creole dialect developed by Africans brought to the United States as slaves, which puts English words into a syntax similar to many African languages. Another explanation sees it as a version of a regional English dialect spoken by early English settlers on the East Coast. Gullah is still spoken by some residents of the Sea Islands off the Carolina coast, and while many of the distinctive features of black English are similar to Gullah, black English is also similar to other dialects spoken by European whites in some rural areas of the United States. Indeed, some scholars have found that similarities outweigh differences when comparing black English with standard English (Wolfram, Adger, & Christian, 1999).

Rural English, sometimes called mountain English, is a dialect spoken primarily in Appalachia and is derived from the language of early English settlers in the area. People from Appalachia are often ridiculed for their speech, but some linguists say that mountain English is the "purest" English spoken in the United States and the closest to the English spoken in Shakespeare's time. It has been preserved, in part, because of the isolation of mountain people, in the same way that Gullah has been preserved off the coast of the Carolinas.

Finally, middle-class European Americans may be surprised to learn that so-called standard English is also a dialect of the English language. Although the term "standard English" is usually taken to mean that version of the English language most acceptable or most "correct," there are, in fact, many varieties of standard English. Gollnick and Chinn (2005) note that "the speech of a certain group of people in each community tends to be identified as standard" (p. 253). Moreover, standard English as it is spoken in countries such as Australia, India, Nigeria, and England differs significantly from standard English as it is spoken in the United States (Tiedt & Tiedt, 1995). Standard English, as the term is used in U.S. schools, usually refers to that dialect spoken by educated middle and upper classes and to the formal written and oral English that dominates print and broadcast media.

Bidialectalism

Bidialectalism refers to the ability to speak two (and sometimes more) dialects and to switch back and forth easily. Examples of people engaging in bidialectalism are the country boy who has become an executive in a large city and switches dialects when he goes back to his hometown, or the African American woman who has become a professor and speaks standard English but switches to Ebonics when speaking informally to African American colleagues, students, or friends. The ability to "code-switch" is often encouraged in schools as a way of enabling youngsters to both broaden their language horizons and receive the perceived economic and social benefits of speaking standard English. Although research does not support the belief that it is necessary to speak standard English in order to read or write it, it is often the case that prejudice against those who speak nonstandard dialects may lead to economic and social discrimination (Grossman, 1995). In Martina's class, Ritchie is able to switch back and forth between Ebonics and standard English easily and does so often.

Code-switching

Sign Language

Although sign language is often thought of as nonverbal communication, it is also a form of verbal expression. One form of sign language is the language of signs spoken by the deaf. Several varieties of signed communication exist, notably **American Sign Language** (ASL), which is the only sign system recognized as a language in the United States (sign languages also exist in other countries); signed English, which translates oral or written English into signs; and finger spelling (sometimes called the manual alphabet), which literally spells out English words letter by letter. Anna acquired ASL in infancy in the same way that her hearing classmates learned oral language. Like other languages, ASL has its own syntax and rhythms. Anna learned to think in it and translates other sign languages and lip reading into ASL. Closely associated with the culture of the deaf, ASL is the subject of often-heated debate in educational circles.

Sign Language

Some educators believe that all deaf or hearing-impaired children should learn to speak orally; others believe that signed communication is not only sufficient but that these individuals—both hearing and hearing-impaired—are bilingual in ASL and English. Such is the case with Anna, who has learned to speak oral English but much prefers to use sign.

Nonverbal Communication

Nonverbal Communication

Nonverbal communication, used by both hearing and hearing-impaired individuals, refers to body movements, facial expressions, and a variety of word replacement strategies. It has been estimated that nonverbal communication accounts for 50 to 90% of the messages we send and receive (Barnlund, 1968). In 1973 Leubitz identified four functions of nonverbal communication: (1) to convey messages; (2) to augment verbal communication; (3) to contradict verbal communication; and (4) to replace verbal communication. For purposes of analysis, three aspects of nonverbal behavior are usually studied: **proxemics** (the culturally determined comfortable distance between people when they are speaking with one another), **kinesics** (the study of body movements), and **paralanguage** (sounds made by the voice that are not words such as crying, sighing, and word substitutes such as "Shhh") (as cited in Gollnick & Chinn, 2005, pp. 218–219). It is well to remember, however, that these nonverbal aspects of communication are seldom used or experienced individually; rather, they combine in various ways with one another and with verbal language to produce the innumerable nuances we take for granted in ordinary communication.

Culture, Language, and Learning Style

A third important area of language concerns its relationships to culture and learning styles. Language provides the names for ideas, people, and things that enable us to make sense of the world around us, and it does so at such an early age that it helps to structure the very ways in which we think. The language that students and teachers bring with them to school inevitably affects the mental processes by which they perceive, think, solve problems, learn, and approach learning. Language is also both a product and a shaper of culture. The two are inextricably intertwined.

Originally conducted in the 1950s by psychologists interested in perception and other forms of cognition, learning style research has in the past decades become increasingly available to educators interested in the variation they see in patterns of learning. Definitions of learning style vary, but the National Task Force on Learning Style and Brain Behavior has adopted the following tentative definition:

> Learning style is that consistent pattern of behavior and performance by which an individual approaches education experiences. It is the composite of characteristic cognitive, affective and psychological behaviors that serve as relatively stable indicators of how a learner perceives, interacts with, and responds to the learning environment. It is formed in the deep structure of neural organization and personality [that] molds and is molded by human development and the cultural experiences of home, school, and society. (Keefe & Languis, 1983, p. 1)

Components of Learning Style

Perhaps the most widely used dimension of learning style was also the first to be investigated. Studying variations in perception, Witkin (1962) discovered that most individuals could be grouped according to whether they were field dependent or field independent. An individual who is **field independent** easily perceives discrete parts, is good at abstract analytical thought, tends to be individualistic and less dependent on others, has less well-developed social skills, prefers working alone and self-organizes information to be learned, and tends to be intrinsically motivated and unresponsive to social reinforcement. In contrast, an individual who is **field dependent** (now more often referred to as field sensitive) perceives globally or holistically, does less well at analytical problem solving, tends to be sensitive to the social environment with well-developed social skills, prefers an observational approach to learning and will accept information to be learned as it is presented, and tends to be extrinsically motivated and responsive to the social environment (Bennett, 2006).

A second dimension of learning style has to do with an individual's preferred sensory mode for learning. Although, barring physical disability, all six senses (sight, sound, smell, touch, taste, and movement) are normally open to learning stimuli, some individuals tend to learn most easily and efficiently through one of the sensory modes. There is also some evidence that preferred modes change as a factor of age. Some research, for example, suggests that younger children make efficient use of taste, smell, and touch, whereas older children come to rely on movement, hearing, and vision.

Other variations in learning style include differences in response to the immediate environment, emotionality, social preferences, and cognitive-psychological orientation (Dunn, Beaudry, & Klavas, 1989). Responses to environmental influences include an individual's preference for quiet or noise, bright or soft illumination, or warm or cool temperatures. Emotionality includes such factors as motivation, persistence at tasks, and sense of responsibility as well as a person's response to the structure of a given context. Social preferences refer to the degree to which the presence of others facilitates learning. Included in this category is the degree to which an individual prefers to work alone, in pairs, in cooperative groups, or with adults. Finally, the psychological dimension refers to the tendencies individuals have to be global or analytic learners, right-brain or left-brain dominant, reflective or impulsive.

Learning Styles

Activity and
Reading 32:
Learning Styles

Multiple Intelligences

Related to the idea of learning style is the idea of multiple intelligences, extensively researched and promoted by Howard Gardner and his colleagues (Gardner, 1983, 1991, 1999). Based on considerable research on the brain and on aspects of cognition, Gardner's concept suggests that human beings have not only preferred learning styles but also different ways of expressing intellectual ability. Initially, Gardner conceptualized seven different kinds of intelligence: visual/spatial, verbal/linguistic, logical/mathematical, bodily/kinesthetic, musical/rhythmic, interpersonal, and intrapersonal. Individuals who have strengths in any (or several) of these kinds of intelligence tend to have preferred modes of thinking. For example, people who are strong in verbal/linguistic intelligence tend to think in words and love reading,

Multiple Intelligences

writing, playing word games, and so on, whereas those who are strong in visual/ spatial intelligence tend to think in images and pictures and love designing, drawing, and even doodling. Since his original works, Gardner (2006) has suggested increasing the "kinds" of intelligence that might be considered in thinking about learning and has also linked the very definition of intelligence with culture:

> Multiple intelligence theory . . . pluralizes the traditional concept [of intelligence]. An intelligence is a computational capacity—a capacity to process a certain kind of information—that originates in human biology and human psychology. . . . An intelligence entails the ability to solve problems or fashion products that are of consequence in a particular cultural setting or community. . . . Only those skills that are universal in the human species are considered. . . . Even so, the biological proclivity to participate in a particular form of problem solving must also be coupled with the cultural nurturing of that domain. For example, language, a universal skill, may manifest itself particularly as writing in one culture, as oratory in another culture, and as the secret language composed of anagrams or tongue twisters in a third. (pp. 6–7)

The importance of multiple intelligences and learning styles in school lies in the ability of teachers to identify preferred modes of learning and to adapt instruction so that all students get to practice learning in multiple ways. Notice that no one recommends that students learn only in their preferred style but rather that they have opportunities to develop learning strategies that can maximize their natural strengths and minimize their weaknesses. It is the teacher's responsibility to understand this and to provide instruction that reaches multiple learners.

Origins of Learning Style

Although the exact origins of a person's particular learning style are still a matter of conjecture, it is clear that learning patterns develop from a combination of biological, psychological, and sociocultural (including linguistic) factors. Also, much research indicates that child-rearing practices and other forms of socialization are heavily implicated in the development of learning style. Because language is the medium through which much socialization occurs in the family, it is not unreasonable to surmise that the relation of language to patterns of learning is considerable. In addition, because language is closely linked to culture, learning style differences may be more readily understood if we look at the connections between language, culture, and learning style.

The Relation of Language and Learning Style to Culture

Geography, history, and cultural experience all influence the way a person acquires language, which language that person learns, what meanings are attributed to words, and what patterns of communication are practiced. The family is normally the first mediator of the culture to a growing child. Nevertheless, language and cultural knowledge are inextricably bound together.

Of primary importance, of course, in the development of language is the acquisition of vocabulary–what are the "right" words for ideas, people, actions, and things. But words themselves are arbitrary. Indeed, the very concept of "word" may differ among language groups. The Japanese word *ikimasu,* for example, may have any of the following English meanings: I (you, he, she, we, they) am (is, are) going. A Japanese listener will decide which of these meanings is correct by the context of the conversation.

Even in the same language, the same words may have different meanings. Consider the word "tip." Tip can mean to push something over or off an edge. It can also refer to payment for some service over and above the stated price. A tip can also refer to a good idea or suggestion that one person might give another, or it can mean a slender point at the end of something. In some parts of the world, a tip refers to a garbage dump. Such common English words as "love," "bread," "chicken," "turkey," "bat," and "top" all have many meanings. Linguists have estimated that the 50 most often used words in the English language can produce over 14,000 different meanings (Samover, Porter, & Jain, 1981).

Language also plays a critical role in the maintenance of subgroups within a larger cultural/language group. Recall that ingroup membership is granted to those with whom the group feels comfortable and with whom the group has perceived similarities. One function of language is to distinguish those who should be considered potential members of the ingroup from those who should not. In this way, language helps people develop a sense of social unity. Thus a variation from a language standard that contributes to a group's sense of identity is nearly as important as the parent language itself.

Language reflects the thought processes of a culture. English writing and thinking, for instance, is relatively linear in comparison to many other languages (Kaplan, 1966). That is, the speaker or writer tries to get right to the point by eliminating reference to issues and topics that seem irrelevant to the message. The task for such a speaker is to communicate the message quickly and efficiently. Speakers who do not keep to the topic can be quite frustrating to English listeners, as is witnessed by the English colloquialism "He just keeps beating around the bush!" On the other hand, speakers of Semitic languages (Arabic and Hebrew) use various kinds of parallels in their thinking. References to past events, for example, are quite common and expected. Another important function of verbal communication among Semitic speakers, as well as many others, is the building of personal relationships through language use.

No pattern of communication is right or wrong; all have evolved to express and satisfy particular cultural patterns and needs. Some, however, may stress the development of interpersonal relationships more than others. If those interpersonal relationships are not expressed in the message (for example, when an American is speaking with an Arab), the person receiving the message may interpret it in a way that the speaker does not intend. Consider the American discussing plans to meet later in the week. While the American is interested in establishing the exact time, place, and purpose of the meeting, the Arab intersperses the conversation with questions about the health of family members, the last time the two parties met, and other significant events in the lives of the two conversants. Both speakers are using language for cultural purposes in cultural ways: the American to get something done, and the Arab to indicate a committed relationship. It would not be surprising, in this instance, if misunderstanding occurred!

Learning style is also developed, in part, as an expression of culture. What we attend to and how we attend to it are culturally shaped adaptations to the physical and social environment. Christine Bennett (1989) recalls a story told by an Anglo-American speech student who had two experiences that illustrate this point, one with a Hopi Indian and the other with Trukee islanders.

> "Look at those clouds!" I exclaimed one afternoon. "We'll probably have rain later today."
> "What clouds?" my Hopi companion asked.
> "Right there!" I responded in amazement, pointing to obvious puffs of white and gray.
> "All I see is the sky."
> "You mean you really don't see those clouds?"
> "There's nothing there but sky." (p. 76)

Several months later, this same student was in the opposite situation with a group of Trukee fishermen.

> I thought we were lost. There had been no sign of land for hours. My companions tried to reassure me that we weren't lost at all. They read the wave patterns like I'd use a map. All I could see were waves. Even when they pointed to specific signs, I couldn't see anything. Here we were looking at the same body of water. It felt strange to know that I simply could not perceive what they actually saw. (pp. 76–77)

Research has indicated that particular patterns of learning (or learning style) can be associated with particular cultural groups. For example, many African Americans and many females tend to be field sensitive, whereas many Japanese and Japanese Americans tend to be field independent. It is important to note, however, that these are examples of cultural generalizations and that there may be more difference within these groups than between them. As discussed in Chapter 3, a large number of factors can contribute to an individual's own particular pattern of culture, and this also holds true for the development of an individual's language and learning style.

Perspectives on Bilingual Education and Second-Language Acquisition

With increasing immigration to the United States in recent decades, schools are being faced with the challenges of large numbers of children for whom English is not their first language. This is not a new phenomenon for American schooling. Contrary to popular belief, **bilingual education** is not a creation of the 1960s, although the civil rights movement gave it renewed emphasis. Indeed, Ohio was the first state to pass a bilingual education law in 1839–allowing German-English instruction if parents requested it. Similar laws were enacted in Louisiana for French and English in 1847 and in the New Mexico territory for Spanish and English in 1850. By the turn of the 20th century, many local districts and nearly a dozen states were providing bilingual education in languages including Norwegian, Italian, Polish, Czech, and Cherokee (History of Bilingual Education, 1998). At that time, at least 600,000 children in primary schools (public and parochial) received part or all of their instruction in German–about 4% of all American elementary students.

Nativist fears stemming from World War I changed the political winds, however, and by the mid-1920s bilingual education provisions were replaced by English-only laws in a majority of states. The ferment surrounding civil rights in the 1960s brought renewed interest in bilingual education. In the 12-year period from 1963 to 1975, private and governmental studies and hearings and a series of lawsuits regarding rights to native language instruction, placement of children with disabilities, and desegregation produced many mandates for the schooling of minority students. Concurrently, new educational strategies and curricula, especially in bilingual and bicultural education, appeared in districts across the nation. The Bilingual Education Act was passed in 1968 as Title VII of the Elementary and Secondary Education Act. President Lyndon Johnson clarified the intent of this law in the following words:

> This bill authorizes a new effort to prevent dropouts; new programs for handicapped children; new planning help for rural schools. It also contains a special provision establishing bilingual education programs for children whose first language is not English. Thousands of children of Latin descent, young Indians, and others will get a better start—a better chance—in school. (as cited in Tiedt & Tiedt, 1995, p. 6)

In 1970, the Office of Civil Rights Guidelines tried to make special training for non–English-speaking students a requirement for public schools that receive federal aid. The office stated:

> Where inability to speak and understand the English language excludes national origin–minority group children from effective participation in the education program offered by a school district, the district must take affirmative steps to rectify the language deficiency in order to open its instructional program to these students. (as cited in Tiedt & Tiedt, 1995, p. 6)

A significant case in the development of multicultural and bilingual education was *Lau v. Nichols,* decided by a 1974 Supreme Court ruling. This decision declared that a San Francisco school district violated a non–English-speaking Chinese student's right to equal educational opportunity when it failed to provide needed English language instruction and other special programs. An important consequence of the *Lau* decision was the declaration that school districts across the country must provide students an education in languages that meet their needs. Other cases followed, making the same arguments for African American and Latino students.

Bilingual Education Legislation and Court Cases

In 1981, a pedagogically sound plan for **limited English proficient** (LEP) students was set by the Fifth Circuit Court in Texas in *Casteñada v. Pickard*. The plan required a sufficient qualified staff to implement the plan, including hiring new staff and training current staff, as well as the establishment of a system to evaluate the programs. It is important to note that a formal "bilingual education" program was not required; however, it did require that "appropriate action to overcome language barriers" be taken through well-implemented programs.

The debate on the requirement that schools provide special programs for English language learners, and the degree of that provision, continues today. In the fall of 2009, for example, the Supreme Court ruled, in *Horne v. Flores,* that Arizona's funding for programs that serve English language learners does not violate the terms of the Equal Educational Opportunities Act, and that states are free to develop their own funding plans for such programs. This case, fought in the courts since 1992, is an example of the debate about "how much funding is enough" to provide sufficient resources for teaching English language learners. In *Flores,* the Supreme Court overturned two lower courts, which had found in favor of those who asserted that, in fact, state funding was insufficient. And the debate goes on.

The Bilingual Education Backlash

The Oakland Ebonics Controversy

Since the 1990s, a growing backlash against teaching students in any language other than English seems to rival the backlash after World War I. Two significant responses surfaced in California. The first one was the largely symbolic decision (since partially amended) of the Oakland schools to recognize the use of Ebonics among some of its students and to attempt to use that fact as a tool to improve student performance. At no time did the Oakland Board of Education plan to teach students in Ebonics. Rather, the policy was part of a larger effort to "stop blaming children and start demanding more accountability from teachers and administrators in a district where the average grade among African American students is a D+" (Diringer & Olszewski, 1996, A17). The idea was to educate teachers to accept Ebonics as the daily language of many African American students and help them learn to use standard English as well. In other words, teachers would begin with the students' own language (or, in this case, dialect) in order to take them more effectively toward the understanding and use of the standard English of the typical American workplace.

So sensitive are some Americans to the bilingual education issue, however, that something of a firestorm erupted when the Oakland board announced its plans. What most critics missed was that such an approach was only part of a process of teaching standard English, not its aim.

A second major response had more far-reaching consequences in California, Arizona, and in the rest of the country as well. In 1998, voters in California passed Proposition 227, which required California public schools to teach limited English proficient (LEP) students in special classes that were taught almost entirely in English. It also shortened the time that most LEP students would stay in special classes, normally not longer than one year. Arizona's Proposition 203 followed in 1999. Similar measures under consideration in Massachusetts, Oregon, Colorado, and Rhode Island (Anderson, 2001) resulted in the ending of bilingual education in Massachusetts, but the defeat of such legislation in the three other states.

Research conducted by University of California researchers 2 years after Proposition 227 offers several insights into the early impact of the revised approach to language instruction. First, the number of English learners in special classes dropped by 29% to 12% statewide. Second, in part due to confusion regarding the responsibilities of districts in informing parents of their rights to seek waivers from the English immersion program, only 67% of districts formally so notified parents. Third, teachers' initiatives in their own classrooms seemed to depend on what they had done prior to Proposition 227, and on their own skills, experience, and beliefs about students' learning. However, it was rare to encounter a teacher who contended that his or her instruction and class organization had not been affected (Hakuta, Butler, & Witt, 2000). Moreover, research conducted by members of the same University of California research team at Stanford suggests that oral proficiency in English may take 3 to 5 years, and proficiency in academic English may take 4 to 7 years (Gándara et al., 2000).

Given the debate among proponents and opponents of bilingual education, it is perhaps worthwhile to inquire why people become so upset about bilingual education. Two major factors seem to be at work here. The first is whether children will suffer if they participate in bilingual instruction. Advocates for Proposition 227 argued that although bilingual education began with good intentions in the 1970s, it has failed in actual practice and that Latino immigrant children are its principal victims, as evidenced by their high failure and dropout rates. The assumption here is that bilingual education results in students not learning to speak, read, and write English and thus being injured for life both economically and socially. A subtext of this argument—a fear of overwhelming numbers of unassimilated students entering the adult American world—is reminiscent of arguments for assimilationist practices at the beginning of the 20th century. A second, related issue deals with the effects of a bilingual education. The assumption of many parents and teachers is that children cannot achieve as much in a bilingual context. Children, it is thought, cannot cope with the demands of schooling in two languages.

Other Bilingual Education Issues

Bilingual education is further complicated by the difficulty of defining just who is and who is not bilingual. Although someone may be able to speak in two languages, use of one of those languages may be restricted to a particular setting. People may use their native language, for example, only at home or among other speakers of that language, whereas they use their second language at school or at work. The 1984 Bilingual Education Act defines LEP individuals as those not born in the United States, those whose native language is not English, those from environments in which English is not the dominant language, and those from the various Native American groups where languages other than English are commonly used. According to the U.S. Department of Education, there are more than 5 million English language learners in American public schools (Spellings, 2006), a 60% increase from 1995 to 2005 (Thompson, 2009). Clearly, helping our young people learn to be academically successful in English is an important challenge.

Perspectives on Second-Language Acquisition

Since the modern beginning of bilingual education in the 1960s, the terminology has changed somewhat. Schoolchildren, for example, whose first language is not English are most often called **English language learners** (ELLs). According to the National Association for Bilingual Education (2004), bilingual education consists of a variety of approaches in the classroom for the purpose of

- teaching English,
- fostering academic achievement,
- acculturating immigrants to a new society,
- preserving minority group's linguistic and cultural heritage,
- enabling English speakers to learn a second language,
- developing national language resources, or
- any combination of the above.

Thus both students whose first language is English and those whose first language is other than English can benefit from acquiring a second (or third!) language.

Stages in Second-Language Acquisition

Years of research on the factors involved in learning a second language have produced agreement that second-language learners will move sequentially through these predictable stages of language acquisition (North West Regional Education Laboratory, 2003):

1. *The silent/receptive or preproduction stage,* in which students may understand as many as 500 words in the new language, but which they are not comfortable using. This stage can last from 10 hours to 6 months.

2. *The early production stage,* in which students have developed nearly 1,000 words that they understand and can use in one- or two-word phrases. This stage can last an additional 6 months.

3. *The speech emergence stage,* lasting up to another year, in which students have developed about 3,000 words and can use short phrases and simple sentences to communicate.

4. *The intermediate language proficiency stage,* in which students have developed nearly 6,000 words and can make complex statements, state opinions, share their thoughts, and so forth. This stage may take another year.

5. *The advanced language proficiency stage,* in which students have developed some specialized content-area vocabulary and can participate fully in grade-level classroom activities, sometimes with some support. To achieve this stage often takes 2 to 5 years.

Other Important Concepts in Second-Language Acquisition

Considerable agreement has also been achieved on several contextual factors involved in acquiring a second language. One of these is the "affective filter hypothesis" (Krashen, 1981; Krashen & Terrell, 1983), which suggests that emotions are a factor in the ease or difficulty in learning another language. In particular, negative emotions such as anxiety, embarrassment, or anger produced by early attempts to speak a second language can produce a kind of filter that gets in the way of the learner's ability to process new or difficult words.

Other important contextual factors are (1) the linguistic distance between two languages (how different they are from one another), (2) the student's level of proficiency in his or her first language (including not only speaking but also reading and writing), (3) the dialect of the first language (whether it is standard or nonstandard), (4) the relative status of the student's first language in the community, and (5) social attitudes toward the student's first language (Waiqui, 2000).

Of particular importance in English language acquisition is the need to build upon the child's knowledge of his or her *first* language. Recent research on the role of the first language demonstrates the relationship between language acquisition and the overall personal and educational development of children (Baker, 1988; Cummins, 2000). This research has resulted in the following findings:

- Developing abilities in two or more languages throughout the primary school years provides a deeper understanding of language and how to use it effectively.

- The level of development of children's first language is a strong predictor of their second-language development.

- School acceptance and promotion of various first languages helps develop not only the first language but also the majority school language.
- Instructional time taken in a child's first language does not inhibit development in the majority school language.
- First languages are fragile and easily lost in the early years of school.
- To reject a child's language in the school is, in large measure, to reject the child.

As Cummins (2000) notes,

In short, the cultural, linguistic and intellectual capital of our societies will increase dramatically when we stop seeing culturally and linguistically diverse children as "a problem to be solved" and instead open our eyes to the linguistic, cultural, and intellectual resources they bring from their homes to our schools and societies.

Ethical Issues: Local and Global

Teaching linguistically diverse students also entails ethical and moral issues. Martina Chandler, for example, is aware that students who speak another language, or who speak dialects of standard English, are likely to be stigmatized by other students as well as by school policies, particularly in schools without well-developed programs for English language learners.

Most U.S. schools, and a majority of the general public, are committed to the proposition that all students learn and perform effectively in standard English, which is the language of choice by the dominant social group. Therefore, debates about bilingual education and English as a second language revolve as much around issues of cultural domination and subordination as they do around what is best for individual students. In short, the debate about bilingual education is part of a larger debate about who controls the school curriculum and for what purposes.

Another ethical issue is the degree to which assessment of student progress is measured by culture-biased tests that favor students who are already fluent in standard English. It is likely, for example, that a student may be quite knowledgeable about a subject matter but cannot express his or her knowledge in the manner required by certain kinds of tests. Similarly, most traditional assessment instruments tend to favor students who are field independent rather than global learners, who are visual learners rather than auditory or kinesthetic learners, and who prefer to work alone rather than in cooperative groups. In recent years, alternative forms of performance-based assessment have been designed that enable teachers to accurately assess progress for those students who do better with other styles of learning. However, such assessments are relatively slow in being incorporated into statewide, government-mandated tests. In the meantime, teachers like Martina Chandler must find ways to demonstrate that their students are, in fact, learning effectively according to current, proficiency-based assessment strategies.

A third ethical issue is a global one and concerns the degree to which language provides the keys to understanding other people in an increasingly interdependent world. Globalization, worldwide television (especially cable news networks such as CNN), and the Internet have tended to make English a worldwide standard language. Indeed, more than 60 countries now use English in an official capacity. Moreover, globalization of communication, a growing world urbanization, the spread of Western cultural and media products, and a disdain for the traditional all contribute to the loss of small, community-based languages (Wallmont, 2003).

International Perspectives: What's Happening Elsewhere in the World?

Bilingual Educational Policy in Georgia

Shalva Tabatadze
Director, Center for Civil Integration and Inter-Ethnic Relations, Republic of Georgia

This brief essay provides an overview of the educational policy for the integration of ethnic minorities in the Georgian mainstream. The first section describes the importance of bilingual education based on the political and legislative context of Georgia. The second section analyzes the problems of bilingual educational policy in the Georgian reality. The third section sets up special recommendations to promote implementation of proper bilingual educational policy.

Political and Legislative Context of Bilingual Education in Georgia

The Political Context

The political context of bilingual education of Georgia can be divided into three main parts: (a) demographics and geographical settlement of ethnic minorities, (b) the Soviet heritage and collapse of the Soviet Union, and (c) educational reform.

Georgia is a multiethnic country. According to the 2002 population census, ethnic Georgians make up 83.8% and ethnic minorities are 15.2% of the population of Georgia. There are four regions with minority compact settlements in Georgia: Abkhazia, South Ossetia (Shida Kartli), Kvemo Kartli, and Samtskhe-Javakheti. All these regions are located on Georgian borders with Armenia, Azerbaijan, and the North Ossetia Autonomous Republic of Russian Federation. These demographics and geographical settlement make the political context for bilingual educational policy even more crucial.

Georgia gained independence in 1991 after the collapse of the Soviet Union. Communist policies of forced migration have engendered difficult multilingual problems in the former Soviet Union countries (Hogan-Brun & Ramoniene, 2004). The language of communication of ethnic groups between and within the republics was Russian during the Soviet era. As a result of Soviet educational and language policy, the residents of the Republic of Georgia with other ethnic origins—Russians, Armenians, Azerbaijanis, Abkhazians, Ossetians, Greeks, Kurds, and others—became members of the Russian political and language society. The collapse of the Soviet Union and the coming of independence required that Georgia build a new strategy toward ethnic minorities.

Georgia has 343 minority public schools in which the language of instruction is not Georgian but either Azeri (150 schools), Armenian (133 schools), Russian (55 schools), Ossetian (4 schools), or Ukrainian (1 school) (Department of Statistics of Georgia, 2004). The Ministry of Education and Science implemented several projects to address the language problems of ethnic minority education: (1) new curriculum and textbooks for teaching Georgian as a second language were developed; (2) Georgian language teachers in the region of Kvemo Kartli and Javakheti were retrained, along with the importation of qualified teachers from the capital; and (3) a new teaching module was created for teaching Georgian as a second language, which prepares teachers for ethnic minority schools. However, experience has shown that these measures are not enough. More important radical and strategic decisions need to be made to enable ethnic minority students to have equal opportunity to succeed. The only strategic and crucial tool seems to be the establishment of bilingual programs in schools of ethnic minorities.

The Legislative Context

The legislative context for bilingual education is very interesting in Georgia. The legislation is mainly twofold: the legislature of Georgia clearly underlines the importance of a state language, and at the same time guarantees the rights of ethnic minorities, including the right to receive education in a native language. Nowadays, it is crucial to develop instruments for effective implementation of both directions of our legislative framework. Both state governance legislation and legislation for human/minority rights and nondiscrimination can be successfully implemented if there are appropriate educational policies for ethnic minorities. Development and implementation of bilingual educational policy can make both legislative approaches capable and workable in reality.

The Problems of Bilingual Educational Policy in Georgia

There are several problems in implementing a bilingual educational policy in Georgia. Since the initiative for bilingual educational (the teaching of Georgian as a second language) comes from the government, it is perceived as a violation of the educational rights of ethnic minorities by the representatives of ethnic minorities. Several important institutional problems for bilingual education policy exist as well. The first is financial in nature, and the second relates to human resources, namely, teachers. The Ministry of Education and Science has had problems finding qualified teachers to teach Georgian as a second language. The solution has been to send teachers from other regions of Georgia into the regions in which large numbers of ethnic minorities reside. This policy cannot work in a bilingual educational policy context. Local teachers will never allow teachers from other regions to substitute for them. Third is the problem of a teaching curriculum and textbooks. In general, subject-matter curriculum does not take into account the ethnic background of the students. There are also concerns regarding textbooks. The Ministry of Education and Science in Georgia introduced a new system of textbook distribution in schools based on principles of a market economy, thus turning the cost of these books over to consumers. This system will not work in ethnic minority schools, where the ethnic minority population is used to having school textbooks provided in their mother country (Armenia and Azerbaijan). Resistance from the ethnic minority population is especially likely because the texts are designed to teach in Georgia, which ethnic populations are not too happy about in the first place.

Possible Solutions and Main Strategic Recommendations

The implementation of bilingual educational policies includes three important dimensions: (1) systemic bilingual education, which requires the formation of a bilingual educational policy on a central level; (2) institutional bilingual education, which requires the implementation of a bilingual educational policy at the institutional level; and (3) pedagogical bilingual education, which requires structuring bilingual education in the classroom setting.

Systemic Bilingual Education

Systemic bilingual educational policy refers to the political issues involved in implementing bilingual educational policies. The most important issue in the development of bilingual educational policy is to provide a clear message about the objectives of bilingual education. As Hornberger (2000) notes, bilingual education should be defined "as a resource to be developed rather than a problem to be overcome" (p. 173). The policies of bilingual education should clearly underline five important goals of bilingual education proposed by Trillos (1998):

> 1) biculturalism, or the ability to act appropriately both in the national society and in . . . [one's] own community; 2) bilingualism, or proficiency in more than one language; 3) knowledge of the main values of both cultures; 4) positive attitudes to different linguistic and cultural groups; and 5) equality of opportunity for children from minority communities.

Clarity in objectives is crucial for successful implementation of the bilingual educational programs (Nieto, 2005). The second important strategy on a systemic level should be the implementation of the program stage by stage. The third important issue on a systemic level is financial provision for the bilingual educational program. Last but not least of the political issues is to ensure that bilingual educational policy is a part of a larger civil integration strategy rather than an isolated policy.

Implementation of Bilingual Education on an Institutional Level

Three important components for effective implementation of bilingual educational policy on an institutional level can be identified: (1) school involvement in the implementation of bilingual educational policy; (2) involvement and commitment of local communities, which can help us deliver the message of equal educational opportunity to ethnic minorities and enhance the prospect of a democratic process; and (3) parental involvement, which is crucial for the success of the programs related to ethnic minority education (Hogan-Brun & Ramoniene, 2004; Perna & Swail, 2000).

Pedagogical Aspects of the Implementation of Bilingual Education

There are important shifts among educational theorists about the development of curriculum, especially for bilingual schools (Mejia & Tejada, 2003). Now more focus is placed on the development of curriculum not by the professionals and experts in the field but by the practitioner teachers, who are closer to students, parents, and communities (Hornberger & Ricento, 1996). This observation is especially true in the Georgian context, where the issue of ethnic minority education is politically sensitive and requires a more careful attitude.

Teacher preparation and training is one of the most important components of bilingual education reform, especially with respect to preparation for the highly politicized and debated nature of bilingual education (Varghese, 2004). At the same time professional roles of bilingual education teachers are influenced by societal forces created by local context and their personal life and experience. If we put all these ideas in a Georgian context, it will be clear how bilingual teachers' professional roles are complicated. On one hand, the bilingual education context is very much politicized and the local societal context is complicated, as there are a lot of local "players" who are against bilingual educational policy. On the other hand, teachers in ethnic minority schools are not bilingual (they cannot speak the state language, Georgian) themselves, and bilingual educational policies will be an additional pressure on them. They should start learning the state language to be able to teach in public schools of ethnic minorities. A complex approach is needed for the formation of teachers' professional roles. Ideally, teachers should be fully liberated from the political context and have only professional characteristics. Teacher retraining programs should be focused on three aspects: (1) defining the professional roles of teachers in bilingual education, (2) establishing teacher preparation courses in the Georgian language, and (3) teaching the teachers interactive methods in bilingual schools.

The issue of textbook distribution is important as well. As mentioned earlier, the existing system of market economy

(continued)

cannot work for ethnic minority schools, at least in the beginning. The Ministry of Education and Science of Georgia has several other options. The first option is achieving an agreement with the Ministries of Education of Armenia and Azerbaijan. Armenia and Azerbaijan can purchase textbooks developed within the national curriculum of Georgia. The second solution can be involvement of local government in the process of purchasing textbooks for students of ethnic minorities. The whole education in Georgia is funded by the central budget and not from local budgets. Thus districts in which ethnic minority populations are large can be involved in the process of financing education through purchasing textbooks for students. The third solution enlists active and successful involvement of international organizations in this process.

There is no empirical evidence regarding teachers' beliefs, language policy, or community language policy in a Georgian context. However, it is clear that some resistance against bilingual education exists among teachers, schools, and communities of ethnic minorities. In terms of classroom configuration, it is clear that classrooms in these districts consist mainly of students of ethnic minorities. Based on the above-mentioned observation, it is obvious that the starting point for establishing bilingual educational policies is less than optimal. Thus policy formation in the area of bilingual education has to take into account this reality and first focus on creating positive attitudinal change among teachers, schools, and communities. Without such changes, bilingual education will be unsuccessful and will further deepen the gap between majority and minority and facilitate the process of disintegration instead of integration. The creation of a democratic process for bilingual education policies rather than imposition of them is the only solution of successful reform of ethnic minority schools.

Critical Incident

Martina's Dilemmas

Many of the students in Martina Chandler's classroom speak a second language or a dialect other than standard English–especially at home. She also realizes that many of them are likely to be stigmatized by other students as well as by school policies, particularly in schools without well-developed programs for English language learners.

- What should she do given this reality in her classroom?
- What should she do for her students as individuals?
- What would you do?

Increasingly, especially since the No Child Left Behind legislation was enacted, children are faced with demonstrating their competence and achievement using standardized tests, which may not be as effective at accurately assessing children from some backgrounds. In the meantime, teachers like Martina must find ways to demonstrate that their students are, in fact, learning effectively according to current, proficiency-based assessment strategies.

- How might she approach this dilemma?

Summary

Classrooms that are learning communities seem to be at the heart of effective teaching and learning in the 21st century. Of particular importance in this regard is attentiveness to the language or languages of students and teachers and to the ways in which all individuals naturally approach teaching and learning. Clearly, language structures the very thoughts and ideas we have as human beings. Not only do we have particular vocabularies that have meaning for us, but we also structure our sentences and pronounce our words in particular ways that we have learned as part of our primary socialization as young children and that therefore seem comfortable and "right" to us.

In classrooms where children of diverse backgrounds attempt to learn a prescribed curriculum, teachers must pay attention to the students' linguistic backgrounds so that they can be certain that all children are effectively understanding and participating in all learning activities. Teachers who are working with children whose first language is not English must remember that each child's language is an integral part of that child's personhood, and must make every attempt to regard that personhood with respect. Both the proponents and opponents of bilingual education want children to learn; they disagree—sometimes profoundly—on the best means (and the best language) to achieve that goal. Because of the history of the bilingual education debate and because of the increasing interconnectedness of today's world, teachers must be clear in their own minds about the relative merits of bilingual education.

Chapter Review

Go to the Online Learning Center at www.mhhe.com/cushner7e to review important content from the chapter, practice with key terms, take a chapter quiz, and find the Web links listed in this chapter.

Key Terms

accent 269
American Sign
  Language 271
black English 270
bidialectalism 271
bilingual education 276
dialect 270
Ebonics 270

English language
  learners (ELL) 279
field dependent 273
field independent 273
kinesics 272
limited English
  proficient (LEP) 277
mountain English 276

paralanguage 272
proxemics 272
rural English 270
standard English 270

Active Exercise

Additional Active Exercises are available online at www.mhhe.com/cushner7e.

Interviewing Non–Native English Speakers About Their Experiences in This Country

Purpose: To raise awareness and sensitivity and learn about the problems faced by new speakers of English.

Instructions: Interview a person who first came to the United States speaking limited or no English. This person might be an international student on campus, or a student or parent who came to the United States speaking minimal English (feel free to adjust the following questions accordingly to accommodate the person you are interviewing).

1. Describe some of the initial difficulties or problems you encountered when you first arrived in this country. To what would you attribute the problems?

2. What significant cultural differences did you encounter in the early stages of your adjustment to this country? How did you overcome these?

3. What primary language did you speak before coming to the United States? Describe your competency as a speaker of your home language. Describe your competency as a speaker of English today.

4. What communication problems did you experience when you first came to this country? How did you handle these?

5. What kinds of communication difficulties, if any, do you or your children currently face?

6. What might people (or schools and/or teachers if interviewing a child or parent) in the United States do that would help to reduce adjustment and communication difficulties for new immigrants?

7. What messages do you have for other non-English speakers that might make their adjustment and communication easier?

8. What can you conclude about communication, culture shock, and adjustment that would be useful for teachers?

Classroom Activities

1. In the elementary classroom, experiment to see what the "comfort zone" of each student is. Draw a circle with a diameter of about three feet on the floor with chalk, and ask students to take turns standing in the middle of the circle. Then, ask another student to stand with his or her toes on the outside of the line. Does the student in the circle feel comfortable with another student standing this close to him or her? Can the "outside" student move closer (cross the line) without making the "inside" student uncomfortable? Do this until all students have had a chance to be "inside" and "outside." Keep track of the results. Discuss with students the importance of proxemics and whether or not their experience with this activity can be in any way attributed to cultural ideas.

2. Another nonverbal form of communication is called kinesics, and relates to the way in which human beings communicate with body movements. Ask for six volunteers to stand in front of the class and try to communicate the following ideas to the rest of the class without saying anything: anger; sadness; excitement; disgust; sympathy; boredom. Give each student a piece of paper with the feeling or idea he or she is to demonstrate. As each student adopts the stance, facial expression, or other body movement for his or her term, ask the rest of the class to describe what they see in the demonstrator's body movement. When each feeling or idea has been expressed and noted, discuss with the class how they "knew" what the student was demonstrating.

3. In a high school classroom, students can be assigned to research the way or ways in which their school district deals with English language learners. Ask students to find out the history of the program or policy in that district, how many ELL students there are, how successful the program appears to be, and any debates surrounding the program or policy. If there is no program or policy, ask students to interview a school board member, or someone in the superintendent's office to find out why there is no program or policy.

4. Another activity for high school students is to ask a faculty member or parent or community member who speaks another language fluently to come to class and begin speaking to the students in that language.

Teachers might provide a little more stress by first telling the students that the visitor will be giving them instructions on a project that will be a part of their unit grade. Ask the speaker to speak for at least five minutes. When he or she is finished speaking, ask all students to write a short essay on how the experience affected them, and what it might be like to be an English language learner in their school.

Reflective Questions

Clearly, establishing a learning-community classroom like Martina Chandler's 10th-grade English class is fraught with both difficulties and possibilities. Put yourself in Martina's place, at this early point in the school year, and answer the questions Martina is asking herself:

1. How am I going to create a democratic, interactive learning community when my students come from such different backgrounds?

2. How am I going to discourage standard English speakers from stigmatizing those students like Tran and Dontae whose language differences are often rejected in American schools?

3. How am I going to provide ways in which Anna, with Mrs. Thomas's help, can participate fully in the life of the classroom?

4. How am I going to create a classroom environment in which students can teach each other effectively?

5. How am I going to organize instruction so that students with different learning styles can have equal access to the material at hand?

6. How many of my students' parents are able and willing to come into the classroom to assist in teaching? How do I find that out?

7. Can my non–standard English speaking students learn to write in standard English without also learning to speak standard English?

Endnote

1. Some of the material used by Martina Chandler in the Case Study at the beginning of this chapter was adapted from the following sources: Siccone, F. (1995). *Celebrating diversity: Building self-esteem in today's multicultural classroom*. Boston: Allyn & Bacon, pp. 14–16; Carnes, J. (1994, spring). An uncommon language. *Teaching Tolerance*; Tiedt, P. L. & Tiedt, I. M. (1995). *Multicultural teaching: A handbook of activities, information, and resources*, 4th ed. Boston: Allyn & Bacon, pp. 34, 162.

References

Anderson, L. (2001, May 29). Bilingual debate reaches boil point. *Chicago Tribune*.

Baker, C. (1988). *Key issues in bilingualism and bilingual education*. Clevedon, UK: Multilingual Matters.

Barnlund, D. (1968). *Interpersonal communication: Survey and studies*. Boston: Houghton Mifflin.

Bennett, C. L. (1989). Teaching students as they would be taught: The importance of cultural perspectives. In Barbara J. Robinson Shade (Ed.), *Culture, style, and the educative process*. Springfield, IL: Charles C Thomas.

Bennett, C. L. (2006). *Comprehensive multicultural education: Theory and practice* (6th ed.). Boston: Allyn & Bacon.

Berger, P., & Berger, B. (1972). *Sociology: A biographical approach*. New York: Basic Books.

Broudy, H., & Palmer, J. R. (1965). *Exemplars of teaching method*. Chicago: Rand McNally.

Butts, R. F. (1978). *Public education in the United States: From revolution to reform*. New York: Holt, Rinehart & Winston.

Castañeda v. Pickard, 648 F2d 989 (1981).

Cummins, J. (2000). *Bilingual children's mother tongue: Why is it important for education?* Retrieved from http://www.iteachilearn.com/cummins/mother.htm

Department of Statistics of Georgia. (2004). *Statistics on population of Georgia*. Retrieved from www.statistics.ge

Diringer, E., & Olszewski, L. (1996, December 21). Critics may not understand Oakland's Ebonics plan: Goal is to teach black kids standard English. *San Francisco Chronicle*, p. A17.

Dunn, R., Beaudry, J., & Klavas, A. (1989, March). Survey of research on learning styles. *Educational Leadership, 46,* 6.

Gándara, P., Maxwell-Jolly, J., Garcia, E., Asato, J., Gutiérrez, K., Stritikus, T., & Curry, J. (2000, April). *The initial impact of Proposition 227 on the instruction of English learners*. Davis, CA: University of California Linguistic Minority Research Institute Education Policy Center, University of California at Davis.

Gardner, H. (1983). *Frames of mind: The theory of multiple intelligences*. New York: Basic Books.

Gardner, H. (1991). *The unschooled mind: How children think and how schools should teach*. New York: Basic Books.

Gardner, H. (1999). *Intelligence reframed: Multiple intelligences for the twenty-first century*. New York: Basic Books.

Gardner, H. (2006). *Multiple intelligences: New horizons*. New York: Basic Books.

Gollnick, D. M., & Chinn, P. C. (2005). *Multicultural education in a pluralistic society* (7th ed.). New York: Macmillan.

Gonzalez, G. (1974). Language, culture, and exceptional children. *Exceptional Children, 40,* 8.

Grossman, H. (1995). *Teaching in a diverse society*. Boston: Allyn & Bacon.

Hakuta, K., Butler, Y. G., & Witt, D. (2000, January). *How long does it take English learners to attain proficiency?* Stanford, CA: University of California Linguistic Minority Research Institute, Stanford University.

History of bilingual education. (1998, spring). *Rethinking Schools, 12,* 3. Retrieved from http://www.rethinkingschools.org/archive/12_03/langhst.shtml

Hogan-Brun, G., & Ramoniene, M. (2004). Changing levels of bilingualism across the Baltic. *Bilingual Education and Bilingualism, 7*(1), 62–77.

Hornberger, N. (2000). Bilingual education policy and practice in the Andes: Ideological paradox and intercultural possibility. *Anthropology & Education Quarterly, 31*(2), 173–201.

Hornberger, N., & Ricento, T. (1996) Unpeeling the onion: Language planning and policy and the ELT professional. *TESOL Quarterly, 30*(3), 401–428.

Horne v. Flores 129 S.C. 2579 (2009).

Kaplan, R. (1966). Cultural thought patterns in inter-cultural education. *Language Learning, 16,* 1 & 2.

Keefe, J. W., & Languis, M. (1983, summer). [Untitled article]. *Learning Stages Network Newsletter, 4,* 2.

Krashen, S. D. (1981). Second language acquisition and second language learning. New York: Pergamon Press.

Krashen, S. D., & Terrell, T. D. (1983). *The natural approach: Language acquisition in the classroom.* Englewood Cliffs, NJ: Prentice Hall.

Lau v. Nichols, 414 U.S. 563 (1974).

McCaleb, S. P. (1994). *Building communities of learners: A collaboration among teachers, students, families, and community.* New York: St. Martin's Press.

Mejia, A., & Tejada, H. (2003). Bilingual curriculum construction and empowerment in Colombia. *International Journal for Bilingual Education and Bilingualism, 6*(1), 37–51.

National Association for Bilingual Education. (2004). *What is bilingual education?* Retrieved from http://www.nabe.org/education/index.html

Nieto, S. (2005). Public education in the twentieth century and beyond: High hopes, broken promises, and an uncertain future. *Harvard Educational Review, 75*(1), 1–20.

North West Regional Education Laboratory. (2003). *Overview of second language acquisition theory.* Retrieved from http://www.nwrel.org/request/2003may/overview.html

Perna, L. W., & Swail, W. S. (2000). A view of the landscape: Results of the national survey of outreach programs. *Outreach program handbook 2001* (pp. xi–xxix). New York: The College Board.

Samover, L., Porter, R., & Jain, M. (1981). *Understanding intercultural communication.* Belmont, CA: Wadsworth.

Spellings, M. (2006). Letter to chief state school officers announcing an LEP initiative of the U.S. Department of Education. Retrieved from http://www.ed.gov/policy/elsec/guid/secletter/060727.html

Stone, E. (1989). *Black sheep and kissing cousins: How our family stories shape us.* New York: Viking Penguin.

Thompson, G. (2009). Where education and assimilation collide. New York Times Series, online at http://www.nytimes.com/2009/03/15/us/15immig.html?pagewanted=1.

Tiedt, P. L., & Tiedt, I. M. (1995). *Multicultural teaching: A handbook of activities, information, and resources* (4th ed.). Boston: Allyn & Bacon.

Trillos, M. (1998). Conclusiones. In M. Trillos (Ed.), *Educación Endógena Frente a Educación Formal.* Bogotá, Universidad de los Andes: Centro Colombiano de Estudios de Lenguas Aborígenes.

Varghese, M. M. (2004). Professional development for bilingual teachers in the United States: A site for articulating and contesting professional roles. *Bilingual Education and Bilingualism, 7*(2/3), 222–238.

Waiqui, A. (2000). Contextual factors in second language acquisition. *CAL Digests.* Retrieved from http://www.cal.org/resources/digest/0005contextual.html

Wallmont, M. (2003). Extinction fear for languages. *CNN online.* Retrieved from http://www.cnn.com/2003/TECH/science/05/22/extinct.language

Witkin, H. A. (1962). *Psychological differentiation.* New York: Wiley.

Wolfram, W., Adger, C., & Christian, D. (1999). *Dialects in schools and communities.* Mahwah, NJ: Prentice-Hall.

Wood, G. H. (1992). *Schools that work: America's most innovative public education programs.* New York: Penguin Books.

Religious Pluralism in Secular Classrooms

Focus Questions

1. Do you remember a time when you attended a religious service with someone of a different denomination or faith? What was it like? Did it feel strange to you? Why?

2. Do you know anyone who attended, or did *you* attend, a parochial school? How did it differ from a secular public school?

3. How and in what ways do you think religious knowledge should be a part of public schooling?

4. Do you believe public funds should be used in support of parochial schools?

5. Why do you think the framers of the Constitution prohibited the establishment of a state religion and also guaranteed the free exercise of religious beliefs?

❝ Without knowledge, the people perish. ❞

BOOK OF PROVERBS

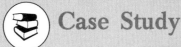

Religion in a Secular Classroom

Melissa Morgan had been teaching fifth grade in a small town in her home state of Georgia for 4 years, and she loved it. She had been married for 2 years, lived only five blocks from the school, and walked to work most mornings, passing on her way the principal's house, the local Baptist church, and the drugstore on the town square. Two evenings a week she attended classes at the local university where she was almost finished with her master's degree in reading. On Sundays she and her husband sang in the Methodist church choir, where many of her students' families also attended. It was a peaceful life in a town known primarily for the neatness of its surrounding farms, the beauty of its old magnolia trees, and the computer technology developed at the university where her husband taught English. Or, at least, it had been a peaceful life until last year.

It all started during the spring semester a year ago when she took a children's literature course taught by a colleague of her husband's, a woman who, prior to becoming a professor, had been a youth minister in Chicago. One of her assignments had been to select several books written at the upper elementary level that could be used to introduce common themes from several of the world's major religions. From subsequent class discussions on ways in which children's literature could be used for a variety of purposes, Melissa had begun to develop an idea that seemed to solve one of her recurring problems. Because her school was in a university town, her students often represented a greater variety of cultural backgrounds than one would normally expect to find in a small southern town. In the past 4 years, she had had students from Japan, South Africa, and Ireland as well as a number of students from various parts of this country; all were the children of university faculty or graduate students. As a result, her own classroom sometimes reflected the same split between local people and newcomers that now and then caused misunderstanding and strife in the community. For the most part, she had been able to help students who were new to the town (and, indeed, the country) adjust to life in Georgia. But there was one element of the cultural differences in her classroom that had stumped her, and that was the difference in religion that had created a number of overt conflicts in the past.

Armed with some new insights about using literature for purposes in addition to reading instruction, Melissa spent the summer developing a series of lessons designed to take advantage of the religious diversity in her class by not only using books and other materials about different religious faiths but also by planning activities that would lead children to discover more about their own religious backgrounds.

When school began in the fall, she was ready—convinced that it would be a wonderful year. She was doubly excited because students in her class represented a wider variety of religious backgrounds than had been the case the year before. Along with the usual Southern Baptists, Methodists, and Presbyterians were a Catholic student who had come to the United States from Brazil 3 years ago, three local Jewish students, five African American students who attended the African Methodist Episcopal church in town, four Muslim children from Iran whose parents were professors at the university, and two children who had been schooled at home until this year by parents who belonged to a conservative evangelical church. She also had students whose families were part of a small Unitarian congregation made up almost entirely of university faculty and their families.

The year began calmly enough, and her initial efforts to weave information about various religions into class discussions seemed to go well. During the month of September she had made home visits to each of her students' families, some of whom she already knew. In the course of these visits she was able to talk informally with parents and other family members, interact with her students in their home settings, and learn something about the cultural and religious backgrounds of those she did not know well. The father of one of her Iranian students turned out to be a professor of architecture and promised to come in to her class one day to talk about both the mathematics and the art in Islamic mosque architecture. She was thrilled!

Near the end of October, the school held its annual open house for parents and community members. Her class was eager for everyone to see the exhibit they had been working on since the beginning of school—models of houses of worship from around the world that

included a mosque, a Jewish synagogue, a stone Gothic cathedral, a Greek Revival Congregational church, a brick African Methodist Episcopal church, a clapboard Southern Baptist church, and a Quaker meeting house. Each model stood against a map of other parts of the world where such a building might be found, and each display was surrounded by pictures and books related to that particular place of worship.

About a week after the open house, Melissa's principal asked her to stop in the office after school. After a little small talk, the principal got to the point: "We've had some complaints about the fact that you're dealing with religion in your class."

She was astonished. "Who's complained?" she asked. "And what about?"

"It seems," continued the principal, "that there are two kinds of complaints. Some parents object to their children talking about religion in school at all, and others believe their children are being exposed to ideas that they believe are not Christian. One family wants to come in and look at the books we have in the library to see if there are any offensive materials there."

"Well," said Melissa, "you know what the children and I have been doing; you've seen the models and maps. Did you explain our project to the parents who called? I really didn't intend to upset anyone, you know."

"Yes, I do know," said the principal, "but I'm afraid we've got something of a problem here. At least one of these families has a history of suggesting that the school might not be 'purely' Christian. They're part of the small group of parents in this school who objected so strenuously to celebrating Halloween because they felt it encouraged pagan beliefs and devil worship. As you know, several years ago we did away with the Halloween Party in favor of a 'Dress Up As Your Favorite Book Character' Day every fall."

"What do you think I should do?" Melissa asked.

"I'm not sure," replied the principal. "Perhaps you should put your models away and let it just die down."

(continued)

A little shaken, Melissa went home that evening wondering if all her ideas about building on religious diversity would be stalled. She certainly hadn't intended to find herself in the middle of a battle over religion! She also didn't want to stop the discussions and activities in class that had led to such a good project as the models; her students were learning a great deal and seemed to be loving it. On an impulse, she called her own minister to talk about the problem. She asked if Rev. Thomas could suggest anything.

"Indeed I can," said Maggie Thomas. "The clergy in the area all belong to a regional clergy council that meets next week. Let me bring this up and see what they say. Perhaps you'd like to attend and tell us about what you're doing in class so everyone can hear it at the same time."

Melissa agreed, and the next week she met with the clergy council, where she carefully explained that although she wasn't teaching any particular religious beliefs, she did think that learning about other religions was a good thing for students. She told them that the idea for building the models had come from the students, and that she had been able to bring mathematics and geography as well as both reading and writing into the project, and she told them how proud the students were of their work. At the end of the meeting, each member of the council agreed that what she was doing was a good thing, even if it had never been done before. Several expressed a desire to see the models for themselves, and Melissa promptly issued an open invitation to all. She was pleased that one of those who wanted to see the exhibit was the pastor of the church attended by several of the families who had complained. "Perhaps," she thought as she drove home, "there is an ecumenical spirit in this town after all." And then she found herself thinking about the coming holidays. "I wonder if we should talk about the way we emphasize Christmas at school?"

Rationale for Attending to Religion in Public Schools

Religion in the American Colonies

Citizens of the United States have, since our national beginnings, been deeply concerned with the role of religion in matters of state. Some of our earliest settlers came to this continent to escape religious prejudice, and all who have come in the years since have brought with them their religious ideas, beliefs, rituals, and habits of mind. Even those who profess to be agnostic or atheist have formed their spiritual values in express rebellion *against* varieties of formalized religion that exist or existed in their particular cultural worlds.

In addition, much of the **cultural capital** of human societies emerges from philosophical, literary, musical, and artistic attempts to answer fundamentally religious questions: Who are we? Where did we come from? What is our purpose on earth? and What happens when we die? Thus, whether individuals see themselves as "religious" or not, religious references and allusions permeate their lives. In most if not all societies, religious references are used in everyday language; families, schools, and other institutions organize time around religious observances; and places of worship exert influence in community affairs. Even money often has religious symbols and language on it.

In part, this connection to religious ideas and symbolism emerges from a seemingly universal human need to be associated with a spiritual dimension. In some societies that connection permeates not only the ways in which the society is organized but also nearly every minute of daily life. When religion plays a large role in society, as it did in our own history in the Massachusetts Bay Colony and

294

as seen recently in such places as Afghanistan and Iran, the society is called a **theocracy.** In other societies, the connection is looser, with some degree of separation between secular and religious life. That was the intention of the founders of the United States, who wrote such a separation into the Constitution in the First Amendment, which reads:

> Congress shall make no law respecting an establishment of religion [**establishment clause**], or prohibiting the free exercise thereof [**prohibition clause**]; or abridging the freedom of speech, of the press; or the right of the people peaceably to assemble, and to petition the Government for a redress of grievances. (1791)

U.S. Constitution

Notice that while the writers of the Constitution did not *establish* a religion as a dimension of the state, they also were careful to ensure that religion could be freely practiced by individuals, that religious speech (as well as other forms of speech) was protected by the Constitution, and that peaceable assembly to practice religious beliefs (as well as for other purposes) was guaranteed. It was, however, passage of the **Fourteenth Amendment** in 1868, which granted to citizens of the states all the rights they had as citizens of the nation, that caused the issue of separation of church and state to have a direct influence on schooling (Uphoff, 1993, p. 95).

Definitions of Religion

Uphoff (1993) notes that religion is a concept that seems easily definable until one actually tries to define it. We have available to us definitions of religion that are both universal (those that apply to all religions) and sectarian (those that apply only to a specific denomination or sect). Yinger (1970), for example, defined religion broadly as "a system of beliefs and practices by means of which a group of people struggle with . . . the ultimate problems of human life (p. 7). The sociologist Durkheim (1969) defined it a bit more concretely but still in a universal manner when he said, "A religion is a unified system of beliefs and practices relative to sacred things, that is to say, things set apart and forbidden–beliefs and practices which unite into one single moral community called a church [*sic*], all those who adhere to them" (p. 46). Similarly, Berger and Berger (1972) viewed religion as "an overarching view of reality concerned with ultimate meanings which provides a cohesive view of the world, explains evil and prosperity, and offers guidelines for social action in the secular realm" (pp. 348–352). Most broad definitions of religion encompass concepts of a deity, of shared values and an orientation toward the sacred, and of a sense of community.

On the other hand, narrower, sectarian definitions of religion (e.g., Presbyterian, Catholic, Muslim, Jewish, Buddhist, Seventh-Day Adventist, Mormon) will have relatively different answers to the following questions:

World Religions

1. What theological outlook or point of view does this religion acknowledge?
2. What kinds of religious practice do the people who belong to this religious denomination accept as expressive of proper worship and devotion?
3. What kind of religious experience–feelings, perceptions, and sensations–ensures that some contact will be made with ultimate reality (i.e., a supernatural agency)?
4. What knowledge about the basic tenets of faith, scriptures, and traditions are necessary to the practice of this particular religion?

5. What are the consequences of this religious belief, practice, experience, and knowledge on an individual's daily life?

6. What are the consequences of falling away from the practice, experience, and knowledge of this particular religion?[1]

Answers to these questions in large measure determine the differences between one religious group and another. Furthermore, it would be a mistake to regard these differences as simply "interesting" variations on a theme. Rather, a person's very identity and relationship with God and other human beings are vested in these beliefs, which are generally regarded by members of a particular faith as true in some ultimate sense. Thus, for example, religious beliefs about the proper kinds of food to eat, the proper way to prepare and eat it, the relative place of males and females in society, and the kinds of rituals required to receive the deity's blessing as well as the number and relative importance of deities themselves, all have a bearing on how an individual conducts his or her daily life. These ideas are so strongly held and so central to a religious person's sense of individual and collective identity that conflicts of belief among different religious groups can–and often have–led to war.

As is clear from today's news, going to war for religious beliefs is just as likely to happen now as it has been throughout history. Indeed, for some contemporary Muslim extremists, terrorist actions are based on and justified by long-remembered people and the battles they fought during the Crusades 700 years ago, as well as by perceived injustices perpetrated more recently. Indeed, it is not unusual for some extremists to refer to all modern Westerners as "Crusaders." Similarly, historically violent insurgencies in Northern Ireland based on centuries-old disputes between Catholics and Protestants, and the torture and horrific murder of thousands of Muslims by Serbian Christians in Kosovo, speak to the potential depth and danger of religious identity.

The experiences of religious pluralism in the United States are not new, but some things have changed over time. First, the degree to which religious belief has been deemed a necessary part of *public* life has changed. In periods of fundamental social change, human beings often turn to the comfort and security of an organized faith and set of absolute values, and many believe that these values should be actively incorporated into the larger society. Second, the advent of technology– especially computer technology–means that it is no longer necessary to actually *attend* a religious service other than your own to obtain knowledge of it. Most faiths, and many individual synagogues, mosques, and churches, have numerous websites on which they can display and promote their religious ideas. Third, the increasing interdependence of the world's social systems means that what happens in one part of the world quickly affects what happens in another part of the world. This connectivity is no less true of religious systems than it is of economic ones.

Religious Pluralism in the United States

Religious Pluralism in the United States

Religious pluralism in the United States is so great that a complete accounting is not possible in a short chapter, but it is possible to describe major religious groups that flourish here and to give a brief summary of their histories. Prior to colonization by Europeans in the 16th century, the Americas were home to a wide variety of religious practices by native peoples. Although Native American societies differed widely in various aspects of culture, in language, and in appearance, all shared a fundamentally religious outlook that emphasized the centrality of a Creator, a reverence for the natural world, and a belief that human beings were a part of nature and were obligated to preserve and protect it. Interestingly, this interest in the human condition as a part of nature, and the importance of living in such a way that our natural world is both preserved and conserved, is, at the beginning of the 21st century, being adopted by a number of contemporary religious groups, including many members of evangelical denominations.

European Influences on Religion in the United States

As Europeans began to explore and colonize the Americas, they brought with them another set of religious variations–Christianity and Judaism–as well as a belief quite contrary to the native religions: that human beings were *apart from* nature and were intended to conquer and control it. This difference in worldview with respect to the place of human beings in the natural world is perhaps the most significant and profound difference between so-called Western religions and most indigenous or "native" ones.

In New England, a puritan form of Protestantism took hold as a dominant theme; in the middle colonies, greater diversity of religious belief, including Catholic, Quaker, and Anabaptist, as well as others, meant that no particular denomination prevailed; in the South, the dominant religion stemmed from the Anglican Church of England. Jews also were among the earliest immigrants: first came Sephardic Jews from Spain and Portugal and then German Jewish immigrants, until by the American Revolution, there were about 3,000 Jews in the colonies (Sowell, 1980, p. 77). Religious diversity continued to expand in the late 18th century. In the 19th century, large numbers of Catholics from Ireland and Italy and Jews from Russia and eastern Europe immigrated to the United States, each group containing within it great diversity of belief and practice. In the 20th century, particularly since the 1960s, the United States saw increasing Catholic immigration from Cuba, the Caribbean, Mexico, and Central America.

African Influences on Religion in the United States

In the 17th, 18th, and 19th centuries, large numbers of Africans were brought to the United States as slaves, and they brought with them not only a large set of their own **nativist religions,** but Islamic influences as well. As noted in the Amherst College Documentary History Project on African-American Religions,

> Working its way down from the Sahara long before Christianity began to touch the West African coast, Islam like Christianity interacted in complex ways with the traditional religions of Africa. Brought to the Americas by enslaved African Muslims, Islam struggled with difficulty to preserve itself in an inhospitable, Christian-controlled environment. Meanwhile, ordinary believers of all sorts, eager to mobilize any resources that might aid them in coping with life's daily hardships, everywhere tended to borrow freely from one another's traditions of religious practice. In sixteenth-century Mexico, for example, there was a complex intermingling of African, Mesoamerican, and European practices of divination. (AARDOC, 2006)

Activity 6:
Proverbs as a Window into One's Culture

Activity and Reading 7:
Cultural Values in American Society

Indeed, the creativity with which Africans interpreted and utilized Protestant scriptures and music to make their daily lives more bearable and to further the cause of freedom produced a unique contribution to American religious and political life. Negro spirituals, for example, were very often used as a form of clandestine communication to spread news of slave activities. After slavery was finally abolished in the middle of the 19th century, African American churches continued to have an immense influence on the cultural and educational lives of their members and are today still central to African American culture and African American social and political struggles.

Middle Eastern Influences on Religion in the United States

Although the importation of Muslim African slaves brought Islam to the Americas very early, it has been in the late 19th and 20th centuries that a growth in the Muslim faith in the United States has reached influential proportions. This is the case in part through conversion and in part through immigration. In fact, Islam is presently one of the fastest growing religions in the United States.

The converted Muslim population is primarily African American and often identifies itself as the Nation of Islam, a group whose history in the United States goes back to the 1930s and grew out of the works of W. D. Fard and Elijah Muhammad. The Nation of Islam was, and in some respects still is, a separatist group that emphasizes freedom, justice, and equality for African Americans and actively discourages intermarriage with whites. Perhaps its best-known leader was Malcolm X, the converted son of a Baptist minister who, as a result of his experience during a pilgrimage to Mecca (a hajj) and shortly before his assassination in 1965, began to shift his beliefs away from separatism and toward kinship among all human beings (Al-Ani, 1995).

The earliest Muslim immigrants–largely rural, poor, and uneducated–came to the United States between 1875 and 1912 from what is known as Bilad ash-Sham, or Greater Syria–an area that after World War I was Jordan, Lebanon, Palestine, and Syria, and also from Turkey, Albania, India, and elsewhere. The second wave, that immigrated after World War II, particularly from the Middle East and North Africa, were primarily educated professionals uprooted by political changes including the creation of the states of Israel and Pakistan.

The third wave, which continues today, began in the 1960s with the liberalization of American immigration laws (Al-Ani, 1995). These individuals came not only from the same areas as their earlier counterparts, but also from the former Yugoslavia. In addition, beginning in the 1970s, the oil-producing countries of the Middle East have sent many Muslim students to study in the United States, and these students have played an active role in Muslim communities. Like their European counterparts, many Muslims have come to the United States as a result of social and political unrest in their native countries.

Today, Islam in the United States–like Christianity and Judaism–has a global face. Highly educated Sunni and Shi'ite Arab Muslims comprise a large proportion of the Islamic community. In addition, however, Muslims from Turkey, eastern Europe, and many African nations continue to enrich the Islamic community, and serious challenges continue to face Islamic residents. Life for Muslim Americans has never been particularly easy, but the attack on the World Trade Center in September 2001 and the war in Iraq have increased both attention and a backlash of negative feelings toward Muslims in general. Jane I. Smith (n.d.), professor of Islamic Studies at the Hartford Seminary in Connecticut, writes about other challenges facing American Muslims:

> Questions of identity, occupation, dress, and acculturation are particularly significant for many American Muslims. Other major issues include the relationships among different racial and ethnic Muslim groups as well as with other American Muslims; how and where to provide an Islamic education for one's children; and appropriate roles and opportunities for women. Many are moving from a phase of dissociation from mainstream American life to much more active participation in political and social arenas. American Muslims appear to be moving into another stage of identity in which these kinds of issues are being confronted and resolved in new and creative ways. The result may well be that a truly American Islam, woven from the fabric of many national, racial, and ethnic identities, is in the process of emerging.

In the United States, any discussion of religion must include a willingness to concede the complexity of American religious ideas and practices. In the introduction to a report on their recent national survey on religion conducted by the Baylor Institute for Studies of Religion, Bader et al. (2006) stated:

> In fact, under the surface American religion is startlingly complex and diverse. Americans may agree that God exists. They do not agree about what God is like, what God wants for the world, or how God feels about politics. Most Americans pray. They differ widely on to whom they pray, what they pray about, and whether or not they say grace. A vast majority of Americans are Christians, but attitudes amongst those Christians regarding the salvation of others, the role of religion in government, the reality of the paranormal, and their consumption of media are surprisingly diverse.

Clearly, while the United States has always been a religiously pluralistic country, today that pluralism is greater than it has ever been. Along with ethnic and racial pluralism, to which it is closely related in a variety of ways, religious pluralism has become a daily experience in classrooms all over the country—a fact that has educational implications in terms of curriculum materials, subject matter, school rules and customs, student services, school calendar decisions, scheduling of student activities, cafeteria offerings, holiday celebrations, teaching methods, and school financing (Uphoff, 1993). Rather than looking at these educational implications as problems, however, some teachers and schools are finding that such diversity of religion offers unique opportunities for teaching and learning.

Characteristics of a Classroom That Attends to Religious Pluralism

How, then, might an educator design a classroom not only to affirm religious pluralism but also to build on it?

Pedagogies: Old and New

Good teaching in a classroom that is sensitive to religious diversity, like good teaching in any classroom, is in large measure a matter of getting to know the children with whom you are working, their families, and the communities in which they live. Most teachers quickly learn the individual idiosyncrasies of their students with respect to psychological issues and traits: attention span, motivation, perceived intelligence, and so on. What is often less well known is the sociocultural background of students. Yet we know very well that the best context for learning is when students are able to build on what they already know. Knowing as much as possible about your students' backgrounds is also central to everything else that happens because you will be designing your classroom around *your* students and the experiences they bring with them to school.

Because formal religious teachings and values may or *may not* be a part of each of your students' lives, it is important to know something about the religious composition of your class. Chances are good that you will not have an overwhelming number of different religions represented in one room, so you need to know something about only those that are represented at any given time. However, you do need to know something about the worldview of those particular religions as well as the worldview of those students who do not subscribe to any religious tenets, particularly with respect to issues of gender and to the relationship between young people and elders. It is also wise to know whether a particular religious group values such skills as critical thinking and questioning for their children because some do not. In some contexts, a child simply does *not* question authority, religious doctrine, or their elders.

Knowledge about religious groups does not, of course, mean that you must design a classroom to match each child's unique experience. Indeed, one of the purposes of schooling in a democracy is to help students expand their experience beyond the relatively small world in which they live. However, it is important that you know something about the religious values of your students so that you can know how to approach new learning, where conflicts may develop, and when you can intercede to help students (and often parents) bridge the gap between their own experience and what they are learning in school. At the same time, you must understand and respect the community's primary values so that you do not go too far beyond the readiness level of community members.

Teachers who want to build on religious diversity must vary the instructional methods used in the classroom. The culture of the traditional American public school stresses certain teaching methods, patterns of instructional interaction, and assessment strategies. For example, teachers talk while students listen, individual students answer teacher-directed questions, individual students give oral reports to their class, students follow detailed, teacher-given instructions on how to carry out a task, and teachers issue paper-and-pencil tests. In the United States, these patterns emerge from a Western cultural worldview that emphasizes individualism, middle-class values, and a generally Protestant Christian belief system that stresses the importance of the minister as teacher and the individual's direct relationship with God. These teaching patterns may be relatively or totally unfamiliar to some students. Native American students, for example, whose religious worldview emphasizes communal patterns of interaction and individual choice, may be more interested in the activities of their peers than of the teacher and may feel that the teacher must earn their respect rather than simply get it by virtue of his or her position. That is, these students may believe that they should follow a teacher's directions because they have chosen to rather than because they are compelled to do so. Another example is African American students whose churches use an emotive "call and response" or a choral pattern of inter-action; these students may respond to teachers' questions with emotion, with hand gestures, with changes in vocal tonality, or in chorus because those are patterns they have learned. In general, what may be *new* about pedagogy for a classroom that pays attention to religious diversity is the subtle but important ability of the teacher to vary and alter instructional patterns so that all students find both familiar and new ways of learning.

Roles: Old and New

Sensitivity to potential and real areas of conflict among students of different religious backgrounds requires that teachers adopt the role of interpreter and, sometimes, mediator. Once again, teachers must learn as much as they can about the religions represented in the classroom not only so that they can help students find the commonalities among different religious beliefs but also so that they can help students interpret differences. Parents and community members are often helpful in this regard, so long as they understand that their role is to explain rather than to convert. Indeed, perhaps more dissention regarding religious tenets has been caused by the failure of teachers to communicate closely with parents about what they are trying to accomplish in class than by any other single factor. Generally speaking, if parents understand that their children will not be deprived of either respect or affirmation because of their religious beliefs, most will be happy to help teachers in any way they can. Students, too, if they are old enough, can serve as teachers to their peers, as can other school staff and members of the community.

Another set of issues to consider in a religiously sensitive classroom is the role of school rules and customs. Attendance, for example, should be flexible for students involved in religious celebrations and/or duties, and policies such as dress codes should take account of religiously based regulations and customs. Dress codes that stipulate that students cannot wear hats in school must exempt the Orthodox Jewish boy who wears the yarmulke as a token of respect to God or the Amish girl who wears a dimity bonnet and long dress as a gesture of modesty.

Similarly, the fact that the school calendar conveys the importance of religious diversity is significant. For example, vacation times scheduled on traditional school calendars, as well as celebrations usually held in schools, tend to be based on the Christian holidays of Christmas and Easter. Moreover, common practices such as scheduling games on Friday nights (when many Jewish families begin the celebration of the Sabbath) or homecoming activities early in the autumn (which may fall on the Jewish High Holidays) should also be seriously reconsid-ered. Later in the school year, teachers need to be sensitive to the demands placed on older Muslim students who observe Ramadan and refrain from eating and drinking during the daylight hours. The customs involved in these special cases must be discussed openly in terms of their religious significance so that other students both learn about different traditions and come to respect the reasons for them. Much of this kind of discussion can take place in the context of learning about religious beliefs and customs as a part of more general cur-ricular study.

Religion in the Curriculum

Place of Content Knowledge: Old and New

When religion is the cultural focus of your thinking, it is well to remember that religion, unlike some other kinds of difference, has a powerful element of "truth" built into it. That is, it may be more difficult for a student to stand apart from his or her religious worldview and look at other religions because religious "truth" is often linked to fundamental ideas of the relationship between individuals and a supernatural power. Nevertheless, religious history and traditions, architecture, art, music, and ideas can become the basis for an enriched and affirming classroom. Although in recent years educators have been reluctant to consider teaching about religion in public schools, the study of the contributions of various religions to world civilization is worthwhile. Indeed, in 1964 the American Association of School Administrators published a book called *Religion in the Public Schools* in which the authors assert that

> a curriculum which ignored religion would itself have serious implications. It would seem to proclaim that religion has not been as real in men's lives as health, or politics, or economics. By omission it would appear to deny that religion has been and is important in man's history—a denial of the obvious. In day by day practice, the topic cannot be avoided. As an integral part of man's [*sic*] culture, it must be included. (as cited in Uphoff, 1993, p. 95)

The study of religion generally can be incorporated into a variety of places in the curriculum; often the best place is the most obvious. Religious dietary regulations might be included in a home economics class, for example, or the intricate, geometrical designs of an Islamic mosque might be part of a math or art class. Because religion is and has been so fundamental to human life and history, locating its study in the context of a variety of subject matters is not difficult. At the same time, separate courses in the study of comparative religion or interdisciplinary courses that study the impact of religion on history, law, and art can be instituted, particularly at the secondary level.

Regular curriculum materials and resources in a religiously sensitive classroom should be carefully screened for bias of various kinds, including omission, not so much in order to exclude those materials as to point out the bias to students and let the bias, itself, become the subject of inquiry, discussion, and debate. At the same time, curricular resources–including books, articles, paintings, music, sculpture, maps, and artifacts such as wearing apparel and icons–that represent various religions can be made available for examination by students. Similarly, students who belong to particular religious groups may educate their classmates about their own religious beliefs and values. In all cases, the basis of study and discussion should be inquiry, not evangelism.

Assessment: Old and New

When you are teaching or learning about a belief system like religion, you must focus not only on assessing the knowledge that has been acquired but also on the form of that assessment. Uphoff (1993) offers a good example of religious sensitivity when he writes about creating exam questions having to do with the concept of evolution. As you may be aware, the teaching of evolution is the subject of much controversy in some communities, with many people calling for balancing the curriculum by including the study of so-called intelligent design in biology and other classes. The following test questions illustrate the difference between showing respect for those families who accept as fact the story of creation as it is written in the Bible and giving the impression that those families are wrong:

Evolution and Creation Science

> *Poor.* It took millions of years for the earth to evolve to its present state. (True/False)
> *Better.* Evolutionists believe that it took millions of years for the earth to evolve to its present state. (True/False) (Uphoff, 1993, p. 104)

In the first question, the student must agree with a factual statement, while in the second, the student can agree that one group (not necessarily one to which he or she belongs) asserts that something is the case. You might agree that this makes a subtle but powerful difference.

Another issue concerns such assessments as psychological testing and health screening and care. Some families—generally those who profess a fundamentalist Christian faith—believe that psychological assessment by school personnel is an invasion of family rights, a corruption of values based on strict adherence to Biblical teaching, or an attempt on the part of school officials to alter or interfere with the religious beliefs of students. These families tend to think that psychological interventions to raise self-esteem or encourage self-expression—such as classroom games or the use of puppets as a way to enable children to speak freely—are suspect, sometimes in the extreme.

Similarly, health screenings and assessments, especially when they involve somewhat invasive procedures such as tine or PPD (purified protein derivative, or Mantoux) tests for tuberculosis, are often the focus of parental objections on a variety of religious grounds. Some parents also may have religious reasons for objecting to their children giving blood in high school blood drives. As schools increasingly become a source of health and social services for children, the number of objections raised by families from a variety of religious backgrounds may increase as well.

Pang and Barba (1995) noted that culturally affirming instruction should include culturally familiar interaction patterns, culturally familiar strategies, a culturally familiar environment, culturally familiar content, culturally familiar materials, and culturally familiar analogies, themes, and concepts. The next section explores some of the ways Melissa Morgan's classroom followed these guidelines with respect to religious sensitivity and appreciation.

Case Analysis

Educators who have been involved in school disputes about religion might think that this Case Study has an improbably positive resolution. Certainly many schools have become the center of highly emotional and long-lasting acrimony about issues such as using counseling techniques to build self-esteem in children and have experienced major attempts at censorship of library and other materials.

Yet Melissa demonstrates several attributes of a good teacher in a religiously sensitive classroom. First, she takes advantage of her students' idea to build models as a way to get them to cooperate in a hands-on activity and to encourage individual students from different religious backgrounds to bring their own specialized knowledge to their classmates. Second, she skillfully integrates several aspects of the curriculum into the project so that students can see that knowledge is interrelated. Rather than listening to dry lectures about different religions, the students learned about various religious beliefs by studying the meaning that underlies different parts of the place of worship itself.

When objections come, Melissa does not try to withdraw, nor does she get angry, nor does she dismiss the objections as unreasonable. Rather, she goes to her own minister as a way to perhaps create linkages with the religious leaders of the community. That there happened to be a clergy council meeting the next week and that she happened to be a persuasive speaker might be viewed as fortuitous. However, many communities have organizations to which various clergy belong, and the notion of enlisting help from community members is always a good one.

As diversity of all kinds is increasingly prevalent in schools and as teachers like Melissa learn to appreciate and build on those differences, experiences like Melissa's will also increase. Thus future teachers will want to consider both the opportunities and possible implications of being an educational leader in the classroom and in the community.

Perspectives on Religion and Schooling in the United States

Court Decisions Related to Religion and Public Schooling

Because a religious or spiritual dimension is so close to the cognitive and emotional lives of human beings and because the founders of the United States believed that religion was so important that it should be addressed in the Constitution, the few words in the First and Fourteenth Amendments have been both the source of religious freedom and the source of educational battles around religion in the schools ever since. In schooling, the fundamental problem has been—and continues to be—how to resolve the tensions created by seemingly opposing principles: (1) the need for schools, as an arm of the state, to support a basic freedom guaranteed by the Constitution, and (2) the need for schools, also as an arm of the state, to uphold the **separation of church and state.** Throughout our history, these tensions have resulted in continually shifting opinions about a number of issues, and because ours is a nation of laws, the courts have been a decisive element in defining the relationship between religion and schools.

In an analysis written many years ago, Butts (1978) cast these issues into two broad categories that help to sort out the confusion that often results when people begin to talk about the role (or absence) of religion in public education. The first category is education's role in protecting *private freedoms,* or "those that inhere in the individual, and therefore may not be invaded or denied by the state." He writes,

> In the most general terms, freedom was sought for parents and their children on the grounds that every human being has the right, and should have the opportunity and the ability, to live one's own life in dignity and security. Further he or she is entitled to a chosen cultural or religious group without arbitrary constraint on action or coercion of belief by the state or by other community pressures.
> (p. 272)

"Most often," he notes, "appeal was made to the free exercise of religion guaranteed by the First Amendment of the Constitution (and as applied by the

Fourteenth Amendment to the states) as a protection against coercion of belief or action by school or government authorities" (p. 272).

Butts's second category is education's role in guaranteeing *public freedoms,* "that is, those that inhere in the welfare of the democratic political community and which the . . . state is obligated actively to safeguard, protect, and promote whether threatened by a majority or minority in the community" (p. 272). He describes the ground for public freedoms for teachers and students as the belief that every person in his or her capacity as a teacher, learner, and citizen had the right and should have the opportunity to speak, to read, to teach, to learn, to discuss, and to publish without arbitrary constraint on action or coercion of belief by the state or by other pressures.

This approach to protection of public freedoms has run into opposition by people who see it as a threat to the established order, in other words, a threat to the dominance of Protestantism as the foundation of public schooling. It has also been opposed by people for whom the protection of private freedoms is paramount; that is, those who see in the protection of *public* welfare a threat to *private* freedoms of parents to control the education of their children.

Several of the more important concrete issues over which these debates have raged are compulsory attendance, freedom to practice religious beliefs with respect to the Pledge of Allegiance, salutes to the flag, prayer and Bible reading in schools, release time for religious instruction, and the use of public funds for religious schools. Each of these issues has reflected the tension between private and public freedoms.

Private Freedoms: Religion and Compulsory School Attendance

The history of schooling in the United States is characterized by a continually expanding effort to include all children. One way in which this has been accomplished is by requiring all children to go to school until a certain age. This requirement was little regarded in the early years of the country; indeed, for much of our history, schooling was not only not required but also not really necessary to earn a living and develop a good life.

Beginning in the 19th century with the advent of industrialization and the major waves of immigration, compulsory schooling gained acceptance largely as a way of protecting young children from exploitation in factories and keeping children off the urban streets. In general, however, the move toward compulsory schooling can be seen as part of a larger movement toward the establishment of a social institution (the common school) that would provide the means to ensure a common citizenship and loyalty to the state among diverse individuals. Thus, early on the issue of compulsory schooling was seen by some Americans as an issue of the rights of parents versus the rights of the state.

In 1922, the state of Oregon narrowly passed an initiative requiring that all children between 6 and 18 must attend a *public* school, or be granted permission to attend a private school by the county superintendent of schools. Fearing that such a law would destroy parochial schools, a Roman Catholic teaching order filed suit to have the law declared unconstitutional. In 1925, the Supreme Court did just that in *Pierce v. Society of Sisters,* saying,

The fundamental theory of liberty upon which all governments in this Union repose excluded any general power of the State to standardize its children by forcing them to accept instruction from public teachers only. The child is not the mere creature of the State; those who nurture him and direct his destiny have the right, coupled with the high duty, to recognize and prepare him for additional obligations.

Although affirming the right of parents to send their children to private religious schools, the Court also stipulated that the state had a right to require children to go to *some* school and that the state could also regulate all schools. Thus the precedent was set for the development of a protected parochial school system alongside the public schools.

As is often the case, however, support for compulsory schooling ebbs and flows. By the 1960s and 1970s, many educators had doubts about requiring attendance of all children to the age of 16 or 18. Again, religious beliefs provided the means for the Supreme Court to further the cause of private freedoms and parental rights. In *Wisconsin v. Yoder* (1972), the Court upheld the decision of the Wisconsin Supreme Court that stipulated that Old Order Amish parents could disobey Wisconsin's compulsory schooling law and remove their children from school at the end of the eighth grade. The Court held that:

a state's interest in universal education, however highly we rank it, is not totally free from a balancing process when it impinges on other fundamental rights and interests, such as those specifically protected by the Free Exercise Clause of the First Amendment and the traditional interest of parents with respect to the religious upbringing of their children so long as they, in the words of *Pierce*, "prepare [them] for additional obligations."

Today, interest in compulsory schooling is once again on the rise, in part because of the perceived interest of the state in a new kind of workforce that can compete economically with other nations and in part because of the requirements of the No Child Left Behind reauthorization of the Elementary and Secondary Education Act of 2001. Although there is some debate on the actual number of high school completions, it seems to be the case that high school dropout rates have been relatively stable since the early 1980s, standing at roughly 20%. Since more states have established graduation tests, however, there is increasing debate about how many students actually graduate on time, and about how such rates are measured. Increased attention to graduation rates has revealed some wide discrepancies, depending on geographic location in the country and between urban and suburban districts (National Center for Higher Education Management Systems [NCHEMS], 2007).

Private Freedoms: The Practice of Religious Beliefs in Classrooms

Public sentiment regarding the role of religion in public schools, like public opinion on other issues, is often easier to understand when it is seen in a historical context. In the decisions cited in the previous section, for example, the right of parents to foster religious beliefs in their children versus the right of the state to compel school attendance was part of the larger questions of child labor and the development of schools as the primary socialization agents of citizenship in a democracy.

Similarly, the debates over the practice of religious beliefs in classrooms have often been part of the larger question of loyalty to the United States and the debate about the role of the state to protect a citizen's rights to equality. In the beginning of the common school movement, there was little question that religious practice–and indeed, religious sources of instruction–was a fundamental part of public schooling. Such practices as school prayer and the reading of the Bible on a daily basis were common, if not universal, and curricular materials such as the widely used McGuffy readers taught moral values derived from Christian Protestantism along with vocabulary and grammar. Although the influence of particular religious ideas and values on schooling has always been (and continues to be) partly a matter of the religious composition of the community in which a school is located, the basic structure of public schooling in the United States emerged from an allegiance to a Judeo-Christian heritage as much as it did from the development of an economically capitalist state. Indeed, the Judeo-Christian God has been (and is) a more or less involuntary party to a wide variety of legislative and judicial meetings, deliberations, and decisions at the federal, state, and local levels. Note that although Americans say they separate church and state, it is still common practice for the president of the United States to place his hand on the New Testament when taking his oath of office.

The question of loyalty to the government usually arises in times of major political disagreement or war. In 1919, for example, in the wake of World War I and fears of involvement with world affairs, Nebraska passed a law requiring that all instruction in the public schools be given in English and prohibiting the teaching of any foreign language to children younger than the ninth grade. In *Meyer v. Nebraska* (1923), however, the Supreme Court ruled that such a law was unconstitutional, stating that the right of parents to guide their children's education is a constitutional right.

Similarly, during World War II, the Minersville, Pennsylvania, board of education enacted a policy that required all teachers and students in the public schools to incorporate the Pledge of Allegiance and a salute to the flag on a daily basis. One set of parents, who were Jehovah's Witnesses and prohibited by their religion from worshiping images, objected that the requirement set aside their First Amendment rights to free exercise of religion. In *Minersville v. Gobitis* (1940) the Supreme Court ruled in favor of the state's right to impose the flag salute rule. The dissent to this ruling was written by Justice Stone, who, on becoming chief justice 3 years later, reversed the *Gobitis* decision in *West Virginia State Board of Education v. Barnette* (1943), saying, in effect, that while the state could require the study and teaching of civic matters, it did *not* have the right to impose an ideological discipline that "invades the sphere of intellect and spirit."

The debate about the role of the state in providing equality of opportunity, on the other hand, has influenced other decisions regarding religion in the public schools. For example, a widely known and still heatedly debated controversy revolves around the issue of prayer and Bible reading in public schools. In a widely referenced case in 1963–*Abington v. Schempp*–the Supreme Court ruled that *requiring* student participation in sectarian prayers and reading from the Bible, particularly the New Testament, violated the First Amendment prohibition of separation of church and state. The argument here was that school prayers were fundamentally Christian (and usually Protestant), that all students were not Christian, that so-called nonsectarian prayers satisfied no one, and that therefore the removal of all religious practice from public school classrooms was necessary.

More recently, the Supreme Court has ruled that sectarian prayers at high school graduations (*Lee v. Weisman,* 1992) and on the football field before a game (*Santa Fe Independent School District v. Doe,* 2000) are also unconstitutional. Still, because religious beliefs are so much a part of the identities of many people, the law and the practices of individual schools and people may be somewhat far apart.

Unfortunately, many people, including the national and local media, confused the argument in *Abington* with the actual decision, which did not "ban" prayer in schools but only said that *requiring* students to participate in sectarian prayers and Bible reading was unconstitutional. Indeed, in the majority opinion written by Justice Clark, the Court strongly supported the study of religion in public schools:

> It might well be said that one's education is not complete without a study of comparative religion or the history of religion and its relationship to the advancement of civilization. It certainly may be said that the Bible is worthy of study for its literary and historic qualities. Nothing we have said here indicates that such study of the Bible or of religion, when presented objectively as part of a secular program of education, may not be effected consistent with the First Amendment. (1963)

Uphoff (1993) suggests that it was the self-censorship of educators and publishers based on both an inadequate reading of the Court decisions and a desire for equal representation for non-Christian religions that is responsible for the relative removal of religion from public schools in recent years. The vacuum created by this removal has enabled a strong challenge from the so-called religious right to reinstate religious practices into classrooms.

In 1993, Congress passed the Religious Freedom Restoration Act, which laid down several principles about the exercise of religion in schools and elsewhere. In part, the act stated that the government cannot "burden" an individual's exercise of religion unless that exercise conflicted with a compelling government interest and/or if that burden was the least restrictive means of furthering such compelling interest.

Public Freedoms: Public Funding for Religious Schools

Arguments for public funding for religious schools stem from the doctrine contained in the *Pierce v. Society of Sisters* decision previously discussed. As Butts (1978) notes,

> If parents have a private *right* to send their children to religious and private schools to meet the compulsory attendance requirements of the state, then distributive justice requires that the state provide parents with public funds to enable them to do what they have the private right to do. (p. 286)

Arguments against public funding for religious schools, on the other hand, stem from the establishment clause of the First Amendment on the grounds that the taxpayer has a right to be free of taxation that promotes a religious doctrine.

Until about the middle of the 20th century, the American public in general was inclined to believe that both national and religious interests were better served if public funds were not used for religious schools. The debate arose again, however, at midcentury, with Americans taking positions about both *direct* and *indirect* aid. Proponents of direct aid argued that since compulsory attendance laws served the state and since parochial schools contributed to the ability of those laws to be enforced, parochial schools should also benefit from public financial support. Further, they argued that since all citizens were required to pay taxes to support public education, those parents who wished—*and had a right*—to send their children to religious schools would have a double financial burden. In addition, they argued that the provision of separation of church and state in the Constitution said nothing about the ability of public and parochial schools to *cooperate* with one another.

A more moderate view favored *indirect aid* to religious schools. As early as 1930, precedent was set for such aid when, in *Cochran v. Louisiana State Board of Education,* the Supreme Court upheld a Louisiana law that affirmed the purchase of texts for use in private sectarian schools on the grounds that the books benefited the children and thus the state. After World War II, however, a variety of religious groups began to push the limits of *Cochran* by asking for public support for health and medical services and school lunches as well as for books. The greatest demand was for help with transportation of parochial students to their schools.

Perhaps the most cited and argued-over case regarding religion and public education, *Everson v. Board of Education* (1947), was the landmark case with respect to busing parochial schoolchildren. Emerging from a New Jersey case in which the state allowed public funds to be used to transport Catholic children to parochial schools, the Court ruled that payment for such transportation essentially benefited the children (and thus the state, as it had said in *Cochran*) rather than the school. The vote was 5 to 4, however, with the minority arguing that such support did, indeed, help children and parents to maintain religious instruction at public expense.

A third position, generally taken by Protestant, Jewish, and civil libertarian supporters of the public school, as well as by many professional educators, argues that both direct aid and indirect aid to parochial schools are unconstitutional. Those who take this position base their argument on a strict separation of church and state. At the middle of the 20th century, both the National Education Association and the American Association of School Administrators adopted this position, asserting that although religious schools had every right to exist, they should be supported entirely by those who use them.

Over the next three decades, the action regarding federal aid to private schools moved from the courts to the legislature. At the federal level, the School Lunch Act of 1948, the National Defense Education Act of 1958, the Higher Educational Facilities Act of 1963, the Higher Education Act of 1965, and the Elementary and Secondary Education Act of 1965 provided financial support for school lunches in parochial schools; massive funding in a variety of areas for private, often sectarian, colleges; and funds for school libraries, textbooks, and secular instructional materials for private as well as public schools. Courts, however, continued to cut down state statutes supporting direct and indirect services to parochial schools, although they did create some conditions under which such aid would be permissible. Thus, in *Zorach v. Clauson* (1952) the Supreme Court ruled that schools could release students during public school hours to attend religious instruction off the school premises.

Charter Schools, Home Schooling, and Voucher Programs

Today, the debate about tax support for parochial education continues, made perhaps even more strident because of current efforts to provide competition for the public education system. Charter schools, home schooling, and voucher programs are often promoted by those who have religious reasons for wanting their children educated by alternative means. While these initiatives are often cyclical, it is the case that over the past few years there has been an increasing demand for and support of faith-based initiatives in many areas of public life.

Children who receive school vouchers, especially in urban areas where voucher programs are most likely to occur, quite often attend parochial schools. Although many have objected that redirecting public school funds to private, religious schools is a violation of the First Amendment's establishment clause, in 2002 the U.S. Supreme Court found that this was not the case with respect to the Cleveland, Ohio, school voucher program. In this case, the Court reversed a lower court decision that struck down the program on the grounds that nearly all students receiving vouchers attended parochial schools. But in a 5 to 4 decision, the majority found that Cleveland parents had a "sufficient range of choices among secular and religious schools that Ohio's voucher plan does not violate the First Amendment prohibition against the establishment of religion" (Frieden, 2002).

Clearly, a growing number of citizens in the United States appear to want to "blur" the boundaries between church and state. That those who promote these ideas are also interested in promoting a particular version of "church" may, in fact, be the catalyst for increasing debate in the years ahead.

Public Freedoms: The Provision of Religious Instruction

Current charges that public schools are too secular and lack the moral tone that will help children grow up to be better citizens are not new. At the end of the 19th century, a consensus had developed that religious instruction should not be a responsibility of public schools; but after World War I and II, many citizens thought that the schools were "godless" and that some sort of religious instruction should be returned to public classrooms. Throughout the 1940s and 1950s, efforts were made to get around Court decisions regarding the separation of church and state, but those efforts were largely unsuccessful. Two arguments were offered.

Some people—mostly Protestants and Catholics—sought a revival of sectarian instruction, usually through the demand for released time in the school day so that students could receive religious instruction from teachers of their own religious faith. Most often, this instruction was to be offered apart from the school building, usually in a nearby church. Others—primarily Protestants—urged that more attention be paid to a nonsectarian religious instruction through daily reading of the Bible and recitation of nonsectarian prayers in school. Both propositions were denounced by many people as an infringement of the separation of church and state.

While a number of states and the U.S. Supreme Court had ruled in various ways on the issue of released time for religious instruction, the Supreme Court finally decided in *Zorach v. Clauson* in 1952 that students leaving the school building for religious teaching was permissible under the First Amendment because the school did not actively promote a sectarian form of instruction and because no public funds were expended for the effort.

The issue of Bible reading has also been decided variously. By the 1970s, a number of states had decided it was *not* religious instruction. At least six state courts, however, ruled that the Bible *was* a sectarian document, at least to Catholics, Jews, and nonbelievers. For Catholics, the King James version of the Bible was thought to be Protestant sectarianism; for Jews, reading the Bible does not hold the same significance that it does for Christians; families of unbelievers objected to any religious practices at all. Nonsectarian prayers were usually objected to by everyone on the grounds that they watered down any real religious belief in an effort at compromise among belief systems and also on the grounds that such prayers nevertheless promoted religion against the establishment clause of the First Amendment. In 1963, the Supreme Court did away with most of these arguments in the previously discussed cases that declared *required* prayer and Bible reading to be unconstitutional even while they affirmed the value of teaching *about* religion in public schools.

In the past 30 years, new issues have arisen that bring religious pluralism in the classroom once again into sharper focus. First, immigration from various parts of the world by people whose religious structures and beliefs are very different from Christianity and Judaism has populated public school classrooms with students from a wide variety of religious backgrounds. Second, changes in the institutions of the family and the economy have weakened the social cohesion that normally helps bind communities together and provide the common socialization processes necessary to raise the next generation. In such circumstances, young people often feel rootless, answerable to no one, and alienated from a system that no longer really exists except in the minds of their elders. One result of these societal conditions is the increase in violence we are now witnessing in all segments of society, but particularly among our youth. Finally, the growth and importance attached to science and technology in our society tends to mask the smaller, more human dramas that contain the very essence of religious questions and meaning. It is small wonder that, in response, the call for religious instruction and moral values in public schools has become a widespread demand.

Perspectives on Religious Identity

Religion as a Form of Personal Identity

Of all the groups to which a person can claim loyalty, religion is perhaps the most common. Indeed, some researchers suggest that Americans are more likely to identify themselves as members of a religious group than as a member of any other group. People who identify themselves as members of a religious group often associate themselves closely with an ethnic group as well. For example, an Irish Catholic may consider her- or himself substantively different from an Italian Catholic, and a Russian Jew may feel quite different from a German Jew. We are reminded in this regard of a story related by a colleague who was teaching about diversity at an urban university in a highly ethnic city. After several class sessions on the subject, a student came up after class to tell her that she (the student) could, indeed, relate to the lesson. "You know," the student said, "I went all through Catholic school in my own Irish neighborhood, and it wasn't until I got to college that I met some Italian Catholics. You're right, they sure are different!"

This differentiation results in part from differences in ethnic histories and in part from differences in the development of religious practices among members of the same general faith. An individual has only to attend services at churches of three or four different Protestant denominations (e.g., Presbyterian, Southern Baptist, high Episcopalian) to know that there is great diversity *within* the same religious tradition. This diversity is even more true for the world's major religions. The diversity within Christianity, or within Islam, or within Judaism is in many respects far greater than the diversity among them. Moreover, people who identify themselves with a particular religious group also usually have placed themselves in a particular social as well as geographical location. The very term *Southern Baptist,* for example, says a great deal about the geographical roots of a person's religious identity, and the term *high Episcopalian* may indicate something about the social class to which a person belongs.

Religious identity has its strongest roots in the family, and many families not only encourage but demand that their children follow in their religious traditions. Indeed, some families will go so far as to deny the existence of a child who breaks with the faith, and some religious groups, such as the Old Order Amish, will occasionally invoke the practice of "shunning" (never speaking to or acknowledging the presence of the person being shunned) when a community member strays from the fold. The belief that a person's religious identity is an integral part of that person's essential self can be seen in the reaction of parents whose children join a cult of some kind. Such parents believe that their child has been brainwashed and often will hire an expert to "deprogram" their child.

Religious identification also places a person in a particular relationship with the deity (e.g., Catholics as part of a community of believers, Protestants in a one-to-one relationship with God). That relationship may determine a person's view of the possibility of a life after death, that person's set of moral codes for living, and the nature of rewards or punishments for the life that person has, in fact, led. Given the profound nature of these issues, it is not surprising that individuals, families, and communities react strongly to perceived threats to their religious beliefs.

At the same time (and perhaps paradoxically), in a religiously heterogeneous society such as the United States, people often switch from one religion to another, and an increasing number of people—estimated at about 14% by some surveys—declare no religion at all. The move from one religious affiliation to another may involve a formal conversion process, or it may be a move from a conservative to a more liberal branch of the same church (or vice versa). It may occur as the result of marriage between people of two faiths, or it may occur in an individual as an outgrowth of intellectual analysis. According to the latest poll by the Pew Research Center's Forum on Religion and Public Life (2009),

Religious Affiliation in the United States

> large numbers of Americans engage in multiple religious practices, mixing elements of diverse traditions. Many say they attend worship services of more than one faith or denomination—even when they are not traveling or going to special events like weddings and funerals. Many also blend Christianity with Eastern or New Age beliefs such as reincarnation, astrology and the presence of spiritual energy in physical objects. And sizeable minorities of all major U.S. religious groups say they have experienced supernatural phenomena, such as being in touch with the dead or with ghosts. (p. 1)

Those who declare no traditional religious affiliation may, in fact, be members of one of a growing number of religious bodies led by charismatic leaders such as Rick Warren (Saddleback Church in California) or Joel Osteen (Lakewood Church in Houston, Texas). Many of these so-called Megachurches (those having memberships of over 2,000 people) are employing television and the Internet to reach more and more potential congregants who would otherwise not be involved in any religious enterprises.

Clearly, the fastest growing churches in the United States tend to be conservative, sometimes evangelical or pentecostal, Protestant denominations, with an

accompanying decline in membership of so-called mainline churches. There are probably a variety of reasons for this trend, not least among them the desire of many people for a solid, unquestioning, and dependable religious orientation at a time when change in all institutions means a dissolution of traditional rules for living. Observers might also argue that the trend toward conservatism reflects, in part, the shrinking of the middle class and the increasing economic gap between those who are wealthy and those who are not. If switching to liberal religious affiliations is a function of upward mobility, then the opposite is perhaps also true. For the first time in American history, there is a general perception that children may not "do better" than their parents, and the real or perceived fact of downward mobility can be related to an increasing desire and need to be a part of a community in which an individual can identify with virtue and righteousness.

Organized Religion and the Net Generation

Still another factor in religious affiliation in the United States is the changing role that technology is playing in attracting new generations of members to religious organizations. Those churches that are attracting large numbers of young people are also quite often those churches that have adopted new forms of worship, especially digital storytelling and contemporary Christian music (Sample, 1998; Wilson & Moore, 2002). Referring, for example, to young Catholics, Arthur Jones (2001) writes that "the medium that communicates the message of these [religious] traditions has changed radically. Many young adults are pursuing a form of spirituality that is subtle, individual and hence unrecognizable to the older generations."

As it is with other social institutions, religion is having to confront the dawn of a new age, populated with young people for whom the "new age" is not new at all but rather is the context in which they have grown up. Speaking to an older generation, Wilson and Moore (2002) give some indication of the dimensions of this wired world:

> A whole new digital world is emerging today. Can you see it? If you can, you know it is a world built on emotional, virtual, holographic, decentralized, holistic, empowered, one-by-one, borderless, bottom-up, global/local, and egalitarian characteristics. Such a world will play by totally different rules than the rules of modernity. In the twenty-first century to *not be digital* will be the new form of illiteracy. (p. 11)

Others suggest that young people—often called Millennials—want to return religiously to a more stable time, adopting traditions from very early times. For Christians, this often means more use of ritual and symbol, more spaces for quiet and contemplation, more authenticity, and a convergence of musical styles (Webber, 2001).

Ways in which all organized religions will experience transformation in the years ahead, as well as ways in which religious ideas will be played out among the peoples of the world will be the subject of much discussion and debate—as will the role that religion plays in schooling in the United States and around the world.

The Influence of the Religious Right

Although the so-called religious right in this country is composed of a politically oriented and loosely connected set of relatively fundamentalist Christians, it would be a mistake to think that conservatism is the "property" of the Christian faith. Indeed, **fundamentalism** is gaining strength in all the religions of the world as people begin to feel the effects of globalization and institutional change. In the United States, however, the determinedly *political* nature of a coalition of conservative Protestants has had a profound effect on the direction of American government and its legislative and judicial processes. National issues such as the size of the federal government, the need to reduce the incidence of crime, abortion, and violence in and out of schools are the issues of choice of the religious right. Information and exhortations about these issues are carried to millions of people through televangelists, through radio networks sponsored by such organizations as Dr. James Dobson's Focus on the Family, and through national figures such as Pat Robertson and Pat Buchanan as well as through numerous websites. The influence of the religious right is also observable in the rhetoric of otherwise more moderate politicians, and political campaigns at all levels will in the future undoubtedly be driven in large measure by conservative and even fundamental beliefs.

Nowhere is the influence of the religious right felt more strongly, however, than at the local and grassroots level, and no institution is of more concern than the school. The tension produced by the constitutional separation of church and state has meant a continual debate regarding the part played by schooling in both protecting religious liberty and enabling religious practice. As it has been in the past, the issue of school prayer is once again at the forefront of public debate, fueled in part by vocal participation of those who believe that the *absence* of regular prayer in schools is one of the elements of what they see as a lack of morality in American society. The current status of prayer in schools, as determined in part by Supreme Court decisions, is that prayer is individual and voluntary (some wit remarked that as long as there is academic testing, there will be prayer in schools!), but conservative groups continue to press for a return of mandated school prayer with the stipulation that individuals can choose not to participate.

Similarly, the issue of funding for private and parochial schools is also the subject of much debate, this time using the language of tuition tax credits. Some proponents argue (again) that because student enrollment in private schools reduces the pressure on public schools and contributes to the overall education of America's children, financial support for private tuition is justified. They argue further that parents should not have to pay twice for the education of their children and that support for private schools encourages pluralism. Interestingly, unlike the Great School Wars in the 19th century in which Protestants opposed parochial schools in general, those proponents of public funding for private schools who are members of the religious right would now like public support for private Christian schools. Opponents, on the other hand, argue that allowing such a use of public funds would weaken the public school system, facilitate the ability of parents to avoid integrated schools, and create a dual system of education that is antithetical to the ideal of a democratically educated citizenry.

Interestingly, a small but growing group of people—teachers and students—are involved in high school elective courses in which the Bible is the text. The emergence of these kinds of classes is based on three arguments: teaching the Bible as an object of study rather than as "received word" in schools is constitutional (see the argument of the Supreme Court in *Abingdon v. Schempp*), the Bible is so much a part of Western culture that consideration of at least its key passages is an important factor in what it means to be an educated person, and, finally, that in the current political climate, so-called religious literacy is critical to a citizen's ability to negotiate claims based on largely Christian religious texts (Van Biema, 2007).

Perhaps the most serious challenge by the religious right to public education, however, lies in the area of censorship. Conservative and fundamentalist religious groups are not the only groups to advocate censoring the materials to which schoolchildren have access, but they are among the most vocal. Gollnick and Chinn (2004) described the seriousness of this challenge in the following way:

> Censorship, or attempts at censorship, have resulted in violence: involved parties have been beaten and even shot. It has resulted in the dismissal or resignation of administrators and teachers. It has split communities and in the past thirty years has created nearly as much controversy as the desegregation of schools. (p. 230)

Most people would not doubt that those who urge the censorship of school materials are sincere and fully convinced that they are espousing a cause that is morally right, but the question arises as to whose morality is to be the basis for whatever guidelines are selected. In a religiously pluralistic society, the public schools have an obligation to educate as broadly as possible. Moreover, the issue of academic freedom for teachers to select the materials they deem most suitable is an important one. Of particular concern to many conservative religious groups are those books and materials that deal with alternative family lifestyles and with sex or sex education, that contain realistic language, and that are written about ethnic minority groups. Indeed, some people object to any materials that do not portray the ethnocentrically patriotic, small-town, middle-class, family-oriented values of Norman Rockwell.

Among the targets of self-styled censors have been books such as Mark Twain's *Huckleberry Finn* and John Steinbeck's *Of Mice and Men;* curricula such as Man—A Course of Study (a social studies curriculum developed by the National Science Foundation) and biology texts that do not give equal space to creation science; dictionaries containing words deemed offensive; the holding of school Halloween parties, which are believed by some people to encourage the worship of devils and witches; and, more recently, the immensely popular Harry Potter books. Further, many conservative groups object to any materials and practices that seem to them to represent secular humanism, which they define as thought and action not based on a God-centered universe. Often referred to as a religion by conservative religious groups, secular humanism does not have a church, a set of rituals and practices, or a set of doctrines and dogma. Rather, humanism is a movement begun in the Renaissance that centers its intellectual attention on human beings and their affairs, including the many ways in which they engage in religious endeavors. Nevertheless, some determined religious groups believe that secular humanism exists as a religion and are committed to defeat it.

Clearly, those who claim to be part of a religious revival in the United States are currently in a strong position. It is difficult to argue that we as a society should not be concerned about crime, about the high rate of unwed parents, or about raising the next generation to be respectful of the traditions of this country. Indeed, many people who do not profess affiliation with conservative religious groups are deeply concerned about those issues and many others. Furthermore, if the United States is to be a truly religiously pluralistic society, people who profess fundamentalist beliefs have every right to hold them and every right not to be discriminated against because of them. What seems to separate the religious right from more moderate citizens, however, is the belief, based on a strict interpretation of one book–the Bible–that they have the one and only, true, and virtuous answer and that it should be applied to everyone. This very problem, of course, is what led the writers of the Constitution to stipulate that while citizens of a free country should be allowed to practice whatever religious beliefs they espoused, the *government* (and thus, the public schools) should not establish one particular religion as the religion of the state. This belief, incidentally, reflects the level of defense proposed in the developmental model of intercultural sensitivity presented in Chapter 5.

This issue is even more urgent today because we have learned firsthand and tragically to what lengths a rigid fundamentalist belief system may lead its followers. Indeed, perhaps one of the *good* things that may emerge from the devastation of the attacks on the World Trade Center and the Pentagon is a deeper understanding in and support for the tradition of the separation of church and state that is written into the United States Constitution.

Ethical Issues

This chapter has emphasized that teachers who address religious issues in their classrooms must understand their communities and not go too far beyond the values that the community holds. This advice may appear to be common sense and carries with it a certain degree of self-preservation, but it also importantly suggests the belief that *all* deeply held religious beliefs are worthy of respect.

Within the classroom, teachers must be on the lookout and intercede for religious prejudice, particularly as it might be expressed in the casual name-calling that children do so easily. Like all other forms of prejudice, religious prejudice is learned–and can be unlearned (though not easily). Respectful behavior toward others, however, can and should be insisted upon.

Another ethical issue concerns the responsibility of teachers to be familiar with federal and state laws with respect to religion and schooling. The classroom teacher often must serve in the role of instructor to parents and community members as well as to students and should be knowledgeable about the development of and debates about religious differences that are a part of the fabric of law and judicial decision in the United States.

With respect to relations with parents and the community, teachers should also be knowledgeable about the bases of different religious beliefs and should be as ready and willing as possible to answer questions and discuss objections calmly. There are times when it is not possible to reach consensus, and finding effective ways of agreeing to disagree is both useful and wise.

International Perspective: What's Happening Elsewhere in the World?

Addressing Religious Pluralism in European Schools

Barry van Driel
Curriculum Consultant, Ann Frank House, Amsterdam, Netherlands

Leyla Sahin was a very bright young medical student in Istanbul, Turkey, in the late 1990s; she was, in fact, at the top of her class. Like most people in Turkey, she was also Muslim. Because of her religious beliefs, she felt that she should cover her hair with a hijab (headscarf) when attending class and taking exams. The University of Istanbul, however, had passed a law in 1998 banning students with beards and students wearing the Islamic headscarf from attending lectures, courses, and tutorials. When Leyla attempted to take a key exam, she was told to remove her hijab. She refused and was subsequently not allowed to take the exam. Leyla took her case to the Turkish courts and eventually to the European Court of Human Rights. The Court ruled in 2004 that although freedom of religion issues were at stake, other principles had to be given priority. These principles included the protection of the rights and freedoms of others, the protection of the public order, the importance of upholding the principle of secularism, ensuring the neutrality of Turkish universities, and the importance of protecting Turkey from those who use religious symbols for political purposes. Leyla lost her case.

The fight for religious freedom and the right to be protected against discrimination is not new in Europe. This very populated and diverse continent has a long history of both religious conflict and religious compromise. Many wars have been fought over faith issues, and this has led to the migration of communities to safer and more tolerant areas. One only needs to think of the history of persecution of the Jews throughout the centuries, the recent genocide in Bosnia, or the continuing religious tensions in Northern Ireland to grasp the intensity of some of these conflicts.

Table 9.1 Percentage of Population That Claims to Go to Church or Other Place of Worship at Least Once a Week

USA 41%	Spain 20%	Germany 9%
	Austria 19%	Czech Republic 9%
Ireland 56%	Britain 13%	France 8%
Poland 54%	Netherlands 12%	Norway 5%
Italy 32%	Belgium 11%	Sweden 5%
Portugal 29%	Switzerland 11%	
Greece 26%	Hungary 11%	

Source: Gallup, 2001, and European Social Survey, 2003.

On the whole, religion is less important to people in Europe than in the United States at the beginning of the 21st century. Fewer Europeans than Americans claim to visit a place of worship as can be seen in Table 9.1.

Also, whereas 59% of Americans indicate that their religion is very important to them, a comparable study in Europe shows that only 21% feel that their religion is very important to them (Pew Forum on Religion in Public Life and European Value Survey). Some 70% of Poles pray at least once a week, while only 4% of Danes do. There has been a steady and marked decline of religiosity in Europe during the last few decades, although there are some indications that this trend is being subtly and slowly reversed.

Religion in European Secular Schools

Like the United States, European countries have long debated the role of religion in society and in secular schools, and this had led to very different outcomes. The importance of religion in public life, for example, is reflected in the constitutions of the various countries.

The Polish Constitution: Preamble

We, the Polish nation . . . for our culture rooted in the Christian heritage of the Nation and in universal human values. . . . Recognizing our responsibility before God or our own consciences . . . establish this Constitution of the Republic of Poland.

The Irish Constitution: Preamble

In the name of the Most Holy Trinity. . . . We, the people of Eire, humbly acknowledging all our obligations to our Divine Lord, Jesus Christ . . . do hereby adopt, enact and give ourselves this Constitution.

The French Constitution: Article 1

France shall be an indivisible, secular, democratic and social Republic. It shall ensure the equality of all citizens before the law, without distinction of origin, race or religion. It shall respect all beliefs.

Though efforts are currently under way, Europe has not yet agreed on a joint constitution. Nevertheless, the guiding documents on religion in secular schools at the European Union level all stress freedom of religion as a human right, interreligious understanding, the importance of dialogue, and tolerance of each others' belief systems. They also stress the need to combat intolerance and discrimination.

The general long-term trend in Europe is increasing secularism, but new migration patterns in Europe due to refugees, labor recruitment (so-called guest workers), and histories of colonialism have all led to increasing debates about religion and its place in the education system.

Historically, confessional education (that is, education in denominational or sectarian schools and colleges) has been the dominant approach in many west European countries. The boundaries between secularism and faith are blurred in these cases because the intention is to raise children in a particular religious tradition, whether Catholicism, Protestantism, or Orthodoxy. The dominant religion is viewed as being a key aspect of a country's history and culture and often the path to Truth. Teachers of religion are expected to be believers themselves. Seeing priests or nuns in the hallways of secular schools is not uncommon. Those that do not want to partake in religious lessons can opt out. Poland is a good example of where such an approach still dominates in secular schools.

Most European educational systems have been moving away from confessional education as societies have become religiously diverse and increasing secularism has taken hold. For instance, there are now approximately 9–12 million Muslims in Europe (out of a total population of 450 million). Muslim immigrants tend to be quite religious and find "values and morals" education to be extremely important. Many are displeased about having their children taught Christianity in school. In some places, they find somewhat unlikely supporters among the Jewish communities across Europe.

A key issue in eastern and central Europe has been how to deal with religion in secular schools since the collapse of the Soviet Union in 1989. Before 1989, religion and religious education was banned in all schools, and religion was viewed as irrelevant and undesirable. With the Soviet restrictions gone, traditional churches are presently trying to gain a firmer grip on how religion is dealt with in schools.

Islam has become the second largest religion in Europe in a relatively short time. The arrival of millions of people from traditional communities has led to many debates and tensions in educational systems across western Europe. Schools and Muslim communities have clashed around issues such as appropriate health and sex education, religious holidays, food requirements, mixed PE lessons, but most of all around the symbolic issue of wearing the hijab.

The rejection by the European Court of Human Rights of the Leyla Sahin complaint in Turkey has allowed other countries to also move toward banning the hijab. We encounter such initiatives, for instance, in France, Belgium, Germany, and the Netherlands. France passed a very controversial law in 2004 called the Law on Secularity and Conspicuous Religious Symbols. It bans all conspicuous religious symbols in schools, such as hijabs, kippahs, large crosses, turbans, and so forth. The main aim of the new law, however, was clearly to ban the hijab. The tendency to keep all matters of religion out of French schools is not new. France has had a strict separation of church and state since 1905. Due to this law, the government may not recognize or fund any religion.

The heated debate about the hijab is largely absent in Britain, where it is felt that wearing the hijab is a freedom of religion issue (much like it would be in North America). Unlike France, the British authorities feel it is critical to teach about religion in schools, precisely because of the multicultural, changing, and dynamic nature of present-day society. The British Education Reform Act 1988 requires that all British students in secular schools be taught a basic curriculum of religious education. The aims of the curriculum are, among others, to promote pupils' spiritual, moral, social, and cultural development and to prepare all pupils for the opportunities, responsibilities, and experiences of life. The actual curriculum used in schools reflects a process in which the local government, local religious communities, and other stakeholders cooperate to develop a curriculum for students that is solid, respectful, and that removes religious stereotypes.

Critical Incident

Celebrating the Holidays

Allie McNeal was a classmate of Melissa's; the two went through high school and then college together. Allie now teaches third grade at Thomas Edison Elementary School, located in a diverse community in a suburb of Denver. She is a member of the school planning committee for all special events in the school, including the celebration of holidays. Her committee had sent a survey to all the parents, explaining that the school was exploring the possibility of removing "Christmas" from the annual December activities–substituting instead activities having to do with winter–and asking the parents what they thought. The rationale was that because the school has a large number of children from different religious backgrounds, celebrating Christmas spoke to only some of the children, but not all.

319

Allie has just received an impassioned phone call from one mother, demanding that they not only *keep* Christmas in the holiday schedule, but that they also eliminate Halloween. The mother expressed—in no uncertain terms—the belief that the United States is a Christian country and that other people had just better get used to it. She went on to say that she was the spokesperson for a large number of other parents who would be asking for an appointment with the principal to discuss the matter. She was especially adamant about Halloween, saying that it was a form of devil worship, and that her group did not want their children to participate in any celebration that included pagan signs and symbols.

Allie was quite taken aback at the intensity of the mother's appeal. She knew she had better speak to the principal about the forthcoming visit, and she also knew she had to make some recommendations to her committee.

- If Allie telephoned you asking for advice, how would you suggest she handle this situation?

Critical Incident

Suggested Reading?

George Manson, a seventh-grade English teacher in the middle school just down the road from Melissa, received a call from the father of one of his students, Rema Assadi, a Muslim girl who had brought home a novel she had selected from George's list of recommended books. The novel, one that had been chosen by librarians in the state as among the best modern fiction for middle schoolers, concerned an American girl going to school in London whose 11-year-old brother had been killed by a bomb detonated by a Muslim girl attempting to avoid an arranged marriage to a man in his 50s who already had two other wives. The book contained numerous stereotypes of Muslims, portraying them as abusers of women, anti-Semitic, under the control of their religious leaders, and prone to violence. Both Rema and her family were upset and frightened at the thought that

other students in the class would be reading this book. After the violent attacks on September 11, 2001, the family feared a major backlash against Muslims.

Mr. Assadi told George that his religious community was mounting a letter-writing and e-mail campaign aimed at the publisher of the book, trying to persuade the company to recall it. In the meantime, he asked, would George please take the book off his recommended reading list? And would he talk to his students about the book, making sure they understood how biased it was?

• If you were George, what would you do?

Summary

Because the United States was founded on the principle of religious liberty, the framers of the Constitution built into the First Amendment both a prohibition against a state religion and a prohibition against limiting the free expression of religious beliefs and practices. That ambiguity has led to considerable dispute over the role of religion in American society and particularly in American schools.

The principle of separation of church and state has not prevented many people from believing that schools should be a repository of morality; the question has always been "Whose morality are we talking about?" Because we are a nation of laws, much of the "action" regarding religion and schooling has been in the courts, which have struggled with this issue over the years, often reversing previous decisions, but always trying to come to a reasonable balance between competing views.

This balance has been impeded by the myth that teachers may not talk about religion in schools; this myth is not true. Indeed, the decision that "banned" school prayer explicitly notes that exposure to the story of the world's great religions is necessary for a complete education. This chapter describes the nature of the debate over religion in public schooling and the importance of attending to the diverse religious backgrounds of American students. In an increasingly interdependent world, it is both necessary and prudent that we understand and respect the religious impulse that influences human identity and guides human behavior.

Chapter Review

Go to the Online Learning Center at www.mhhe.com/cushner7e to review important content from the chapter, practice with key terms, take a chapter quiz, and find the Web links listed in this chapter.

Key Terms

cultural capital 294
establishment clause
   of the First
   Amendment 295
Fourteenth
   Amendment 295

fundamentalism 315
nativist religions 297
prohibition clause of the
   First Amendment 295

separation of church
   and state 304
theocracy 295

Active Exercise

Additional Active Exercises are available online at www.mhhe.com/cushner7e.

Understanding Religious Diversity

Purpose: To assist you with gaining greater understanding and reducing stereotypes of the major religions that may be encountered in schools and communities.

Instructions: Derive a series of interview questions using the guidelines below. Then conduct interviews with individuals who represent religions other than your own.

1. In small groups, generate potential interview questions you could use to help gain greater understanding and reduce misperceptions about religions other than your own.

2. Discuss these questions with the class and determine which among them will help to uncover stereotypes, attitudes, perceptions, and misperceptions of a particular group.

3. Agree as a class upon 5–7 questions that will generate the most useful information.

4. Using the same questions, individually or in pairs, interview at least two individuals from religious groups other than your own. You should try to find representatives from at least the five major world religions (Christianity, Judaism, Islam, Buddhism, and Hinduism), as well as any other groups of interest and available in your region.

5. Individually, summarize key points of your interviews.

6. As a class, discuss the following questions:

   a. Did the questions you asked provide you with the information you had hoped for?

   b. Discuss at least one response that you found surprising or interesting. What did you find especially intriguing about this response?

   c. Was there anything the interviewee said that led you to reconsider any of your views?

   d. Did you learn anything significant from the interviewee about the religion?

   e. Were any stereotypes you might have held about this religion challenged?

   f. Now that the interviews are complete, are there any questions you wished you had asked?

   g. What did you learn in this exercise that will influence your teaching?

Classroom Activities

1. In an elementary classroom, an interesting activity might be to have students research religious holidays for a variety of religious traditions, for

example, Jewish, Muslim, Christian, Buddhist, Hinduism, Taoism, and so forth, with the goal of creating an annual calendar of religious festivals and holidays from around the world. Much material for such a study is available online and students will learn, among other things, that the world's major religions probably have as much in common as they have differences.

2. Elementary students might also be interested in reading stories about world religions; some of these might include both folktales from various religious traditions and explanatory books written for children.

3. High school students might research some (or all!) of the Supreme Court cases discussed in Chapter 9, studying the arguments used in the case and the rationale used by the judges in deciding on the case. A variation of this activity might be for a whole class to study one or two seminal cases and then participate in a mock court in which the arguments are presented and the judges discuss aspects of the case prior to writing their decisions. Students would take the roles of attorneys and each of the judges in the actual case.

4. Organizing, researching, and participating in a debate is an activity that high school students usually enjoy. In this case, students could debate any of a number of "propositions" that are currently matters of debate surrounding religion and schools. For example, Should Public Funding Be Awarded to Support Private, Parochial Schools? Or, What Are the Pros and Cons of Using Christmas as the Focal Point of a Winter Break Holiday for Schools? Or, What Difficulties Are Presented by the First Amendment's Establishment and Free Exercise Clauses Regarding Religion in the United States?

Reflective Questions

Quite unintentionally, indeed with the very best of intentions, Melissa Morgan found herself in the center of a controversy that could have turned into a major issue both in her classroom and in her community. On reflection, it is likely that Melissa might have asked herself the following questions. Think about how you would answer these questions if you were in Melissa's place.

1. Having grown up in a town very much like the one in which she taught and having taught in her school for 5 years, how is it that Melissa didn't think about what she knew to be a streak of deep-seated conservatism present in the community?

2. Once her students' project was under way, are there strategies she could have used that might have forestalled the objections voiced by some parents after they saw the exhibit at the open house?

3. As is evident in other examples in this book, acting as an agent of change can be a tricky business, particularly when the school in which you teach is a very traditional one. Certainly, it is often easier to go with the flow of traditional school culture than to try to change it. It does not appear, however, that Melissa thought of herself as a change agent; rather, she was attempting only to utilize existing human and intellectual resources in a better way for the sake of her students. What are some of the factors that turn a seemingly innocent curricular activity into a potential source of protest?

4. Melissa attempted to resolve the issue by going to a number of community leaders. Are there dangers in this strategy? What might some of those dangers be?

5. Melissa could have simply dismissed the objections raised to her use of religious information in the classroom as ignorant, unenlightened, or prejudiced behavior. How would that view have undermined her strong belief in religious pluralism?

6. When the episode was over, Melissa began to think about some of the long-standing practices of American schooling, such as the way most schools use Christian holidays—particularly Christmas and Easter—as sources for both curricular and extracurricular activities. Are such traditional practices fitting subjects for review and rethinking?

7. In her meeting with the clergy council, Melissa did not mention that, according to the most recent Supreme Court decisions, she was well within her rights to teach *about* religion in her classroom. Should she have raised that issue? Might there have been some negative results if she had?

Endnote

1. This list was adapted and extended from R. Stark & C. Y. Glock, "Dimensions of Religious Commitment," in R. Robertson, *Sociology of Religion*, p. 46; cited in Donna M. Gollnick and Philip C. Chinn, *Multicultural Education in a Pluralistic Society*, 3rd ed. (New York: Macmillan, 1990), p. 175.

References

AARDOC. (2006). African-American religion: A documentary history project. *Atlantic World*. Retrieved from http://www.amherst.edu/~aardoc/Atlantic_World.html

Abington Township District School v. Schempp, 374 U.S. 203 (1963).

Al-Ani, S. H. (1995). Muslims in America and Arab Americans. In C. L. Bennett, *Comprehensive multicultural education: Theory and practice* (3rd ed.). Boston: Allyn & Bacon.

Bader, C., et al. (2006). *American piety in the 21st century: New insights to the depth and complexity of religion in the US.* The Baylor Religion Survey, Baylor Institute for Studies of Religion. Retrieved from http://www.baylor.edu/content/services/document.php/33304.pdf

Berger, P. L., & Berger, B. (1972). S*ociology: A biographical approach.* New York: Basic Books.

Butts, R. F. (1978). *Public education in the United States: From revolution to reform.* New York: Holt, Rinehart, & Winston.

Cochran v. Louisiana State Board of Education, 281 U.S. 370 (1930).

Durkheim, E. (1969). The social foundations of religion. In R. Robertson (Ed.), S*ociology of religion.* Baltimore: Penguin Books.

Everson v. Board of Education, 330 U.S. 1 (1947).

Frieden, T. (2002). Supreme Court affirms school voucher program. Retrieved from http://archives.cnn.com/2002/LAW/06/27/scotus.school.vouchers

Gollnick, D. M., & Chinn, P. C. (2004). *Multicultural education in a pluralistic society* (6th ed.). Upper Saddle River, NJ: Pearson.

Jones, A. (2001, March 30). Engaging, keeping new Catholic generations. *National Catholic Reporter.* Retrieved from http://www.natcath.com/NCR_ Online/archives/033001/033001s.htm

Lee v. Weisman, 112 S. Ct. 2649 (1992).

Meyer v. Nebraska, 262 U.S. 390 (1923).

Minersville v. Gobitis, 310 U.S. 586 (1940).

National Center for Higher Education Management Systems. (2007). *Public high school graduation rates: 2004.* Retrieved from http://www.higheredinfo.org/ dbrowser/index.php?measure=23

Pang, V. O., & Barba, R. H. (1995). The power of culture: Building culturally affirming instruction. In C. A. Grant (Ed.), *Educating for diversity: An anthology of multicultural voices.* Boston: Allyn & Bacon.

Pew Research Center's Forum on Religion and Public Life (2009). Many Americans mix multiple faiths. Retrieved from http://www.pewforum.org/ docs/?DocID=490

Pierce v. Society of Sisters, 268 U.S. 510 (1925).

Sample, T. (1998). *The spectacle of worship in a wired world: Electronic culture and the gathered people of God.* Nashville, TN: Abingdon Press.

Santa Fe Independent School District v. Doe, 530 U.S. 290 (2000).

Smith, J. I. (n/d). *Patterns of Muslim immigration.* Bureau of International Information Programs, U.S. Department of State. Retrieved from http://usinfo. state.gov/products/pubs/muslimlife/immigrat.htm

Sowell, T. (1980). *Ethnic America: A history.* New York: Basic Books.

Uphoff, J. K. (1993). Religious diversity and education. In J. A. Banks & C. A. McG. Banks (Eds.), *Multicultural education: Issues and perspectives* (2nd ed.). Boston: Allyn & Bacon.

Van Biema, D. (2007, April 2). The case for teaching the Bible. *Time Magazine,* pp. 40–46.

Webber, R. E. (2001). How will the millennials worship? A snapshot of the very near future. *Reformed Worship: Resources for Planning and Leading Worship, 59,* 1. Retrieved from http://www.reformedworship.org/magazine/ issue.cfm?id=59

West Virginia State Board of Education v. Barnette, 319 U.S. 624 (1943).

Wilson, L., & Moore, J. (2002). *Digital storytellers: The art of communicating the gospel in worship.* Nashville, TN: Abingdon Press.

Wisconsin v. Yoder, 406 U.S. 213 (1972).

Yinger, J. M. (1970). *The scientific study of religion.* New York: Macmillan.

Zorach v. Clauson, 343 U.S. 306 (1952).

Chapter

10

Developing a Collaborative Classroom

Gender and Sexual Orientation

Focus Questions

1. If you were buying clothes for a newborn, how would you select the color?

2. What do you think about girls who often use vulgar language? How about boys who do?

3. If you were babysitting for a 3-year-old boy whose favorite toys were dolls, what might you do?

4. How might you feel if your favorite cousin–or your sister–suddenly declared that she was a lesbian?

5. In school, would you rather work closely with others (in pairs or small groups) or work by yourself?

6. Has anyone (parent, friend, guidance counselor) ever told you that certain subjects were not "suitable" for you because of your gender?

7. What do you think about the increasing number of males who are nurses? What about females who work in construction?

“ Prejudices, it is well known, are most difficult to eradicate from the heart whose soil has never been loosened or fertilized by education; they grow there, firm as weeds among rocks. ”

CHARLOTTE BRONTE

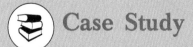

Gender and Sexual Orientation in a Collaborative Classroom

It's the beginning of April in Spokane, Washington, and Tom Littleton's combined biological/ environmental science class is in full swing.[1] The 27 juniors and seniors in the class are working together in twos, threes, and fours at a variety of tasks—putting together a large display unit, cataloging leaf and bark samples at the two stone-topped lab benches, looking at water samples under a microscope, taking notes from a well-illustrated botany book, and working at a computer in the corner. Three adults who come into the class regularly—Steven's father, a journalism teacher, and a staff member from the local Environmental Protection Agency—are working with some of the students while Tom moves from one group to another watching, listening, answering questions, and giving advice.

Since school started in late August, these students have turned the classroom into what they call a working land lab. Its purpose is to study the ecological characteristics of the land, water, plants, and animals that make up a wooded plot of ground behind the school. They have taken and tested water samples for toxic chemicals, tested the soil for its chemical compounds, identified and cataloged all the trees and plants (including several rare species), and noted the presence of animal and bird life. In short, they have developed a "map" of the ecological system in this area and have come to understand the living relationships existing there. In the process, they have decided to formally request that the school board set aside this land as a nature preserve for use by students and members of the community.

The project began somewhat haphazardly last summer when several of the students noticed that the creek running through the property looked cloudy. When school started, they asked Tom about it, and he showed them how to take and test water samples. Since then, the creek area has not only become the catalyst for teaching and learning the subject matter in Tom's class, but has provided an opportunity to accomplish other worthwhile goals. As the school year ends, the class is preparing displays of their findings and writing a report they intend to present to the school board in May. The report contains their recommendations for establishing the nature preserve. On one long wall is a hand-lettered chart that says:

Natural History Perspectives: Goals

- To appreciate the universality of change and the dynamic processes of the physical and biological sciences.
- To obtain a personal standard of scientific literacy that allows for reasonable assessment of the local and global condition in terms of economic, social, legal, and applied science concepts.
- To achieve the ability to distinguish between science, personal opinion, and **pseudoscience** through inquiry, investigation, research, and interpretation of data.

Next to this chart on the same wall is a brightly colored poster of flying geese, with a printed text superimposed on the drawings. It reads:

Lessons From Geese

1. As each bird flaps its wings, it creates an "uplift" for the bird following. By flying in a "V" formation, the whole flock adds 71 percent greater flying range than if the bird flew alone. The lesson to be learned is that people who share a common direction and sense of community can get where they are going quicker because they are traveling on the thrust of one another.
2. Whenever a goose falls out of formation, it suddenly feels the drag of trying to fly alone, and quickly gets back into formation to take advantage of the "lifting" power of the bird immediately in front. The lesson to be learned is that if we have as much sense as a goose, we will stay in formation with those who are headed where we want to go. We should be willing to accept their help and give them ours.
3. When the lead goose gets tired, it rotates back into the formation and another goose flies at the point position. The lesson to be learned is that it pays to take turns doing the hard tasks, and sharing leadership. With people, as with geese, we are interdependent.

4. The geese toward the rear honk to encourage those up front to keep up their speed. The lesson to be learned is that we need to make sure our honking from behind is encouraging, not something else.

5. When a goose gets sick, wounded, or shot down, two geese drop out of formation and follow it down to help and protect it. They stay with it until it is able to fly again or dies. They then launch out on their own, with another formation, or catch up with the flock. The lesson to be learned is that if we have as much sense as geese we, too, will stand by each other in difficult times as well as when we are strong (McNeish, 1972).

Seeing that all the students are occupied and that no one seems to have a question at the moment, Tom moves over to his small, crowded desk, sits down, and takes a spiral-bound notebook out of one drawer. That same drawer also contains portfolios that document the accomplishments of individual students. Tom's notebook is a reflective journal in which he notes observations of students, details of the work they are all doing, and records ideas for future teaching. In a way, the journal is Tom's portfolio, his assessment of himself as a teacher in this class. "One of the great things about this class," he writes, "is that as the year goes by the students need me less and less. They really are learning to work together and to solve their own problems."

When the year began, Tom had two major objectives apart from—although related to—the curriculum. The first was to systematically encourage the girls in this class to actively participate, to willingly put forth their ideas and speculations, and to be outwardly as well as inwardly proud of their accomplishments. For several years he had been encouraging ninth- and tenth-grade girls to take this class, and this year the class was nearly half female. Tom thought that a science class might be the perfect place for girls to exercise their collaborative skills. After all, discoveries in science are nearly always the result of group effort involving scientists, lab technicians, social scientists, and often students. The process of actually doing science, he thought, should be a particularly fitting one for girls, who were usually socialized to collaborate with others.

Unfortunately, he also knew that girls were often guided away from scientific and technical classes by parents and counselors who believed that they were less suited to such subjects. He knew that girls (and boys) usually thought that science and math were "male" activities. His second goal was to fully integrate three students from the fairly large Gypsy community that lived in Spokane. These students, Steven, Rebecca, and Ian, had been part of a long-term effort by the Spokane schools to build relations of trust between the schools and Gypsy (or, more accurately, Romani) parents. Because of a long history of persecution by the wider community in both Europe and the United States, these Romani parents were hesitant about sending their children to school.

Steven and Rebecca had been in school since they were 7; Ian moved to Spokane when he was 10. All three began school in a program especially designed to accommodate cultural factors within the Roma community such as its close family structure, its respect for age, its highly male-dominated society, and its resistance to change. Also, these children were expected to assume responsibility in the community at an earlier age than were European American middle-class children and were thus somewhat more mature than their age-mates.

Some aspects of the program were very different from traditional school practice. For instance, because the Roma community was a male-dominated society, boys had to be served lunch first, and female teachers were expected to wear "female" attire—dresses and skirts. Because parents were afraid for their children, phones had to be installed in every classroom so that parents could have direct access to teachers and to their own children regarding after-school activities. Because the community's goal was English literacy but not cultural literacy, the classrooms were explicitly not assimilationist. Because change was feared on a deep level, bus drivers had to keep the same routes, and teachers had to stay with the same children. Because respect for elders had to be maintained, illiterate parents could not be taught along with their children but needed separate instruction, younger children could not serve as tutors

(continued)

for older children, and teachers were expected to be over 30 years old. Teachers also needed to be flexible regarding school goals and schedules to allow for participation in community events and rituals.

Although the Romani children had originally been separated from other children in this program, the goal was to eventually build enough trust in the community that they would allow their children to be placed in regular classrooms. Steven, Rebecca, and Ian had gone into regular classes when they began the ninth grade. At this point, the three were still inclined to stay together, but Tom had noticed that they all had become deeply involved in the work of the land lab and that even Rebecca seemed willing to venture forth with a suggestion now and then.

As Tom leafed through his notebook and watched the students at work, scenes from the past several months floated through his mind. He remembered the first day of class, when he had introduced the students to the concept of prediction by doing an exercise called Future's Window (see the Active Exercise in Chapter 7). In this activity, students divide a piece of paper into quarters and label the top half "Self" and the bottom half "World." The left side of each half is labeled "5 Years," and the right half represents "20 Years" into the future. Students are then asked to make at least five entries in each quadrant, things they expect themselves to have accomplished or to be dealing with in 5 years and in 20 years, and things they expect the world to be confronting in 5 and 20 years. Students do this activity at first by themselves and then with two or three others. They have about 10 minutes to come up with a compilation of the groups' responses to the activity, after which the whole class discusses what they have generated. Tom remembers that the list generated by this class was typical:

Self

5 Years	20 Years
In college	Well into my career
Own a car	Have a graduate degree
Married	Married, with children
Have a good job	Traveled overseas
Live on my own	Own a business
Have a good stereo	Own a vacation home
Graduated from college	

World

5 Years	20 Years
More pollution and global warming	Still polluted
Increase in AIDS	Cure for AIDS
Many conflicts and war	Human beings on Mars
Decrease in crime	World hunger still a problem
Homelessness still a problem	Still many people without homes and work
Nuclear arms in the hands of terrorists	
Spread of antibiotic-resistant viruses	Nuclear explosions have occurred in a few places on the planet
Another Chernobyl-like disaster	Criminals more sophisticated

He also remembers that, like most students this age, this class had a hard time realizing that there was a connection between their own lives and the life of the larger community and world. He remembers that not one of the Roma contributed to the discussion and that only one girl said anything at all. How different they are now!

Tom's eyes glance at a page in his journal and he recalls the day, about a month after school started, when he saw Steven's mother standing in the hall watching the class through the partially open door. He had invited her in and she came, somewhat hesitatingly, saying that she only wanted to see that Steven and the other two students from their community were all right. Tom didn't know at the time that she had been one of the first parents involved in the Spokane outreach to Romani children. In fact, it had been Steven's mother and grandmother who had been primarily responsible for convincing the entire community that "those school people" could be trusted with their children.

Tom also remembered the day that all his careful work to create collaborative working relationships in the class was almost destroyed. For several months, Tom had noticed that many of the students had been avoiding one of their peers, a young man named Kurt. Although he was not overtly excluded from participation in class activities, the boys interacted with him only when necessary and did not include him in the informal conversation and laughter that was often a part of their group work. One rainy Saturday morning in November, Tom had taken Kurt with a group of other boys out to the land area behind the school to finish identifying and tagging trees. In dividing the group into pairs, Tom put Kurt with Jimmy, who immediately objected, saying he would rather work with two other boys. Not paying too much attention, Tom told him that since the work would be accomplished much faster if they divided up and since it was raining and they all wanted to get inside, he'd appreciate it if Jimmy would just go along with Kurt and get to work. He was totally unprepared for Jimmy's loud reaction: "I'm not going off alone with that fag, and you can't make me!"

There was a dead silence in the group. All eyes were down except Jimmy's, who stared defiantly at Tom. Tom looked around the group and said, "Okay guys, I guess there is something more important going on here than cataloging trees. Let's go into the school and see if we can sort this out." Somewhat reluctantly the boys followed him into their classroom where they spent the rest of the day talking about what had happened and what they were going to do about it. Tom had told them two things: (1) he was not going to tolerate homophobic (or any other kind of) name-calling; and (2) since it seems likely that homosexuality has a biological basis, hating a person because of sexual orientation was a lot like hating someone because he or she had brown eyes, or was left-handed, or was very tall. Thinking about it now, Tom knew that the discussion didn't change the boys' minds and hearts all at once—homophobia is too emotional and too strong for that. But he did think that the air had been cleared, and in fact, several of the boys were intrigued to learn that sexual orientation was not a simple matter of sexual choice. Afterward, there had been no more name-calling, and Kurt's expertise with the computer earned the admiration of his classmates. He even wrote some programs that enabled the class to classify their data more easily. Although Jimmy was still obviously antagonistic toward Kurt, and Ian and Steven looked at him now and then with some distrust, most of the class seemed to accept him as just another member of the class, and several had become his good friends.

Tom thought about many other incidents during the year: the day the students had finally settled on the three basic goals of the class that were now hanging on the wall; the time Rebecca's father had joined them on one of their field explorations and had told them the name and habits of every bird they saw; the excitement generated by a group of four girls who had been the first to identify the source of the cloudy water; the time Eric had told Penny that she should take the notes in a class meeting because she was a girl; the arguments and the discoveries made by each student in collaboration with others. It had certainly not been a perfect year, but it had been a good one.

And now they were almost ready to present their case to the school board. Tom didn't see how they could fail. In fact, he thought, even if the school board refuses to act on their request, nothing can stop their interest in their project now.

Case Analysis

Tom Littleton's class and its land lab provide numerous examples of a collaborative and **gender-sensitive** classroom in action. It also illustrates the importance of dealing effectively with nonacademic problems that threaten the existence of a learning-community atmosphere. Key elements of a collaborative learning environment that are evident in Tom's classroom include the following.

1. Students have been encouraged to work together on a project that they helped design. During the year, each student had an opportunity to work with others on a variety of tasks that were part of a larger group goal.

2. The use of collaborative teaching and learning has encouraged the girls in the class to think of themselves as equal partners in the group endeavor.

3. Other adults (teachers and parents) have been encouraged to bring their own expertise and experience into the classroom for students' benefit.

4. By combining his own knowledge with that of collaborating teachers, Tom has been able to show how solving real-world problems requires integrating knowledge from a variety of subject areas. His nature study project required measurements and calculations (math); report writing (English); consideration of social, political, and economic issues (social studies); and the preparation of drawings and displays (art).

5. Students have been actively involved in setting their own goals and in planning strategies for accomplishing them.

6. Students have learned how specialized tasks, such as testing water and writing up the results of the tests, are interdependent subgoals that are part of a larger, more holistic goal.

7. Students have learned that their individual successes depend, in part, on the successes of those with whom they are working.

As he reflected on the goals that he had set for this particular class, especially those related to gender and cultural difference, Tom Littleton realized that he needed more than biological and environmental knowledge: he needed a firm grasp on the basis of collaborative teaching and learning. Furthermore, he realized now how closely related such issues as gender and cultural difference are to both in-school and out-of school learning. In this chapter we discuss issues of collaborative learning, gender, sexual orientation, and education from a variety of perspectives, including the differences between collaborative and traditional teaching and learning, the importance of socialization to gender roles, the relation of middle-class values to the creation of gender identity, and the role of the school as a gender-socializing agent.

Rationale for Collaborative Teaching and Learning

The rationale for collaborative teaching and learning rests on many of the same ideas as does the rationale for democratic communities of learners and developmentally appropriate and inclusive classrooms. In addition, support for increasing collaboration in schools and classrooms emerges from two other major sources.

First, as has been said throughout this text, we are members of an interdependent global economic and political community, and many theorists suggest that we must learn to live cooperatively with one another rather than continue to engage in the kinds of destructive competition that produce hunger, disease, and war. As the world's population increases, issues such as natural resources, food, and human problem solving become critical. We must choose between competing for such resources, which has been a major cause of war, and sharing them, which means cooperative efforts at problem solving. Some of the traditional values espoused by the mainstream culture in the United States (e.g., individualism, materialism, an emphasis on technology) may be intensifying rather than ameliorating the major problems we confront (e.g., global warming, preservation of the environment, increasing poverty, and loss of community). Solutions to such complex social problems demand collaboration and cooperation.

A second and very different source of support for collaborative classrooms emerges from 30 years of research on gender and on the degree to which boys and girls have different experiences in school. Such research suggests two important points: (1) girls and women tend to focus on preserving relationships whereas boys and men tend to focus on principles of behavior (Gilligan, 1982; Noddings, 1984); and (2) girls and women tend to learn more effectively when collaboration rather than competition is central to the teaching-learning process (Belenky, Clinchy, Goldberger, & Tarule, 1986; Clinchy, Belenky, Goldberger, & Tarule, 1985). This research is discussed in more detail later in the chapter. The point to be made here is that gender researchers have developed instructional models based on classroom collaboration and cooperation rather than competition and that these models are currently available for classroom use.

Both of these rationales for collaborative classrooms suggest a shift away from the values of individualism and competition that are so deeply woven into both our political and our economic culture and the school curricula that transmit that culture. Although teachers and the school curriculum are not the only means of socializing youngsters, they are critical elements in helping students attain the understanding and the skills needed to live cooperatively and comfortably with others.

Characteristics of a Collaborative Classroom

Collaborative Classrooms

Fortunately, teachers, parents, and supporting school personnel are beginning to recognize both the opportunity and the obligation they have to effect change toward more collaborative classrooms.

First, although competition is not absent from collaborative classrooms (nor should it be), cooperation and collaboration are woven throughout both instructional and evaluative processes. Similarly, while group activities and group performance are clearly in evidence, individual acquisition of knowledge and skills and individual performance are still stressed. Indeed, one of the primary goals of collaboration is the enhancement of individual learning. In U.S. schools, competition has often been blindly equated with rigor and quality, both of which are regarded as exemplifying American values of hard work and individual achievement. When a competitive environment threatens classroom equity, however, it becomes problematic. Clearly, we need both. As John Goodlad (1984) correctly predicted more than 20 years ago, "Equality and quality are the name of the game. These two concepts will frame dialogue, policy, and practice regarding schooling for years to come" (p. 45).

Second, collaborative classrooms involve teachers and other school personnel, parents, and other community members working together to plan and implement instructional goals. In traditional schools, teaching is often a lonely activity that involves little or no interaction with other adults. This isolation is unfortunate on many accounts, not the least of which is that in order to grow professionally, teachers must work in collaboration with others. By observing other teachers in their classrooms, teachers gain new ideas, fresh strategies, and new perspectives on their professional lives.

Third, because teachers in collaborative classrooms work closely with other adults in the school, many of whom have different areas of expertise, lessons and other activities tend to benefit from the integration of different disciplines and skills. Students thus begin to see connections between the subjects they study and their learning gains relevancy.

Fourth, collaborative classrooms also extend beyond the school, most obviously to the home. Interest in home–school collaboration, often referred to as "parent involvement," initially emerged from concerns about increased student failure and dropout rates among minority groups, particularly in immigrant families, many of whom were unfamiliar with the culture and practices of U.S. schools. In truly collaborative classrooms, however, the involvement of parents is perceived as central to effective education, not as a response to difficulties in an otherwise effective schooling system. In short, parents are regarded as the child's first and continuing teachers and, as such, are natural partners in a collaborative relationship with classroom teachers.

Finally, in collaborative classrooms students cooperate with one another in planning their activities. Students may be organized (or organize themselves) in project teams or in dyads and triads, depending on the nature of the work to be done. The assumption here is that students bring to school useful knowledge from a variety of backgrounds and experiences and that they are competent to assist one another in acquiring new knowledge.

Pedagogies: Old and New

Schools have always sponsored a variety of collaborative activities. Think, for example, of sports teams, choirs, dramatic productions, and school newspapers and yearbooks, not to mention a wide variety of social and fund-raising activities carried out by students and teachers. Each of these activities requires the skills of teamwork, cooperation, and interdependence. However, each of these activities is also either co-curricular or extracurricular.

In collaborative classrooms the teaching processes and strategies so necessary to co-curricular and extracurricular activities are applied to the very heart of schooling itself; that is, to the formal curriculum. Teachers find themselves working together to plan units and often teach in teams. One excellent example of this collaboration is a middle school in which four teachers have 100 students. During the course of the school day, one teacher may be working with all 100 students while the other three meet to plan future lessons. At other times each teacher may be working with 25 students on separate aspects of a unit. The possible combinations of teachers and students, as well as the possible uses of time, are really unlimited.

One of the most widely known pedagogical strategies found in most collaborative classrooms is called *cooperative learning*. Like other instructional strategies, cooperative learning encompasses a variety of instructional techniques. In general, cooperative learning environments are characterized by what is called *positive goal interdependence*. That is, individuals share the same group goals, and members of the group are accountable to one another. In short, the group sinks or swims together as it works in concert in the attainment of a particular instructional goal. Group cohesiveness thus becomes paramount in the attainment of the specific instructional objective or goal.

In discussing his interest in cooperative learning, Kagan (1989-1990) related some findings from his early research on children's play in Mexico. One finding that intrigued him was that children from rural parts of Mexico were more cooperative with one another than were their peers in urban settings. Somewhat bothered by this finding, Kagan extended his work to look at cooperation and competition among children in other parts of the world. What he discovered appears to be nearly universal and has to do with differences between students who live in rural and urban areas. That is, worldwide, regardless of the continent or culture, children in urban environments are more competitive than their rural counterparts. This finding, coupled with the fact that the world is becoming increasingly urban, raised considerable concern in Kagan's mind. Out of fear that the social character of the nation and world would become increasingly competitive, Kagan began exploring ways to help reverse the tendency children had to become more competitive with age. He found that using cooperative teams in the classroom, often referred to as cooperative learning, worked quite well.

Slavin (1995) and Cooper and Slavin (2004) identified two factors that seem to account for the effectiveness of cooperative learning. The first is that cooperative groups must work to achieve a group goal that cannot be mastered unless each member performs his or her assigned task. The second critical factor is that each individual in the group must still be held accountable for learning the required content. That is, members must work together to make certain that all have mastered the assigned content and have earned satisfactory grades or other forms of recognition. The group's success depends on each individual learning the required material. Evidence of group success might be seen in the sum of the individual members' test scores or in the presentation of a group report. In other words, each individual in the group must have differentiated tasks whose successful performance is critical to achieving the group goal. Secondary characteristics of cooperative learning include an emphasis on face-to-face interpersonal interaction, development of social skills, and group reviews that help members analyze how well they are functioning.

Cooperative learning groups may be used to teach specific content (information or skills), to ensure active cognitive processing of information during a lecture, or to provide long-term support and assistance for academic progress. Basically, any assignment in any curriculum area for a student of any age can be accommodated through cooperative learning.

Cooperative learning does not imply either devaluation of individual contributions or lack of individual accountability. Instead, when individuals of diverse

cultural backgrounds and differing physical characteristics have the opportunity to work together in pursuit of a common goal, the barriers of stereotype that prevent people from knowing each other as individuals are likely to be broken down. Friendships are more likely to form. Individual accountability is explicitly addressed in cooperative learning strategies in either of two ways: *task specialization,* or determination of *group scores* for team assignments, or both.

Task specialization, or assignment of a specific subtask to each member of a team or group, is particularly effective in ensuring that students with disabilities, for example, contribute significantly to the group effort. In some instances, a student with a disability may be uniquely able to carry out a certain task because students with physical, academic, cognitive, or emotional-behavioral differences are also people with *abilities*. Thus, not only can the self-image and identity of students with disabilities be enhanced, but all students can, through firsthand experience, realize this fundamental truth.

The corollary to collaborative learning, of course, is collaborative teaching, which refers to interactions among students who are teaching one another, to interactions between teachers and students, and to interactions between teachers engaged in collaborative efforts. In classrooms where collaboration is the norm, teachers do some of the talking but are not necessarily the center of attention even the majority of the time. Students work in teams, discuss issues, engage in group problem solving, and help one another understand the material at hand. Teachers and other adults work with students by encouraging them to inquire, to reflect, and to share and modify ideas (Thousand et al., 2002).

Roles: Old and New

The traditional roles of teacher as teller and student as listener change in a collaborative classroom. Rather than always being the expert, the teacher often acts as coach, encouraging and assisting students to complete the assigned tasks. Students also serve as coaches for one another and, not infrequently, find themselves acting as experts in particular areas. One of the most obvious examples of this phenomenon is the native Spanish, French, or German speaker in a foreign-language classroom. There are, however, many other ways in which students of all ages can provide expert knowledge and skills to their fellow students. For instance, the student who actively uses the computer at home or one who has a well-developed skill in playing a musical instrument can become active as a peer-tutor in these areas.

One of the most important role changes in a collaborative classroom, however, is that of parents. In traditional elementary classrooms, parents ordinarily serve in various "motherly" capacities, such as providing goods for a bake sale, bringing treats on birthdays, and acting as planners for holiday celebrations. Parents also are expected to ensure that homework assignments are completed and to attend open houses and parent-teacher conferences. In traditional middle and high school classrooms, the role of parents is often limited to these latter functions.

In collaborative classrooms, however, parents (and grandparents, and other community members with some interest or expertise) are often central to the instructional program, helping to make and implement curricular and instructional decisions. For example, parents and others may take an active role in elementary reading instruction by organizing various small group activities. Or they may work with small groups of students in math-related activities, thus providing greater opportunity for children to be actively engaged in classroom content.

It is not always easy to encourage such collaboration. Indeed, McCaleb (1994) has explored various reasons for the lack of parental involvement particularly among nondominant groups. One reason she offers for a lack of involvement among minority parents centers on the perceived inequality between students from non–standard English home environments and students from the dominant culture. She argues that most young children, understandably, identify strongly with their families–their primary teachers. If students happen to come from families with minimal or no schooling or if the educational experience of parents differs significantly from that which is normally experienced by the American middle class, children quickly sense the contradictions between their home and school lives. Seeing many books at school, for example, and few at home, they may begin to question their own potential for educational success. A similarly negative self-attribution may be made by parents if they, in turn, believe that they have little to teach or share with their children. In Hawaii, however, a successful curricular innovation involves grandparents and other community elders regularly coming into elementary classrooms to teach children Hawaiian culture and language from their traditionally oral approach.

The situation in which many immigrant families find themselves may be another obstacle to parent collaboration, particularly if parents do not speak English and if they are unfamiliar with the somewhat pervasive role that American schools play in the lives of children. Families in which parents are linguistically isolated, defined as those in which no family member 14 years of age or older speaks English very well, (Kids Count, 2007), are families in which teachers will have to reach out to parents to encourage them to become involved in the classroom.

Greenspan, Niemeyer, and Seeley (1991) conducted a study of how principals perceived parental involvement in school affairs. They cite four reasons for the lack of parental involvement in schools.

1. *A significant transient population.* Many schools have children whose families move frequently, thus forcing their children to attend new schools.

2. *Alienation between the home and school.* Social class differences, for one, tend to separate families from teachers and administrators. Such differences may be accentuated by racial factors. Most of the principals interviewed for the study, however, concurred that poor parents were just as concerned about education and wanted the same things for their children (a good education, good behavior, respect for authority) as other parents. What they did not understand was how to assist their children in attaining these goals.

3. *School-generated problems.* In some instances teachers and other school staff are simply insensitive to the needs and problems of students and their families.

4. *Disintegration of the family.* The researchers inferred this point from the large number of children who seem to be cared for by adults other than their natural parents. McCaleb (1994), on the other hand, suggests that the perceived "broken family" issue might be a classic case of misunderstanding and misattribution. She suggests that such nonparental caring arrangements do not represent a disintegration of the family but rather a reinterpretation of the concept "family" because many of these families consist of an extended network of caregivers.

To summarize, in collaborative classrooms parents and other community members share with teachers and other school staff the responsibility for educating children. This partnership model views parents as resources and contributors to the education of their children and helps integrate the school and the community. Oakes and Lipton (2003) suggest that real changes in schools will take place only when the relationships of power begin to change and when the voices and concerns of parents and the community are heard, engaged with, and acted upon.

Place of Content Knowledge: Old and New

In collaborative classrooms where teachers, parents, other school personnel, and students work together, boundaries between academic disciplines tend to become less defined as cooperative teams pool their knowledge in the pursuit of integrated projects. As teachers learn about what other teachers are doing, they begin to see ways of integrating their efforts. In such classrooms, the language arts and social studies may begin to merge, and the arts may be put to use in the service of scientific and geographical knowledge.

A good example of this "blurring" of disciplinary boundaries is given by Charles Fowler (1994). He writes:

> If, for example, students are studying the Grand Canyon, and we want to give them a general idea of it without actually going there, we often resort to a verbal description: "The Grand Canyon, the world's largest gorge, is a spectacle of multicolored layers of rock carved out over the millennia by the Colorado River." If we want to convey its vastness, we use measurements: "The Grand Canyon is over 1 mile deep, 4 to 18 miles wide, and more than 200 miles long." Each of these

symbolic systems—words and numbers—permits us to reveal important aspects, but a picture or a painting can be equally telling.

The arts—creative writing, dance, music, theater/film, and visual arts—serve as ways that we react to, record, and share our impressions of the world. Students can be asked to set forth their own interpretation of the Grand Canyon, using, say, poetry as the communicative vehicle. While mathematics gives us precise quantitative measures of magnitude, poetry explores our disparate personal reactions. Both views are valid. Both contribute to understanding. Together, they prescribe a larger overall conception of, in this case, one of nature's masterpieces. (pp. 4–5)

In a collaborative classroom, content knowledge not only becomes something to be learned but, more important, becomes something meaningful to students who learn to make connections between areas of knowledge that, after all, blend together in the world outside school.

Assessment: Old and New

Methods of evaluating student performance should be compatible with the types of learning activities that characterize a particular classroom. For example, traditional forms of evaluation such as standardized paper-and-pencil tests, answering questions posed by the teacher in a large group format, and student reports all seek to determine what and how much students "know" about a particular subject such as math or English. Each evaluation assumes that subject matter knowledge can be "given" to students who are then able to "give" such knowledge back as a sign that it has been learned. Perhaps the most efficient form of instruction for transmitting subject matter knowledge is that in which teachers talk and students listen, read, and are evaluated on the degree to which they have retained what they have heard and read.

In collaborative classrooms, however, learning is less dependent on teacher talk and more dependent on group activities (projects, problem-solving situations, study groups) that take place over time. In such classrooms compatible evaluation techniques are those that measure performance over time, such as the creation of artifacts and portfolios and demonstrations of individual and group problem-solving ability. Although all these evaluation techniques will be discussed in more detail in Chapter 13, the point to make here is that these forms of assessment are a good match with instructional methods that emphasize collaborative teaching and learning.

With the currently mandated standardized testing contained in the No Child Left Behind law, some of these assessment methods are being questioned by both teachers and parents, who may see them as irrelevant when the only thing that really counts is test scores. However, most experts in evaluation and assessment suggest that assessment must go beyond standardized tests. Assessments, for example, should (1) include a variety of techniques, (2) encourage students to go beyond simple recall of data or facts, (3) close the gap between the classroom and the real world, and (4) include opportunities for students to perform tasks and solve problems.

Indeed, as we move further into the 21st century, models of assessment from around the world are increasingly of interest to American educators. Indeed, a number of high-performing countries have done away with the kind of standardized, relatively low-level testing system used in the United States and replace it with "highly trained teachers and curriculum and assessments focused on problem solving, creativity, independent learning and student reflection" (Finnish National

Board of Education (2007, November 12); Lavonen, (2008). As states in America seek to create world-class educational systems, the kind of collaborative classroom described in this chapter may become more the norm than the exception, and both teaching and assessments in those classrooms will change.

Activity 21:
**Gender Role
Socialization**

Perspectives on Gender Identity

One of Tom Littleton's first goals for his science class was to systematically encourage girls to enroll in and to participate actively in the class. His goal stems from the realization that science is often not considered a "suitable" subject for girls and that girls often do not take higher level science classes in high school for that reason, thus effectively preventing them from pursuing the sciences in

college. The reasons for this state of affairs are many and complicated, but central to all of them is the reality of **gender role socialization.**

One of the earliest and most important learning experiences in any society is the development of a sense of self-identity–the knowledge that one is separate from mother, father, and family. This perception begins when an infant is 7 or 8 months old and continues throughout an individual's life. It is not unusual for a person's sense of identity to undergo significant changes as new experiences are encountered during the course of that person's life.

An extremely important part of an individual's identity, and one that begins at least at birth, is gender. It is thought that identification in terms of sex begins at about 18 months of age and by the age of 3 is clearly internalized. But sexual identity is more complex than simply "knowing" that you are male or female. More important to your sense of self is your identification as a member of a gender group–"I am a girl"; "I am a boy." Whereas sex is a biological characteristic, gender is a social one. In all cultural groups, gender identity includes knowledge of a large set of rules and expectations for what boys and girls should wear, how they should speak and act, and their "place" in the overall structure of society. Knowledge of these rules is knowledge of our role as a member of a particular gender group and provides us with the ability to deal with many social situations without having to stop each time to figure out what to do. Gender role identity, however, also limits us in terms of our range of choices and, sometimes, the very quality of our lives.

Gender Role Socialization

The rules associated with a person's gender role may vary by race, ethnicity, social class, religion, and even geographical region. Such socialization takes place in a variety of different ways, many of them small and incremental–simple routines of daily life and language. Early in the study of gender roles, Weitzman (1975) described the process of such learning as having three parts:

1. The child learns to *distinguish* between men and women, and between boys and girls, and to know what kinds of behavior are characteristic of each.

2. The child learns to express appropriate gender role *preferences* for him- or herself.

3. The child learns to *behave* in accordance with gender role standards. (p. 109)

Although this process of internalizing knowledge of and identification with gender role is a part of all children's lives, it has been most studied in the lives of middle-class white children, especially girls. This concentration is significant for at least two reasons. First, it reflects the predominant characteristics of the researchers themselves, many of whom have been not only white, middle-class university scholars but also feminists interested in rediscovering the reality of women's lives. Because the focus has been on girls, the consequences of gender role socialization on boys, which are great, often have been minimized.

Second, studies primarily located in the white middle class have reflected the dominant social group in the United States. Because dominance is often equated with universality, norms related to the gender role socialization of middle-class whites are often thought to apply to *all* American girls and boys–indeed, to *all* girls and boys everywhere. Researchers who have looked at gender role socialization in terms of racial, ethnic, religious, and national groups over the last 30 years have discovered significant differences in value and orientation between white, middle-class socialization practices and those of other groups. This finding is important because the role of the school in teaching gender role attitudes and behavior is second only to the role of the family. Schools normally represent the **dominant culture,** and gender role is no exception. Thus schools often unconsciously attempt to "mold" boys and girls into dominant (white, middle-class) gender roles while ignoring the different orientations and behaviors regarding gender that students bring with them to school.

Gender Role Socialization in the Middle Class

For American families, differences in socialization practices for boys and girls are many and obvious. More than 30 years ago, Howe (1974) described some of them in the following way. See whether you think things have changed all that much:

> We throw boy babies up in the air and roughhouse with them. We coo over girl babies and handle them delicately. We choose sex related colors and toys for our children from their earliest days. We encourage the energy and physical activity of our sons, just as we expect girls to be quieter and more docile. We love both our sons and daughters with equal fervor, we protest, and yet we are disappointed when there is no male child to carry on the family name. (p. 27)

Kramer (1988) has suggested a number of socialization agents in early childhood that reflect middle-class values, and these, too, have remained relatively constant. The first, of course, is parents. Studies have demonstrated not only that infant boys are handled more roughly than their sisters and that infant girls receive more verbal attention, but also that young boys are given more freedom to explore than are young girls, who are often kept closer to the supervising parent. In addition, girls receive more help on tasks than do boys, who are encouraged to "figure it out for yourself." Research also shows that parental reaction to the behavior of their children tends to be more favorable when girls and boys are behaving in ways traditionally associated with their gender (Dronsberg, Fagot, Hagan, & Lleinback, 1985; Fagot, 1978). Thus parents shape the expectations and abilities of their children not only by overt behavior but also by rewarding them with approval when they behave "appropriately."

Gender Role Socialization in Popular Culture, Books, and Toys

In contrast to the usually more traditional socializing influence of the family is another powerful socializing agent–television. Although there is much that is still stereotypical about the images of boys and girls and women and men on television– particularly the sexual images on networks such as MTV–there has been a significant change in the nature of gender role images to be found in commercials. Indeed, males and females of all ages are shown in roles unheard of even 15 years ago: young women are competing in sports, and young men are taking care of their infants in a variety of commercial messages. Similarly, this kind of change can also be seen in the roles played by older people on television commercials, who are, today, climbing mountains, fording streams in the wild, and going on cruises rather than sitting on front porches telling stories to their grandchildren.

It is still the case, however, that images of girls and boys on television, in video games, on music videos, and in movies provide strong messages about gender. In May of 2007, the National Organization for Women surveyed parents, other caregivers, teachers, and, indeed, anyone who cares about children, looking for feedback on the influence of media and pop culture on raising children today (Grunberg, 2007). The survey suggested five major challenges related to the gender socialization of both boys and girls:

1. Media's sexualization of young female performers/celebrities.
2. Marketing of unrealistic beauty standards through fashion magazines and the beauty/diet industry.
3. Video games that promote violence and negative stereotypes.
4. Music lyrics and music videos that promote negative stereotypes and violence.
5. Sex stereotypes in kids' TV programs and movies.

At the very least, we can say that media messages regarding gender are mixed: Dora the Explorer as a role model for little girls when they are 4 years old competes with the Disney Princesses, and they morph into the Bratz line of dolls-with-an-attitude at 8, and the slightly ditzy Hannah Montana at 12. After that, it's on to the larger pop culture. For boys, Diego or the Little Einsteins' Quincy and Leo give way to alien action figures like transformers or movie characters from *Pirates of the Caribbean,* and after that it's pretty much the NFL, the NBA, and major league baseball. In all cases, popular culture has a lot to say about gender roles.

A third influence on young children's development of gender role identity is children's books. Although many nonsexist books are being published today, the classics are still read with enthusiasm. Traditional fairy tales, such as Cinderella, Little Red Riding Hood, Snow White and Rose Red, and Sleeping Beauty present "heroines" who are browbeaten, tricked, chased, put to sleep by wicked witches (another ever-popular female character), and/or eaten. Release from such vicissitudes, when it occurs, is always at the hands of a (handsome) young man who finally shows up at the end of the story to whisk the young girl away on *his* horse, to live out her days in *his* castle (Kolbenschlag, 1981).

A fourth important gender socializer of children is toys. If the inclination of parents and relatives to buy "gender-appropriate" toys is not sufficient to the task, manufacturers provide on their packaging useful clues to the gender of the child expected to use the toy. This influence also extends to the placing of such toys in store aisles. Go to any large toy store and observe the placement of toys (and colors of the signs) for girls and boys. Ordinarily, blocks, cars, trains, manipulative games, chemistry sets, doctor's kits, work tools, building games, and of course, balls of all kinds show boys on the package. Dolls, kitchen or cleaning toys, needlework, craft, or sewing equipment, and nurse's kits show girls on the package. No matter how many Barbie dolls come with briefcases, astronaut helmets, and computers, Barbie is still a *very* well-endowed young lady who is very much into clothes, and who has been known to say that "Math is hard!"

Boys' toys are relatively more complex, more varied, and more expensive than girls' toys and frequently have no counterpart for girls. Consider, for example, the range of remote-control cars, boats, and airplanes for sale as well as electronic sports and adventure games that are marketed for boys. Take a look at a store that sells electronic games for boys and girls in the preteen years: there are a wide variety of action-oriented games (jungle adventures, space travel) for boys and a good many Barbie dress-designing games, Disney Princess games, Fashion Girls, and, for the Wii Cooking Mania and Hannah Montana, plus the occasional Nancy Drew mystery game for girls of the same age. There is no *law* preventing parents and others from buying cross-gender toys, but most people still feel a bit uncomfortable doing so. Even in the 21st century, we buy toy lawn mowers for little boys and toy shopping carts for little girls, and seldom do the reverse.

Other socializing influences of young children may be found in a variety of everyday places and activities. From nursery rhymes we learn that young girls are frightened of spiders and that young boys are nimble and quick. In Bible stories we observe that young boys are brave and able to do away with giants, whereas women have a tendency toward evil actions such as cutting off a man's hair and robbing him of his strength. From familiar proverbs and sayings we become aware that objectionable behavior on the part of boys sometimes must be excused on the grounds that "boys will be boys" (did you ever hear "girls will be girls"?) and that "it's a man's world." And from children's songs we learn that John Henry built a railroad while Suzannah was waiting for her young man to return from Louisiana.

Masculine and Feminine Behavior

If middle-class gender roles seem to limit girls more than boys, it may be only that our society favors the active, the adventurous, and the aggressive and that

Activity 22:
**Observing Gender
Differences**

those traits are largely associated with boys. However, there is a high price to be paid by boys for all their "freedom." First of all, boys are socialized much earlier to what is perceived to be "manly." A girl who participates in boys' activities, plays with boys' toys, is impatient with dresses and ribbons and lace, and in general eschews "girlish" things is called a "tomboy" and is regarded with some tolerance by most adults, at least until adolescence. At that point, according to conventional wisdom, chances are good that she will "grow out of it." At the same time, from the age of 3 onward, boys who want to play with dolls, spend time with their mothers in the kitchen, cry easily, like to stay clean, and avoid contact sports are called "sissies"–a much more negative label. Adults viewing such behavior even in very young boys often become enormously uncomfortable and worried that "he is moving in the wrong direction." Adult intervention in these "girlish" activities is usually swift, direct, and unmistakable.

Second, boys are punished much more harshly for deviation from the norms of "masculine" behavior. Moreover, such punishment occurs at an age when they are too young to really understand the source of their "problem" or the reasons for adult distress. To make matters more difficult, the desired behavior is rarely defined positively as something the child *should* do; rather, undesirable behavior is indicated negatively as something he should *not* do or be–anything, that is, that the parent or other people regard as "sissy." Thus very early in life the boy must either stumble on the right path or bear repeated punishment without warning when he accidentally enters the wrong one.

One result of this socialization is that boys very early come to regard anything having to do with girls' play and behavior as something to be avoided at all costs, and this attitude increases during the elementary years until most boys would rather "drop dead" than play with girls. Thus little is done to alter practices

that lead to separation of the sexes and the masculine disdain for the "feminine," which often lasts a lifetime.

That such lessons are well learned is without doubt, and little has changed in the responses of a representative group of boys (8 and 10 years old) when asked to describe what boys and girls have to be able to know and do (Hartley, 1974). Boys, they said,

> have to be able to fight in case a bully comes along; they have to be athletic; they have to be able to run fast; they must be able to play rough games; they need to know how to play many games—curb-ball, baseball, basketball, football; they need to be smart; they need to be able to take care of themselves; they should know what girls don't know—how to climb, how to make a fire, how to carry things; they should have more ability than girls . . . they are expected to be noisy; to get dirty; to mess up the house; to be naughty; to be "outside" more than girls are; not to be cry-babies; not to be "softies;" not to be "behind" like girls are; and to get into trouble more than girls do. (p. 90)

Thinking about the roles boys must assume, it is hard not to question, with Hartley, "not why boys have difficulty with this role, but why they try as hard as they do to fulfill it" (p. 27).

Perspectives on Gender and Schooling

One answer to why boys try hard to fulfill their role is that gender roles are **normative**–that is, the ideas about what attitudes, values, and behavior are associated with sex or gender have been coded by the social group into norms or, often, stereotypes. A *norm* is a rule of conduct based on attitudes and values that are usually internalized through socialization until they become "of course" statements.

Schools as Socializing Agents

Schools have an important though little discussed function as socializers to societal norms, particularly those associated with the middle class. Because these norms are so much a part of what most people in schools believe is correct, they seem "normal" and "right" and are usually taken very much for granted. That sense of "normality" is probably the most powerful force operating to encourage obedience to norms. However, other factors are involved in encouraging normative thought and behavior as well. In all societies, there are *sanctions,* or punishments, for deviation from norms.

These sanctions operate in schools on a daily basis, and most of them are particularly *social* sanctions. Consider again, for example, that girls may avoid taking advanced science or math classes because they don't want boys to think they're "too smart." The assumption of some girls is that the boys will "sanction" them socially for appearing to compete with them academically. Or consider the overt social sanctioning of boys who are gay by those boys who are straight, which is perhaps the most intense sanctioning that occurs. A number of lesser normative rules are broken every day in schools, by both males and females, and it appears that as gender roles change (which they are doing, but slowly), the social sanctions are also becoming less severe. Nevertheless, the power of gender role stereotypes is enormous and frequently costly to both males and females.

Gender Stereotypes in School

Although it is slowly changing, in our society, **gender role stereotyping** most often includes the belief that boys and men are (and should be) aggressive, independent, strong, logical, direct, adventurous, self-confident, ambitious, and not particularly emotional. Girls and women are passive, weak, illogical, indirect, gentle, and very emotional. Boys, the stereotypes say, are good at math and science, and girls are good at language and writing. Boys are loud and girls are quiet. Girls play with dolls and boys play with balls. Although it is true that not every single boy or girl believes or adheres to these stereotypes, it is generally true that *society,* in part through schooling, attempts to enforce them. Moreover, these stereotypes are reinforced even in the face of contrary evidence, such as the fact that girls and women are now participating in nearly every aspect of life once "owned" by boys and men.

Gender role stereotypes vary not only in their content but also in the value ascribed to the content. In other words, not only are boys and men perceived to be *different* from girls and women, but their learned behavior is generally more highly valued. Thus gender role stereotypes are the basis for **genderized traits,** traits that any person may be *able* to display but that are assigned value when displayed by people of the appropriate sex. Often, these stereotypes are genderized in favor of men because many of the personality traits valued by society— think of self-reliance, adventurousness, ambition, and directness—are those traits that quite often are socialized into boys and not girls. Gender role stereotypes are hard on males as well, but in a somewhat different way.

As the women's movement has succeeded in opening up to women public roles that had been traditionally associated with men, women have learned to assume those roles more or less well, and the gender role socialization of young girls has changed somewhat to accommodate their broader life chances. The same is not as true of boys and men, although traditionally "women's work" careers such as nursing have opened up for men, and more men are being encouraged to think about early childhood and elementary education as a fulfilling career. In both areas, men are sorely needed and greatly appreciated!

Definitions of masculinity held by boys often are not based on what boys *should* do but rather on what they *should not* do, and that what they should not do is to be anything like a girl. Two forces in our society that help to enforce male and female stereotypes are misogyny and homophobia. Simply stated, **misogyny** is the hatred of women, and **homophobia** is the fear of homosexuality and homosexuals. Homophobia is the irrational fear or hatred of, aversion to, or discrimination against homosexuals or homosexual behavior. More specifically, homophobia is an irrational fear of feminine qualities in men, whereas misogyny is the hatred of feminine qualities in women. In both cases, the assumption is that feminine qualities are less valued, even contemptible.

There are, however, important distinctions between sex-role stereotypes, sex bias, and sex discrimination. *Stereotypes* are present whenever specific behaviors, abilities, interests, or values are attributed to one sex or another. Sex *bias* generally results from an underlying belief in sex-role stereotypes. And discrimination based on sex occurs when any action or rule or law denies opportunities, privileges, or rewards to members of a particular sex (Carelli, 1988).

Calling another boy a *fag* because he is exhibiting "female" qualities is an example of gender bias—an action based on gender role stereotypes. If that boy were prevented from, say, taking art classes on the grounds that drawing is a "feminine" activity and that all artists are fags, that would be gender discrimination because denying access to specific educational activities is against the law.

Clearly, the power of gender role stereotypes is great, and the cost is high for everyone: boys and girls, women and men. Gender role stereotypes serve to prevent girls and boys from having valuable human experiences; they limit growth and development both by denying such experiences and by creating anxiety in children. They also create social and institutional barriers against the development of interests, goals, and talents in young people that may be outside gender role "parameters." The human cost in terms of discouragement, sadness, fear, and alienation is incalculable. Gender role stereotypes also contribute to the organization of schooling and to the subtle and not-so-subtle messages that boys and girls absorb about their identities, their expectations, and their futures.

Gender as an Issue of Legal Equity in Schools

As with laws and court cases involving issues of race, language, and later, of disability, gender became a legal issue in Congress and the courts.

Legislation and Court Cases

Inspired by the civil rights movement during the 1960s and early 1970s, members of the women's movement began to pressure Congress to enact legislation that would guarantee equitable educational experience for girls and women. The result was Title IX of the Education Amendments of 1972. This statute was intended to prohibit discrimination in elementary and secondary schools on the basis of sex; its preamble reads:

> No person in the United States shall, on the basis of sex, be excluded from participation in, be denied the benefits of, or be subjected to discrimination under any education program or activity receiving federal financial assistance.

Not until 1975, however, were the rules and regulations enforcing Title IX published and sent to state departments of education and to school districts. In the interim, there was heated controversy; several bills were introduced in Congress to take the teeth out of the legislation (all of which were defeated); and many thousands of citizens sent in written comments. The initial government agency responsible for enforcing Title IX was the Department of Health and Human Services.

In 1980, the U.S. Department of Education was created, and the responsibility for Title IX was given to them through the Office of Civil Rights. All was not smooth sailing, however. In the now-famous *Grove City v. Bell* (1984) case, Grove City College in Pennsylvania attempted to evade compliance with Title IX (and all other civil rights mandates directed toward schools and colleges receiving federal funds) on the grounds that the college took no money from the federal government (although their students did receive college loans from the federal government). In 1984, the Supreme Court agreed with Grove City

College and removed the applicability of Title IX in athletics programs by finding that only those programs or activities that receive *direct* federal assistance can be held accountable to Title IX.

The victory was short-lived because in 1988 Congress passed the Civil Rights Restoration Act, overriding President Reagan's veto. This act overrode the decision in *Grove City v. Bell* by establishing that all educational institutions that receive *any* federal funding–direct or indirect–are bound by Title IX legislation. By 1990, the Office of Civil Rights of the U.S. Department of Education had published an investigation manual to aid in enforcement, and in 1994, Congress passed the Equity in Athletics Disclosure Act, which requires coeducational institutions of higher education to disclose, on an annual basis, information regarding its intercollegiate athletics program.

For the most part, regulation and interpretation of Title IX has affected middle school, high school, and college athletics programs. Lower courts have seen numerous cases involving the participation of girls in athletics, the requirement that expenditures on male and female athletic programs be "substantially" the same, and the canceling of boys' athletics programs to better balance expenditures on athletics. In most cases, Title IX has been enforced.

Other cases have been brought in the area of sexual harassment–both adult-and-student cases and student-and-student cases. Court decisions have been mixed in this area. For example, in two cases involving sexual harassment by teachers of students, the decisions were opposite. In *Franklin v. Gwinnett County Public Schools* (1992), the Supreme Court ruled that petitioners may claim punitive damages under Title IX when intentional action to prevent Title IX compliance is established. In *Alida Star Gebser and Alida Jean McCullough v. Lago Vista Independent School District* (1998), a California court denied compensatory and punitive damages from both the teacher involved and the school district. However, in the first student-on-student sexual harassment case to be decided successfully under Title IX in federal court–*Doe v. Petaluma Unified School District* (1995)–the plaintiff was awarded $250,000. Clearly, the whole story of unequal educational opportunity for girls has not been written, but progress has been made, particularly in athletics, under Title IX.

In 2005, the liability under Title IX was extended by the Supreme Court, allowing those who report violations of Title IX (usually school personnel) to sue for remedy against retaliation by school districts. In 2006, in an interesting reversal of position, however, the federal government–through the U.S. Department of Education–relaxed the rules governing single-sex education so that public school classes (and sometimes whole public schools) can create and maintain single-sex populations. Title IX has always allowed single-sex education under certain circumstances, but this ruling broadens those circumstances. Citing the need for flexibility, the Secretary of Education noted that:

> Research shows that some students may learn better in single-sex education environments. . . . The Department of Education is committed to giving communities more choices in how they go about offering varied learning environments to their students. These final regulations permit communities to establish single sex schools and classes as another means of meeting the needs of students. They also establish that enrollment in a single sex class should be a completely voluntary option for students and their families and they uphold the prohibitions against discrimination of Title IX. Every child should receive a high quality education in America and every school and district deserves the tools to provide it. (Spellings, 2006)

Contemporary Concerns About the Education of Boys

In part, the relaxation of Title IX regulations with respect to single-sex classes and schools reflects a concern among African American parents and all educators about the so-called achievement gap between white students and African American students, particularly boys. Currently, 91 completely single-sex public schools exist in the United States, and more than 5 times that many offer some single-sex classrooms (NASSPE, 2010). However, evidence for the improvement of the education of African American boys has been mixed (Cooper, 2006). On the other hand, there is considerable evidence, accumulated over the past 20 years, that single-sex education does benefit girls (Standen, 2007).

A second, and perhaps more compelling reason for interest in single-sex education is that it is put forth as one solution to the perception that there is a major crisis in the education of boys in general (Pollack, 1998; Slocumb, 2004; Sommers, 2000). Fueled by major "reports" in national news magazines (Tyre, 2006; Von Drehle, 2007), this perception has grown so fast and spread so far that, as David Berliner and Bruce Biddle (1995) noted in another context, "Lots of intelligent people believe things that aren't true" (p. 9). A widely quoted *Newsweek* article (Tyre, 2006), for example, cites the following argument:

> By almost every benchmark, boys across the nation and in every demographic group are falling behind. In elementary school, boys are two times more likely than girls to be diagnosed with learning disabilities and twice as likely to be placed in special-education classes. High-school boys are losing ground to girls on standardized writing tests. The number of boys who said they didn't like school rose 71 percent between 1980 and 2001, according to a University of Michigan study. Nowhere is the shift more evident than on college campuses. Thirty years ago men represented 58 percent of the undergraduate student body. Now they're a minority at 44 percent. This widening achievement gap, says Margaret Spellings, U.S. Secretary of Education, "has profound implications for the economy, society, families, and democracy."

Missing from much of this discussion is the question, "Which boys?" (Weaver-Hightower, 2005). Indeed, there is considerable evidence to suggest that white, middle-class boys (and girls!) are doing just fine, and that race and class are much more important predictors of weak educational achievement than is gender (Mead, 2006). Using data from the National Assessment of Educational Progress (NAEP), which has tracked American students' achievement since 1971, a report from the independent think-tank Education Sector notes that "boys are scoring significant gains in elementary and middle school and are much better prepared for college" (Mead, 2006). In addition, the report asserts that "much of the pessimism about young males seems to derive from inadequate research, sloppy analysis and discomfort with the fact that although the average boy is doing better, the average girl has gotten ahead of him" (Matthews, 2006).

The debate about the education of boys reflects what is probably a "success story" in the decades-long push for equity for girls and women: as a nation, we have become truly interested not only in gender as a factor in the education of our young people, but also in the relationships between gender, social class, and race, as well as religion and a number of other factors as they affect teaching and learning in our schools. The reality is complex, but we are beginning to understand that there are some differences, in some circumstances, that do make a difference in education—and we're beginning to try to act on this understanding.

Gender and Sexuality

Perspectives on Gender and Sexuality

Although the number of sexually active teenagers is lower than it was 10 or 15 years ago, it is still very high, and the United States has the highest teen pregnancy and birthrates in the industrialized world. The likelihood of sexual activity among teens increases with age: more than half of 17-year-olds are sexually active, and close to 98% report using some form of contraception–notably condoms and birth control pills (Kaiser Family Foundation, 2005).

Although we might like to believe that these issues are not part of everyday life in school, we would be wrong. Sexual images are all around us, most with very specific "criteria" for how males and females should look, feel, want, and need. In addition, the increase in AIDS cases among both the homosexual and heterosexual population and the increase in other sexually transmitted diseases means that teenagers are thinking about a great many things besides history, English, math, and science.

Among the most difficult problems facing teachers and students is the relationship between heterosexual and homosexual students. As public awareness of homophobia increases, largely as a result of gay and lesbian activism engendered by tragedies such as the murder of Matthew Shepard in 1998, some professional educators are beginning to consider the need to address issues of homosexuality in schools. Some studies suggest that the more students know about homosexuality, the less homophobic they will be and the more accepting they will be toward homosexual people (Wells & Franken, 1987). However, cognitive knowledge about homosexuality sometimes fails to neutralize deep-seated attitudes of anger and guilt that accompany the issue (Ernulf & Innala, 1987). Tolerance is also complicated by the gender-related issues that are involved. For example, anger, hostility, and violence are more often directed toward gay men than toward lesbian women, although less physical forms of violence against lesbians, such as losing jobs or being evicted from housing, are common. Furthermore, within the homosexual community, differences in masculine and feminine traits among individuals are wide. The belief that gay men are "feminine" and lesbian women are "masculine" is a stereotype that bears little resemblance to reality, as is reflected by the surprise often expressed by parents, friends, and acquaintances when a person "comes out." Indeed, one of the most difficult aspects of being homosexual in a homophobic society is the separation of sexuality and gender role.

Gay, Lesbian, Bisexual, and Transgendered Rights Are Human Rights

The Human Rights Resource Center at the University of Minnesota (2004) has developed a series of activities in which students can "listen" to the real-life stories of peers and others who are gay and lesbian, and then discuss what they have heard. Here are a few of these testimonials:

Student, 17, Lesbian

I'm 17 and I'm gay. Adolescence is hell for me. I am told that my sexuality is something to be ashamed of, something to hide, something evil. I have cowered in my closet in shame and fear. I found myself lying to my parents and friends, being constantly afraid of discovery, and censoring my words and actions with paranoid concentration. I remember hiding books from my parents because I was ashamed of them discovering about me. In short, I hated my sexuality and myself. My closet wasn't a refuge; it was a prison and it was destroying me. By staying silent, I was confirming the emotions that were killing me inside. I am not just a statistic. I live in a Boston suburb in a white house with black shutters. I go to school every day, feeling that I can't be honest, that I have no right to be proud, that I am a second-class citizen. Just this past week, as I was walking down my street in my town where I have lived all of my life, a pick-up truck full of guys ran me off the road, screaming, "You lesbian!" at me. Homophobia is everywhere, and bigotry is inexcusable. It's time to start showing you care.

Student, 16, Lesbian, Attending Boarding School

I wish I could be more open with my parents, but having realized that my father might cause me physical harm, I realize that this is not an option. I live in utter dread that someone will let something slip, or that they'll see or find something that will tell them I'm a lesbian. Before they arrived for the weekend, I scoured my room, jamming the newspapers, the buttons, the pins, anything with the word "gay" on it in the bottom drawer under every item of summer clothing I could jam in there. When they arrived—early—they spent a moment or two in my room, unguarded. Luckily, they didn't find anything. Nor, luckily, did they find anything when my mother cleaned my desk out at home. But when I'm with people I'm not out to, I'm always on guard against what might slip out. It makes me very tense.

Student, 18, Gay

I think it's fair to say I grew up without any real role models. There aren't Asian-Americans on TV—Connie Chung and a few Fu Manchu rip-offs don't really count. There are even fewer gays and lesbians. Experiencing life as a double minority has given me insight into how people focus on the parts of a person rather than on the whole. About a year and a half ago, I came out. Being involved in a support group helped me overcome my confusion and helped me to become proud of my sexuality. But I began to distance myself from my cultural heritage. The Chinese family sees homosexuality as abnormal and immoral. This caused me to hate myself for being yellow. Reconciling and integrating my sexual identity and cultural background is a major obstacle for me. I am not "out" to my parents, who highly value Chinese traditions. This puts an incredible barrier between us. I am afraid they will be deeply hurt and confused when I decide to share this part of my life with them.

Student, 16, Straight

Two years ago my parents got divorced and my mother started to have a lesbian relationship. This scared and confused me. She tried to talk to me about it, but I always pushed her away. As far as I was concerned, that topic was off-limits. I know I shouldn't push her away, but it's so hard for me to deal with. After hearing a speaker on LGBT issues at school, I called her to tell her about it and I felt like what I was really saying was "I realize and accept your relationship." It was likely I was finally admitting that my mother is a lesbian. I don't really know though, because I still haven't really talked to her about it. And I still don't think I can. That's the worst part. But I feel like that phone call was the first step. I feel like I'm carrying this big burden on my shoulders. I don't think any of my friends could understand or, worse still, they wouldn't want to get to know my mother and she's such a great person. My best friend adores my mom—in fact, she just invited Mom to her graduation. And I wonder, would she feel the same way if she knew about my mom's relationship? I remember learning: Don't expect the worst in people. But it's hard—it's hard to know who to trust.

Teacher

At 3:40 today Tracy called me and told me she had slashed her wrists and taken two bottles of pills. Tracy is a brave young woman who has struggled to come to terms with her sexual orientation and has bravely taken the lead in raising awareness on our campus as one of the heads of our Gay-Straight Alliance. She said to me on the phone, "I always thought when I reached the breaking point, that it would be some big thing that pushed me over the edge. But it's not." Later at the hospital, while waiting for her father to arrive from out of town, she said to me, "What do I say when he asks me why I did it?—Dad, I just don't fit in with the world?" As Tracy convulsed in her hospital bed, her stomach torn to bits by the pills she had taken, I murmured, "I know, I know" and in fact I do know because—yes, just like you Tracy—I took 140 aspirin one night in high school because I couldn't see a way out. I couldn't see a future. I couldn't see a way to go on. You see, when you're a gay teenager, you don't need some big thing to push you over the edge, as Tracy discovered. . . . You get the message every day in your life, just like Tracy did, that you just don't fit in with the world. You get it driven through your skull. Sooner or later you get the message. You get the point. Tracy got the point at about 3:40 this afternoon. Wonderful, brave Tracy, whom everybody thinks has it so together with her student leadership position and her 1420 on her SATs. Yeah, Tracy got the point today.

It is very clear that the culture of the school is overwhelmingly heterosexist. State laws that have an impact on school environments and school safety have been summarized by the Gay, Lesbian, and Straight Education Network (GLSEN, 2005). Their report, which is the first systematic measurement and analysis of statewide policy, found that 42 states do not meet minimum criteria for protecting all students, particularly gay, lesbian, bisexual, and transgendered students.

Given that six states allow same-sex marriages, while at least 36 states have either a state constitutional ban on or legislative statutes banning same-sex marriage, and while some interest groups are still working for a federal constitutional ban on such marriages, there is an even greater need for teachers and other school people to seriously consider school climate and curriculum issues that may help to make schools safe for all students, including gay, lesbian, bisexual, and transgendered (GLBT) students.

Safe Zone programs in a number of schools and other organizational settings have been used to reduce homophobia in the environment. Using a list suggested by Youth Pride, Inc. (2007), the Safe Zone program (2007) at Case Western Reserve University suggests the following "how-tos":

1. *Make no assumption about sexuality.* If a student/peer has not used a pronoun when discussing a relationship, don't assume one. Use neutral language such as "Are you seeing anyone" instead of "Do you have a boyfriend." Additionally, do not assume that a female who confides a "crush"

on another girl is a lesbian. Labels are often too scary and sometimes not accurate. Let students label themselves.

2. *Have something gay-related visible in your office*–a sticker, a poster, a flyer, a brochure, a book, a button. This will identify you as a safe person to talk to and will hopefully allow a gay, lesbian, bisexual, or questioning youth to break his or her silence. SAFE ZONE campaign stickers and resources can provide this visibility.

3. *Support, normalize, and validate a person's feelings about his or her sexuality.* Let them know that you are there for them. If you cannot be supportive, please refer them to someone who can be. Then work on your own biases by reading, learning, and talking to people comfortable with this issue. And always remember, the problem is homophobia not homosexuality.

4. *Do not advise students to come out to parents, family, and friends* as they need to come out at their own safe pace. Studies show that as many as 26% of gay youth are forced to leave their homes after they tell their parents. IT IS THEIR DECISION, and they have to live with the consequences. Help them figure out what makes sense for them.

5. *Guarantee confidentiality with students.* Students need to know their privacy will be respected or they will not be honest about this important issue. If you cannot maintain confidentiality for legal reasons, let students know this in advance.

6. *Challenge homophobia.* As a role model for your students, respond to homophobia immediately and sincerely. Encourage in-service training for staff and students on homophobia and its impact on gay and lesbian youth.

7. *Combat heterosexism in your classroom.* Include visibly gay and lesbian role models in your classroom.

8. *Learn about and refer to community organizations.* Familiarize yourself with resources and call them before you refer to make sure they are ongoing. Also, become aware of gay-themed bibliographies and refer to gay-positive books.

9. *Encourage school administrators to adopt and enforce antidiscrimination policies* for their schools or school systems that include sexual orientation. The language should be included in all written materials next to race, sex, religion, and so forth.

10. *Provide role models.* Gay and straight students benefit from having openly gay teachers, coaches, and administration. Straight students are given an alternative to the inaccurate stereotypes they have received, and gay students are provided with the opportunity to see healthy gay adults. You, as teachers, can help by making gay and lesbian students feel more welcome.

Utilizing these and other strategies to encourage discussion and planning among school staff and students, homophobia *can* be reduced. It is well to remember that homophobia is a learned behavior; it can thus be *unlearned*.

Ethical Issues

Clearly, there are many ethical issues involved in the consideration of gender and sexual orientation in the classroom. One important issue has to do with the degree to which all students, regardless of their beliefs and attitudes, are encouraged to be open, reflective, and critical thinkers. Children and adolescents are all in various stages of physical, intellectual, and moral development. It is unwise and unfair for teachers either to impose their own judgments on students or to differentially favor those students whose beliefs and attitudes are most nearly like their own. Rather, students should be enabled and encouraged to discuss all aspects of these issues in a context of thoughtful inquiry.

A second and related issue is the degree to which such inquiry may place students in direct conflict with the values of their families or the communities in which they live. Teachers should exercise a great deal of judgment in this regard, particularly when the family and community context is fairly rigid. It is quite possible for teachers to insist on an equitable set of language and behaviors while still recognizing and affirming contrary beliefs. To do otherwise is to set up a climate of "political correctness" that usually does more harm than good and does not do anything at all to promote self-reflection or inquiry.

Equity as a value is consistent with democracy, but so is pluralism. In a society as diverse as the one in the United States, it is not possible—nor is it useful—to insist on a single set of attitudes, beliefs, and values. Rather, the role of the school should be to help students negotiate differences, to understand their origins, and to appreciate what is valuable about them. One of the goals of a collaborative classroom is to nurture *both* similarities and differences among people by enabling them to work together in ways that benefit everyone.

International Perspective: What's Happening Elsewhere in the World?

Challenging Homophobia in Conservative Times: Nurturing a Safe School Environment for All

Darren E. Lund

Associate Professor, Education, University of Calgary, Alberta, Canada

As easy as it is to talk about promoting fairness for all students, it is often difficult to stand up for what we know is right as educators. We know from daily observations and a growing body of research that students are often discriminated against based on their sexual orientation or gender identity. This dangerous situation is well documented in U.S. schools (Boshenek & Brown, 2001) and here in Canada where I teach and do research in social justice (Grace & Wells, 2001; Pruegger & Kiely, 2002). When asked for their opinions on the current situation in schools, some gay, lesbian, bisexual, transgendered, and transsexual (GLBTT) students in Calgary, Alberta, reported that they "did not think they could get any support from the school due to teachers who were homophobic and a school system reluctant to educate others on these issues" (Pruegger & Kiely, 2002, p. 29). I believe that many fair-minded people wishing to promote acceptance on this issue may simply need a bit of encouragement to take the first steps.

The reluctance by many educators to address sexual orientation is particularly understandable if you are living and teaching in a community with especially conservative values. Now imagine that your community is one often associated with extremist views and actions, and that one of the politicians representing your city is a staunch conservative who regularly expresses anti-gay sentiments (Kossowan, 1994).

I hope that the experiences of educators and students in Canadian schools might offer some helpful guidance. To inform this chapter[1] I have spoken with some fellow activists in this field, as well as drawing on some of my own recollections from helping to form Alberta's first *Gay Straight Alliance* (GSA) program in a high school in quite a conservative community. A group of student and teacher activists in the small city of Red Deer—with a population of about 72,000 at the time—has shown that they have been able to make a positive difference toward acceptance in their school and community in the face of apparently long odds. Thankfully, there are a number of other courageous students, teachers, and educational leaders in many communities who are willing to take risks to ensure that schools are safer places for all students.

Promoting Diversity in a Conservative Climate

A voluntary student group formed to promote diversity in schools and society might be expected to face an insurmountable uphill climb in central Alberta. Surprisingly, this was not the case for our student activist group. Formed in 1987 by accident in one of my grade 10 English classes, the *Students and Teachers Opposing Prejudice* (STOP) program thrived in a Red Deer high school for the better part of two decades with the goal of creating an atmosphere of accepting differences. The group attracted much media attention, no doubt in part because of Central Alberta's unfortunate national reputation for extremist hate group activity (see Kinsella, 2001), but the STOP program has also received regional and national honors for its work in countering discrimination (Alberta Human Rights and Citizenship Commission, 2000; Canadian Race Relations Foundation, 2001).

When we began our project to promote acceptance on issues of sexual orientation and gender identity, members of STOP were concerned that raising awareness about homophobia would be an overwhelming task. Over the years, the STOP program has undertaken activities including awareness campaigns on First Nations issues and violence against women, various presentations to government officials, drama presentations to children, local protests, international human rights advocacy, public debates with political leaders on government policies, and a variety of other projects (see Lund, 1998). Each of these initiatives has involved students and teachers collaboratively tackling contentious issues on social justice themes. On occasion, the group and its organizers have been the recipients of some strong expressions of hatred (see Lund, 2003, 2006).

As much as our school community had come to embrace STOP's antiracist messages over the years, one of my colleagues and a STOP co-adviser, Kirsten Spackman, feels that the high school is not yet a healthy place for some students:

> The school was not a safe environment for homosexual or perceived homosexual students. And by this I don't mean physically dangerous—although I know of one incident where a boy was assaulted at the downtown bus stop—but instead, emotionally and mentally torturous. Students frequently used degrading language such as "fag" and "dyke" and calling negative things "gay." As well, the most hurtful male insults attacked their sexuality. This created an environment of fear among students who were gay or even perceived to be gay.

Sadly, this is a fairly common occurrence in contemporary Canadian and American schools; for all of the gains that have been made in eliminating racist slurs from the public discourse, derogatory comments against the GLBTT community are commonplace in many of the school hallways I have visited across Canada and the United States in recent years.

(continued)

Raising Awareness and Acceptance on Sexual Orientation

Late during the 1999–2000 school year, two conversations initiated a new activist group's formation in our high school. A student in grade 11 named Rebecca[2] approached me in the spring to ask why the STOP group did not do more to counter prejudice based on sexual orientation. I encouraged her to share her idea with the STOP group. At the same time, one of the school administrators raised her concerns with me about the increasingly dangerous situation for GLBTT students in our school. Events came together in June of 2000 when members of STOP decided unanimously to form a *Gay Straight Alliance* (GSA) committee, the first ever such group in Alberta. They first sought the principal's approval, and then sent out a call for student volunteers. Meeting once a week and organized mainly by students, the GSA was intended to deal specifically with reducing the discrimination faced by students on the basis of sexual orientation and gender identity.

Rebecca remembers that the school could be a cruel place for particular students among her peer group and talks about her reasons for wishing to form the GSA group:

> I do remember it was fueled in particular when I discovered that my gay friend, Tim, was being harassed about his sexuality, and the counselor who was supposed to deal with it simply didn't. I remember he said something along the lines of "If Tim would 'flaunt' his sexuality less, he would be harassed less" as though it was Tim's fault that he was being harassed and his sole responsibility to stop the bullying. I was totally outraged by this response. The GSA, in the beginning, was a response or protest to this teacher's attitude. Also, I was interested in sexuality, human rights and gender issues, and I hoped that all of these issues could be addressed within the GSA.

Surprisingly, there was very little initial backlash to the group in the large high school (student population of about 1,800 students) or in the central Alberta community. Even a front-page newspaper story on the group in the *Red Deer Advocate* (Kennedy, 2000) elicited not a single negative reaction from the community. My colleague, Kirsten, pointed out that "our group has experienced remarkably little resistance or hostility from the school and community," a situation she attributes to the careful groundwork built by student leaders. We knew we would require their guidance along the way, as two straight allies who were trying hard to learn the best way to help our students organize effective school efforts to challenge homophobia.

Early in the GSA group's existence, one of its student members, Roberto, had the courage to volunteer to address a staff meeting of about 150 adults, at which he offered a moving and poignant account of growing up gay in central Alberta. He explained his fear of the violence that would come from his being exposed as a gay teenager, and he talked about the important role teachers can play in fostering acceptance in schools. He asked them to help him and the GSA help make the school a safer place for all students, and I remember him receiving the first standing ovation I had ever seen at a staff meeting.

Kirsten reflected on Roberto's courageous comments and the lasting effect that she thinks he had on the staff:

> One of our more confident students spoke with staff about his experiences in school. He actually came out to staff, which was a surprise because we didn't ask any of the students about their orientation. He finished his speech by imploring staff to do something about the problem because he just didn't want to be afraid anymore. The staff applauded a long time and understood, I think, how important their role was in engaging students who were using discriminatory language in their classes.

Other GSA members took care to get school administration and staff on their side from the outset, seeking the principal's approval before making any plans. As Rebecca recalls, "I didn't think that it would be approved by the school—that was a surprise. I really hoped that it would start people discussing sexuality and diversity." Student members regularly reminded staff and their fellow students that they were not a "sexuality" club or a support group, but a collective of students striving to create a safe and respectful learning environment. When she is asked how important it was to have teachers involved in the formation of the GSA committee, Rebecca answers:

> It was very important. I couldn't and wouldn't have done it without the help and encouragement of you and Ms. Spackman. That support was necessary for both practical and emotional reasons. It also helped to know that other staff members were supportive of the idea, if not directly involved.

Some of the activities to raise awareness in the school were provocative; the GSA group organized a "Sexual Orientation Awareness and Acceptance Week" in 2002 that featured a poster campaign with administration-approved posters offering thought-provoking messages such as "Closets are for clothes," "Why do you care who I love?" and "I don't care whether you're gay, straight, or Australian." Some of the posters were torn down, but GSA members strongly suspected a small number of students were to blame.

During the GSA's second school year of existence, members drafted a formal looking and oversized *GSA Declaration of Acceptance*, modeled on the *Canadian Charter of Rights and Freedoms*, and displayed it by the school library during lunch hours. About 200 students and staff signed the declaration, promising to refrain from using derogatory language related to sexual orientation. Once framed, the document was placed in a prominent display in the high school. In addition, STOP members gave a rainbow ribbon to each person who signed the declaration to wear during the week to signify their commitment to the GSA's ideals.

Other ongoing activities have helped the GSA group to promote an atmosphere of acceptance in the school. Facts and myths about sexual orientation were included in the student bulletin at regular intervals. One lunch hour saw a local guest speaker, a protestant pastor from a popular local church, offer a biblically based talk on homosexuality to dozens of staff and students. The reverend facilitated a discussion of sexual orientation from a Christian perspective that was neither hateful nor condemning.

On a designated "Day of Silence" about 20 students refrained from speaking for the entire day to symbolize the silence surrounding the issue of discrimination against people based on their sexual orientation. They had prepared printed cards with information about the activity to give to their teachers or to any students who asked them about it. Rebecca emphasizes that the protection of the dignity of each student being promoted by the GSA is a basic human rights issue:

> I think the most important argument [for forming a GSA] is taken from a human rights standpoint. The fact is that queer students are being harassed and marginalized in the public school system and by their peers and that's totally a violation of their rights. I think schools have a responsibility to protect and empower *all* students and, as much as possible, to create an environment that is safe, comfortable, and based on the idea of respect and dignity for all. Encouraging queer students to keep their sexuality quiet, even if it is in a subtle or indirect way, violates their right to express a fundamental aspect of their identity and beliefs.

Another group of students produced a haunting audio recording featuring historical moments of hatred including the Nazi treatment of Jews and civil rights struggles in the United States. The tape ended with a scenario involving the all-too-common expressions of hatred toward homosexuals and issued a strong challenge to encourage young people to make positive choices in their treatment of others. The recording was played for the entire staff, over the school intercom, and additional copies were available through the guidance office as a resource for any teachers who wanted to address these and other discrimination issues in their classes.

When asked if typical bullying programs might be implemented to address the discrimination faced by GLBTT students in our schools, the students and teacher with whom I spoke are adamant that these programs are inadequate. As Kirsten explains, there are some specific reasons more general antiviolence initiatives miss the mark in dealing with homophobia:

> Everyone can agree in principle that violence and bullying are wrong. You won't, however, get the same consensus about homosexuality. There are many people who consider homosexuality a disease, an abomination and even a criminal act. It is, therefore, very different. Adults in the community who say they don't support bullying may support anti-gay sentiments.

It becomes necessary, then, for the school community to make it clear that even if a person disagrees with a particular belief that she or he has no right to take away that person's ability to feel safe in the school environment. As well, there are a whole series of myths that travel around about homosexuality that involve a whole different approach to awareness.

On the same topic, Trina, an activist student who recently graduated from a high school in Calgary, expresses this view:

> Traditional anti-violence and anti-bullying programs are not enough in schools because they are too simplistic. The issues behind, or motivating the bullying (homophobia, racism) are never addressed. The anti-bullying programs that were presented when I was a student simply said that violence was bad and a cause of the perpetrator's low self-esteem. No discussion, no safe space, just end bullying.

Clearly a more comprehensive and specific program of awareness raising and resistance is needed in schools, and the formation of a GSA can be an important first step in mobilizing activist students and teachers to begin to work collaboratively on approaches that will work best for each school context.

The Work Must Continue

It would be naive to imagine that central Alberta no longer has residents who hold narrow views about sexual orientation, or that there are still people who wish to deny human rights to certain groups of citizens based on their gender identity. In fact, despite the best efforts of human rights supporters in the region, there are ample public examples of homophobia in recent years. As an example, in 2002 the *Red Deer Advocate* chose to publish letters to the editor expressing extremist views against homosexuality. However, following the resolution of a human rights complaint against them, the newspaper now includes a statement on their "Letters" page that reads, in part: "The *Advocate* will not publish statements that indicate unlawful discrimination or intent to discriminate against a person or class of persons, or are likely to expose people to hatred or contempt because of . . . sexual orientation."

I must also report that I have personally been subjected to hate mail and job threats over the years for my work on diversity issues (see Knapp, 2006). In the past 4 years I have been the target of costly legal action—namely, a $400,000 nuisance defamation lawsuit that was subsequently dropped—that I believe was designed to intimidate me into no longer supporting the fair treatment of gay, lesbian, bisexual, and transgendered students. Another more violent reminder of the dangers of hatred came in the form of a vicious attack on a Red Deer teenager in July 2002 (Zielinsky, 2002). The victim, a 17-year-old male, was attacked by a man who used derogatory slurs against his perceived sexual orientation, asking him, "You're a faggot, right?" before shattering his cheekbone.

(continued)

Teachers and students in Alberta are very fortunate to be supported by a forward-thinking Alberta Teachers' Association (ATA) that provides a number of materials on teaching about sexual orientation and other matters related to promoting fairness in public schools. Numerous resources are available free of charge online (see ATA, 2006). Their Diversity, Equity and Human Rights Web page includes teaching materials, a newsletter, workshop information, relevant publications, videos and media resources, and an annual grant program supporting diversity efforts in schools in the province. Especially helpful is a booklet entitled, *Safe and Caring Schools for Lesbian and Gay Youth*, also published by the ATA. I would strongly encourage teachers, parents, and students from every jurisdiction to check with their local teachers' association and community groups for relevant policy, curricular, and programming materials on this and other diversity issues.

As Rebecca noted, bringing up these issues appropriately with young people, either in a GSA or with the larger student body, is a challenging and complex task given the pervasiveness of homophobia in the larger community. She recognizes that "all students need to be told that they cannot harass or bully queer students, even if they seem to have the larger population backing them up in their behavior." However, she acknowledges the fact that this means "dealing with the sometimes touchy subject of sexuality. I think that many high school students, even the straight ones, are not sure of themselves as sexual people and so the question of homosexuality is not going to be entirely easy or comfortable for them to talk about." She recommends overcoming this discomfort for the safety and dignity of all staff and students.

My GSA staff co-adviser, Kirsten, offers this advice in dealing with those who may oppose addressing these issues in schools:

> The best arguments are the ones that are personal. A person would find it difficult to argue with someone who honestly and emotionally tells a story of harassment. Avoid arguments that deal with whether or not homosexuality is wrong and stick with the point that discriminating against and harassing homosexuals is wrong.

Conclusion

Everyone is not expected to share the same ideas or opinions on controversial matters surrounding sexual orientation and gender identity, but we can all agree that our public schools should be safe places for all students to learn. Kirsten remembers having both hopes and fears when we first started the GSA: "I had great hopes that we might be able to educate people about the hurtfulness of discriminatory language and attitudes. I had some fears that some of the more adamant staff and students might be verbally and/or personally abusive." I am pleased to report that her hopes came to fruition and her fears did not materialize, and the GSA thrived for a few strong years in the high school where we both worked. Kirsten is now at another high school, working with a new student social justice group to address a range of diversity issues, and I am working at the university level to continue teaching, studying, and fostering social justice activism in schools.

Reassuringly, my research reveals that many school-based activists continue their important work in the face of extremist backlash against diversity initiatives, a growing political and social conservatism, and other potential inhibitors to social justice efforts. Keeping our focus on the goal of keeping schools as safe learning environments will ensure that staff and student organizations and educational campaigns to challenge homophobia and promote the acceptance of differences will continue to flourish and spread to schools across our country and beyond.

Notes

[1] Revised portions of this chapter originally appeared in the following works and are included here with the kind permission of the publishers: D. E. Lund (2005), Promoting dignity and respect in Red Deer: Forming Alberta's first Gay/Straight Alliance. In N. O'Haire (Ed.), *Lessons learned: A collection of stories and articles about bisexual, gay, lesbian, transgender issues* (pp. 57–62). Ottawa, ON: Canadian Teachers Federation; and D. E. Lund (in press), Challenging homophobia in conservative Canada: Forming Alberta's first gay/straight alliance in Alberta. In B. van Driel & L. van Dijk (Eds.), *Challenging homophobia: Educating about sexual diversity.* The author gratefully acknowledges the generous support of the Killam Trusts for this and other related work.

[2] Student names used here are pseudonyms.

Critical Incident

Responsibilities at Home

Some of the students in Tom Littleton's class were talking about going to the movies on Friday night when two of the Romani students, Steven and Rebecca, walked by. "Hey, Steve," called out one of the boys, "do you want to go to the movies with us on Friday?"

Steven stopped and looked at them. He seemed about to accept their invitation, but then said, "Oh, I can't. My grandmother is coming over that night, and I'm going to help my mother fix dinner."

"Aw, come on!" said one of the students. "You can see your grandmother anytime."

"No," said Steven. "I have a responsibility to be there."

• Why do you think Steven refused an invitation that he might otherwise have wanted to accept?

• Why do you think part of Steven's responsibilities included fixing dinner?

Critical Incident

Should She Go to College?

Anamarie was an extremely bright young Latina in her junior year of high school. Mr. Jordan, her English teacher, thought she should be thinking seriously about going to college. He knew, however, that if she did go, she would be the first in her family to continue school after high school. He also knew that her parents, who owned a very successful restaurant, expected her to help with the business when she finished high school.

One afternoon in April, Mr. Jordan asked Anamarie to come to his office after school. She was a little nervous; what had she done wrong?

When Anamarie sat down, Mr. Jordan came right to the point. "I'd like to talk to you about college," he said. "You have a very good mind, and you're an excellent writer. I'd be very happy to help you look at different college opportunities and to write a good recommendation for you."

Anamarie was astonished. She didn't say anything for a minute; then she said, "Oh, Mr. Jordan, I couldn't do that! My parents want me to help them with the restaurant. They're not getting any younger, you know, and I need to be looking out for them."

She hesitated a moment, and then added, "You know, I think I might really *like* to go to college . . . but I just can't."

• Do you think Mr. Jordan should have considered any ethical issues before talking to Anamarie?

• Would you have handled the situation any differently?

Critical Incident

Who's Using the Computer?

Joan Thompson is a math education professor at a local university who was working with teachers in a nearby elementary school on incorporating computer technology into their classrooms. In every session of the 12 biweekly meetings she had with these teachers, she stressed the need to include girls in computer work and gave them some background on the need to encourage girls in math, science, and technology.

At the end of the semester, the teachers and students prepared a culminating presentation to demonstrate what they'd learned. In the presentation, students were to be paired in male and female dyads, a fact that the teachers were quick (and proud) to point out. Some students were going to use the computer to find specific information while others were going to write that information on the board. Joan really looked forward to seeing the results of all their work.

When she got there, everyone was excited to show what they'd learned. As the presentation progressed, Dr. Thompson was astounded to observe that, in every dyad, the boys were using the computers and the girls were writing on the board!

- If you were Dr. Thompson, how would you respond to the teachers and students?

- Why do you think the event was planned in just this way?

Summary

In this chapter, we explained the importance of gender role socialization to a person's identity through discussion of the ways in which children learn to "become" members of a gender group. The part played by the school and by teachers, administrators, and other adults as socialization agents was also discussed, as was the particular *type* of socialization—generally middle class—exercised by the school and the relation of that socialization to mainstream American values.

Traditional gender role stereotypes are both harmful and changing. Indeed, it is the very *change* in the nature of gender roles, as exemplified by Title IX, that is likely to cause some difficulties for students and teachers. In the same way, collaborative classrooms are particularly good vehicles for engendering understanding among both male and female students.

Finally, the issue of sexuality was addressed, in part as a studentwide phenomenon—at least in middle and high schools—and in part in terms of an increasing need to attend to issues raised by students who are gay and lesbian and to issues created by the relations between homosexual and heterosexual students.

Chapter Review

Go to the Online Learning Center at www.mhhe.com/cushner7e to review important content from the chapter, practice with key terms, take a chapter quiz, and find the Web links listed in this chapter.

Key Terms

dominant culture 341	gender-sensitive 332	pseudoscience 328
gender role socialization 340	genderized traits 346	task specialization 336
gender role stereotyping 346	homophobia 346	
	misogyny 346	
	normative 345	

Active Exercise

Additional Active Exercises are available online at www.mhhe.com/cushner7e.

Sexual Orientation: A Matter of Experience?

Purpose: To examine potential classroom situations that reflect others' as well as your own responses to issues surrounding sexual orientation.

Instructions: The term *sexual orientation* refers to the preference one exhibits in terms of sexual partners. There is increasing evidence that one's sexual orientation is genetically based; that is, it may be "'hard-wired" into the individual, and therefore resistant, if not impossible, to change. Other beliefs attribute early experience to later sexual preference. Regardless of the explanation you are most comfortable with, in your role as an educator you will encounter situations that will require your action and intervention on behalf of a child, either in making accurate attributions concerning a child's behavior at a given moment, or on behalf of a child who is experiencing strained relationships with her or his peers.

1. How would you explain the following scenarios to the concerned individual?

   a. Four-year-old Jeremy heads right to the doll corner as soon as he arrives at the day-care center each morning. His father is concerned that this behavior is not appropriate for a little boy. How would you respond to the father?

   b. Seventeen-year-old Patricia (who prefers to be called Pat) wears her hair cut very short and tends to dress like the boys. You walk by a group of her female classmates and hear them refer to her as a lesbian. How would you respond to this group of girls?

   c. Five-year-old Suzanne plays with blocks and trucks during most of her free time in kindergarten. Her mother asks you if this is "normal" behavior? How would you respond to the mother?

   d. In addition to his theater performances, 13-year-old Robert takes ballet classes 3 days a week after school. Other boys often ridicule him in class. He comes to you and asks you to intervene. What would you suggest to Robert? What would you say to the other boys in Robert's class?

   e. Fifteen-year-old Shauna, who has few friends, lifts weights and seeks out all the opportunities she can to play typical boys sports. She has also been having conflicting and confusing sexual feelings. She comes to you after school one day, initially to seek your advice about what to do about friends, but soon begins to talk about her confusion and fear of talking to her parents. What advice would you give her?

   f. Sixteen-year-old Joseph's stated goal in life is to become a nurse. You overhear a group of boys teasing him and laughing about his "gay" behavior. You find Joseph sulking in a corner of the room and approach him. What do you say to him?

Reflect on your responses to the above scenarios. Do you notice any patterns in the way you answered the questions? Did you respond differently to the scenarios involving girls than you did for the scenarios involving boys? Did you respond differently to parents than you did to the child? If so, to what do you attribute this?

Classroom Activities

1. Ask elementary students who their "heroes" are–both male and female. Who do they look up to? What characteristics do these "heroes" have? Do the female "heroes" have different characteristics than the male "heroes"? Do they have some of the same characteristics? Students can then make posters about their "heroes" with a written description of who they are and why they are "heroes," putting the posters up around the classroom as a "Hall of Fame Display."

2. In an elementary classroom, have students read the language of Title IX: *"No person in the United States shall, on the basis of sex, be excluded from participation in, be denied the benefits of, or be subjected to discrimination under any educational program or activity receiving federal financial assistance."* Discuss with students the implications of Title IX in their school: Should girls and boys both play sports? What other areas of school life could Title IX be applied to? Ask students to write a short essay describing their ideas about gender equity in school.

3. Using two flip charts, in a high school class, ask students to brainstorm characteristics that demonstrate manly behavior and ladylike behavior. On one flip chart, write students' suggestions for "manly" behavior and draw a box around the responses. Write "Manly Characteristics" at the top of the chart. On the other flip chart, write students' suggestions for "ladylike" behavior, again drawing a box around the responses, and writing "Lady-like Characteristics" at the top of the chart. Discuss the two sets of responses in terms of stereotypes and ask students where they think they learned these ideas, where in society we find these messages, and to what extent they think these "characteristics" reflect reality in their lives.

4. Ask high school students to be "gender detectives," visiting large local toy stores or big box stores with large toy departments. Students should take notebooks and pencils with them. In the store, or toy department, look for sections that display boys' and girls' toys and describe what kinds of toys are in each section. Then look at the packaging around the toys and describe what words and figures are on the packaging. Finally, see if the store (or department) has a section of "gender neutral" toys (e.g., blocks, stuffed animals) and describe what kinds of toys are in that section. Ask students what they conclude about toys as gender socializers.

Reflective Questions

As Tom Littleton reads his journal, he probably asks himself some of the following questions. Put yourself in Tom's place, and think about how you would answer these questions.

1. Both competition and individualism are deeply held values in American society. Have I stressed collaboration in a way that omits these values from the students' lives or in a way that weaves them together?

2. All people need to feel that they belong, that they have a reliable sense of alliance with others. Has this class fostered such feelings?

3. The culture of some students centers on individualism and the culture of others centers on a collective spirit. Is there a balance here? For example, are students given enough opportunity to be assessed individually as well as in groups?

4. Have I gone too far with Rebecca in stressing equity for girls? Have I put her in a position where she feels she has to choose between her community's emphasis on the male and my encouragement of her individual talents? How can I help her bridge these two sets of values and still maintain her family's trust in me?

5. To what extent has the collaborative structure of this class resulted in individual learning for all students? How can I measure that? How can I be sure that real learning is going on for everyone?

6. I can't keep all these students together with me all day or for the rest of their schooling. How are they doing, and how will they do, in more traditional classrooms that stress competition and individual performance? Is this class just a unique experience that will fade from memory as they get older?

It is obvious that Tom can have few definitive answers for these questions, but the fact that he asks them is important. He clearly believes that a collaborative classroom is both necessary and valuable. Yet he knows that this approach to schooling is not shared by everyone, either in the school or outside it. The decisions he makes as he thinks about these issues are always tempered by what he knows about his school and his community. Still, he will probably continue to modify and improve his approach, knowing also that change is incremental and does not come all at once. It is a great challenge.

Endnote

1. More than a few elements of this Case Study, in particular the land discovery project, are adapted from the real experience of Bill Elasky and his students at Amesville Elementary School in Amesville, Ohio, and Dan Bisaccio and his students at Thayer Junior/Senior High School in Winchester, New Hampshire. Both are described in G. Woods (1992), *Schools That Work* (New York: Penguin Books). Elements of Gypsy education are taken from *The First S.T.E.P. (Systematic Training and Early Prevention) Program,* prepared by Sam Chandler and Rebecca Boglione, Tacoma Public Schools, 1992.

References

Alberta Human Rights and Citizenship Commission. (2000, May). *Tools for transformation: Human rights education and diversity initiatives in Alberta.* Edmonton, AB: Government of Alberta.

Alberta Teachers' Association. (2006). *Diversity, equity and human rights.* Retrieved February 9, 2006, from http://www.teachers.ab.ca/ Issues+In+Education/Diversity+and+Human+Rights/

Alida Star Gebser and Alida Jean McCullough v. Lago Vista Independent School District, 524 U.S. 274 (1998).

Belenky, M. F., Clinchy, B., Goldberger, N., & Tarule, J. (1986). *Women's ways of knowing: The development of self, voice, and mind.* New York: Basic Books.

Berliner, D. C., & Biddle, B. J. (1995). *The manufactured crisis: Myths, fraud, and the attack on America's public schools.* Cambridge, MA: Perseus Books.

Boshenek, M., & Brown, W. (2001). *Hatred in the hallways: Violence and discrimination against lesbian, gay, bisexual and transgender students in U.S. schools.* New York: Human Rights Watch. Retrieved April 10, 2006, from http://www.hrw.org/reports/2001/uslgbt/

Canadian Race Relations Foundation. (2001). *CRRF 2001 best practices reader.* Toronto, ON: Author.

Carelli, A. O. (1988). Introduction. In A. O. Carelli (Ed.), *Sex equity in education.* Springfield, IL: Charles C Thomas.

Clinchy, B. M., Belenky, M. F., Goldberger, N., & Tarule, J. (1985). Connected education for women. *Journal of Educational Thought, 167*(3).

Cooper, K. J. (2006, November 30). Scholars debate effectiveness of single-sex classes. *Diverse Online.* Retrieved from http://www.diverseeducation.com/artman/publish/printer_6718.shtml

Cooper, R., & Slavin, R. E. (2004). Cooperative learning: An instructional strategy to improve intergroup relations. In W. G. Stephan & W. P. Vogt (Eds.), *Education programs for improving intergroup relations: Theory, research and practice* (pp. 55–77). New York: Teachers College Press.

Doe v. Petaluma Unified School District, 54 F.3d 1447 (9th Cir., 1995).

Dronsberg, S., Fagot, B., Hagan, R., & Lleinback, M. D. (1985). Differential reactions to assertive and communicative acts of toddler boys and girls. *Child Development, 56*(6), 1499–1505.

Ernulf, K. E., & Innala, S. M. (1987). The relationship between affective and cognitive components of homophobic reaction. *Archives of Sexual Behavior, 16*(6).

Fagot, B. (1978). The influence of sex of child on parental reactions to toddler children. *Child Development, 49*(2), 459–565.

Finnish National Board of Education. (2007, November 12). Background for Finnish PISA success. Retrieved from www.oph.fi/english/SubPage.asp?path=447,65535,77331

Fowler, C. (1994). Strong arts, strong schools. *Educational Leadership, 52*(3), 4–5.

Franklin v. Gwinnett County Public Schools 503 U.S. 60 (1992).

Gay, Lesbian, and Straight Education Network. (2005). *State of the states: A policy analysis of lesbian, gay, bisexual, and transgender (LGBT) safer schools issues.* Retrieved from http://www.glsen.org/cgi-bin/iowa/all/news/record/1687.html

Gilligan, C. (1982). *In a different voice.* Cambridge, MA: Harvard University Press.

Goodlad, J. I. (1984). *A place called school: Prospects for the future.* New York: McGraw-Hill.

Grace, A. P., & Wells, K. (2001). Getting an education in Edmonton, Alberta: The case of queer youth. *Torquere: Journal of the Canadian Lesbian and Gay Studies Association, 3,* 34–44.

Greenspan, R., Niemeyer, J. H., & Seeley, D. (1991). *Principals speak: Report #2, parent involvement.* New York: Research Foundation of City University of New York.

Grove City v. Bell, 465 U.S. 555 (1984).

Grunberg, J. (2007). *Media's influence on raising kids: Moms sound off.* National Organization for Women. Retrieved from http://www.now.org/issues/media/070802momresults.html

Hartley, R. E. (1974). Sex role pressures and the socialization of the male child. In J. Stacey, S. Bereaud, & J. Daniels (Eds.), *And Jill came tumbling after*. New York: Dell.

Howe, F. (1974). Sexual stereotypes start early. In O. L. Johnson (Ed.), *Nonsexist curriculum materials for elementary schools*. Old Westbury, NY: Feminist Press.

Human Rights Resource Center, University of Minnesota. (2004). *Lesbian, gay, bisexual, and transgendered rights: A human rights perspective*. Activity 7. Retrieved from http://www1.umn.edu/humanrts/edumat/hreduseries/TB3/act7/act7f.html

Kagan, S. (1989–1990). The structural approach to cooperative learning. *Educational Leadership, 47*(4), 12–15.

Kaiser Family Foundation. (2005). *Fact sheet on teen sexual activity*. Retrieved from http://www.kff.org/youthhivstds/upload/U-S-Teen-Sexual-Activity-Fact-Sheet.pdf

Kennedy, C. (2000, November 20). New student group fights anti-gay bias at local high school. *Red Deer Advocate,* p. A1.

Kids Count: A project of the Annie E. Casey Foundation. (2007). One out of five U.S. children is living in an immigrant family. *Data Snapshot*, March.

Kinsella, W. (2001). *Web of hate: Inside Canada's far right network* (2nd ed.). Toronto, ON: HarperCollins.

Knapp, S. (2006, April 10). Prof battles injustice despite threats. *OnCampus, 3*(16), 7 [Electronic version]. Retrieved from http://www.ucalgary.ca/oncampus/weekly/march3-06/lund.html

Kossowan, B. (1994, April 15). Sex with children "next step": Pedophiles may seek rights–Day. *Red Deer Advocate*, pp. A1–2.

Kolbenschlag, M. (1981). *Kiss sleeping beauty goodbye: Breaking the spell of feminine myths and models*. New York: Bantam Books.

Kramer, S. (1988). Sex role stereotyping: How it happens and how to avoid it. In A. Carelli O'Brien (Ed.), *Sex equity in education* (pp. 5–23). Springfield, IL: Charles C Thomas.

Lavonen, J. (2008). Reasons behind Finnish students' success in the PISA Scientific Literacy Assessment. Conference presentation. Helsinki, Finland, University of Helsinki. Cited in Darling-Hammond, L. *The flat world and education: How America's commitment to equity will determine our future*. New York: Teachers College, Columbia University, 5.

Lund, D. E. (1998). Social justice activism in a conservative climate: Students and teachers challenging discrimination in Alberta. *Our Schools/Our Selves, 9*(4), 24–38.

Lund, D. E. (2003). Facing the challenges: Student antiracist activists counter backlash and stereotyping. *Teaching Education Journal, 14,* 265–278.

Lund, D. E. (2006). Social justice activism in the heartland of hate: Countering extremism in Alberta. *Alberta Journal of Educational Research, 52,* 181–194.

Matthews, J. (2006, June 26). *Study casts doubt on the "boy crisis."* Retrieved from Washingtonpost.com

McCaleb, S. P. (1994). *Building communities of learners*. New York: St. Martin's Press.

McNeish, Robert. (1972). *Lessons from geese*. Retrieved from http://suewidemark.netfirms.com/lessonsgeese.htm#nutshell#nutshell

Mead, S. (2006, June 27). The truth about boys and girls. *Education Sector*. Retrieved from http://www.educationsector.org/analysis/analysis_show.htm?doc_id=378705

National Association of Single Sex Public Education (NASSPE). (2010). Single-sex schools/single sex classrooms: What's the difference? Retrieved from http://www.singlesexschools.org/schools-schools.htm

Noddings, N. (1984). *Caring*. Berkeley: University of California Press.

Oakes, J., & Lipton, M. (2003). *Teaching to change the world* (2nd ed.). Boston: McGraw-Hill.

Pollack, W. (1998). *Real boys: Rescuing our sons from the myths of boyhood*. New York: Henry Holt.

Pruegger, V., & Kiely, J. (2002). *Perceptions of racism and hate activities among youth in Calgary: Effects on the lived experience*. Calgary, AB: City of Calgary.

Safe Zone Program. (2007). *Reducing homophobia*. Case Western Reserve University. Retrieved from http://www.case.edu/provost/lgbt/safezone/reduce.html

Slavin, R. E. (1995). *Cooperative learning: Theory, research, and practice* (2nd ed.). Englewood Cliffs, NJ: Prentice Hall.

Slocumb, P. D. (2004). *Hear our cry: Boys in crisis*. Highlands, TX: aha! Process, Inc.

Sommers, C. H. (2000). *The war against boys: How misguided feminism is harming our young men*. New York: Touchstone.

Spellings, M. (2006). Secretary Spellings announces more choices in single-sex education amended regulations give communities more flexibility to offer single sex schools and classes. [U.S. Department of Education Press Release]. Retrieved from http://www.ed.gov/news/pressreleases/2006/10/10242006.html

Standen, A. (2007). Gender matters: Dividing boys and girls. *Edutopia.org*. Retrieved from http://www.edutoia.org/node/3148/print

Thousand, J. S., et al. (2002). *Creativity and collaborative learning: The practical guide to empowering students and teachers* (2nd ed.). Baltimore, MD: Brookes.

Tyre, P. (2006, January 30). The trouble with boys. *Newsweek* [Electronic version]. Retrieved from http://www.msnbc.msn.com/id/10965522/site/newsweek/

Von Drehle, D. (2007, July 26). The myth about boys. *Time* [Electronic version]. Retrieved from http://www.time.com/time/magazine/article/0,9171,1647452-1,00.html

Weaver-Hightower, M. (2005, February 14). Dare the school build a new education for boys? *TC Record* [Electronic version]. Retrieved from http://www.tcrecord.org/PrintContent.asp?ContentID=11743

Weitzman, L. J. (1975). Sex-role socialization. In J. Freeman (Ed.), *Women: A feminist perspective*. Palo Alto, CA: Mayfield.

Wells, J. W., & Franken, M. L. (1987, December). University students' knowledge about and attitudes toward homosexuality. *Journal of Humanistic Education and Development, 26*(2).

Youth Pride, Inc. (2007). Retrieved from http://www.youthpride.org/

Zielinsky, S. (2002, July 4). Gay teenager beaten: Victim fearful attackers could return. *Red Deer Advocate*, p. A1.

Chapter

11

Creating Developmentally Appropriate Classrooms

The Importance of Age and Developmental Status

Focus Questions

1. How can culture, and schooling, affect students' development?
2. Are there really stages in children's and adolescents' development? If so, are some of those stages critical?
3. How do teachers determine what is developmentally appropriate for their students?
4. How can teachers reconcile demands for educational performance standards and accountability with the goal of education for understanding?

" The blunt fact is that the American high school was designed for fifteen- to eighteen-year-olds who were children only beginning their journey to adulthood. It is now filled with young adults of the same age. One does not have to subscribe to a Freudian theory of human development to accept the sharp distinction between the years before and after sexual development. And likewise, one does not need to be a professional psychologist to recognize that the way in which one deals with a prepubescent youngster is quite different from the way in which one deals with one in the early stages of puberty. "

LEON BOTSTEIN

" Much of the story of human development must be written in the light of cultural influences in general and of the particular persons, practices, and paraphernalia of one's culture. And chief among these, of course, in any complex culture will be such educational institutions as apprenticeships or formal schools. "

HOWARD GARDNER

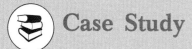

Age in Developmentally Appropriate Classrooms

It was a coincidence that Sally Dougherty and Tony Stuart—both recent graduates of the same midwestern university—were hired in the same month at Garfield Elementary School in Asheville, West Virginia.[1] What was not a coincidence was that both Sally and Tony had wanted to come back to the Appalachian Mountains where they had been born.

Settled in waves of people moving westward, Appalachia is ordinarily defined as a set of 397 counties in 12 states, running from southern New York to Mississippi, with a population of some 18 million people. Its population has been comprised predominantly of a mixture of English, German, Welsh, Scots-Irish, and French who, upon their arrival, met major civilizations of Iroquois and Shawnee in the north and Creek, Cherokee, Choctaw, and Chickasaw in the south.

Historically, Appalachia has been a hiding place for Native Americans, runaway slaves, and whites escaping from indentured servitude in the early colonies or from privation and persecution in Europe. Cut off from the rest of the world by geography, traditional conservatism, economic hardship, and fear, the people of Appalachia have developed a culture that values kinship, independence, and tradition. They tend to distrust and avoid involvements with social institutions, such as schooling. Strangers are often regarded with suspicion or disinterest, including all those outsiders who had recently descended upon the area in an effort to "fix" it.

Sally and Tony, however, were not outsiders. They knew that out of the experience of poverty and the pride of independence (some might say the curse of individualism) has come a people who are accustomed to making do or doing without, whose experience with the outside world has been largely one of repeated disappointment, who refer to themselves proudly as "highlanders" or "mountain people," and who have produced beautiful folk art in wood carvings, quilts, dulcimer and fiddle music, baskets, and pottery. Indeed, it was because of their sense of loyalty to and admiration for the people and places in which they had grown up that the two new teachers wanted to return to bring the best education they had to offer to a new generation of mountain children.

Garfield Elementary School, with about 350 children in grades K–8, is typical of many schools in the region. Constructed of cement block, it was built in 1968 as part of a "modernization" effort. It has 12 classrooms painted in pastel colors, tiled floors, a cafeteria with a kitchen, a library, modern restrooms, dependable heating, and adequate lighting. It serves a number of surrounding communities, has about a 10% absentee rate, and has a low budget for books and materials. About 40% of its children qualify for free lunches. Most teachers in the school have been there for 20 or more years, and many are nearing, or have reached, retirement, accounting for Sally and Tony being hired at the same time.

Other changes had occurred as well, perhaps the most important one being the conversion of the sixth, seventh, and eighth grades into a middle school housed in the same building as K–5. Sally was hired to teach kindergarten, and Tony had been hired to teach music to the sixth, seventh, and eighth graders. Although they had known one another slightly in college, neither realized that they were going to be teaching in the same school until the week before school began, when they met at the trash bins behind the school. Each was there getting their rooms ready for the first day of school.

Surprised and excited by their meeting, the two neophyte teachers compared notes. "I've been planning all summer for this," confided Sally. "I didn't get to see much of the place when I came to be interviewed, but I wanted to get here early so I could arrange my room the way I wanted it. Come and see!"

She practically dragged Tony to her classroom, where she was beginning to organize furniture into activity centers like those she had used in student teaching. Already discernible was a block area, with several kinds of blocks for construction; a part of the room for active games and other large muscle activity; a science center, with a terrarium; an area for counting, sorting, and measuring; a listening center; and also a quiet area, where children could stretch out with picture books. "I had hoped to have a computer and a sand table," she said, "but maybe I can figure out how to get those later. At least I have a sink in my room for cleaning up after painting, washing hands, and getting water for our classroom pets."

Not to be outdone, Tony was also eager to show off his room. One of the first at their university to graduate with licensure in middle childhood, Tony knew that the concept of middle school had been devised in part to allow young people more time to explore before committing themselves to futures foreordained by the type of curriculum they chose to pursue. For this reason, there were a lot of things to explore in Tony's room. He had arranged the usual chairs in a semicircle at one end of the room for choral rehearsals and singing, thereby leaving the rest of the rather large room available for bookshelves, tables, and—his pride and joy—a large workbench on which were tools and materials for making and repairing musical instruments.

"I got a lot of these from my grandfather," he explained, pointing to the tools. "He makes both hammered and lap dulcimers and knows just about everything there is to know about mountain music. I'm going to have him come in several times this year and help teach the kids how to play and repair them."

"That's great!" exclaimed Sally. And then, thinking about her own situation, she asked, "Is that part of your curriculum? I didn't get to talk with the principal about the school philosophy, and the kindergarten curriculum is certainly laid out without a lot of room for extra stuff!"

"Well, I'm supposed to do both vocal and instrumental music, and many of these kids are already familiar with the sound of dulcimers, even if they don't know how to play them. And I thought that dulcimers and flutes could be good introductions to other stringed and wood-wind instruments. And the songs of the mountains are also familiar, and I hope they'll get the kids interested in other kinds of singing."

"Sounds good to me," said Sally as she headed back to her room. But she wondered what these folks will think about "developmentally appropriate practice" as she thought about the district's goals, which were clearly spelled out for the subjects comprising the kindergarten curriculum, the scope and sequence of which left little to the teacher's, or the children's, imagination.

On the first day of school it was hard to tell who was more excited, Sally and Tony or the new kindergartners. In the kindergarten room, there were a few difficult separations and some tears. Although several children had had preschool experience, most had not. Familiarizing herself with background information that was available, Sally had learned that four of the boys were "late starters" whose kindergarten entry had been delayed based on readiness testing. She wondered fleetingly whether the tests had been accurate assessments. During her student teaching experience, she had witnessed an incident in which a young boy had failed a read-ing readiness test, although he was fully able to read, because the teacher had never used workbooks or dittos and her students had not had much practice in what she called "the skills test makers want—filling in small dots, sitting for hours." When the teacher had gone to the administrator with samples of the boy's work and the books he was reading in class, the administrator had again referred her to the boy's test scores, which indicated that he wasn't ready to learn to read. When the teacher pointed out that there was no reading on the "reading readiness" test, the administrator retorted that perhaps she should spend more time getting her students ready to read than in having them read!

Looking across the hall at the other kindergarten classroom, Sally saw that Mrs. Conrad had already passed out worksheets to the quietly waiting children seated around five rectangular tables. She also saw a gaily decorated but otherwise empty bulletin board with the words GOOD WORK at the top ready to receive the children's efforts. Principal Wilson had told Sally that Mrs. Conrad would be a good mentor for her. "She's an excellent teacher," the principal had said. "She always has things under control and she has a quiet, friendly manner with the children."

As she invited her charges to look around their room, Sally spent some time observing them as a group. Three other children, two girls and a boy, had "borderline birthdates," but their parents were adamant that they not be held back. Altogether, the group represented more varied ethnicity than Sally had expected, certainly more than she had experienced in her

(continued)

own elementary schooling. This class included four African American and two Asian American pupils; the latter's families had recently immigrated to the United States. Both were just beginning to speak a little English, and one girl spoke scarcely at all. As Sally quickly learned, this girl was by no means the only child in the group that would be difficult to bring out. And that small boy with the sad expression—David; what could be on his mind?

Meanwhile, in Tony's room was a kind of organized chaos. Because Tony was a "special" teacher, his students came to him on a rotating basis. His first group was seventh graders, scheduled for music three times a week, and they were definitely not yet ready to settle into any kind of routine! Remembering his own alarming entry into puberty, Tony grinned at the interplay between boys and girls. Like most young people at this age, the girls were well ahead of the boys in all domains, though most obviously physical development. And like all preteens and early teens, they came in all shapes and sizes and were at diverse points along the road to being grown up. He also knew that some had already tried out "adult" behaviors, including sexual and substance-related ones.

Noticing that the students were all clustered around the workbench, Tony went behind it and began to talk with them about what was on the bench. "Might as well begin where they are," he thought to himself. "Here's where my career begins!"

As the year progressed, Sally's room acquired a variety of children's art work, some of it not perfect by any means, some of it unlike anything anyone had ever seen before, but all of it respected and valued because it had been produced by the children's own imaginations. In one corner was the class fairy-tale museum complete with a gingerbread house, and on a low table was a carousel with photographs of each child riding a horse. By January, there was also a list of rules for the classroom hanging on the wall, developed by the children. Rule 1 was "No smoking," and Rule 2 was "No throwing books at the lights." Mrs. Conrad had commented more than once that the list of rules seemed a little silly, but Sally believed that the room was the children's space as well as hers and that the experience of deciding what rules should be followed by everyone was an important step toward building the sense of community she wanted in her class.

Knowing that play is the young child's work and natural mode of expression, Sally had developed a schedule that balanced child-selected activity in especially arranged interest centers with whole-group circle activities. Following opening circle routines—who was here, who would be helpers, today's weather—she introduced a theme through an intriguing "lesson" based on a story or finger play. Afterward, each child was asked to choose from among various centers where that theme could be pursued in different ways, as Sally became a participant-observer, moving from center to center and encouraging children to explore with different media. As new themes were introduced, centers were changed accordingly, but they always enabled children to have experiences with language and other modes of expression, quantities and physical attributes, cause-effect relationships, social interactions, and other curriculum content appropriate for 5-year-olds. Noting what each child chose and how each child played, Sally supported mutual helping and other prosocial behavior, intervening as unobtrusively as possible. Then, bringing the children back to the circle, she returned to the theme, urging them to talk about what they had done, often helping them frame this activity in the form of a story in which each child was an important character.

Tony also was learning about his students, and as he was quick to point out to Sally, he had a much wider age range to deal with than she did. Even in a single class, students' interests and needs were far from uniform. Furthermore, while Tony had anticipated needing to establish his own authenticity (and authority), the students at first had seemed to him to be compliant but apathetic. After the first week they had little apparent interest in either the workbench or any of the other activities he planned. Even their singing of familiar songs had a tendency to be dirge-like. Clearly, he thought, he was failing to connect with their concerns and their priorities.

Toward the end of September, a tragic fire in a cabin up in the hills brought the children out of their lethargy. Two children had died in the fire, and a third child was very badly burned. The family had little money, nothing to wear, and no place to live except with cousins down the road who already had cramped quarters. Help came from all the communities in the school district: a hundred families met to fell trees and raise a new cabin, clothes were provided, and money was collected to tide the family over. But the burned child faced months of hospitalization, and her parents were faced with not only medical bills but also the expenses of traveling back and forth to the city in which she was hospitalized, 60 miles away.

As his students continued to talk about the family's plight, Tony got an idea. Perhaps his classes could raise some money for the family themselves by staging a country music fair, performing in a musical review, and selling space for local musicians and craftspeople to sell their wares. Why not?

Tony's classes were excited by the idea. He formed a grade 6–8 chorus and organized students into groups to write the review, decide on the music, make costumes and build sets, talk with Principal Wilson and other community leaders about finding space for the fair, write an article for the local newspaper to publicize the event, take orders from craftspeople for booth space, and attend to all the other necessary details. Soon most of the school was involved one way or another: middle school teachers were using the event to teach English, social studies, and math, and even Sally's kindergartners were drafted to help paint large pieces of scenery. The event itself was scheduled to be held just before Thanksgiving in a local church.

The students decided to write a pageant about the history of the community, which enabled them to choose from a wide variety of music—colonial church hymns, patriotic anthems, and 200 years' worth of folk music from many countries that had been adopted and adapted over the years until it became true "mountain music."

Tony found himself stretched to provide enough music history—let alone the music itself— for the students' eager needs. He very quickly learned who in the community could be called upon to help (his own grandfather was, of course, one of the first to be asked), and the project became a community effort. Nearly every minute of Tony's time was devoted to advising, guiding, rehearsing, and teaching his students what they needed to know. Everyone had a job (most had several!), and all the students felt that they were participating in something important.

A number of youngsters truly "came out of themselves" during the weeks before the event. Tony's favorite was a boy named Tim, a diminutive, prepubescent loner who strove mightily to affect a grunge persona. Tim, it turned out, had a talent for limericks that could be set to music. Tim's favorite, his signature piece, went as follows:

My name is Tim Bandles
I eat lighted candles
I eat them for lunch
I eat them in a bunch
Oh, how I wish they had handles!

This little limerick was the source of much teasing and giggling among his peers, but it also gave Tim something to call his own and, in fact, provided a name for the combined chorus— The Lighted Candles. "That's good!" exclaimed Tony when the students suggested it. "Light a candle where you are is just what we're all doing."

And they were: when the music fair was all over, Tony's students had raised $5,000 to help the stricken family. By the end of that first year, both Sally and Tony were tired. Sally still did not have a computer or a sand table, the district curriculum was still confining, and Mrs. Conrad was still using photocopied worksheets. Tony had a hard time coming up with activities that were as interesting and exciting as the music fair had been, and his students were still afflicted with adolescent moods and quick mouths. Still, Sally's students had discovered that school was a happy and productive place to be, that they could, in fact, learn to read, and that first grade was something to look forward to. Tony's students had learned a great deal about the history of Appalachian music and instruments and quite a bit about themselves as caring, collaborating, and capable people, which, as the two teachers agreed, is what developmentally appropriate practice is all about.

Rationale for Developmentally Appropriate Educational Practice

Age is one of the two most obvious dimensions of diversity among human beings, and clearly Sally's kindergartners and Tony's "middlescents" are at very different points on the journey to adulthood. In fact, although Tony's specialization of music education is a multiage field (preschool through high school), his middle school licensure identifies him also as an age-specialist, as is Sally (whose licensure in fact qualifies her to teach children from preschool to Grade 3). Both these novice teachers were fortunate in being assigned to children of an age group, and within a cultural context, for which they felt a particular affinity. The teachers also recognized that, those commonalities notwithstanding, each of their students was a unique person making her or his own way along that journey to becoming an adult.

During the 20th century, patterns of schooling were radically influenced by increased knowledge of distinctive phases of human development. A striking example was the emergence of junior high schools, a trend greatly influenced by G. Stanley Hall's child study movement. Based on questionnaires, interviews, and teacher observations, Hall had argued that early adolescence is a particularly vulnerable and malleable period and that schooling for that age group ought to be quite different from that provided in high schools. The first American "intermediate school," as it was called, was established in 1909, and by 1930 there were about 4,000 junior highs in the United States.

The attempt to apply what is known about children's development to school organization is even more sharply reflected in today's middle schools, a refinement of the concept of a transitional school experience between primary and secondary schooling. It is also reflected in those local school districts that have established early childhood centers, often housing child care and Head Start programs, as well as school-administered kindergarten, prekindergarten, and early childhood special education services.

In brief, **developmentally appropriate practice (DAP)** involves providing learning environments, instructional content, and pedagogical practices that are responsive to the major attributes and salient needs and interests that characterize a given life period in order to facilitate continuing developmental progress. Whatever learners of a given age and stage may have in common, however, the principle of developmentally appropriate practice recognizes both each child's uniqueness and the diversity of the social and cultural contexts that affect children's socialization. This recognition is captured in the definition that follows.

Developmentally appropriate practices result from the process of professionals making decisions about the education and well-being of children based on at least three important kinds of information or knowledge:

Developmentally Appropriate Practice

1. *what is known about child development and learning*–knowledge of age-related human characteristics that permits general predictions within an age range about what activities, materials, interactions, or experiences will be safe, healthy, interesting, achievable, and also challenging to children;

2. *what is known about the strengths, interests, and needs of each individual child in the group* to be able to adapt for and be responsive to inevitable individual variation; and

3. *knowledge of the social and cultural contexts in which children live* to ensure that learning experiences are meaningful, relevant, and respectful for the participating children and their families.

"Furthermore, each of these dimensions of knowledge—human development and learning, individual characteristics and experiences, and social and cultural contexts—is dynamic and changing, requiring that teachers remain learners throughout their careers" (Bredekamp & Copple, 1997, p. 9).

Striking examples of such changes in knowledge have involved the preadolescent and adolescent years. Neuroscientists have long known that the first years of life are characterized by amazingly rapid brain development, with the brain attaining about 95% of its adult size by age 6. It has also been recognized that this early development is characterized by an *overproduction* of cells and neural connections, followed by a period of "pruning," during which the brain continues to be highly malleable. But what neuroscientists have recently discovered is that a "second wave" of overproduction occurs prior to puberty, making the teen years a period of continuing development in the refinement, and malleability, of higher cognitive processes. This suggests an explanation of the neural substrates underlying marked changes in the way adolescents think as described by developmental psychologists such as Jean Piaget. Yet, although adolescent learners may *appear* to be "full-grown," their decision-making, planning, judgment, and organizational skills are very much "works in progress." Moreover, as in the early childhood years, continued development of areas of skill requires use of these skills, and brain malleability is also highly vulnerable to harmful influences, such as drugs or alcohol (e.g., Thompson, Giedd, & Woods, 2000).

A second area of new understanding involves adolescent sleep patterns. Although altered circadian timing patterns at puberty, as well as social expectations, result in later bedtimes for most teens, adolescents have been found to require *more,* not less, sleep than either younger children or adults. Consequentially, many–perhaps most–high school students arrive at school and move through their school day–especially if theirs is a school that starts early in the day–in a state of sleep deprivation (e.g., Wolfson & Carskadon, 1998). The situation becomes even more serious when we consider that accidents, the leading cause of death among American adolescents, are often directly or indirectly attributable to sleep deprivation, and suicide, a second leading cause of adolescent death, is often precipitated by depression, to which sleep deprivation may be a contributing factor.

What implications do these areas of new and emerging knowledge have for educational policy and practice? Better understanding of adolescent sleep needs and patterns should, at the very least, influence teachers and parents to be less judgmental, but it has also encouraged many high schools to experiment with later start times, despite the complications (e.g., for after school sports or jobs) that may entail. Better understanding of adolescent brain structure and function implies a renewed conviction that teachers indeed can play a highly influential role, not only in their students' acquisition of knowledge but in their continuing cognitive development.

We must also ask what impact cultural changes, notably the pervasive presence of electronic technology in children's lives, have on their development. How are young learners of the 21st century cognitively and socioemotionally *different* from those of the 20th?

Economic Aims for Schooling

Leon Botstein (1997), president of Bard College, has offered the "modest proposal" of replacing the American high school and ending secondary education with what is now the 10th grade. If schooling were more age-appropriate, he argued, it could be more efficient as well as far more effective. His argument is essentially for faith in the potential of the American educational system–for, in his phrase, "the language of hope"–but his critique of what's wrong with the system essentially concerns developmentally inappropriate curriculum and pedagogy. "The challenge," he writes, "is to find ways to engage the early onset of adolescence and its attendant freedoms and habits" (p. 85). Botstein maintains that if we are able to do that and also to capitalize on the learning potential of younger children, what today's 18-year-olds have imperfectly learned most students can master by age 16, when they can move on to postsecondary academic or technical preparation.

National Education Goals

The currently high profile of early childhood education can be attributed to a combination of factors, especially mounting evidence of the critical importance of early educational experiences in influencing children's subsequent development. Recognition of such evidence was reflected in Goal 1 identified by the National Education Goals Panel (1996) that, by the year 2000, all American children would enter school "ready to learn." Although there is evidence of progress in reducing the glaring discrepancies in participation in quality preschool programs between high- and low-income families, no one would assert that that goal was achieved, especially for the nearly one American child in five who lives in poverty. Moreover, as the Children's Defense Fund 2001 report, *The State of America's Children,* stressed, the discrepancy persists when children enter school, reflected in "the dramatic disparity in resources provided to the poorest children" (p. 62). Jonathan Kozol (1991) depicted this disparity as reflecting "savage inequalities" in the educational opportunities provided in American schools.

Some early 20th-century Progressive reformers had considered kindergarten "the one thing needful" to redress societal inequities and equalize opportunity. The growth since the 1960s of prekindergarten programs has arguably been directed toward that same goal. Yet despite the call for all children to have access to developmentally appropriate preschool programs as an important means for achieving the goal of entering school "ready to learn," do educators attempting to meet this goal face a danger of placing developmentally *inappropriate* cognitive, perceptual-motor, and social-emotional demands on young children?

Concerned observers cite two sources of danger. The first is an economic view of educational aims; that is, the view that the

major purpose of schooling is to prepare students to enter the workforce. The second concern emerges from higher education, which now enrolls many students who might otherwise not have considered college but have found that a college degree is required for an increasing number of jobs. Such a view begins with the business community and the professorate, and the sequence of attribution goes something like this: employers concerned about workers' literacy skills, and professors concerned about students' "readiness" for college work, blame high school teachers, who attribute responsibility to middle school teachers for failing to prepare students for the rigors of concentrated academic study. Those teachers in turn think intermediate-level instruction must have been weak, for students lack grounding in the basics (mathematical operations, paragraph construction, reading for meaning), but those problems, alas, are the fault of primary instruction. The ultimate blame doesn't stop with the kindergarten teacher (who ought to better ensure children's readiness for first grade); it gets passed on to parents.

If the ultimate goal is international competitiveness and if American graduates fare poorly when compared to their counterparts in other industrialized nations, one kind of logic argued for "more! earlier! faster!" And that logic inevitably, as advocates for young children maintain, results in inappropriate practices that actually impede children's development in the attempt to accelerate the notion that "more" will speed up children's development and adolescents' readiness for college has been very evident in connection with homework, as many parents will attest. However, what is known about development suggests to experts like Cathy Vatterot (2009) that "more" isn't necessarily better. In addition to out-of-school factors that differentially affect children's lives, she stresses the differential readiness of each successive developmental level, endorsing the "10-Minute Rule": ten minutes per night per grade level.

Early Childhood Education and Developmentally Appropriate Practice

Although the principle is relevant to all levels of schooling, *developmental appropriateness* emerged in the 1970s and 1980s as a particular concern in the rapidly growing field of early childhood education. This field encompasses infant and toddler services, preschool programs, kindergarten, and primary grades; that is, from birth through about age 8. As Rebecca New and Bruce Mallory (1994) summarized, the resulting publication of the National Association for the Education of Young Children (NAEYC), *Developmentally Appropriate Practice*, was—like many other reform ideas—an important political statement:

> The NAEYC effort was motivated primarily by the need to respond to the increasingly pervasive pressure for early childhood programs to conform to an academic model of instruction typical of programs designed for older children. Throughout the document, there is also evidence of the intent to advocate for the field's long-standing core values of respect for and nurturing of young children as among the necessary means to achieve the democratic goals of a just and compassionate society. (p. 1)

Constructivist Thought in Developmentally Appropriate Practice

Cognitive Development Theories

The resulting document and its subsequent revisions have a scientific as well as an ideological basis. Developmentally appropriate practice (DAP) is not itself a theory of education (or of child development); it reflects a tradition of child pedagogy that, while centuries old, gained scientific support in the 20th century largely because of Jean Piaget's highly influential theory of cognitive development. Thus developmentally appropriate practice is often described as based on, or at least congruent with, *cognitive developmental theory,* especially Piagetian theory. Also reflecting the social constructivist theory of Lev Vygotsky, DAP is clearly congruent as well with the ideas of cross-cultural psychology, which posits that the ways in which individuals construct their world are strongly influenced by cultural factors. Rebecca Williams (1994) described the pedagogical implications of the theoretical orientation intended by the term **constructivism** in this way:

> Children are understood to be active constructors of their own knowledge. Mental activity is enhanced by wide experience with people, materials, and events, through which children form concepts and develop perceptions. Children's skills also are refined through repeated experience. Curriculum is therefore expected to provide multiple opportunities for children's direct and concrete engagement. This view of children's learning places the locus of control of the process within children themselves. Adults are not the pivotal factor in the process. They can provide a conducive setting, but it is the children's inner structures that impel them to learn. (p. 158)

Activity 4: Childhood Experiences

The word *structure* in this context refers to the concepts, ideas, and understandings that children *construct* through their transactions with their social and physical environment. Some scholars call this a *frame* or a *lens* or—after Vygotksy—a *scaffold,* but all agree that it is through this construction that individuals filter information and make sense of the world in which they live.

Thus, from a constructivist perspective, knowledge is "made" by the knower, who (to use Piaget's terms) assimilates new experiences within knowledge structures already present and accommodates to experiences that do not fit neatly into those structures. Imagine the cognitive manipulation that takes place when a small child who knows the class "dog" as four-legged creatures with bushy tails and so on encounters a stub-tailed or pointy-tailed dog . . . or a pony!

Motivation to learn emerges from the fact that children's **cognitive structures** are continuously challenged, and the child's inherent need to understand– *epistemic curiosity,* in philosophical terms–provides the impetus for acquiring new knowledge. Note that this need to understand is an *internal* motivating factor and is significantly different from such external factors as the praise of adults or the awarding of candy and gold stars or stickers. Since some conditions are more likely than others to elicit that motivation, the teacher's task is to solve "the problem of the match" between what each child is ready, cognitively and motivationally, to learn and what is made available to the child to learn. (Vygotsky [1978] called the range of experiences that are sufficiently challenging yet manageable the **zone of proximal development.**)

Although the NAEYC's DAP guidelines emphasize the uniqueness of the early childhood years, both the concept of developmentally appropriate teaching and its underlying constructivist theory of learning and knowing are relevant to the instruction of older children, adolescents, and even adults. Many (most?) college students, experiencing a small epiphany of understanding of some concept or idea, remember that it was introduced in a high school course, but they "didn't get it" then. Many also remember lack of interest and boredom with material presented in high school classes that was already too familiar.

The constructivist view differs from the traditional notion of readiness–used as a criterion for determining when a child should enter kindergarten, move on to first grade, and so on–in that constructivists emphasize that cognitive readiness is not determined simply by biological maturation, a kind of natural unfolding. It is rather an interactional–better, a *transactional*–matter. At any point in time, every individual is ready to learn, if learning experiences are at an optimal level of novelty or incongruity. Clearly, what is optimal for one learner is not necessarily optimal for another, even among learners of the same age. Though each of us functions within a particular social-cultural context, everyone undertakes as an individual the *tasks* of development (Havighurst, 1972) associated with each successive life stage.

Characteristics of a Developmentally Appropriate Classroom

Pedagogies: Old and New

Though they have historical antecedents, constructivist notions gained scientific support and integrity as a coherent theory through the work of Piaget and other theorists, notably Vygotsky and Jerome Bruner, both of whom placed greater emphasis than did Piaget on the social-cultural context of children's development.[2]

Constructivist ideas were actually advanced much earlier by a succession of educational theorists and reformers, including Comenius in the 17th century, Condillac and Rousseau in the 18th, Pestalozzi and Parker in the late 19th, and John Dewey in the 20th. Sharply critical of the old methods used to teach reading in the schools—memorization based on recitation from the New England Primer—Horace Mann argued that children could best master reading and writing if instruction were guided by, and built on, the language base a child had. (Does that argument sound like today's *whole language* approach?) Pestalozzi's object teaching emphasized the child's experience and perceptions as the basis for organizing knowledge and developing powers of reasoning—a "faculty" the authoritative educational psychology of his day considered not available to young children!

In Francis Parker's child-centered approach, school subjects and practical arts were correlated—that is, integrated—as pupils worked eagerly, without coercion or control by the teacher, at their individual and cooperative jobs. In contrast to the traditional faculty psychology, which portrayed the mind as comprised of a number of discrete faculties, and pedagogy as mental discipline to strengthen them, Parker viewed children's learning as holistic and, like Piaget, inseparable from development. Yet, turn of the century classrooms—with few exceptions, such as Parker's Quincy (Massachusetts) System and Dewey's laboratory school at the University of Chicago, and kindergartens (which were still quite separate from public schools)—were as described by Larry Cuban (1993):

> Generally, teachers taught the entire class at the same time. Teacher talk dominated verbal expression during class time. Classroom activities revolved around teacher questions and explanations, student recitations, and the class's working on textbook assignments. Except for laboratory work in science classrooms, teachers sought uniformity in behavior. The social organization of the turn-of-the-century classroom, then, was formal, with students sitting in rows of bolted-down desks facing the teacher's desk and chalkboard, rising to recite for the teacher, and moving about the room or leaving it only with the teacher's permission. The academic organization of the classroom hinged upon the whole class's moving as one through the course of study, text, recitations, and homework. Those who worked, succeeded; those who didn't, failed. (p. 37)

Does that picture sound familiar to you? Based on his study of American classrooms from 1880 to 1990, Cuban concluded that teacher-centered instruction continued to be the dominant pattern, although at the elementary level and in some secondary schools "a hybrid version of student-centered practices, begun in the early decades of this century, has spread and is maturing" (p. 272). Such practices have included the use of small group organization, activity centers, projects, more provision for student choice, joint teacher–student planning of learning activities, and integration of content.

The notion of intrinsically motivated, child-directed learning is, for many, epitomized in the approach developed by Maria Montessori, whose injunction, "Don't *tell, teach!*" summed up her view of how classrooms for students of any age should be conducted: The teacher planfully arranges, models, and monitors, as students, within limits defined by the learning materials, follow their inborn inclination to discover and to understand. Yet Montessori's tardy popularity in the United States, in contrast to many other nations, has been attributed to its proposal of a highly individualized approach at a time when Dewey, Kirkpatrick, and other leaders in the American progressive education movement stressed cooperative projects and group problem solving. Paradoxically, since her work had begun with children considered intellectually deficient or living in the slums of Rome, the relatively few Montessori programs in the United States by the 1950s were viewed by many as desirable for exceptionally capable or (perhaps because only privately available) more privileged children. Today, some American public schools and a number of independent schools offer Montessori education, some at least through the eighth grade.

A few other educational approaches have, like Maria Montessori, maintained that teaching the *whole* child must not only take account of characteristics associated with major stages of development but also of the child's *spiritual* nature. Among the best known of these, the Waldorf approach, evolved from a school Rudolph Steiner established in 1919 for the children of workers in the Waldorf Astoria cigarette factory in Stuttgart, Germany. Waldorf schools, while not presently as numerous as Montessori programs, are similar in certain respects, but strikingly different in others. Each reflects a pedagogical theory inseparably linked to its founder, views learning holisti-

cally and of a piece with development, attempts to respond to the learner's spiritual nature, and purposefully eschews competitiveness, but there is much greater emphasis in the Waldorf approach on such areas as art, music, and foreign language, and on the critical role in human development of *imagination*. Although both systems provide for secondary schooling, most Montessori and Waldorf schools in the United States are limited to prekindergarten through Grade 8.

One fairly coherent constructivist model that has attracted much interest among American educators is the Reggio Emilia approach. Rather than having a philosophy linked to a single founder, it is named for the town in the Emilia Romagna region of northern Italy where it has been developed and refined from its post–World War II origins (Edwards, Gandini, & Foreman, 1993). The system's distinctive qualities include some familiar constructivist ideas: learning occurs within the context of an emergent curriculum organized around projects carried out over extended periods of time (determined by children's activity and choice rather than adult-controlled time schedules) that integrate diverse areas of learning and elicit children's expression, in all of their "hundred languages," including words, movement, drawing, painting, building, sculpture, shadow play, collage, dramatic play, and music. Leading children to surprising levels of symbolic skills and creativity, the approach takes place not in an elite and sheltered setting of private education but rather in a municipal system of full-day child care open to all, including children with special needs (Edwards et al., pp. 3–4).

Perhaps the most striking feature of Reggio Emilia may be the most difficult to translate from one cultural setting to another: the view, shared by parents and educators, of the school as an extension of the home. This deeply embedded

Reggio Emilia Approaches

understanding is a legacy of its origins in a parent cooperative movement that emerged in the region during the years of post–World War II reconstruction. A second distinctive feature perhaps difficult to translate is, as in the Waldorf approach, the centrality of artistic expression. Although this approach, like DAP and the progressive and open education movements, was explicitly designed for preprimary and primary schools, some of the key concepts seem valid and applicable with older learners:

- Conscious awareness of the important role of physical space and especially of aesthetic properties of the physical environment in inviting learning
- Not holding students' motivation and accomplishment hostage to the tyranny of the clock, curriculum guide, or textbook
- The importance of true team collaboration, over time, marked by shared ownership of the educational process and continued inquiry on the part of teachers, learners, families, and leaders (principals, supervisors)
- Elimination of artificial compartmentalizations among subjects and between science and the arts, knowledge and creativity, effort and enjoyment
- Trust in and respect for students, expressed through responsibility combined with empowerment, opportunity to work cooperatively as well as independently, and valuing of diverse modes of expression
- A concept of development as a dynamic process rather than as static levels

Middle Schools

The shift from the traditional junior high to the **middle school** is another example of DAP being put into practice and uniting an understanding of development of young people with principles of learning. Each age level seems to have a set of characteristics that distinguishes it from all others, and one of the most marked is that of children who are in the transition into adolescence. Actually, as discussed in Chapter 7, the transition begins well before the onset of puberty for most Western children, with increased cognitive flexibility and awareness of perspectives of others. Whereas administrative organization and grade-level content are the focus in secondary schools, in middle schools a focus on broadly defined needs of the learner that, as in Waldorf education, encompasses the full range of intellectual as well as social, emotional, and other developmental needs is fundamental. Moreover, the challenge of middle school education is, as the National Middle School Association (1992) states, "to develop an educational program that is based on the needs and characteristics of a most diverse and varied population" (p. 4).

Although *middle childhood* is usually defined as spanning the years from about age 8 to age 12, American middle schools are generally intended to address developmental issues associated with early adolescence. The essential elements of a true middle school, according to the National Middle School Association, are: (1) educators knowledgeable about and committed to young adolescents; (2) a balanced curriculum based on the needs of young adolescents; (3) a range of organizational arrangements; (4) varied instructional strategies; (5) a full exploratory program; (6) comprehensive advising and counseling; (7) continuous progress for students; (8) evaluation procedures compatible with the nature of young adolescents; (9) cooperative planning; and (10) positive school climate.

Persistent concerns about drops in academic performance among students, as well as declining self-esteem, bullying, and other antisocial behavior have prompted some educators to favor eliminating middle schools and returning to the K–8 and 9–12 grade structure. Others believe children of this age group would benefit from older role models. Modifying school structures is a continuous process as communities attempt to respond to perceived local needs. Increasingly, you may find preschool through primary age groupings served in early childhood centers, or Grades 5 and 6 housed separately from Grades 7 and 8, or schools returning to a K–8 structure, or a return to the grades 7–9 junior high model, or–as Leon Botstein proposes–a two-tiered (K–6 and 7–10) structure. However, differential organizational structures represent but one way in which schools respond to developmental diversity among students.

Roles: Old and New

Although constructivism (in both its old and new forms) places the student at the center of the learning process and acknowledges that much important learning is done by students entirely on their own or with peers, the teacher's role is of key importance. In the 1997 revision of the NAEYC DAP guidelines, Bredekamp (1997), affirmed the basic responsibility of teachers as well as the principle that a child's sense of competence and worth is the essential foundation for learning and development:

> The goal is for teachers to support the learning and development of all children. To achieve this goal, teachers need to know children well and use everything they know about each child—including that individual's learning styles, interests and preferences, personality and temperament, skills and talents, challenges and difficulties. Children are more likely to achieve a positive sense of self if they experience more success than failure in the early school years. The teacher must support a positive sense of self-identity in each child. (p. 40)

The one word that best captures the most fundamental change in the teacher's role is *collaboration*. Because the field of early childhood education has been a major influence in bringing about a reexamination of the teacher's role, another look at its history may be instructive.[3]

Soon after Friedrich Froebel's notion of "child-gardening" was brought to America by Margarethe Meyer Schurz in the wake of the great German immigration, Elizabeth Peabody described the role of kindergartner (the term referred to the kindergarten teacher) as a partner and adviser for parents in nurturing young children. Although kindergartens have been around since the mid-19th century, prekindergartens as such have been in existence only about half as long. The common school (not exactly "common," considering that most 19th-century American children received very little instruction, many none at all) enrolled pupils as young as 3 years old, but they were mixed in with older brothers and sisters with no provisions for early childhood's uniqueness. Nursery schools, like those Margaret MacMillan started for English children of poor families, and kindergartens spread as a facet of the British and American settlement movements of the early 20th century, and they had a particular focus on health and nutritional concerns.

Two other important movements fostered the expansion of early childhood education in the United States: child study and mental hygiene. G. Stanley Hall,

History of
Kindergarten

often called the founder of child psychology, was a key influence in both movements. He influenced the latter by introducing to American intellectuals and professionals psychoanalytic theories of the formative significance of early childhood experiences (and introducing them to Freud himself at the historic conference at Clark University in 1909!). Arnold Gesell, Hall's student, had by 1930 led the growth of nursery education, in his words, "from a no man's land to an every man's land" (p. 143), although of course nursery teachers, like "kindergartners," were invariably women. What Gesell meant was that a broad range of professionals—psychologists, physicians, social workers, public health workers—had become involved. Universities had established laboratory programs, like Gesell's own Guidance Nursery at Yale, as centers for child development research and teacher training. He and other professionals viewed programs for young children as important both in identifying problems early in life so that timely ameliorative measures could be provided and in promoting the healthy development of mind and body.

The Great Depression halted the spread of nursery education, but when the Second World War called multitudes of women to defense industry work, the Lanham Act created another role for such programs: day care. The years since World War II and especially since the 1960s have witnessed an enormous increase in the need for outside-the-home child care in many industrialized nations. In the United States, this need was exacerbated by welfare reform requirements instituted under the Clinton administration, which created a crisis for many families, as well as providers and policymakers. Parents and child advocates insist that child care, including before- and after-school care for school-age children, must be more than custodial, but is it "education"? In the United States, the NAEYC joined forces with other major child advocacy groups such as the Children's Defense Fund in working for policies to ensure that child care is accessible and affordable yet also adheres to high-quality standards of professional nurture and guidance that are in the interests of children and, consequently, of society itself. That is, whether provided in a center or in someone's home, child care must be *developmentally appropriate.*

Children's Defense Fund

Growth in families' need for child care led to new discoveries about young children and, consequently, to a redefinition of adult roles. Conventional wisdom in the burgeoning field of child psychology had held that group experiences were of no value for children until at least age 3. But as necessity truly became the mother of invention, caregivers (and psychologists) discovered that toddlers were quite interested in each other, and even babies were, in their fashion, social creatures. Such discoveries implied a (developmentally appropriate) teacher role for adults caring for infants and toddlers, and a number of roles (model, partner in parallel play, friend, leader) for very small children themselves. These new roles became ever more influential in the course of children's development through and beyond the early childhood years. Educators who observed the ways children learn from and with each other sought to reapply Parker's and Dewey's less teacher-centered concepts through such strategies as cooperative learning and small-group activity. From birth through all the years of schooling, learners have a central role in their own learning and an instrumental role in the learning of their peers.

Early childhood programs, especially Project Head Start and Early Start, emphasize collaborative relationships with families to promote optimal development during the most formative years. For school-age children and youth, the teacher's role has increasingly become a collaborative one in other respects. Rather than being expected to function on their own, teachers can anticipate the support of peers through building-level planning and problem-solving teams and actual team teaching. And, of course, working collaboratively with others—fellow professionals, parents and other family members, and community resource persons—requires a unique set of sensitivities and skills.

Head Start Programs

Place of Content Knowledge: Old and New

Developmentally appropriate practice means a change in the place of content knowledge in schooling that involves rediscovery of some old wisdom under-girded by new knowledge about human development. What is often called the "cognitive revolution" in American psychology that began in the 1950s and 1960s brought new respect for children's intellectual resources and for the potential of schooling to influence the course of development. But it also contributed to an unduly narrow emphasis and raised what Piaget called the "American question": How much can we accelerate the pace of children's cognitive learning in order to create smarter adults?

The discourse concerning DAP is more concerned with process than with content, which Bernard Spodek (1991) attributes to the fact that "early childhood educators are more concerned with the effects of early childhood education on a child's development than with what a child comes to know as a result of that education" (p. 1). What Piaget called "social knowledge" (information)—imparted by parents, teachers, *Sesame Street,* siblings, and peers—is important, but cognitive development is an active, transactional process, not a passive one. The deductive reasoning basic to mathematical understanding and the inductive questioning that is the hallmark of scientific inquiry are inherent capabilities of children as they strive to reconcile incongruities and impose structure on their constantly expanding experiential world. In related fashion, literacy learning begins in early childhood—in fact, in earliest infancy—and is fostered to the degree that the child's active and creative use of language, and pleasure in its use, continue to be encouraged (Vacca, Vacca, & Gove, 1987). However, to put basal readers or phonics worksheets in the hands of all 3-year-olds would be developmentally inappropriate.

In the constructivist perspective, learners of any age generate content knowledge, not just receive it. As Howard Gardner (1991) has emphasized, the goal of effective education is not merely transmitting information, but ensuring understanding. Moreover, Gardner emphasizes that since understanding is itself a developmental process—proceeding from sensorimotor, to intuitive, to application of logical reasoning—school instruction must support this progression if learners are ultimately to gain mastery of content disciplines.

Assessment: Old and New

When we consider assessment in the context of learners' developmental status, we need to distinguish different purposes of assessment. Statewide proficiency or graduation tests and international comparisons of educational achievement indeed reflect urgent American concerns for accountability and a national effort to identify and maintain educational standards as essential for educational reform.

"Setting the bar" higher, some educators argue, will only widen the gap between the more and the less advantaged children and schools. Yet conversely, several decades of research have demonstrated the strong link between adult expectations and student (and school) performance: expectancy becomes a self-fulfilling prophecy (Botstein, 1997). Whatever standards are agreed upon for progression through the educational system and ultimate graduation, there must be some means of assessing the status of individual students in terms of those standards. Although often it may be imperfectly implemented, assessment is essential to educational accountability.

But assessment of student progress vis-à-vis performance standards should not be confused with sorting, a questionable and potentially invidious use of assessment. In the past, assessment often was used to validate beliefs about the limited learning potential of children of poor and low-income families and immigrants, children of color, and children with disabilities. Although inappropriate assessment procedures also have been used to identify which children are ready for school and which ones are not, the DAP guidelines are quite explicit about the responsibility of schools to be "ready" for all children. As Samuel Meisels (1981) has written, screening and assessment should never be used to close educational doors for a child but to open them.

A 21st-century view of educational assessment goes beyond reliance on narrow and fallible tests in linking knowledge about individual learners with instructional planning and decision making. This view is frequently identified by the term **authentic assessment.** Noting the limited value of traditional, norm-referenced assessment procedures with young children, DAP guidelines emphasize the importance of observation of children in natural activity contexts, collections of children's work, and ongoing communication with parents "for the purpose of improving teaching and learning" (Bredekamp & Copple, 1997, p. 17). To Gardner (1991), with students of any age, understanding can only be meaningfully assessed through opportunities to apply learning to new situations:

> Whereas short-answer tests and oral responses in classes can provide clues to student understanding, it is generally necessary to look more deeply if one desires firm evidence that understandings of significance have been obtained. For these purposes, new and unfamiliar problems, followed by open-ended clinical interviews or careful observations, provide the best way of establishing the degree of understanding that students have obtained. (p. 145)

Perspectives on Age and Development

School experiences both profoundly influence and are influenced by people's development as human beings. That statement may seem on the surface so obvious that it scarcely deserves mention. But consider it more closely. What is "development," and precisely what implications does it have for learning and teaching in schools? As David Shaffer (1993) summarizes, "Simply stated, development refers to systematic changes in the individual that occur between the moment of conception . . . and the moment the individual dies" (p. 4). You are probably familiar with important concepts involving patterns of change that humans experience over time, such as nature versus nurture, sensitive or critical periods, individual differences, and developmental stages and domains. What implications do such concepts have for schooling?

Sensitive Periods and Developmental Crises

Since critically important systematic changes occur before schooling begins (indeed, from the moment of conception) as well as afterward, it may appear that development proceeds relatively independently of schooling. While the so-called **nature versus nurture debate** has revolved more around what young children experience at home than what older children and youth experience in school, major social programs such as Project Head Start have reflected the awareness that education can indeed alter the course of children's development. Moreover, as described in Chapter 7, middle childhood is also a period of heightened receptiveness to developmental influence, when teachers can encourage children's desires to process new experiences and foster their awareness of the perspectives of others. And, as noted previously, recent neuroscientific findings confirm that the adolescent years also constitute a period of significant cognitive change, and thus a period of sensitivity and responsiveness to the influence of others, teachers as well as parents and peers. Probably most people believe their own lives have been affected in crucial ways by school experiences that occurred at some point in their lives when they were particularly receptive or particularly vulnerable.

Although those points of receptivity and vulnerability are to a great extent an individual matter—associated with a major change in an individual's family situation like parental divorce, separation, or death; a person's own or a family member's illness; a move to a new community and a new school; a new friendship; even a certain teacher or coach—some are fairly universal. In Erik Erikson's (1963) familiar formulation, the development of *ego identity* is a lifetime enterprise, involving eight stages of psychosocial development, each marked by a conflict to be resolved. The adolescent identity crisis is preceded by successive childhood crises, or turning points, emerging from conflicting influences or needs: basic trust versus mistrust, autonomy versus shame and doubt, initiative versus guilt, industry versus inferiority. Everyone remembers—happily, painfully, or ruefully—their own adolescent years and the changes they brought. For centuries, in fact, adolescence, though not identified as such, was assumed to be the critical period for learning, and schooling often didn't begin until then. Infancy, traditionally the first 7 years of life, was accorded little importance.

Clearly, the kinds of experience that are critical will change in the course of development. Yet, as Howard Gardner (1991) noted in *The Unschooled Mind,* formal instruction often fails to challenge students to move beyond the intuitive modes of knowing that served them well as young children and use the cognitive resources they have acquired. Matching instruction to the developmental level of learners requires, he reminds us, challenging students to demonstrate understanding by applying knowledge to new situations.

Individual Differences and Developmental Domains

Developmentally appropriate practice is based not only on age and stage differences but also on another key concept in the psychology of human development: individual differences. Many such differences are culture-related; others are situational, influenced by circumstances in a person's life and quite idiosyncratic. Wide variations, even within cultures, are to some degree attributable to built-in factors, certainly to biological heredity. Arnold Gesell (1949), well-known for his detailed descriptions of nearly universal characteristics of infants, children, and youth that are virtually programmed in humans as in other species, asserted, "No two infants were ever born alike" (p. 530). While the nature side of the nature versus nurture debate involves both common (i.e., maturational) and highly idiosyncratic (i.e., hereditary) influences, development involves the subtle interaction of these influences with a host of environmental influences, many cultural and many specific to the individual. All the characteristics or traits that distinguish everyone's unique personality reflect some interactive mix of biological and environmental influences. This impact is true even of some physical attributes, such as skeletal structure, although others (e.g., eye color) are entirely biologically influenced.

Human development proceeds on many fronts, often referred to as *developmental domains* (e.g., motor, cognitive, language/communication, social/emotional). The notion of domains in some ways involves arbitrary distinctions, for babies, children, youth, and adults are whole beings, not just composites of discrete parts. Language development, for example, is virtually inseparable from cognitive and social development. During the critical period for language acquisition—the first 3 years of life—language is also mightily influenced by sensory and motor development. But language can be analyzed on the basis of domain-specific concepts (phonology, morphology, syntax, semantics, and pragmatics). Appropriate educational practice requires knowledge of such concepts and patterns of change associated with major domains. It is not developmentally appropriate to expect 3-year-olds to cut expertly with scissors or know (in the adult sense) what clouds are, to expect 5-year-olds to be physically inactive for extended periods or argue the merits of a bicameral legislature, or to expect 10-year-olds to do grueling labor or solve algebraic equations. Nor is it developmentally appropriate, Gardner reminds us, to fail to challenge learners to apply their developing powers of understanding.

Because milestones, such as first words and independent walking, as well as transitions from one stage to another are reached by different children at different times, it is necessary to be aware of normal ranges of variation in the timing and sequencing of developmental changes. Such variations are attributable to many factors, including gender, geography (e.g., climate), genetics, specific environmental influences, and differential cultural values and expectations. And for some children, such as a child who is blind or one who has cerebral palsy, developmental processes may differ qualitatively, rather than quantitatively, from their typical peers. It makes no sense to say, for example, that a child who cannot see has "delayed" visual development or that a child with cerebral palsy who cannot walk independently has "delayed" motor development. The first child learns to complement functional vision with other sensory information more than do most children; the second child may accomplish mobility with the aid of adaptive equipment, such as a wheelchair.

The Importance of Developmental Knowledge

What should teachers know about children and adolescents in order for their instruction to be developmentally appropriate? Until the latter half of the 19th century, most American and European teachers and school officials knew very little because not much attention was paid to the unique features of successive stages. In some common schools, children as young as 3 or 4 were instructed along with older students, even adolescents, seated on hard benches inappropriate for all, awaiting their turn to recite. Age-grading supplanted such arrangements, however, and though instruction could be more age-appropriate, it rarely took into account individual variations. Pupils who deviated considerably from the norm—who didn't "fit"—presented problems that were addressed through grade repetition or ungraded classes and classes for "unrulies" (forerunners of special education classes, which are discussed in Chapter 11).

The **child study movement,** while promoting more positive awareness of differential rates of development among children, mainly inspired more age-appropriate practices, such as the introduction of the junior high school. From the child study tradition, through the work of Gesell and his associates, a generation of aspiring teachers who were trained in the 1940s and 1950s also learned about the terrible 2s, trusting 3s, and general attributes characteristic of successive ages and stages of childhood and adolescence. What they didn't always learn about development was the extent to which, and the ways in which, it is influenced by experience and the wide variability among children that can be expected within each of the successive stages. Nor did they learn about variability associated with diverse cultural norms, expectations, and values.

Stage theories of human development emphasize the universality of developmental milestones and the manifestations of specific attributes of successive stages. In addition to Gesell's normative descriptions, some well-known theorists have focused on personality development (Sigmund Freud, Anna Freud, Erik Erikson), on cognitive development (Jean Piaget), on language (Noam Chomsky), and on moral development (Lawrence Kohlberg). Although many of these aspects of development may emerge in much the same way among the world's children, it is also the case that they may be differentially valued and expressed in different cultural settings.

One instance of culturally different values placed on developmental skills involves the notion of *independence,* or autonomy, and developmental domains labeled on assessment scales as *self-help, adaptive,* or *social-emotional.* Noting aspects of the Reggio Emilia early childhood approach that may be culture-specific, Rebecca New (1994) commented on a standard routine that children in American day-care centers quickly learn: how to put on one's jacket when it's time to go home or for outdoor play by flipping it, arms in sleeves, over one's head. This maneuver may require concentration and involves occasional mistakes, but the pleasure in accomplishment and sense of mastery youngsters experience is apparent in their expression. "Few Italian 2-year-olds have been taught how to put their coats on unassisted," she notes, for "adults . . . enjoy the opportunity to assist children, even as they encourage children to also help one another" (p. 72). This example illustrates a difference in culturally valued independence versus cooperation that is expressed in various ways. What implications do such differences have for developmentally appropriate expectations concerning children?

The concept of *developmentally appropriate practice* emerged in a political context, with a certain agenda, of establishing consensus concerning the uniqueness of early childhood, defined as the first 8 years of life. But age, stage, or developmental status cannot be the sole determinant of *educational* appropriateness, in the early childhood years or beyond. The guidelines as they were originally formulated and generally understood may have been insufficiently responsive to diverse cultural values, a concern addressed in the revised version of DAP. For example, Leslie Williams (1994) contrasts widely shared Native American traditions of interconnectedness, interdependence, and respectful listening with DAP's original strong emphasis on individualism, independence, and overt expression of language. The constructivism underlying DAP's guidelines, as originally formulated, has thus been criticized as being ethnocentrically narrow and inadvertently legitimizing social and educational inequities by expressing a preconceived and prescribed version of what is developmentally appropriate.

A broader social constructivism, on the other hand, implies a more inclusive and collaborative perspective of educational practices that not only considers family and culture but recognizes their primacy in the lives of children and respects children in both their uniqueness and interconnectedness. In the Reggio Emilia educational approach, for example,

> the child is understood as having not only needs but competencies and rights as well. . . . Implicit in this view is the recognition of the child's embeddedness in a family, a community, a culture, and a society. It is thus the responsibility of the teachers, in active collaboration with parents and other members of the community, to acknowledge and respect those rights, to identify and understand those competencies, and respond collectively to those needs. In order to fulfill this role, teachers in Reggio Emilia become researchers in their own classrooms, regularly making and sharing hypotheses about learning and development rather than reifying existing conceptions. (Williams, 1994, p. 158)

There are in fact different "constructions" of what constructivism entails, ranging from those that encompass applied behavior analysis and direct instruction to those that consider teaching, if the term implies adult direction and management of children's learning, a "dirty word" (Harris & Graham, 1994). Exclusive commitment to any doctrinaire approach in teaching risks blinding a teacher to the differences among students at any particular stage of development or level of schooling. In its essence, constructivist teaching recognizes that learning, though it occurs in and is supported by social contexts, is an individual affair. Developmentally appropriate practices are those that respond to each student's uniqueness.

Critical Incident

Responding to a Concerned Board Member

Things seemed to take a positive turn for Tony once he and his students began planning for the music program; many of the students seemed to be actively engaged and interested in the program planning and in the variety of preparatory activities that needed to occur. Then one morning, about 3 weeks before the scheduled program, Tony was called into Principal Wilson's office. One of the members of the school board, a rather influential individual who was quite supportive of the existing school band, had complained that Tony might be setting a bad example for other teachers—especially ones new to the school. While this board member acknowledged that it was of benefit to raise money to assist the family with their expenses, it was pretty clear to him that this activity was outside the standard music curriculum and that it was setting a bad precedent. And besides, he reasoned, there was a pretty good music curriculum in place that was approved by the state. The principal wanted to let Tony know of the concern because the board member was coming in to discuss the issue in 2 days,

International Perspective: What's Happening Elsewhere in the World?

Please Journey With Me Across and Within Cultures

Kofi Marfo, PhD

Professor of Educational Psychology & Director, Center for Research on Children's Development & Learning, University of South Florida, Tampa

The stories you are about to read are real personal experiences I have used in my classes over the years to illustrate, as well as trigger class discussions on, important concepts and issues in human development and learning. Unlike my own students, however, you have the benefit of seeing these stories in print. Of course, this also means that you have the misfortune of not experiencing firsthand the drama and cultural cadence with which these stories are "performed" in my classes. I have selected these stories to help you think both conceptually and concretely about the meaning and real-world implications of the principle of developmental appropriateness. All three dimensions of developmental appropriateness to which you have been introduced in this chapter find expression in these stories and the accompanying reflections. However, highlighted more pivotally and purposefully is the cultural and contextual dimension, which is often missing in conceptualizations of DAP.

Let's start the journey with a chapter out of my primary school years in my home country of Ghana, West Africa. Permit me to title this chapter "Face to face with teaching outside the sociocultural radar of the poor learner." You may be familiar with the children's song that begins as follows:

One man went to mow,
Went to mow a meadow,
One man and his dog,
Went to mow a meadow
Two men went to mow
Went to mow a meadow
Two men, one man and his dog. . . .

I was most likely taught this "Tweenies Song Time" selection early in my primary school experience—at an age and in a cultural setting where two words that are central to understanding the lyrics meaningfully (*mow* and *meadow*) were utterly foreign to little children ages 6 to 9 (and most likely to some of the teachers who taught this song routinely as well). Here is a little intercultural mental exercise for you. In place of every occurrence of "a meadow," insert "Ahmadou." In the shared recollection of the many classmates with whom I have had the opportunity to share reflections on this early schooling experience in my hometown, "Went to mow Ahmadou" is what was sung out aloud by the numerous children who learned to sing this song in the lower primary grades. Now, pretending that this is the first time you are being exposed to

this song, try to figure out what meaning you would attach to the lyrics with "Ahmadou" in place of "a meadow." Next, see if the song makes better sense after this clue: Ahmadou, a common Moslem name (as I would learn later on), was typically associated with ethnic groups with roots in the Northern part of Ghana. Thus in the minds of many young children growing up in my hometown in the same era, the one man who went to mow was Ahmadou. The word "mow" was still foreign—and for that matter the true meaning of the song was never captured—but at least thinking that this one man, called Ahmadou, went to "do something" brought some semblance of meaningfulness, even if deceptively so, to an otherwise culturally meaningless song. As we transition to another intriguing chapter in my life, think of what constitutes meaningful learning and try to answer the following questions: Are there "Ahmadou" moments in North American classrooms? What factors are likely associated with children's experiencing of Ahmadou moments in their learning? To what extent are teachers aware of their potential to create Ahmadou moments for some, if not all, of the students in their classrooms?

Now travel with me to the Canadian city of Edmonton in the western province of Alberta, where I arrived in the fall of 1979 to begin graduate studies. For now, let's skirt the intriguing question of why and how a young man who grew up in a very warm and humid tropical country with only two seasons (wet and dry) ended up in one of the coldest regions of the world. I had been told so many scary stories about Alberta's biting winters that I remember owning more than four heavy coats and several heavy boots long before the cold weather actually arrived. The experiences I am about to share occurred during the waiting period of pleasant weather—the calm before the storm, so to speak. It was midafternoon on a clear and sunny day. I had walked about three blocks to the neighborhood Safeway grocery store to stock up on food supplies before the beginning of another busy week of classes. Returning home with two big bags of groceries (one on each shoulder), I found myself caught in something that I was to discover later to be a hail storm. With no warning whatsoever, and with no accompanying rain, impressively sized pellets "rained" on me for a period that I'm sure lasted for no more than 30 seconds; but it felt as if a gate to the skies had been opened to give me a "Welcome to Alberta" taste of precipitational pelting. Relieved by the brevity of the experience, I quickened my steps home and opened the door to the old house I shared with four other African students. Three of them sat in the living room watching television. "Boy, this snow really comes down on you with no warning," I remarked rather

(continued)

authoritatively. The sight of three friends rolling on the floor and laughing their lungs out sent a clear signal that I had had a significant cultural moment. With near-choreographed syncopation, all three of them blurted out, "Kofi, that was not snow!"

As one of them proceeded to explain that what I experienced was hail, I found myself debating him. "We get hail in West Africa too, but it always comes with rain; as a child, I used to enjoy running around in the rain collecting and eating the ice falling from the skies; it always came with the rain!" Rather than feel embarrassed by my apparent ignorance, I celebrated the deposit of new entries into my knowledge base, but there was more to come! One October morning, I left the house for the office, traversing the same heavily wooded street. There was something different that morning. I noticed little particles of "something" coming down but there was nothing noticeable on the ground. I kept looking up at the trees and down on the ground in search of what this was all about. I continued to experience this phenomenon throughout the wooded portion of my walk. I concluded that these must be particles falling from the trees. However, long after I left the wooded street—and all the way to the bare parking lot by the six-storey Education building—the little particles of "something" were still in the air, but there was still nothing noticeable on the ground.

Somehow, I managed to toss out of my mind this puzzle that made this morning different from all others I had experienced so far in my now 6-week sojourn. My research assistantship and my classes filled my time on campus with enough excitement, so once I entered the building my mind was on to other things. That evening, I returned home to find only one of my African friends in the living room. I had barely entered the house when Kashoro asked, "So Kofi, what did you think about the snow today?" "What snow?" My response tickled him, of course, but this time I was spared the drama of a band of three to four other African students having fun at the expense of the latest addition to household lore. I knew the word *snow* many years before leaving Ghana for Canada, but it is obvious from these remarkable encounters that I certainly did not have a *concept* of snow, a reality that I have drawn upon in my *cognition and education* class to help my students distinguish between having a label and having a concept. Here is one more mental exercise for you. See if you can offer a plausible explanation (or two) for how a supposedly "knowledgeable" young scholar with the word *snow* as part of his lexicon for many years could confuse hail with snow and fail to identify snow the very first time he encounters real snow?

You might be interested in one explanation I have considered plausible through a historiographic, sociocultural analysis of my own cognition. This analysis led me to blame two principal agents for my predicament: Christina Georgina Rossetti (1830–1894), whose 1872 poem "In the Bleak Mid-Winter" became a popular Christmas carol, and my primary grades teachers who taught this carol to their students. (Ghana's education system is deeply rooted in the British

tradition.) I present the first stanza of this carol as Exhibit One for my case against these culprits:

In the bleak mid-winter
Frosty wind made moan
Earth stood hard as iron
Water like a stone
Snow had fallen, snow on snow
Snow on snow
In the bleak mid-winter
Long ago

I have conjectured that in addition to the many pictures of frozen, snow-capped mountains to which I was exposed in textbooks throughout my education in the primary and middle grades (including my favorite Mount Kilmanjaro in East Africa), the images of snow imprinted in my young mind by this carol were somehow suggestive of snow as solid and icy. These images, coupled with the experience of growing up in a part of the world where hail rarely (or never) falls without rain, may very well explain my quick characterization of hail as snow during the opening weeks of my Alberta experience. By the way, much to the chagrin of my wife and daughters, who would have me save them the embarrassment of displaying my "musical challenge" in public, I do actually sing this carol to my class whenever I use it to explore the role of prior knowledge in cognitive processing and new learning!

What has all this got to do with DAP? I want you to remember more than just the stories, so let's examine their broader instructional implications. In the story of the meadow-mowing song, I'm sure you find evidence of age-based or stage-based developmental appropriateness. Very young children enjoy songs and stories in this kind of genre. They excite and motivate as much as they teach children about the world around them. However, there is also evidence of cultural inappropriateness. You can create a song out of nonsense syllables and children will have fun learning and singing it— and that is important for children's development—but there is little educational value to it. With the profoundly foreign nature of "mowing" and "meadow," the images the song was intended to conjure fell outside the children's cognitive radar.

Many insights can be drawn from the "snow" carol story. The first is the central importance of prior knowledge to the processing of new experiences. Development and learning occur within a sociocultural context, and prior knowledge is shaped by the day-to-day experiences children have accumulated over time. Misconceptions regarding the nature of snow, in this case, appear to be rooted, in part, in geographic differences in the learning context. Acquiring the concept of snow in a context where there is no direct encounter with snow requires appropriate instructional ingenuity on the part of teachers. When learning occurs predominantly in abstraction, children are more prone to developing misconceptions about the phenomena or events at the center of the learning process. Perhaps even more poignant is the deleterious impact that misconceptions from early learning experiences can have on meaningful learning and problem solving in later years. Consider the potential impact that my implicit conception of snow could have had on my ability to write an essay or solve a word problem relating to snow. Better still, consider the ramifications of an instructional context in which a teacher, in planning a lesson on any related topic, makes assumptions about what students know or should know about snow solely on the basis of the students' chronological or developmental age. A student of any age or developmental level with the kind of misconception my story portrays would certainly be "left behind." Thus while we may draw on our knowledge of developmental theory to plan or develop curricula to ensure that the right material is taught at the right age or stage of development, we cannot lose sight of differences—at the idiosyncratic, individual level as well as at the broader sociocultural level—that may determine instructional success for the teacher and accomplishment of optimal learning on the part of the student.

It is extremely important that we be able to think about these issues beyond comparisons between our own cultural contexts and those in far away places in other parts of the world. All too frequently, researchers and practitioners alike do a better job acknowledging and appreciating cultural differences between peoples of different nations or regions of the world than they do about cultural differences within their own society or ethno-racial group. I have implied in some of my scholarly works (Marfo & Boothby, 1997; Pence & Marfo, in press) that this picture reveals a syndrome of *differential*

cultural relativism in North American thinking about cultural influences on human development. Simply defined, North American developmental specialists and educators do not appear to approach sociocultural differences within their own society with the same rules of understanding and application they apply to differences between white, middle-class North American society and the cultures of other nations, especially those with comparable economic and political structures.

Therefore, before you walk away from these pages thinking that the stories I have shared here help North American teachers to understand and work with students who come to us from cultures of far away places with non-Western traditions, I would like you to think more deeply. By virtue of the profound cultural limitations in much of the seminal research in North American developmental psychology, most of us have come to think about the conditions necessary for optimal development and learning as those associated with white, middle-class cultural norms. As Robert LeVine (1989) so aptly pointed out, deviations from patterns of development commonly found in white, middle-class environments "are interpreted not as alternative pathways for normal child development but as conditions of deficit or deprivation, representing less adequate environments in which to raise children" (p. 54). In our increasingly diverse cultural landscape, this image of development must be overcome if the true intent of developmentally appropriate practice is to manifest itself in developmental and instructional practice in school and other community settings.

and he had asked to speak with Tony. The principal asked Tony to think about how he might best present his argument and rationale for the activities in which he and the students were presently engaged.

- If you were Tony, how would you best structure your meeting with the board member?
- Given the developmental status of the students involved, what particular justification do you see for such an activity that would make it worth advocating for?

Critical Incident

The Disgruntled Parent

A few weeks into the school year, Mrs. Johnson, a parent of one of the children in Mrs. Conrad's class, stopped Sally in the hallway after school, sounding both excited and concerned. It seemed that her son, Ronald, had complained to her about school, saying that it was boring and hard and that he didn't want to go anymore. Mrs. Johnson seemed certain that her son's unhappiness in school was related to Mrs. Conrad's reliance on worksheets and excessive seatwork, and the mother was going to ask for a meeting with Principal Wilson to discuss the issue.

Mrs. Johnson wondered if Sally might have a talk with the principal with the hope of encouraging Mrs. Conrad to have a greater variety of activities in her teaching.

- If you were Sally, how would you respond to Mrs. Johnson?
- If you were, in fact, called in to speak with the principal, what would you say?

Summary

The concept of developmentally appropriate practice, or structuring an educational program that is sensitive to factors of age, individual differences, and culture-influenced life experience, is introduced in this chapter. In particular, the concept of constructivist learning is introduced as a pedagogical approach that integrates both development of the learner and practice of the teacher.

Chapter Review

Go to the Online Learning Center at www.mhhe.com/cushner7e to review important content from the chapter, practice with key terms, take a chapter quiz, and find the Web links listed in this chapter.

Key Terms

authentic
  assessment 386
child study
  movement 389
cognitive structures 379

constructivism 378
developmentally
  appropriate
  practice (DAP) 374
middle schools 382

nature versus nurture
  debate 387
zone of proximal
  development 379

Active Exercise

Additional Active Exercises are available online at www.mhhe.com/cushner7e.

Childhood Experiences

Purpose: To identify early socialization experiences that have influenced one's cultural values, beliefs, and practices held today.

Instructions: For culture to be a shared phenomenon, it must be effectively transmitted to the young. There oftentimes exist clear childhood experiences that individuals can identify that help to develop and teach particular values and practices. Identify three examples of cultural beliefs, values, and practices that are expected of "successful" representatives of American culture (or another culture with which you are familiar). Your list will include desirable beliefs, values, and behaviors.

Beliefs	Values	Behaviors
_____	_____	_____
_____	_____	_____
_____	_____	_____

Next, consider an example from each column. What childhood experiences did you have that may have helped you to develop the cultural traits that are expected of you? (For instance, a paper route helps one develop responsibility, individuality, business sense, initiative, and so forth.) Describe early childhood experiences that may have helped you to achieve the desired and expected outcome.

Classroom Activities

1. Ask each (primary-grade) student to choose a character in a story (book, TV cartoon) they especially like (or assign a character familiar to the student) and use any, or several, of various media (crayon drawing, descriptive words, mime, cooperative role-playing) to illustrate some of the character's important characteristics. Ask other class members to interpret their classmate's representation of what the character is like, is feeling, and so on, or (if appropriate) guess who the character is and why they think so.

2. In assigning tasks or activities to be carried out at home, try to apply the "10-minute rule." Let parents (and students) know what you are attempting and why. Reflect to determine whether or how this affects your efforts to achieve instructional objectives, including objectives imposed by state or district standards or requirements, such as standardized achievement testing.

3. Ask high school students, perhaps in an English or social studies class, to write brief descriptions of fairly specific ways they are different now than they were as a young child. Ask volunteers to share their descriptions or examples with the class. Encourage discussion of similarities or differences. As a follow-up—or as an alternative—ask students to do this individually or in groups of 3–4 based on real or fictional characters from their own or common reading.

4. Possibly quoting from your text, share with your students the experiences Kofi Marfo describes in adjusting to a significant cultural change when he was in school. Ask them to discuss how other students in a new setting can affect such a transition. Possibly one or more class members who might have had similar experiences will volunteer to talk about them—even if the transition had "only" been from one community in the U.S. to another.

Reflective Questions

1. Consider for a moment what it might mean to integrate developmentally appropriate practice into a variety of content-area disciplines. Give an example of developmentally appropriate practice when considering (a) a physical education class on basketball for students in grades 3, 7, and 10; (b) a social studies class discussion related to the topic of slavery in the United States for children in Grade 6 versus Grade 10; and (c) basic literacy and reading readiness activities for a class of nonreading 6-year-olds compared to a class of nonreading adults in a basic literacy evening class.

2. How does the more recent development of middle schools address developmentally appropriate practice differently than the more traditional junior high schools, even though they both are designed to serve children of similar ages?

Endnotes

1. The setting for Garfield Elementary School as well as elements of Sally Dougherty's classroom have been incorporated from a true story related by George Wood about a first-grade classroom in southern Ohio in *Schools That Work: America's Most Innovative Public Education Programs* (New York: Penguin Books, 1992, pp. 9–12).

2. Unless otherwise noted, the source consulted for historical background information discussed in this chapter is Philip L. Safford and Elizabeth J. Safford, *A History of Childhood and Disability* (New York: Teachers College Press, 1996).

3. See Lillian Weber, *The Kindergarten: Its Encounter with Educational Thought* (New York: Teachers College Press, 1969), for an excellent analysis of the impact of the progressive movement on the philosophy and goals of the American kindergarten.

References

Bredekamp, S. (1997). Developmentally appropriate practice: The early childhood teacher as decisionmaker. In S. Bredekamp & C. Copple (Eds.), *Developmentally appropriate practice in early childhood programs*. Washington, DC: National Association for the Education of Young Children.

Bredekamp, S., & Copple, C. (Eds.). (1997). *Developmentally appropriate practice in early childhood programs* (Rev. ed.). Washington, DC: National Association for the Education of Young Children.

Botstein, L. (1997). *Jefferson's children: Education and the promise of American culture*. New York: Doubleday.

Children's Defense Fund. (2001). *The state of America's children: A report from the Children's Defense Fund, Yearbook 2001*. Boston, MA: Beacon Press.

Cuban, L. (1993). *How teachers taught: Constancy and change in American classrooms, 1890–1990* (2nd ed.). New York: Teachers College Press.

Edwards, C., Gandini, L., & Foreman, G. (Eds.). (1993). *The hundred languages of children: The Reggio Emilia approach to early childhood education*. Norwood, NJ: Ablex.

Erikson, E. H. (1963). *Childhood and society* (2nd ed.). New York: Norton.

Gardner, H. (1991). *The unschooled mind: How children think and how schools should teach*. New York: Basic Books.

Gesell, A. (1930). A decade of progress in the mental hygiene of the preschool child. *The Annals of the American Academy of Political and Social Sciences 151*, 143.

Gesell, A. (1949). Human infancy and the ontogenesis of behavior. *American Scientist, 37*, 529–553.

Harris, K. R., & Graham, S. (1994). Constructivism: Principles, paradigms, and integration. *Journal of Special Education 28*(3), 233–247.

Havighurst, R. J. (1972). *Developmental tasks and education* (3rd ed.). New York: David McKay.

Kozol, J. (1991). *Savage inequalities: Children in America's schools.* New York: Crown.

LeVine, R. A. (1989). Cultural environments in child development. In W. Damon (Ed.), *Child development today and tomorrow* (pp. 52–68). San Francisco: Jossey-Bass.

Marfo, K., & Boothby, L. H. (1997). The behavioral sciences and special education research: Some promising directions and challenging legacies. In J. Paul, M. Churton, H. Rosselli-Kostoryz, W. Morse, et al. (Eds.), *Foundations of special education: Basic knowledge informing research and practice in special education* (pp. 247–278). Pacific Grove, CA: Brooks/Cole.

Meisels, S. J. (1981). Testing four- and five-year olds: Response to Salzer and to Sheppard and Smith. *Educational Leadership 44*(3), 90–92.

National Education Goals Panel. (1996). *Profile of 1994–95: State assessment systems and reported results.* Washington, DC: Author.

National Middle School Association. (1992). *This we believe.* Columbus, OH: Author.

New, R. S. (1994). Culture, child development, and developmentally appropriate practice: Teachers as collaborative researchers. In B. L. Mallory & R. S. New (Eds.), *Diversity and developmentally appropriate practice: Challenge for early childhood education.* New York: Teachers College Press.

New, R. S., & Mallory, B. L. (1994). Introduction: The ethic of inclusion. In R. S. New & B. L. Mallory (Eds.), *Diversity and developmentally appropriate practice: Challenges for early childhood education.* New York: Teachers College Press.

Pence, A. R., & Marfo, K. (in press). Early childhood development in Africa: Interrogating constraints of prevailing knowledge bases. *International Journal of Psychology.*

Safford, P. L., & Safford, E. J. (1996). *A history of childhood and disability.* New York: Teachers College Press.

Shaffer, D. R. (1993). *Developmental psychology: Childhood and adolescence* (3rd ed.). Pacific Grove, CA: Brooks/Cole.

Spodek, B. (1991). Early childhood curriculum and cultural definitions of knowledge. In B. Spodek & O. N. Saracho (Eds.), *Issues in early childhood curriculum: Yearbook in early childhood education* (Vol. 2, pp. 1–20). New York: Teachers College Press.

Thompson, P. M., Giedd, J. N., & Woods, R. P. (2000). Growth patterns in the developing brain detected by using continuum mechanical tensor maps. *Nature, 404*(6774), 190–193.

Vacca, R., Vacca, J., & Gove, M. (1987). *Reading and learning to read.* Boston: Little, Brown, 1987.

Vatterot, C. (2009). *Rethinking homework: Best practices that support diverse needs.* Washington, DC: American Society for Curriculum Development.

Vygotsky, L. S. (1978). *Mind in society: The development of higher psychological processes.* Cambridge, MA: Harvard University Press.

Weber, L. (1969). *The kindergarten: Its encounter with educational thought.* New York: Teachers College Press.

Williams, L. R. (1994). Developmentally appropriate practice and cultural values: A case in point. In B. L. Mallory & R. S. New (Eds.), *Diversity and developmentally appropriate practice: Challenges for early childhood education.* New York: Teachers College Press.

Wolfson, A. R., & Carskadon, M. A. (1998). Sleep schedules and daytime functioning in adolescents. *Child Development, 69,* 875–887.

Wood, G. (1992). *Schools that work: America's most innovative public education programs.* New York: Penguin Books.

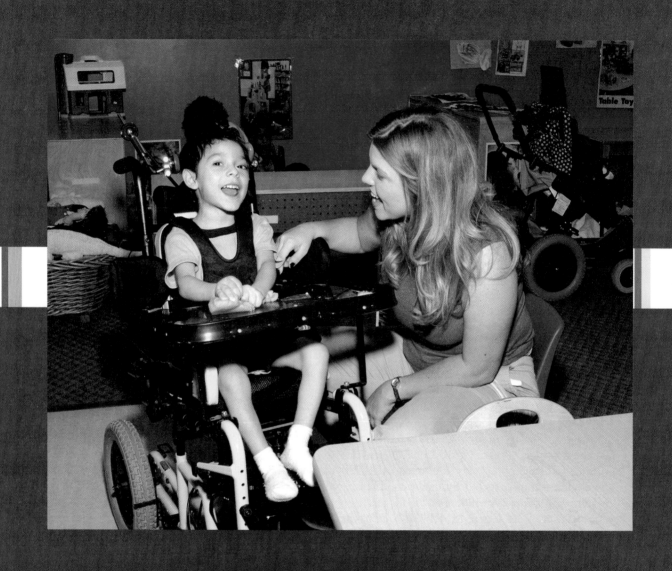

Chapter 12

Creating Inclusive Classrooms

The Ability/Disability Continuum and the Health Dimension

Focus Questions

1. What determines which students are "exceptional"?
2. What is meant by the term *inclusion* of exceptional students?
3. What is the philosophical basis of inclusion? Its legal basis?
4. What is its educational basis?

" Wow! I would love to be able to show yesterday to others and say, THIS
is inclusion! . . . I really enjoyed visiting Tim's class. . . . It's good to see
him in the classroom environment, so mature and confident. "

A PARENT

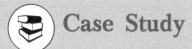

Case Study

Schools That Include All Students

Located in Burlington, a suburb of a large midwestern city, John Dewey Elementary School serves the children of predominantly middle- and upper-middle-class families.[1] The community is relatively conservative, but its citizens want what is best for their children and have shown they're willing to pay for it through consistent passage of operating levies. Inspired by a state initiative encouraging schools to develop alternative models to include students with disabilities in the regular school program, the John Dewey faculty, with the administration's blessing, developed a plan designed to enhance the educational opportunities of all students.

The program initially focused on including primary-age children with suspected or identified **specific learning disabilities** in regular classrooms with their same-age peers. Planning for this was accomplished through regular meetings of the participating classroom teachers and a special educator, who was present in each classroom during the 75 minutes scheduled daily for the Language Arts block, the area of greatest difficulty for most of the identified students.

In subsequent years, all John Dewey students with disabilities, including those with significant delays and multiple impairments as well as those with disabilities requiring less intensive intervention, were served in inclusion classes. These classes comprised typical pupils experiencing no particular difficulties, pupils considered at risk for learning or behavior problems, and pupils with identified disabilities ranging from mild to severe. For each student eligible for special education, the instructional goals and most related services identified in the student's **individual education program (IEP)** would be implemented within the context of regular classroom activity. Joint planning is continuous, and each Inclusion Team meets once each month to review progress and consider needs to modify strategies. All teams come together for periodic Building Inclusion Meetings, joined by the school psychologist, counselor, speech-language pathologist, art and physical education teachers, and school librarian.

All classes reflect a common philosophy and basic strategy of collaboration and individualized adaptation, but each is a unique community in many respects, including the specific needs presented by its members who have disabilities. The extent to which a special educator participates directly in instruction is determined by individual students' needs for varying degrees of support, which also determines class size, ratio of typical students to those with special needs, and whether a classroom aide is assigned. **Related services** are integrated within ongoing class routines (e.g., physical therapy in the context of physical education, occupational therapy in art and other activities), except where certain objectives (e.g., self-care for a child with **cerebral palsy**) suggest the need for brief, unobtrusive pullout for work with a therapist.

Carol is a fully accepted member of Mr. Tom Beeman's first-grade class, even though her IEP indicates a label of "multihandicapped." The supports she needs have also become an integral part of the classroom routine; that is, as Carol needs assistance, everyone knows help will be provided, whether by a classroom aide, by Mr. Beeman, or by another student.

On this day, the class is learning about units of measurement. Working in small learning groups, the children are engaged in such tasks as determining how many "hands" it takes to measure the width of a doorway or length of a table. Today's lesson also involves walking heel-to-toe across the room to determine its length and width in "feet." Mr. Beeman instructs the students in the group with Carol, who uses a wheelchair, to place a piece of tape on the wheel of her chair and determine the number of rotations required as she moves from one side of the room to the other. The children view this simply as part of their lesson on units of measurement, and Carol is happy to have yet another opportunity to participate with her peers in the ongoing classroom activities. Mr. Beeman considers such an adjustment "no big deal. Isn't that what being 'included' should be?"

Carol's parents have been gratified by her teachers' willingness to regard her as just another one of the students. Prominent in her file is the letter they wrote last year to the principal:

> Watching our daughter go off to kindergarten was the beginning of a new adventure. The anticipation of riding the "big yellow school bus" and entering a world of all new learning was thrilling! As the year progressed, each day brought much joy. She loved making new friends and learning new skills.

Carol's confidence and willingness to learn is only enhanced by the surrounding of real life with real children of all walks of life. It has been fulfilling to watch her grow in a classroom where the teacher reaches out to all the children's potential. All children deserve to discover their abilities and develop their talents regardless of their circumstances. It has been a positive experience for Carol to be given the opportunity to expand her mind in an exceptional classroom . . . where all children are encouraged to pursue their academic and social challenges.

Since teachers' participation has been voluntary, some negotiation has been involved. Elizabeth Sims, a first-grade teacher with 19 years of experience, recalls being "very apprehensive" when Sheila Marks, a special education colleague, approached her. "She assured me it would be fun and listed the benefits: a full-time aide's help with running off papers and monitoring recess, a hand-selected class with fewer children, specials such as art and gym at the time we would choose, and the largest classroom in the building. After listening to her litany, being one who does not say no easily, I agreed." Mrs. Sims continues,

It was a wonderful decision. . . . I am a teacher who has done a 180-degree turn! I had always felt "those children" needed to be in a class by themselves with teachers who were trained to meet their needs. I saw no benefit to including them in regular classes and felt a disservice was being done to the typical child. Now, I see the advantages far outweigh the disadvantages for everyone involved. The children are accepting of differences and very helpful to each other, whether they are typically developing or have special needs. I also feel that the children with special needs try more challenging things when seeing what their peers can do.

Margaret Burns stresses the importance of meeting the needs of the children in her kindergarten class.

My one overview special education course gave me little specific knowledge about the children our inclusion program might serve. As it has turned out, my preparation as a regular teacher, combined with the expertise of the specialist I'm privileged to work with, has combined to create an effective and positive learning environment for all of the children.

Our class is composed of 20 typical children and 4 with disabilities identified as **"low-incidence."** The teaching team this semester includes a student teacher, as well as the special education teacher, a classroom aide, and myself. Several factors are critical to the success of this type of program, most basic of which is having a team with the same philosophy and vision for all the children served. Since hands-on time is fundamental at the kindergarten level, where every child has very immediate needs, a workable teacher–pupil ratio is essential. Specific numbers would vary as do the profiles of the children from year to year. Having an experienced and knowledgeable special educator on the team is important, but our greatest strength as a team is the flexibility visible every single day in our classroom. Knowing that our bottom line is meeting the emotional and educational needs of each of our students gives us the freedom to exchange roles, modify plans, and adapt as situations warrant.

Ms. Burns emphasizes that "it is critical that the class be a truly representative sample of a normal population distribution. Placing many identified children in one room and calling it 'inclusion' would defeat its most important purpose—to be a model for the world we live in outside the school walls." To underscore this point, she shares a letter expressing the feelings of parents about their boys' experiences:

Our fourth grade son was in a homeroom with several multiple-handicapped children last year. This year our first grade son has been in an inclusion room. Both boys have had wonderful learning experiences as a result of being involved directly on a day-to-day basis with special children. We as adults have not been exposed to this! Imagine how great it has been for their learning environment to know that not all people are alike. Everyone has special gifts, and at such a young age my children have been able to realize this! I think it has brought out in them responsibility, increased sensitivity to others and a sense of pride in being involved with these special children. As parents we have been very pleased with the inclusion environment for all these reasons. Our children are receiving an excellent education . . . both scholastically and socially.

(continued)

As the Burlington inclusion program progressed, the model was extended to the middle and high schools. As anyone familiar with middle schools knows, defining what is "normal" can be difficult. In 15-year-old Marty's school, 800 students are grappling with the developmental tasks of adolescence. Prior to his family's move to Burlington, Marty had spent his elementary school years in a self-contained, special class with other similarly labeled children, where much professional effort had been invested in implementing **behavior management plans** to address his displays of inappropriate social behaviors and incessant drooling and to ensure that Marty made it to the bathroom and avoided accidents. On entering middle school, with the inclusion program in place, his school experiences changed dramatically. Interestingly, within a short time the drooling lessened significantly, and his ability to monitor his own bathroom schedule improved markedly, both greatly enhancing Marty's social success.

One of the intended by-products of being included in typical classroom settings is involvement in the ongoing social milieu of the school and community, an outcome truly realized for Marty the day he was hanging out with other students after lunch. When an exchange of taunting and teasing with members of the opposite sex escalated, he and several of his "regular" classmates were taken to the assistant principal, who determined that all involved would be subject to in-school suspension. Neither Marty's parents nor his resource teacher viewed this negatively, but instead were gratified that he was an integral member of the group being disciplined.

James, whose various diagnoses over the years have included **autism spectrum disorder**, spent much of his childhood in segregated residential facilities and special schools, but his life had recently changed dramatically. Now 17, James lives in a foster home and attends Burlington High, where he is enrolled in regular classes. One of the first assignments in his Public Speaking class required reciting a poem, a challenge for James, but a resourceful teacher turned into a teaching strategy James's tendency to repeat phrases or sentences addressed to him. James's poem was recorded by another student, who left a pause between each line and stanza. When the time came to recite, he was given the tape recorder and a headset, and as the voice on the tape recited a line into James's ears, he repeated it flawlessly. This continued until he had recited the entire poem. As he finished reciting, the classroom erupted into applause and cheers, his classmates sharing in the joy of his accomplishment.

It would be misleading to suggest there have been no problems, or that Burlington's inclusion program has been greeted with universal enthusiasm. The first 2 years, in fact, saw some heated exchanges at Board of Education meetings, and two families, concerned that classmates with special needs would detract from their own children's learning, opted for home schooling. And Marty, the middle-schooler, wasn't always just "one of the guys," certainly not at first; his acceptance by peers was hindered by the fact that he was older and bigger, as well as "different."

Moreover, in Burlington as throughout the United States, the No Child Left Behind (NCLB) legislation brought with it special academic proficiency concerns involving students with disabilities. Some tension is inevitable between the requirement that the educational progress of most students with disabilities must be assessed based on the same benchmarks as for their peers and the IDEA (Individuals With Disabilities Education Act) philosophy of assessments tailored to individualized goals and objectives. Since, by definition, students eligible for IEPs have disabilities that adversely affect educational performance, a concern for schools that welcome student diversity, including diversity reflected in the ability/disability and health dimensions, involves meeting aggregated student performance criteria. However, assessment requirements for these students are not affected by placement, and inclusion in regular classrooms is intended to increase their access to curricular content addressed in general performance measures.

Rationale for Inclusive Classrooms

From its inception, a fundamental characteristic of American schooling has been its intended inclusiveness, across social boundaries of gender, class, and—belatedly—race. Today, the term **inclusion** refers to the practice of including another group of students in regular classrooms: students with physical, developmental, or social-emotional disabilities, and those with chronic health problems.

Educational inclusion has both a philosophical and legal basis. Philosophically, proponents believe that groups of learners are ideally inclusive communities— cohesive groups with common goals, each of whose members is a unique individual, different from every other member, but sharing with every other member the characteristics that distinguish the age (e.g., middle school), affinity (e.g., computer club), or other basis for forming that particular community. All members have their individual contributions to make, and each derives his or her own benefits from membership. The philosophical basis of inclusive education does not rest on the manifestly wrong notion that everyone is the same or learns in the same way. It rests, instead, on the principles that heterogeneity within a group is both unavoidable and desirable and that differences in ability—to read printed material or use Braille, to speak or use signs, to walk or use a wheelchair, to acquire skills rapidly or slowly, to express thoughts with pen and paper or with a keyboard—are not marks of greater or lesser worth.

Another key philosophical basis for inclusive education is the concept of **normalization,** an idea that emerged in work with persons with cognitive disabilities in the Scandinavian countries in the 1960s. It was originally defined as "making available to all mentally retarded people patterns of life and conditions of everyday living which are as close as possible to the regular circumstances and way of life of society" (Nirje, 1969, p. 231; see also, Wolfensberger, 1972). Subsequently extended to all areas of disability, normalization means that the

Inclusion

403

lives of exceptional individuals of any age should be characterized as much as possible by the same kinds of experiences and daily routines and rhythms as those of persons who do not have disabilities.

For a person living in an institution, rather than with a family in the community, that implied radical changes in practice–a shift from institutional care to community-based services, such as **group homes** and **supported employment.** This principle also has had important implications for exceptional children and youth in school, not in suggesting they do not need supportive services, but concerning *how* assistance is provided. The idea is to provide whatever adaptations are needed as unobtrusively as possible, ensuring that the student can participate in all classroom experiences and, as much as possible, in the same manner as everyone else.

Civil Rights Legislation Related to Disabilities

While philosophical principles transcend the letter of the law, civil rights legislation represents their expression in public policy. In the legal sense, an inclusive classroom is one from which no "otherwise qualified" student, who would ordinarily be a member, has been *excluded* because of a disability, if the student's needs can be addressed through "reasonable accommodations." Those key phrases–"otherwise qualified" and "reasonable accommodations"– were contained in two pieces of civil rights legislation. First, Section 504 of the Rehabilitation Act of 1973 prohibited discrimination based on disability on the part of agencies receiving federal funds (including public schools). This mandate was extended to the private sector by the Americans With Disabilities Act (ADA) of 1990.[2] As a practical matter for schools, that means no *a priori* policies can be adopted consigning pupils who have, have had, or have been thought to have a certain "type" of disability to a certain "type" of program. It means pupils with impairments affecting major life functions cannot be deprived of access to learning opportunities by architectural or attitudinal barriers, and that all pedagogical decisions, including placement, must be based on individual, rather than categorical, considerations. This legal protection from discrimination also affects pupils who have disabilities but who have not been found eligible for special education (including many with special health-care needs, such as asthma, sickle cell disease, and HIV/AIDS) as well as those who are eligible for special education.

Least Restrictive Environment

The other legal cornerstone of inclusive education is the principle of **least restrictive environment (LRE),** expressed in Public Law 94-142, federal legislation that was reauthorized in 1990 as the Individuals With Disabilities Education Act (IDEA).[3] While recognizing a continuum of potential school placements, this principle states that, to the maximum extent appropriate, students with disabilities must be educated in a regular classroom, with nondisabled peers, and be removed from such settings only if the student's needs cannot be met there, even with supportive aids and services. Moreover, each student's individual education program (IEP) must include a statement of the extent to which the student will participate in regular education and an explanation of why any needed services cannot be provided in a regular class. Although this law, like Section 504 and the ADA, was most compellingly based on the need to prohibit *exclusion,* in this instance of children from public schooling, its intent was also to promote *inclusion* of exceptional children in the learning experiences shared by other children. Congress clearly meant to ensure that each student found eligible receive specialized instruction and related services (e.g., speech, physical, or occupational therapy; adapted physical education; counseling; and **adaptive equipment** or technology) appropriate to his or her individual needs in the most normal setting considered feasible for that student.

Although the legal basis for inclusion–nondiscrimination and LRE–has not changed, changes in language used by educators, advocates, and exceptional individuals themselves reflect philosophical changes. *Mainstreaming,* a term used in the 1970s, implied movement out of a special placement, often for limited periods of time, and into regular school experiences–the "mainstream." In the 1980s, reflecting the legacy of the civil rights movement, the word on the lips of many educators and parents was *integration,* sometimes merely physical, preferably social, and ideally instructional.

Like societal *inclusion,* inclusive education implies shared participation of diverse individuals in common experiences. As one might expect, this concept is interpreted somewhat differently by different people and, therefore, is implemented with varying degrees of inclusiveness. The most straightforward interpretation of *full inclusion,* which many educators and parents endorse as the standard, is that a pupil, like those in the Burlington School District, should attend the school she would attend if she did not have a disability, with her neighbors and siblings, and be enrolled with whatever groups of learners she would be part of if she did not have a disability. A key proviso is that any needed supportive aids or services are provided, including those requiring the direct service or consultative expertise of specialists, so that special education is defined as a *service,* not a *place.*

What Is Exceptionality?

Ability/disability and health are distinct dimensions. They do not necessarily overlap except in certain conditions such as **muscular dystrophy** that entail high risks for health problems. People who are in any way "exceptional" with respect to ability/disability, such as those with cerebral palsy, a hearing loss, impaired vision, or who are intellectually gifted or cognitively impaired, are not necessarily "exceptional" with respect to health. Like everyone else, these people may experience health problems. As stated, the inclusive classroom is one in which class members *include* some who are considered exceptional on either of these two dimensions; they have not been *excluded* because of their exceptionality.

The Ability/Disability Continuum

Defining childhood exceptionality is a circular affair: exceptional children and youth are those eligible for special educational services, which in turn are services provided for exceptional pupils. However, this definition restricts the scope of human differences, which may include the following factors:

- Sensory differences (vision and hearing)
- Other physical differences (e.g., those affecting mobility or other voluntary control of motor activity, vitality, and such basic life functions as eating)

- Communication differences (speech and language)
- Cognitive, or intellectual, and information processing differences
- Emotional and behavioral differences

Federal guidelines under IDEA delineate 13 disability categories based on these dimensions (e.g., *deaf* is distinguished from *hard of hearing*; some children are both deaf and blind or are otherwise multiply impaired; and autism spectrum disorder and **traumatic brain injury (TBI)** are now distinct categories).

Explicit definitions of each classification are important because allocation of financial resources is involved, and schools must ensure that eligible pupils receive services to which they are entitled. But since many such differences occur along a continuum (e.g., cognitive, social-emotional, communication, as discussed in Chapter 11), differentiating exceptionality from normality in the course of children's development is often a matter of judgment and somewhat arbitrary. Although some disabilities, and some special health-care needs, involve qualitative differences that must be considered and addressed, most exceptional children have the same needs, interests, and concerns that their "typical" peers have, and the same right to public education.

Historical Perspectives on Special Education

Samuel Gridley Howe

Horace Mann believed the goal of education as preparation for citizenship in a democracy applied to all children.[4] Accordingly, Massachusetts's compulsory attendance law of 1851 explicitly encompassed "crippled" children, and Boston's Horace Mann School was named in recognition of Mann's efforts to provide day classes so that deaf children could live at home and interact with hearing children. His staunch ally, Samuel Gridley Howe, was 19th-century America's most influential special educator. Though he founded the world-renowned Perkins Institute, now located in Watertown, Massachusetts, and was an important figure in the spread of residential institutions, Howe later wrote that such segregated facilities could be justified only, in his words, as "a last resort. The practice of training . . . blind and [deaf] children in the common schools . . . will hardly come in my day; but I see it plainly with the eye of faith and rejoice in the prospect of its fulfillment" (as cited in Richards, 1909, p. 25).

Pioneers in Research and Treatment of Disabilities

Special education's history is studded with tales of pioneers like Howe, the first to teach a pupil (Laura Dewey Bridgman) who was both deaf and blind; like Jean-Marc Gaspard Itard, the physician who taught Victor, the "wild boy of Aveyron"; and like Edouard Seguin, who defied received wisdom by undertaking to instruct persons who were thought unable to learn, fated to be beggars, dependents, or a threat to society.

Significantly, the historical record also reveals that many of the key breakthroughs were made by persons who themselves had disabilities. Arguing that in blindness lay a key to understanding human reason, the Enlightenment philosopher Denis Diderot advised that to understand blindness one must consult blind persons themselves. Valentin Hauy, who founded the world's first school for blind students in Paris in 1784, heeded Diderot's counsel and learned from his first pupil, Francois Lesueur, how reading could be accomplished through touch. Since then, the pantheon of "greats" has included persons with visual impairment such as J. W. Klein, Louis Braille, Helen Keller, Thomas Cutsforth, and Robert Irwin. Deaf persons have had a critical role in gaining recognition of Deaf culture and the legitimacy of signed languages. Although deaf education has had hearing pioneers, their own "teachers" were their deaf pupils, many of whom, most notably Laurent Clerc, became influential leaders in that field.

Special education emerged in the context of social reform, inspired by belief in natural rights and individual worth, and the conviction that, through education, every person can contribute to society. In important respects, it began as a rescue mission. In 1860 nearly two thirds of the countless "unfortunates" who languished in American almshouses were children with sensory or other physical or cognitive impairments. By the 1870s, state Boards of Charities, supporting the work of local benevolent societies, had undertaken a major "child-saving" effort, organized nationally as the National Conference of Charities and Corrections. In some families of more privileged circumstance, parents advocated for schooling for their children, a tradition of parent advocacy that since has been pivotal in bringing about major policy reforms.

Early programs based in centralized residential facilities represented an important step in enabling children with disabilities "to share in the blessings of education," as Howe (1848) eloquently persuaded the Massachusetts legislature in 1848. Although early reformers' most urgent concern was to provide proper care and at least rudimentary instruction, the goal then, as now, was to achieve maximum independence and integration in society (a goal sadly for a time abandoned for many persons with mental or physical abnormality, such as epilepsy, as attitudes toward deviance became less accepting). Although 19th-century facilities were often called asylums, they were originally intended as extensions of the common schools. But they were training schools, employing a highly utilitarian pedagogy to enable pupils to become, as much as possible, able to support themselves through certain prescribed trades, such as boot-making.

History of Disability and Special Education

Specialized instruction had begun its gradual move into the common schools by the beginning of the 20th century. At the same time, school officials, pressed by Settlement leaders like Lillian Wald and Jane Addams, were struggling to meet the challenge of pupil diversity compounded by massive immigration from southern and eastern Europe. Special classes were a facet of a more general diversification effort: so-called steamer classes to expose immigrant youngsters to the English language (which led to programs for children with actual speech impairments); separate classes for "unrulies" or troublesome students; "fresh air" schools for pupils with tuberculosis or who were "physically weak" (which led to classes for children with other health impairments); and "ungraded classes" for those who "just didn't fit" (from which classes for pupils with cognitive disabilites evolved). Excepting deafness and blindness, and speech training for "young stammerers," special pedagogy was usually secondary to the perceived need to separate pupils who were different as a way of making schooling more manageable.

The Settlement House Movement

By the first decades of the 20th century, day classes were increasingly a component of the common school. The first public day school program for blind children, in Chicago, involved them in many ways with seeing peers, a model emulated in other cities. In rural areas, because blindness is a low-incidence impairment, many children, even those using Braille, have long been enrolled in regular classrooms, receiving periodic assistance from itinerant specialists. Many schools made "reasonable accommodations" for pupils with other physical impairments long before that was legally mandated. But as American attitudes toward differentness grew increasingly negative, special education increasingly became a system within a system, separated physically and administratively. Segregating students who "didn't fit" in special classes, and excluding altogether those who "didn't fit" in those classes, schools seemingly tried to manage pupil diversity by making it go away.

By the 1930s, with widespread adoption of IQ testing, the basis for separation of students who had difficulty learning presumably became more scientific and less arbitrary. However, the specialized instruction provided differed from regular instruction mainly because classes were somewhat smaller and comprised pupils of various ages: urban versions (in most instances) of the one-room schoolhouse. However, an emphasis on practical life skills emerged in these programs. For children with physical impairments, chronic health problems, and (by the 1960s) serious emotional disturbance, special pedagogy was truly an afterthought, decidedly secondary to the medically oriented *treatment* focus. Until the parent-led learning disability movement gathered force in the 1960s, special education was more likely to mean special place than special pedagogy. And with implementation of systematic exclusionary policies, the place was often likely to be somewhere other than public school: home, an expensive private facility if families could afford it, or an institution.

Yet even as special education expanded, most students with special needs who were not excluded from schooling altogether were "mainstreamed" because their problems had not been identified or services were not available. For those who had difficulty learning, and also those who were exceptionally capable, there was a downside. Pupils who needed more time, or less time, than their peers, or who could succeed only with some adaptation in the way material was taught or assignments could be completed, often paid a considerable price for being treated like everyone else. In 1975, a watershed year from the standpoint of social policy, the Education of All Handicapped Children Act (P.L. 94-142, reauthorized in 1990 as P.L. 101-476, the Individuals With Disabilities Education Act) required schools to identify all students whose disabilities adversely affected their educational functioning and provide them, excluding none, with a Free Appropriate Public Education (FAPE). Even earlier, some special educators (and parents) questioned whether special education must mean special placement, and many regular educators and parents were concerned about students who experienced difficulties but were not found eligible for special education.

Special Education Law

In the 1920s, a few leaders, like Leta Hollingworth (1924), were concerned also that gifted children were not being challenged to realize their potential. During this period, some large urban school districts initiated provisions, such as Cleveland's Major Work Program, for students identified as academically gifted using the special class model. Since then, support for special programs for gifted students has waxed and waned, with advocates concerned that the brightest students are insufficiently challenged in inclusive classrooms, while many opponents argue that what is presented as appropriate for gifted students would be desirable for *all* students. Two other major concerns involve gifted students who are hard to identify, including ethnic and linguistic minority students and students with disabilities who are also gifted, and each schools', or each state's, definition of giftedness. The latter is problematic not only with respect to determining criteria for academic giftedness (usually based on measures of school learning ability, or IQ, and of academic achievement) but also because giftedness can take various forms, including leadership, artistic endeavors, motor performance, and creativity that is not necessarily reflected in academic measures.

What constitutes an appropriate education for a student who is identified as gifted? Most programs involve enrichment, acceleration, "pull-out," specialized tracking strategies, or combinations thereof. For students with disabilities, IDEA defines *appropriate* on the basis of the IEP developed for each student, stipulating that the student's educational placement must be in the least restrictive environment. In some states, such as Pennsylvania, identification and education requirements for children and youth who are gifted are the same as those with disabilities, although federal legislation addresses only the latter.

Subsequent amendments to the original federal legislation (P.L. 94-142) extended the law's provisions to children as young as age 3 who demonstrate significant delays in one or more areas of development; added a family-focused early intervention component for infants and toddlers; stipulated a required **transition plan** (by age 14) in anticipation of a student's leaving school and entering the adult world of work and community living; clarified definitions; and distinguished autism and traumatic brain injury as distinct areas of disability. No doubt the legislation will continue to be amended as it is revisited by the Congress for periodic reauthorization. Many advocates for gifted and talented students hope that eventually an *individually appropriate education* will be mandated on a national basis for these students as well.

The Health Dimension

Although certain forms of disability may involve greater vulnerability to health problems (for example, many people with **Down syndrome** tend to experience cardiac difficulties and middle ear and upper respiratory infections), health is a dimension encompassing everyone. Some disabilities, such as **spina bifida,** may involve health services such as **clean intermittent catheterization (CIC).** A child with cerebral palsy may have significant motor, sensory, communication, and possibly cognitive impairment, yet experience no health problems, whereas a child with no such neuromotor involvement may experience, for example, chronic asthma. Most of us enjoy reasonably robust good health most of the time, but all of us will probably, at some times in our lives, experience debilitating illness. Were it not for anticonvulsants or other forms of medication, special diets, or other adaptations, some of us would experience continuous, significant disruption in our daily lives or impairment of critical life functions of self-care, working, and going to school. And for some of us, supplemental oxygen, kidney dialysis, or adaptations make it possible to take in nourishment or eliminate waste, which are essential life functions. Children with leukemia or other forms of cancer may experience times of great fatigue; those with **sickle cell disease** may experience times of excruciating pain.

Although they represent a very small proportion of students eligible for special services, children with significant health care needs are often a matter of concern in discussions of inclusion. Actually, a great many American children, estimated at more than 1 in 10, experience some form of chronic illness, although the number with relatively severe conditions is much less. However, several factors have led to increased prevalence in recent years: interventions that sustain life in utero and facilitate the survival of newborns at very low birth weight and with related biological risk factors, such as respiratory distress; medical advances in bringing certain childhood diseases that were once fatal into remission during the vulnerable first year of life; marked increases in drug-affected pregnancies; and HIV transmission to newborns. Given these factors, the National Center for Health Statistics (2000) estimated that at least 2% of all surviving American newborns were likely to have conditions implying special health care needs, with the risk factors twice as great for babies born to African American mothers than for babies born to European American mothers.

Some conditions involve *established risk* (that is, the condition is known to involve lasting impairment), but much more often the future of a newborn at *biological risk* (e.g., very young gestational age at birth, very low birth weight) cannot be reliably predicted, for much depends on the quality of nurture the child will have. Although many of the great numbers of children born each year who were prenatally exposed to alcohol, lead, crack or powder cocaine, or other toxic agents continue to have special needs, biology is not destiny. These and other biological factors interact in subtle ways with environmental ones, most crucially the quality of nurture and of health care.

After a brief period of time in the neonatal intensive care unit, a still tiny infant is likely to come home, dependent on life-support equipment parents will need to manage as they attempt to normalize the baby's life and their own.

Many young children soon cease to be technology dependent, but some will continue to need a respirator, perhaps, or require nasogastric or gastrostomy tube feeding. Although the term *medically fragile* is really inappropriate considering the struggle a newborn may need to put forth just to survive, some children who may require no special adaptations to support life functions may be particularly susceptible to infection, experience debilitating allergies, or have other special health care needs throughout their school careers, perhaps throughout their lives.

Historically, the belief that children with special health care needs needed special school arrangements originated with efforts to contain the spread of tuberculosis. Fresh air classes were first established in the United States in Providence, Rhode Island, in 1908. In Europe open air schools were often located, like adult sanitoriums, in the mountains or forests. However, American fresh air schools were usually in large cities where the disease was epidemic, with classes sometimes conducted on tenement roofs. (Tragically, little effective intervention was done in the reservations and boarding schools established for Native Americans, where tuberculosis decimated tribal populations.) In eastern states, siblings of infected children were often removed to "preventoriums." Where children were thus gathered, school districts collaborated with charity groups and health agencies to provide arrangements for instruction, mild exercise, and rest. Although worldwide public health measures eventually halted the spread of tuberculosis, reducing the need for segregated programs, the special class or special school model established in response to tuberculosis was adopted for children with other health care needs, such as heart defects.

Also, for children experiencing lengthy hospital stays for any reason, the convention of establishing a hospital school, introduced in Europe, was adopted in the growing number of pediatric hospitals and pediatric units in general hospitals. Increasingly, public education agencies assumed operation of such schools, especially in large metropolitan communities. For many children believed unable to manage the physical demands of school attendance, whether hospitalized or at home, state departments of education or local school districts established tutoring for "homebound and hospitalized children."

Health needs of children and youth have changed with the presumed conquest (in industrialized nations) of tuberculosis, poliomyelitis, and a number of diseases, such as smallpox, scarlet fever, and diptheria, to which children had been particularly vulnerable. And philosophies of medical care have changed also. Extended periods of hospitalization are now rare for children (as for adults), and while that has been influenced by crass realities of cost and insurance coverage limits, it also reflects awareness of the importance for children to experience conditions of growing up that are as normal as possible. Most children who in times past would have been excluded, either by formal policy or assumed dependency, weakness, or vulnerability, now go to school with their siblings, neighbors, and friends.

What are the implications for inclusive education? First, we should remember three basic, and obvious, principles: (1) we can all expect to experience serious health problems at some time in our lives, for they are part of the universal human condition; (2) serious health impairment in childhood is certainly not a new phenomenon, historically speaking, evidenced in epidemics and pandemics of the past to which children were especially vulnerable; and (3) a health problem

Children with Multiple Health Problems

is, for a child or an adult, certainly not a person's only, or primary, identifying characteristic or need.

Our own vulnerability helps to explain an element of fear, particularly of contagion, that for centuries focused on leprosy, a century ago on tuberculosis, then on poliomyelitis, and today on AIDS even though other conditions (e.g., hepatitis B) are more readily transmitted than is the HIV virus. Today, all school personnel are advised to employ **universal health precautions** to lessen the risk to themselves or to pupils of any form of infection, especially if there is possible exposure to blood or any body fluids. The need for such precautions is not affected by whether or not a school adopts an inclusive education philosophy. While contagious disease is understandably feared, it is conquered not by avoidance, ignorance, or blaming the victim. This point is certainly the message of AIDS awareness.

Another source of fear has to do with a different type of vulnerability, implied by terms such as *medically fragile*. Teachers neither want a child to be endangered nor want themselves to be vulnerable to guilt feelings or even to a lawsuit should a pupil in their charge incur injury or even die. As with many human fears, these are best allayed by information, availability of appropriate resources and supports, and most important, personal experience. Teachers can feel vulnerable whether they are dealing with a child who has a condition that is actually life threatening or has no chronic special health care needs per se but significant physical impairment. A fourth-grade teacher participating in an inclusion project in Virginia spoke of "fear of the unknown. . . . You're afraid they might hurt you or you might hurt them" (Janney, Snell, Beers, & Raynes, 1995, p. 436). Rachel Janney and her co-authors, reporting on the success of that project, summarized:

> Teachers who initially had been hesitant to get involved . . . judged that their original fears and expectations were based on inaccurate perceptions about the integrated student's needs and abilities. By getting to know the students with disabilities on an individual basis, they had gained knowledge of the student's unique abilities and a new perspective on disabilities in general. "I guess we just really had never thought about them being 'normal.' They really are," explained the junior high math teacher in District C. These general education teachers' attitudes toward integration also had been changed by finding that it was personally and professionally rewarding to work with the integrated students, a sentiment expressed in these words by the high school physical education teacher in District A: "These kids seem to appreciate you a lot more . . . and that's a little pat on the back for the teacher." (p. 438)

Characteristics of an Inclusive Classroom

The discussion in the preceding section, although it gives a sense of what inclusion in this specific sense means, is likely to raise questions in a teacher's, or prospective teacher's, mind about how, or even whether, inclusion actually works. Inclusive schools and classrooms do not just happen, nor do they require each individual teacher to be "all things to all students." Some of the major ideas reflected in this chapter's Case Study are based on legal requirements, but most derive from or are congruent with emerging principles and practices in general pedagogy and in the way many schools now operate.

Inclusion and Human Diversity

One fundamental idea is an old one, and it is that a major purpose of schooling is to prepare the young for citizenship in a democracy that is increasingly heterogeneous. Another idea is relatively new: that the young must be prepared for successful participation in a global economy. The fact that the world children will enter is not one in which everyone is like themselves has important implications for the necessary learning experiences of any child, with or without a disability or health impairment. The former will not live in a society comprised only of other people with cerebral palsy, mental retardation, autism, dyslexia, diabetes, and so forth; the latter will not live in a society comprised only of people who do not have these conditions or characteristics. Related to that societal reality is another that can be seen in any school and in any classroom: even if it were desirable to eliminate heterogeneity in a group of learners by putting anyone who is "different" in another group, it is impossible, for every group is necessarily heterogeneous; *all* children are "different."

Activity 20:
**What Does It Feel
Like to Be Excluded?**

Another major idea emerging in general pedagogy, *collaboration*, involves new kinds of teacher–specialist relationships and team models, more mutually supportive school–family relationships, and new awareness of the important role of interactions among learners. Each of these sets of relationships is multifaceted. For example, Marlene Pugach and Lawrence Johnson (1995) have described four different roles–*supportive*, *facilitative*, *informative*, and *prescriptive*–underlying relationships of adults within schools. The IDEA legislation implies such relationships with respect to the education of students with disabilities, but the concept of collaboration goes beyond the legal requirements:

1. The law requires multidiscipline participation in assessing a student's current functioning and planning and monitoring the student's IEP, but collaboration suggests continuing *interdisciplinary* teamwork on the part of regular and special educators and other specialists in implementing the student's program.

2. The law requires parents' **informed consent** prior to multifactored evaluation, participation in developing the IEP, and right to procedural

due process in the event of disagreement; collaboration suggests going beyond these bare legal requirements to ensure that a student's IEP reflects the family's concerns and priorities, that a student's home and school expectations and experiences are mutually supportive, and that professionals respect the primacy and continuing influence of families on children's development.

3. The law requires that students with disabilities be educated as much as is appropriate with peers who do not have disabilities; collaboration implies optimizing the potential benefits for both by fostering positive classroom interactions and creating opportunities for students to respect and learn from each other and to develop feelings of group identification.

Policy requirements have a critical role in determining how students with disabilities are educated, but as in all aspects of schooling, other factors such as research findings influence pedagogical practices. The next sections summarize some contrasts between old and new characteristics. Keep in mind that, in one sense, everything before the IDEA legislation was enacted is "old," and what is "new" continues to emerge.

Pedagogies: Old and New

Although traditional methods of teaching are incorporated in pedagogies for inclusion, a major influence on inclusive pedagogy is *constructivism,* a way of understanding students' learning as a process of cognitive development influenced, but not controlled, by adult instruction. Constructivist perspectives are fundamental to current conceptions of developmentally appropriate practices for young children,[5] but they are also reflected in current discussions of elementary, middle school, and even high school curriculum and instruction, especially in the areas of literacy, mathematics, social studies, and science. Is all genuine and meaningful learning–though externally influenced by family and peers, as well as teachers and textbooks–internally motivated and internally organized? And if so, is it true of all learners? Beliefs about *how* children learn are key determinants of *what* is taught.

This issue is critical with respect to the pedagogy of inclusion because special education, strongly influenced both by a *medical model* of treatment and a *behavioral model* of learning, has traditionally placed great emphasis on skill acquisition, through training strategies employed by teachers and therapists. The assumption has been that most children "naturally" learn important skills, such as language skills, and generalize what they have learned to new situations, but that children with developmental delays or disabilities for which they must learn to compensate require more direct adult intervention. This is far from a simple issue considering the wide variation among children with disabilities, and such distinctions have certainly been unduly emphasized; generally speaking, children with disabilities, and certainly children with health impairments, are more *like* other children in the way they learn, and in what they need to learn, than they are *different* from their peers.

Moreover, some constructivist practices were actually introduced or readily adopted by special education pioneers like S. G. Howe, Seguin, and early educators of deaf children. Edouard Seguin, Maria Montessori, and Ovide

DeCroly were convinced that the experiential methods they developed in working with children with cognitive disabilites based on faith in every child's ability and motivation to learn, should be extended to instruction of all children. Some learners do require more adult direction and adult-imposed structure than others, but the same can be said of many students who do not have disabilities. Arguably, the diverse needs present in any learning group can more effectively be accommodated with constructivist approaches than those that assume all pupils learn the same things at the same pace. Individualized pedagogy represents an important legacy of special education that is applicable for all students.

Roles: Old and New

The most dramatic difference between old and new affecting the education of children with disabilities is that today most live at home with their families and attend public schools, which was not the case in the era of centralized, residential institutions. That fact implies fundamental changes in the roles of both families and educators, and critically important changes in their relationships. Moreover, the increasing number of students with disabilities who participate to some degree or totally in regular education suggests fundamental changes in the roles of both special and regular educators, and critically important changes in their relationships. To appreciate the significance of these changes, consider other contrasts between old and new roles of regular and special educators.

The special educator of the past was indeed a specialist, not only as a special educator but as a teacher of a specific category of students. As children were segregated, so too were their teachers. Early special educators were trained in residential schools, following a medically oriented, preceptor model, which was quite unlike the preparation their counterparts were provided in normal schools. Even as preparation for both types of educators moved to degree-granting colleges and universities, special and general educators were most often prepared separately and taught different content, by different instructors. Those barriers, like those separating regular and special education in schools, have been gradually receding.

Except in schools for deaf students, which had a strong pedagogic tradition, the special educator was a clinician, albeit a junior one, increasingly likely to be a woman, as Edouard Seguin (1880) insisted, "supervised by a competent [male] physician." In school and in clinical settings, special education teachers were (and are today) members of teams, collaborating with (or carrying out the recommendations of) psychologists; sometimes physicians or social workers; and physical, occupational, and speech-language therapists. In medical settings—hospitals, rehabilitation centers, and residential treatment facilities—the team was often led by a physician, in schools by a school psychologist or special education supervisor. Because team members were expected to work together, each applying her or his own expertise, the model was termed *multidisciplinary.* To the extent diverse perspectives on the child as patient, or client, were integrated within a unified plan (difficult because members had been trained in their respective disciplines in relative isolation from each other), teams increasingly evolved an *interdisciplinary* approach. In clinical settings a social worker often provided the only link teachers had with parents, but in schools home–school cooperation and consistency were often seen as critical. A more integrated, *transdisciplinary team* model has recently emerged, characterized by *role exchange* and *role release,* in which professionals share and synthesize perspectives on an ongoing basis (Rainforth, York, & Macdonald, 1997).

Like their fellow team members, then, and quite unlike regular education teachers, special educators were imbued with a clinical orientation influenced more by a medical than an educational model. Just as their preparation was relatively distinct from that of elementary and secondary teachers, their work environment was often in relative isolation from other teachers. Older special educators recall that their classrooms were located next to the boiler room. Their pupils were usually transported on separate buses, used the playground at separate times, and often ate lunch in their classroom, with their teacher, rather than the cafeteria. Like their students, many special educators perceived themselves as outsiders, and in fact were more likely to be accountable to a central office supervisor, or "inspector," than to the building principal.

Regular educators, for their part, were often the first line of identification of children experiencing difficulty in school, as well as those who might be gifted. Their principal role vis-à-vis exceptional students was to identify suspected problems and, as IDEA stipulates, to attempt to address such problems within the regular classroom. Only if their attempts are unsuccessful should a referral be made for **multifactored evaluation**, with parents' informed consent, to determine whether a student is eligible for special education. However, the federally mandated **placement continuum** of possible school arrangements implies that nearly all exceptional pupils would have varying degrees of involvement in regular education, either pulled out for special help or provided supportive aids and services within the regular education program.

Place of Content Knowledge: Old and New

As suggested in the previous section, *what* was to be learned has long been a key issue in special education, and it is a key issue in discussions of inclusion. Generally, content issues have involved the same fundamental question, posed by Herbert Spencer (1859/1963), that has been raised for all learners: What knowledge is of most worth? In the case of blindness, deafness, and other physical impairment, the answer to that question was knowledge that could enable one to be maximally independent and self-supporting as an adult. In the past, such knowledge generally implied training in a trade. Although their societal role later shifted from instruction to containment, facilities for persons with cognitive disabilites and epilepsy also originally were intended to be training schools, a designation that was maintained even though residents were "trained" based on the expectation of lifelong institutionalization. As the European day class model was introduced in the United States, at first in the form of ungraded classes for relatively undifferentiated low achievers, the goal of economic self-sufficiency shifted to imply that pupils with cognitive disabilities needed to develop habits that would make them reliable workers as well as good citizens. Consequently, the distinctive curricular tradition that emerged in special classes focused on relatively generic and social *employability skills.* With extension of schooling under the **zero exclusion mandate** of P.L. 94-142, a "criterion of ultimate functioning" was advanced as the basis for curriculum for students with severe disabilities, including severe cognitive disability. This criterion means that what is taught must be age-appropriate, future-oriented, functional, and community-referenced (Snell, 1993).

The advent of the concept of specific learning disabilities (SLD), which today comprises more than half the special education enrollment, brought a greater focus on differential instructional strategy than on curricular content. Based on an educational diagnostic profile showing specific areas of strength and of difficulty, or intraindividual differences—differences *within* an individual student—a plan of remediation or compensatory instruction could be devised for each pupil, usually within the context of the standard curriculum. This distinctive feature, individually tailored instruction, was subsequently mandated for all eligible students with disabilities, through the IEP, which specifies individual annual goals and short-term objectives for each area in which a student is to receive special education. Although not required by federal law, as noted previously, in some states an IEP and other provisions also are required for students identified as gifted.

Assessment: Old and New

With respect to children with disabilities, assessment has both a general and a specific meaning. Emerging trends in educational assessment (general) are relevant for all learners, but two assessment concerns (specific) have unique importance: the determination, as a result of assessment, of eligibility for special education services, and the determination of how accountability for those services is demonstrated. The former concern also pertains to possibly gifted and talented students, but for those with "suspected handicaps" IDEA requires that, to be eligible for special education services, a pupil must have a disability (as defined in the law) that adversely affects educational functioning. Such determination cannot be based on only one measure, or one criterion, but is based instead on a multifactored evaluation, conducted with informed parental consent by appropriately qualified, multidisciplinary professionals, using appropriate and nondiscriminatory procedures.

IDEA broadly defines criteria for each disability "category," but individual state standards may specify what types of assessment must be carried out, such as medical or psychological evaluations. In the case of gifted and talented programs, mandated in some states but not in others, state or local district policies stipulate criteria and identification processes. In both cases, norm-referenced, standardized tests (e.g., IQ tests) play an important role but must be used in combination with other appropriate procedures (e.g., criterion-referenced tests of academic skills, teacher reports, and ratings).

With respect to outcome as well as process, the IEP is an accountability document. It states what services the pupil will be provided, and for each goal that is listed it delineates the evaluation procedure that will be used and who is responsible. These two key functions reflect the legacy of a medical and of a behavioral model, the former in such concepts as *screening* (to identify indications of need for thorough diagnostic evaluation) and *diagnosis*, the latter in stipulating that objectives must be stated in the form of observable, measurable behavior.

Individualized Education Plan (IEP)

Although medically oriented diagnostic evaluation may be essential in determining eligibility, it has limited value as a guide to the individualized instruction that is the hallmark of special education.

Although the term *diagnostic/prescriptive teaching,* a legacy of the medical model tradition, has been closely associated with special education, more instructionally relevant types of assessment have been developed. Moreover, whether special learning difficulties are believed to reflect underlying *process* differences (e.g., in information processing or visual-motor coordination) or are viewed as specific *skill* deficiencies to be identified and remediated, the most useful types of assessment are criterion-referenced rather than norm-referenced. The purpose of such assessment is to ascertain a pupil's current status and progress on the basis of age or stage expectations (developmental assessment), the school's or state's curricular expectations (curriculum-based assessment), systemic observation of functioning in the classroom (behavioral assessment), skill acquisition (task-analytic assessment), or in accomplishing skills required to function in present and/or future environments (ecological assessment).

Increasingly, educators have been implementing an alternative method to determine a student's need for special education services, called *response to intervention* (RTI). This approach is intended to address key concerns associated with past practice, specifically with reference to the identification of specific learning disabilities by means of an ability/achievement discrepancy model: (1) that model's inability to identify children's learning problems early in their school careers; (2) an overreliance on standardized tests, which may be subject to cultural bias or other limitations; (3) inconsistency in determining eligibility criteria; and (4) overidentification and labeling of students as SLD who could respond to regular instruction more attentively tailored to their individual learning characteristics. While RTI may be variously implemented and its effectiveness is still being researched, the approach has certain common elements, all of which are associated with "new" assessment practices:

- It involves "tiers" of assessment rather than a single decision point and continuous monitoring of the individual student's progress.
- It involves curriculum-based, criterion-referenced assessment.
- It is collaborative, usually assigning a major role to regular education personnel in the initial stage, with increasing specialist participation in successive tiers.
- It ensures continuing instruction for students as they are being assessed.
- It requires implementation of evidence-based instructional practices at each successive tier.

With young children diagnostic profiles are often based on *developmental domains* as described in Chapter 10. For older students and those with severe or multiple impairments, diagnostic profiles often are based on *functional domains*; that is, important life functioning areas, such as work and leisure skills. For children with visual impairments, assessing how the child uses his or her vision, orients in space, and progresses in achieving independent mobility are critical concerns. For those with hearing impairments, use of residual hearing or of compensatory (hearing aid augmentation, lipreading) or alternative (sign language) communication modes are critical. In both instances, progress in communication and literacy, as well as in general curricular areas, are continuously assessed. For children with impaired mobility or communication, specific assessment concerns involve possible needs for adaptive equipment or procedures.

Each student is unique, and some indeed have differences that require certain adaptations or support services in order to receive an appropriate education as required under federal law. Can these be provided within normalized classroom settings in which they learn side by side with typical peers? That is the challenge of inclusive education.

Making Inclusive Teaching Work

The Importance of Collaboration

Students with and without disabilities are intended to benefit from participation in inclusive classrooms. Perhaps the greatest benefits are the positive self-esteem of all the students and the fact that more students have their needs met than in a conventional classroom. The special education student doesn't experience the stigma and confusion associated with the daily journey to a "special" room for "special" instruction. The day is less fragmented, and the student doesn't feel different or left out. Also, special education teachers have hands-on experience with their interventions—applying them to real, daily learning situations—and can make more precise changes in those interventions as they are needed. With a co-teaching situation, there is always a teacher available to help a student. Also, co-teaching provides two perspectives on any situation and increases creativity in teaching.

Mutual understanding and respect are essential elements in any true collaboration. The teachers at John Dewey Elementary agreed that the special educator and the regular educator should acknowledge that both have specialized knowledge and skills but that their perspectives and knowledge bases may differ. For example, special educators should recognize that the regular educators' instructional and behavior management techniques often can be effective in working with students with special needs. They must also understand that teachers in regular classrooms must respond to the needs of many students and cannot devote disproportionate time and attention to any one student. They must also recognize that some techniques that may be successful in a separate special education class may not be appropriate for the regular classroom environment.

At the same time, the regular educator should recognize that his or her special education colleague may be responsible for supporting many students in a variety of settings and therefore have a limited amount of time to devote to each student. She or he must also realize that a new intervention strategy is unlikely to have an immediate effect and that a fair trial is needed before judging it ineffective. Acknowledging that students differ in the extent of instructional adaptations they need, regular classroom teachers should understand that many of the adaptations that the specialist recommends will be extensions of regular education techniques. They should also maintain familiarity with each exceptional student's IEP, sharing responsibilities for determining how goals and objectives can be reinforced during the course of classroom activities.

Accordingly, the teachers at John Dewey Elementary developed the following set of principles to guide their collaborative team functioning:

- Establish a system for ongoing communication.
- Discuss each placement together.
- Assist each other in individualizing instruction.
- Work together to adapt subject matter.
- Share materials.
- Assist each other in adapting evaluative procedures.
- Exhibit characteristics of flexibility, dedication, reliability, organization, imagination, energy, initiative, and enthusiasm.
- Involve others by sharing plans and ideas.
- Seek support and suggestions from others.
- Set realistic goals.
- Work to improve interpersonal relations.
- Be happy and proud about working with students with special needs.
- Remember that presenting a positive attitude will change attitudes about inclusion both inside and outside the school.

What Does Flexibility Involve

Burlington teachers often use the word *flexibility* in describing their inclusion programs. While flexibility is important in any teaching situation, as they note, it is critical to the success of inclusion of students whose learning characteristics and needs may require adaptations, both planned and spontaneous, in the instructional program. They concluded that classroom adaptations to accommodate differential needs among *all* students can be delineated in terms of four basic parameters: curriculum materials, instructional strategies, classroom organization, and behavior management.

Curriculum Materials

Within the context of the regular curriculum, learning experiences can be adapted in a wide variety of ways, as suggested by these examples:

- When working with fractions, provide recipes that include measurements and have student identify all the fractions on the recipe.
- When teaching about time, help student develop a personal schedule showing daily activities matched to a clock face showing the time of the activity.
- When working with adding two columns of numbers and regrouping, help students practice balancing a checkbook or compile a shopping list with prices, using a calculator to add.
- When administering a spelling test, have student practice identifying functional words.
- When identifying U.S. presidents, have student practice keyboarding skills by locating letters of presidents' names.

Instructional Strategies

Examples of instructional adaptations include the following:

- The way instruction is delivered (e.g., visual or auditory aids, learning centers, cooperatively structured activities, cooperative learning, small group instruction).
- The way the learner can demonstrate knowledge (e.g., oral vs. written response, pictures that can be pointed to, using a computer, augmentative communication devices such as picture boards, tape recorder, language master, calculators).
- Modifying the number of items the learner is expected to complete (e.g., spelling words, math problems).

Classroom Organization

Adaptations can be made in aspects such as the following:

- The skill level, problem type, or rules on how the learner may approach the work (e.g., using calculators or computer, simplifying task directions, changing rules to allow for participation, breaking a task down to sequential steps, providing more planned opportunities to achieve success).
- The amount of individual instruction with a specific learner (e.g., peer partner, use of teaching assistant).
- The time allotted (e.g., extra time to practice new skills, individualized timelines for work completion, flexible class schedules) and/or the location (e.g., specific classroom area, home, school library or media center) for completing a task.

Behavior Management

Examples of adaptations that can be used to anticipate and prevent inappropriate or disruptive behavior include the following:

- Have student assist with visual aid equipment while some other students are being instructed.
- Have student take on a teacher role by sharing a favorite activity or interest.
- Individualize goals or outcome expectations while using the same materials (e.g., a language arts activity of diagramming a sentence can be, for some students, a verbal language activity of hearing and speaking in full sentences).

As a way of conceptualizing variations in individual students' needs for instructional adaptation or curricular modifications, the Burlington teachers devised a continuum of levels, each defined by a question for the team to resolve through discussion.

Level I. What can the student learn in the regular program of instruction with the same performance standards as nondisabled peers?

Level II. What can the student learn with nondisabled peers, but with adjustments in performance standards according to the student's needs as identified through curriculum-based assessment?

Level III. What can the student learn with adjustments in pacing, method of instruction, or special materials or techniques provided with consultant support to the teacher?

Level IV. What can the student learn with adjustments in pacing, method of instruction, or special materials or techniques provided jointly with regular and support or ancillary staff?

Level V. What can the student learn with adjustments in the content of the classroom curriculum to be taught jointly by regular and special support or ancillary staff?

Level VI. What classroom curriculum content must be modified significantly and taught by special staff?

Level VII. In what situation is some or all of the content of the classroom curriculum inappropriate for this student? What alternative curriculum program will be used to address this student's educational needs?

Ethical Issues in Inclusive Education

Federal legislation does not mandate inclusion, as defined earlier in the chapter, although it does forbid exclusion. The legal basis for inclusion continues to be the least restrictive environment (LRE), the requirement that education occur "as much as appropriate" in a regular classroom setting, with supportive aids and services, as may be needed. Some professionals, organizations, and also parents have reservations about any concept that could be interpreted to suggest "one size fits all," especially if legislators and school officials construe inclusion to mean less costly services. (Although individual needs differ widely, the cost per year of educating a student with disabilities is, on average, about twice the cost of educating other pupils, only a part of which is provided through IDEA.)

The American Federation of Teachers, in fact, had called for a moratorium on inclusion until all schools were provided with the kinds of supports (resource specialists and classroom aides) and other provisions (such as manageable class size) that they needed. But advocates compare such proposals to similar situations in the civil rights movement, in which a moratorium on school desegregation was suggested until all European Americans fully "accepted" their African American fellow citizens. The question in both situations is, Should the crucial years of childhood be allowed to pass irretrievably while children's elders await optimal conditions?

How many children with disabilities are currently included in regular classrooms? Based on data compiled for the U.S. Department of Education's 2003 annual report to Congress, about 96% of all students with disabilities are taught in regular school buildings, almost half of whom are included in regular classrooms for most if not the entire school day. For some students, resource rooms to which the pupil is either pulled out for certain purposes or included in

regular classrooms only for selected subjects or activities continue to be a common arrangement. This may seem to offer the best of both worlds–normalizing experiences supplemented by more intensively individualized instruction by specialists. But Joanne Yatvin (1994), a superintendent, found that many students dislike "being sent 'down the hallway' to learn." Moreover, she adds, "When students return to their classrooms, their regular teachers, believing that they have had their daily dose of 'special education,' feel little need to modify other instruction. . . . Under such a system, students get far less instruction than they would if they were grouped with their peers, by age and interest, in regular classrooms with teachers who knew that they had to modify instruction for everyone" (p. 484).

Many educators, parents, and persons with disabilities themselves maintain that if the society of the 21st century is to be inclusive and human differences are recognized and celebrated, it must begin with inclusive schools and inclusive classrooms. They point out that it is not inclusion that needs to be justified but rather separation, even for part of the school day. That is precisely what the

IDEA legislation requires: a student with a disability may not be removed from the regular classroom unless it has been demonstrated that that student's needs cannot be met within the regular classroom, even with supportive aids and services. Policies and practices that segregate children on the basis of a categorical label, whether the label refers to ability/disability, health, or race, are in violation of the U.S. Constitution.

Can every individual child with special needs receive an individually appropriate education without having to be segregated in a special place? Can these students still get the services they need? And what about the typical students? As such questions are debated in local schools like those in the Burlington Case Study, many teachers in collaboration with parents are making inclusive education a reality. From such examples, the Advocacy Board for the Center on Human Policy (1994) at Syracuse University has developed the following statement:

Inclusion Means

1. Educating all children with disabilities in regular classrooms regardless of the nature of their disabling condition(s).
2. Providing all students enhanced opportunities to learn from each other's contributions.
3. Providing necessary services within the regular schools.
4. Supporting regular teachers and administrators (e.g., by providing time, training, teamwork, resources, and strategies).
5. Having students with disabilities follow the same schedules as nondisabled students.
6. Involving students with disabilities in age-appropriate academic classes and extracurricular activities, including art, music, gym, field trips, assemblies, and graduation exercises.
7. Students with disabilities using school cafeteria, library, playground, and other facilities along with nondisabled students.
8. Encouraging friendships between nondisabled and disabled students.
9. Students with disabilities receiving their education and job training in regular community environments when appropriate.
10. Teaching all children to understand and accept human differences.
11. Placing children with disabilities in the same schools they would attend if they did not have disabilities.
12. Taking parents' concerns seriously.
13. Providing an appropriate individualized educational program.

Inclusion Does Not Mean

1. "Dumping" students with disabilities into regular programs without preparation or support.
2. Providing special education services in separate or isolated places.
3. Ignoring children's individual needs.
4. Jeopardizing students' safety or well-being.

International Perspective: What's Happening Elsewhere in the World?

Special Education: The Case of Kenya

Kagendo Mutua, PhD
University of Alabama

In this era of increased globalization, it is important that teachers be increasingly aware of how such issues as human exceptionality are treated in other countries. In this section, I present a focus on special education in Kenya. In doing so, I begin from the standpoint of international policies on education and how those international decrees, such as Education for All, have influenced national policy on education in Kenya. Further, I examine how national education policy translates into practices within Kenyan schools, and specifically how national education policy in Kenya addresses the needs of learners with disabilities. By understanding this, I hope teachers become aware of the need to understand the similarities and differences in the way persons with disabilities are treated in cross-cultural contexts and how policies affecting their service provision have evolved within countries. Additionally, through this understanding, I hope teachers will have a global consciousness of the social inequities that exist in other countries and how the experiences of such inequities may indeed be at the heart of the challenges that teachers often face when they are attempting to extend educational services to children from other cultures immigrating into the United States.

The role played by the United States and other industrialized countries (often referred to as the G-8 countries) in shaping social policies and practices within developing countries cannot be overstated. Their influence extends from providing policy models to directly or indirectly funding programs that support the implementation of their proposed models of education, government, and other areas that affect social infrastructures within countries. Within many developing countries, education is one of the areas that have been greatly affected by policies and practices in the United States and other leading industrialized countries of the West. While the impact on education by the West is easily identifiable in general education practices at the primary (elementary) level all the way to the tertiary (postsecondary) level, the practices in the education of individuals with disabilities in Kenya has not changed tremendously from the colonial period. This section provides a discussion of special education policy and practices within Kenyan schools, highlighting the particular issues that relate to inclusion of children with disabilities in Kenya's public schools.

Kenya is a signatory to numerous international commitments on the provision of education for all such as the Universal Declaration of Human Rights adopted in 1948, World Declaration on Education for All adopted in 1990, and the Dakar Conference of 2000. Despite these commitments, access to education for all children in Kenya remains a problem. The efforts of education stakeholders' since independence, including the recent introduction of the Free Primary Education (FPE) program by President Mwai Kibaki, the third and current president of Kenya, have not sufficiently addressed the key issues of access, retention, quality, completion, and the smooth transition from lower to higher educational levels. In no other sector of education in Kenya have the inequities been more obvious than in the area of special education. The attitudes of both policymakers and the general public toward special education continues to be shaped by a colonial legacy that was typified by meritocracy and a quest to provide higher levels of education only to the brightest and the best as determined by one's high performance in national graduation examinations. Within such a colonial and postcolonial arrangement, the education of individuals with disabilities has continued to be marginalized despite the progress that has been made in adopting more culturally appropriate policies to govern education for all.

The Education Act under which Kenya is currently operating was enacted in 1968 with minor revisions in 1970 and 1980. It does not accord its citizens with disabilities rights to education despite the fact that Kenya recently passed the Children's Act, which provides every Kenyan child with a disability the right to be treated with dignity and to be accorded appropriate medical treatment, special care, education, and training free of charge or at a reduced cost. Currently an Education Bill is being debated in the parliament that is intended to close the gaps in the Education Act. However, even within the Education Bill that is currently under consideration by the Kenyan Parliament, the needs of children with disabilities continue to be neglected. Many shortcomings have been identified within the bill, including the failure to address such critical issues as the need for a comprehensive policy framework on special education, for instance by specifying definitions of the population; the contexts and content of instruction; the identification processes; and even more critically important, issues of funding. Currently many children with disabilities who attend public schools in Kenya are forced to adhere to an academic curriculum that is typified by national primary and secondary graduation examinations that even the brightest and the best often find difficult. Additionally, the bill does not address the need for special education that is public, free, and

(continued)

mandatory for all children with special needs. By addressing these shortcomings, the Education Bill would be in concert with the Children's Act and the proposed Disability Bill, both of which accord civil and human rights to persons with disabilities.

Currently, the Kenya Institute for Special Education (KISE) provides special education teacher training in a 3-month course or a 2-year course in special education for visually impaired children. KISE was established under the sponsorship of the Danish International Development Agency (DANIDA). In addition, since 1995, Kenyatta University has been offering a 4-year course in special education. While these are commendable markers of progress in the area of education of children with disabilities in Kenya, still much remains to be done. Currently large disparities in service provision exist between urban and rural areas where the majority of individuals with disabilities live. The majority of children with intellectual disabilities do not attend school. Indeed studies have found that in Kenya, as the severity a child's disability increases, so does the likelihood that the child will not be enrolled in school. Those children with hearing and visual impairments who attend school often do so in separate schools, with the largest number of such schools being located in large urban areas. In general, such children pursue the same academic goals as their same-age peers without disabilities, but they are provided with instruction by specially trained teachers who are knowledgeable about manual communication or proficient in Braille, respectively. As for children with physical disabilities, depending on the severity of the disability, they may be included in the general education classrooms with same-age peers to pursue an academic curriculum without supports in terms of accommodations or modifications, or they may be placed in a special school where many learn a trade in addition to learning academics.

Children with intellectual disabilities are classified by severity of the disability. There are four levels of labels assigned children with mental retardation in Kenya. These are borderline, mild, moderate, and severe and profound mental retardation. Children labeled as having borderline and mild mental retardation are typically placed in Special Units (analogous to a separate class in the regular school within the U.S. special education service model). These children do not deviate very much from their typically developing peers. They are seen as having the ability to learn within the same school environments as other typically developing children. However, there are typically no Special Units at the secondary (high) school level in Kenya. Students' entrance into a secondary school in Kenya is not automatic, but rather it is predicated on successful performance in the primary (elementary) school graduation examination, called Kenya Certificate of Primary Education (KCPE). This examination is academic in nature and measures skills that require high cognitive ability. Therefore, within this model, a student with mental retardation is seldom successful, and thus, Special Units are not needed at the secondary school level. Further, in many rural area schools, Special Units are not available. Therefore, students with borderline to mild and sometime moderate intellectual disabilities who attend school are often included in general education classrooms to pursue academics without supports in terms of accommodations or modifications. Additionally, those with severe to profound intellectual disabilities, if they attend school at all, often do so in an institution or may be placed in a separate classroom for the disabled, if such a classroom exists in a particular school. The curriculum comprises self-help skills instruction. In all, the education of children with disabilities in Kenya is an area that continues to be marginalized from the standpoint of educational research, policy, and practice.

5. Placing unreasonable demands on teachers and administrators.

6. Ignoring parents' concerns.

7. Isolating students with disabilities in regular schools.

8. Placing students with disabilities in schools or classes that are not age-appropriate.

9. Requiring that students be "ready" and "earn" their way into regular classrooms based on cognitive or social skills.

Perhaps the most important ethical issues involved in inclusion, however, are the degree to which it benefits an individual student and the degree to which educators are committed to seeing that positive effect occur. Consider the case of Stevie, a student in Burlington Elementary School, and his school experience as described by his parents:

Stevie ends each day by asking if it's a school day tomorrow. When it is, he picks out his clothes promptly for the next day so that he won't be late. . . . We believe that his eagerness reflects his joy in being included in a kindergarten classroom just like every other child in his neighborhood. In so many ways, Stevie is just like all of the other children. But he does face extra challenges due to his diagnosis of Down syndrome. We recognize that Stevie's learning style and ability does differ when compared to his typically developing peers. What we have found critical, though, is not the differences in style and ability, but the desire to do what his peers are doing. We believe that this desire is shared by all children. And for Stevie, this desire becomes his greatest source of motivation and thereby his success.

In an inclusive classroom, Stevie's classmates become his positive role models. In the last six months, Stevie has made considerable progress in his academic and fine motor skills. He is now able to write his name with minimal prompting, count to five with meaning and begin to identify the beginning letters of words by their sounds. His speech, self-help and social skills continue to improve because he wants and expects to interact with the other children. . . . Probably one of the most important benefits of an inclusive classroom is that our life is just *more normal*. As parents, we volunteer in the classroom and participate in school-sponsored events just like every other parent. Thus, we are constantly talking to other parents about mutual parenting concerns. For Stevie's younger brother, it gives him the opportunity to follow the footsteps of his big brother just like other siblings do. And, for Stevie, he has *friends*. Stevie's friends include classmates who are both typically developing and others who have special needs. This too we believe will become the norm for all children because of inclusion. Thus, inclusion leads us to focus our attention on the *child* first and his disability second. Stevie needs that focus. We will always strive to maintain it.

Critical Incident

Integrating the New Student With a Disability

As a new second-grade teacher in Burlington Elementary School, you are assigned to a classroom that is directly across the hall from Mr. Beeman's. You have been watching him closely throughout the year and are particularly intrigued by the degree of comfort he seems to have with Carol, the student who uses a wheelchair. At mid-year, a new student is assigned to your classroom. Stephen is a boy from out of state who has a degenerative orthopedic disorder that requires him to use a walker on most days and a wheelchair on some of the more difficult days. You are not certain how you will integrate him into the classroom, but you are concerned that his first day is most positive.

- How will you go about introducing Stephen to the other students in your class?

- What will you do to familiarize your students with disabilities in general and with Stephen's in particular?

Critical Incident

The Reluctant Parents

Not long after Stephen moves into your classroom, several parents approach you expressing concerns that their children may be missing out on valuable time with you as the primary teacher and may not themselves develop as fully as the parents expect. You, of course, are concerned that all students receive the education to which they are entitled.

- How will you go about addressing the parents' concerns?
- What issues would you want to be certain they understood?
- In what kinds of activities might you engage them so they become better informed and more positive about the opportunities their children will have?

Summary

This chapter has described both the historical foundations of the field of special education and current practices in the inclusion of children with disabilities or who may be identified as gifted in regular education programs. In addition, it addresses issues related to the health of children and the responsibility of teachers and schools to consider the means by which children with a variety of special health care needs can be integrated into the regular classroom. Of most importance is the critical role the teacher can play in ensuring that all children are fully integrated into the life and activities of today's classroom while they develop the skills necessary to function effectively in the society at large.

Chapter Review

Go to the Online Learning Center at www.mhhe.com/cushner7e to review important content from the chapter, practice with key terms, take a chapter quiz, and find the Web links listed in this chapter.

Key Terms

adaptive equipment 405
autism spectrum
  disorder 402
behavior management
  plans 402
cerebral palsy 400
clean intermittent cath-
  eterization (CIC) 409
Down syndrome 409
group homes 404
inclusion 403
individual education
  program (IEP) 400

informed consent 413
least restrictive
  environment
  (LRE) 404
low-incidence 401
multifactored
  evaluation 416
muscular dystrophy 405
normalization 403
placement continuum
  416
related services 400
sickle cell disease 409

specific learning
  disabilities 400
spina bifida 409
supported employment
  404
transition plan 409
traumatic brain injury
  (TBI) 406
universal health
  precautions 412
zero exclusion
  mandate 417

Active Exercise

Additional Active Exercises are available online at www.mhhe.com/cushner7e.

The Student With Special Needs

Purpose: To assist future teachers in gaining greater understanding and insight into the probable expectations and responsibilities toward children with special needs.

Instructions: Full inclusion of all children in all classrooms is likely to be a major emphasis in the years to come, thus making it essential that all teachers are well-versed in ways to accommodate the needs of children with special needs. The following exercises will assist you in developing a greater understanding of your role and responsibilities.

1. Arrange to do an observation of a classroom that has children who have special needs. What do you notice about the manner in which the teacher interacts with the children who have special needs compared to those without special needs? What needs do the children seem to have that are unique to this group? Common to other children? What modifications in instructional approach are evident?

2. Interview a parent of a child who receives special educational services. In what ways has the child been helped? What improvements are still needed in the education the child receives? What recommendations does the parent have for you, as a future teacher, regarding what you might provide for children who have special needs?

3. Interview a teacher, focusing on how she or he has been affected by educational policy directed at children with special needs. What modifications has the teacher made in teaching? What special preparation has she or he received to help make the necessary changes? What does the teacher still feel is needed?

4. Ask to observe a conference where an individual educational plan (IEP) is developed for a student with special needs. Analyze the perspectives and needs of each of the parties at the meeting. What concerns did parents address? Teachers? Administrators? Psychologists? Students? What concerns did you have that were not addressed?

Classroom Activities

1. Aided by information you are able to obtain, describe what, if any, adaptations you would want to make to enable any of the following students to participate fully and most successfully in a lesson you plan to implement:

   - A class member whose *low vision* often requires the use of high-contrast or otherwise-adapted print materials in order for her to participate optimally.

   - A class member who is an avid and generally successful achiever, even though his behavioral characteristics are consistent with the autism spectrum disorder/Asperger's disorder diagnoses he has received.

   - A class member who uses a wheelchair.

   - A class member who, although experiencing no hearing loss, demonstrates particular difficulty processing auditory information.

2. Depending on the instructional level at which you plan to teach, begin a bibliography or resource file (e.g., films) that will help your future students better understand and interact comfortably with others, including their peers, who experience special health care needs, difficulties in learning or social behavior, mobility or sensory impairments, or other special needs. For each item, describe your possible classroom use.

Reflective Questions

1. Can every student with special needs receive an individually appropriate education without having to be segregated in a special place? Using information about these conditions accessible via the Internet or other sources, suggest how a teacher might endeavor to accomplish this for:

   - Madeline, a 13-year-old middle school student whose *Asperger's syndrome* involves difficulties in social interactions and sometimes in self-control, along with strong, although sometimes atypical, intellectual interests.

   - Marcus, age 7, who is one of a growing number of young children given a diagnosis of *bipolar disorder* and whose parents and pediatrician rely on his teacher's communication in order to monitor his medication and guide the therapeutic counseling he receives.

2. How can Madeline's and Marcus's teachers make certain that these students' classmates not only are not detrimentally affected but derive benefit from their inclusion in regular education?

Endnotes

1. The Case Study in this chapter is a composite that reflects the experiences of children, parents, and educators in two communities. The authors extend appreciation to the educators who, with parents' consent, provided material for this Case Study. The names of all children and adults are pseudonyms.

2. Vocational Rehabilitation Act of 1973 § 504, P. L. 93–112, 29 U.S.C. § 794 (1973); Americans With Disabilities Act of 1990, 42 U.S.C. § 12101 (1990).

3. Individuals With Disabilities Education Act of 1990, P. L. 101-476, 20, U.S.C. §§ 1400–1485 (1990, reauthorized in 1995).

4. The source for this and subsequent historical information in this chapter is Philip Safford and Elizabeth Safford, *A History of Childhood and Disability.* (New York: Teachers College Press, 1996).

5. See Chapter 11 for a comprehensive discussion of constructivism as reflected in the concept of developmentally appropriate practice.

References

Advocacy Board, Center on Human Policy. (1994). Inclusion (Inclusion in education: A choice for your child). *Newsletter, TASH: The Association for Persons with Severe Handicaps, 20*(9), 27.

Hollingworth, L. S. (1924). Provisions for intellectually superior children. In M. V. O'Shea (Ed.), *The child: His nature and his needs* (pp. 277–299). New York: The Children's Foundation.

Howe, S. G. (1848). *Report of Commission to Inquire into the Conditions of Idiots of the Commonwealth of Massachusetts.* Boston, MA: Senate Document No. 51.

Janney, R. E., Snell, M. E., Beers, M. K., & Raynes, M. (1995). Integrating students with moderate and severe disabilities into general education classes. *Exceptional Children, 61*(5), 425–439.

National Center for Health Statistics. (2000). Births: Final data for 1998. *National Vital Statistics Reports 48*(11).

Nirje, B. (1969). The normalization principle and its human management implications. In R. B. Kugel & W. Wolfensberger (Eds.), *Changing patterns in residential services for the mentally retarded* (pp. 179–188). Washington, DC: President's Committee on Mental Retardation.

Pugach, M., & Johnson, L. (1995). *Collaborative practitioners, collaborative schools.* Denver, CO: Love.

Rainforth, B., York, J., & Macdonald, C. (1997). *Collaborative teams for students with severe disabilities: Integrating therapy and educational services* (2nd ed.). Baltimore, MD: Paul H. Brookes.

Richards, L. E. (1909). *Letters and journals of Samuel Gridley Howe, the servant of humanity* (Vol. 2). Boston: Dana Estes.

Safford, P. L., & Safford, E. J. (1996). *A history of childhood and disability.* New York: Teachers College Press.

Seguin, E. O. (1880). *Report on education (U.S. Commissioner on Education at the Vienna Universal Exhibition).* Washington, DC: U.S. Government Printing Office.

Snell, M. (Ed.). (1993). *Instruction of students with severe disabilities* (4th ed.). New York: Macmillan.

Spencer, H. (1963). What knowledge is of most worth? *Education: Intellectual, Moral & Physical* [Essays, 1854–1859] (pp. 21–96). Patterson, NJ: Littlefield, Adams, & Co. (Original work published 1859)

U.S. Department of Education. (2003). *Twenty-fifth annual report to Congress on the implementation of the Individuals With Disabilities Education Act.* Washington, DC: U.S. Government Printing Office.

Wolfensberger, W. (1972). *The principle of normalization in human services.* Toronto, Ontario: National Institute of Mental Retardation.

Yatvin, J. (1994). Flawed assumptions. *Phi Delta Kappan, 76*(6), 482–484.

Improving Schools for All Children

The Role of Social Class and Social Status in
Teaching and Learning

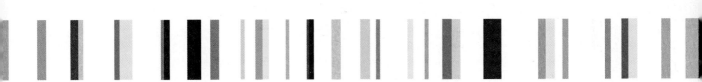

Focus Questions

1. Do you believe that all children can learn?
2. Do you believe that all children should be educated to the same level?
3. What factors do you think may hinder reforms that promote learning for all children?
4. What role do you think social class and social status might have had in your own education?
5. Are you the first in your family to go to college?
6. Can you think of some examples in which a person might have high status but not be a member of a higher social class?
7. Do you believe that those who are born into the lower classes can rise in the U.S. class system if they really work hard?

" An imbalance between rich and poor is the oldest and
most fatal ailment of all republics. "

PLUTARCH

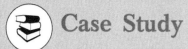

Fulfilling the Promise in the Northeast Kingdom[1]

"Well, they've done it!" exulted Steve Rogers as he pushed the "print" button on his computer. It was a snowy Saturday in January, and Steve and his wife were working in their study.

"Who's done what?" asked his wife, Anne.

"The Vermont Society for the Study of Education (VSSE, 2007) has affiliated with an organization called Education Roundtable in promoting a petition to dismantle the No Child Left Behind Act. Look at this: the petition says that "We, the educators, parents, and concerned citizens whose names appear below, reject the misnamed No Child Left Behind Act and call for legislators to vote against its reauthorization."" He handed the two-page document to his wife.

"Do you think such a petition has a chance?"

"I don't know. There are certainly more states that are trying to opt out of NCLB and several lawsuits currently in the courts."

"Do you think it's a good idea?"

"Well, the Roundtable petition is based on 16 'findings,' backed up with research, that they claim make NCLB 'too destructive to salvage'" (Educator Roundtable, 2007).

"I know that in 2004, the Vermont Superintendents Association published a Position Paper asking the legislature to review the costs of 'truly leaving no child behind' and, if the federal government can't or won't come up with adequate resources to assure that goal, to 'carefully review the federal obligations and federal revenues, and determine whether the federal NCLB law is in the best interest of the state or of Vermont's children.'"

"In other words, they were thinking they might tell the federal government to keep its Title I money and let Vermont manage its own education system?"

"Yes, they were. That hasn't happened yet, but Vermont has been a national leader in trying to equalize funding for all its school districts, and, hopefully, those who believe that school policies should be set at the local, or at least the state level, will continue putting their arguments forward."

Later that day, Steve found himself alone in the house, his wife having gone off to run errands. He wandered back into the study and picked up the Roundtable petition. Sitting at his desk, staring at the still-snow-covered mountains that surrounded his house, Steve remembered when they first came to this part of the country. It was nearly 25 years ago that they answered an ad for a high school English teacher and a speech therapist. What they found here in what was called "the Northeast Kingdom" was both more and less than they had expected, but all of it was thought provoking.

Encompassing three counties in northeastern Vermont (Caledonia, Essex, and Orleans), the Northeast Kingdom is bordered 20 miles away on the north by French Canada (Quebec), and on the east by northern New Hampshire. It has almost no industry but is a region of glacial lakes, broad forests, dairy farms, a surprising lack of quaintness, a statistical lack of sunshine in the winter, and a noticeable degree of poverty.

Its name, the Northeast Kingdom, was given it by then Vermont Senator George Aiken, who said: "You know, this is such beautiful country up here—it should be called the Northeast Kingdom." And so it has been and still is. The richness of its landscape contrasts sharply with the degree of economic development in the area, and—at least to some—mediates the effects of little money. Indeed, a wide variety of people have called this area home, including a fair number of French Canadian descendants, some residents of communes founded by counterculture folks in the 60s and 70s, farmers, artists, entrepreneurs, and a few fugitives from the fast life in cities down the eastern seaboard.

In spite of this variety of people, Steve thought, most kids in the Northeast Kingdom have lived here all their lives, mostly on farms. And they're all a bit isolated, both because of the circumstances of their lives and because the rest of America is woefully ignorant of, not to say indifferent to, its rural populations. Even some of his students' real deprivations don't "count" in the larger scheme of things, he thought; "real" poverty is most often equated with urban poverty!

Steve rummaged in his files and brought out the original Vermont Superintendents Association Position Paper from which the major criticisms of this current petition were, in part, derived. He glanced at the first of the asserted "shortcomings" in the Position Paper:

The Purpose of Education—Vermont's Constitution requires our children be taught civic virtue. Thus, teaching and learning encompass more than what NCLB measures on limited paper and pencil tests in a few areas. To reach our broader goal, we must maintain a broader curriculum and ways of measuring school progress than NCLB envisions. To reach this end, we must strengthen and embrace (rather than diminish) our unique Vermont heritage of direct and continuous accountability through locally elected boards to assure a high quality and cost-effective education for all children.

He thought immediately of his first encounter with the Future Farmers of America in his high school. He had been asked to be a judge for the annual F.F.A. Creed Speaking Contest, an event that demonstrated the great emphasis the organization placed on public speaking. There was a very good reason for this emphasis: living in a rural community, a farmer will in all likelihood be called upon to participate in self-government—often more likely than his urban and suburban counterparts. He had been impressed with the seriousness and the skill of the students, in their blue corduroy jackets, with F.F.A. written on the back, as they conducted meetings according to Roberts' Rules of Order. Civic virtue, he thought . . . yes, that was an important element of education for our kids. Was it more important than math?

Steve read again the second "shortcoming" in the Position Paper:

The Growth of the Whole Child—VSA is further concerned that NCLB does not acknowledge essential family, poverty, and social issues. The schools are held solely responsible for the education of our most needy and neglected children. Furthermore, adequate programs to address these human needs such as effective pre-school programs, nutrition, medical care, parental support, and expanded intellectual and social opportunities are not substantively addressed by the federal law. Many children from impoverished backgrounds arrive at the school-house door unprepared to prosper or to learn.

Steve thought of the new girl who arrived in his study hall last week. He'd been warned about her in advance: she'd been abused for years . . . had had her bare feet held in boiling water by her father, or her mother's boyfriend, or someone. There was some thought that she might have some trouble relating to men. "Oh, really!" he said out loud. "How do I tell her that I will scold her if she creates a disturbance but that I couldn't really blame her if she opened my head with a hatchet?"

"Or, what about the 5-year-old who can hardly finish a sentence?" Steve went on, talking aloud to himself. "He just met his first teacher the other day, and hated her for trying to show him how to bounce a ball. It was too hard for him. He lives in garbage and dog dung with his brother, mother, and a man who lost his own children for molesting them. The heat has gone off in the house. A car motor sits in the bathtub. The mother sits near the kitchen stove with a black eye and won't answer the door when a social worker comes by. The social worker never returns. Only the school bus comes by faithfully, and in a decade, if the boy is still alive, he will come to my school."

Steve's wife came into the room. "What did you say?" she asked.

"Oh, I'm sorry. I didn't hear you come in. I was just thinking out loud about the way we treat our children in this society. The legislature passes a tougher child-support law and adjourns. The lawyers pull out the law's teeth and run for the legislature. The sociology professors discuss changing trends in the family and order another salad. But every day the girl with the scalded feet and the boy who has no one to speak for him get out of bed and come to school."

"Oh, Steve . . . I know it's hard, sometimes. But there are students that make you glad, too, I know there are!" said Anne.

(continued)

Steve looked back at the Position Paper. The third "shortcoming" had to do with testing.

Measuring Schools—Learning should be measured by looking at how much students grow in their knowledge, civic values, and skills from the time they enter a school until the time that they leave the school. Instead, the Act requires that judgments be made by comparing how much students know in one year with how much a different group of students know in other years. This is like evaluating an employee based on the work of the person who previously held the job. It makes even less sense in Vermont's small schools and classes where the performance of a single student can dramatically affect the entire school's label.

"That's true," he answered his wife. "There are lots of satisfactions. Remember the time we took the students to Boston to see a real Shakespearean production? George Dalton couldn't get over all the people. 'Now,' he said, 'whenever I go to sleep, I think of all those people behind all those windows—people I'll never know, with their own lives—and they're going to sleep, too.'"

"Or, remember when Ruth's mother told me how she had reacted to music I played in class? Ruth went home that day saying, 'Mr. Rogers comes into homeroom and he asks if we'd like to hear some music, and we don't think nothing of it, so we say Okay. And what does he put on? The opera! I thought I'd die. Well, I got to listening to it there, and you know, it weren't half bad.' I guess maybe playing that music—actually it was a Brandenburg Concerto—might be one of the best things I've done in all these years of teaching! But it sure wouldn't be 'measured' on a graduation test!"

Steve put down the Position Paper and the NSSE petition and sat back in his chair. "You know," he said to Anne, "all this talk about educational excellence is, in some ways, a way of avoiding the real issue in this country, which is inequality of educational opportunity. I can give my students the most challenging assignment imaginable—and I try to do just that—but as long as Tommy's father needs him to keep the farm going, or Linda's mother needs her to help with the baby, that assignment is not going to get done. We can print our commitment to equality of educational opportunity on every scrap of stationery that comes out of the superintendent's office, or wave the flag on government websites, but what does it mean when a few of my students will get iPods for Christmas while the rest are lucky to bring an apple for lunch? Surely there must be a better way!"

No Child Left Behind Act of 2001

With the passage of the **No Child Left Behind Act of 2001,** the federal government of the United States entered into the most far-reaching, controversial, and potentially expensive effort to reform public education in the history of the country. Actually a reauthorization of the Elementary and Secondary Education Act of 1965 (ESEA), No Child Left Behind (NCLB) has imposed a whole series of conditions on public schooling, with sanctions if those conditions are not met. These conditions are based on two major ideas: (1) that the nation's education system needs subject area standards for what students should know and be able to do, and (2) that the nation's students, teachers, and schools should be held accountable for reaching those standards.

Under No Child Left Behind, accountability is enforced by testing all children in Grades 3 through 8 in reading and mathematics, with some other subject area testing done in middle and high school. Indeed, it is this assessment of progress that is believed by proponents to be the engine of reform—serving both to measure achievement and to compel it.

Other aspects of the law include the provision that every classroom will be staffed by a "highly qualified" teacher, that further support for reform will be aided by introducing competition into education by encouraging parental choice through the establishment of charter schools and through school voucher programs for low-income families, that all schools must meet "adequate yearly progress" toward the goals of proficient education, and that such progress (or lack of it) must be reported to the public in the form of a state "report card."

Central to this effort is a debate about assessment—of students, of curricula, of teachers, of school administrators. The debate surrounds the following questions: What kinds of assessment? Who should be assessed, and how often? How much time should be given to assessments? How is the implementation of assessments affecting the curriculum at the state level? and Who decides the answers to all of the above?

In this chapter, we ask—in addition—what role does social class and social status play in the outcomes, not only of assessments but of teaching and learning as well?

Case Analysis

Steve's experience teaching in the Northeast Kingdom is typical of many teachers who work in schools where there is significant poverty, but it is somewhat different from those whose students live in urban areas. Rural poverty is just as devastating, but it often doesn't get the attention that urban poverty does. The counties of the Northeast Kingdom are 3 of 2,052 such counties defined as rural by the federal census; these counties comprise about 75% of the nation's land. In 2003, 49 million people lived in rural areas—about 17% of the total population of the United States (Kusmin, 2006).

Residents of the Northeast Kingdom, like other residents of rural areas, are also keepers of important American history and traditions, and significant caretakers of the environment. These roles are reflected in the Vermont superintendents' emphasis on the need for "civic virtue" as a critical goal of education in the state. It also explains, in part, why the superintendents want to preserve the power of locally elected boards of education to set standards and maintain accountability.

What is difficult for many residents is their isolation, which often contributes to a lack of access to good-paying jobs and to education and health care. Small farmers, largely dairy farmers, often have a hard time too, especially as they are being squeezed by "megafarms" in other parts of the country. Indeed, in the United States over half a million small farmers have incomes below the poverty level (Economic Research Service, 2004). In Vermont, there's an old joke about the farmer who won the lottery. "What are you going to do now?" he was asked. "Well, I guess I'll just keep on farming till it's gone!"

Over the years, Steve has tried in many different ways to adapt his own ideas about education and his English curriculum to the needs of the students of the Northeast Kingdom.

Pedagogies: Old and New

Like many teachers of rural children, Steve is determined not to "dumb down" his curriculum. He plans to introduce his students to classic literature, and to engage them in it in meaningful ways.

My freshman English classes read *Antigone, The Odyssey, Macbeth*, Hardy's *Return of the Native*—none of them abridged or paraphrased. I will not pretend

that the books are not difficult, and I will not pretend that they are without passages which most modern readers will find tedious—but I will also not pretend
that tripe is profound or that people lack sensibility simply because they are
fifteen and live "in the sticks." (Keizer, 1988, p. 9)

But a classical curriculum is not enough if it means the same old pedagogies.
One of the hallmarks of a "classic" is its ability to relate to any time period,
including our own. So, Lady Macbeth complains about the lack of gratitude in
children: "How sharper than a serpent's tooth it is to have an ungrateful child!"
And today's young people know what that means because their parents have
said the same thing. Or, while Odysseus nearly succumbs to the call of the
Sirens, Steve's students can tell you a thing or two about the temptations of sex
and drugs.

"If a child can't spell, have him write a book," says Steve. "If a kid can't
clear the low hurdles, give him a shot at the high" (Keizer, 1988, p. 10). This
approach is often in direct opposition to the beliefs of some educators in deficit
models—that is, that children from low-income families are perceived as culturally deprived or disadvantaged and cannot be taught the same things in the same
ways as middle-class children.

By characterizing the environment of lower-class children as deprived, disorga-
nized, or pathological, the cultural deprivation argument [shifts] attention away
from the failings of the schools and of biased testing instruments to the
supposed failure of poor people to bring up their children correctly. (Hurn,
1993, p. 152)

Such attitudes are counterproductive at best and harmful to both students and
teachers at worst. Not surprisingly, low expectations of students quite often produce low performance, thus engaging in what is called a self-fulfilling prophecy
(see below). And research has demonstrated that:

The instruction available to students lower down on (any) social-class scale is, on
average, academically less challenging, more repetitive, and more dominated by a
concern for social control than that offered to students of higher-social-class background. (Knapp & Woolverton, 2003, p. 672)

In contrast, when teaching is respectful, exciting, engaging, and challenges the
real and human needs of the learner, great things often happen. Of course, this
is the case in *any* classroom, regardless of *who* is in it!

Roles: Old and New

Social class influences the nature of the teaching force just as it influences the
nature of the student population in any school. Teaching as a profession occupies
a middle rung in the hierarchy of occupations, and, in fact, many teachers come
from middle-class backgrounds. But not all do, and for those from working-class
backgrounds, teaching offers the possibility of "moving up" the social ladder a
bit. This upward mobility differs somewhat, however, for men and women, as
there is a long history in U.S. schools of what is often called the feminization of
teaching (Knapp & Woolverton, 2003). This phenomenon divides the labor market of school people into a kind of within-the-profession stratification in which
men manage and women teach (Tyack, 1981).

Not surprisingly, teachers bring their own class-based knowledge, attitudes, and values with them into the profession, just as students do. Metz (1990) studied variations in teachers' social class backgrounds and found the following:

> Teachers participate in communities and in kinship and friendship networks that also are part of the social class system. While teachers have formally similar educational credentials. . . . they not only come from a range of social class backgrounds but participate as adults in networks that vary significantly in their social class. (p. 94)

In this study, this variance had an effect on how teachers defined their work. Those whose background was more middle and upper-middle class tended to think of their responsibilities in terms of being sure to do a good job. Those from lower-class backgrounds tended to think of their work in terms of "conscientiously putting in required hours" (Metz, 1990, p. 95).

There is also some evidence that social class helps to subtly shape faculties within and between schools (Anyon, 1980, 1981; Metz, 1990). As Knapp and Woolverton (2003) point out, while social class is not the most powerful variable influencing where teachers are assigned or find work, and while teachers are not passive participants in their search for employment, it is still the case that

> Teachers are likely to gravitate to teaching situations in which their colleagues' social class sensibilities resemble their own. . . . Thus, the cadre of teachers at a typical working-class school and those serving predominantly upper-middle-class students are likely to look very different. (p. 666)

When teachers—regardless of their own social class backgrounds—are consciously prepared to be aware of, to think, and to act in multicultural ways, they are more likely to be effective in teaching students from a variety of backgrounds. This will be even more the case in the years ahead as student populations in the United States become more and more diverse.

Place of Content Knowledge: Old and New

In her now-classic study of the work fifth-grade children do in schools representing different social classes, Jean Anyon (1980) documented the role of curriculum in preparing students for different roles in life based on their social class. In general, for children in working-class schools, work is procedural and teacher-directed and involves little choice or decision making. For children in middle-class schools, work is demonstrated by getting the right answer, which is usually based on following directions. Accumulating right answers results in good grades. However, in middle-class schools, following directions often includes some figuring out, some choice, and some decision making. In upper- or professional-class schools, work is quite often carried out independently and involves creative and/or critical thinking. Suggesting that her study (and others) finds the nature of schoolwork is "tacit preparation for relating to the process of production in a particular way," she noted that by emphasizing different cognitive and behavioral skills related to academic content, children are learning the expectations the society has with respect to their relation to authority and to work.

In many ways, these distinctions are part of a "hidden" curriculum. The *formal* curriculum teaches little about the experiences of people living at either end of the social class scale, and teaches quite a bit about the experiences and worldview of middle-class America. The public school is, after all, a middle-class institution.

What does seem to be the case, however, is a differentiation of actual content by social class along several dimensions: emphasis on "advanced" versus "basic" skills, emphasis on conceptual understanding, range and variety of academic tasks, degree of repetition, extent of topical coverage, and attention to "practical" or vocational knowledge (Knapp & Woolverton, p. 673). By the time students reach high school, selection into various "tracks" (e.g., college-bound, vocational, commercial), can be fundamentally related to social class patterns, with the result that students from different social class backgrounds often leave public schooling with quite different educations. It is, in part, this phenomenon that the No Child Left Behind Act seeks to redress. Indeed, it is this effort to redress social class and other differences in the education of American children that the Vermont superintendents justly called a "noble purpose."

Assessment: Old and New

Similarly, the goal of measuring student achievement in terms of standardized testing is, in part, an effort to avoid the kind of differentiation of assessment by class that has allowed many lower-class students to fall through the cracks of public education. For example, in Anyon's (1980, 1981) study of fifth-grade classrooms in schools catering to different social classes, students in working-class schools tended to be evaluated on whether or not they had followed the correct steps rather than on whether or not their answers were right. Middle-class students tended to be evaluated on whether they had done the assignment and "understood it." In contrast, students in upper-class schools tend to be evaluated on their ability to think critically, express themselves well, and apply ideas and concepts.

One criticism of the one-size-fits-all use of standardized tests, as articulated by the Vermont Society for the Study of Education (2007) and others (Meier & Wood, 2004), is that judgments are made by comparing how much students

know in one year (e.g., the fourth grade *this* year) with how much a different group of students (e.g., the fourth grade *next* year) know in other years. Increasingly, however, educators and planners are becoming interested in different approaches. Such changes are suggested, in part, because it is becoming increasingly clear that the skills needed in the 21st century may very well not be amenable to paper-and-pencil tests. For example, a government report even 15 years ago ("What Work Requires of Schools," 1991) suggested that the following skills will be needed in the workforce in the future: the ability to identify, analyze, plan, and allocate resources; the ability to work effectively with others; the ability to acquire and evaluate information; the ability to understand complex interrelationships; and the ability to work with a variety of technologies.

In her recent book, The Flat World of Education, Linda Darling-Hammond (2010) lists six sets of skills that are already required in the work world of the 21st century—the capacity to: design, evaluate, and manage one's own work so that it continually improves; frame, investigate, and solve problems using a wide range of tools and resources; collaborate strategically with others; communicate effectively in many forms; find, analyze, and use information for many purposes; and develop new products and ideas.

To assess these kinds of skills and competencies, many educators today are calling for several changes in the assessment system, notably:

> encouraging the use of state and local assessments designed to improve curriculum and teaching, including multiple measures of learning and progress in assessing school progress and success, and evaluating gains using "value-added" approaches that assess the progress of individual students, not changes in average student scores. (Darling-Hammond, 2004, pp. 30–31)

Regardless of their social class backgrounds, all students in the United States will increasingly be required to participate in jobs that have any number of the above requirements. Thus it seems necessary that no students be allowed to "disappear" into a composite or average or group assessment. Rather, teachers need to know how each student is doing as he or she progresses through schooling. Sometimes called **growth measures,** these approaches to assessment entail enlarging the time window in which students are evaluated from a single class year to the whole of the student's academic career and then measuring how that student is learning and growing. Coupled with fast feedback of test results to teachers, these approaches enable timely encouragement and intervention, as well as allowing for natural differences in development among children.

Perspectives on Social Class and Social Status

Previous chapters have suggested that differences in school achievement may be attributed to a variety of cultural influences. Two of those influences are the cultural aspects of social class and social status.

Most Americans believe they live in a relatively classless, egalitarian society. At the least, American ideology promotes the idea that through proper attention, diligent effort, and some luck (which Americans also believe in), an individual may "rise above" his or her social class. Part of what has been called an "American religion" (Bellah, 1976), this faith in the reality of upward mobility may account for the relative lack of attention given to the concept of social class in much of the educational and psychological literature in the United States (Brislin, 1988).

Certainly it accounts for the difficulty encountered by sociology professors in helping young people understand the bases of class differences in this society. Nevertheless, as we all know, there are significant variations in economic standard of living, status of occupation, and extent of expectations for upward mobility among U.S. citizens.

Definitions of Social Class

Social class has been defined in a number of ways, all of which refer in some sense to a hierarchical stratification or "layering" of people in social groups, communities, and societies. Assignment to social class categories is one of several stratification systems that can be used to distinguish one individual or group from another in such a way as to assign "worth." The urge to organize people in layers almost appears to be a human characteristic. Indeed, it has been said that whenever there are more than three people in a group there will be stratification; someone will be more respected, more powerful, or more "worthy" than the rest. Although many Americans would identify class membership in terms of income (Gilbert & Kahl, 1982), it is important to understand that money alone does not determine a person's social class. Rather, social class standing depends on a combination of prestige, power, influence, and income (Webb & Sherman, 1989).

Traditional class markers in the United States include family income, prestige of one's father's (and recently, one's mother's) occupation, prestige of one's neighborhood, the power one has to achieve one's ends in times of conflict, and the level of schooling achieved by the family head. Among other nations and cultures, markers of one's social class may include such determiners as bloodline and status of the family name, the caste into which one was born, the degree to which one engages in physical labor, and the amount of time that one might devote to scholarly or leisurely activities of one's choosing (Brislin, 1988).

One reason that social class is so difficult to talk about and truly understand is that while class distinctions are real and observable in concrete daily experience, they are also highly abstract. It is no accident that social class categories are mostly "assigned" by others (often sociologists), for social class in the real world is often in the eyes of the beholder. Nevertheless, for purposes of analysis, American society can be divided into five social classes.

At the top is a very small upper class, or social elite, consisting of people who have generally inherited social privilege from others. Second is a somewhat larger upper-middle class whose members often are professionals, corporate managers, and leading scientists. This group usually has benefited from extensive higher education, and while family history is not so important, manners, tastes, and patterns of behavior are. The third (or middle) social class is generally comprised of people employed in white-collar occupations earning middle incomes—small business owners, teachers, social workers, nurses, sales and clerical workers, bank tellers, and so forth. This class is the largest of the social classes in the United States (although some claim that it is shrinking rapidly) and encompasses a wide range of occupations and incomes. Central to the values of the "typical" middle class is a "desire to belong and be respectable . . . friendliness and openness are valued and attention is paid to 'keeping up appearances'" (Webb & Sherman, 1989, p. 407).

Fourth in the hierarchy of social class is the **working class,** whose members are largely blue-collar workers (industrial wage earners) or employees in low-paid service occupations. Working-class families often have to struggle with poor job security, limited fringe benefits, longer hours of work, and more dangerous or "dirtier" work than people in the classes above them. It is not surprising, then, that members of the working class often feel more alienation from the social mainstream. Finally, fifth in the hierarchy is the lower class, which includes both the so-called **working poor** and those who belong to what has been termed the **underclass**–a designation that refers to people who have been in poverty for so long that they seem unable to take any advantage at all of mobility options and thus lie nearly outside the class system. Clearly, poverty is both the chief characteristic and the chief problem of this group.

While it is the case that social class membership involves more than income, it is also the case that incomes in the United States have become considerably more *unequal* since the late 1970s. As Iglitzen and Hill (2007) note:

> Currently the top 10 percent of income earners in the United States own 70 percent of the wealth and the wealthiest 1 percent own more than the bottom 95 percent, according to a Federal Reserve Study. In 2005, the top 300,000 Americans collectively enjoyed almost as much income—21.8 percent—as the bottom 150 million Americans, more than double their share of income in 1980.

Indeed, it is possible that the prospects of individuals to move up the social ladder have, themselves, declined in recent decades due to the loss of manufacturing jobs as the economy globalizes, and the consequent growth of minimum-wage, service jobs, and a labor market divided between those who have a 4-year college degree and those who do not.

Social Class and Child-Rearing Practices

Those people who share similar socioeconomic status, whatever its level may be, also share similar cultural knowledge, attitudes, and values. These similarities can be seen in various patterns of child rearing; various attitudes toward and expectations about dress, food, and shelter; and various beliefs about the necessity and value of schooling. Of prime interest to educators is the influence social class has on educational opportunity, behavior, and achievement in schools.

Brislin (1988) reviewed a number of sources in this area that are useful. Kohn (1977), for example, argued that parents from different class backgrounds emphasize different values when raising their children. Parents in the middle classes tend to emphasize intellectual curiosity, self-control, and consideration of others. This emphasis leads to adult characteristics of empathetic understanding and self-direction. Working-class parents, on the other hand, stress neatness, good manners (often involving quietness and invisibility when adults are present), and obedience (Gilbert & Kahl, 1982). These emphases lead to a concern with external standards, such as obedience to authority, acceptance of what other people think of as good manners, and difficulty in articulating one's wishes to authority figures. The middle-class emphasis leads to adolescents and adults who are relatively comfortable with self-initiated behaviors and at ease when interacting with others outside their immediate family or friendship networks. Kohn (1977) suggests that the skills learned by children of the middle classes prepare them to assume professional and managerial positions that demand intellectual curiosity and good social skills. In addition, Argyle (1980) suggests that social skills, such as those learned by children of the middle classes, may be central to success in the professions because they may take precedence over purely intellectual skills in many promotion and hiring decisions.

In contrast, the skills learned by working-class children lead them to take wage labor jobs that are closely supervised and demand physical effort. The implication is that these jobs are taken partly as a result of less emphasis on intellectual curiosity and partly as a result of parental concern for external standards and obedience to the expectations and demands of a visible supervisor. However, jobs involving strictly physical labor have all but disappeared, a fact that makes life for lower-class individuals only that much more frustrating.

Lindgren and Suter (1985) suggest many reasons students from middle-class backgrounds may do better in school than their working-class peers. One difference can be attributed to perceived parental expectation. Students from working-class backgrounds may think their parents expect less of them with regard to future school achievement, even when those parents don't really have lower expectations. Children of parents who have attended college or participated in other forms of postsecondary education are more likely to encourage their children to attend college than are parents who have not. Family income may be a factor that discourages college attendance among the lower classes, but the cultural context of schooling may also discourage many lower-income and inner-city children (Boykin, 1986). Success in school, for example, demands linguistic competence, and children from working-class backgrounds tend to have less exposure, less expertise, and less confidence with language skills.

Another view, however, is taken by Knapp and Shields (1990), who seriously question the efficacy of emphasizing the so-called deficits of so-called disadvantaged children. To do so, they assert, is to

> risk making inaccurate assessments of children's strengths and weaknesses. . . . [to] have low expectations . . . and set standards that are not high enough to form the foundation for future academic success . . . [and, in] focusing on the deficits of students from disadvantaged backgrounds . . . [to risk] overlooking their true capabilities. Finally, a focus on the poor preparation of disadvantaged children often distracts attention from how poorly prepared the school may be to serve these youngsters. (p. 754)

Social Status

As discussed in Chapter 3, the term **social status** refers to a hierarchical position determined not so much by one's wealth (or lack of it) but by the prestige, social esteem, and honor accorded one within one's own social milieu. It is quite possible, in fact, to have high social status without having commensurate money. Members of the clergy are good examples of this condition, as are, quite often, teachers. Conversely, it is also possible to have a great deal of money but occupy a low-status position, at least in terms of general community norms, for example, drug lords and leaders of gangs.

In the social hierarchy of schools, individual students usually achieve high status because of roles they assume, such as star athlete, academic achiever, cheerleading captain, and so forth. Interestingly, the social status of a particular student often differs from the point of view of students and of teachers. Thus students may often accord athletes with high status, whereas teachers generally accord high status to students who achieve well academically. In neither case are economic considerations necessarily predominant.

All of which, of course, is not to say that social class and social status don't necessarily go hand in hand. To the extent, for example, that teachers believe that middle- and upper-middle-class students will achieve more than working- and lower-class students, such expectations are often reflected in reality.

The Importance of Teacher Expectations

Teacher expectations regarding the possibilities and potential of academic success for individual students are a critical factor in student achievement. **Teacher expectation** refers to the attributions that teachers make about the future behavior or academic achievement of their students, based on what they presently know about them. Teacher expectation effects refer to student outcomes that occur because of the actions taken by teachers in response to their own expectations (Good & Brophy, 1987).

As noted previously, an important type of teacher expectation is the self-fulfilling prophecy. In this effect, a false or untrue belief leads to specific behavior that causes that expectation to become true. For instance, if false rumors begin to spread that the stock market is going to crash and if millions of people then rush to sell off their stock holdings, the market may in fact crash. The outcome, however, is not due to any event that was predicted accurately but because people responded to the false information that was rumored.

In the classroom setting, teachers may tell themselves about the potential for success or failure of the students in their charge. For instance, assume that a teacher looks at her roster for the upcoming year and sees that she will have in her classroom a particular student, named Sandra, whose sister, Sally, was in the

same classroom 2 years earlier. Assume further that Sally had a difficult year. Not only did she struggle academically, but (perhaps as a result of academic failure) she also had behavior problems. This teacher, vividly remembering her problems with Sally, may expect that Sandra will repeat the pattern. When Sandra walks into the classroom at the start of the year, the teacher may greet her in a cool manner, may be hesitant to approach her, and may even avoid personal contact with her as much as possible. Such behavior on the part of the teacher may alienate Sandra, may make her feel as if she doesn't belong, and may generate many feelings of anxiety and uncertainty. These feelings may, in turn, result in certain acting-out behaviors on Sandra's part. The teacher may then have set the stage for a self-fulfilling prophecy.

Just the opposite can also be true. A teacher may, for whatever reason, believe a certain child will be a good student when in fact he or she may be just about average. This belief may translate into particular actions on the part of the teacher that demonstrate care and concern and an expectation of success to the student. The teacher may call on this particular student to read more than other students, may trust this student with particular responsibilities, and may afford greater attention and privilege to this student, which may, in turn, result in increased gains in achievement. This outcome may not have happened if the teacher did not have high expectations for this student.

The Culturally Responsive Teacher

Culturally Responsive Teaching

Although Americans are not used to thinking (or talking) about social class as a cultural category, it is relatively easy to think about the relationship between social class and school achievement because there is so much data on the subject, particularly with respect to poverty. Indeed, the phrase *culture of poverty* (Banfield, 1970) has frequently been used as a kind of vague reason for achievement gaps between middle- and lower-class children in school. Nevertheless, there is a class aspect of culture observable in different forms in both rural and urban settings around the world. In the United States, we might think of all but middle-class children as living in "another country," from which, at the age of 5, they are suddenly transported every day to a highly middle-class setting–the school–where they are expected to not only have but also honor the knowledge, attitudes, and values of this new place. This conception is as true for upper-class children as it is for lower-class children, although many upper-class children attend private rather than public schools, in part for this very reason.

For the culturally responsive teacher, however, any aspect of a student's social context–class, race, ethnicity, gender, language, and so forth–is important to note and to take into consideration when planning instruction as well as assessment. Villegas and Lucas (2007) list six characteristics of a culturally responsive teacher:

- *They understand how their learners construct knowledge.* They are interested in how students connect new knowledge to prior knowledge and beliefs, and help students "build bridges between what they already know about a topic and what they need to learn about it" (p. 29).
- *They learn about their students' lives.* To understand how learners construct knowledge, culturally responsive teachers make it a point to learn about their students' family makeup, their interests, concerns, strengths, and problem-solving strategies.

- *They are socioculturally conscious,* defined as "the awareness that a person's world view is not universal but is profoundly influenced by life experiences, as mediated by a variety of factors, including race, ethnicity, gender, and social class" (p. 31).

- *They hold affirming views about diversity* rather than having a deficit perspective. This is especially important when it is related to the idea of self-fulfilling prophesies because the expectations of teachers are critical to student success.

- *They use appropriate instructional strategies* such as "asking them to discuss what they know about a given topic . . . embedding new ideas and skills in projects that are meaningful to the students . . . and . . . using pertinent examples and analogies from students' lives" (p. 32).

- *They are advocates for all students,* thus "seeing themselves as part of a community of educators working to make schools more equitable for all students" (p. 32).

As Villegas and Lucas (2007) note, "Teaching is an ethical activity and teachers have an ethical obligation to help all students learn" (p. 32).

Social Class and School Funding

One of the most visible ways in which social class in American schooling plays itself out is the way public schools are funded. Public schooling is a responsibility of the states, and the states have traditionally turned over control of school finances to local districts, which generally fund schools through taxing property. As local districts vary widely in the value of their property, the ability to raise money for education also varies widely. Although most states also have some sort of funding formula through which state money is allocated to local districts, and although federal funding is still available for specific programs in schools (e.g., Title I, special education), it is still the case that the value of local property sets the parameters for how much funding is available for public schools. Neither state funding formulae nor federal dollars make up for disparities in funding among schools (Harp, 1992; Verstegen, 1990).

In the past 35 years, numerous court cases have been filed in both state and federal courts seeking in one way or another to change the way in which schools are funded. In one of the earliest cases, *Serrano v. Priest* (1971), the California Supreme Court declared that the state's dependence on property taxes to support schools was a violation of equal protection principles in the state constitution. In response, the state legislature put a cap on potential revenues in wealthy districts and increased state aid to poorer districts. Some say that this decision contributed to the California tax revolt of 1978, which resulted in the passage of Proposition 13, an amendment to the state constitution that reduced property taxes by 57% and drastically cut funding for public services, notably, public schools.

In the *Rodriguez* case in Texas (*San Antonio Independent School District v. Rodriguez,* 1973), the school district argued that using the property tax as the basis for school funding disadvantaged poor children because poor districts didn't have the tax base that wealthier districts had. Thus, the Fourteenth Amendment, which guarantees equal protection under the law, had been violated. The U.S. Supreme

Court disagreed, stating that since there is no federal constitutional right to education, and since the Texas system did not discriminate systematically against all poor people, the equal protection clause of the Fourteenth Amendment was not violated. The amendment, it was noted, did not require absolute equality.

These cases did not end the battle for changes in school funding policy. As of 2005, only five states have not filed court cases challenging school funding policies, and only seven have not had such cases decided. In general, these cases have had decidedly mixed results. A more successful outcome was experienced in Kentucky (*Rose v. Council for Better Education,* 1989), when the Kentucky Supreme Court affirmed a lower court decision that found

> that the system of school financing provided for by the General Assembly is inadequate; places too much emphasis on local school board resources; and results in inadequacies, inequities and inequalities throughout the state so as to result in an inefficient system of common school education in violation of Kentucky Constitution, Sections 1, 3 and 183 and the equal protection clause and the due process of law clause of the 14th Amendment to the United States Constitution. Additionally the complaint maintains the entire system is not efficient under the mandate of Section 183.

What is clear is that as education costs continue to rise, due to a number of factors, including federal and state unfunded mandates, growth of the need for special services for students, and increases in health insurance and transportation costs, the problem of equitably funding schools will undoubtedly become more critical.

The Role of Social Class in Student Progress: Problems and Issues

The task of assessing student progress has always been of central importance to educators, but in the last decade or so schools, teachers, and students have felt increasing pressure to demonstrate competence in their teaching and learning. Indeed, since the publication of *A Nation at Risk* in 1983, the debate about how well our children are learning has become both ubiquitous and emotional.

New Language for Considering Public Education

The federal role in the accountability and standards movement increased tremendously in 2002 with the signing of the reauthorization of the Elementary and Secondary Education Act (ESEA) called No Child Left Behind. This law emphasized several concepts that have become watchwords in any contemporary discussion of American schooling: standards, accountability, highly qualified teachers, annual yearly progress (AYP), and failing schools.

The Standards Movement

The current standards-based movement emerged in response to the 1983 Report of the National Commission on Excellence in Education, *A Nation at Risk,* as well as from the publication, from 1983 to 1986, of numerous state-of-the-schools reports funded or sponsored by groups with widely divergent interests. The general assertion in all of these reports was that American students were losing

The Standards Movement

the race for academic superiority to the rest of the industrialized world, and, it was said, so also would Americans lose the economic battle for superiority in a new global economy. Despite considerable criticism of the data upon which these reports were based (Berliner & Biddle, 1995), it became something of a truism that U.S. schools were a disaster and must be fixed (Meier, 2000).

In 1989, then President George H. W. Bush convened the nation's governors for an education summit, out of which came a set of national education goals–Goals 2000–designed to improve America's schools in eight specific areas, including improvement in reading and math, and graduating 90% of America's high school students by the year 2000. In 1992, Congress convened a 32-member panel of educators, business leaders, and public officials, called the National Council on Education Standards and Testing. That panel concluded that creating national standards and assessments was both highly desirable and feasible.

One important aspect of the problem of setting national standards for education is that it implies a national curriculum, something that states have resisted mightily over a long period of time. Questions that arose across the nation with respect to national standards included not only how to decide on specific definitions of standards in major academic subjects, but also how the standards would be tied to some reasonable assessment of what students really needed to know to be good citizens and productive workers, how student learning would be measured, and how the standards would affect poor and minority children, children with special needs, and children for whom English was not their primary language (Hilliard, 1998).

This concern with children who are not white, middle-class children reflects the reality that substantial changes must occur in the way we "do" school if all children are really to succeed. If the public school is a middle-class institution, then part of its role in a democratic society is to provide access to middle-class knowledge, attitudes, and values to all children. That is, in part, what the standards aim to accomplish. When it fails to do so, when the school, in fact, reproduces class stratification through its curriculum, its learning activities, its testing, and the hidden curriculum in its halls, then the society as a whole will suffer from a lack of the human resources it could otherwise count on. This is no small matter in an interdependent and somewhat fragile world where change occurs rapidly. Indeed, a large and healthy middle class, actively involved in forming a political community, is deemed by many to be a social necessity if we are to have a sustainable society (Tilkidjiew, 1998).

Despite these legitimate reservations or, perhaps, because of them, there is currently a movement to establish common curriculum standards for the nation. This effort has been approved by 48 states and is being led by the Council of Chief State School Officers. Called the "Common Core," these standards have been developed in draft form for language arts and mathematics and are now being studied by individual state legislatures for adoption. Whether or not these (and additional ones for science and social studies) will survive the debates that are sure to come, and what form they will eventually take, there is considerable political "push" for them and the debate will be both interesting and informative in terms of the nation's ideas about curriculum for the 21st century.

Accountability

In 1994, President Clinton signed the Goal 2000: Educate America Act, which awarded states additional money for education and granted them considerable

**The Accountability
Movement**

flexibility as to how that money would be spent. Central to the whole idea was the belief that states and local districts should set high standards for achievement, should test to see how well students were achieving, and should hold schools, teachers, and students accountable for the results. Thus was the **accountability movement** born, but decision-making power about how it would be implemented resided in the states.

With the passage of No Child Left Behind, however, the federal government assumed at least oversight responsibility for state plans for accountability. Although there has been considerable debate about the ways in which the law is, or should be, implemented, every state, the District of Columbia, and Puerto Rico have submitted approved accountability plans. In these plans, states must describe how they will reduce achievement gaps among various student groups and make sure that all students, including disadvantaged students, will achieve academic proficiency. The assumption here, of course, is that by instituting standards and accountability through testing, educational progress for all students will be achieved.

The argument for standardized testing as the central mechanism for accountability rests on a belief that U.S. students, in comparison with students in other industrialized nations, lack basic skills, particularly in literacy and mathematics. Such insufficiency, the argument goes, is due to two factors. First, American education suffers from too much child-centered educational practice and the wide latitude of curriculum in U.S. schools that has been commonplace. Second, children from racial minority groups, poor children, and those for whom English is a second language routinely score lower than white, upper- and middle-class children on tests of basic skills. Proponents argue that these combined factors only prove that U.S. schools were not doing their job with respect to basic knowledge.

At the same time, an increasing number of teachers, parents, administrators, and policymakers are questioning the nature and outcomes of traditional evaluation practices as well as the uses to which these are put. Particularly called into question is the primary use of standardized objective tests—called high-stakes tests—to make decisions about students with respect to placement and graduation.

Those who find the one-size-fits-all umbrella of standardized testing to be both educationally frustrating and generally counterproductive argue that there is poor validity between the stated purpose of a given test and what it might actually measure; that the reliability and comparability of test scores is low; that there is often cultural bias in the design and use of tests; and that the narrow approach and application of tests—although they provide easy quantitative analysis—tend to measure out-of-context learning while downplaying actual student performance.

Additionally, citing the need for small, local communities to be the source of both standards and accountability, Deborah Meier (2000) writes:

> Standardized tests are too simple and simpleminded for high-stakes assessment of children and schools. Important decisions regarding kids and teachers should always be based on multiple sources of evidence that seem appropriate and credible to those most concerned. These are old testing truisms, backed even by the testing industry, which has never claimed the level of omniscience many standards advocates assume of it. The state should require only that forms of assessment be public, constitutionally sound, and subject to a variety of "second opinions" by experts representing other interested parties. (p. 17)

Testing for accountability plans set by states do not, in general, take into account differences in social class or any other population characteristics. Indeed, it is a matter of principle under NCLB that all students should learn, and part of accountability is measuring the learning of racial and ethnic groups, economically disadvantaged students, students with disabilities, and students whose first language is not English. Nevertheless, a number of scholars have offered effective ways to cross the bridge between standards and **assessment** that are designed to help teachers help all students be successful (Gentile & Lalley, 2003; Wiggins & McTighe, 1998).

Highly Qualified Teachers

Beginning with the 2005–06 school year, every district receiving money under NCLB was required to have "highly qualified teachers" in all core subjects. (Charter school teachers do not need the same qualifications unless such qualifications are part of their state charter.) Core subjects are English, reading or language arts, mathematics, science, foreign languages, civics and government, economics, history, arts, and geography. To be "highly qualified," all new teachers must hold at least a bachelor's degree and be certified or licensed by their state on the basis of rigorous tests in subject matter and pedagogy. Veteran teachers must demonstrate, in ways determined by each state, their competence in the subjects they teach.

As of March 2004, some new flexibility was built into the requirements for highly qualified teachers. Because it has proved difficult to recruit and retain teachers for both rural and urban schools, and in several subject areas such as foreign languages, mathematics, and science, teachers in those settings and in those subjects have been given a bit more leeway in demonstrating their "highly qualified" status. This flexibility is generally in the length of time or manner in which teachers may "become" highly qualified, as well as in the definition of certain subject matter categories. For example, rural teachers who may be teaching subjects for which they do not have specific degrees now have 3 additional years in which to become highly qualified in all teaching areas, and science teachers who may have previously been required to demonstrate competence in all areas of science (e.g., biology, physics, chemistry) may now demonstrate competence in "broad field" science ("No Child Left Behind Flexibility," 2004).

It is interesting to speculate on the relation of social class (as well as ethnicity) to the need for these more flexible rules. One could argue, for example, that the nature of class differences in rural and urban poverty when compared to the overwhelmingly middle-class status of most teachers might account for the difficulty in recruiting them to teach in these settings in the first place. In addition, because the United States has—at least for the past half-century—resolutely avoided the need for any of its citizens to actually speak a foreign language, and has, of late, experienced one of its recurring bouts with "English Only" propositions, one could argue that the dearth of foreign language teachers is somehow related to these American cultural choices.

Annual Yearly Progress and Failing Schools

A major emphasis in NCLB has been the idea that students in all schools will progress each year, until by 2014 all American students will be proficient in all subjects. Key to this result is the concept of "annual yearly progress," or AYP. Annual yearly progress is defined by each state in such a way that states can measure progressive achievements of schools and districts over time, and then report results on an annual basis to school districts and the public. Schools that do not meet AYP for 95% of their students, or for 95% of students in specified subgroups, for 2 consecutive years begin receiving a series of increasingly severe sanctions, including the ability of parents to take their children out of such schools (transportation to be provided out of Title I money of the inadequate school) and, after 5 years, with the complete reorganization of the school in question.

Schools that do not meet AYP for several years are termed "failing schools." There are some who believe that NCLB was written in such a way as to ensure that all schools will be "failing schools" by 2014, and indeed, in the 2005–06 school year more than a quarter (26%) of the nation's schools, or 24,470 schools, fell into that category (Basken, 2006). In the 2004–05 school year, the percentage was about 22%, and in 2003–04 it was about 35% (Paulson, 2004). Thus the "story" of failing schools is mixed. What is clear, however, is that poverty, or social class, is a large factor in whether or not schools "make" AYP. Consider, for example, this report from rural Vermont:

> Looking at Vermont, forty-three schools have been identified as not making "adequate yearly progress." What do we know about these Vermont school communities?
>
> - The poverty rate in communities with schools identified as not making adequate yearly progress is 50% higher than the state average.
> - The child poverty rate (below 18 years old) is double the state average.
> - The child poverty rate (below 5 years of age) is more than double the state average.
> - The percent of households on public assistance is 67% higher.
> - The percent with less than a ninth grade education is 35% higher.
> - The percent without a high school diploma is 40% higher.
> - Per capita income is 20% lower.
>
> Perhaps our state tests measure poverty rather than the quality of our schools. What we simply don't know from our test scores is whether the schools are doing a great job or a bad job of teaching our children. (Mathis, 2004)

The Future of No Child Left Behind: Moving Away From "One Size Fits All"

As this book goes to press, the debate over the reauthorization of NCLB continues, and draft bills are emerging from Congress that are stimulating considerable discussion. What seems to be the case is that proposals for more flexibility and a broadening definition of "what counts" as valid assessments of student progress–particularly so-called growth models that measure individual student progress across a year–will be a part of the new law. One element of the reauthorization of the Elementary and Secondary Education Act will probably be a reversal of the format for school reform. Whereas, under the No Child Left Behind Act, achievement goals were left to the states, while the process for achieving those goals was strictly proscribed, under the new guidelines the achievement goals are to be set by the federal government, while the process of achieving them in each state is left open to encourage ingenuity and creativity, and to enable states to craft the process in ways that accommodate each state's circumstances.

What will not have changed is the problem of educating children who are poor, nonwhite, or who do not speak English as a native language, nor the problem of how to assess the education of these children, who currently comprise a growing segment of the U.S. public school population. Critics of plans for the reauthorization of NCLB argue that giving increasing flexibility in AYP will largely affect suburban schools and will thus continue to leave lower-class children behind (Petrilli, 2007).

Perspectives on Multiple Forms of Assessment: Demand Versus Support

The belief that *all* children can and should learn is, in essence, at the heart of the idea of multiple forms of assessment, and a number of scholars have looked at ways in which this philosophical position can be translated into classroom practice.

Kohn (1999) suggests that certain classroom orientations distinguish between what we as educators expect that students ought to be able to do and how we as educators can support students' development, thereby helping them to learn. He calls these opposing approaches "demand" versus "support."

In the demand model, students are perceived as workers who are obligated to do a better job. Students who do not succeed are said to have chosen not to study or not to have earned a given grade. Under such an approach, responsibility is removed from the teacher and attention is deflected away from the curriculum and the context under which learning is meant to occur. In reporting to parents, teachers state whether students did what they were supposed to do. Even programs that reportedly emphasize performance objectives often adopt such an approach under the guise of the common buzzword—outcomes. Unfortunately, in the context of the demand model, many working- and lower-class students appear to choose not to study and thus earn lower grades.

The support model, on the other hand, assumes that students are active contributors to the learning process, or as Nichols and Hazzard (1993) put it, the "adventure of ideas." Under such an approach, the teacher has a major responsibility to guide and stimulate all students' natural curiosity and desire to learn and explore the unfamiliar, to construct meaning in their world, and to develop the competence for using words, numbers, and ideas. Teaching and learning become child-centered or student-centered, and the goal becomes helping students build on their desire to make sense of, and to become competent in, their world. Student evaluation becomes, in part, a way to determine how effective we have been as educators. We seek to measure improvement in students because it indicates that we have been successful in engaging students and in creating a context in which they become motivated. Assessment, then, becomes supportive.

Kohn (1999) offers five principles of assessment that follow a supportive model.

1. Assessment should not be overdone. The United States seems to be a test-happy nation, and American young people are the most tested in the world. When students become preoccupied with how they are doing, they begin to lose interest in what they are doing. An excessive concern with

Alfie Kohn

performance can erode curiosity and thus reduce the quality of performance. Students excessively concerned with their performance may tend to avoid difficult tasks so they can avoid any negative evaluation.

2. The best evidence we have of whether we are succeeding as educators is to observe the behavior of children. Test scores only tell us if students perform well on that specific test. Most tests are not true indicators of a student's subsequent ability to perform a specific task. When we observe children actively engaged in dialogue or conversation about a given topic, seeking out answers to their own questions, or reading on their own, we know that we have sparked their interest and that skills are often subsequently acquired.

3. Schools must be transformed into caring, safe communities. Such characteristics are critical for helping students become good learners willing to take risks and seek guidance and support. Only when there is no fear of humiliation or punitive judgment will children be free to acknowledge their mistakes and take the guidance of others. When the environment stresses grades and standardized testing or when teachers feel that a certain amount of curriculum must be covered, pressures increase and, subsequently, learning diminishes.

4. Any responsible discussion about assessment must attend to the quality of the curriculum. The easy question to answer is whether the student has learned anything. The more difficult question to answer is whether the student has been given something worth learning. Research has supported the notion that good teachers already know. That is, when students have interesting things to do, artificial inducements to boost their achievement are not necessary. If the need to evaluate students has directed the design of the curriculum, students will not be actively engaged in their learning.

5. Students must become part of the discussion in determining the criteria by which their work will be judged and then play a role in that judgment. Such participation gives students greater control over their own education, makes evaluation feel less punitive, and provides an important learning experience in and of itself.

To the extent that educators consider adapting both instructional and assessment strategies in such a way that all children are encouraged and supported in their learning, the public schools will truly continue to be what they have always been in the United States—a place where doors open to children who may not even know those doors are there, and a boost up the social class ladder. As Lugg (2005) noted about the theme of *The American Dream and the Public Schools* by Jeffiner Hochschild and Nathan Scovronick, "regardless of the numerous flaws, public schools are essential to maintaining a vital U.S. democracy, as well as ensuring that the pursuit of the American dream is available for all."

Ethical Issues

Regardless of the specific means of communicating performance to others, assessment is inherently a subjective process. Ornstein (1994) has suggested that the more detailed the reporting method and the more analytic the process, the more likely it is that subjectivity will influence the results. Subjectivity, however, is not always a negative factor. After all, teachers who truly know their students understand their progress in far greater detail than any test might uncover.

It is when subjectivity turns into bias that educators get into trouble. Teachers' perceptions and subsequent expectations can significantly influence their judgments of scholastic performance. Students with behavior problems, for instance, often face the obstacle that their infractions will overshadow their performance. These effects are especially evident with boys. Such aspects as a student's handwriting, dress, family background, and so forth can all influence a teacher's judgment.

The official labeling of children and identification of cognitive difficulties happens chiefly in the elementary years. Public schools typically label children as mentally retarded when their measured IQ is below 79. Children with African American and Spanish surnames are more likely to score below 79 than are European American counterparts and subsequently are more likely to be placed in special education classes. Children with African American and Spanish surnames are overlabeled as mentally retarded by public agencies; European Americans are underlabeled when compared to the general population. Such a situation suggests that educators are using tools of analysis that favor some students over others or that actively discriminate against some groups. The special education literature is replete with evidence of individuals wrongfully identified as in need of special education services when all that was really at issue was their inability to communicate as expected in the English language at the time the exam was administered. How many children have been cheated or wrongfully labeled as failures because of an inadequate means of assessment?

Imagine, for a moment, that you are viewing the files of the following two students. What kinds of judgments would you make about these children? What kind of academic program would you recommend? Would you expect them to fit in with your regular class program? Would you suggest any special intervention, such as special classes for gifted or handicapped students? Would you recommend any extracurricular activities that would help develop special skills in these children?

Sam Edder did not begin speaking until he was 3 years old. He has always had trouble with school, often remaining withdrawn and unsociable. He was even removed from school at one time because of his emotional instability. Sam's test scores are well below average except for his performance on creativity measures. In this area he shows some potential. Other than reading intently and playing a musical instrument, Sam seems to have few interests and expresses little in the way of personal or vocational goals. Sam's parents are of European descent, with high school educations.

Bill Ridell has never spent much time in school. He started late because of an illness and was withdrawn several times because of continued sickness. Bill has been labeled "backward" by school officials. He has suffered from a variety of ailments and is going deaf. Although his creative performance shows some promise, Bill's IQ score is low (81), as are his scores on other achievement indices. However, Bill enjoys building things and mechanical pursuits, has good manual dexterity, and would like someday to be a scientist or railroad mechanic. Although Bill's mother is well educated, his father has no formal schooling and is unemployed.

What do you think? What judgments are you able to make about these two children, given this descriptive information? As a teacher, what other information would you like to have? How might you go about working with these children?

International Perspective: What's Happening Elsewhere in the World?

Changes in the Social Class Structure of China: The Rise of a Viable Middle Class

Guangyu Tan
Kent State University

The Traditional View of Social Class in China

It was recorded in early Chinese mythology that the right to govern was originally based on the ability to reason, the goodness of one's innate nature, virtue, wisdom, and merit. This lasted until the Xia Dynasty (2000 BC—1600 BC), when the throne was passed on by ascription. Since then, over the expanse of China's 5,000 year history, despite numerous changes in dynastic succession, there has been an uninterrupted continuity of a two-class system: the ruling class of nobles, and the rest of the populace.

The "divine" nobles traced their origins to descent from a god, or deified ancestor, whereas the populace were merely royal subjects. Among the populace, there were subdivisions held in descending order of social status: the scholar-officials or bureaucratic elite (*shi*), who were able to administer the government and acted as the guardians of the laws, were the ruling gentry. The next rung on the social ladder comprised the peasants (*nong*), who provided substance to the kingdom. Ranked below the peasants were artisans and craftsmen (*gong*), who made the necessities of life. At the bottom of the strata were businessmen or trades people (*shang*), and the ordinary soldiers of the military (*bing*).

It is notable that the social order was based on political power that was related to the position one held in the bureaucracy, rather than on the ownership of wealth and land. This order of *shi, nong, gong, shang*, and *bing* has been acknowledged as the accepted class ranking since the establishment of a unified state in China in 221 BC through at least the late Qing Dynasty in the 1800s AD (Watson, 1984; Wortzel, 1987).

The Chinese Communist's View of Social Class

From 1949 when the People's Republic of China (PRC) was founded, until 1979, when economic reforms and a more open policy were launched, the Chinese communist view on class was dominated by Mao's thoughts (*Mao Zedong si xiang*). Mao (1926) listed six classes in his work, including (1) a landlord and comprador class, (2) a middle bourgeoisie, (3) a petty bourgeoisie, (4) a semi-proletariat, (5) a proletariat, and (6) a lump proletariat. Mao did not analyze class by the ownership of property; rather, he categorized Chinese people into two camps based on a dogmatic epistemology: "Who are our enemies?" and "Who are our friends?"

Mao summarized the criteria for identifying "friends" and "enemies" as follows:

> To sum up, our enemies are those in league with imperialism— the landlords, the bureaucrats, the comprador class, the big landlord class, and the reactionary section of the intelligentsia attached to them. The leading force in our revolution is the industrial proletariat. Our closest friends are the entire semi-proletariat and petty-bourgeoisie. As for the vacillating middle bourgeoisie, their right-wing may become our enemy and their left-wing may become our friends—but we must be constantly on our guard and not let them create confusion in our ranks. (pp. 8–9)

After the PRC was founded, the Chinese Communist Party claimed to have eliminated antagonistic class relations by ensuring that the proletariats are the owners and masters of the state power, and they look after the interests of the workers. Since most of the means of production were no longer privately owned, everyone (except the enemies, who were again the dictatorship of the proletariat) belonged to the working class or the proletariat.

The Rising Middle Class in Contemporary China

The Rise of the Middle Class

The concept of "middle class" did not emerge in China until the 1990s. In the 1960s, when equalitarianism prevailed in China, people lived in the context of state-ownership, which meant everyone sharing ownership of the means of production. In 1979, when economic reforms and a more open policy were launched, a market-oriented economy was introduced in China, and Marxism and Maoism were jettisoned in favor of so-called socialism with Chinese characteristics (Luard, 2004). The knowledge-based economy in China today, in addition to the central government's strategy of building on science and technology, has encouraged the rapid development of higher education, which is the incubator of the middle class. People with both luck and a good educational background have quickly claimed their position and the result has been a rising middle class in China.

Professor Zhou Xiaohong (2005), Department Chair of Sociology Studies at Nanjing University, defines middle class in China as people "with a monthly income of 5000 Yan (about US $617), with a bachelor's degree or above, and who work as civil servants, company managers, technicians or private business owners." Meanwhile, BNP Paribas, a French bank, defines members of China's middle class as well-educated professionals and white-collar employees with per capita annual income between 25,000 Yuan (US $2,010) and 30,000 Yuan (US $3,610), or household incomes between 75,000 Yuan (US $9,040) and 100,000 Yuan (US $12,050) (People's Daily Online, 2004).

The expansion of the urban middle class in major cities is obvious. A study by the Chinese Academy of Social Sciences (CASS) in 2004 (as cited in Xin, 2004) reported that the middle income class in China accounted for 15% of the total population in 1999, and then it rose by 1% annually until it reached 19% of the total population of 1.3 billion in 2003. Furthermore, it was estimated that about 13% of the country's urban households, of 24.5 million households, with a total of 75 million people, would achieve middle-class status in 2005. This number is expected to amount to 25% in 2010, indicating 57 million households with 170 million people classified as middle class. It is projected that the middle-class community will amount to 40% of the whole society by 2020. This will transform the society from an "onion" shaped structure to an "olive" shape.

The Role of the Middle Class in Social Changes

Studies of social structure have shown that an "olive-shaped" society is always more stable than an "onion-shaped" one in which wealth is polarized (Weber, 1924; Wright, 2003). Li Qiang (1999), a sociologist at Tsinghua University, suggested that the expansion of the middle class is conducive to social development. On one hand, the middle class can help ease contradiction and conflict between the upper and lower strata. On the other hand, the moderate and conservative ideologies of the middle stratum tends to be accepted as the mainstream ideology of a society as a whole, and thus helps safeguard social stability by forcing out extremism.

Li further pointed out that the existence of a vast middle class also will facilitate the upward movement of individuals into higher strata. With China's rapid industrialization and urbanization, there will be more opportunities for upward movement of people into the large middle class. For instance, CASS (as cited in Xin, 2004) found that compared to 1992, in the year 2000 the proportion of lower-layer employees (industrial and agricultural workers) had dropped by 8.17%, and middle-class employees increased by 7.2%. This further suggests that in the coming 8 to 10 years, China will witness a leap in its professionalism level, a huge expansion of the middle class, and a sharp reduction in agricultural workers. Hope, at least, is definitely high.

This rosy picture of the rising middle class has been criticized as "journalistic hype" by other sociologists, who warn that such an overoptimistic prediction betrays the real situation in China's development. For example, He Qunglian (2005), a renowned sociologist in China, concedes that the mythic rise of a nascent Chinese middle class will probably make little difference in the country's political ecology. She identifies three characteristics of the Chinese middle class. First of all, like the middle class in the West, the wealth of the middle class in China is related to political power, though its role in decision making in Chinese government should not be overstated. Second, China's middle class has no group consciousness, and therefore has no independent ideas, and it has no way to express itself in public affairs. Finally, because the middle class is dependent on political powers, and because it has no means to express itself, it cannot initiate or promote political reforms in the short term.

In the same vein, Unger (2006) argued that China's conservative middle class "tends to accept and approve of the status quo, and see the strained circumstances of China's peasants and workers as the necessary price to be paid for China's modernization" (p. 126). Unger further concludes that the Chinese middle class has been a part of the current regime, and that the rise of China's middle class has, in fact, blocked the path to social changes and democratization. As Chen and Lu (2005) put it, "those who perceive themselves to belong to the middle class and who are government bureaucrats are more likely to support the incumbent authorities" (p. 12).

Top Chinese leaders have recognized that the expansion of the middle class has already come to a crucial juncture. As Jiang Zemin, the former Secretary-General of the Communist Party of China (CPC) said in his report to the 16th Party Congress in 2002, "Bearing in mind the objective of common prosperity, we should try to raise the proportion of the middle-income group and increase the income of the low-income group." Sociologists say that the CPC's call reflects the authorities' determination to foster a large middle stratus in a bid to achieve the ultimate goal of building a well-off society in an all-round way. If the transition is done well, a fair, reasonable, and open social structure will eventually be able to come into being. Otherwise, social change will come to a standstill, and the social structure will be developed in a morbid way.

To facilitate the transition of the Chinese social structural pattern into a fair, reasonable, open, and modernized one, the Chinese government has taken measures in making economic policies that have favored fostering a middle class. With the reforms to deepen gradually, the stock and securities markets have been opened and promoted, and large-scale campaigns to transform enterprises into joint-stock corporations have been launched. The private sector has been encouraged to grow, and hi-tech private companies have been started up. High salaries have been offered to returning overseas students, and salaries have been raised for civil servants and teachers. All of these measures have promoted the growth of the middle class in China.

(continued)

Conclusion

Social class has a specific meaning in the context of Chinese society. For thousands of years, the Confucian social strata—which was the hierarch of *shi, nong, gong, shang,* and *bing*—dominated Chinese social structure. Between 1949 and 1979, Mao's ideas on class greatly influenced the Chinese Communist Party's view of social class.

However, reforms launched in 1979 have welcomed capitalists into the ruling party and formed the so-called socialism with Chinese characteristics. Since then, a middle class has emerged and been growing fast. There are currently intense debates among scholars about whether the growing middle class is a myth or a reality, and what role the middle class is playing in changing the social structure. Clearly, there are still many problems to be solved and many barriers to be overcome. China must resolve the major problems of growing income inequality and the uneven regional development it is experiencing. Only by equitably addressing these problems can Chinese society be transformed into the desired "olive-shaped" society. Much will depend, it seems, on changes in education that will produce the next generation, more used to the idea of the middle class, and more able to participate in it.

This exercise can be used to check the accuracy of your attributions as well as the assumptions you are making. The descriptions of Sam Edder and Bill Ridell are actually case studies of real people. Sam Edder's file is that of Albert Einstein and Bill Ridell's is that of Thomas Edison. How quickly did you make faulty attributions about the potential for success of these students? How many other potential geniuses have been overlooked or have slipped through the cracks because of our narrow approaches to assessing and judging students?

Increasingly, teachers are searching for more effective ways to communicate performance to both students and parents. Many issues converge as we consider what it is, exactly, that we wish to communicate to others. Clearly, it is well to remember that—as is the case with all forms of student and teacher differences—social class differences require that attention be paid to subtle and often relatively invisible beliefs and values. Because the United States *professes* to be a classless society doesn't make it so; indeed, the combination of ethnicity and social class may, in the end, give us our most perplexing and most important problems.

Critical Incident

The Pull of Home

Beth Thomas, one of Steve Rogers's students, homesick for her small town life and confused by all the strange ways of the university, was ready to leave the place that enormous amounts of student loans had let her leave home to attend. The last straw had been when her roommate's car had been broken into and robbed of nearly $500 of clothing, cosmetics, and cash. Beth's roommate told her father that she'd lost $1,000 worth of belongings, and her dad had quickly sent her a check to cover the losses. The check arrived just as Beth was leaving for her job waiting tables in one of the university dining halls, and her roommate was leaving to buy a satisfyingly large batch of new clothes.

Beth's younger sister came to see Steve, begging him to write to Beth to encourage her to stay in college. He agreed to write, although he didn't think it would mean much.

• If you were Steve, what would you say in such a letter?

Critical Incident

Too Much Traveling[2]

Tommy's dad is a career Army man, and Tommy is a quintessential "Army brat," having lived 10 places in 20 years. Although he has gotten used to the traveling, he has a hard time adjusting to the sharp changes in his social status that come with each move. Until the age of 10 he was oblivious to class differences, but when he hit middle school, he began to notice how he was perceived by others.

For a while the family lived in a small town in western Pennsylvania, where Tommy's father, a colonel, was considered part of the local elite. Tommy fondly remembers country club parties with his friends who were the sons and daughters of the local banker and lawyer. But then his father was posted to the Pentagon, where colonels are a dime a dozen. He moved to rental housing in a Virginia suburb and felt excluded from the golden inner circle at his new high school. The family couldn't get into the "best" country club, his clothes seemed out of fashion, and he developed a sense of resentment that has begun to erode his relationship with his parents.

Tommy has struck up the beginnings of a friendship with his social studies teacher, Mr. Gordon. One day after school, he tells Mr. Gordon some of what is bothering him.

- If you were Mr. Gordon, what might you do to help him understand what he is experiencing?
- What advice might you give Tommy to help him feel that he "belongs" in the new environment?

Summary

In this chapter we explored the concepts of social class and social status in terms of their relation to schooling—to its curriculum, both hidden and explicit, to the ways in which schools are funded, and to its implications for No Child Left Behind, particularly in terms of assessment. Social class is difficult to discuss in the United States because the American "story" presupposes that one's social class is not important—one can always rise up the social ladder by keeping one's "nose to the grindstone."

The degree to which this is not as easy as it sounds is a pervasive theme in the chapter, and the role of assessment is presented as a critical part of both the debate and the substance of school reform issues today. Arguments for and against standardized testing and the arguments for the use of multiple forms of assessment are presented as subjects for discussion, and suggestions are made for a model of supportive assessment as an approach that will help all students learn.

Chapter Review

Go to the Online Learning Center at www.mhhe.com/cushner7e to review important content from the chapter, practice with key terms, take a chapter quiz, and find the Web links listed in this chapter.

Key Terms

accountability
movement 450
assessment 451
growth measures 441

No Child Left Behind
Act of 2001 436
social class 442
social status 444

teacher expectations 445
working class 443
working poor 443
underclass 443

Active Exercise

Additional Active Exercises are available online at www.mhhe.com/cushner7e.

Institutional Discrimination: Social Class in Focus

Purpose: To distinguish between individual and institutional practices that may discriminate against certain social classes.
Instructions: Institutional discrimination refers to policies and practices of institutions that allow certain discriminatory practices to persist. In this exercise you are presented with a number of situations and are asked to determine if these policies or practices systematically privilege members of certain groups while discriminating against members of other groups. Complete the three questions that follow for each situation that you determine to be an example of institutional discrimination.

1. Children of teachers employed in this private school receive free tuition. Is this an example of discrimination?

    a. Against which groups, if any, might this policy discriminate?

    b. What is the purpose of the policy?

    c. If the purpose is valid, how else might it be achieved?

2. A local religious school offers reduced tuition for members of its faith. Is this an example of discrimination?

    a. Against which groups, if any, might this policy discriminate?

    b. What is the purpose of the policy?

    c. If the purpose is valid, how else might it be achieved?

3. Because a recent school levy failed, a new school policy states that children who wish to participate in sports or musical performing groups must pay for their own uniforms. Is this an example of discrimination?

    a. Against which groups, if any, might this policy discriminate?

    b. What is the purpose of the policy?

    c. If the purpose is valid, how else might it be achieved?

4. A teacher awards 10 points out of 100 to boys who wear a jacket and tie and to girls who wear a full-length dress during an oral presentation as part of the final grade in a business speech class. Is this an example of discrimination?

   a. Against which groups, if any, might this policy discriminate?

   b. What is the purpose of the policy?

   c. If the purpose is valid, how else might it be achieved?

Classroom Activities

1. In an upper elementary classroom, ask students to read the first chapter in Barbara Ehrenreich's book, *Nickel and Dimed*, about one woman's experiment in living on minimum wages. (This chapter can be found online at http://www.nytimes.com/books/first/e/ehrenreich-01nickel.html). Ask them to make a list of all the things she set out to do—find housing, find a job, and so forth, and what her financial limitations were. Discuss their observations with them and then ask them to write a short essay describing their ideas about the "real life" of people living with few financial resources.

2. Engage elementary students in a discussion of what they understand about a classmate's circumstances from looking at what they wear. In order to make it less "personal" in the class, a teacher might want to use pictures of students of the same age in various kinds of dress. List their reactions on the board, and discuss, being sure to include in the discussion the notion that some students really don't pay much attention to what they wear, or don't much care what others think. Then, ask students whether or not a school dress code might be helpful to children whose families could not afford to buy them many clothes, or to follow the "in" styles that change so often in children's clothing. Ask students to list pros and cons of a dress code.

3. Ask students in a high school classroom to discuss the assessments they are familiar with from their own experiences in school. Do they think these assessments actually measure what they know? Which of the various types of assessments (e.g., multiple choice, essay, short answer questions) they think produce a good representation of their knowledge and skills. Ask them "why" or "why not"? Engage students in a discussion of alternate forms of assessment, for example, portfolio, oral, knowledge application. Do students think alternate forms of assessment should be included in the assessment mix? Ask students to research various forms of assessment and bring findings back to the classroom. What do they conclude?

4. It is very difficult to discuss social class in the United States, because most people believe that they are "middle class" or will soon become so. One way to get the idea of social stratification across to high school students is to ask students to describe the informal but identifiable social "groups" in their school and who "belongs" to each group. Write the names of these groups on the board as they come in from the students. Then ask students to rank these groups in terms of which are "better" or "worse" to be identified with. Then ask students how easy or difficult it would be for a member of a "lower" group to "move up" to a more prestigious group. Discuss this phenomenon in terms of social class and social status in the wider society.

Reflective Questions

1. Several criticisms of the No Child Left Behind Act are cited in the Case Study. Do you think these criticisms are valid? Why or why not?

2. Steve Rogers believes that the isolation of the students in the Northeast Kingdom is one of their greatest problems. For those students who are working class, how does that isolation create barriers to achieving middle-class status, if that is something they desire?

3. Do you think Steve is from a different social class background than his students? What makes you think so?

4. How is poverty in rural Vermont different from what you know about urban poverty?

5. How might tests be an impediment to effective instruction (that is, instruction that results in student learning)?

6. A common criticism of multiple forms of assessment is that two teachers using the same assessment procedures may arrive at different evaluations of students' achievement. Assuming that this criticism has some validity, how might conditions be set so that variation in teachers' evaluations might be minimized?

Endnotes

1. This Case Study is based on two texts. One is the work of Garret Keizer, a teacher and minister who wrote of his experiences teaching in northeastern Vermont, an area popularly referred to as the "Northeast Kingdom" (see Keizer, 1988, *No place but here: A teacher's vocation in a rural community.* New York: Penguin Books). The second is the text of a Position Paper on the No Child Left Behind Act, published by the Vermont Superintendents Association in April 2004 and the subsequent work of the Vermont Society for the Study of Education (see http://www.vsse.net/)

2. "Two Much Traveling" is an incident adapted from the PBS presentation, People Like U*s: Social Class in America.* A companion website to the program, well worth exploring, is http://www.pbs.org/peoplelikeus/

References

A nation at risk: The imperative for educational reform. (1983). Washington, DC: National Commission on Excellence in Education.

Anyon, J. (1980). Social class and the hidden curriculum of work. *Journal of Education, 162*(1), 67–92.

Anyon, J. (1981). Social class and school knowledge. *Curriculum Inquiry, 11*(1), 3–42.

Argyle, M. (1980). Interaction skills and social competence. In J. Orford & M. P. Feldman (Eds.), *Psychological problems: The social context.* New York: Wiley.

Banfield, E. C. (1970). *The unheavenly city: The nature and future of our urban crisis.* Boston: Little Brown.

Basken, P. (2006). States have more schools falling behind. *Washington Post* [Online]. Retrieved from http://www.washingtonpost.com/wp-dyn/content/article/2006/03/28/AR2006032801794.html

Bellah, R. N. (1976). Civil religion in America. In A. Wells (Ed.), *American society: Problems and dilemmas* (pp. 351–368). Pacific Palisades, CA: Goodyear.

Berliner, D. C., & Biddle, B. J. (1995). *The manufactured crisis: Myths, fraud, and the attack on America's public schools.* Cambridge, MA: Perseus Books.

Boykin, A. W. (1986). The triple quandary and the schooling of African-American children. In V. Neisser (Ed.), *The school achievement of minority children: New perspectives.* Hillsdale, NJ: Lawrence Erlbaum.

Brislin, R. (1988). Increasing awareness of class, ethnicity, culture, and race. In I. Cohen (Ed.), *The G. Stanley Hall lecture series* (Vol. 8, pp.137–180). Washington, DC: American Psychological Association.

Chen, J., & Lu, C. (2005). *Does China's middle class think and act democratically?* Paper presented at the annual meeting of the American Political Science Association, Washington, DC. Retrieved July 17, 2007, from http://www.allacademic.com/meta/p42669_index.html

Darling-Hammond, L. (2004). From "separate but equal" to "no child left behind": The collision of new standards and old inequalities. In D. Meier & G. Wood (Eds.), *Many children left behind.* Boston: Beacon Press Books.

Darling-Hammond, L. (2010). *The flat world and education: How America's commitment to equity will determine our future.* New York: Teachers College, Columbia University, p. 2.

Economic Research Service, U.S. Department of Agriculture. (2004). *Enhanced quality of life for rural Americans: Overview.* Retrieved from http://www.ers.usda.gov/Emphases/Rural/overview.htm

Educator Roundtable. (2007). *A petition calling for the dismantling of the No Child Left Behind Act.* Retrieved from http://www.educatorroundtable.org/

Gentile, J. R., & Lalley, J. P. (2003). *Standards and mastery learning: Aligning teaching and assessment so all children can learn.* Thousand Oaks, CA: Corwin Press.

Gilbert, D., & Kahl, J. (1982). *The American class structure: A new synthesis.* Homewood, IL: Dorsey.

Good, T., & Brophy, J. (1987). *Looking in classrooms* (4th ed.). New York: Harper & Row.

Harp, L. (1992). School-finance suits look beyond money to issues of quality. *Education Week, 11*(39), 1–2.

He, Q. (2005). *Will a growing Chinese middle class bring about change in China?* Retrieved July 17, 2007, from http://en.epochtimes.com/news/5-8-13/31208.html

Hilliard, A. (1998, Summer). The standards movement: Quality control or decoy? *Rethinking Schools Online, 12,* 4. Retrieved from http://www.africawithin.com/hilliard/standards_movement.htm

Hurn, C. (1993). *The limits and possibilities of schooling* (3rd ed.). Boston: Allyn & Bacon.

Iglitzen, D., & Hill, S. (2007, August 30). Income inequality threatens America. *The News Tribune* [Online]. Retrieved from http://www.thenewstribune.com/opinion/insight/story/100240.html

Keizer, G. (1988). *No place but here: A teacher's vocation in a rural community.* New York: Penguin Books.

Knapp, M. S., & Shields, P. M. (1990, June). Reconceiving academic instruction for the children of poverty. *Phi Delta Kappan, 71*(10).

Knapp, M. S., & Woolverton, S. (2003). Social class and schooling. In J. A. Banks & C. A. McG. Banks (Eds.), *Handbook of research on multicultural education* (2nd ed.). San Francisco: Jossey-Bass.

Kohn, A. (1999). *The schools our children deserve: Moving beyond traditional classrooms and"tougher standards."* Boston: Houghton Mifflin.

Kohn, M. L. (1977). *Class and conformity* (2nd ed.). Chicago: University of Chicago Press.

Kusmin, L. D. (2006). *Rural America at a glance: 2006 edition.* Washington, DC: U.S.D.A. Economic Research Service. Retrieved from http://www.ers.usda.gov/publications/eib18/eib18.htm#head1

Li, Q. (1999). The market transition and the generational change of China's middle class. *Strategy and Management, 3.*

Lindgren, H. C., & Suter, W. N. (1985). *Educational psychology in the classroom* (7th ed.). Monterey, CA: Brooks/Cole.

Luard, T. (2004). China's middle-class revolution. Retrieved October 19, 2005, from http://news.bbc.co.uk/1/hi/world/asia-pacific/3732914.stm

Lugg, C. A. (2005, May). *The American dream and the public schools* [Book review]. *American Journal of Education, 423.*

Mao, Z. D. (1926). *Selected Works of Mao Zedong, 1*(19), 8–9.

Mathis, W. J. (2004). *What are we measuring: School quality or poverty?* National Education Association. Retrieved from http://www.nea.org/lawsuit/mathis.html

Meier, D. (2000). *Will standards save public education?* Boston: Beacon Press.

Meier, D., & Wood, G. (Eds.). (2004). *Many children left behind: How the No Child Left Behind Act is damaging our children and our schools.* Boston: Beacon Press.

Metz, M. H. (1990). How social class differences shape teachers' work. In M. W. McLaughlin, J. E. Talbert, & N. Bascia (Eds.), *The context of teaching in secondary schools: Teachers' realities* (pp. 40–107). New York: Teachers College Press.

Nichols, J. G., & Hazzard, S. P. (1993). *Education as adventure: Lessons from the second grade.* New York: Teachers College Press.

No child left behind flexibility: Highly qualified teachers. (2004). *Fact sheet.* Retrieved from http://www.ed.gov/print/nclb/methods/teachers/hqtflexibility.html

Ornstein, A. C. (1994). Grading practices and policies: An overview and some suggestions. *NASSP Bulletin, 78,* 55–64.

Paulson, A. (2004, November). A shortening list of failing schools. *Christian Science Monitor, 23.* Retrieved from http://www.csmonitor.com/2004/1123/p01s02-uspo.html

People's Daily Online. (2004). Retrieved from http://english.people.com.cn/90833/90836/review/

Petrilli, M. J. (2007). *The suburban schools relief act.* The Thomas B. Fordham Foundation. Retrieved from http://fordhamfoundation.org/foundation/gadfly/issue.cfm?id=305&CFID=9143125&CFTOKEN=16968814#3571

Rose v. Council for Better Education, 790 S.W.2d 186 (1989).

San Antonio Independent School District v. Rodriguez, 411 U.S. 1 (1973).

Serrano v. Priest, 487 P.2d 1241 (Cal. 1971).

Tilkidjiew, M. (1998). *The middle class as a precondition of a sustainable society.* Sofia, Bulgaria: AMCD-LIK.

Tyack, D. B. (1981). *Women and men in schools: A history of the sexual structuring of educational employment.* Washington, DC: National Institute of Education.

Unger, J. (2006). China's conservative middle class. In S. Ogden (Ed.), *Global studies: China* (5th ed., pp. 125–127). Dubuque, IA: Contemporary Learning Series.

Vermont Society for the Study of Education. (2007). Retrieved from http://vsse.net/

Verstegen, D. A. (1990). Invidiousness and inviolability in public education finance. *Educational Administration Quarterly, 26*(3), 205–234.

Villegas, A. M., & Lucas, T. (2007, March). The culturally responsive teacher. *Educational Leadership,* 28–33.

Watson, J. L. (Ed.). (1984). *Class and social stratification in post-revolution China.* Cambridge, London: Cambridge University Press.

Webb, R. B., & Sherman, R. R. (1989). *Schooling and society* (2nd ed., pp. 397–398). New York: Macmillan.

Weber, M. (1924). *Economy and society.* Berkeley: University of California Press.

What work requires of schools: A SCANS report for America 2000. (1991). Washington, DC: Secretary's Commission on Achieving Necessary Skills (SCANS), U.S. Department of Labor, U.S. Department of Education.

Wiggins, G., & McTighe, J. (1998). *Understanding by design.* Upper Saddle River, NJ: Merrill Prentice Hall.

Wortzel, L. M. (1987). *Class in China: Stratification in a classless society.* New York: Greenwood Press.

Wright, E. O. (2003). Social class. In G. Ritzer (Ed.), *Encyclopedia of social theory.* Thousand Oaks, CA: Sage.

Xin, Z. (2004). *Dissecting China's middle stratum.* Retrieved October 19, 2005, from http://www.chinadaily.com.cn/english/doc/2004-10/27/content_385952.htm

Zhou, X. (2005). *Middle class on rise in China: Survey.* Retrieved October 19, 2005, from http://en1.chinabroadcast.cn/2238/2005-9-2/148@269568.htm

Glossary

A

Ability/disability A dimension encompassing the range of individual differences with respect to the physical, cognitive, socioemotional, and other (e.g., aesthetic) domains characterizing human behavior.

Accent The pronunciation habits of the standard language acquired by people from a particular geographic region.

Acceptance Acceptance is the first ethnorelative stage of the Developmental Model of Intercultural Sensitivity and represents an individual's ability to recognize and appreciate cultural difference in terms of both people's values and their behavior.

Accountability movement The national interest in and reform of schooling that began in the 1980s, continues to the present time, and rests on the idea that schools, teachers, and students are responsible for meeting standards of learning in all major subjects.

Acculturation The changes that take place as a result of continuous firsthand contact between individuals of different cultures; usually refers to the experiences of adults.

Adaptation The ability of organisms, including human beings, to successfully negotiate the requirements of their environment.

Adaptive equipment The range of electronic, mechanical, and other devices that may enable a child or adult with a sensory, motoric, or other disability to perform tasks, such as those required for self-care, mobility, and classroom and work participation.

Age The chronological index of developmental change from conception to death.

American Sign Language Recognized as a distinct and legitimate language employing manual signs, facial expression, and other visual information according to a shared system of symbols and rules, ASL is the official signed system of communication in North America.

Anglo-conformity The belief that all immigrant children must be socialized into the culture and worldview of the dominant Anglo society in the United States.

Assessment A comprehensive, individualized evaluation of the student's strengths, as well as areas that are in need.

Assimilation The process whereby an individual or group is absorbed into the social structures and cultural life of another person, group, or society.

Assimilationist model The practices by which children were socialized into the culture and worldview of the dominant Anglo society.

Authentic assessment A form of assessment in which students are called upon to perform real-world tasks that demonstrate understanding and application of essential knowledge and skills.

Autism spectrum disorder (autism) A brain disorder that to varying degrees typically affects a person's ability to communicate, form relationships with others, and respond appropriately to the environment.

B

Behavior management plan A formal plan for classroom organization and instruction designed to elicit good behavior on the part of all students, as well as to plan for adaptations required for children with disabilities.

Bidialectalism The ability to speak and understand two (and sometimes more) dialects and to switch back and forth among them.

Bilingual education An education program for children whose native language is not English. Children are taught for some portion of the day in their native language, with the goal of moving them into mainstream English classes as quickly as possible, usually within two to three years.

Black English (Ebonics) A dialect of English spoken primarily by urban African Americans.

C

Categorization The process of dividing stimuli into classes or groups according to a particular system. In the cultural context, the manner by which one's culture teaches one to view the world around him or her.

Cerebral palsy An administrative term for a range of impairments caused by nonprogressive damage to the brain incurred pre-, peri-, or post-natally and reflected in impaired voluntary use of specific muscle groups.

Child study movement Pioneered by G. Stanley Hall at the turn of the 20th century, the child study movement was an aspect of the (then) new discipline of psychology, which defined childhood as a distinct stage of life and set about to study it.

Clean intermittent catheterization (CIC) A process by which a hollow plastic tube (catheter) is inserted into the bladder to drain it; CIC is normally done on a regular schedule during the day and night to assist children and adults who, for one reason or another, cannot control bladder function.

Cognitive structures The ways in which individuals organize or scaffold knowledge so as to learn, remember, think, and otherwise use it.

Constructivism The belief that all knowledge is built or "constructed" by individual learners; it is thus important when teaching and learning *new* knowledge to connect it to knowledge already known.

Cross-cultural awareness Perception of significant differences among cultural groups that leads to greater understanding and ability to interact effectively with members of different groups.

Cultural capital The accumulation of both subjective and objective cultural knowledge that one uses to advance or be a leader in one's society.

Cultural pluralism A system of social or political organization that stresses and promotes mutual understanding and respect among disparate ethnic, religious, and racial groups existing in a society.

Culture The totality of socially transmitted behavior patterns, arts, beliefs, institutions, and all other products of human work and thought characteristic of a community or a population.

Culture-general approaches Cross-cultural concepts that apply to the kinds of interactions and experiences people are likely to encounter regardless of the groups that are interacting.

Culture-specific approaches Cross-cultural concepts that apply to people who live and/or work with people of a particular culture or group.

D

Defense Defense is the second stage of the Developmental Model of Intercultural Sensitivity and is characterized by a recognition of cultural difference coupled with negative evaluations of those whose culture is different from one's own.

Demographics Vital statistics that characterize human populations, including age, gender, ethnicity, and so forth. Demographics, often generated from population census data, can be used to project future trends and needs of relevance to educators.

Denial Denial is the first stage of the Developmental Model of Intercultural Sensitivity and refers to an inability to see cultural differences, usually evidenced when individuals isolate or separate themselves in homogeneous groups.

Developmentally appropriate practice (DAP) Instructional practices that are organized and designed on the basis of the age and development of the student.

Dialect A variation of some "standard" language form that includes differences in pronunciation, word usage, and syntax; such differences may be based on ethnicity, religion, geographical region, social class, or age.

Dominant culture The culture of the social/political group that holds the most power and influence in a society.

Down syndrome A genetically inherited condition caused by extra genetic material (genes) from the 21st chromosome, resulting in a combination of features including some degree of mental retardation, or cognitive disability, and other developmental delays.

E

Ebonics A systematic and rule-governed variety of English (dialect), with regular grammar and pronunciation patterns; spoken by many African Americans in the United States. This variety of speech is also known as "African American Vernacular English" (AAVE) and "Vernacular Black English."

Empathy A psychological sense of understanding and "feeling for" another person's situation.

Enculturate The process of raising a child to be a member of a particular culture or culture group.

English language learners (ELL) English language learners (ELLs) are children or adults whose first language is other than English and who are involved in school or other programs in which they are learning English.

Establishment clause of the First Amendment The clause that prohibits the government from establishing a state religion.

Ethnic group A group that shares a common heritage and reflects identification with some collective or reference group, oftentimes in a common homeland. A feeling that one's own destiny is somehow linked with others who share this same knowledge.

Ethnic identity A sense of belonging and identification with one's ancestral ethnic group.

Ethnicity/nationality Ethnicity is culturally defined according to the knowledge, beliefs, and behavior patterns shared by a group of people with the same history and perhaps the same language. Nationality is culturally defined on the basis of a shared citizenship, which may or may not include a shared ethnicity.

Ethnocentrism The tendency people have to evaluate others from their own cultural reference point.

F

Field dependent The ability to learn best when given a larger context or "field" in which to embed new learning.

Field independent The ability to learn material that is separated from its context. An example might be learning the Table of Elements without an explanation of its history or purpose or where it "fits" into the larger scientific enterprise.

Fourteenth Amendment Constitutional amendment prohibiting states from abridging rights granted to all U.S. citizens, born or naturalized in the United States; it also guarantees that no person shall be deprived of life, liberty, or property without due process of law, and that all persons shall be guaranteed equal protection under the law.

Freedmen's Bureau Officially known as the Bureau of Refugees, Freedmen, and Abandoned Lands, the Freedmen's Bureau was established by Congress on March 3, 1865, to supervise all relief and educational activities relating to refugees and freedmen, and to assume custody of confiscated lands in the former Confederate States, border states, District of Columbia, and Indian Territories.

Fundamentalism A movement or attitude stressing strict and literal adherence to a set of basic principles, usually religious ones.

G

Gender role socialization The process by which young children acquire the knowledge and internalize the values of socially determined sex roles.

Gender role stereotyping The process of attributing specific behaviors, abilities, interests, and values to one sex.

Genderized traits Traits such as aggression or empathy that are differentially valued by a society when displayed by males and females.

Gender-sensitive Instructional and other practices that take differences in gender into account.

Generalization The tendency of a majority of people in a cultural group to hold certain values and beliefs, and to engage in certain patterns of behavior. Thus, this information can be supported by research and can be applied to a large percentage of a population or group.

Genotype The whole complex of genes inherited from both parents and determines the potentials and limitations of an individual from embryonic formation through adulthood.

Geographic location/region Geographic location and region are culturally defined by the characteristics (topographical features, natural resources) of the ecological environment in which a person lives. Geographic location may include the characteristics of a neighborhood or community (rural, urban, suburban) and/or the natural and climatic features of a region (mountains, desert, plains, coastal, hot, cold, wet, dry).

Global perspective A worldview that takes into account the fact that individuals and societies are a part of a larger, worldwide system.

Globalization The process by which nations of the world become connected and interdependent through ties created by electronic communication, rapid means of travel, and interlocking economies.

Group homes Supervised, family-style residential arrangements accommodating small numbers of adults with disabilities.

Growth measures An approach to assessment of students that uses computerized tests in several subjects to identify where individual students are at a particular time, for the purpose of intervening exactly where the student is in mastering a particular subject. The test questions "adjust" to each student and, when given to that same student again, can measure growth.

H

Health The dimension encompassing acute and chronic physical and psychological illness, on the one hand, and physical and psychological vigor, stamina, and general well-being on the other.

Homophobia The irrational fear of homosexuality and of those whose sexual orientation is homosexual.

Hypodescent A way to categorize racial membership in which any amount of biological inheritance from a group considered to be a socially "lower" or minority group automatically places one in that group.

I

Immigrants People who voluntarily move to a country of which they are not a native with the purpose of taking up permanent residence.

Inclusion The belief in and practice of creating heterogeneous classrooms; more particularly, the practice of teaching students with disabilities in "regular" classrooms.

In-context learning Learning that takes place through direct participation in real-world events.

Indigenous people Those living in an area generally since prehistoric (or pre-European contact) times. Related terms include aboriginal people (particularly in Australia) and first nation people (particularly in Canada).

Individual education program (IEP) A formal plan for instruction mandated by laws governing special education that sets forth the educational needs of a student, the goals and objectives that direct his or her program, the educational programming and placement, and the evaluation and measurement criteria that have been agreed upon by a team encompassing appropriate school personnel, parents, and when appropriate, the individual student her- or himself.

Informed consent The legal requirement for parents' informed consent prior to multifactored evaluation, participation in developing an IEP, and right to procedural due process in the event of disagreement.

Integration The coming together of ideas, things, people, or objects in such a manner to form a common unit that cannot be distinguished from the original parts. In the educational context, it refers to the positive interaction of all people along equal lines of power, authority, status, and involvement in the school process.

K

Kinesics The study of nonverbal communication in the form of body movements, often called "body language"; kinesics includes gestures, posture, facial expressions, and eye contact.

L

Language Language is often defined as a system of shared vocal sounds and/or nonverbal behaviors that enables members of a particular group to communicate with one another.

Least restrictive environment (LRE) The requirement of federal special education legislation that requires that students with disabilities be educated as much as is individually appropriate in "regular" or "typical" learning environments along with peers who do not have disabilities.

Limited English proficient (LEP) Those individuals who do not speak English as their primary language and who have a limited ability to read, speak, write, or understand English.

Low-incidence A type of disability that does not occur very often, for example, blindness.

M

Marginalization The practice of excluding a social group from the mainstream of the society; placing that group—legally or socially—on the "margins" of the society.

Microculture A social group that shares distinctive traits, values, and behaviors that set it apart from the parent macroculture of which it is a part. Microculture seems to imply a greater linkage with the parent culture and often mediate the ideas, values, and institutions of the larger political community.

Middle schools Schools at a level between elementary and high school; middle school can include grades 5 through 8, but more typically includes grades 6 through 8; devoted to enhancing the education of young adolescents, who are perceived to have particular needs apart from either elementary or high school students.

Minimization The last ethnocentric stage in the Developmental Model of Intercultural Sensitivity begins when people recognize and accept superficial cultural differences such as eating customs, money, and so forth, yet continue to hold the belief that all human beings are essentially the same.

Misogyny An irrational hatred and fear of women.

Mountain English A dialect of English spoken largely in Appalachia.

Multicultural education An education that is designed and shaped by several cultural perspectives.

Multifactored evaluation An evaluation that looks at many possible aspects of the learning problems of children with disabilities; may include cognitive, physical, social, and psychological factors.

Muscular dystrophy An inherited disease that causes increasing weakness in muscle tissue. The muscles affected are the skeletal muscles and, occasionally, the muscles of the heart.

N

Nativist religions Religions practiced by native peoples, often based on a sense of oneness with the earth.

Nature versus nurture debate A long-standing argument about whether a set of inborn and immutable characteristics or education is more important in the outcome of an individual's development.

No Child Left Behind Act of 2001 The name given the reauthorization of the Elementary and Secondary Education Act of 1992.

Normalization A philosophical view that the lives of exceptional individuals, of any age, should be characterized as much as possible by the same kinds of experiences, daily routines, and rhythms as those of persons who do not have disabilities.

Normative The norms of a society influence and regulate an individual's beliefs and behavior.

Norms Accepted ways of agreed-upon behavior that enable similar groups of people to function in a similar manner.

O

Objective culture The tangible, visible aspects of a culture, including such things as the artifacts produced, the foods eaten, and the clothing worn.

Out-of-context learning Learning that typically occurs in the abstract as opposed to learning using concrete objects and references.

P

Paralanguage A form of nonverbal communication that is concerned with vocalizations that are not words.

People of color Nonwhite minority group members, but reflects recent demographic realities of the United States. The phrase *people of color* refers to groups such as African Americans, Mexican Americans, Puerto Ricans, and Native Americans and is often preferred over *ethnic minority* because these groups are, in many schools and communities, the majority rather than the minority.

Perception The process by which people are aware of stimuli in the world around them.

Perspective consciousness The awareness (consciousness) of the perspectives of others who are different from oneself.

Phenotype All the observable characteristics of an organism, such as shape, size, color, and behavior, that result from the interaction of its genotype (total genetic inheritance) with the environment. The common type of a group of physically similar organisms is sometimes also known as the phenotype; the phenotype may change constantly throughout the life of an individual.

Placement continuum The degree to which students with disabilities are involved in "regular" education.

Prejudice Nonreflective judgments about others that are harsh, discriminatory, or involve rejection.

Prohibition clause of the First Amendment The clause that says that Congress shall make no laws "prohibiting the free exercise" of religion or religious beliefs.

Proxemics The normal physical distance between speakers when they are communicating with one another, which is normally acquired as part of one's culture; it is sometimes referred to as "social space."

Pseudoscience A set or system of beliefs claiming to be "scientific" without the benefit of the scientific method used to make further inquiries that might suggest that the belief system is wrong in any particular way.

R

Race Race is an imprecise term: biologically, it is defined as the clustering of inherited physical characteristics that favor adaptation to a particular ecological area; culturally it is defined according to the particular set of physical characteristics emphasized by different cultural groups.

Racial identity An individual's sense of belonging and identification with a racial group; may also refer to the categorization of an individual in terms of a racial group by society or other social groups.

Racial profiling The practice of constructing a set of characteristics or behaviors based on race and using that set of characteristics to decide whether or not an individual might be guilty of some crime and therefore worthy of investigation or arrest.

Racism Discriminatory or abusive behavior toward members of another race; and/or the belief that members of one race are inherently superior to members of other races.

Refugees People who flee for safety to another country.

Related services Defined in the Individuals with Disabilities Education Act (IDEA) as services an eligible student between the ages of 3 and 22 requires in order to benefit from special education. These services, such as transportation, adapted physical education, counseling, speech-language pathology, or occupational or physical therapy services, are identified in the student's IEP and provided by the school at no cost to the student's family.

Religion/spirituality Religion and spirituality are culturally defined on the basis of a shared set of ideas about the relationship of the earth and the people on it to a deity or deities and a shared set of rules for living moral values that enhance that relationship.

Rural English A dialect of English, sometimes called "mountain English," spoken primarily in Appalachia and derived from the language of early English settlers in the area.

S

Segregation The act of separating or setting apart from others. In the educational context, it may refer to the establishment of separate schools for students of different races or abilities/disabilities.

Separation Situations in which two social groups voluntarily decide that it is of value for each to maintain its own cultural identity but not considered a value to maintain relationships with other groups.

Separation of church and state The philosophical belief that religion and government should not be conjoined; in the United States this belief is codified in the First Amendment to the Constitution.

Sex/gender Sex is a biological category referring to a set of human reproductive physical characteristics. Gender, on the other hand, is culturally defined on the basis of what it means to be male or female in a given society or cultural group. Thus, gender is expressed in terms of socially valued behaviors of males and females.

Sexuality Sexuality is culturally defined on the basis of particular patterns of sexual self-identification, behavior, and interpersonal relationships.

Sickle cell disease A genetic abnormality, affecting more individuals of African descent than other groups, causing intermittent or chronic severe and debilitating pain and impaired physical functioning.

Social class A way to categorize individuals in a stratified social system; social class characteristics are often related (but may not be limited) to child-rearing practices, beliefs, values, economic status, prestige and influence, and general life chances.

Social institution A formal, recognized, established, and stabilized way of pursuing some activity in society.

Social status The degree to which an individual has power, influence, or leadership in his or her social group.

Socialization The process whereby individuals learn what is appropriate to be a functioning member of a particular group, such as a family, work, or social group.

Sojourner A person who stays in a place for a relatively brief period of time; often used in reference to tourists or short-term visitors or strangers to a country.

Specific learning disabilities (SLD) A significant difficulty in one or more areas of school achievement, such as reading, writing, mathematical calculation, spelling, or listening, that is not caused by general cognitive disability (mental retardation); hearing, vision, or motor impairment; emotional disturbance; or social or cultural disadvantage. SLD is reflected in a discrepancy between intellectual ability and academic achievement that may be caused by impairment in one or more basic neurological processes underlying linguistic functioning.

Spina bifida A condition in which there is a congenital cleft or opening in the vertebral column.

Standard English A dialect of the English language, usually taken to mean that version of the English language most acceptable or most "correct," used by educated middle and upper classes, and thus the dialect taught in public schools; standard English may vary by geographical location, but in general it is the dialect used in formal writing and in the broadcast and print media.

State of the planet awareness Awareness (consciousness) of the ways in which human beings are acting in ways that endanger the ecological life of the planet as well as knowledge of ways in which such dangers can be averted.

Stereotypes Beliefs about the personal attributes of a group based on the inaccurate generalizations used to describe all members of the group, thus ignoring individual differences.

Subculture A social group with shared characteristics that distinguish it in some way from the larger cultural group or society in which it is embedded. Generally, a subculture is distinguished either by a unifying set of ideas and/or practices (such as the corporate culture or the drug culture) or by some demographic characteristic (such as the adolescent culture or the culture of poverty).

Subjective culture The invisible, intangible aspects of a group, including such things as attitudes, values, norms of behavior—the things typically kept in people's minds.

Supported employment A range of methods used to enable individuals with significant disabilities to engage in regular productive and remunerative employment in various work settings in the community, rather than within traditional, segregated settings.

T

Task specialization The practice of assigning a specific subtask to each member of a collaborative learning team or group.

Teacher expectations The relation between what a teacher believes a student can do and what the student can actually do; generally, the more a teacher believes a student can do, the higher the achievement of the student, without respect to such factors as measured intelligence, social class, or family background.

Theocracy A system of government in which a particular set of religious beliefs, or an organized religion, is completely intertwined with the processes of government.

Transition plan A formal education plan, mandated by federal special education legislation, that elaborates the steps to be taken to move a student with disabilities into adult and working life.

Traumatic brain injury An injury to the brain causing subsequent cognitive or psychomotor disability; usually the result of an accident, but sometimes can be sustained at birth.

U

Underclass The class of people belonging to the lowest and least privileged social stratum or a group which is in some sense outside the mainstream of society.

Universal health precautions Observing common hygienic practices as precautions against contracting infection or disease, especially frequent hand-washing and avoiding skin contact with human bodily fluids. These precautions should be observed whether or not it is known that a communicable disease is present.

W

Working class Most often refers to the social class of those who work for wages rather than salaries, who do manual or manufacturing work, and who, in the United States at least, also can be perceived (and perceive themselves) as lower middle class.

Working poor This usually refers to that group of people in a society who although gainfully employed, do not earn enough to rise out of poverty.

Z

Zero exclusion mandate The section of Public Law 94-142 that requires that all children with disabilities be provided a free, appropriate, public education; local school systems do not have the option to decide whether to provide needed services.

Zone of proximal development Russian psychologist Lev S. Vygotsky uses this phrase to refer to learning experiences that allow an individual learner to build upon what is already familiar, yet sufficiently novel to be interesting and challenging.

Photo Credit

Chapter 1 p. 2 Andersen Ross/Getty Images, p. 5 BananaStock/PictureQuest, p. 12 Getty Images, p. 17 Photodisc Collection/Getty Images **Chapter 2** p. 30 Library of Congress, p. 34 Library of Congress, p. 35 Library of Congress, p. 37 Library of Congress Prints and Photographs Division [LC-USZ62-120532], p. 39 Library of Congress Prints and Photographs Division [LC-USZ62-68344], p. 52 BananaStock/PictureQuest **Chapter 3** p. 64 Image Source/Getty Images, p. 77 © Getty Images, p. 83 Erica Simone Leeds 2007 **Chapter 4** p. 108 David Buffington/Getty lmages, p. 113 © Gaetano Images Inc./Alamy, p. 124 The McGraw-Hill Companies, Inc./John Flournoy, photographer, p. 128 © Royalty-Free/CORBIS **Chapter 5** p. 144 Don Hammond/Design Pics/Corbis, p. 152 Comstock/Picture-Quest, p. 160 © Pixland/PunchStock **Chapter 6** p. 174 BananaStock/JupitorImages, p. 188 © Greatstock Photographic Library/Alamy, p. 194, © Greatstock Photographic Library/Alamy, p. 197 © Greatstock Photographic Library/Alamy **Chapter 7** p. 210 © image100 Ltd., p. 217 Erica Simone Leeds 2007, p. 226 Ingram Publishing/age Fotostock, p. 230 © Digital Vision/PunchStock **Chapter 8** p. 254 © Photodisc Collection/Getty Images, p. 257 © Photodisc Collection/Getty Images, p. 266 © Digital Vision **Chapter 9** p. 290 Royalty-Free/CORBIS, p. 293 © Digital Vision/Getty Images, p. 308 The McGraw-Hill Companies, Inc./Jill Braaten, photographer, p. 313 Digital Vision/Punchstock, p. 320 © image100 Ltd **Chapter 10** p. 326 Digital Vision/Getty Images, p. 336 © Creatas/PunchStock, p. 340 © Stockbyte/PunchStock, p. 344 BananaStock/Picture-Quest, p. 353 The McGraw-Hill Companies, Inc./Jill Braaten, photographer **Chapter 11** p. 368 Bananastock/AGE Fotostock, p. 375 © 2004 image100 ltd, p. 377 Laurence Mouton/Photoalto/PictureQuest, p. 381 © Brand X Pictures/PunchStock **Chapter 12** p. 398 Getty Images/Collection Mix: Subject RF, p. 402 Digital Vision/Punchstock/Punchstock, p. 410 Photodisc Collection/Getty Images, p. 413 © Creatas/PunchStock, p. 423 © Digital Vision **Chapter 13** p. 432 The McGraw-hill Companies, Inc./Jill Braaten, photographer, p. 440 © Getty Images, p. 445 © image100 Ltd

Name Index

Subject Index